QUICK START GUIDE

LSAT Premier

Get familiar with all the features of your multimedia test prep experience.

1 REGISTER YOUR ONLINE COMPANION

2 TAKE THE ONLINE DIAGNOSTIC QUIZ AND ESSAY PROMPT

3 CREATE YOUR STUDY PLAN

4 FAMILIARIZE YOURSELF WITH THE LSAT

SCORE HIGHER!

Turn the page for more details

Kaplan
Quick Start Guide
for the
LSAT Premier Program

The **KAPLAN LSAT PREMIER PROGRAM** is *your*

program — flexible and customizable to your test

prep needs. Kaplan's test prep strategies have

been the industry standard for over 70 years. These

time-tested, proven strategies are presented in

a clear, easy-to-grasp format for this interactive

program.

KAPLAN

FOUR EASY STEPS TO CREATING YOUR PERSONALIZED LSAT STUDY PLAN

These four easy steps will help you quickly work out your study plan from now until test day.

1 Register Your Online Companion

To begin your Kaplan LSAT test prep experience, you must first log on to your ONLINE COMPANION. Go to **kaptest.com/LSATbooksonline**. Have your book in front of you because you'll be prompted to retrieve important information from it for the registration process.

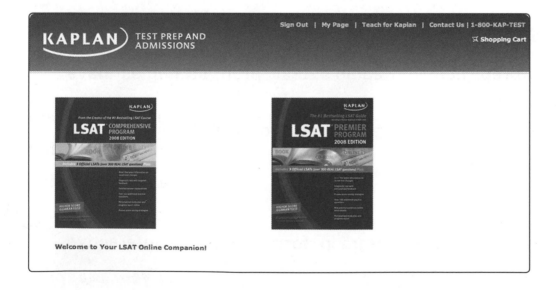

You can return to your Online Companion 24/7 through any Internet browser by going to **Kaptest.com** and selecting the "My Page" link.

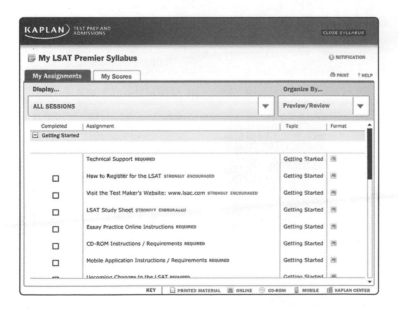

The Online Companion gives you access to LSAT Premier Program components that are not included between the covers of this book, including your Diagnostic Quiz, fresh new quizzes monthly, downloadable on-the-go prep content, and more!

② Take the Online Diagnostic Quiz and an Online Essay Prompt

The Diagnostic Quiz and a practice essay serve as a baseline so you can see how much you improve as you go through the lessons, skill-building practice sets, practice quizzes, and practice tests included in this program.

▶ The Diagnostic Quiz

After logging in to your Online Companion, go to the "Diagnostic Quiz" session, and click on the "LSAT Diagnostic Quiz" link that appears. This will prompt a separate window to appear with the quiz.

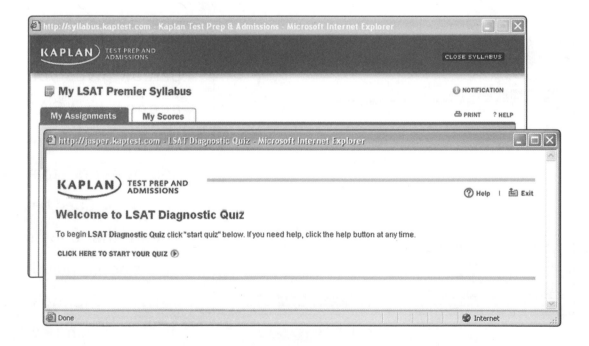

The LSAT Diagnostic Quiz is half the length of the real test. It includes samples of each question type found in the LSAT. When you complete the quiz and submit your answers,

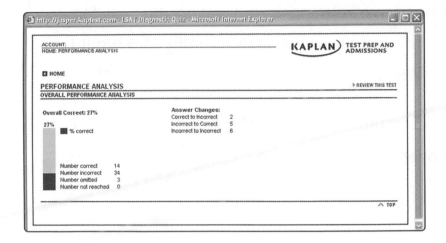

you will see a summary of your performance on the "Performance Analysis" page.

In the upper-right-hand corner of the "Performance Analysis" page, you'll see a link that says "Review This Test." When you click on this link, you'll see a detailed summary of how you did. You can also access the questions and answer explanations by clicking the "GO" link in the last column on the right.

▶ **Two Easy Steps to Diagnosing Your Results**

STEP 1: Evaluate your general performance

Look at the summary of your performance on the "Performance Analysis" page to see what your scaled score would be, and to get a sense of:

- The number of questions you got right, wrong, skipped or didn't answer overall and by section

- How long it took you to answer each question

- How much you changed your mind

STEP 2: Identify your strengths and weaknesses

Now look at the detailed summary of your performance on each question in the "Review This Test" page, as well as the answer explanations. Make a list of your *personal* strengths and weaknesses by identifying whether or not:

- You know and understand the concepts being tested

- You find certain question types especially challenging

- You are answering questions quickly enough

▶ Online Essay Prompt

Select a writing prompt from your Online Companion. You'll be prompted to click on a link, and a separate window will appear:

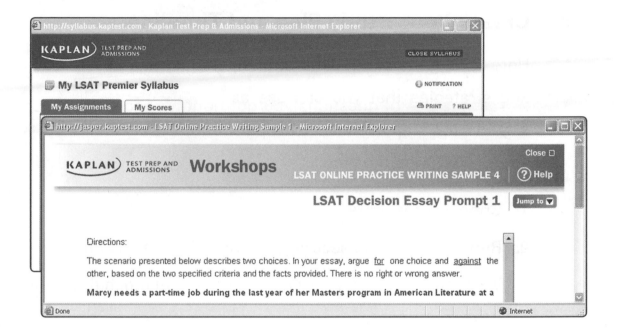

Read the directions and the prompt, and then write your essay on a separate piece of paper, following the timing guidelines provided. When you are finished:

- Read the model essay provided.

- Compare your essay to the model essay.

- Make a list of your *personal* strengths and weaknesses by identifying:

  - If your argument was coherent

  - If your writing flowed fluently from one paragraph to the next

- If your use of grammar and spelling was correct

- If you finished the essay in the allotted time

③ Create Your Study Plan and Timeline

Here is a general timeline with tips
and strategies that you can use as
a guide for creating your own personal LSAT prep timeline:

1. Choose a test date.

2. Register! This will secure your spot in the test center.

3. Work back from your test date to figure out much time you
    have to prepare.

4. Divide that preparation time in half.

In the first half, concentrate on your weaknesses

Study and Review

▸ If you had trouble with concepts:

- Review and master the essential concepts you struggled with.

▸ If you had trouble with question types:

- Go through the lessons for the question types you struggled with. Learn the Kaplan methods and strategies.

Practice and Reinforce

- Complete practice sets. Use the diagnostic tool to asses your performance.

- When you feel comfortable that you've made significant progress, take a full-length practice test. Use the diagnostic tool to asses your performance.

> **ONLINE COMPANION**
>
> Fill in the completion dates for your lessons you've reviewed in the book, so you can keep track of your progress.

In the second half, reinforce your strengths

Study and Review

- Review and master the Kaplan methods and strategies for all question types. This will increase your overall speed and accuracy.

> **ONLINE COMPANION**
>
> Fill in the scores for your practice sets in your Online Companion, so you can chart your progress.

Practice and Reinforce

- Complete practice sets.

- Complete sample writing prompts.

- Use full-length practice tests as milestones.

Three days before the test

- Don't take a full-length practice LSAT less than 48 hours before the test.

- Figure out how you're getting to the test center, and how long it will take to get there.

ONLINE COMPANION

Download the one-page study sheet of key strategies for study on the go.

The day before the test

- Instead of studying, prepare in other ways, like:

  - Do some relaxation and visualization techniques. Read a magazine, take a long hot shower or bath, and/or watch TV.

  - Get together a "Test Day Kit" containing items such as your admission voucher, your picture ID, a watch, and a snack.

  - Get a full night's sleep.

The morning of the test

- Don't eat anything too heavy or greasy for breakfast. Also, remember that too much caffeine may make you jittery — plus bathroom breaks will cut into your test-taking time!

- Dress in layers so that you can adjust to the temperature of the testing room.

- Read something. Don't let the test be the first thing you read this morning.

- Allow yourself extra time for traffic, mass transit delays, and detours.

4 Familiarize Yourself with the LSAT

Review chapters 1 and 2 in the book to get familiar with important details about the test, including structure, registration, scoring, and format.

ONLINE COMPANION

Once you have finished reading chapters 1 and 2, visit the "About the LSAT 1" session in your Online Companion, and record your completion dates.

NAVIGATING AROUND YOUR ONLINE COMPANION

Here are some quick tips for navigating around your Online Companion.

To add completion dates

1. Go to the corresponding session.

2. Click on the box to the left of the task you completed.

3. A pop-up will appear allowing you to select the date.

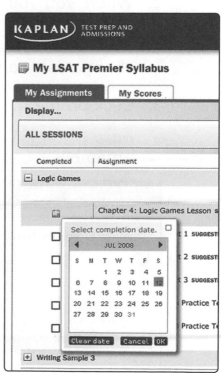

To add scores and completion dates

1. Go to the corresponding session.

2. Click on the box to the left of the task you completed.

3. A pop-up will appear allowing you to select the completion date, as well as enter a score or percentage of correct answers.

To start a quiz or online prompt

1. Go to the corresponding session.

2. When you roll your mouse over the name of the test or prompt, the name will turn into a "hyperlink" (it will change color and become underlined).

3. Click on the hyperlink. A separate window will appear.

4. Click the "Click Here to Start..." link.

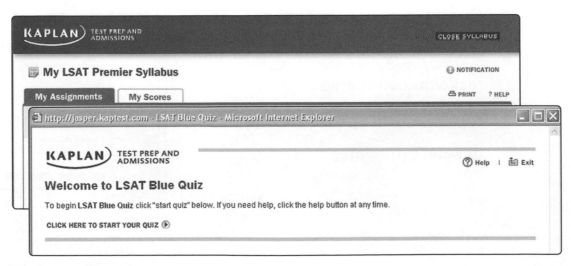

To suspend a quiz at any time

Click on the "Suspend" button at the bottom left side of the quiz window.

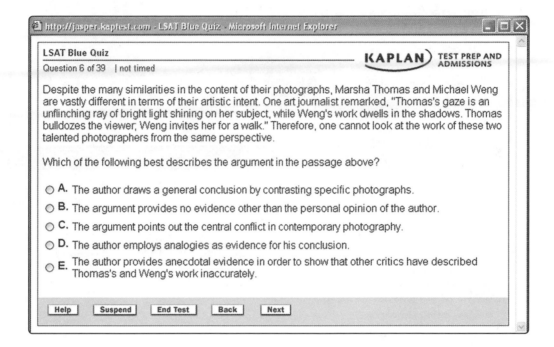

To resume a quiz

1. Select the quiz from the corresponding session.

2. A pop-up will appear with a table showing the status.

3. Click the "Resume" button in the right-hand column of the table.

To start a quiz over again

1. Select the quiz from the corresponding session.

2. A pop-up will appear with a table showing the status.

3. Click the "Click Here to Start..." link.

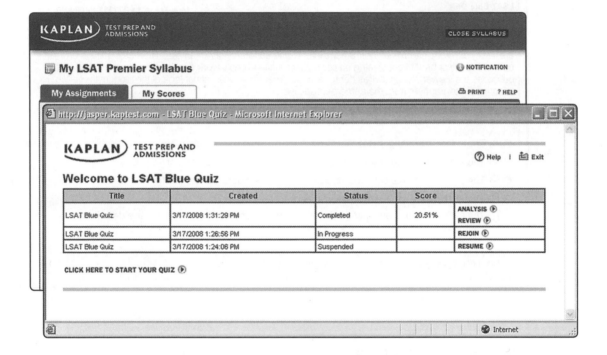

CUSTOMIZING THE ORGANIZATION OF YOUR ONLINE COMPANION

After logging in to your Online Companion, you will arrive at the default "My Assignments" page with the default "Preview/Review" category. This category presents all the assets for *every* session.

To see all the assets of *just one* session:

- Go to the "Display" pull-down menu

- Click on the "ALL SESSIONS" option.

- Select the title of the session you want.

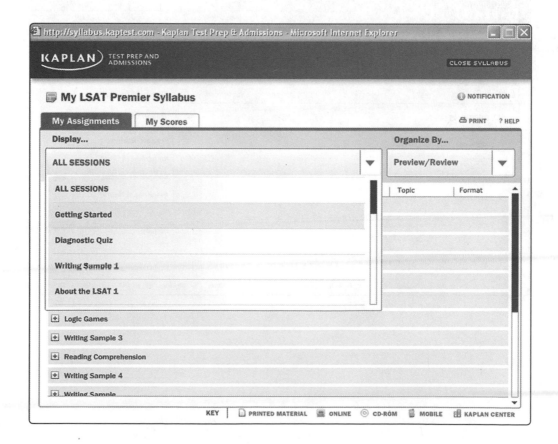

▶ Reorganize Display by Category in Your "My Assignments" Page

There are six categories: Preview/Review, Requirement Level, Completion Status, Assignment Name, Topic, and Format.

Requirement Level

1. Go to the "Organize by..." pull-down menu.

2. Select the "Requirement Level" option

3. Each asset will be listed by a requirement level: Required (in red); Strongly Encouraged (in green); Suggested (in blue)

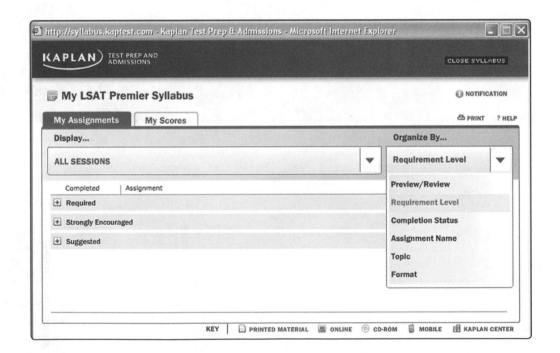

Completion Status

1. Go to the "Organize by..." pull-down menu.

2. Select the "Completion Status" option.

3. Each asset will be listed by a completion status: Completed; In Progress; Incomplete.

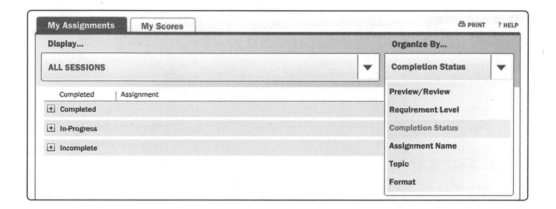

Assignment Name

1. Go to the "Organize by..." pull-down menu.

2. Select the "Assignment Name" option.

3. Each asset will be listed alphabetically (not by session).

Topic

1. Go to the "Organize by..." pull-down menu.

2. Select the "Topic" option.

3. Each asset will be listed by topic, such as "Review," "Skill-building, or "Practice Test."

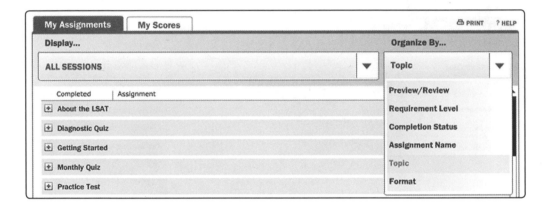

Format

1. Go to the "Organize by..." pull-down menu.

2. Select the "Format" option.

3. Each asset will be listed by format.

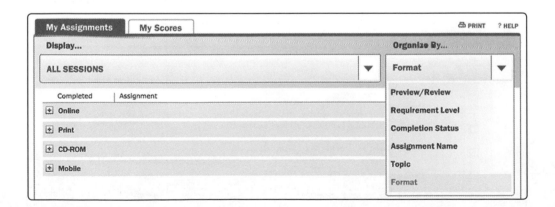

▶ View a Summary of Your Scores in Your "My Scores" Page

- Click on the "My Scores" tab next to the "My Assignments" tab.

- The scores from the online assets will automatically appear here. Scores you fill in from other assets will appear here, too!

Completed	Assignment	Score
☐ Diagnostic		
☑	LSAT Diagnostic Quiz	Percentage ▭ 27
☐ Linear Practice Test		
☑	Practice Test 1	Percentage ▭ 57
☑	Practice Test 2	Percentage ▭ 78
☐	Practice Test 3	Score ▭ NA

➡ NAVIGATING AROUND YOUR CD-ROM

The CD-ROM you receive with this LSAT Premier Program contains: quizzes focusing on each LSAT question type; two full-length practice tests; and full answer explanations for every question.

▶ System Requirements

The software on this CD-ROM is Windows-compatible only. It was NOT designed to operate on Apple Macintosh (MAC) computers. You will be able to take the maximum advantage

KAPLAN

of all facets of the CD-ROM if you use it on a computer with the following features: Windows 98/98SE / NT4.0/ME / 2000 / XP / Vista ◆ Pentium 266 MHz or higher ◆ 4x CD-ROM ◆ 16 MB RAM ◆ 15 MB free hard disk space ◆ Sound card ◆ 640 x 480 screen resolution ◆ 256 colors (thousands of millions recommended)

▶ Installation

1. Check that your PC meets the system requirements

2. Start your PC.

3. Insert the LSAT Companion CD into the CD drive. You should get an installer menu immediately; if you do not (or if you have an Autorun disabled), go to Step 4.

4. From the Start menu, select Run and type x:/gmtsetup.exe (where "x:" is your CD-ROM drive).

▶ Tutorials on Your CD-ROM

- After installing the CD software, you'll hear a brief introduction to the software's features.

- Before beginning a quiz or a test, a pop-up window will appear asking if you'd like to run through the optional tutorial. If you would like to use the tutorial, click "YES." If you'd like to continue with the quiz or test, click "NO."

→ HELPFUL HINTS IN THE BOOK

We've added icons throughout the book to highlight important points:

📖 **Read More** – Suggestions for additional study materials

▶ **Go Online** – More information and practice online

💿 **Check out the CD** – More tests and practice on your CD-ROM

📱 **Mobile Help** – More practice on a mobile application

♟ **Kaplan Strategy** – Proven strategies to master the LSAT

KAPLAN) EXCLUSIVE – Methods to score higher on the LSAT

→ TAKE ADVANTAGE OF THE KAPLAN COMMUNITY

Visit us at **Kaptest.com/LSAT** to become part of the Kaplan Community!

- **Online Discussion Boards** —Share experiences and information with others just like you! Join in on or start a discussion and search the extensive archives for topics like: deciding to go to law school, preparing applications, and choosing a school.

- **Law Edge e-Newsletter** — Sign up to get this free e-mail newsletter delivered to your inbox every month. You'll get fantastic resources like timely information and insider tips to help you maximize your law school applications, interactive questions and full explanations to help you score higher on the LSAT, and much more!

- **Exclusive Offers** — Be among the first to learn about and register for special career and admissions events. Receive exclusive discounts on products from Kaplan and our affiliated partners.

HOW DID WE DO?

After you have completed the LSAT Premier Program and have taken the test, go back to the Online Companion and fill out the online survey. We want to know how you did on the exam—and how we did in helping you to prepare.

Good luck!

LSAT®

2009 Edition

Premier Program

FEATURING OFFICIAL LSAT QUESTIONS AND 3 OFFICIAL LSAT PRACTICE TESTS

The Staff of Kaplan Test Prep and Admissions

KAPLAN

PUBLISHING

New York

This publication is designed to provide accurate and authoritative information in regard to the subject matter covered. It is sold with the understanding that the publisher is not engaged in rendering legal, accounting, or other professional service. If legal advice or other expert assistance is required, the services of a competent professional should be sought.

© 2008 Kaplan, Inc.

Published by Kaplan Publishing, a division of Kaplan, Inc.
1 Liberty Plaza, 24th Floor
New York, NY 10006

Materials used in this book were adapted from the following sources:

Dr. Ed Newman and Bob Verini, "The Kaplan Advantage™ Stress Management System"© 1996, Kaplan, Inc.

Martin V. Melosi, "Hazardous Waste and Environmental Liability: A Historical Perspective," *Houston Law Review*, Volume 25: 741, 1988. Reprinted by permission.

Wendy S. Zeligson, "Pool Coverage, Press Access, and Presidential Debates: What's Wrong with This Picture?" *Cardozo Law Review*, Vol. 9, 1988. Reprinted by permission.

Dan W. Brock and Allen E. Buchanan, "The Profit Motive in Medicine," *Journal of Medicine and Philosophy*, Vol. 12, 1987. Reprinted by permission.

Fred Anderson, "The Republic Reborn by Steven Watts," *American Historical Review*, Vol. 94, No. 2 (April 1989), p. 516. Reprinted by permission.

Judith Olans Brown, Phyllis Tropper Baumann, and Elaine Miller Melnick, "Equal Pay for Jobs of Comparable Worth: An Analysis of the Rhetoric," *Harvard Civil Rights & Civil Liberties Review*, No. 1, Winter 1986. © 1988, the President and Fellows of Harvard College. Reprinted by permission.

Ward & Trent, et al, *The Cambridge History of English and American Literature*. New York: G.P. Putnam's Sons, 1907–21.

National Cancer Institute, "Molecular Test Can Predict Both the Risk of Breast Cancer Recurrence and Who Will Benefit From Chemotherapy." Posted 12/10/2004. *www.cancer.gov/newscenter*

Anne Reynolds, "Nazi Looted Art: The Holocaust Records Preservation Project, Part 1" Prologue, Fall 2002, Vol. 34, No. 3. Viewed 24 December 2004, U.S. National Archives and Records Administration at *www.archives.gov/publications*.

Mary Wollstonecraft, *A Vindication of the Rights of Woman*. Printed at Boston by Peter Edes for Thomas and Andrews, Faust's Statue, No. 45, Newbury Street, 1792.

Printed in the United States of America

June 2008
10 9 8 7 6 5 4 3 2 1

ISBN-13: 978-1-4195-5208-3

Kaplan Publishing books are available at special quantity discounts to use for sales promotions, employee premiums, or educational purposes. Please email our Special Sales Department to order or for more information at kaplanpublishing@kaplan.com, or write to Kaplan Publishing, 1 Liberty Plaza, 24th Floor, New York, NY 10006.

Table of Contents

PART ONE

The LSAT

Chapter 1: **An Introduction to the LSAT**

The LSAT is probably unlike any other test you've taken in your academic career. Most tests you've encountered in high school and college have been content-based—that is, they required you to recall and be conversant with a certain body of facts, formulas, theorems, or other acquired knowledge.

But the LSAT is a skills-based test. It doesn't ask you to repeat memorized facts or to apply learned formulas to specific problems. In fact, all you'll be asked to do on the LSAT is think—thoroughly, quickly, and strategically. There's no required content to study!

Sound too good to be true? Well, before you get the idea that you can skate into the most important test of your life without preparing, let's clarify the very important distinction between study and preparation.

ABOUT THE LSAT

The LSAT is designed to test the critical reading, data management, and analytical thinking skills that have been deemed necessary (by the governing bodies of law schools themselves) for success in the first year of law school.

These are skills that you already possess to some extent. But what you probably haven't yet acquired is the know-how to use these skills to your best advantage in the context of a standardized, skills-based test, requiring careful time management.

The LSAT is also an endurance test—175 minutes of multiple-choice testing, plus a 35-minute writing sample. Add in the administrative details at both ends of the test, and a 10- to 15-minute break midway through, and you can count on being in the test room for at least four and a half hours.

It's a grueling experience, and if you can't approach it with confidence and rigor, you'll quickly lose your composure. That's why it's so important to take control of the test, just as you've been taking control of the rest of your application process.

Our content is as up-to-date as possible at the time of this printing, but ETS test specifications may change at any time. To accommodate this, please check our website *www.kaptest.com/LSAT* where Kaplan will be continually posting the latest news and updates.

Study vs. Preparation

And that's where test preparation comes in. While you can't technically study for a standardized, skills-based test like the LSAT, you can and must prepare for it.

The Kaplan LSAT program will teach you to tailor your existing skills to the very idiosyncratic tasks required by the LSAT, and how to use your critical reading skills most effectively to unlock dense but highly structured arguments and passages. Similarly, while you've probably developed plenty of sound, logical ways to analyze problems in everyday life, the Kaplan program will teach you to apply those deductive and analytical skills to the unusual demands of Logical Reasoning and Logic Games.

The LSAT Question Types

The LSAT consists of five multiple-choice sections: two Logical Reasoning sections, one Logic Games section, one Reading Comprehension section, and one unscored "experimental" section that will look exactly like one of the other multiple-choice sections.

At the end of the test, there will be a Writing Sample section in which you'll have to write a short essay. Here's how the sections break down:

Section	Number of Questions	Minutes
Logical Reasoning	24–26	35
Logical Reasoning	24–26	35
Logic Games	23–24	35
Reading Comprehension	26–28	35
"Experimental"	23–28	35
Writing Sample	n/a	35

The five multiple-choice sections can appear in any order, but the Writing Sample comes last. A 10- or 15-minute break will come between the third and fourth sections of the test.

Each question type is covered in its own chapter. You'll be answering roughly 125 multiple-choice questions (101 of which are scored) over the course of three intense hours. That's an average of just a little over a minute per question, not counting the time required to read passages and set up games. Clearly, you're going to have to move fast. But don't let yourself get careless. Taking control of the LSAT means increasing the speed only to the extent you can do so without sacrificing accuracy. Good time management involves maximizing the use of each second of your time by working strategically—for example, skipping questions and passages that slow you down and coming back to them if you have time, and determining which questions you can answer and which you should guess on. There are questions in the test designed solely to see whether you will get bogged down in them and questions that may be especially challenging to you personally. No one question is worth more than any other, so over-commitment to any one question can be fatal.

 CHECK OUT THE CD

Your CD Companion includes targeted practice quizzes for each test section.

First, just familiarize yourself with the kinds of questions asked on each section.

Logical Reasoning

What It Is: Each of the two scored Logical Reasoning sections consists of 24–26 questions based on short passages called *stimuli*. Most stimuli involve an **argument**—a conclusion based on evidence. You need to understand the stimulus argument to answer the one or two questions based on it. Many, perhaps most, Logical Reasoning stimuli aren't full arguments; they're a series of facts from which you must make logical deductions. Although you don't need to know the technical terms of formal logic, you do need the critical reasoning skills that enable you to analyze a stimulus and make judgments accordingly.

Why It's on the Test: Law schools want to see whether you can understand, analyze, evaluate, and manipulate arguments, and draw reliable conclusions—as every law student and attorney must. This question type makes up half of your LSAT score, so you know that the law schools value these skills.

What It's Like: Here are the directions to the section, along with a sample question:

Directions: This test consists of questions that ask you to analyze the logic of statements or short paragraphs. You are to choose as the answer to each question the one choice you consider best on the basis of your commonsense evaluation of the statement and its assumptions. Although a question may seem to have more than one acceptable answer, there is only one best answer, and it is the one that does not entail making any illogical, extraneous, or conflicting assumptions about the question.

1. One of the requirements for admission to the Lunnville Roller-Skating Club is a high degree of skill in roller-skating. The club president has expressed concern that the club may have discriminated against qualified women in its admissions this year. Yet half of the applicants admitted to the club this year were women. This proves that there was no discrimination against qualified women applicants in the club's admissions this year.

    Which one of the following is an assumption on which the conclusion of the argument depends?

    (A) Only a few applicants were found to be qualified and were admitted to the club this year.

    (B) No more than half of all the roller skaters in Lunnville are women.

    (C) No more than half of all the roller skaters in Lunnville are men.

    (D) This year no more than half of the applicants who met all the qualifications for admission to the club were women.

    (E) This year no more than half of the members of the club's committee that makes decisions about applicants' qualifications were men.

 READ MORE

When you finish this program, there's more practice on the tougher questions, games, and passages in Kaplan's *LSAT 180*.

Choice (D) is correct.

Logic Games

What It Is: There are 22–24 questions in the Logic Games (a.k.a. Analytical Reasoning) section, based on four games with 5–7 questions each. They require an ability to reason clearly and deductively from a given set of rules or restrictions, all under tight time restrictions. Games are highly susceptible to systematic technique and the proper use of scratchwork.

Why It's on the Test: The section tests your command of detail, your formal deductive abilities, your understanding of how rules limit and order behavior (which is the very definition of law itself), and your ability to cope with many pieces of data simultaneously to solve problems.

What It's Like: What follows are directions to the Logic Games section with a short sample game and two questions:

Directions: Each group of questions is based on a set of conditions. You may wish to draw a rough sketch to help you answer some of the questions. Choose the best answer for each question and fill in the corresponding space on your answer sheet.

Questions 2–3

Ron washed a total of seven objects after eating his lunch. Two of the objects were pieces of china: a mug and a plate. Two were pieces of glassware: a water glass and a juice glass. Three were utensils: a fork, a knife, and a spoon. Ron washed the two pieces of china consecutively, the two glasses consecutively, and the three utensils consecutively. He washed the objects as follows:

He washed each of the objects exactly once.
He washed the glassware after either the china or the utensils but not after both.
He washed the knife before the spoon, and he washed the mug before the plate.
He did not wash any two objects at the same time.

2. Which one of the following statements CANNOT be true?
    (A) Ron washed the fork first.
    (B) Ron washed the fork second.
    (C) Ron washed the mug first.
    (D) Ron washed the plate second.
    (E) Ron washed the plate third.

3. If Ron washed the spoon immediately before the fork, then which one of the following statements can be true?
    (A) He washed the knife second.
    (B) He washed the knife third.
    (C) He washed the plate third.
    (D) He washed the plate sixth.
    (E) He washed the plate seventh.

For question 2, the answer is (E); for 3 it's (E). You'll see an explanation for this game in the Logic Games chapter.

Reading Comprehension

What It Is: The Reading Comprehension section consists of four passage sets: three single passages, each 450–550 words long, and a pair of passages that together total approximately 500 words. Each passage set is followed by 5–8 questions. The topics are chosen from the areas of social sciences, humanities, natural sciences, and law.

Why It's on the Test: The purpose of the section is to see whether you can quickly get the gist of long, difficult prose—just as you'll have to do in law school and in your law career.

What It's Like: Here are the directions and a sample single passage with one question.

 GO ONLINE

There's no substitute for practice. Be sure to take each new online quiz.

Directions: Each selection in this test is followed by several questions. After reading the selection, choose the best response to each question and mark it on your answer sheet. Your replies are to be based on what is *stated* or *implied* in the selection.

Modern architecture has been criticized for emphasizing practical and technical issues at the expense of aesthetic concerns. The high-rise buildings constructed throughout the industrialized world in the 1960s and 1970s provide ample evidence that cost-efficiency and utility have become the overriding concerns of the modern architect. However, Otto Wagner's seminal text on modern architecture, first published in Germany in 1896, indicates that the failures of modern architecture cannot be blamed on the ideals of its founders.

Wagner's *Modern Architecture* called for a new style based on modern technologies and modes of construction. He insisted that there could be no return to traditional, preindustrial models; only by accepting wholeheartedly the political and technological revolutions of the nineteenth century could the architect establish the forms appropriate to a modern, urban society. "All modern creations," Wagner wrote, "must correspond to the new materials and demands of the present...must illustrate our own better, democratic, self-confident, ideal nature," and must incorporate the new "colossal technical and scientific achievements" of the age. This would indeed seem to be the basis of a purely materialist definition of architecture, a prototype for the simplistic form-follows-function dogma that opponents have identified as the intellectual basis of modern architecture.

But the picture was more complex, for Wagner was always careful to distinguish between art and engineering. Ultimately, he envisaged the architect developing the skills of the engineer without losing the powers of aesthetic judgment that Wagner felt were unique to the artist. "Since the engineer is seldom a born artist and the architect must learn as a rule to be an engineer, architects will in time succeed in extending their influence into the realm occupied by the engineers, so that legitimate aesthetic demands can be met in a satisfactory way." In this symbiotic relationship essential to modernism, art was to exercise the controlling influence.

No other prospect was imaginable for Wagner, who was firmly rooted as a designer and, indeed, as a teacher in the classical tradition. The apparent inconsistency of a confessed classicist advising against the mechanical imitation of historical models and arguing for new forms appropriate to the modern age created exactly the tension that made Wagner's writings and buildings so interesting. While he justified, for example, the choice of a circular ground plan for churches in terms of optimal sight lines and the technology of the gasometer, the true inspiration was derived from the centralized churches of the Italian Renaissance. He acknowledged as a rationalist that there was no way back to the social and technological conditions that had produced the work of Michelangelo or Fischer von Erlach, but he recognized his emotional attachment to the great works of the Italian Renaissance and Austrian baroque.

4. Which one of the following best expresses the main idea of the passage?

   (A) Modern architecture has been criticized for emphasizing practical and technical issues and for failing to focus on aesthetic concerns.

   (B) Critics have failed to take into account the technological innovations and aesthetic features that architects have incorporated into modern buildings.

   (C) Wagner's *Modern Architecture* provides architects with a chronicle of the origins of modern architecture.

   (D) Wagner's *Modern Architecture* indicates that the founders of modern architecture did not believe that practical issues should supersede the aesthetic concerns of the past.

   (E) Wagner's seminal text, *Modern Architecture*, provides the intellectual basis for the purely materialistic definition of modern architecture.

The answer is (D). Of course, actual passages will be longer and will have as few as five or as many as eight questions. We'll show you how to approach this passage and its questions in the Reading Comprehension chapter.

The Experimental Section

The experimental (unscored) section allows LSAC to try out questions for use on future tests. This section will look just like one of the others—Logical Reasoning, Logic Games, or Reading Comp—so don't try to figure out which section is experimental and cruise through that section. That's an extremely risky proposition. Just do as well as you can on every section.

KAPLAN STRATEGY ─────────────────────────

Know the test sections, their relative value, and what they test.

Logical Reasoning
- Accounts for 50 percent of your score.
- Tests ability to understand, evaluate, and manipulate arguments.

Logic Games
- Accounts for just under 25 percent of your score.
- Tests logic, ability to organize and manipulate data, and attention to detail.

Reading Comprehension
- Accounts for just over 25 percent of your score
- Tests ability to quickly break down dense material, identifying structure and reasoning.

The Writing Sample

What It Is: The Writing Sample comes at the end of your LSAT day. You'll have 35 minutes to write an argument.

Why It's on the Test: The Writing Sample shows law schools whether you can argue for a position while breaking down the argument of an opponent. This essay isn't graded but is sent to law schools along with your LSAT score.

What It's Like: Here's a sample topic:

> The program director of a television station must select the guest for the first edition of *Timewaves*, a new talk show. Write an argument in favor of selecting one of the guests over the other, with the following considerations in mind:
> - *Timewaves* must have enough mass appeal to attract a significant viewing audience in a competitive time slot.
> - *Timewaves* must continue the company's tradition of providing serious commentary on current topics.
>
> Jeanne Josephs—a popular writer—is known for her sharp analysis of national issues. Her most recent article, published in a widely read news magazine, was entitled "Success: Who's Got It and Why." In the article, Josephs interviews celebrities in various fields, including sports, business, and the arts, about their views on success and how they achieved it. Josephs has not appeared on a television talk show in several years. Last year, however, she won a prestigious journalism award for "The Private Pain of Politics," a series of articles on the toll

public office has taken on the family lives of prominent politicians. At that time reports about Josephs and her work appeared in many major newspapers.

Dr. Kingston Evans—a prominent psychologist—recently led an expert panel in a study of drug use in several affluent suburban communities. The panel's controversial final report, "Drugs in Suburbia," is to be published as a book soon after the first edition of *Timewaves* is shown. The report is said to expose establishment figures, including public officials, as narcotics suppliers to the suburban market. The study received some media attention after the panel's conclusion—that drugs are more prevalent though less visible in the suburbs than in the inner city—was inadvertently revealed. At the same time, there have been accusations that the study is an inaccurate, sensationalized account of a serious issue. Dr. Evans, however, is a distinguished professor with a well-respected body of academic research to his credit.

Topics are chosen and set up so that there can be no right or wrong answer, but there can be good and bad responses. You'll see one possible response to this topic in the Writing Sample chapter.

HOW THE LSAT IS SCORED

You'll receive one score for the LSAT ranging between 120 and 180 (no separate scores for Logical Reasoning, Logic Games, and Reading Comprehension). Here's how it's calculated.

There are roughly 101 scored multiple-choice questions on each exam:

- About 52 from the two Logical Reasoning sections
- About 22 from the Logic Games section
- About 27 from the Reading Comprehension section

Your **raw score**, the number of questions that you answer correctly, will be multiplied by a complicated scoring formula (different for each test, to accommodate differences in difficulty level) to yield the **scaled score**—the one that will fall somewhere in that 120–180 range—which is reported to the schools.

Because the test is graded on a largely preset curve, the scaled score will always correspond to a certain percentile, which will also be given on your score report. A score of 160, for instance, corresponds roughly to the 80th percentile, meaning that 80 percent of test takers scored at or below your level. The percentile figure is important because it allows law schools to see where you fall in the pool of applicants.

All scored questions are worth the same amount—one raw point—and there's no penalty for guessing. That means that you should always fill in an answer for every question, whether you get to that question or not.

What's a "Good" LSAT Score?

Of course, what you consider a good LSAT score depends on your own expectations and goals, but here are a few interesting statistics:

If you got about half of all of the scored questions right (a raw score of roughly 50), you would earn a scaled score of roughly 147, putting you in about the 30th percentile—not a great performance. But on the LSAT, a little improvement goes a long way. In fact, getting only one additional question right every 10 minutes would give you a raw score of about 64, pushing you into the 60th percentile—a huge improvement.

KAPLAN EXCLUSIVE

Never let time run out on any section without filling in an answer for every question.

SAMPLE PERCENTILES		
Percentile	Approx. Scaled Score (Range 120–180)	Approx. Raw Score
99th percentile	174	~94 correct out of 101
95th percentile	168	~88 correct out of 101
90th percentile	164	~82 correct out of 101
80th percentile	160	~76 correct out of 101
75th percentile	157	~71 correct out of 101
50th percentile	152	~61 correct out of 101

Note: Exact percentile-to-scaled-score relationships vary from test to test.

So you don't have to be perfect to do well. On most LSATs, you can get as many as 28 wrong and still remain in the 80th percentile or as many as 20 wrong and still be in the 90th percentile. Most students who score 180 get a handful of questions wrong.

Although many factors play a role in admissions decisions, the LSAT score is usually one of the most important. And—generally speaking—being average won't cut it. The median LSAT score is somewhere around 152. And if you're aiming for the top, you've got to do even better. The median LSAT scores accepted by the best law schools in the country, such as Yale, Stanford, and Columbia, range from the high 160s to the low 170s. That translates to a percentile figure of 95 and up.

 MOBILE PREP

Your downloadable mobile application lets you practice when you travel.

In the next chapter you'll start to learn how to approach—and master—the test in a general way. As you'll see, knowing specific strategies for each type of question is only part of your task. To really do your best, you have to approach the entire test in the proper spirit, and the proactive, take-control kind of thinking it inspires—the LSAT mindset.

LSAT Checklist

BEFORE THE TEST

Get the *LSAT/LSDAS Registration and Information Book.*

☐ It's available at most colleges and law schools; you can also get a copy at www.LSAC.org or order it by phone at (215) 968-1001.

Choose a test date.

☐ June is best (that is, 14–15 months before your anticipated law school entrance date), October second best (see chapter 8).

Complete your LSAT/LSDAS Registration.

☐ You can register online, by mail, or by phone.

☐ Make sure you list a first- and second-choice test center. If you register online, you can confirm test center availability in real time.

☐ If you register by mail, don't forget to sign the form and include payment.

☐ Download the free PrepTest and order additional practice tests.

Receive your LSAT admission ticket.

☐ If you register online, you can print out your ticket immediately (and can reprint it if it is lost).

☐ Be sure you have your ticket before the late registration date.

☐ Check it for accuracy; correct any errors promptly.

Create a test-prep calendar to ensure that you're ready by the day of the test.

☐ If you skipped it, go back and read "How to Use the LSAT Comprehensive Program."

☐ On a calendar, block out the weeks you have to prepare for the test.

☐ Based on your strengths and weaknesses, establish a detailed plan of study. Don't forget to include some days off for stress control.

☐ Reevaluate your strengths and weaknesses from time to time and revise the plan accordingly.

Check out your test center.

☐ Know the kind of desk you'll be working on and whether the room is likely to be hot or cold.

☐ Know the directions to the building and room where you'll be tested.

☐ Use Kaplan's exclusive "Test Center Rater" at *www.kaptest.com/testsites* for information from former test takers about desk space, noise, levels, proctors, and more..

THE DAY OF THE TEST

☐ Make sure you have your LSAT admission ticket and acceptable ID.

☐ Make sure you have your LSAT Survival Kit (see chapter 7)

Chapter 2: **Take Control of the Test**

To do your best on the LSAT, keep in mind that it's like no other test you've taken. If you took a test in college and got a quarter of the questions wrong, you'd probably receive a pretty low grade. But on the LSAT, you can get a quarter of the questions wrong and still score higher than the 80th percentile. The test is geared so that only those who exercise strong time-management skills are able to finish every section.

What does this mean for you? Just as you shouldn't let one bad game or passage ruin an entire section, you shouldn't let what you consider a below-par performance on one section ruin your performance on the rest of the test.

If you feel you've done poorly on a section, it could be the experimental. And even if it's not, chances are it's just a difficult section—a factor that will already be figured into the scoring curve. Remain calm; do your best on each section, and once a section is over, forget about it and move on. Losing a few extra points won't do you in, but losing your head will.

> **KAPLAN** **EXCLUSIVE**
>
> Never, ever try to guess which section is experimental. Handle each section as if it counts.

LSAT MINDSET

The Strategy and Practice chapters will arm you with the tools you need to do well on the LSAT. But you must wield those tools in the right spirit. This involves taking a certain stance toward the entire test.

The Right Attitude

Those who approach the LSAT as an obstacle and rail against the necessity of taking it don't fare as well as those who see the LSAT as an opportunity to show off the reading and reasoning skills that law schools are looking for—to distinguish themselves from the rest of the applicant pack.

With that in mind:

- Look at the LSAT as a challenge, but try not to obsess over it; you certainly don't want to psyche yourself out of the game.
- Remember that the LSAT is important, but this one test will not single-handedly determine the outcome of your life.

- Try to have fun with the test. Learning how to match your wits against the test makers can be very satisfying, and the skills you'll acquire will benefit you in law school and in your career.
- Remember that when you've trained with Kaplan, you're more prepared than most people. You have the tools you need and the know-how to use those tools.

Confidence

Confidence feeds on itself, and unfortunately, so does self-doubt. Confidence in your ability leads to quick, sure answers and a sense of well-being that translates into more points. If you lack confidence, you end up reading sentences and answer choices two, three, or four times, until you confuse yourself and get off-track. This leads to timing difficulties that perpetuate the downward spiral, causing anxiety and a tendency to rush.

If you subscribe to the LSAT mindset, however, you'll gear all of your practice toward taking control of the test. When you've achieved that goal—armed with the principles, techniques, strategies, and methods in this book—you'll be ready to face the LSAT with confidence.

Stamina

The LSAT is a grueling experience, and some test takers simply run out of gas before it's over. To avoid this, take full-length practice tests in the weeks before the test. That way, five sections plus a writing sample will seem like a breeze (well, maybe not a breeze, but at least not a hurricane). On the other hand, don't just rush from one practice test right into another. Learn what you can from your review of each test; then work on your weaknesses and build your strengths before tackling another full-length test.

 READ MORE

Get as much test practice as possible. Order PrepTests from LSAC to use as your final practice tests.

In addition to the practice tests included in the Kaplan Program, you can buy PrepTests published by LSAC. The available PrepTests are listed in the *LSAT Registration and Information Book*. Send away for them early, since they can take several weeks for delivery. You can also download a single free PrepTest from the LSAC website.

TEST EXPERTISE

It's one thing to answer a Logical Reasoning question correctly, and quite another to answer 25 of them correctly in 35 minutes. Time pressure affects virtually every test taker. So when you're comfortable with the content of the test, your next challenge will be to manage your time.

On most tests you take in school, you wouldn't dream of not taking at least a try at every one of the questions. If a question seems particularly difficult, you spend significantly more time on it, since you'll probably earn more points for correctly answering a hard question.

Not so on the LSAT. Every LSAT question, no matter how hard, is worth a single point. And since there are so many questions to do in so little time, it's foolish to spend three minutes getting a point for a hard question and then not have time to get a couple of quick points from two easy questions later in the section.

Given this combination—limited time, all questions equal in weight—you've got to develop a way of handling the test sections to make sure you get as many points as you can, as quickly and easily as you can. Here are the principles that will help you do that.

Answer Questions in the Order That's Best for You

One of the most valuable strategies to help you finish sections in time is to recognize and deal first with the questions, games, and passages that are easier and more familiar to you. Temporarily skip those that promise to be difficult and time-consuming—come back to them at the end, and if you run out of time, you're much better off not getting to questions you may have had difficulty with, rather than missing easier ones. (Since there's no wrong-answer penalty, always fill in an answer to every question on the test, whether you get to it or not.)

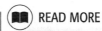 **READ MORE**

Come back and reread this section occasionally, to be sure you don't overlook any strategies.

Remember, LSAT questions, games, and passages are not presented in order of difficulty; in fact, the test makers scatter easy and difficult questions throughout the section, in effect rewarding those who get to the end. If you find sequencing games particularly easy, seek out the sequencing game on the Logic Games section and do it first.

Know That There Will Be Difficult Questions

It's imperative that you remain calm and composed while working through a section. Don't be rattled by one hard logic game, logical reasoning question, or reading passage. Part of the job of a top-notch test taker is to recognize those tough questions, games, and passages and leave them for last, making sure to pick up all of the quicker, easier points before investing time where the payoff is questionable. Expect to find at least one difficult passage or game on every section; you won't be the only one to have trouble with it. The test is curved to take the tough material into account. Understand that part of the test maker's goal is to reward those who keep their composure.

Control Time Instead of Letting Time Control You

The last thing you want is to have time called on a section before you've gotten to half the questions. It's essential, therefore, that you pace yourself. Don't spend exactly one-and-one-quarter minutes on every Logical Reasoning question. But you should have a sense of the average time you have to do each question, so you know when you're exceeding the limit and should start to move faster.

Keeping track of time is also important for guessing. It pays to leave time at the end to guess on any questions you couldn't answer. For instance, let's say you never get a chance to do the last logic game in the section. If you leave the grids for those questions blank, you'll get no points for that entire game. If, on the other hand, you give yourself a little time at the end to fill in a guess for each of those questions, you'll have a very good chance of getting lucky on one or two questions.

Grid In Answers Efficiently

You not only have to pick the right answers, you also have to mark those right answers on the answer grid in an efficient and accurate way. It sounds simple, but it's extremely important: Don't make mistakes filling out your answer grid! When time is short, it's easy to get confused going back and forth between your test book and your grid. Here are a few methods of avoiding mistakes:

1. Always Circle Answers You Choose: Circle the correct answers in your test booklet, but don't transfer the answers to the grid right away. That wastes too much time. Circling your answers in the test book will also make it easier to check your grid against your book.

2. Grid About Five Answers at Once: Transfer your answers after every five questions, or at the end of each Reading Comp passage or Logic Game, or at the end of a two-page spread in your test booklet (find the method that works best for you). You won't keep breaking your concentration to mark the grid, so you'll save time and improve accuracy.

3. Always Circle Questions You Skip: Put a big circle in your test book around the number of any question you skip (or circle the whole question). When you go back, it will be easy to locate them. And if you accidentally skip a box on the grid, you can more easily check your grid against your book to see where you went wrong.

4. Save Time at the End for a Final Grid Check: Take time at the end of every section to check your grid. Make sure you've got an oval filled in for each question in the section. Remember, a blank grid has no chance of earning a point.

 KAPLAN STRATEGY

To meet the LSAT's stringent time demands, cultivate:

- A sense of timing
- A system that enables you to skip around without getting confused
- An ability to assess the difficulty level of a question, passage, or game

SECTION MANAGEMENT

Logical Reasoning

Time per Question

Tackling 24–26 questions in 35 minutes works out to roughly a minute and a quarter per question. Keep in mind that this is only an average; there are bound to be questions that take more or less time. It's okay if the occasional question takes you two minutes, if you're able to balance it out with a question that takes 45 seconds.

Remember, too, that every question is worth one point, so don't get hung up on any one question. No single point on this section is worth three minutes of your valuable time. And if a question is that hard, there's a good chance that you may get it wrong anyway and have nothing to show for that extra time.

Managing the Section

What kind of Logical Reasoning questions should you skip? You'll develop your own answer to this question as you learn your strengths and weaknesses. Skip questions containing stimuli that are indecipherable to you after a quick reading. Questions containing extra-long stimulus arguments may be good to skip initially as well, especially if you're running out of time. But don't automatically be intimidated by the sheer length of a stimulus; often, the long ones are uncomplicated and easy to understand.

As you'll see in chapter 3, the Kaplan Method is to read the question stem first; you may be able to single out questions to postpone based solely on question type. If a question involves finding a principle that lends credence to an argument, and you know that principle questions are a problem for you, then that's a good question to postpone.

A good stimulus to tackle early is one that comes with two questions attached. There are usually anywhere from two to four double-question stimuli on each Logical Reasoning section. Working through these, as opposed to single question arguments, saves a little time, as you can potentially rack up two points for reading only one stimulus.

KAPLAN) EXCLUSIVE

If you decide to skip a question you've already spent some time on, be sure to cross out answers you already know are wrong.

Logic Games

Time per Game

Four games in 35 minutes means roughly eight and a half minutes per game. Remember, just as in Logical Reasoning, this is an average—games that are harder or have more questions should take a little more time than others.

Managing the Section

First, and most important, preview the section. Literally flip through the pages, having a glance at each game in order to decide which games look the easiest and most familiar to you. Previewing is not foolproof; a game that looks fairly straightforward at first glance can turn out to be challenging. However, if you look for game-type familiarity, concrete rules, and straightforward actions, and attack those games first, your efficiency will improve.

The goal is to tackle the games in order of difficulty, from easiest to hardest. But if you achieve nothing more than saving the hardest game for last, the strategy is a winner.

The best way to know which games may be difficult is to be familiar with the game types discussed in chapter 4, and to have a sense of which types you're strongest in.

A game that doesn't look familiar at all could be an oddball game—a good candidate to postpone. But don't necessarily be scared off by games with a lot of rules; sometimes, this works to your advantage. If you're given numerous rules that are clear and concrete, your setup will be more complete and the questions will be easier to answer. By the same token, a game with few rules, especially if they're conditional rules, may take little time to set up but also give you little to work with. When it comes to rules, quality is more important than quantity.

If you have several Logic Games to practice on, you may wish to build gradually to the point where you're ready to take full-length sections. First attempt one game in 8–9 minutes. Next, try two games in 16–18 minutes. When you're ready to move on, try three games in 24–27 minutes, until finally you can reliably handle a full four-game section in 35 minutes.

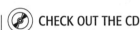
CHECK OUT THE CD

Improve your pacing with more timed practice—there are two full-length practice tests on your CD Companion.

Finally, remember the way the test makers test efficiency. They're crafty—they'll sometimes throw an intentionally time-consuming question at the end of a game, possibly one involving a rule change that requires you to backtrack and set the game up all over again. When this happens, they may not be testing who's smart enough to get the right answer, but rather who's clever enough to skip the troublesome question in order to devote precious time to the next game, with a possible payoff of six or seven new points.

Reading Comprehension

Time per Passage

Reading Comp is similar in structure to the Logic Games section: Four passages in 35 minutes means about eight and a half minutes per passage. But don't apply this timing too rigidly; denser passages and those with more questions should take a little more time than others. Kaplan's Reading Comp strategies and techniques will help you to get through each passage as quickly as possible, but here are a few additional points about tackling a full section.

Managing the Section

It may seem more difficult at first to choose which Reading Comprehension passages to attack first, but as you become familiar with the passage types and with reading for structure, you'll know what to look for: clear topic, scope, and purpose and a clear passage structure. And if you start working your way through a passage and find that you've made a mistake, you're not chained to it—move on to a different passage as soon as you recognize the difficulties. As in Logic Games, the goal is to save the most difficult for last, so if you can't get a handle on the passage's structure, move on.

Quite often, you'll encounter Reading Comp passages that contain technical details or difficult concepts, only to find that few if any questions deal with the part of the passage that's so dense. Just as in the Logic Games, the test makers aren't necessarily testing who's smart enough to understand that passage; they may want to see who's clever enough to skim past those details. Chapter 5 prepares you for the Reading Comp section.

MANAGING STRESS

Some test stress is normal and good; it's a motivation to study and the adrenaline that gets pumped into your bloodstream helps you stay alert and think more clearly. But high stress levels can make it difficult to concentrate, and you can't work under stress for prolonged periods without exhausting yourself. Practice using techniques to get stress under control, and learn which of them will work best for you during the test.

> **KAPLAN) EXCLUSIVE**
>
> Never practice for more than about three hours at a stretch; take breaks and come back refreshed.

Take Control

Research shows that if you don't have a sense of control over what's happening in your life, you can easily end up feeling helpless and hopeless. Try to identify the sources of the stress you feel. Which of these can you do something about?

Set Realistic Goals

Facing your problem areas give you some distinct advantages. What do you want to accomplish in the time remaining? Make a list of realistic goals. You can't help feeling more confident when you know you're actively improving your chances of earning a higher test score.

Focus on Your Strengths

Make a list of your strengths that will help you do well on the test. Recognizing your own strengths is like having reserves of solid gold. You'll be able to draw on your reserves as you need them. And every time you recognize a new area of strength, solve a challenging problem, or score well on a practice test, you'll increase your reserves.

Imagine Yourself Succeeding

Close your eyes and imagine yourself in a relaxing situation. Breathe easily and naturally, and think of a real-life situation in which you scored well on a test or did well on an assignment. Focus on this success. Now turn your thoughts to the LSAT, and keep your thoughts and feelings in line with that successful experience. Don't make comparisons between them; just imagine yourself taking the upcoming test with the same feelings of confidence and relaxed control.

Exercise

Whether it is jogging, biking, yoga, or a pickup basketball game, physical exercise stimulates your mind and body and improves your ability to think and concentrate. A surprising number of students fall out of the habit of regular exercise, ironically because they're spending so much time prepping for exams.

Eat Well

Good nutrition helps you focus and think clearly. Eat plenty of fruits and vegetables, low-fat protein such as fish, skinless poultry, beans, and legumes, and whole grains such as brown rice, whole wheat bread, and pastas. Don't eat a lot of sugar, high-fat snacks or salty foods.

Keep Breathing

Conscious attention to breathing is an excellent way to manage stress. Most of the people who get into trouble during tests take shallow breaths: They breathe using only their upper chests and shoulder muscles and may even hold their breath for long periods of time. Breathe deeply in a slow, relaxed manner.

Stretch

If you find yourself getting spaced out or burned out as you're studying for or taking the test, stop for a brief moment and stretch. Stretching will help to refresh you and refocus your thoughts.

Avoid Drugs

Using drugs (prescription or recreational) specifically to prepare for and take a big test is self-defeating. Mild stimulants like coffee or cola can sometimes help as you study because they keep you alert. But too much of them can lead to agitation, restlessness, and insomnia.

SUMMARY

- LSAT questions are not presented in order of difficulty; answer them in any order that seems effective.

- There is no penalty for wrong answers; always guess if you can't answer a question.

- All questions are worth the same amount; don't spend excessive time on one of them.

- In Logical Reasoning, spend an average of 12 minutes on each block of 10 questions, save for last any question types that give you trouble, and look for the double-questions to get more points for your minutes.

- In Logic Games, preview the section for the most familiar games, spend an average of eight and a half minutes per game, and save for last any rule-change questions or others that are especially time-consuming for you.

- In Reading Comp, skip passages that are slowing you down too much, and spend an average of eight and a half minutes per passage.

- Practice stress management throughout your preparation to maximize your effectiveness.

PART TWO

Strategies and Practice

Chapter 3: **Logical Reasoning**

- The 6 basic principles of Logical Reasoning
- Formal Logic in Logical Reasoning
- The 9 Logical Reasoning question types and their strategies
- Kaplan's 4-Step Method for Logical Reasoning

The fact that Logical Reasoning makes up half of your LSAT score is actually good news because you already have most of the skills you need for the section. In fact, we all do. But the LSAT tests your ability to use those skills thoroughly, quickly, and strategically.

THE 6 BASIC PRINCIPLES OF LOGICAL REASONING

On the LSAT, in law school, and in your law career, you'll need the ability to understand complex reasoning. It's not enough to sense whether an argument is strong or weak; you'll need to analyze precisely why it is so. This involves an even more fundamental skill—the ability to isolate and identify the various components of any given argument. Assumption, Strengthen, Weaken, and Flaw questions, which make up about half of the Logical Reasoning sections, call on these skills. (Other Logical Reasoning question types, such as Paradox and Parallel Reasoning questions, draw on other skills and plans of attack specific to those question types, which will be discussed later.)

 GO ONLINE

Your downloadable study sheet summarizes these principles, strategies, and methods.

Understand the Structure of Arguments

Success in Logical Reasoning depends on the ability to break an argument down into its core components.

In Logical Reasoning, the word *argument* doesn't mean a conversation in which two or more people are shouting at one another. It means any piece of text in which an author puts forth a set of ideas and a point of view and attempts to support them.

Most LSAT Logical Reasoning stimuli—and all arguments—involve two parts:

- The **conclusion** (the point that the author is trying to make)
- The **evidence** (the support that the author offers for the conclusion)

Success on this section hinges on your ability to identify these parts of the argument. There is no general rule about where conclusion and evidence appear in the argument—the conclusion could be the first sentence, followed by the evidence; or it could be the last sentence, with the evidence preceding it; or it could be any sentence in between.

 GO ONLINE

As you read through the basic principles, consider how each might have improved your Diagnostic Quiz performance.

Keywords

Use structural signals or keywords when attempting to isolate evidence and conclusion. Words in the stimulus such as *because, for,* and *since* usually indicate evidence is about to follow, while words such as *therefore, hence, thus,* and *consequently* usually signal a conclusion. Keywords are also important in recognizing formal logic concepts like *if/then* statements and in distinguishing what is *necessary* from what is *sufficient.*

Single Sentence Test

Consider the following short stimulus:

> The Brookdale Public Library will require extensive physical rehabilitation to meet the new building codes passed by the town council. For one thing, the electrical system is inadequate, causing the lights to flicker sporadically. Furthermore, there are too few emergency exits, and even those are poorly marked and sometimes locked.

Suppose that the author of this argument were allowed only one sentence to convey her meaning. Do you think that she would waste her lone opportunity on the statement: "The electrical system at the Brookdale Public Library is inadequate, causing the lights to flicker sporadically"? Would she walk away satisfied that she got her main point across? Probably not. Given a single opportunity, she would have to state the first sentence: "The Brookdale Public Library will require extensive physical rehabilitation. . . ." This is her conclusion. If you pressed her for her reasons for making this statement, she would then cite the electrical and structural problems with the building.

But does that mean that the statement, "The electrical system at the Brookdale Public Library is inadequate" can't be a conclusion? No; it's not the conclusion for this particular argument. Every statement must be evaluated in the context of the stimulus. For the sake of argument (no pun intended), see what a stimulus would look like in which the statement above serves as the conclusion:

> The electrical wiring at the Brookdale Public Library was installed over 40 years ago and appears to be corroded in some places (evidence). An electrician, upon inspection of the system, found a few frayed wires as well as some blown fuses (evidence). Clearly, the electrical system at the Brookdale Public Library is inadequate (conclusion).

The explanations of the Practice Tests in this book discuss the structure of of the Logical Reasoning arguments contained there; read them carefully, even for the questions you get right.

 READ MORE

To keep improving, reread these principles from time to time. Which are you using effectively? Which are you overlooking?

Paraphrase the Author's Point

As you read the stimulus, restate the author's argument in your own words. Frequently, authors in Logical Reasoning (and in Reading Comp) say pretty simple things in complex ways. In the library argument, for instance, you probably don't want to deal with the full complexity of the author's stated conclusion:

> The Brookdale Public Library will require extensive physical rehabilitation to meet the new building codes just passed by the town council.

Instead, carry a simpler form of the point in your mind, something like:

> The library needs fixing up to meet new codes.

You can concentrate on only a certain amount of information at one time. Restating the argument in your own words will not only help you get the author's point in the first place, but it'll also help you hold on to it until you've found the correct answer.

Judge the Argument's Persuasiveness

You must read actively, not passively, on the LSAT. Active readers question whether the author's argument seems valid. Since many of the questions deal with finding flaws in the author's reasoning, it's imperative to read with a very critical eye.

How persuasive is the argument in the library stimulus? Well, it's pretty strong, since the evidence certainly seems to indicate that certain aspects of the library's structure need repair. But without more evidence about what the new building codes are like, you can't say for sure that the conclusion of this argument is valid. So this is a strong argument, but not an airtight one.

Don't allow yourself to fall into the bad habits of the passive reader—reading solely for the purpose of getting through the stimulus. Those who read this way invariably find themselves having to read the stimuli twice or even three times. Then they wonder why they run out time on the section. Read the stimuli right the first time—with a critical eye.

Answer the Question Being Asked

It's disheartening when you fully understand the author's argument and then lose the point by supplying an answer to a question that wasn't asked. For example, when you're asked for an inference supported by the argument, it does you no good to jump on the choice that paraphrases the author's stated conclusion. Likewise, if you're asked for an assumption, don't be fooled into selecting a choice that looks vaguely like a piece of the author's stated evidence.

When asked why they chose a particular wrong choice, students sometimes respond by saying such things as, "Well, it's true, isn't it?" and "Look, it says so right there," pointing to the stimulus. Well, that's simply not good enough. The question stem doesn't ask, "Which one of the following looks vaguely familiar to you?" It asks for something very specific. It's your job to follow the test makers' line of reasoning to the credited response.

Also, be on the lookout for "reversers"—words such as *not* and *except,* which are easy to miss, but entirely change what you're looking for among the choices.

Remember the Scope of the Argument

One of the most important Logical Reasoning skills, particularly when you're at the point of actually selecting one of the five choices, is the ability to focus in on the scope of the argument. The majority of wrong choices on this section are what the test makers call **distracters** (tempting wrong answers) because they are "outside the scope." In everyday language, that simply means that these choices contain elements that go beyond the context of the stimulus.

Some common examples of scope problems are choices that are too narrow, too broad, or literally have nothing to do with the author's points. To illustrate this, look again at the question above:

> The author's argument depends on which of the following assumptions about the new building codes?

Say one of the choices reads as follows:

> (A) The new building codes are far too stringent.

Knowing the scope of the argument would help you to eliminate this very quickly. That argument is just a claim about what the new codes will require—that the library be rehabilitated. It's not an argument about whether the requirements of the new codes are good, or justifiable, or ridiculously strict. That kind of value judgment is outside the scope of this argument.

 GO ONLINE

Reinforce your skills each month with your new quiz.

Recognizing scope problems is a great way to eliminate dozens of wrong answers quickly. Pay special attention to the scope issues discussed in practice set and Practice Test explanations.

Eliminate Wrong Choices First if You Have to Guess

One or more of the wrong answer choices on any question will fall into patterns that, with practice, you'll quickly recognize. Any wrong choice you can eliminate improves your chance of choosing the correct answer. On Logical Reasoning questions, common wrong answer types are:

- **Outside Scope:** As you just saw, these are very common.
- **Extreme:** Unless the language of the argument is extreme, choices using words like *always, never, none, all,* and *every* are most likely wrong.
- **Distortion:** Some choices use language or ideas from the stimulus, but misapply them conspicuously; you can eliminate those.

- **Half Right, Half Wrong:** Some choices join a correct statement with an incorrect one; don't be hasty and choose your answer without reading the entire choice.
- **180:** Choices that are exactly the opposite of the correct one are common, especially on questions that ask for exceptions or on Strengthen/Weaken questions.
- **Irrelevant Comparison:** These often involve statistical evidence that compares apples and oranges: e.g., a statistic about all of a school's students in one statement may be compared to a statistic about freshman students in another.

 KAPLAN STRATEGY ─────────────────────────

Kaplan's principles for success in Logical Reasoning are:
- Understand the structure of arguments.
- Paraphrase the author's point.
- Judge the argument's persuasiveness.
- Answer the question being asked.
- Remember the scope of the argument.
- Eliminate wrong choices first if you have to guess.

FORMAL LOGIC IN LOGICAL REASONING

The manner in which formal logic is tested on the LSAT has evolved. Gone (at least for now) are the days when the test makers would line up formal *if/then* and *all/some/none* statements and ask you what *can, must,* or *cannot* be true on the basis of them. Nowadays, the test makers bury formal statements in the context of a casual argument, asking for one or more inferences that can be drawn. You may not easily recognize formal logic when you see it, and questions of this nature are fewer in number than in the past. But formal logic is tested in Logic Games as well, so it's best to get a solid handle on it.

Look at an example:

> Ian will go to the movies only when his wife is out of town. He'll go
> to a matinee alone, but will see a movie at night only if accompanied
> by Ezra and Mabel.

This simple stimulus looks like any other casual argument in Logical Reasoning, but in fact, it's made up of a couple of formal logic statements, each fraught with its own implications. Formal logic statements resemble rules in Logic Games. Be on the lookout for Logical Reasoning stimuli that contain sentences that can be boiled down to such hard and fast rules, and apply the following principles of formal logic to help you arrive at the correct answer.

The Contrapositive

The **contrapositive** of any *if/then* statement is formed by reversing and negating the terms. The general model goes like this:

Original: If X, then Y.

Contrapositive: If not Y, then not X.

KAPLAN EXCLUSIVE

Formal Logic is usually tested in the context of causal arguments that hinge on the differences between what is *sufficient* and what is *necessary*.

For any *if/then* statement (or any statement that can be translated into *if/then* form) the contrapositive will be equally valid. This is a nice shortcut to employ when faced with formal logic. Consider the following strict formal logic statement:

If the building has vacancies, then the sales office will be open.

To form the contrapositive, reverse and negate the terms:

If the sales office is NOT open, then the building does NOT have vacancies.

This would be a valid inference based on the original statement. The contrapositive, while quite a fancy term, is nothing more than everyday common sense. Now apply the contrapositive to the first sentence of the earlier example. Here's the original:

Ian will go to the movies only when his wife is out of town.

You can translate this statement into an *if/then* statement without changing its original meaning:

If Ian goes to the movies, then his wife must be out of town.

If that statement is true, what statement must also be true? Its contrapositive, of course:

If Ian's wife is not out of town, then Ian does not go to the movies.

One caveat: Wrong answers often result from either forgetting to switch around the terms before negating them, or negating only one of the terms. For instance, if Ian doesn't go to the movies, you can't infer anything about whether his wife is in or out of town. Similarly, if Ian's wife is out of town, you can't tell for sure whether Ian goes to the movies or not.

If one part of the formal logic statement contains a compound phrase, then both parts of the phrase must be taken into account. For example, take the other part of the stimulus above:

Ian will see a movie at night only if accompanied by Ezra and Mabel.

- **Translation:** If Ian sees a movie at night, then he's accompanied by Ezra and Mabel.
- **Contrapositive:** If Ian is not with Ezra and Mabel, then he does not see a movie at night.
- **Correct Interpretation:** If either Ezra or Mabel is missing, then Ian can't go to a night movie.

Finally, if one part of a formal logic statement is already in the negative, the same rules that apply to math apply to forming the contrapositive: Negating a negative yields a positive.

If the sun is shining, then Samantha does not wear green.

- **Contrapositive:** If Samantha is wearing green (if she's not not wearing green), then the sun is not shining.

Necessary versus Sufficient Conditions

For success in formal logic, it's crucial that you distinguish clearly between necessary and sufficient conditions. Here are examples of each:

- **Sufficient:** If I yell loudly at my cat Adrian, he will run away.
- **Necessary:** The TV will work only if it is plugged in.

My yelling loudly is a sufficient condition for Adrian to run away. It's all I need to do to get the cat to run; it's sufficient. But it's not necessary. My cat might run if I throw water at him, even if I don't yell loudly.

The TV's being plugged in, on the other hand, is a necessary condition for it to work. My TV won't work without it, so it's necessary. But it's not sufficient. Other conditions must apply for the TV to work (for example, the electricity to the house must be on).

You must be clear on what kinds of deductions you can and can't make based on statements of necessary and sufficient conditions. For instance, sufficient conditions are usually signaled by an *if/then* statement, which means that the contrapositive can be used.

> If I yell loudly at my cat Adrian, he will run away.

Given that the above statement is true, which one of the following statements must also be true?

- **Not Valid:** If I don't yell loudly at my cat Adrian, he will not run away.
- **Not Valid:** If my cat Adrian has run away, then I yelled loudly at him.
- **Valid:** If my cat Adrian has not run away, then I did not yell loudly at him.

The third statement, the contrapositive, is the only one of the three that's inferable from the original. My yelling loudly is sufficient to make Adrian run away, but it's not necessary; it'll do the trick, but it's not the only possible thing that will make him head for the hills. If I squirt him with a water gun, he'll also run away. This is why the first two statements are not inferable from the original statement.

Necessary conditions, on the other hand, are usually signaled by the keyword *only*:

> The TV will work only if it is plugged in.

If that statement is true, which of the following statements must also be true?

- **Not Valid:** If my TV is plugged in, it will work.
- **Not Valid:** If my TV is not working, then it must not be plugged in.
- **Valid:** If my TV is working, then it must be plugged in.
- **Valid:** If my TV is not plugged in, then it won't work.

 MOBILE PREP

Practice the same concepts in your downloadable mobile application.

True, the TV won't work without plugging it in, but plugging it in is not a guarantee that the TV will work. Maybe the picture tube is broken or my electricity is out. So the first two statements above are not inferable from the original statement, while the last two are.

THE 9 CRUCIAL LOGICAL REASONING QUESTION TYPES

Now that you're familiar with the basic principles of Logical Reasoning, look at the most common types of questions you'll be asked. Of the types discussed below, the first three predominate on most Logical Reasoning sections, but become familiar with the others as well.

 GO ONLINE

As you read through the question types, think about which you had trouble with on your Diagnostic Quiz. Learn your strengths and weaknesses.

Assumption Questions

An **assumption** bridges the gap between an argument's stated evidence and conclusion. It's a piece of support that isn't explicitly stated but that is required for the conclusion to be valid. Whenever you find that a central term appears only in the conclusion, there's one or more assumptions at work.

When the question stem specifically asks for a *necessary* assumption, you can use the **Denial Test**. Simply negate the statement and see if the argument falls apart. If it does, that is the correct assumption. If, on the other hand, the argument is unaffected, the choice is wrong. Consider this simple stimulus:

> Allyson plays volleyball for Central High School. Therefore, Allyson must be more than six feet tall.

Based on the keyword *Therefore*, you should recognize the second sentence as the conclusion, and the first sentence as the evidence. But is the argument complete? No; the piece that's missing—the unstated link between the evidence and conclusion—is the assumption. You could probably predict this one pretty easily:

> All volleyball players for Central High School are more than six feet tall.

To test whether this really is an assumption necessary to the argument, apply the Denial Test by negating it. What if it's not true that all volleyball players for Central High School are more than six feet tall? Can you still logically conclude that Allyson must be taller than six feet? No, you can't. Sure, it's possible that she is, but just as possible that she's not. By denying the statement, then, the argument falls to pieces; it's simply no longer valid. And that's our conclusive proof that the statement is a necessary assumption of this argument.

You can often predict the answer to an Assumption question. In more difficult Assumption questions, the answers may not be as obvious. When the question stem asks for a necessary component of the argument, you can use the Denial Test to verify your prediction, or to test answer choices. However, don't forget that the Denial Test only works when the question stem is looking for a necessary element—not all Assumption questions can be attacked this way.

Sample Stems

Here are some of the ways that Assumption questions are worded:

- Upon which one of the following assumptions does the author rely?
- Which one of the following, if added to the passage, will make the conclusion logical?
- The validity of the argument depends on which one of the following?

Strengthen or Weaken Questions

Determining an argument's necessary assumption, as you've just seen, is required to answer Assumption questions. But it also is often necessary for two other common question types— Strengthen and Weaken questions.

One way to weaken an argument is to break down a central piece of evidence. Another way is to attack the validity of any assumption the author is making. The answer to many Strengthen questions provides additional support by affirming the truth of an assumption or by presenting more persuasive evidence.

Consider the stimulus used before, but look at it in the context of these other question types:

> Allyson plays volleyball for Central High School. Therefore, Allyson must be more than six feet tall.

The assumption holding this argument together was that all volleyball players for Central High School are more than six feet tall. So, if the question asked you to weaken the argument, the answer might attack that assumption:

> Which one of the following, if true, would most weaken the argument?

Answer: Not all volleyball players at Central High School are more than six feet tall. But what about strengthening the argument? Again, the key may be a necessary assumption:

> Which one of the following, if true, would most strengthen the argument?

Answer: All volleyball players at Central High School are more than six feet tall. Here, by making explicit the author's central assumption, you've in effect bolstered the argument.

Weaken questions tend to be more common on the LSAT than Strengthen questions. But here are a few concepts that apply to both question types:

- Weakening an argument is not the same thing as disproving it, and strengthening is not the same as proving the conclusion true. A strengthener tips the scale towards the validity of the conclusion, while a weakener tips the scale in the other direction.

- The wording of these questions often takes the form "Which one of the following, if true, would most [weaken/strengthen] the argument?" The *if true* part means that you have to accept the truth of the choice right off the bat, no matter how unlikely it may sound to you.

- Don't be careless. Wrong answer choices in these questions often have exactly the opposite of the desired effect. That is, if you're asked to strengthen an argument, it's quite likely that one or more of the wrong choices will contain information that actually weakens it.

Sample Stems

The stems associated with these two question types are usually self-explanatory. Here are some alternate forms you can expect to see on the test:

Weaken:

- Which one of the following, if true, would most seriously damage the argument above?
- Which one of the following, if true, casts the most doubt on the argument above?

Strengthen:

- Which one of the following, if true, would provide the most support for the conclusion in the argument above?
- The argument above would be more persuasive if which one of the following were found to be true?

Flaw Questions

This question type asks you to recognize what's wrong with an argument. There are two basic types.

In the **general** type, the correct choice will critique the reasoning by pointing out a classic fallacy (e.g., "The argument attacks the source of an opinion, rather than the opinion itself"). In this case, the flaw falls into a general, well-defined category.

In the **specific** type, the correct answer will attack a specific piece of the argument's reasoning. An example of this would be: "It cannot be concluded that the number of male turtles has increased simply because the percentage of turtles that are male has increased." Notice that the subject of this statement isn't turtles; it's the author's faulty reasoning about turtles. The most common specific flaws in Logical Reasoning are unwarranted assumptions, ignored alternative possibilities, and scope shifts.

In each case, the required skill is the ability to identify the structure of the author's argument—and where the argument goes wrong. Use your practice to become familiar with each of these types.

Inference Questions

Another of the most common question types in Logical Reasoning is the Inference question. Drawing an **inference** is a matter of considering one or more statements as evidence and then drawing a conclusion from them. (This same concept, also known as **deduction**, is central to Logic Games, as well.)

Sometimes the inference is very close to the author's main point. Other times, it deals with a less central point. A valid inference is something that must be true if the statements in the passage are true—an extension of the argument rather than a necessary part of it.

For instance, take a somewhat expanded version of the volleyball team argument:

> Allyson plays volleyball for Central High School, despite the team's rule against participation by nonstudents. Therefore, Allyson must be over six feet tall.

Inference: Allyson is not a student at Central High School. If Allyson plays volleyball *despite* the team's rule against participation by nonstudents, she must not be a student. Otherwise, she wouldn't be playing despite the rule; she'd be playing in accordance with the rule. But note that this inference is not an essential assumption of the argument, since the conclusion about Allyson's height doesn't depend on it.

So be careful; unlike an assumption, an inference need not have anything to do with the author's stated conclusion.

Sample Stems

Inference questions probably have the most varied wording of all the Logical Reasoning question stems. Some question stems denote inference fairly obviously. Others are more subtle, and still others may even look like other question types entirely. Here's a sample of the various forms that Inference questions can take:

- Which one of the following is implied by the argument above?
- The author suggests that . . .
- If all the statements above are true, which one of the following must also be true?
- The author of the passage would most likely agree with which one of the following?
- The passage provides the most support for which one of the following?
- Which of the following is probably the conclusion towards which the author is moving?

Method of Argument Questions

Method of Argument questions ask you to demonstrate an understanding of how an author's argument is put together. Unlike Flaw questions, Method of Argument questions don't always involve faulty logic. The key skill—once again—involves being able to analyze the structure of an argument.

There are two types of Method of Argument questions. The **general** type deals with classic argument structures, such as, "arguing from a small sample to a larger group," or "inferring a causal relationship from a correlation." The **specific** type gives you a description of the argument in much more specific terms. An example of this might read, "The author presents the case of his mother in order to show that not all astronauts are men."

KAPLAN EXCLUSIVE

Understanding argument structure is key in Flaw, Method of Argument, and Parallel Reasoning questions.

The questions you should ask yourself in order to determine the author's method of argument are: What is the evidence? What is the conclusion? How does the author link the evidence and conclusion together?

Parallel Reasoning Questions

Parallel Reasoning questions require you to identify the choice that contains the argument most similar to that in the stimulus. To do this, you need to grasp the distinction between an argument's form and its content.

"A causal relationship concluded from a correlation" is a form—a type—of reasoning. Arguments with this form can contain virtually any content. Your task is to abstract the argument's form, with as little content as possible, and then locate the choice that uses the same form. Don't let yourself be drawn to a choice based on its subject matter. A stimulus about music may have an answer choice that also involves music, but that doesn't mean that the reasoning in the two arguments is similar.

A good approach to these questions is to see first if the argument can be symbolized algebraically, using X's and Y's. Take the following example:

All cows eat grass. This animal eats grass. Therefore, it must be a cow.

This (flawed) argument can be symbolized in the following way:

All X do Y. This does Y. Therefore, this must be an X.

If the stimulus can be symbolized this way, your job will be to search for the choice that can be symbolized in the same way. Your answer might look something like this:

Every politician (all X) tells lies (does Y). Stegner is lying (this does Y). So he must be a politician (therefore, this must be an X).

Notice that the wording doesn't have to match exactly ("all X" means "every X"), and that the subject matter doesn't have to match in the least. What's important is the parallel structure.

Sometimes, though, an argument's reasoning isn't amenable to symbolization. In such a case, see if you can put a label on the type of argument being used, such as "Arguing from a Part to a Whole," or "Circular Reasoning" (evidence and conclusion are identical). Naming the argument will often help eliminate two or three choices that don't even come close to this general form.

KAPLAN) EXCLUSIVE

The right choice in a Parallel Reasoning question mimics the structure, not the content, of the stimulus.

As long as you can summarize the argument's form without including content, you're well on your way to finding the parallel argument among the choices.

Here are a few general tips on parallel reasoning:

- All elements of the original argument must be present in its parallel. For example, if the original argument made a generalization to a specific case, a second argument, no matter how similar in structure otherwise, cannot be parallel unless it makes a comparable generalization.

- Stay away from answer choices written about the same subject matter as the original. This is an old trick of the test makers.

- To be logically parallel it isn't necessary that all logical elements be in the same sequence, as long as all elements of the first argument exist in the second.

Paradox Questions

A paradox exists when an argument contains two or more seemingly inconsistent statements. You'll know you're dealing with a paradoxical situation if the argument ends with what seems to be a bizarre contradiction. In a typical Paradox question, you'll be asked either to find the choice that "explains the paradoxical result" or "resolves the apparent discrepancy." The correct answer will reconcile the seemingly inconsistent statements while allowing them all to still be true.

Take the following question:

Fifty-seven percent of the registered voters in this district claimed to support the Democratic candidate, and yet the Republican candidate won the election with 55 percent of the vote.

Which of the following would resolve the apparent discrepancy above?

The stimulus seems paradoxical since the Republican won the election, even though more registered voters preferred the Democrat. But do all registered voters vote? No. So a correct answer for this question might read something like this:

> Because of an intensive get-out-the-vote effort in traditionally
> Republican neighborhoods, a disproportionate number of registered
> Republicans actually voted in the election.

This statement reconciles the seemingly contradictory elements of the argument by showing that the group of registered voters is not identical to the group of people who actually voted in the election.

Here are a few tips for handling this question type:

- Before attempting to resolve it, make sure you have a good grasp of what the paradox is.
- Resolving paradoxes is often a matter of recognizing that the things being compared aren't really comparable. Read critically to note these subtle distinctions.
- In Paradox questions, avoid choices that merely amplify points already raised in the argument.

> **KAPLAN** EXCLUSIVE
>
> The correct choice in a Paradox question will often involve realizing that two groups presented as identical are actually different.

Principle Questions

Principle questions—the closest question type to the actual practice of law—involve fitting a specific situation into a global generality (or, occasionally, vice versa). Usually, you'll be given an argument and asked to find the principle that seems to justify the author's reasoning. For example, suppose that an author's evidence leads to this conclusion in the final sentence of the stimulus:

> Therefore, Marvin should provide a home for his ailing
> grandmother until she gets back on her feet.

The question stem might read: "The author's position most closely conforms to which one of the following principles?" In other words, what principle best accounts for or justifies the author's position? The answer could sound like this:

> If a close relative is in need, one should always do one's best to help
> that person, regardless of personal inconvenience.

On the other hand, the question stem might read: "Which one of the following principles would justify Marvin's refusal to follow the author's recommendation?" In this case, the answer may be something like this:

> No person should be obligated to provide support for another
> person, even if that other person is a close relative.

Notice the general nature of both principles. Whereas they don't specifically mention Marvin or his grandmother, or the exact conditions of the stimulus per se, the general situation (helping a relative in need) is addressed in both.

The correct answer to Principle questions is usually the one that expresses the key concepts and contains the key terms that the other choices leave out. Be extremely wary of choices that are outside scope. Most of the wrong choices contain principles that sound very formal and look good on the page by themselves, but that don't address the author's main concern.

Point at Issue Questions

A relatively new question type, these always involve a stimulus with two or more expressed opinions, and your task is to identify the issue on which they take differing positions. To see where two arguments differ, separately compare their conclusions and their evidence. The trick is to stay within the scope of both speakers' arguments; the point at issue can't be something that one speaker raises, but the other doesn't address at all. The correct answer will describe a point addressed by both speakers and about which the speakers hold conflicting views.

Sample Stems

The stems associated with these questions are usually self-explanatory. Here are a couple of examples:

- A and B disagree over which of the following
- The point at issue between A and B is

Now that you've learned the basic Logical Reasoning principles and have been exposed to the full range of question types, it's time to learn how to orchestrate all of that knowledge into a systematic approach to Logical Reasoning.

KAPLAN'S 4-STEP METHOD FOR LOGICAL REASONING

1. Read the Question Stem First.

Preview the stem so that you know exactly what you're looking for in the stimulus. For example, say the question attached to the original library argument above asked the following:

> The author supports her point about the need for rehabilitation
> at the Brookdale Library by citing which of the following?

By previewing this question stem, you know what to look for—evidence, the support provided for the conclusion. If the question asked you to find an assumption, you would read looking for a crucial missing piece of the argument. Previewing the stem allows you to set the tone of your attack on each stimulus, saving time.

2. Untangle the Stimulus.

With the question stem in mind, read the stimulus, paraphrasing as you go. Read actively and critically, pinpointing evidence and conclusion, and forming a sense of how strong or weak the argument is.

3. Think Critically About the Answer.

If you've read the stimulus critically enough, you may know the answer without even looking at the choices. It's much easier to find the correct choice if you have a sense of what you're looking for.

But don't ponder the question for minutes until you're able to write out your own answer—it's still a multiple-choice test, so the right answer is there on the page. Just get in the habit of framing an answer in as much detail as possible first. For instance, say a question for the library argument went like this:

> The author's argument depends on which of the following assumptions about the new building codes?

Having thought about the stimulus argument, an answer to this question may have sprung to mind immediately—that the new codes apply to existing buildings as well as to new buildings under construction. After all, the library will have to be rehabilitated to meet the new codes, according to the author. So an assumption is that the codes apply to existing buildings, and that's the kind of statement you would look for among the choices.

KAPLAN) EXCLUSIVE

Your prephrase of an answer need not be elaborate or specific. Your goal is to get an idea of what you're looking for in the correct answer.

By the way, don't be discouraged if not all questions are good candidates for predicting answers. Some questions just won't have an answer that jumps out at you. But if used correctly, predicting (or **prephrasing**—a word Kaplan uses to mean "get a general sense of what the answer will contain or look like") will really boost your confidence and increase your speed on the section.

4. Evaluate the Answer Choices.

Skim the choices looking for something that sounds like what you have in mind. If you couldn't prephrase very specifically, read and evaluate each choice, throwing out the ones that are outside scope. After settling on an answer choice, you may wish to double-check the question stem to make sure that you're answering the question that was asked.

Now try this approach on a genuine Logical Reasoning item:

> One of the requirements for admission to the Lunnville Roller Skating Club is a high degree of skill in roller-skating. The club president has expressed concern that the club may have discriminated against qualified women in its admissions this year. Yet half of the applicants admitted to the club this year were women. This proves that there was no discrimination against qualified women applicants in the club's admissions this year.
>
> Which one of the following is an assumption on which the conclusion of the argument depends?
>
> (A) Only a few applicants were found to be qualified and were admitted to the club this year.
> (B) No more than half of all the roller skaters in Lunnville are women.
> (C) No more than half of all the roller skaters in Lunnville are men.
> (D) This year no more than half of the applicants who met all the qualifications for admission to the club were women.
> (E) This year no more than half of the members of the club's committee that makes decisions about applicants' qualifications were men.

 CHECK OUT THE CD

Get more practice with Kaplan's Method in a CD Companion Logical Reasoning quiz.

1. Read the Question Stem First.

Like most Assumption questions, this one is easy to identify—the stem uses the word *assumption* directly. Before you even look at the stimulus, you know there's a piece missing between the evidence and the conclusion.

2. Untangle the Stimulus.

The language introducing the conclusion helps identify it: "This proves that . . ." The author concludes that there was no discrimination against qualified women. Why does he think that? Because half of the applicants admitted were women. That's his evidence. Look for the gap.

3. Think Critically About the Answer.

We're missing something here—as we knew we would be as soon as we saw that this was an Assumption question. The conclusion says there was no discrimination, but the evidence is just about the percentage of new admits who are women. What don't we know? We don't know what percentage of *qualified applicants* were women—if that doesn't match the 50 percent of admission, there may still have been discrimination. The author assumes, then, that the percentages DO match. That is, he assumes that no more than half of the qualified applicants were women.

4. Evaluate the Answer Choices.

You already know what you're looking for. Skim the choices and try to find it. Answer choice (D) is what we were expecting. Don't let the other choices distract you!

So there you have it—a quick demonstration of how to use the strategies and techniques outlined in this chapter to work through the complete Logical Reasoning process. Apply these techniques on the following practice sets and in the Logical Reasoning sections of your Practice Tests in this book. Pay careful attention to all of the written explanations, even for the questions you got right.

SUMMARY

The basic principles of Logical Reasoning are:

- Understand the structure of arguments.

- Paraphrase the author's point.

- Judge the argument's persuasiveness.

- Answer the question being asked.

- Remember the scope of the argument.

- Eliminate wrong choices first if you have to guess.

The 9 crucial Logical Reasoning question types are:

- Assumption questions: Identify unstated, necessary support for the conclusion.

- Strengthen or Weaken questions: Support or challenge evidence or assumptions in the stimulus.

- Inference questions: Know what must be true if statements in the stimulus are true.

- Flaw questions: Focus on general classic fallacies or specific pieces of the argument.

- Method of Argument questions: Identify the structure of arguments.

- Parallel Reasoning questions: Mimic the structure, not the context, of the stimulus.

- Paradox questions: Reconcile apparent inconsistencies.

- Principle questions: Identify or apply underlying principles.

- Point at Issue questions: Identify how two or more arguments differ.

Kaplan's 4-Step Method for Logical Reasoning

1. Read the question stem first.

2. Untangle the stimulus.

3. Think critically about the answer.

4. Evaluate the answer choices.

LOGICAL REASONING PRACTICE

Set One

Directions: This test consists of questions that ask you to analyze the logic of statements or short paragraphs. You are to choose as the answer to each question the one you consider correct on the basis of your common sense evaluation of the statement and its assumptions. Although a question may seem to have more than one acceptable answer, there is only one answer, and it is the one that does not entail making any illogical, extraneous, or conflicting assumptions about the question. These questions do not presuppose any knowledge of formal logic on your part.

1. Educational television is a contradiction in terms. While a classroom encourages social interaction, television encourages solitude. School is centered on the development of language, but television depends upon constantly changing visual images. And in a classroom, fun is merely a means to an end, but television is the end in itself.

    Upon which one of the following assumptions does the author rely in the passage?

    (A) The classroom should not be a place where anyone has fun.

    (B) Only experiences that closely resemble what takes place in the school environment can be educational.

    (C) Television programs reinforce some of the values of the school environment.

    (D) Educational television programs are qualitatively better than most other television programs.

    (E) The potential of television as a powerful learning tool has not yet been realized.

2. Some people have questioned why the Homeowners Association is supporting Cooper's candidacy for mayor. But if the Association wants a mayor who will attract more businesses to the town, Cooper is the only candidate it could support. So, since the Association is supporting Cooper, it must have a goal of attracting more businesses to the town.

    The reasoning in the argument is in error because

    (A) the reasons the Homeowners Association should want to attract more businesses to the town are not given

    (B) the Homeowners Association could be suporting Cooper's candidacy for reasons unrelated to attracting businesses to the town

    (C) other groups besides the Homeowners Association could be supporting Cooper's candidacy

    (D) the Homeowners Association might discover that attracting more businesses to the town would not be in the best interest of its members

    (E) Cooper might not have all of the skills that are needed by a mayor who wants to attract businesses to a town

3. High-technology medicine is driving up the nation's health care costs. Recent advances in cataract surgery illustrate why this is occurring. Cataracts are a major cause of blindness, especially in elderly people. Ten years ago, cataract surgery was painful and not always effective. Thanks to the new technology used in cataract surgery, the operation now restores vision dramatically and is less expensive. These two factors have caused the number of cataract operations performed to increase greatly, which has, in turn, driven up the total amount spent on cataract surgery.

    Which one of the following can be inferred from the passage above?

    (A) Ten years ago, few people had successful cataract surgery.

    (B) In the long run, the advantages of advanced medical technology are likely to be outweighed by the disadvantages.

    (C) The total amount spent on cataract surgery has increased because the increased number of people electing to have the surgery more than offsets the decrease in cost per operation.

    (D) Huge increases in the nation's health care costs are due primarily to increased demand for surgery for older people.

    (E) Ten years ago, cataract surgery was affordable for more people than it was last year.

4. It is not known whether bovine spongiform encephalopathy (BSE), a disease of cattle invariably deadly to them, can be transmitted directly from one infected animal to another at all stages of the infection. If it can be, there is now a reservoir of infected cattle incubating the disease. There are no diagnostic tests to identify infected animals before the animals show overt symptoms. Therefore, if such direct transmission occurs, the disease cannot be eradicated by ____.

    Which one of the following best completes the argument?

    (A) removing from the herd and destroying any diseased animal as soon as it shows the typical symptoms of advanced BSE

    (B) developing a drug that kills the agent that causes BSE, and then treating with that drug all cattle that might have the disease

    (C) destroying all cattle in areas where BSE occurs and raising cattle only in areas to which BSE is known not to have spread

    (D) developing a vaccine that confers lifelong immunity against BSE and giving it to all cattle, destroying in due course all those animals for which the vaccine protection came too late

    (E) developing a diagnostic test that does identify any infected animal and destroying all animals found to be infected

5. Lucien: Public-housing advocates claim that the many homeless people in this city are proof that there is insufficient housing available to them and therefore that more low-income apartments are needed. But that conclusion is absurd. Many apartments in my own building remain unrented, and my professional colleagues report similar vacancies where they live. Since apartments clearly are available, homelessness is not a housing problem. Homelessness can, therefore, only be caused by people's inability or unwillingness to work to pay the rent.

Maria: On the contrary, all recent studies show that a significant percentage of this city's homeless people hold regular jobs. These are people who lack neither will nor ability.

Maria responds to Lucien's argument by

(A) challenging the accuracy of the personal experiences he offers in support of his position

(B) showing that a presupposition of his argument is false

(C) presenting evidence that calls into question his motives for adopting the view he holds

(D) demonstrating that the evidence he offers supports a conclusion other than the conclusion he draws from it

(E) offering an alternative explanation for the facts he cites as evidence supporting his conclusion

6. When a study of aspirin's ability to prevent heart attacks in humans yielded positive results, researchers immediately submitted those results to a medical journal, which published them six weeks later. Had the results been published sooner, many of the heart attacks that occurred during the delay could have been prevented.

The conclusion drawn above would be most undermined if it were true that

(A) the medical journal's staff worked overtime in order to publish the study's results as soon as possible

(B) studies of aspirin's usefulness in reducing heart attacks in laboratory animals remain inconclusive

(C) people who take aspirin regularly suffer a higher-than-average incidence of stomach ulcers

(D) the medical journal's official policy is to publish articles only after an extensive review process

(E) a person's risk of suffering a heart attack drops only after that person has taken aspirin regularly for two years

7. Slash and burn agriculture involves burning several acres of forest, leaving vegetable ash that provides ample fertilizer for three or four years of bountiful crops. On the cleared land nutrients leach out of the soil, however, and the land becomes too poor to support agriculture. New land is then cleared by burning and the process starts again. Since most farming in the tropics uses this method, forests in this region will eventually be permanently eradicated.

The argument depends on the assumption that

(A) forests in the tropics do not regenerate well enough to restore themselves once they have been cleared by the slash and burn method

(B) some other methods of agriculture are not as destructive to the environment in tropical regions as the slash and burn method is

(C) forests in the tropics are naturally deficient in nutrients that are needed to support the growth of plants that are not native to those regions

(D) slash and burn agriculture is particularly suit able for farming in tropical areas

(E) slash and burn agriculture produces a more bountiful crop than do other agriculture methods for the first year

8. Broadcaster: Our radio station has a responsibility to serve the public interest. Hence, when our critics contend that our recent exposé of events in the private lives of local celebrities was excessively intrusive, we can only reply that the overwhelming public interest in these matters makes it our responsibility to publicize them.

Which one of the following is a flaw in the broadcaster's defense of the radio station's practice?

(A) assuming without argument that there is a right to privacy

(B) ignoring grounds for criticism of the exposé aside from intrusion into people's private lives

(C) intentionally failing to specify what is meant by "excessively intrusive"

(D) confusing legal responsibility with moral obligation

(E) improperly exploiting an ambiguity in the phrase "public interest"

9. G: The group of works exhibited in this year's Metropolitan Art Show reveals a bias in favor of photographers. Equal numbers of photographers, sculptors, and painters submitted works that met the traditional criteria for the show, yet more photographs were exhibited than either sculptures or paintings. As you know, each artist was allowed to submit work in one medium only.

   H: How could there have been bias? All submitted works that met the traditional criteria—and only those works—were exhibited in the show.

Which one of the following, if true, most strongly supports G's allegation of bias?

(A) If an artist has had one of his or her works exhibited in the Metropolitan Art Show, that artist has an advantage in getting commissions and selling works over artists who have never had a work exhibited in the show.

(B) The fee for entering photographs in the Metropolitan Art Show was $25 per work submitted, while the fee for each painting or sculpture submitted was $75.

(C) The committee that selected from the submitted works the ones to be exhibited in this year's Metropolitan Art Show had four members: one photographer, one sculptor, one painter, and one who works in all three media but is the least known of the four members.

(D) Reviews of this year's Metropolitan Art Show that appeared in major newspapers and magazines tended to give more coverage to the photographs in the show than to the sculptures and paintings that were exhibited.

(E) In previous years, it has often happened that more paintings or more sculptures were exhibited in the Metropolitan Art Show than photographs, even though the total number of works exhibited each year does not vary widely.

10. The foreign minister of Zeria announced today that her country was severing diplomatic relations with Nandalo because of Nandalo's flagrant violations of human rights. But Zeria continues to maintain diplomatic relations with many countries that the minister knows to have far worse human-rights records than Nandalo does. Therefore, despite the foreign minister's claim, this latest diplomatic move cannot be explained exclusively by Zeria's commitment to upholding human rights.

The argumentative structure of which one of the following most closely parallels that of the argument in the passage?

(A) Henry's parents insist that he eat breakfast before leaving for school because not doing so would be bad for his health. But his parents themselves almost never eat breakfast, so their insistence cannot be completely explained by their concern for his health.

(B) Professor Walsh says that only typed term papers will be accepted because most handwriting is difficult to read. But since she lectures from handwritten notes, her policy cannot be exclusively explained by any difficulty she has with handwritten material.

(C) James claims that he stole only because he was hungry. But although hunger could account for stealing if food could not be readily obtained in any other way, in this case food was otherwise readily available, and so James's theft cannot be completely explained by his hunger.

(D) Armand declined Helen's invitation to dinner on the grounds that socializing with coworkers is imprudent. But since Armand went to a movie with another coworker, Maria, that same evening, his expressed concern for prudence cannot fully explain his refusal.

(E) It is often asserted that there are fewer good teachers than there used to be because teachers' salaries have reached a new low. But teachers have always been poorly paid, so low salaries cannot fully explain this perceived decline in the effectiveness of teachers.

11. Someone's benefiting from having done harm to another person is morally justifiable only if the person who was harmed knew that what was done could cause that harm but consented to its being done anyway.

    Which one of the following judgments most closely conforms to the principle above?

    (A) Attempting to avoid being kept after school as punishment for breaking a window, Sonia falsely claimed that her brother had broken it; Sonia's action was morally unjustifiable since it resulted in both children being kept after school for something only Sonia had done.

    (B) Since Ned would not have won the prize for best model airplane if Penny's brother had not inadvertently damaged her entry while playing with it, Ned is morally unjustified in accepting his prize.

    (C) Wesley, a doctor, persuaded Max to take part in a medical experiment in which a new drug was being tested; since Wesley failed to warn Max about the serious side effects of the drug, and the drug proved to have no other effects, Wesley was morally unjustified in using the results obtained from Max in his report.

    (D) Because Roger's mother suffered severe complications as a result of donating a kidney to him for a lifesaving kidney transplant, it was morally unjustifiable for Roger to receive the transplant, even though his mother, herself a doctor, had been eager for the transplant to be performed.

    (E) James, was convicted of having defrauded a large number of people out of their savings and wrote a book about his scheme while in prison. For James to be denied the profits from his book would be morally unjustifiable since he has already been punished for his crime.

12. For democracy to survive, it is imperative that the average citizen be able to develop informed opinions about important policy issues. In today's society, this means that citizens must be able to develop informed opinions on many scientific subjects, from ecosystems to defense systems. Yet, as scientific knowledge advances, the average citizen is increasingly unable to absorb enough information to develop informed opinions on many important issues.

    Of the following, which one follows logically from the passage?

    (A) Scientists have a duty to educate the public.

    (B) The survival of democracy is threatened by the advance of scientific knowledge.

    (C) Every citizen has a duty to and can become scientifically literate.

    (D) The most effective democracy is one that is the most scientifically unsophisticated.

    (E) Democracy will survive if there are at least some citizens who are capable of developing informed opinions on important scientific issues.

13. J. J. Thomson, the discoverer of the electron and a recipient of the Nobel Prize in physics, trained many physicists, among them seven Nobel Prize winners, 32 fellows of the Royal Society of London, and 83 professors of physics. This shows that the skills needed for creative research can be taught and learned.

Which one of the following is an assumption on which the argument depends?

(A) J. J. Thomson was an internationally known physicist, and scientists came from all over the world to work with him.

(B) All the scientists trained by J. J. Thomson were renowned for their creative scientific research.

(C) At least one of the eminent scientists trained by J. J. Thomson was not a creative researcher before coming to study with him.

(D) Creative research in physics requires research habits not necessary for creative research in other fields.

(E) Scientists who go on to be the most successful researchers often receive their scientific education in classes taught by renowned research scientists.

Set Two

1. Data from satellite photographs of the tropical rain forest in Melonia show that last year the deforestation rate of this environmentally sensitive zone was significantly lower than in previous years. The Melonian government, which spent millions of dollars last year to enforce laws against burning and cutting of the forest, is claiming that the satellite data indicates that its increased efforts to halt the destruction are proving effective.

Which one of the following, if true, most seriously undermines the government's claim?

(A) Landowner opposition to the government's antideforestation efforts grew more violent last year in response to the increased enforcement.

(B) Rainfall during the usually dry six-month annual burning season was abnormally heavy last year.

(C) Government agents had to issue fines totaling over $9 million to 3,500 violators of burning-and-cutting regulations.

(D) The inaccessibility of much of the rain forest has made it impossible to confirm the satellite data by direct observation from the field.

(E) Much of the money that was designated last year for forest preservation has been spent on research and not on enforcement.

2. High-technology medicine is driving up the nation's health care costs. Recent advances in cataract surgery illustrate why this is occurring. Cataracts are a major cause of blindness, especially in elderly people. Ten years ago, cataract surgery was painful and not always effective. Thanks to the new technology used in cataract surgery, the operation now restores vision dramatically and is less expensive. These two factors have caused the number of cataract operations performed to increase greatly, which has, in turn, driven up the total amount spent on cataract surgery.

Each of the following, if true, would support a challenge to the author's explanation of the increase in the number of cataract operations EXCEPT:

(A) The overall population of the nation has increased from what it was 10 years ago.

(B) Any one individual's chance of developing cataracts is greater than it was 10 years ago.

(C) The number of older people has increased during the last 10 years.

(D) Today, health insurance covers cataract surgery for more people than it did 10 years ago.

(E) People who have had unsuccessful cataract surgery are left with more seriously impaired vision than they had before the surgery.

3. People who accuse the postal service of incompetence and inefficiency while complaining of the proposed five-cent increase in postal rates do not know a bargain when they see one. Few experiences are more enjoyable than reading a personal letter from a friend. Viewed in this way, postal service is so underpriced that a five-cent increase is unworthy of serious debate.

The reasoning in the argument is flawed because the argument

(A) suggests that the postal service is both competent and efficient, but does not establish how competence and efficiency should be measured

(B) claims that the proposed increase is insignificant, but does not say at what level the increase would be worthy of serious debate

(C) confuses the value of the object delivered with the value of delivering that object

(D) appeals to an outside authority for support of a premise that should be established by argument

(E) fails to establish whether or not the critics of the postal service are employees of the postal service

4. Advertisement: Attention pond owners! Ninety-eight percent of mosquito larvae in a pond die within minutes after the pond has been treated with BTI. Yet BTI is not toxic to fish, birds, animals, plants, or beneficial insects. So by using BTI regularly to destroy their larvae, you can greatly reduce populations of pesky mosquitoes that hatch in your pond, and you can do so without diminishing the populations of fish, frogs, or beneficial insects in and around the pond.

Which one of the following is an assumption on which the argument depends?

(A) The most effective way to control the numbers of mosquitoes in a given area is to destroy the mosquito larvae in that area.

(B) Populations of mosquitoes are not dependent on a single body of water within an area as a place for their larvae to hatch and develop.

(C) There are no insect pests besides mosquitoes that pond owners might want to eliminate in and around their ponds.

(D) The effectiveness of BTI in destroying mosquito larvae in a pond does not require the pond owner's strict adherence to specific application procedures.

(E) The fish, frogs, and beneficial insects in and around a pond-owner's pond do not depend on mosquito larvae as an important source of food.

5. A survey of alumni of the class of 1960 at Aurora University yielded puzzling results. When asked to indicate their academic rank, half of the respondents reported that they were in the top quarter of the graduating class in 1960.

Which one of the following most helps account for the apparent contradiction above?

(A) A disproportionately large number of high-ranking alumni responded to the survey.

(B) Few, if any, respondents were mistaken about their class rank.

(C) Not all the alumni who were actually in the top quarter responded to the survey.

(D) Almost all of the alumni who graduated in 1960 responded to the survey.

(E) Academic rank at Aurora University was based on a number of considerations in addition to average grades.

6. Mayor of Plainsville: In order to help the economy of Plainsville, I am using some of our tax revenues to help bring a major highway through the town and thereby attract new business to Plainsville.

   Citizens' group: You must have interests other than our economy in mind. If you were really interested in helping our economy, you would instead allocate the revenues to building a new business park, since it would bring in twice the business that your highway would.

   Which one of the following principles, if accepted, would most help the citizens' group to justify drawing its conclusion that the mayor has in mind interests other than Plainsville's economy?

   (A) Anyone really pursuing a cause will choose the means that that person believes will advance the cause the furthest.

   (B) Any goal that includes helping the economy of a community will require public revenues in order to be achieved.

   (C) Anyone planning to use resources collected from a group must consult the members of the group before using the resources.

   (D) Any cause worth committing oneself to must include specific goals toward which one can work.

   (E) Any cause not pursued by public officials, if it is to be pursued at all, must be pursued by members of the community.

7. All students at Pitcombe College were asked to label themselves conservative, liberal, or middle-of-the-road politically. Of the students, 25 percent labeled themselves conservative, 24 percent labeled themselves liberal, and 51 percent labeled themselves middle-of-the-road. When asked about a particular set of issues, however, 77 percent of the students endorsed what is generally regarded as a liberal position.

   If all of the statements above are true, which one of the following must also be true?

   (A) All students who labeled themselves liberal endorsed what is generally regarded as a liberal position on that set of issues.

   (B) More students who labeled themselves middle-of-the-road than students who labeled themselves liberal opposed what is generally regarded as a liberal position on that set of issues.

   (C) The majority of students who labeled themselves middle-of-the-road opposed what is generally regarded as a liberal position on that set of issues.

   (D) Some students who labeled themselves conservative endorsed what is generally regarded as a liberal position on that set of issues.

   (E) Some students who labeled themselves liberal endorsed what is generally regarded as a conservative position on that set of issues.

KAPLAN

8. Criticism that the press panders to public sentiment neglects to consider that the press is a profit-making institution. Like other private enterprises, it has to make money to survive. If the press were not profit-making, who would support it? The only alternative is subsidy and, with it, outside control. It is easy to get subsidies for propaganda, but no one will subsidize honest journalism.

    It can be properly inferred from the passage that if the press is

    (A) not subsidized, it is in no danger of outside control

    (B) not subsidized, it will not produce propaganda

    (C) not to be subsidized, it cannot be a profit-making institution

    (D) to produce honest journalism, it must be a profit-making institution

    (E) to make a profit, it must produce honest journalism

9. Crimes in which handguns are used are more likely than other crimes to result in fatalities. However, the majority of crimes in which handguns are used do not result in fatalities. Therefore, there is no need to enact laws that address crimes involving handguns as distinct from other crimes.

    The pattern of flawed reasoning displayed in the argument above most closely resembles that in which one of the following?

    (A) Overweight people are at higher risk of developing heart disease than other people. However, more than half of all overweight people never develop heart disease. Hence it is unnecessary for physicians to be more careful to emphasize the danger of heart disease to their overweight patients than to their other patients.

    (B) Many people swim daily in order to stay physically fit. Yet people who swim daily increase their risk of developing ear infections. Hence people who want to remain in good health are better off not following fitness programs that include swimming daily.

    (C) Most physicians recommend a balanced diet for those who want to remain in good health. Yet many people find that nontraditional dietary regimens such as extended fasting do their health no serious harm. Therefore, there is no need for everyone to avoid nontraditional dietary regimens.

    (D) Foods rich in cholesterol and fat pose a serious health threat to most people. However, many people are reluctant to give up eating foods that they greatly enjoy. Therefore, people who refuse to give up rich foods need to spend more time exercising than do other people.

    (E) Many serious health problems are the result of dietary disorders. Yet these disorders are often brought about by psychological factors. Hence people suffering from serious health problems should undergo psychological evaluation

10. Infants younger than six months who have normal hearing can readily distinguish between acoustically similar sounds that are used as part of any language—not only those used in the language spoken by the people who raise them. Young adults can readily distinguish between such sounds only in languages that they regularly use. It is known that the physiological capacity to hear begins to deteriorate after infancy. So the observed difference in the abilities of infants and young adults to distinguish between acoustically similar speech sounds must be the result of the physiological deterioration of hearing.

The reasoning in the argument is flawed because the argument

(A) sets an arbitrary cutoff point of six months for the age below which infants are able to distinguish acoustically similar speech sounds

(B) does not explain the procedures used to measure the abilities of two very different populations

(C) ignores the fact that certain types of speech sounds occur in almost all languages

(D) assumes that what is true of a group of people taken collectively is also true of any individual within that group

(E) takes a factor that might contribute to an explanation of the observed difference as a sufficient explanation for that difference

11. English and the Austronesian language Mbarbaram both use the word *dog* for canines. These two languages are unrelated, and since speakers of the two languages only came in contact with one another long after the word *dog* was first used in either language, neither language could have borrowed the word from the other. Thus, this case shows that sometimes when languages share words that are similar in sound and meaning, the similarity is due neither to language relatedness nor to borrowing.

The argument requires that which one of the following be assumed?

(A) English and Mbarbaram share no words other than *dog*.

(B) Several languages besides English and Mbarbaram use *dog* as the word for canines.

(C) Usually when two languages share a word, those languages are related to each other.

(D) There is no third language from which both English and Mbarbaram borrowed the word *dog*.

(E) If two unrelated languages share a word, speakers of those two languages must have come in contact with one another at some time.

12. Using clean-coal technologies to "repower" existing factories promises ultimately a substantial reduction of polluting emissions and will affect the full range of pollutants implicated in acid rain. The strategy of using these technologies could cut sulfur dioxide emissions by more than 80 percent and nitrogen oxide emissions by more than 50 percent. The emission of a smaller quantity of nitrogen pollutants would in turn reduce the formation of noxious ozone in the troposphere.

    Which one of the following statements is an inference that can be drawn from the information given in the passage?

    (A) Sulfur dioxide emissions are the most dan gerous pollutants implicated in acid rain.

    (B) Noxious ozone is formed in factories by chemical reactions involving sulfur dioxide.

    (C) Twenty percent of the present level of sulfur dioxide emissions in the atmosphere is not considered a harmful level.

    (D) A substantial reduction of polluting emissions will be achieved by the careful design of new factories.

    (E) The choice of technologies in factories could reduce the formation of noxious ozone in the troposphere.

13. Older U.S. automobiles have been identified as contributing disproportionately to global air pollution. The requirement in many jurisdictions that automobiles pass emission-control inspections has had the effect of taking many such automobiles out of service in the United States, as they fail inspection and their owners opt to buy newer automobiles. Thus, the burden of pollution such older U.S. automobiles contribute to the global atmosphere will be gradually reduced over the next decade.

    Which one of the following, if true, most seriously weakens the argument?

    (A) It is impossible to separate the air of one country or jurisdiction from that of others, since air currents circle the globe.

    (B) When automobiles that are now new become older, they will, because of a design change, cause less air pollution than older automobiles do now.

    (C) There is a thriving market for used older U.S. automobiles that are exported to regions that have no emission-control regulations.

    (D) The number of jurisdictions in the United States requiring automobiles to pass emission-control inspections is no longer increasing.

    (E) Even if all the older automobiles in the United States were retired from service, air pollution from U.S. automobiles could still increase if the total number of automobiles in use should increase significantly.

Set Three

1. Until he was dismissed amid great controversy, Hastings was considered one of the greatest intelligence agents of all time. It is clear that if his dismissal was justified, then Hastings was either incompetent or else disloyal. Soon after the dismissal, however, it was shown that he had never been incompetent. Thus, one is forced to conclude that Hastings must have been disloyal.

   Which one of the following states an assumption upon which the argument depends?

   (A) Hastings's dismissal was justified.

   (B) Hastings was a high-ranking intelligence offcer.

   (C) The dismissal of anyone who was disloyal would be justified.

   (D) Anyone whose dismissal was justified was disloyal.

   (E) If someone was disloyal or incompetent, then his dismissal was justified.

2. Four randomly chosen market research companies each produced population estimates for three middle-sized cities; the estimates of each company were then compared with those of the other companies. Two of the cities had relatively stable populations; and for them, estimates of current population and of projected population in five years varied little from company to company. However, for the third city, which was growing rapidly, estimates varied greatly from company to company.

   The passage provides the most support for which one of the following?

   (A) It is more difficult to estimate the population of middle-sized cities than of smaller cities.

   (B) Population estimates for rapidly growing cities can be accurate enough to be useful for marketing.

   (C) The rate of change in population of rapidly growing cities does not fluctuate.

   (D) The market research companies are likely to be equally reliable in estimating the population of stable cities.

   (E) Estimates of a city's future population are likely to be more accurate than are estimates of that city's current population.

3. When the economy is in a recession, overall demand for goods and services is low. If overall demand for goods and services is low, bank interest rates are also low. Therefore, if bank interest rates are not low, the economy is not in a recession.

   In which one of the following does the reasoning most closely parallel the reasoning in the argument above?

   (A) If the restaurant is full, the parking lot will be full, and if the parking lot is full, the restaurant is full; so if the parking lot is not full, the restaurant is not full.

   (B) If the fish is ready, it is cooked all the way through, and if it is cooked through it will be white; so if the fish is not white, it is not ready.

   (C) If pterodactyls flew by flapping their wings, they must have been warm-blooded; so if they were cold-blooded, they must have flown only by gliding, if they flew at all.

   (D) If you want to put in pleats, you will have to double the amount of material for the skirt, and that means you will have none left for the top; so if you put in pleats, you will not be able to make the top.

   (E) If economic forecasters are right, there will be inflation, and if there is inflation, the governing party will lose the election; so if it does lose the election, the economic forecasters were right.

4. Naturalist: For decades we have known that the tuatara, a New Zealand reptile, have been approaching extinction on the South Island. But since South Island tuatara, were thought to be of the same species as North Island tuatara, there was no need to protect them. But new research indicates that the South Island tuatara are a distinct species, found only in that location. Because it is now known that if the South Island tuatara are lost an entire species will thereby be lost, human beings are now obliged to prevent their extinction, even if it means killing many of their unendangered natural predators.

   Which one of the following principles most helps to justify the naturalist's argumentation?

   (A) In order to maximize the number of living things on Earth, steps should be taken to preserve all local populations of animals.

   (B) When an animal is in danger of dying, there is an obligation to help save its life, if doing so would not interfere with the health or well-being of other animals or people.

   (C) The threat of local extinction imposes no obligation to try to prevent that extinction, whereas the threat of global extinction does impose such an obligation.

   (D) Human activities that either intentionally or unintentionally threaten the survival of an animal species ought to be curtailed.

   (E) Species that are found in only one circumscribed geographical region ought to be given more care and attention than other species, because they are more vulnerable to extinction.

5. Animals with a certain behavioral disorder have unusually high levels of aluminum in their brain tissue. Since a silicon-based compound binds to aluminum and prevents it from affecting the brain tissue, animals can be cured of the disorder by being treated with the compound.

    The argument is based on which one of the following assumptions?

    (A) Animals with the disorder have unusually high but invariable levels of aluminum in their brain tissue.

    (B) Aluminum is the cause of the disorder rather than merely an effect of it.

    (C) Introducing the compound into the brain tissue has no side effects.

    (D) The amount of the compound needed to neutralize the aluminum in an animal's brain tissue varies depending upon the species.

    (E) Aluminum is never present in normal brain tissue.

6. Recently, highly skilled workers in Eastern Europe have left jobs in record numbers to emigrate to the West. It is therefore likely that skilled workers who remain in Eastern Europe are in high demand in their home countries.

    Which one of the following, if true, most seriously weakens the argument?

    (A) Eastern European factories prefer to hire workers from their home countries rather than to import workers from abroad.

    (B) Major changes in Eastern European economic structures have led to the elimination of many positions previously held by the highly skilled emigrants.

    (C) Many Eastern European emigrants need to acquire new skills after finding work in the West.

    (D) Eastern European countries plan to train many new workers to replace the highly skilled workers who have emigrated.

    (E) Because of the departure of skilled workers from Eastern European countries, many positions are now unfilled.

7. Waste management companies, which collect waste for disposal in landfills and incineration plants, report that disposable plastics make up an ever-increasing percentage of the waste they handle. It is clear that attempts to decrease the amount of plastic that people throw away in the garbage are failing.

    Which one of the following, if true, most seriously weakens the argument?

    (A) Because plastics create harmful pollutants when burned, an increasing percentage of the plastics handled by waste management companies are being disposed of in landfills.

    (B) Although many plastics are recyclable, most of the plastics disposed of by waste management companies are not.

    (C) People are more likely to save and reuse plastic containers than containers made of heavier materials like glass or metal.

    (D) An increasing proportion of the paper, glass, and metal cans that waste management companies used to handle is now being recycled.

    (E) While the percentage of products using plastic packaging is increasing, the total amount of plastic being manufactured has remained unchanged.

8. College professor: College students do not write nearly as well as they used to. Almost all of the papers that my students have done for me this year have been poorly written and ungrammatical.

    Which one of the following is the most serious weakness in the argument made by the professor?

    (A) It requires confirmation that the change in the professor's students is representative of a change among college students in general.

    (B) It offers no proof to the effect that the professor is an accurate judge of writing ability.

    (C) It does not take into account the possibility that the professor is a poor teacher.

    (D) It fails to present contrary evidence.

    (E) It fails to define its terms sufficiently.

9. Roses always provide a stunning display of color, but only those flowers that smell sweet are worth growing in a garden. Some roses have no scent.

    Which one the following conclusions can be properly drawn from the passage?

    (A) Some flowers which provide a stunning display of color are not worth growing in a garden.

    (B) All flowers with no scent provide a stunning display of color.

    (C) Some flowers which are worth growing in a garden have no scent.

    (D) Some roses which smell sweet are not worth growing in a garden.

    (E) No sweet-smelling flower is worth growing in a garden unless it provides a stunning display of color.

10. No one knows what purposes, if any, dreams serve, although there are a number of hypotheses. According to one hypothesis, dreams are produced when the brain is erasing "parasitic connections" (meaningless, accidental associations between ideas), which accumulate during the day and which would otherwise clog up our memories. Interestingly, the only mammal that does not have rapid eye movement sleep, in which we humans typically have our most vivid dreams, is the spiny anteater, which has been seen as anomalous in that it has a very large brain relative to the animal's size. This fact provides some confirmation for the parasitic connection hypothesis, since the hypothesis predicts that for an animal that did not dream to have an effective memory, that animal would need extra memory, space for the parasitic connections.

    The parasitic connection hypothesis, if true, most strongly supports which one of the following?

    (A) The animals with the smallest brains spend the most time sleeping.

    (B) Immediately after a person awakens from normal sleep, her or his memory contains virtually no accidental associations between ideas.

    (C) When a mammal that would normally dream is prevented from dreaming, the functioning of its memory will be impaired.

    (D) Insofar as a person's description of a dream involves meaningful associations between ideas, it is an inaccurate description.

    (E) All animals other than the spiny anteater dream.

11. Purebred dogs are prone to genetically determined abnormalities. Although such abnormalities can often be corrected by surgery, the cost can reach several thousand dollars. Since nonpurebred dogs rarely suffer from genetically determined abnormalities, potential dog owners who want to reduce the risk of incurring costly medical bills for their pets would be well advised to choose nonpurebred dogs.

    Which one of the following, if true, most seriously weakens the argument?

    (A) Most genetically determined abnormalities in dogs do not seriously affect a dog's general well-being.

    (B) All dogs, whether purebred or nonpurebred, are subject to the same common nongenetically determined diseases.

    (C) Purebred dogs tend to have shorter natural life spans than do nonpurebred dogs.

    (D) The purchase price of nonpurebred dogs tends to be lower than the purchase price of purebred dogs.

    (E) A dog that does not have genetically determined abnormalities may nevertheless have offspring with such abnormalities.

12. When butterfat was considered nutritious and healthful, a law was enacted requiring that manufacturers use the term "imitation butter" to indicate butter whose butterfat content had been diminished through the addition of water. Today, it is known that the high cholesterol content of butterfat makes it harmful to human health. Since the public should be encouraged to eat foods with lower rather than higher butterfat content, and since the term "imitation" with its connotations of falsity deters many people from purchasing products so designated, manufacturers who wish to give reduced-butterfat butter the more appealing name of "lite butter" should be allowed to do so.

    Which one of the following, if true, most seriously undermines the argument?

    (A) The manufacturers who prefer to use the word "lite" instead of "imitation" are motivated principally by the financial interest of their stockholders.

    (B) The manufacturers who wish to call their product "lite butter" plan to change the composition of the product so that it contains more water than it now does.

    (C) Some individuals who need to reduce their intake of cholesterol are not deterred from using the reduced-butterfat product by the negative connotations of the term "imitation."

    (D) Cholesterol is only one of many factors that contribute to the types of health problems with which the consumption of excessive amounts of cholesterol is often associated.

    (E) Most people deterred from eating "imitation butter" because of its name choose alternatives with a lower butterfat content than this product has.

13. Approximately 7.6 million women who earn incomes have preschool-age children, and approximately 6.4 million women are the sole income earners for their families. These figures indicate that there are comparatively few income-earning women who have preschool-age children but are not the sole income earners for their families.

A major flaw in the reasoning is that it

(A) relies on figures that are too imprecise to support the conclusion drawn

(B) overlooks the possibility that there is little or no overlap between the two populations of women cited

(C) fails to indicate whether the difference between the two figures cited will tend to remain stable over time

(D) ignores the possibility that families with preschool-age children might also have older children

(E) provides no information on families in which men are the sole income earners

ANSWERS AND EXPLANATIONS

Set One	11. C	8. D	5. B
1. B	12. B	9. A	6. B
2. B	13. C	10. E	7. D
3. C		11. D	8. A
4. A	Set Two	12. E	9. A
5. B	1. B	13 C	10. C
6. E	2. E		11. A
7. A	3. C	Set Three	12. E
8. E	4. E	1. A	13. B
9. B	5. A	2. D	
10. D	6. A	3. B	
	7. D	4. C	

Diagnostic Tool

Tally up your score and write down your results below.

Total Correct: _____ out of 39

Percentage Correct: # you got right x 100 ÷ 39: _____

Diagnose Your Results

Look back at the questions you got wrong and think back on your experience answering them.

Step 1: Find the Road Blocks

Some questions you struggled to answer. To improve your score, you need to pinpoint exactly what element of these "road blocks" tripped you up. To do that, ask yourself these two questions:

Am I weak in the skills being tested?

Logical Reasoning questions test your skills in evaluating arguments and formulating or assessing a plan of action. Were you unable to identify the various components of any given argument, or digest the dense language? If so, you need more practice with complex reasoning skills. The Kaplan Logical Reasoning principles and methods in this book can help you focus on and develop the specific skills you need to work through these questions thoroughly, quickly, and strategically.

Was it the question type that threw me off?

Then you need to become more comfortable with it! Go back to the beginning of this chapter and review the Kaplan principles and methods. Make sure you understand them, and know how to apply them. These strategies help to improve your speed and efficiency on Test Day. You also need to be very familiar with the nine Logical Reasoning question types. Finally, get as much practice as you can so you grow more at ease with this question type.

Step 2: Find the Blind Spots

Some questions you answered quickly and confidently, but got them wrong anyway! When you come across wrong answers like these, you need to figure out what you thought you were doing right, what it turns out you were doing wrong, and why that happened! The best way to do that is to **read the answer explanations!**

They give you a detailed breakdown of why the correct answer is correct, and why all the other answer choices are wrong. This helps to reinforce the Kaplan principles and methods for each question type, and helps you figure out what blindsided you so it doesn't happen again. Also, just like with your Road Blocks, try to get in as much practice as you can.

Step 3: Reinforce Your Strengths

Read through all the answer explanations for the ones you got right. Again, this helps to reinforce the Kaplan principles and methods for each question type, which in turn helps you work more efficiently so you can get the score you want. Now keep your skills sharp with more practice.

As soon as you are comfortable with all the LSAT question types and Kaplan methods, complete a full-length practice test under timed conditions. In this way, practice tests serve as milestones; they help you to chart your progress! So don't save them all for the final weeks.

If you are aiming for that top score, TRY OUT the *LSAT 180*, Kaplan's advanced workbook that includes only the toughest LSAT questions and most focused strategies.

You can also visit Kaptest.com/LSAT for more details on Kaplan's online and classroom-based options, like LSAT Advanced, LSAT Extreme, and LSAT Crash courses. Kaplan uses real LSAT questions, so you get the most comprehensive, test-like experience.

Set One

1. B

In arguing that educational television is not educational, the author contrasts television with the activity found in a classroom: Since television isn't like school, it's therefore not educational. The argument therefore assumes that a schoollike environment is a prerequisite for educational value. (A) is wrong: The author doesn't suggest that fun in the classroom is inappropriate. In fact, by referring to fun as a "means to an end," the author hints that fun may, in some way, belong in the classroom. (C) is inconsistent; the foundation of the argument is that television lacks a common ground with school. (D) is beyond the scope of the argument. The only television programming discussed in the argument is educational TV. With (E), the author argues that television is not an educational medium. That TV might be a "powerful learning tool" hardly seems consistent with this theme.

2. B

The key phrase is "if the Association wants a mayor who will attract more business," which implies that it's not a foregone conclusion that the Association wants that at all. The argument boils down to "if they want a specific thing, then Cooper is the only viable candidate, and since they're supporting Cooper, then they must in fact want this specific thing." It's altogether possible, based on the wording of the argument, that the Association does not want a mayor who attracts more business, that they're supporting Cooper for other reasons—in which case this circular kind of reasoning falls flat. In flaw questions, as you evaluate the argument, ask yourself, "Assuming that all the premises are true, is this the only conclusion that one could reach?" If the answer is no, look for a choice that deals with the ambiguity.

(A) and (D) confuse the point of the argument, which seeks to explain why the Association supports a candidate, not the reasoning behind its goals or what's in the best interest of its members down the road. (C) goes beyond the scope of the argument. We're only concerned with the Homeowners Association, not with other groups. With (E), if the Association does in fact support Cooper for the reasons given, then this choice addresses a possible flaw in their decision. However, (E) doesn't address the overriding flaw in the argument's structure, and that's the possibility stated in correct choice (B).

3. C

The structure couldn't be laid out more clearly: High-tech medicine is driving costs up (conclusion); the cataract example "illustrate[s] why" (evidence). The example goes on to indicate that now that technology has made the surgery easier and cheaper, more and more people are having it done, thus driving up the total cost. "Hang on a second, back up," you might have said to yourself. "Didn't the author just say that cataract surgery is cheaper now?" Indeed he did, and yet he concludes that total costs are up. It has to be true, then, as (C) says, that whatever money is saved due to the lower price of the procedure is offset by the increased number of patients opting for the surgery.

(A) is wrong; that the surgery was "not always effective" 10 years ago is a far cry from saying that "few" surgeries were effective. For all we know, there were still many effective surgeries back then, even though the surgery is more effective today. (B)'s scope is the future—what is "likely to" happen in the long run—but that cannot be inferred from this argument set in the past and present. In (D), we are explicitly told that what is driving up costs is the elderly's demand for surgery. Cataract surgery—admittedly an ailment of the elderly—is used as an example, not identified as the main culprit. (E) seems to run counter to the fifth sentence: The passage explicitly indicates that the surgery is cheaper now, which strongly suggests that it's more affordable now than it was 10 years ago.

4. A

Read the fragment of the final sentence carefully: The correct choice must describe a program that won't work. Well, if BSE can be transmitted from cow to cow at any and all stages of the disease, then diseased cows without visible symptoms could be passing BSE around unnoticed. And there'd be no way to identify those cows, since no diagnostic test can identify cows with BSE but without symptoms. Our search for the nonsolution doesn't last long, because (A) is it. Removing and destroying cows that actually showed symptoms wouldn't control the disease: Sick cows would already have been passing along the disease before they showed symptoms. So (A)'s plan would not fell the disease.

If you gave (B)'s drug to a cow, it would have no disease-bearing agent to spread to other cows, and the disease couldn't spread. So if you treated all cattle that might have the disease, you could eradicate it. (C) would work like a charm: All the cows that could possibly be carrying the disease would be eliminated. Sad for the cows, but good for eliminating BSE. (D), which would immunize the healthy animals and kill off the diseased ones, would have a solid shot at eradicating BSE. With (E), a diagnostic test that could identify the diseased animals right from the start would solve the problem: All diseased animals could be eliminated before they transmitted the disease. Result? No more BSE.

5. B

Now we have to describe Maria's method of argument; she pointed out that many homeless people work and therefore don't lack the will or ability to do so. As (B) says, her comment demonstrates that a presupposition of Lucien's argument is false. A presupposition is a just a fancy word for an assumption, and in order for Lucien to conclude that homelessness is caused by people's unwillingness or inability to work, he must assume, of course, that the homeless don't work. After all, if he assumed that they did work, he'd have to conclude that homelessness was caused by something else—say, by a shortage of housing that the homeless could afford.

It's pretty clear that Maria's response isn't intended to challenge the accuracy of Lucien's personal experiences, as (A) says. Although his use of anecdotal evidence is another possible weakness in his argument, she doesn't address it. And her evidence doesn't bring up the issue of his motives, so (C) is out. Regarding (D), Maria doesn't point out that Lucien's evidence—his claim that there are many vacant apartments—should lead to a different conclusion; in fact, she never deals with his evidence at all. And as for (E), it's hard to see how her evidence that many homeless have jobs could be interpreted as an alternative explanation for his evidence about vacant apartments. Again, she doesn't address his evidence; she undermines his assumption with her own evidence.

6. E

We need to weaken this argument, and here we'll take the tactic of undermining the conclusion by providing alternative evidence. The author claims that if results concerning a study on heart attacks had been published sooner, then heart attacks that occurred during the delay might have been prevented. We can weaken this conclusion by finding evidence that shows that taking aspirin could not have made a difference during the period in question. (E) does this by explaining that it takes two years for aspirin to have an effect on a patient's risk of heart attack. Thus, heart attacks that took place during this period could not have been prevented by the use of aspirin during the delay period.

(A) has no effect on the conclusion—no matter how hard the staff worked, the assertion that the heart attacks in question could have been prevented is unaffected. (B)'s lab animals, meanwhile, are outside the scope of the argument, so the questionable effect of aspirin on heart attacks in such animals does not affect the logic. Stomach ulcers, (C), are also outside the scope, since they wouldn't necessarily have an effect on those patients who had heart attacks during the delay. (D) is only relevant as an explanation of the reason for the delay.

7. A

If tropical forests do regenerate after they have been subjected to slash and burn, it would be possible that while farmers move from one section of land to another, previously cleared land would ultimately grow back with forest vegetation. This directly conflicts with the conclusion that the forests would be permanently eradicated, so it must be assumed that the forests cannot regenerate well enough to offset slash and burn.

(B) is wrong; at no point does the argument hint at the possibility that another agricultural method would have a more positive—or negative—impact on tropical regions. (C) cannot be a necessary assumption as the growth of foreign plants has no bearing on the argument. With (D) and (E), the author doesn't judge the utility of slash and burn—she's concerned only with the effect that method has on the environment, not its usefulness with respect to farming.

8. E

The radio broadcaster claims that a responsibility to the "public interest" justifies the intrusions into the private lives of celebrities. When the broadcaster speaks of "public interest" in this way, he or she is talking about "serving the public welfare or betterment. However, the broadcaster then goes on to use the term "interest" as in the context of "the public is interested/curious in this matter." The broadcaster's fallacy is in using the term "public interest" in two different ways.

(A) is quite the contrary; the broadcaster actually implies that when the public is interested in a matter, no such right exists. With (B), there's no logical flaw committed by disregarding other grounds for criticism of the exposé. The

argument centers on the invasion of privacy issue; the flaw is in the manner of the broadcaster's defense, not that he or she ignored other issues. With (C), defining the term "excessively intrusive" isn't necessary to the broadcaster's argument. The term belongs to the critics, and the broadcaster was merely repeating it. With (D), in that legality is not discussed and morality is only vaguely hinted at in the critics' argument, there's no confusion of these types of responsibilities and obligations.

9. B

Generally, to strengthen an argument, we want to look for an additional piece of evidence that shores up a key assumption. (B) seems like a clear show of bias since, if it's cheaper to enter a photo in the contest than to enter a painting or a sculpture, a photographer could afford to submit many more entries into the show than a painter or sculptor could. (A) is way off, since it doesn't make any distinction between the different types of artists exhibiting, which is the crux of G's allegation of bias. Even if the committee mentioned in (C) had been stacked with photographers, (C) would be a dubious choice—answer choices impugning people's motives tend to be wrong answers—but the membership (C) actually describes is so inconclusive (in terms of which media predominates) that the choice shouldn't have tempted you much. (D) goes even further astray, having to do with the possible bias of the art show's critics rather than its governing board. And (E)'s art shows from previous years are beyond the scope of the argument between G and H, which is only about what happened this year.

10. D

We can generalize the structure of the argument as: Someone took action A (severing diplomatic relations with Nandalo) in opposition to B (Nandalo's human rights violations). However, action A has not been taken in other cases when B is present. Therefore, opposition to B can't be the full reason that person took action A. (D) follows this same structure: Armand took action A (declined invitation to dinner) in opposition to B (socializing with coworkers). However, he didn't avoid socializing with coworkers when he went to a movie with Maria. The conclusion is that there must be some additional explanation, other than hangups about fraternizing with coworkers, that explains his blowing off Helen's invitation.

With (A), Henry's parents advocate action by one person for that person's benefit while not pursuing the same action themselves. Although a double standard, their reasoning can nevertheless be reconciled with their differing actions—their insistence could be motivated solely by a concern for his health, even if they don't take their own advice. (In rhetoric we call this a tu quoque—"you do it too"—response. You didn't have to know the Latin name, but if you recognized that that's not what's going on in the original, you could have thrown (A) out on that basis.) With (B), Professor Walsh's statement is obviously referring to the handwriting of her students; it's not inconsistent that she would nevertheless rely on her own handwriting for lectures, and no additional explanation is needed. With (C), James's reasoning is inconsistent with other facts. However, it's not parallel since it doesn't show any hypocrisy in James's actions in regard to different circumstances. (E) focuses on the reasoning behind a general proposition rather than an individual's actions, so it can't be parallel.

11. C

We're given a principle of conduct and asked for the real-life scenario that best matches up to it. The issue is: "When is it morally justifiable to benefit from harming someone else?" And the principle cites a two-part necessary condition, signaled as usual by "only if": the victim's awareness that the behavior could be harmful and his/her consent. We must see that in the absence of such awareness and/or consent, the benefits accruing from the harm will not be morally justified. Having done that analysis, we can then proceed with confidence to the choices and see how they stack up:

(A) ignores the issue of awareness and consent, focusing instead on issues (false statements, preventing harm) that the principle never mentions. Besides, Sonia attempts to benefit, but does not—she gets stuck in detention anyway—so the morality test doesn't apply here; no one benefits from harming another. (B) brings in the concept of accidental behavior and again ignores the awareness and consent issues. With (C), Max lacked awareness of the potential harm of the experimental drug. Thus, a necessary condition for the moral justification in Wesley's using the results is lacking. He harmed Max without informing Max of the risks. Thus, according to the principle, it is not morally justifiable for Wesley to benefit from the harm he inflicted on Max, and so the judgment in (C) is right on the money. But for the record, let's examine the remaining choices: With

(D), Roger's mother consented to the operation, and the wording seems to suggest that, as a doctor, she'd be aware of the risks. Since this situation meets the two criteria for moral justification, we cannot use the principle at hand to conclude that Roger was morally wrong to benefit from the transplant. (E) argues that taking the profits from James is unjustifiable, but that can't be correct here: James is the one trying to benefit from having done harm, and the principle in the stimulus certainly wouldn't support that in this case (who, after all, consents to being defrauded?). Denying James the profits would be in line with the principle in the stimulus, but (E) says that denying James is unjustifiable, which conflicts with the principle.

12. B

When a condition necessary for a result does not occur, the result cannot occur. This principle is at the heart of most Logical Reasoning questions that hinge on necessity. "... It is imperative that ... ," "must be able to ... ," "is ... unable to ... ": Phrases like these signal that the author's main interest is in necessary conditions—conditions that are required for some result to occur. Sentence 1 says that a necessary condition of democracy's survival is the average citizen's informed opinions, and sentence 2 narrows that to focus on opinions about science. Sentence 3 comes along to assert that in the face of today's scientific developments, the average Joe or Jane cannot absorb enough info to hold such informed opinions. But as we've already seen, without such opinions, democracy can't survive; so it has to be true, as (B) has it, that today's scientific developments threaten democracy.

(A) fails because the author never mentions scientists, so we cannot infer from her remarks that they have the responsibility to attack the problem. For all we know, other groups such as science writers or educators can help the public form meaningful scientific opinions. (C) isn't correct because democracy's survival requires that the average Joe or Jane, not that *every* Joe or Jane, hold informed opinions on science. Also, the phrase "scientifically literate" isn't used in the stimulus, so we can't be sure that it applies. (D) is a classic extreme choice. The stimulus implies that extremely advanced scientific knowledge threatens democracy, not, as (D) would have it, that any scientific knowledge is bad for democracy. The notion that science may be getting a little difficult for the average citizen to comprehend doesn't lead to the notion that the least scientific knowledge would yield the best democracy. (E) tests necessity/sufficiency confusion in a classic way. Citizens having informed opinions on science are necessary for democracy's survival, but aren't necessarily sufficient for it. In other words, democracy could be destroyed (for other reasons) even if every single citizen becomes scientifically informed and opinionated.

13. C

The conclusion is that the skills needed for creative research are teachable and learnable, but not a single word in the evidence directly mentions skills or creative research. All we're told is that Thomson taught tons of physicists of great distinction, so two key assumptions are at work here. First, the author must assume that Thomson's distinguished students do, in fact, have creative research skills—but this isn't listed as an answer choice. Second, she must assume that at least some of those distinguished students lacked creative research skills before they met up with Thomson. After all, if they were all creative researchers beforehand, then Thomson's influence wouldn't support the conclusion, would it? That second assumption is found in (C).

With (A), the argument could work even if (A) were false even if Thomson were relatively unknown and all his students came out of his own home—town. Thus, the Kaplan Denial Test proves that (A) isn't a necessary assumption. (B) needn't be assumed, because even if Thomson taught some people who were never recognized for any accomplishment, the author still has the eminent students to support her argument. With (D), "other fields" have no role in this argument. (D) raises an unwarranted comparison between other fields and physics, and the validity of the argument does not depend on any such comparison. (E) isn't a necessary assumption either, because Thomson's successful students may be rare exceptions. The author's point is that creative research skills can be taught, and the possibility that few successful researchers are taught by renowned scholars doesn't hinder that argument.

Set Two

1. B

The best way to weaken an argument is either to undermine a central assumption or to provide an alternative explanation for the conclusion. This question is a classic example of the latter strategy. We're told that deforestation

in Melonia was significantly lower this year than in other years—and reliable proof is offered in the form of satellite photographs. The government of Melonia (land of melon?), having spent lots of money to enforce antideforestation laws, is quick to take credit for the drop in forest destruction.

How can we weaken the government's claim? Look for an alternative explanation, like (B). If it's true that the rainfall during burning season was abnormally heavy, then it's possible that the drop in deforestation had nothing to do with the government—it had to do with the rainfall instead. If this were the case, the government's claim would be substantially weakened. (A) tries to show that people protested the government's efforts, but since we don't even know that the government's plan was effective, proof of opposition doesn't help. (C) is beyond the scope, since we have no idea if the number cited was a large or a small number of violations or what effect this would have on the deforestation rate. (D) would weaken the idea that deforestation dropped significantly this year by undermining the proof, the photographs, but that's not what we need to do—we need to weaken the government's claim. (E) is out as well, since the author says that the government spent millions of dollars enforcing the laws. We don't care about how much money was spent in other areas, since it won't touch the government's claim about the cause of the drop in deforestation.

2. E

Four of the choices weaken the explanation of why so many more people are having their cataracts done; therefore the right answer must either strengthen it or be outside the scope. And remember what that explanation is: They're going for the surgery, says our author, because the technology makes it less painful, more successful, and cheaper. There's really no way to prephrase here—we simply have to check the choices, looking for the one that either strengthens the argument or is irrelevant to it.

(A) asserts that there are more people now. More people could lead, in general, to more people needing or wanting surgery, which on its face could explain the increase.

(B) strongly suggests that the prevalence of the disease may have increased. An increased need for cataract surgery would certainly explain an increase in its incidence.

(C) asserts that there are more elderly now, and the author admits that elderly people are prone to cataracts. As with (A), this change in the demographics would suggest another reason besides improved technology for the increase in surgeries.

(D) The fact that more people don't have to pay for the procedure could also reasonably account for an increased number of people opting for it. This, would therefore challenge the author's argument that the increase in cataract operations is due to the benefits conferred by the new technology.

(E) is too vague to challenge the author's explanation. Are these unlucky patients victims of the new technology or the old? We simply don't know. Since (E) doesn't differentiate between unsuccessful surgery then and now, and doesn't even tell us what percentage of surgeries fail, we have to consider the consequences of unsuccessful surgery in general to be irrelevant to the specific line of reasoning here. (E) is therefore the one we want.

3. C

The flaw should have leaped right out at you—the author is comparing apples and oranges. People shouldn't complain about the supposed incompetence and inefficiency of the post office, he says, since a letter from a friend is such a valuable object. Huh? What has the joy of receiving a letter to do with crummy service? The author wants us to accept without question a rate increase because getting a letter is worth the money, but as (C) says, the author is confusing the value of the process of delivery with the value of the actual letter being delivered, and this is the egregious mistake.

(A) wants us to think that the author believes the postal service is competent and efficient, but this just isn't so. He merely suggests that we should overlook such faults, since the object received is so valuable—he never asserts that the service is exemplary. As for (B), the level of the increase is immaterial here, since the flaw resides in the confusion of the service with the object in question. We don't need to know what the author would consider an outrageous price, since the price isn't the crux of the argument. (D) brings up an appeal to an outside authority, but the author never claims that an authoritative voice supports his assertion. And (E) is similarly bizarre since any connection of the critics to the postal service is immaterial—it doesn't have any relevance to the flaw.

4. E

The argument here is that regular use of BTI will destroy mosquito larvae, while preserving the rest of the animal

population in and around the pond. If these animals counted on the mosquito larvae as a food source, then eliminating this source of food could have the effect of reducing—or even eliminating—the fish, frogs, and beneficial insects. (E), by stating that no such dependence exists, is necessary to maintain the argument, and is therefore a valid assumption.

(A) The connection between mosquito larvae and mosquitoes isn't featured at all in the argument, so there's no reason why the argument would necessarily depend on this piece of information.

(B) isn't relevant. Whether larvae need a single body or multiple bodies of water to evolve shouldn't change the effectiveness of BTI, and that's the argument's sole point.

(C) The argument never suggests that mosquitoes are the only insects that pond owners might want to eliminate, so even if there are hundreds of other insect pests that pond owners wish to get rid of, the argument is still unaffected.

(D) is beyond the scope. We have no knowledge as to whether "strict adherence" is necessary: The ad simply recommends using BTI regularly.

5. A

How can 50 percent of the respondents be among the top 25 percent of the class? This only seems to be a contradiction: If the number of respondents was smaller than the total number of graduates, and if many of those who responded were students with high academic rank, then it's quite possible that half the respondents graduated in the top 25 percent of the class. The only puzzle here was if you didn't see that the respondents could be a subset of the total set of graduates, or if you assumed that everyone in the class responded. (Then it'd be a puzzle, all right!—see (D), below.) Anyhow, (A) makes it all clear: The group of respondents included more than its share of people who graduated with high ranks. (B) reinforces the accuracy of the numbers, without making it clearer how 50 percent of respondents fits into 25 percent of graduates. (C) tells us that some of the 25 percent who graduated at the top of the class weren't respondents, which makes it harder to see how 50 percent of the respondents came from the top 25 percent of the class. (D) is even worse than (C); if the number of respondents roughly equals the number of graduates, we'd have more than one-fourth of the graduates saying they were in the top 25th percentile of graduates. Rather than explaining an apparent discrepancy, (D) creates a real one. (E) deals with the criteria for academic rank, which is outside the scope of the argument. It gives us no information that explains how one-half of respondents can be one-fourth of graduates.

6. A

According to the citizens' group, if the mayor wants to attract business he should build a new business park, the best way (in their view) to attract business. Since he supports the highway, which won't attract as much money, the group says he mustn't really be interested in attracting new business at all. (A) sums that up in abstract language: The group reasons that if the mayor were really pursuing the cause of strengthening business, he would choose the means that would strengthen business the most, i.e., the business park. With (B), both plans admit that public revenues are required, so it doesn't advance either argument any further. (C) is irelevant: Nothing in the group's argument implies that they want the mayor to consult taxpayers or that they have done so themselves in considering the new business park. (D) is too vague; it could just as easily justify the mayor's wanting to bring the highway to town. (E) is irrelevant to the group's argument, which concerns the mayor's motivation, not who is responsible for attracting new business; there's no hint of the community building the business park by themselves.

7. D

Though this is nominally an Inference question, the stimulus has the sound of a paradox: There's no conclusion per se, just two facts connected by a "however." First we learn how the Pitcombe students label themselves politically (and notice that the percents—25% conservative, 24% liberal, 51% middle-of-the road—add up to 100%, so everyone's covered). Yet a whopping 77% of the group hold a liberal position on a certain set of issues. Well, we'd expect self-proclaimed liberals to do so, but even if every single Pitcombe liberal plus every single middle-of-the-roader held the liberal position, that would only account for 75% of the students; the remaining 2% would have to come out of the conservative wing. So (D) has to be true: At least some conservatives must hold that liberal position. Otherwise the 77% figure could not be achieved.

(A) is by no means necessarily true because as we've just seen, IF all self-described liberals and middles hold the liberal position, then some conservatives must. And if some of the liberals and middles do NOT hold that position, then that just means that more conservatives must hold it.

With (B) and (C), it's not clear whether "not endorsing" a position is the same as opposing it, but either way, (B) and (C) cannot be inferred. If you assumed that "not endorsing" means opposing, then you may have concluded that only (B) is possible, while (C) is impossible. With (E), just as "opposition" is technically never mentioned, "a conservative position" is also never mentioned. And even if some liberals do not hold the liberal view, it needn't be true that some of them support a conservative stance.

8. D

This is a disguised formal logic question. It's hard to follow, and it helps a lot if you read the question stem first: That way you know enough to read the stimulus looking for what deductions you can make about the press. The heart of the argument is as follows: If the press were not a profit-making institution, it would be subsidized and subject to outside control—there'd be no other alternative. Furthermore, it's easy to get subsidies for propaganda, but it's impossible to get subsidies for honest journalism. We can infer from this last statement that if the press produces honest journalism, it isn't subsidized. Combine that with the statement that the only possible alternatives are a subsidized press and a profit-making press. What's the conclusion? If the press produces honest journalism (and therefore is not subsidized), then it must be profit-making—and that's (D). To check, consider its contrapositive: "If it's not gonna make a profit (i.e., if it's subsidized), then it's not gonna be honest." Just what the author says! An inference, remember, is a statement that is virtually certainly to be true based on the stimulus. And in a large number of cases on the LSAT, the correct answer will be the contrapositive of something the author stated.

You might have been able to pick (D) by quickly scanning the answer choices after unpacking the stimulus. On the other hand, sometimes the only way is to slog through each of the choices one by one. (A) can't be inferred; the argument says that if the press is not profit-making, then it will be subsidized and subject to outside control. This does not mean that if the press isn't subsidized it will of necessity be free of outside control—a profit-making, outside-controlled press is still a possibility. (B) makes a similar mistake—even if it's true that the press that doesn't produce propaganda doesn't get subsidies, that doesn't imply that the press that doesn't get subsidies doesn't produce propaganda. (C) is completely confused—the argument says that if the press isn't subsidized it must be a profit-making institution. Finally, we showed that, as (D) says, the passage implies that if the press produces honest journalism, then it must be profit-making. (E) commits the error of turning this around (affirming the consequent) and concluding that if the press is profit-making, it must be honest. We most definitely can't conclude that!

9. A

There are three pieces to this argument: evidence, counterevidence and conclusion. If that's not obvious, *look at the structural signals* — the counterevidence is signaled by "however" and the conclusion by "therefore." A quick skim down the choices, however, makes it clear that the overall structure won't help us, since all the choices have the same basic form. *For parallel reasoning, an effective technique involves choosing a key piece of the argument (often the conclusion is best), then looking for a parallel among the answer choices.* The stimulus' conclusion says that it's not necessary to enact laws that address handgun-related crimes separately from other crimes. If we look down at the choices, (A) appears correct, since its conclusion — that it's not necessary for physicians to emphasize the danger of heart disease to overweight patients more than to other patients — carries the idea that it's unnecessary to follow a given course based on a certain distinction. *Using a close paraphrase* — like "unnecessary" for the original "no need to" — *is a classic testmaker tactic in parallel reasoning questions*. Others come close, but only (A)'s conclusion is parallel.

(B)'s conclusion recommends that people who want to be healthy avoid swimming for fear of ear infections — the idea of a distinction between two groups is missing here as is the idea of an unnecessary recommendation. (C) clicks on the "not necessary" part, but, again, there's no distinction between groups. (D) is about a group of people, those who eat rich foods, and makes a specific recommendation — but, without the idea that something is unnecessary, there's no parallel. And (E) has a recommendation for certain people, but also leaves out the "unnecessary" aspect. *No need to remind you that you should ignore the subject matter when looking for a parallel* since, in this case, all the choices had similar subject matter, and all were unrelated to the stimulus topic. Keep it in mind for future questions — ETS isn't always this kind

10. E

If you know what you're looking for in advance, a flaw should become readily apparent, if not readily identifiable, as you read the stimulus. Read the question stem first. First, the author compares two groups: infants with normal hearing who can distinguish sounds from any language and not just from the language of the people who are raising them; and young adults, who can only readily distinguish sounds from the languages they use. There's one segment of evidence. The author then points out that hearing begins to deteriorate after infancy. Well, you might say, perhaps that has something to do with the fact that young adults can't distinguish sounds as well as infants can. Perhaps not, though that certainly sounds plausible. Yet the author goes much further, drawing his conclusion based only on these facts. He asserts that the difference between infants' and young adults' sound discrimination abilities must be due to the deterioration of hearing. That's a big leap in logic, and as (E) explains, the author takes a factor that might contribute to an argument and uses it as a sufficient explanation.

(A) accuses the author of using an arbitrary cutoff point, though we have no reason to believe that the six month figure isn't scientifically documented. (B) wants to know more about the methods used in the studies, but we can still find the argument plausible nevertheless. To put it another way, that the author fails to explain the methodology makes it no more and no less likely that those methods were flawed. Clearly we're not concerned with (C)'s sounds that occur in most languages, only with sounds that are unique in different languages. And (D) suggests that the author makes an assumption based on the characteristics of a group and applies the assumption to individuals within the group, and this just doesn't happen. In fact, the argument makes no assumptions about individuals at all.

11. D

The author's conclusion only works if (D) is true: if there's no third language from which these two languages got the word *dog*. If you don't see that, try the Denial Test—the best way of seeing whether something is in fact being assumed. If (D) were false, what effect would it have on the argument? If there were some third language from which English and Mbarbaram borrowed the word *dog*, then that would blow apart the author's conclusion that these similarities can arise without language borrowing having occurred. In this case, language borrowing would have occurred, but indirectly, via a third language. When the denial of a choice counters the argument, then that choice is something that the author has assumed.

The author needn't assume that the only word shared by these languages is *dog*, so (A) is out. Try the Denial Test again: If she assumed the existence of other words like *dog* that supposedly weren't borrowed, then these words would just be more evidence for her conclusion. And if she assumed the existence of words that were borrowed, they'd be irrelevant, because her argument only concerns allegedly nonborrowed words. Contrary to (B), the author needn't assume that any other languages possess the word *dog*. Again, the Denial Test: If no other languages besides English and Mbarbaram used the word *dog*, that wouldn't weaken her argument that the similarity occurred without borrowing—if anything, it'd strengthen it. So (B) is not being assumed. (C) is a possible, but not necessary, assumption. The author could assume that word sharing between two languages usually occurs when the languages are related. But this isn't necessary to her argument, which, if you read carefully, concerns what sometimes happens, not what usually happens. If you don't see that, one more time, try the Denial Test: If she assumed that two languages that share a word usually aren't related (which is kind of counterintuitive), it wouldn't affect her argument either way. Again, she's arguing that word sharing can sometimes occur without language relatedness or word borrowing. Assumptions about when languages are and are not related are beside the point. Finally, (E)'s conclusion implies that the only way unrelated languages can share words is by borrowing them from one another. But if the author assumed this, her argument would be blasted to kingdom come: Her whole point is that it's possible for such languages to share words without borrowing having occurred.

12. E

The paragraph lays out a chain of cause and effect that begins with the overall point made in the first sentence: Using these new "clean-coal technologies" in factories could reduce pollutants and acid rain. How? By cutting a lot of noxious emissions (sentence 2), which in turn would reduce noxious ozone production in the troposphere (sentence 3). You don't have to understand what all of this technical terminology means; you simply have to see that in the author's mind, the factory technology strategy mentioned in sentence 1 could lead to a reduction of

tropospheric ozone in sentence 3, choice (E). Put another way: If one thing (new tech in factories) could lead to another (reduced emissions), and the second (reduced emissions) leads to a third (reduction in noxious ozone), then it's fair to say that the first could lead to the third.

(A) can't be a valid inference; the author is way too vague on which of the pollutants contributes to acid rain. For all we know, sulfur dioxide has little or no impact on the acid rain phenomenon.

(B) Nitrogen pollutants are all that affects noxious ozone formation, as far as this passage is concerned; sulfur dioxide may have little or no role. (And anyway, it says that noxious ozone is formed in the troposphere—don't think there are too many factories there.)

(C) distorts the statistic that these new technologies could cut sulfur dioxide emissions by 80%. For all we know, even 1 % of sulfur dioxide is unsafe.

(D) The concept of "careful design" is never raised here and is so vague that it cannot be part of a proper inference. More importantly, (D) is about designing new factories, while the stimulus is about reconfiguring existing ones.

13. C

American industry strikes again; this time we're responsible for clogging up the world's air supply thanks to old American cars that contribute disproportionately to global air pollution. The problem is decreasing though, according to the author, because many of these older polluting cars are being taken out of service in the United States for failing emissions tests. The conclusion? Over the next 10 years, the amount of air pollution contributed by old American cars will decrease. Did you catch the subtle scope shift? The problem is global, the solution is national. Since the requirement forces these cars out of service only in the U.S., this leaves the argument vulnerable to a weakener the likes of choice (C): If lots of old, retired American cars are being shipped to places that lack emission controls, then the author is overly optimistic. In other words, if (C) is true, then those old junkers aren't as retired as the author thinks, but may still be in service in other countries where they may still contribute significantly to global air pollution.

(A) won't weaken the argument because it merely says that the air of different regions can't be separated. That's precisely the author's point; that's why old American cars contribute disproportionately to global air pollution even though the cars are located, for the most part, in the United

States. Watch out for choices like this that seem to make a valid point. The test for each choice in a Weaken question is not "is this true?" or "does this sound reasonable and familiar?" but rather "does this damage the argument?" The answer must have a definite effect on the argument.

(B) amounts to the claim that newer automobiles are better for the atmosphere than the old ones, which certainly stands to reason—that's why use of newer American autos will lessen pollution.

(D) So what? Even if the number of such jurisdictions isn't increasing, the jurisdictions that have these standards would still be taking old American cars off the road, and that, according to the author, will decrease the amount of air pollution contributed by old American cars.

(E) The argument only predicts a decrease in the air pollution caused by older American cars, not all American cars.

Set Three

1. A

Why must Hastings have been disloyal? Because if his firing was justified, then he must have been either incompetent or disloyal, but the former is ruled out. That seems to leave only the latter, "disloyal"—but all of that rests on the key issue of justification, which merely appears in an "if" clause in the argument. To proceed from that conditional "if" clause to her categorical conclusion, the author must be taking for granted that that "if" clause is confirmed—that Hastings's firing *was* in fact justified. The Denial Test proves it: If contrary to (A) Hastings's firing was *not* justified, then we have no evidence upon which to base a finding of disloyalty.

(B) Hastings's rank, high or otherwise, goes unmentioned, so the author need not be assuming anything about it.

(C) The scope of this argument is Hastings and Hastings only; the author need not assume anything about others.

(D) can't be the assumption we seek. According to the author, someone justifiably dismissed could be loyal—as long as she or he was incompetent. (D) flies in the face of the second sentence.

(E) commits the "fallacy of affirming the consequent," i.e., reversing the if and then terms of sentence 2. The author doesn't do so; she simply takes for granted that her "if" clause is affirmed . . . which, again, is (A).

2.   D

We're looking for an inference that can properly be derived from the stimulus. There are four research companies estimating the population of the same three cities. For two of the cities, all the estimates agree; for the third city, the estimates vary widely. How come? The difference is that the first two cities are stable while the third city is "growing rapidly." There's one thing we can deduce with certainty up front: Since the companies' estimates for the rapidly growing city vary so wildly, someone's got to be wrong. That's not among the choices, however, so as is often the case with Inference questions, we'll have to evaluate the choices, looking for the one that's best supported by the information at hand.

(A) and (E) are unwarranted distinctions. No surveys of smaller cities are made here (A), nor is any mention made about current vs. future estimates (E). Neither of these comparisons is inferable here from the information given.

(B) The paragraph stops short of mentioning, let alone evaluating, the uses to which the data might be put. The usefulness of the data is outside the scope.

(C), if anything, works against the implicit general idea that it's difficult to determine the population of a rapidly growing city. But even if you didn't see that, you should have seen that there's no way to infer anything about the rate of population change here—it very likely may fluctuate.

(D) Since all four estimates are roughly the same for the stable cities in this study, it's reasonable to say that these companies' population estimates for stable cities, in general, will likely coincide. And if they do, then their reliability must be roughly the same, whether they're all right on, or all way off. Notice how correct choice (D) is highly qualified, by virtue of the word "likely." To say that the companies would definitely be equally reliable in their estimates of stable cities might be a bit of a stretch; but to say that it's likely is perfectly in the realm of believability—and perfectly in line with the phrasing of the stem. Of course, (D) also comes to the fore because of the problems with all of the wrong choices. You need not be fully in love with (D) in order to conclude that among the five choices, it's the one that's best supported by the text.

3. B

This Parallel Reasoning stimulus lends itself nicely to an algebraic treatment. If the economy is in recession (X), then demand is low (Y), and if demand is low, then interest rates are low (Z). Combining these statements, we get if X, then Z, and the author concludes with the contrapositive of this—if not Z (if interest rates aren't low), then not X [no recession]. So this is valid logic, paralleled exactly by (B), where X = the ready fish, Y = cooked all the way through, and Z = white. Both arguments conclude correctly that if the Z is not so, the X cannot be so.

(A) starts with an X and Y term that complement each other: A full restaurant means a full parking lot and vice versa. There's no subsequent Z term brought in, so (A) isn't parallel.

(C), too, only gives us an X and Y term: X = flying by flapping wings, and Y = warm-blooded. Then we get negations of these terms: "Gliding" is used as "not X," and "cold-blooded" is, of course, "not Y." As in (A), there's no true Z term. Furthermore, the phrase "if they flew at all" has no parallel in the original anywhere.

(D) Here, we could reasonably say that X = pleats, Y = doubled material, and Z = having none left for the top. The conclusion is that if X (you want pleats) then Z (you won't make the top). This is valid reasoning, but as you'll recall, the original argument doesn't formally combine the statements in this way—it concludes with the contrapositive of the combination of the first two statements. (D) fails to go on to draw this final conclusion. It would be parallel if, instead of the last sentence, it finished with "if you have material left for the top, then you didn't want to put in pleats."

(E) has its X, Y, and Z terms right, but concludes that if Z (the party loses) then X (the forecasters were right). This is classic faulty logic: The forecasters could be wrong, and yet the governing party could still lose for other reasons besides inflation. Bad logic and not parallel.

4.   C

When it was thought that South Island tuatara were the same species as those found on North Island, the naturalist saw no reason to protect them, even though they were approaching extinction. (After all, there would still be tuataras on North Island). But now that it has been discovered that the South Island tuatara are a unique species, the author feels we must save them from extinction, even if it means slaughtering their predators. What principle would justify this change of heart? (C), which boils down to this: If a species is being wiped out only in a given area, there's no obligation to save it, but if a species is to be completely wiped out, then we must save it.

(A) If she were guided by this principle, the naturalist would have wanted to protect South Island tuatara even before she knew they were a different species.

(B) speaks of individual animals rather than species. Secondly, it would grant equal rights to tuatara predators, which the naturalist is ready to kill.

(D) There's no hint that human activity is responsible for the declining numbers of South Island tuatara; the naturalist's remedy points to animal predators as a source of danger.

(E) enjoins us to protect South Island tuatara now that we know they are a separate species, but doesn't justify the idea that when they weren't considered a unique species, it was okay to let them die. Moreover, (E) doesn't mention an "obligation" to save the tuatara, mentioning instead that we should give them "care and attention."

5.   B

A classic case of correlation vs. causation. The fallacy of confusing causation with correlation is common on the LSAT. When the evidence states "whenever A happens, B also happens," all that means is that these two events are correlated. That doesn't necessarily mean "A causes B" or "B causes A." Causation must be explicitly stated. The author cites a correlation between the presence of a certain brain disorder and the presence of a high amount of aluminum in the brain. He then presents a simplistic conclusion: A compound that prevents aluminum from affecting the brain will cure the afflicted animals. The author assumes that the aluminum causes the behavioral disorder, but the evidence only shows a correlation. It's possible that there's no causal connection between the disorder and the aluminum, or even that the connection runs the other way around (the high aluminum level is a result of the disease). Therefore, in order to arrive at the conclusion in the last sentence, the author must assume (B)—that extra aluminum is the cause, and not a result, of the disorder.

(A) is irrelevant. Try the Denial Test: Can the unusually high levels of aluminum vary from one afflicted animal to another? Sure, why not? Denying (A) has no effect on the argument.

(C) is outside the scope: Since the author never makes the claim that the method of cure won't also do some harm, he needn't assume that there will be no side effects. (You could use the Denial Test here, too, by asking yourself whether the appearance of side effects would doom the logic of the argument; since side effects are irrelevant here, the answer is clearly no.)

(D) may or may not be true (we have no way of knowing), but either way, it isn't an assumption. Even if exactly one dose of the compound cures every organism, the logic of the argument still stands.

(E) is wrong: The author speaks of "unusually high levels" of aluminum found in animals with the disorder, which implies that some level of aluminum is normal.

6.   B

Because many highly skilled Eastern European workers have emigrated, the author concludes that there is now great demand for such workers in Eastern Europe. This depends on the idea of supply and demand, the assumption being that the emigration has left a shortage of highly skilled workers in Eastern Europe, which has resulted in a high demand for skilled workers. (B) attacks this assumption by making it likely that the workers who have gone abroad haven't left jobs behind. The jobs are disappearing along with the workers, so there's no shortage of skilled workers for the jobs available and no necessary increase in demand. By weakening the assumption, (B) weakens the argument.

(A) eliminates the possibility that Eastern European countries would hire foreign skilled workers, so it strengthens the argument that the emigration of skilled workers would create high demand for native skilled workers. (C) is irrelevant, because it deals only with the workers who have already left Eastern Europe, while the argument is concerned with the workers still there. (D) and (E) strengthen the argument. If, as (D) says, there are plans to train many new workers to replace the highly skilled ones who left, then apparently there is high demand for skilled workers. And (E) says that many positions are unfilled, which pretty much proves the author's point.

7.   D

Whenever stimuli throw around percent increases or decreases, beware: Percent increases and decreases are not the same as changes in the actual numbers or amount. Here the author signals the conclusion with "it is clear": What is clear is that people are throwing away just as much plastic or even more than ever before. We know that because waste management companies are reporting that

an "ever-increasing" percentage of the waste they handle is plastic. But percentages are deceiving; there may, for example, be a higher percentage of plastic in the waste, but if the total amount of waste is decreasing, then the actual amount of plastic waste may have remained stable or even decreased. (D) gets at this: Waste handlers are receiving less of other types of waste; thus, there is less overall waste; thus, the increase in percent of plastic waste does not necessarily mean that people are throwing out as much or more plastic waste.

(A) sets up an opposition that doesn't exist in the stimulus. There's no difference between plastic incinerated and that sent to a landfill; it's all included in the plastic waste "handled" by the management companies. The point (B) raises—that some plastic isn't recyclable and therefore ends up in the garbage—would strengthen rather than weaken this argument. (C) is irrelevant; whatever people do with plastic at home is not the issue. The question is whether they are putting more of it in the trash. Same thing with (E); the amount of plastic manufactured, or even an increase in the amount of plastic packaging, isn't necessarily connected to how that plastic ends up in the trash.

8.   A

The professor's argument makes the assumption of representativeness without justifying it. She argues that college students in general don't write as well as they used to; her evidence is that almost all of her students' papers were poorly written. She assumes without evidence that the writing produced by her students is representative of the writing produced by college students in general. But it needn't be.

(B) and (C) While it's true that no proof of the professor's competence is offered, this is a much less important omission than that mentioned in (A). If we were given the "proof" that (B) mentions, would the prof's conclusion be stronger? No, because (A)'s crucial assumption would still be unsupported. So (B) is far from the biggest weakness. As for her teaching skills, we don't even know she teaches writing, so we can't argue, as (C) does, that she is responsible for her students' poor abilities.

(D) There is no contrary evidence. If contrary evidence were presented, we could expect the author to address it. We can't, however, fault her for not presenting evidence against herself.

(E) While it's true that writing well and writing poorly may be somewhat subjective terms, they definitely aren't ambiguous. Moreover, the term "ungrammatical" certainly isn't ambiguous. However, even if you did consider some of the terms to be in need of further definition, this clearly isn't as serious a weakness as that described in (A).

9. A

According to the first sentence, a condition necessary for a flower to be worth growing in a garden is that it smell sweet. Some roses, we're told, have no scent at all, sweet or otherwise; they, like all roses, provide stunning color, but are scentless. All in all, then, there must be some flowers—namely the scentless roses—that provide stunning color but aren't worth growing. That's just what (A) says.

(B) The only scentless flowers mentioned are "some roses." Other types of flowers might be both scentless and visually drab.

(C) contradicts the passage's necessary condition. Only flowers that smell sweet are worth growing in a garden, so there can be no flowers worth growing that are scentless.

(D) is possible only: It's possible that some sweet-scented roses might still not be worth growing in a garden, but it's equally possible that all sweet-smelling flowers, roses or otherwise, are worth growing.

(E) Nothing in the stimulus makes stunning color a requirement for cultivation in a garden.

10. C

The argument is based on a link between dreaming and memory, so the correct choice should make reference to this link. The hypothesis suggests that dreaming serves to unclutter the mind, thus freeing up memory. It would follow that when dreaming is interrupted, so too is this process of erasing our brain's meaningless connections, which would in turn negatively impacts our memory space.

(A) is not necessarily true; maybe these dim bulbs have the fewest parasitic connections to dispose of, and therefore need very little time for sleep. Besides, only dreaming time is discussed, not sleeping time. With (B), the hypothesis implies that, after dreaming, a person's memory will contain fewer "accidental associations." However, there's no indication that the erasure process eliminates virtually all meaningless associations. With (D), nothing in the hypothesis implies that we dream only in terms of parasitic connections. There's no reason why a person's dreams

couldn't contain meaningful associations that he or she accurately describes upon waking. With (E), the spiny anteater is described as the only mammal that does not have rapid eye movement sleep. No mention is made of nonmammals in this argument. Also, there's ambiguity relating to the difference between REM sleep and dreaming: Humans typically experience the latter during the former, but we can't be sure that this applies to "all animals."

11. A

One way to weaken an argument is to undermine its central assumption. And this author is assuming that these "genetically determined abnormalities" that afflict purebred dogs are a serious problem. Without that assumption, there'd be no reason for him to argue that potential dog owners should choose nonpurebred dogs in order to avoid having to pay for the expensive surgery needed to correct these abnormalities. If (A) is true, and if the abnormalities don't seriously harm the dog, then the surgery is an unnecessary expense, and potential dog owners needn't worry about having to avoid it.

(B) is a typical wrong answer choice—it falls outside the scope of the argument. The argument only addresses genetically determined diseases, so evidence about nongenetically determined diseases won't weaken it. (C) and (D) provide us with new, and irrelevant, information. Neither the shorter life span of purebred dogs in (C) nor their higher purchase price in (D) speaks to the central issue, which is avoiding the costly surgery the author claims is needed to correct genetic abnormalities in purebreds. At best, (C) and (D) can only strengthen the author's argument by presenting even more reasons to eschew purebreds: Not only are they likely to need surgery, but they tend to die sooner, and they're more expensive to buy. Finally, (E) tries to weaken the case for buying nonpurebreds by pointing out that dogs without genetically determined abnormalities can still have puppies with such abnormalities. Again, irrelevant. The author only claimed that dog owners can avoid costly surgery by buying nonpurebreds. He never said anything about what may or may not happen to the dogs' offspring, so (E)'s information doesn't weaken his argument.

12. E

Here, it can really pay to read the question stem first. If you knew that you were looking for a weakness, it was probably much easier to plow through the text. People used to think that butterfat was nutritious and healthful, and at that time a law was passed requiring that butter that had been diluted with water be labeled "imitation butter." Now, the author says, we know that butterfat is unhealthy, so people should be encouraged to eat foods with lower butterfat content. The term "imitation" deters people from buying diluted butter, so the law should allow this product to be labeled "lite butter," a more appealing name.

We can weaken this by showing that the author's solution won't help the problem, as (E) does. (E) explains that the name "imitation butter" provides a service, because people shy away from it and instead buy products with even lower butterfat contents. This is not so good for the imitation butter industry, but it undermines the author's argument, and so it's correct. Speaking of the industry, (A) tries to explain that the decision to use the word "lite" was motivated by financial greed, but the reason for the decision doesn't have enough of an effect on the argument to be considered a weakener. As so often happens, the motivation behind a plan is not especially relevant to the wisdom of that plan. (B) would have the imitation-butter makers watering their butter even more, which might help people eat even less butterfat, which is a good thing, so (B) strengthens the author's argument, if anything. (C) tells us that some people eat imitation-butter despite its name— well, that's good, but it's the people who are deterred from it and instead eat real butter that the manufacturers are concerned with. And (D) focuses on the detail of cholesterol in butter and its effects on health, which can't weaken the argument—just because it's not the only factor doesn't mean it's not an important factor, and it doesn't mean that the author's plan won't work.

13. B

Notice anything odd about the two groups mentioned in the first sentence? They don't necessarily overlap! One group includes women with preschool-age children, the other sole income earners. Does the latter group include women with preschool-age children? Who knows? Maybe all of them have preschool-age children, maybe none. So how can the author subtract one figure from the other and conclude that there are comparatively very few working women who have preschoolers but who aren't their families' sole supporters? If there is substantial overlap between the two groups cited, this would be reasonable. Since we don't know of such an overlap, this is unreasonable, and the flaw is pointed out in (B). (A) is unreasonable; a decimal point is precise enough.

Also, since the conclusion isn't given in precise language ("comparatively few"), it doesn't require precise figures. As for (C), the argument deals with the state of affairs now; there's no need to predict the future. With (D), older children are irrelevant, plain and simple. (E) is beyond the scope of the argument; there's no need to discuss working men. Even if you didn't see the mistake in this question, you could answer it by process of elimination. (D) and (E) are beyond the scope, which only extends to preschoolers and women. (C) brings in time, which isn't in the stimulus. As for (A), the charge of "imprecise" almost never sticks on the LSAT.

Chapter 4: **Logic Games**

- The 6 basic principles of Logic Games
- Sequencing, grouping, and matching skills
- Kaplan's 5-Step Method for Logic Games

Nothing inspires more fear in the hearts of LSAT test takers than Analytical Reasoning, or Logic Games, because the skills tested on the section are unfamiliar. It may help you to reexamine the reason this section is included on the test—the major analytical skills that the Logic Games section is designed to measure:

- **Organization:** the ability to assimilate efficiently, both in your head and on the page, the formidable amount of data associated with each game
- **Mental agility:** the ability to maintain enough flexibility to shuffle the data around in different ways for each question
- **Memory:** the ability to retain the work done in the setup stage while focusing on the new information in each question stem
- **Concentration:** the ability to keep focused on the task at hand and not let your mind wander

Games are most troublesome to those students who don't have a clearly defined method of attack. And that's where Kaplan's basic principles, game-specific strategies and techniques, and 5-Step Method for Logic Games will help, streamlining your work so you can rack up points quickly and confidently.

 GO ONLINE

Your downloadable study sheet summarizes these principles, strategies, and methods.

THE 6 BASIC PRINCIPLES OF LOGIC GAMES

For many students, Logic Games is the most time-sensitive section of the test. The test makers know that if you could spend hours methodically trying out every choice, you'd probably get everything right. But what does that prove? Who's going to get the sought-after legal position or win the important client—the person who can write the legal brief and prepare the court case in four days, or the person who can do the same job in four hours? It's all about efficiency. And that brings you to the first, and somewhat paradoxical, Logic Games principle.

 KAPLAN

GO ONLINE

As you read through these principles, consider how each might have improved your Diagnostic Quiz performance.

Slow Down To Go Faster

To gain time in Logic Games, spend time thinking through and analyzing the setup and the rules. This is the most important principle for Logic Games success and the one that's most often neglected, probably because it doesn't seem right intuitively. People with timing problems tend to rush to the questions. But spending a little extra time thinking through the stimulus, the "action" of the game, and the rules, helps you to recognize key issues and make important deductions that will save you time.

Games are structured so that, in order to answer the questions quickly and correctly, you need to search out relevant pieces of information that combine to form valid new **deductions** (inferences). You can either do this once, up front, or you can choose to piece together the same basic deductions—repeating the same work—for each question. For instance, what if two of the rules for a Logic Game are:

- If Bob is chosen for the team, then Eric is also chosen.
- If Eric is chosen for the team, then Pat will not be chosen.

You can, as you read through the rules of the game, treat those rules as two independent pieces of information. But there's a deduction to be made from them: If Bob is chosen, Eric is, too. If Eric is chosen, Pat is not. Therefore, if Bob is chosen, Pat is not chosen. And that deduction will undoubtedly be required in more than one question.

The choice is yours; but the rush-to-the-questions method is inefficient, time-consuming, and stress-inducing. Take the game scenario and the rules as far as you can before moving on to the questions.

Common Elements and Deductions

As the Bob-and-Eric example demonstrates, rules that contain common elements often lead to deductions. Consider the following three rules:

- If Sybil goes to the party, then Edna will go to the party.
- If Jacqui goes to the party, then Sherry will not go to the party.
- If Edna goes to the party, then Dale will go to the party.

Rules 1 and 2 have no entities in common—it doesn't appear you can deduce anything by combining them. Note, however, that even when rules have no common elements, their placement or the way they interact with the numbers may lead to something useful. The same goes for Rules 2 and 3. But since Rules 1 and 3 have Edna in common, a deduction is possible (although not guaranteed). In this case, you can deduce another rule: If Sybil goes to the party, then Dale will go also.

Focus on the Important Rules

Not all rules are equal—some are inherently more important than others. Try to focus first on the concrete ones and the ones that involve the greatest number of the entities or otherwise have the greatest impact on the action.

These are also the rules to turn to first whenever you're stuck on a question and don't know how to set off the chain of deduction.

No "Best" Choice

The answers in Logic Games—like answers to math questions—are objectively correct or incorrect. Therefore, when you find an answer that's definitely right, have the confidence to circle it and move on, without checking the other choices. This is one way to improve your timing on the section.

Use Scratchwork and Shorthand

Developing good scratchwork will help your performance on Logic Games. Although some rare games aren't amenable to scratchwork, for most games you'll find it helpful to create a master sketch that encapsulates the game's information in an easy-to-follow form. This gives your eye a place to gravitate towards when you need information, and helps to solidify in your mind the action of the game, the rules, and whatever deductions you made.

Keep scratchwork simple—you get no points for beautiful diagrams, and the less time you spend drawing the more time you'll have for thinking and answering questions. Pay careful attention to the scratchwork suggestions in the explanations to the games in the Practice Tests.

The goal of the scratchwork is to condense a lot of information into manageable, user-friendly visual cues. Jot down a quick, short form of each rule. Shorthand is useful only if it reminds you at a glance of the rule's meaning. You should never have to look back at the game itself once you get to the questions. It's much easier to remember and apply rules written like so:

B → E

No G in 2

than those written like so:

If Bob is chosen for the team, then Eric is also chosen.

Box 2 does not contain any gumdrops.

But such notation is only helpful if you know what the arrow means and use it consistently. If you develop personal shorthand that's instantly understandable to you, you'll have a decided advantage on test day.

Know What a Rule Means, Not Just What It Says

The LSAT measures critical thinking, and virtually every sentence in Logic Games has to be filtered through some sort of analytical process to be of any use. So it's not enough just to copy a rule off the page (or shorthand it); it's imperative that you think through its full meaning, including any implications it might have. And don't limit this to the indented rules; statements in introductions are very often rules that warrant the same meticulous consideration.

Say a game's introduction sets up a scenario in which you have three boxes, each containing at least two of the following three types of candy—chocolates, gumdrops, and mints—and then you get the following rule:

Box 2 does not contain any gumdrops.

What does that rule say? *There aren't any gumdrops in Box 2.* But what does that rule *mean* in the context of the game? That Box 2 *does* contain chocolates and mints. Each box contains at least two of three things. If you eliminate one of the three things from any particular box, the other two things *must* be in that box.

Moreover, part of understanding what a rule means is being clear about what the rule *doesn't* mean. Take the rule you saw earlier:

Rule: If Bob is chosen for the team, then Eric is also chosen.

Means: Whenever Bob is chosen, Eric is, too.

Doesn't mean: Whenever Eric is chosen, Bob is, too.

Remember the discussion of formal logic in the Logical Reasoning chapter, with its *if/then* statements and sufficient and necessary conditions? If I yell loudly at my cat, he will run away. That means that whenever I yell at him loudly, he runs away. But, just as important, it *doesn't* mean that whenever he runs away, I've yelled at him.

 EXCLUSIVE

Don't over-compartmentalize your skills: Those used mainly in one LSAT section may be very helpful in another.

Try to Set off Chains of Deduction

When a question stem offers a hypothetical—an *if-clause* offering information pertaining only to that question—use it to set off a new chain of deductions. Consider the following question. (Since this question is excerpted without the accompanying introduction and rules, ignore its specific logic; it's just presented to make a point.)

If the speedboat is yellow, which one of the following must be true?

(A) The car is green.

(B) The airplane is red.

(C) The train is black.

(D) The car is yellow.

(E) The train is red.

The stem contains a new "if." The wrong approach is to acknowledge that the speedboat is yellow and then proceed to test out all of the choices. The muddled mental thought process accompanying this approach might sound something like this:

"All right, the speedboat's yellow, does the car have to be green? Well, let's see, if the speedboat's yellow, and the car is green, then the train would have to be yellow, but I can't tell what color the airplane is, and I guess this is okay, I don't know, I better try the next choice. Let's see what happens if the speedboat's yellow and the airplane is red. . . ."

Stay focused! The question doesn't ask: "What happens if, in addition to this, the car is green?" or "What happens if this is true and the airplane is red?" So why is this confused test taker intent on answering all of these irrelevant questions? Never begin a question by trying out answer choices. Only if you're entirely stuck should you resort to trial and error.

The Correct Approach

Incorporate the new piece of information into your view of the game, creating a new sketch if it helps. Apply the rules and any previous deductions to the new information in order to set off a new chain of deductions. Play out the deductions just as you would have if this had been one of the original rules, but stop after each new deduction and skim your answer choices. You don't want to waste time on unnecessary work after you've found all you need to answer the question.

Know the Logic Games Question Types

You must have a solid command of the limited number of Logic Games question stems. When you take a few seconds to recognize the question type, characterize the answer choices, and apply the appropriate process, your work becomes more efficient—and more accurate.

Acceptability Questions

If the question asks which choice would be "acceptable," one answer choice will satisfy all the rules; each wrong choice will violate at least one rule.

 GO ONLINE

Start to learn your strengths and weaknesses based on your Diagnostic Quiz results with these question types.

New "If" Questions

When the question adds a new "if" condition, treat the "if" as a new rule and draw a new sketch if necessary.

Complete and Accurate List Questions

Answer the other questions first; their sketches will help you answer these. Use the choices to decide what possibilities you have to test.

Could [not] vs. Must [not] Questions

Focus on the nature of the right and wrong answer choices:

If the question reads . . .	The right answer will be . . .
Which one of the following statements could be true?	a statement that could be true, and the four wrong choices will be statements that definitely cannot be true (that is, must be false)
Which one of the following statements cannot be true?	a statement that cannot be true, and the four wrong choices will be statements that either must be true or merely could be true

Which one of the following statements must be true?	a statement that must be true, and the four wrong choices will be statements that either cannot be true or merely could be true
All of the following statements could be true EXCEPT . . .	a statement that cannot be true, and the four wrong choices will be statements that either could be true or even must be true
All of the following statements must be true EXCEPT . . .	a statement that either cannot be true, or merely could be true, and the four wrong choices will be statements that must be true
Which one of the following statements could be false?	a statement that cannot be true or could be true or false, and the four wrong choices will be statements that must be true
Which one of the following statements must be false?	a statement that cannot be true, and the four wrong choices will be statements that either must be true or merely could be true

You'll have a chance to see these major Logic Games principles in action when you review the explanations to the games in the Practice Tests in this book.

 KAPLAN STRATEGY ——————————————————————

Kaplan's basic principles for success in Logic Games are:

- Slow down to go faster.
- Always use the rules and deductions to work out as much positive, concrete information as you can before moving to the questions.
- Know what a rule means, not just what it says.
- Use scratchwork and shorthand.
- Try to set off chains of deductions.
- Know the Logic Games question types.

 GO ONLINE

Reinforce your skills each month with your new quiz.

THE 3 CRUCIAL LOGIC GAMES SKILLS

Although Logic Games can contain a wide variety of situations and scenarios, certain skills are required again and again. Variations on the following are the most common:

Sequencing

Logic Games requiring **sequencing** skills—those that involve putting entities in order—have long been a test maker's favorite. In a typical sequencing game, you may be asked to arrange the cast of characters numerically from left to right, from top to bottom, in days of the week, in a circle, and so on.

The sequence may be a matter of degree—say, ranking the eight smartest test takers from one to eight. Or it may be based on time, such as one that involves the order of shows broadcast on a radio station. Occasionally, there are two or even three orderings to keep track of in a single game.

Strict and Loose Sequences

There are two types of sequence games. In a **strict** sequence game, the placement of entities is very strictly defined. You may be told, for example, that "A is third," or that "X and Y are adjacent," and so on. These are definite, concrete pieces of information, and the game centers around placing as many people into definite spots as possible. In contrast to this, in a **loose** (or "free-floating") sequence game, your job is to rank the entities only in relation to one another. You're usually never asked to fully determine the ordering of the cast of characters. Instead, the relationships between the entities constitute the crux of the game.

Typical Sequence Game Issues

The following is a list of the key issues in sequencing games, each followed by a corresponding rule—in some cases, with several alternative ways of expressing the same rule. At the end, these rules will be used to build a miniature Logic Game, so that you can see how rules work together to define and limit a game's action.

 GO ONLINE

As you practice, don't forget to track your progress in your online syllabus.

These rules all refer to a scenario in which seven events are to be sequenced from first to seventh.

Issue	Rule
Which entities are concretely placed in the ordering?	K is fourth.
Which entities are forbidden from a specific position in the ordering?	R is not first or last.
Which entities are next to, adjacent to, or immediately preceding or following one another?	M and K are consecutive. M is next to K. No event comes between M and K. M and K are consecutive in the ordering.
What is the relative position of two entities in the ordering?	P comes before L in the sequence. P comes after K and M in the sequence.

How a Sequence Game Works

Now see how rules like the ones we just looked at combine to make up a Logic Game.

There are exactly seven houses on a street. Each house is occupied by exactly one of seven families: the Kahns, Lowes, Muirs, Newmans, Owens, Piatts, and Rutans. All the houses are on the same side of the street, which runs from west to east.

The Rutans do not live in the first or the last house on the street.

The Kahns live in the fourth house from the west end of the street.

The Muirs live next to the Kahns.

The Piatts live east of both the Kahns and the Muirs but west of the Lowes.

$$\cancel{K}LMNOPR$$

West ___ ___ ___ K ___ ___ ___ East

The next most concrete rule is a negative one: Rule 1 tells us the Rutans DON'T live in the first house or the last house. Build it in to your sketch, and also think about what it means in positive terms—there are only four houses in which the Rutans can live . . . the second, third, fifth, or sixth from the west.

$$\cancel{K}LMNOPR$$

West ___ ___ ___ K ___ ___ ___ East
  no R   no R

Rule 3 tells us that the Muirs live next to the Kahns. Be careful! Whenever you see a rule like this, remember that the Muirs could be on *either side* of the Kahns—don't make assumptions about the order.

$$\cancel{K}LMNOPR$$

West ___ ___ ___ K ___ ___ ___ East
  no R   ↖ M ↗   no R

The last rule contains a lot of information. Make sure to break it down and work through it piece by piece. You can't build this one directly into your sketch, but it will help you narrow down the possibilities. For instance, you can see that P can only be fifth or sixth from the west, and L can only be sixth or seventh.

$$\cancel{K}LMNOPR$$

West ___ ___ ___ K ___ ___ ___ East
  no R   ↖ M ↗   no R

          KM . . . PL
              or
          MK . . . P . . . L

This is how the rules work together to build a sequence game. The questions might then present hypothetical information that would set off the "chain of deduction" (fifth basic principle). You'll see how this works in the sequencing games on the Practice Tests; pay careful attention to the written explanations.

Grouping

In a pure grouping game, unlike sequencing, there's no call for putting the entities in order. Instead, you'll select a smaller group from the initial group or distribute the entities into more than one subgroup. You're not concerned with what order the entities are in, but rather who's in, who's out, and who can and cannot be with whom in various subgroups. In grouping games, knowing an entity is rejected is as helpful as knowing one is selected.

Selection and Distribution

In **selection** games, you'll be given the cast of characters and told to select a smaller group based on the rules. For example, a game may include eight music CDs, from which you must choose four. Sometimes the test makers specify an exact number for the smaller group, sometimes they don't. In a common variation, the initial group of entities is itself broken into subgroups at the start of the game: An example would be a farmer choosing three animals from a group of three cows and five horses.

In **distribution** games, you're concerned with who goes where rather than with who's chosen and who isn't. Sometimes, every entity will end up in a group—like placing eight marbles into two jars, four to a jar. A common hybrid game combines selection and distribution. For instance, a game might mandate the placement of three marbles in each jar, leaving two marbles out in the cold.

It's important for you to be aware of the numbers that govern each particular grouping game, because although all grouping games rely on the same general skills, you have to adapt these skills to the specific situation. Like sequencing games, grouping games have a language all their own, and it's up to you to speak that language fluently.

Typical Issues—Grouping Games of Selection

The following is a list of the key issues in grouping games of selection, each followed by a corresponding rule—in some cases, with several alternative ways of expressing the same rule. At the end, again, these rules will be used to build a miniature Logic Game.

These rules all refer to a scenario in which you are to select a subgroup of four from a group of seven entities—F, L, M, O, P, S, and Y.

Issue	Rule
Which entities rely on a different entity's selection?	If M is selected, then Y is not selected. If F is selected, then P is not selected.
Which entities rely on two different entities selection?	If L and O are not selected, then F and S are selected.
Which entities cannot both be chosen?	M and Y won't both be selected. F and P won't both be selected.
	If Y is not selected, then L or O are selected, but not both.

How Grouping Games of Selection Work

Here's how rules like this combine to form a grouping game of selection:

> A park contains at most five of seven kinds of trees—firs, laurels, maples, oaks, pines, spruces, and yews—consistent with the following conditions:
>
>> If maples are in the park, yews are not.
>>
>> If firs are in the park, pines are not.
>>
>> If yews are not in the park, then either laurels or oaks, but not both, are in the park.
>>
>> If it is not the case that the park contains both laurels and oaks, then it contains firs and spruces.

Often, the best way to approach a grouping game of selection is simply to create a list of the entities and then circle the ones you know are to be selected, and cross out the ones that cannot be selected. Remember, though, not to circle or cross out anything in your main list unless it's always going to be true—for individual questions, make a new list.

Numbers are often critical in a selection game; make sure that you clearly note that no more than five types of tree can be selected.

$$F L M O P S Y \qquad (max\ 5)$$

All of the rules in this game are *if/then* rules—there's nothing that tells us directly that a particular type of tree is always selected or is never selected. That means there's nothing you can build straight into the sketch yet. These rules must be understood and noted in useful, consistent shorthand for future use.

KAPLAN EXCLUSIVE

The rule, "If X is selected, then Y is selected" works only in one direction; if X is chosen, Y must be, but if Y is chosen, X may or may not be.

> F L M O P S Y   (max 5)
> If M→No Y
> If F→No P
> If No Y→L or O, No (L O)
> If No L and No O→F and S

Now the rules are broken down and clearly organized for when a question adds a new "if" and triggers a chain of deductions. Let's say, for instance, that a question said:

If maples are selected, which of the following must be true?

The selection of M sets off a chain reaction: The first rule tells us that if M is selected, Y is not.

> F L (M) O P S Y̸   (max 5)

But we're not done. We know now that Y is not selected, and the third rule tells us that if Y is not selected, either L or O must be selected, BUT NOT BOTH.

> F L (M) O P S Y̸   (max 5)
> L or O, No (L O)

If L & O are not both selected, then the last rule tells us that both F and S must be selected.

> (F) L (M) O P (S) Y̸   (max 5)
> L or O, No (L O)

Finally, the second rule tells us that if F is selected, P can't be selected.

> (F) L (M) O P̸ (S) Y̸   (max 5)
> L or O, No (L O)

Now, you've nailed down quite a bit of information about what happens when maples are selected. There are several possible correct answers to this question. For instance, "yews are not selected" or "firs are selected." Don't worry, though—only one of them will be an answer choice!

KAPLAN EXCLUSIVE

In selection games, create a roster of entities. Circle those accepted and X-out those rejected.

Typical Issues—Grouping Games of Distribution

Here are the issues involved in grouping games of distribution—along with the rules that govern them.

These rules refer to a scenario in which the members of another group of nine entities—F, G, H, J, K, Q, R, S, and T—have to be distributed into three different classes:

Issue	Rule
Which entities are barred from a particular group?	H and T cannot be in class 2.
Which entities must be placed in the same subgroup?	F must be in the same class as J.
Which entities cannot be placed in the same subgroup?	G cannot be in the same class as T.
	H cannot be in the same class as R.

How Grouping Games of Distribution Work

Rules like these combine to form grouping games of distribution like the one below:

> Five children—F, G, H, J, and K—and four adults—Q, R, S, and T—are planning a canoeing trip. The canoeists will be divided into three groups—groups 1, 2, and 3—of three canoeists each, according to the following conditions:
>
>> There must be at least one adult in each group.
>> F must be in the same group as J.
>> G cannot be in the same group as T.
>> H cannot be in the same group as R.
>> Neither H nor T can be in group 2.

A good sketch for this game will designate each of the three separate canoes and precisely mark out three seats in each one. Knowing how many slots are available in each group is key in a distribution game. You'll need a list of the entities, too, of course, and you should use a different notation (here we've used capital and lower case letters) to make it easy to tell the adults from the children. Rule 1 is the only one that's concrete enough to go into the sketch. Be sure to think through the numbers, too—there are four adults, so if there must be "at least one" in each canoe, that means one canoe has two adults and each of the other two has one adult.

KAPLAN EXCLUSIVE

For distribution games, draw the subgroups and enter the slots to be filled in for each.

1	2	3	QRST
Adult	Adult	Adult	fghjk
___	___	___	
___	___	___	

Nearly all of the remaining rules in this game revolve around which canoeists can, can't, or must be in the same canoe.

Rule 2 requires F and J to travel together.

1	2	3	QRST
Adult	Adult	Adult	f g h j k
			(f j)

Rule 3 says that g and T CANNOT travel together—the alternating positive/negative statements in grouping game rules can trip you up, so be sure to read carefully.

1	2	3	QRST
Adult	Adult	Adult	f g h j k
			(f j)
			No gT

Rule 4 gives you another pair that can't be together—and another pair that's one adult and one child. Since every child has to be in a canoe with at least one adult, these limitations will help push other combinations together.

1	2	3	QRST
Adult	Adult	Adult	f g h j k
			(f j)
			No gT
			No hR

The last rule gives us something concrete once again: Two of our entities—h and T—are prohibited from traveling in Canoe 2..

1	2	3	QRST
Adult	Adult	Adult	f g h j k
			(f j)
	No h		No gT
	No T		No hR

That's the basics of setting up a grouping game of distribution; you'll see more games like this one in the practice sets.

Matching

As the name implies, **matching** games ask you to match up various characteristics about a group of entities—often many characteristics at once. A game may involve three animals, each assigned a name, a color, and a particular size. It's no wonder test takers get bogged down in these types—there's a lot to keep track of.

Some people dislike matching games because they feel bombarded with information and don't know where to start. Organization is especially crucial. A table or grid can be helpful. Distinguish each characteristic by using CAPS for one category, lowercase for another.

KAPLAN EXCLUSIVE

In matching games, make a list or grid; represent one set of entities in CAPS and one in lowercase. Keep track of the number of slots available.

Remember that thinking must always precede writing. A visual representation of a mental thought process can be invaluable; scribbling thoughtlessly for the sake of getting something down on the page is useless, even detrimental.

Center the sketch around the most important characteristic—the one with the most information attached to it. Going back to the animals example, don't assume that you should organize your sketch around the animals—there may be a better attribute, one that you know more about, that should take center stage. Visualize the action and create a mental picture or a sketch that puts the elements into a logical order. If you think through the scenarios and don't get scared off by their seeming complexity, you can find matching games accessible and even fun.

Typical Matching Game Issues

The following is a list of the key issues in matching games, each followed by a corresponding rule or set of rules.

All these rules refer to a situation in which you have three couples: John and Kate, Lewis and Marie, and Nat and Olive. Each couple consists of one man and one woman, and each person is ordering only one of the following entrees: pork chops, roast beef, swordfish, tilefish, and veal cutlet

Issue	Rule
Which entities are matched up?	J and K are a couple.
	L and M are a couple.
	N and O are a couple.
	M orders a swordfish
	O orders a roast beef.
Which entities are not matched up?	J and N cannot order swordfish or tilefish.
Which entities matchups depend on the matchups of other entities?	J, L ,and N cannot order the same meal
	J and K cannot order the same meal
	L and M cannot order the same meal
	N and O cannot order the same meal.

KAPLAN EXCLUSIVE

Use the contrapositive on all *if/then* rules in Logic Games. It will always yield an important deduction.

How Matching Games Work

Rules like the ones above combine into matching games like this one:

> Three couples—John and Kate, Lewis and Marie, and Nat and
> Olive have dinner in a restaurant together. Kate, Marie, and Olive
> are women; the other three are men. Each person orders one and
> only one of the following kinds of entrées: pork chops, roast beef,
> swordfish, tilefish, and veal cutlet. The six people order in a manner
> consistent with the following conditions:
>
> > The two people in each couple do not order the same kind of
> > entrée as each other.
> > None of the men orders the same kind of entree as any of the
> > other men.
> > Marie orders swordfish.
> > Neither John nor Nat orders a fish entreé.
> > Olive orders roast beef.

A matching game with many entities is best set up in columns, very similar to a grouping game of
distribution. Some matching games lend themselves well to grids, but gridding a game with five or six
of each type of entity is generally too time-consuming and may be confusing.

Here, you have six people, but you're also given pairings—that information has to be reflected in your
sketch as well. You're also told which are men and which are women. It's not immediately apparent
why that's important, but logic games rarely provide superfluous information, so make sure you note
the distinction. You'll also need a list of the possible entrées.

Start with the most concrete rules: In this game, that means Rules 3 and 5. Build "Marie orders
swordfish" and "Olive orders roast beef" right into your sketch.

The first rule tells us that the two people in a couple don't order the same entrée. This can be noted
right at the top of the sketch.

$$J \neq K \quad L \neq M \quad N \neq O \qquad prstv$$
$$\qquad\qquad s \qquad\quad r$$

You may already be noting that the first rule combines with some other information you've been given to make some deductions, but stay focused on working the rules one at a time for a moment—the time for deductions is coming. The second rule says that none of the men orders the same entrée as any other man. This is the most abstract rule in terms of being able to incorporate it into your sketch—you'll probably just want to note it.

$$J \neq K \quad L \neq M \quad N \neq O \qquad prstv$$
$$\qquad\qquad s \qquad\quad r \qquad J \neq L \neq N$$

Finally, neither John nor Nat orders a fish entrée. That means no swordfish and no tilefish. You could note this in your sketch as it's expressed, but there are only five possible entrees and this rules out two of them—it's more relevant to note the three options that ARE available to these two men. Remember, though, that they're only possibilities; note them in a way that you can't possibly confuse them with the definite information already in your sketch.

$$J \neq K \quad L \neq M \quad N \neq O \qquad prstv$$
$$\qquad\qquad s \qquad\quad r \qquad J \neq L \neq N$$
$$pr \qquad\qquad\quad pr$$
$$v \qquad\qquad\qquad v$$

Now you can move on to deductions. Since the two members of a couple can't order the same entrée, you know that Lewis can't have swordfish and Nat can't have roast beef. That narrows Nat's options down to pork chops and veal. Now you're ready to attack the questions.

$$J \neq K \quad L \neq M \quad N \neq O$$
$$\qquad\qquad s \qquad\quad r$$
$$pr \qquad\qquad\quad p\slashed{r}$$
$$v \qquad\quad no\,s \quad\; v$$

Hybrid Games

Many games are hybrid games, requiring you to combine sequencing, grouping, and/or matching skills (one will be used in discussing Kaplan's 5-step Method). It really doesn't matter if you categorize a game as a sequencing game with a grouping element or as a grouping game with a sequencing element, as long as you're comfortable with both sets of skills.

Now that you have some Logic Games background, it's time to see how you can marshall that knowledge into a systematic approach to games.

KAPLAN EXCLUSIVE

In hybrid games, expect to draw a separate sketch for each action, but consider whether you can combine the sketches.

KAPLAN'S 5-STEP METHOD FOR LOGIC GAMES

1. Overview

Carefully read the game's introduction and rules to establish the **situation**, the **entities** involved, the **action**, and the number **limits** governing the game (SEAL).

2. Sketch

Make a mental picture of the situation, and let it guide you as you create a sketch or other scratchwork, to help you keep track of the rules and handle new information.

3. Rules

As you think through the meaning and implications of each rule, you have two choices. You can:

- Build it directly into your sketch.
- Jot down the rule in shorthand.

4. Deduction

Look for common elements among the rules; that's what will lead you to make deductions. Treat these deductions as additional rules, good for the whole game.

5. Questions

Read the question stems carefully! Take special notice of words such as *must, could, cannot, not, impossible,* and *except.* Use new "ifs" to set off a new chain of deduction.

Here's how the approach can work with an actual Logic Game:

CHECK OUT THE CD

You can practice applying Kaplan's Method with a CD Companion Logic Games quiz.

<u>Questions 1–2</u>

Eight people—Jack, Karen, Laura, Mark, Nick, Owen, Peggy, and Ruth—will be placed on two four-person teams—X and Y—for a relay race that is run in four successive legs: first, second, third, and fourth. The teams race concurrently. Each team member runs exactly one of the legs, one team member per leg, according to the following conditions:

Jack is on the same team as Karen.
Karen is not on the same team as Nick.
Ruth runs an earlier leg of the race than Peggy runs, whether or not they are on the same team as each other.
Mark and Nick are both on team Y.
Neither Jack nor Mark runs third.
Karen and Laura both run second.
Owen runs fourth.

1. If Ruth is assigned to team X, which one of the following is a complete and accurate list of the legs that she could run?

   (A) first
   (B) second
   (C) first, second
   (D) first, third
   (E) second, third

2. If Peggy runs third on the same team to which Jack is assigned, which one of the following must be true?

   (A) Jack runs the first leg on the team to which he is assigned.
   (B) Ruth runs the first leg on the team to which she is assigned.
   (C) Owen runs on the same team as Jack.
   (D) Owen runs on the same team as Mark.
   (E) Ruth runs on the same team as Mark.

Though only two questions accompany this game, a typical logic game will have 5–7 questions.

1. Overview

You need to divide eight people—J, K, L, M, N, O, P &, and R—into two equal teams (X and Y) and put them in order to run a relay. This hybrid game requires you to distribute the runners and to sequence them. The introductory paragraph is loaded with information; don't make the mistake of skimming it too quickly. In addition to the tasks and the list of entities, you've learned that the teams each have exactly four members and that each of the runners is used exactly once in the lineup, and that every slot is filled.

2. Sketch

In a hybrid game, your sketch must provide for both of the tasks assigned to you (here, distribution and sequencing). In this case, you'll want the typical four blanks setup to sequence the runners on each team, but you'll also need a sort of holding area for runners assigned to a team but not yet sequenced.

JKLMNOPR

Team X   Team Y

___ ___ ___ ___   ___ ___ ___ ___
1 2 3 4   1 2 3 4

3. Rules

You've already worked through some hidden rules in the introductory paragraph. As you work your way through the indented rules, make sure that you're taking the time to understand and interpret each rule, not simply noting it quickly and moving on without really knowing what it means in terms of the game.

You've already seen the advantage of starting with the most concrete rules. Here, there's also an advantage to starting with the distribution rules. This is where having a handle on the real-life situation is very helpful—if you were splitting a group up into teams and then putting them in order in the real world, you'd have to divide them up before you could sequence them, right?

Start with the fourth rule, which is the most concrete distribution rule. You can build it right into your sketch.

> **KAPLAN) EXCLUSIVE**
>
> The Logic Games expert knows how to press on when more deductions are possible.

JKLMNOPR

Team X   Team Y
               MN

___ ___ ___ ___   ___ ___ ___ ___
1 2 3 4   1 2 3 4

The rest of the distribution rules involve which runners can, must, or cannot be on teams together. Rule 1 says Jack is on the same team with Karen. We can't build that into the sketch—at least, not yet—so note it.

JKLMNOPR

Team X   Team Y   (JK)
                  MN

___ ___ ___ ___   ___ ___ ___ ___
 1   2   3   4   1   2   3   4

The second rule tells us that Karen is not on the same team as Nick. This can be noted in the same way. You may note that this tells you exactly where Karen belongs, but hold that thought for a moment. The key to not overlooking anything in Logic Games is working the rules one by one first, THEN combining them to make deductions.

JKLMNOPR

Team X   Team Y   (JK)
                  MN   No (KN)

___ ___ ___ ___   ___ ___ ___ ___
 1   2   3   4   1   2   3   4

The rest of the rules involve the sequencing element of the game.

Ruth runs earlier than Peggy, even if they're not on the same team. You can note this like you would any other sequencing rule that says one entity comes before another. Think through what this means in terms of legs of the race, too: Ruth can't ever run the fourth leg (because then Peggy couldn't come later), and Peggy can't ever run the first (because then Ruth couldn't come earlier).

JKLMNOPR

Team X   Team Y   (JK)
                  MN   No (KN)
                               R . . . P

___ ___ ___ ___   ___ ___ ___ ___
 1   2   3   4   1   2   3   4

That neither Jack nor Mark runs third can be built right into the sketch. You already know that Mark is on Team Y, so you don't have to bother noting that he can't run third on Team X, but if you didn't catch that here, don't worry. That's what the deduction step is for!

JKLMNOPR

Team X					Team Y					JK
					MN					No (KN)
										R . . . P
1	2	3	4		1	2	3	4		
	No J					No J				
						No M				

That Karen and Laura both run second can be built into your sketch, as well—although you don't know which runner takes spot 2 on which team, you know that each will occupy one of those slots.

JKLMNOPR

Team X					Team Y					JK
	K|L					MN				No (KN)
						K|L				R . . . P
1	2	3	4		1	2	3	4		
	No J					No J				
						No M				

📖 **READ MORE**

Kaplan's *LSAT 180* offers even more Logic Games practice.

Owen runs fourth, but we don't know on which team, so put that in your shorthand list of rules.

JKLMNOPR

Team X					Team Y					JK
	K|L					MN				No (KN)
						K|L				R . . . P
1	2	3	4		1	2	3	4		O = 4
	No J					No J				
						No M				

4. Dedications

Taking the extra moment to work through deductions and understand what you do and don't know sets the prepared test taker apart. You actually know quite a bit that isn't yet in your sketch. One important thing to look for in making deductions is entities (in this case, runners) that appear in more than one rule.

For instance, the concrete fourth rule told us that Nick was on Team Y. Rule 2 told us that Karen is not on the same team with Nick, so what does that mean? She's on Team X! But that's even more concrete, because the sixth rule told us that Laura and Karen both ran second. If Karen is on Team X, she must run second on Team X . . . which means Laura must run second on Team Y.

You also know from the first rule that Jack and Karen must be together. You've just placed Karen on Team X, so Jack must be there, too. Build that into your sketch.

Make sure you take note of what we don't know, too: Five of the eight runners have been assigned to teams, so who's left floating? Only O, P, and R. Here's what your sketch might look like after building in your deductions:

JKLMNOPR

Team X   Team Y   JK
J   MN   No KN
K   L   R . . . P
1   2   3   4   1   2   3   4   O = 4
    No J   No M

5. Questions

This is where you'll see how the work you did up front pays off. The first question on page 90 gives you a new piece of information to build in. Usually, when a new rule is introduced in the question, you'll want to create a new mini-sketch just for that question. Here, though, you've already done so much of the groundwork that you can probably just read the answer off of your sketch. We're told (for purposes of this question only) that Ruth is on Team X. Which legs can she run? We already know she can't run fourth (no room for Peggy after her) and that she can't run second (Karen is already there), so eliminate any answer choice that includes leg 2 or 4. That leaves just (A) and (D)—which brings the question down to this: Can Ruth run third? Nothing in your rules prevents it, so answer choice (D) is correct.

The second question also adds a rule, and will require a new sketch to incorporate the rule. Peggy runs third on Jack's team, and we know that Jack's team is Team X, so fill Peggy right in to the third leg on Team X.

JKLMNOPR

Team X   Team Y   JK
J   MN   No KN
K   P   L   R . . . P
1   2   3   4   1   2   3   4   O = 4
    No J   No M

Now, we're looking for something that MUST be true. If Peggy runs third, what else do we know? That Ruth must run either first or second (whichever team she's on). But wait—the second leg is booked on both teams. That means Ruth has to run first, whatever team she's on. That's answer choice (B).

Taking just a couple of minutes to walk through each of the five steps and thoroughly set up a game and think through its rules will save time when you reach the questions. Don't be afraid to make that investment!

SUMMARY

The basic principles of Logic Games are:

- Slow down to go faster.
- Always use the rules and deductions to work out as much positive, concrete information as you can before moving to the questions.
- Know what a rule means, not just what it says.
- Use scratchwork and shorthand.
- Try to set off chains of deductions.
- Know the Logic Games question types.

Types of Games

Sequencing Games: have been the most popular game type, involving putting entities in order (strict or loose), often in time, space, or degree.

Grouping Games: the number of elements is often crucial; it's action involves deciding what entities are included a group (selection), or which group an entity belongs in (distribution).

Matching Games: often complicated games requiring tables or grids, they may involve *if/then* rules that can be handled by using the contrapositive.

Hybrid Games: often the most difficult games that contain elements of two (or more) of the other game types.

Kaplan's 5-Step Method for Logic Games

1. Overview (SEAL)
2. Sketch
3. Rules
4. Deduction
5. Questions

LOGIC GAMES PRACTICE

Set One

Questions 1–6

Ron washed a total of seven objects after eating his lunch. Two of the objects were pieces of china: a mug and a plate. Two were pieces of glassware: a water glass and a juice glass. Three were utensils: a fork, a knife, and a spoon. Ron washed the two pieces of china consecutively, the two glasses consecutively, and the three utensils consecutively. He washed the objects as follows:

He washed each of the objects exactly once.

He washed the glassware after either the china or the utensils but not after both.

He washed the knife before the spoon, and he washed the mug before the plate.

He did not wash any two objects at the same time.

1. Which one of the following statements CANNOT be true?

   (A) Ron washed the fork first.
   (B) Ron washed the fork second.
   (C) Ron washed the mug first.
   (D) Ron washed the plate second.
   (E) Ron washed the plate third.

2. Which one of the following statements can be true?

   (A) Ron washed the knife second.
   (B) Ron washed the knife seventh.
   (C Ron washed the mug second.
   (D) Ron washed the mug third.
   (E) Ron washed the mug fourth.

3. Which one of the following CANNOT be an accurate list of the objects Ron washed second, third, and fourth, respectively?

   (A) fork, spoon, water glass
   (B) knife, fork, juice glass
   (C) knife, spoon, juice glass
   (D) knife, spoon, water glass
   (E) plate, water glass, juice glass

4. It is NOT possible that Ron washed the knife

   (A) first
   (B) second
   (C) third
   (D) fifth
   (E) sixth

5. If Ron washed the spoon immediately before the fork, then which one of the following statements can be true?

   (A) He washed the knife second.
   (B) He washed the knife third.
   (C) He washed the plate third.
   (D) He washed the plate sixth.
   (E) He washed the plate seventh.

6. If Ron washed a glass and the knife consecutively, but not necessarily in that order, then which one of the following statements must be false?

   (A) He washed the fork before the plate.
   (B) He washed the fork before the spoon.
   (C) He washed the juice glass before the knife.
   (D) He washed the plate before the water glass.
   (E) He washed the spoon before the fork.

Questions 7–12

A newly formed company has five employees F, G, H, K, and L. Each employee holds exactly one of the following positions: president, manager, or technician. Only the president is not supervised. Other employees are each supervised by exactly one employee, who is either the president or a manager. Each supervised employee holds a different position than his or her supervisor. The following conditions apply:

There is exactly one president.

At least one of the employees whom the president supervises is a manager.

Each manager supervises at least one employee.

F does not supervise any employee.

G supervises exactly two employees.

7. Which one of the following is an acceptable assignment of employees to the positions?

President	Manager	Technician
(A) G	H, K, L	F
(B) G	H	F, K, L
(C) H	F, G	K, L
(D) H, K	G	F, L
(E) K	F, G, H, L	—

8. Which one of the following must be true?

(A) There are at most three technicians.

(B) There is exactly one technician.

(C) There are at least two managers.

(D) There are exactly two managers.

(E) There are exactly two employees who supervise no one.

9. Which one of the following is a pair of employees who could serve as managers together?

(A) F, H

(B) F, L

(C) G, K

(D) G, L

(E) K, L

10. Which one of the following could be true?

(A) There is exactly one technician.

(B) There are exactly two managers.

(C) There are exactly two employees who are not supervised.

(D) There are more managers than technicians.

(E) The president supervises all of the other employees.

11. If F is supervised by the president, which one of the following must be true?

(A) G is the president.

(B) H is the president.

(C) L is a technician.

(D) There is exactly one manager.

(E) There are exactly two technicians.

12. If K supervises exactly two employees, which one of the following must be true?

(A) F is supervised by K.

(B) G is a manager.

(C) L is supervised.

(D) There are exactly two managers.

(E) There are exactly two technicians.

Set Two

Questions 1–5

On Wednesday, a physician will have exactly one appointment with seven patients—P, Q, R, S, T, U, and W—one patient per appointment. The schedule of appointments, chronologically numbered 1 through 7, must meet the following conditions:

Q's appointment is at some time before W's appointment.

U's appointment is at some time before P's appointment.

Either R or T has appointment 3.

S's appointment is either the appointment immediately before or the appointment immediately after R's appointment.

1. Which one of the following is an acceptable schedule of appointments in order from 1 to 7?

   (A) Q, S, R, P,W, U, T

   (B) Q, U,W, S, R, T, P

   (C) S, Q, R, T,W, U, P

   (D) T, U, R, S,W, P, Q

   (E) U, Q, T, P, R, S,W

2. If W has appointment 2 and P has appointment 5, then which one of the following must be true?

   (A) R has appointment 6.

   (B) S has appointment 4.

   (C) S has appointment 7.

   (D) U has appointment 1.

   (E) U has appointment 4.

3. If U's appointment is immediately after T's appointment and immediately before R's appointment, then which one of the following must be true?

   (A) Q's appointment is at some time before P's appointment.

   (B) S's appointment is at some time before P's appointment.

   (C) S's appointment is immediately before Q's appointment.

   (D) W's appointment is immediately before P's appointment.

   (E) W's appointment is at some time before S's appointment.

4. If P's appointment is immediately before S's appointment, then each of the following could be true EXCEPT:

   (A) R's appointment is immediately before W's appointment.

   (B) T's appointment is immediately before Q's appointment.

   (C) U's appointment is immediately before P's appointment.

   (D) U's appointment is immediately before Q's appointment.

   (E) W's appointment is immediately before T's appointment.

5. If T's appointment is immediately after P's appointment and immediately before W's appointment, then which one of the following must be true?

   (A) W's appointment is at some time before R's appointment.

   (B) U's appointment is at some time before R's appointment.

   (C) S's appointment is at some time before U's appointment.

   (D) R's appointment is at some time before P's appointment.

   (E) Q's appointment is at some time before S's appointment.

Questions 6–12

Exactly six employees—officers F, G, and H and supervisors K, L, and M—must be assigned to exactly three committees—Policy, Quality, and Sales—with exactly three employees per committee. Committee assignments must conform to the following conditions:

Each committee must have at least one officer assigned to it.

Each employee must be assigned to at least one committee.

All three officers must be assigned to the Policy Committee.

G cannot be assigned to the same committee as L.

K must be assigned to the Sales Committee.

6. Which one of the following is a group of three employees who can be assigned together to the Sales Committee?

   (A) F, G, and H
   (B) F, G, and M
   (C) G, K, and L
   (D) H, K, and L
   (E) K, L, and M

7. If H is assigned to exactly one committee, and if no committee has both F and M assigned to it, then it must be true that

   (A) G and M are both assigned to the Quality Committee
   (B) K and L are both assigned to the Sales Committee
   (C) K is assigned to exactly two committees
   (D) L is assigned to exactly two committees
   (E) M is assigned to exactly two committees

8. Which one of the following CANNOT be true?

   (A) F is assigned to exactly one committee.
   (B) G is assigned to exactly three committees.
   (C) H is assigned to exactly three committees.
   (D) K is assigned to exactly one committee.
   (E) L is assigned to exactly two committees.

9. If F is assigned to exactly three committees and G is assigned to exactly two committees, then which one of the following must be true?

   (A) G is assigned to the Quality Committee.
   (B) G is assigned to the Sales Committee.
   (C) K is assigned to the Quality Committee.
   (D) L is assigned to the Sales Committee.
   (E) M is assigned to the Quality Committee.

10. Which one of the following is a group of three employees who can be assigned together to the Quality Committee?

    (A) F, G, and H
    (B) F, G, and K
    (C) G, H, and K
    (D) G, K, and L
    (E) H, L, and M

11. If L is assigned to exactly two committees, which of the following must be true?

    (A) F is assigned to the Sales Committee.
    (B) G is assigned to the Sales Committee.
    (C) H is assigned to the Quality Committee.
    (D) K is assigned to the Quality Committee.
    (E) M is assigned to the Quality Committee.

12. Which one of the following CANNOT be true?

    (A) F and G are each assigned to exactly one committee.
    (B) F and H are each assigned to exactly one committee.
    (C) G and H are each assigned to exactly one committee.
    (D) F and M are both assigned to the Sales Committee.
    (E) G and K are both assigned to the Quality Committee.

Set Three

Questions 1–5

On Tuesday, Vladimir and Wendy each eat exactly four separate meals: breakfast, lunch, dinner, and a snack. The following is all that is known about what they eat during that day:

    At no meal does Vladimir eat the same kind of food as Wendy.
    Neither of them eats the same kind of food more than once during the day.
    For breakfast, each eats exactly one of the following: hot cakes, poached eggs, or omelet.
    For lunch, each eats exactly one of the following: fish, hot cakes, macaroni, or omelet.
    For dinner, each eats exactly one of the following: fish, hot cakes, macaroni, or omelet.
    For a snack, each eats exactly one of the following: fish or omelet.
    Wendy eats an omelet for lunch.

1. Which one of the following statements must be true?

    (A) Vladimir eats fish for lunch.
    (B) Vladimir eats fish for dinner.
    (C) Vladimir eats fish for his snack.
    (D) Wendy eats fish for dinner.
    (E) Wendy eats fish for her snack.

2. Vladimir must eat which one of the following foods?

    (A) fish
    (B) hot cakes
    (C) macaroni
    (D) omelet
    (E) poached eggs

3. If both Vladimir and Wendy eat macaroni on Tuesday, then which one of the following statements could be true?

    (A) Vladimir eats fish for lunch.
    (B) Vladimir eats hot cakes for lunch.
    (C) Vladimir eats macaroni for dinner.
    (D) Wendy eats hot cakes for breakfast.
    (E) Wendy eats hot cakes for dinner.

4. If Wendy does not eat macaroni on Tuesday, then which one of the following statements could be true?

    (A) Vladimir eats poached eggs for breakfast.
    (B) Vladimir eats fish for lunch.
    (C) Vladimir eats hot cakes for lunch.
    (D) Wendy eats hot cakes for breakfast.
    (E) Wendy eats fish for dinner.

5. If Wendy eats poached eggs for breakfast, then which one of the following statements cannot be true?

    (A) Vladimir eats fish for lunch.
    (B) Vladimir eats hot cakes for lunch.
    (C) Vladimir eats macaroni for dinner.
    (D) Wendy eats hot cakes for dinner.
    (E) Wendy eats macaroni for dinner.

Questions 6–11

At an automobile exhibition, cars are displayed on each floor of a three-floor building. On each floor, the cars are either all family cars or all sports cars, either all new or all used, and either all production models or all research models. The following conditions apply to this exhibition:

If the exhibition includes both family cars and sports cars, then each family car is displayed on a lower numbered floor than any sports car.

The exhibition includes no used research models.

The exhibition includes no research models that are sports cars.

There are new cars on floor 1.

There are used cars on floor 3.

6. If there are sports cars on exactly two floors, then which one of the following statements could be true?

    (A) There are research models on floor 1.

    (B) There are sports cars on floor 1.

    (C) There are family cars on floor 2.

    (D) There are research models on floor 2.

    (E) There are family cars on floor 3.

7. Which one of the following statements could be true?

    (A) The exhibition includes new research model sports cars.

    (B) The exhibition includes used research model family cars.

    (C) The exhibition includes used research model sports cars.

    (D) There are research models on exactly one floor.

    (E) There are research models on all three floors.

8. Which one of the following statements must be true?

    (A) There are production models on floor 1.

    (B) There are research models on floor 1.

    (C) There are production models on floor 2.

    (D) There are production models on floor 3.

    (E) There are research models on floor 3.

9. If there are research models on exactly two floors, then which one of the following statements can be false?

    (A) There are family cars on floor 1.

    (B) There are research models on floor 1.

    (C) There are new cars on floor 2.

    (D) There are research models on floor 2.

    (E) There are family cars on floor 3.

10. If all the new cars in the exhibition are research models, then which one of the following statements must be true?

    (A) All the family cars in the exhibition are new.

    (B) All the family cars in the exhibition are research models.

    (C) All the family cars in the exhibition are used.

    (D) All the new cars in the exhibition are family cars.

    (E) All the production models in the exhibition are family cars.

11. If all the production models in the exhibition are used, then which one of the following statements must be true?

    (A) There are family cars on floor 1.

    (B) There are new cars on floor 2.

    (C) There are research models on floor 2.

    (D) There are family cars on floor 3.

    (E) There are sports cars on floor 3.

ANSWERS AND EXPLANATIONS

Answer Key

Set One	Set Two	Set Three
1. E	1. E	1. E
2. A	2. E	2. D
3. B	3. B	3. D
4. C	4. B	4. B
5. E	5. D	5. B
6. A	6. D	6. A
7. B	7. C	7. D
8. A	8. B	8. D
9. E	9. E	9. E
10. B	10. E	10. D
11. D	11. E	11. A
12. C	12. B	

Diagnostic Tool

Tally up your score and write down your results below.

Total Correct: _____ out of 35

Percentage Correct: # you got right x 100 ÷ 35: _____

Diagnose Your Results

Look back at the questions you got wrong and think back on your experience answering them.

Step 1: Find the Road Blocks

Some Logic Games you simply couldn't wrap your head around. To improve your score, you need to pinpoint exactly what elements of these "road blocks" tripped you up. To do that, ask yourself these two questions:

Am I weak in the skills being tested?

Logic Games are a complex LSAT question type that tests your analytical reasoning skills. They not only assess whether you are able to assimilate the data being presented in each game, they also test your ability to organize the data according to different rules, and to remember the work you did in the setup stage while focusing on the new information in each question stem.

The Kaplan Logic Games principles in this book can help you focus on the specific skills required for tackling the complicated, multifaceted data presented to you in Logic Games. If you need more help in this department, TRY OUT the *Kaplan Logic Games Workbook*. It contains proven methods for improving data organization and concentration, as well as techniques for increasing speed and accuracy on the hardest questions.

Was it the question type that threw me off?

Then you need to become more comfortable with it! Go back to the beginning of this chapter and review the Kaplan principles and methods for Logic Games. Make sure you understand them, and know how to apply them. Also, make sure are you very familiar with the types of Logic Games you are likely to encounter on Test Day.

Also, get as much practice as you can, so you grow more at ease with Logic Games. For even more practice, TRY OUT the *Kaplan Logic Games Workbook*, which includes practice sets for each type of Logic Game, and two full-length Logic Games practice sections!

Step 2: Find the Blind Spots

Some Logic Game questions you answered quickly and confidently, but got them wrong anyway! When you come across wrong answers like these, you need to figure out what you thought you were doing right, what it turns out you were doing wrong, and why that happened! The best way to do that is to **read the answer explanations!**

They give you a detailed breakdown of why the correct answer is correct, and why all the other answer choices are wrong. This helps to reinforce the Kaplan principles and methods for each question type, and helps you figure out what blindsided you so it doesn't happen again. Also, just like with your Road Blocks, try to get in as much practice as you can.

Step 3: Reinforce Your Strengths

Read through all the answer explanations for the ones you got right. Again, this helps to reinforce the Kaplan principles and methods for each question type, which in turn helps you to work more efficiently so you can get the score you want. Now keep your skills sharp with more practice.

As soon as you are comfortable with all the LSAT question types and Kaplan methods, complete a full-length practice test under timed conditions. In this way, practice tests serve

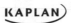

as milestones; they help you to chart your progress! So don't save them all for the final weeks.

If you are aiming for that top score, TRY OUT the *LSAT 180*, Kaplan's advanced workbook that includes only the toughest LSAT questions and most focused strategies.

You can also visit Kaptest.com/LSAT for more details on Kaplan's online and classroom-based options, like LSAT Advanced, LSAT Extreme, and LSAT Crash courses. Kaplan uses real LSAT questions, so you get the most comprehensive, test-like experience.

Set One

Questions 1–6

Here we have a sequencing game within a sequencing game. Three types of dishes, seven objects in all, are being washed: china (a mug and a plate), glassware (a water glass and a juice glass), and utensils (a fork, a knife, and a spoon). Here in the opening paragraph we get another important rule: The objects within each type are washed consecutively. This means, for example, that the fork (a utensil) will not be washed in between the mug and plate (pieces of china). However, within each group, the order in which the objects are washed can vary, thus accounting for the sequence within a sequence. There are only two basic sequencing **key issues** in this one:

1) Which objects are washed in which order?

2) Which objects are washed before and after which other objects?

The Initial Setup

This begs for a simple setup. For now, just separate the dishes into type and wait for the rules.

The Rules

1) is your typical loophole closer. Don't let it worry you. All it means is that Ron won't go back and rewash any of the dishes. Once is enough.

2) This rule has tricky wording, but once you comprehend it, it's quite helpful. The glasses are washed after the china or after the utensils, but not after both. Again, make the information concrete. What are the possibilities? The "not after both" part eliminates C, U, G and U, C, G, so the order will either be C, G, U or

U, G, C. In other words, the two glasses, W and J, will always be washed in the middle of the three types.

3) deals with the internal order of the dish washing. There are only two pieces in the china category, and we now know that the mug is always washed before the plate. Likewise we are told that of the utensils, the knife is washed before the spoon. Note though, that the fork can float around anywhere in relation to the knife and spoon. Write "M . . . P" and "K . . . S" as reminders.

4) Another loophole closer, and again don't give it a second thought. No two objects are washed at the same time (no "Octopus Ron" doing the dishes).

Key Deductions/Final Visualization

We can further flesh out our work with Rules 2 and 3. Thanks to these two rules, there are only two possible options for the order of dishes washed:

$$
\begin{array}{cccccc}
& 1 & 2 & | 3 & 4 & |5 & 6 & 7 & Option\ 1 \\
& M\ .\ .\ .\ P & | (W) & (J) & | K\ .\ .\ .\ S & & K = 5\ or\ 6 \\
& & | (J) & (W) & | (F) & & S = 6\ or\ 7 \\
& 1\ 2\ 3 & | & or & & & F = 5,\ 6,\ or\ 7 \\
K = 1\ or\ 2 & K\ .\ .\ .\ S & | 4 & 5 & | 6 & 7 & Option\ 2 \\
S = 2\ or\ 3 & & | & & & \\
F = 1,\ 2,\ or\ 3 & (F) & | (W) & (J) & | M & P \\
& & | (J) & (W) & | &
\end{array}
$$

And that's it. From this we can see many valuable facts (M can only be washed first or sixth, etc.). These two possibilities are what we will come back to again and again to answer nearly all of the questions. After making the abstract "C, G, U or U, G, C" more concrete, we will have an infinitely better grasp of what's going on.

1. E

By scanning the two possibilities, it's pretty easy to see that the plate can only be washed second or seventh, not third. (A) through (D) all could be true.

2. A

Again, using what we know about the two possibilities, the second option shows that the fork could be washed first, in which case the knife would be washed second. (B) through (E) are all impossible, as we see with our ordering.

3. B

Simply check each choice against the possibilities: knife, fork, juice glass? For 2, 3, and 4? That's way off. The only order close (as we see with our two possibilities) would be knife, fork, spoon in the 1, 2, 3 slots. (A), (C), (D), and (E) are all very possible.

4. C

Again, use our two possibilities. The knife can't be washed third. First, second, fifth, sixth—(A), (B), (D), (E)—yes, but not third.

5. E

Ask yourself, "What does this mean in the context of this game?" The only way for this to be possible is if the utensil order is knife, spoon, fork. Now test out the options using this new restriction. (A) and (B) would relate to the second option, but are both impossible because they violate the K, S, F order. The plate can never be washed third or sixth in either option, so (C) and (D) are out, but the plate can be washed seventh if K, S, and F are washed first, second, and third, respectively.

6. A

Ask yourself, "How can this be possible?" Only if the order by type is C, G, U, our first option, and the knife is washed fifth. The plate is washed second and the fork either sixth or seventh, so (A) is obviously false. (B) and (E) could be true, and (C) and (D) must be true.

Questions 7–12

With this game, we're asked to group five employees—F, G, H, K, and L—(a godsend: more entities would have made this game considerably less manageable) into three categories—president, manager, and technician. There's an extra dimension in this one: Some employees supervise other employees. The **key issues** are:

1) What employees can, must, or cannot be distributed into each group?
2) What employees can, must, or cannot supervise what other employees?

The Initial Setup

This is not an easy setup to get a handle on, because we want to include not only the consideration of position, but also who supervises whom. One way is to mimic a "family tree" type of game, with entities placed above and below each other and connected by lines. This way we can place entities who supervise over those they supervise and connect them with lines.

The Rules

This game has many vital rules built into the opening paragraph: We're told that only the president is not supervised, and that each employee is supervised by one employee who is either the president or a manager. We can infer then that technicians cannot supervise anyone.

We're also told that the supervised employee has a different position than his or her supervisor. Since the supervised employee and the supervisor cannot hold the same position, this means that all managers are supervised by the president and all technicians are supervised by a manager or the president.

These basic rules are just as important as the indented ones. If you missed them, the game is undoable.

1) Only one president means that only one of our employees will go unsupervised. Note how Logic Games tend to reflect real-life situations. It makes sense that there is only one president, just as it makes sense that the employees can only supervise those that are of a lower level.

2) At least one of the people that the president supervises will be a manager. Don't make the mistake of assuming that this rule means that the president must supervise more than one employee; that's not what the rule states. It's quite possible that the president supervises exactly one employee, a manager.

3) This rule will prove vital. We know that the president is unsupervised (opening paragraph) and that a manager cannot supervise another manager (opening paragraph). So if each manager supervises at least one employee, we now know that *there must be at least as many technicians as managers*.

4) Don't just write "F supervises no one." Consider what that means. We learned from the setup that only technicians do not supervise anyone, so instead of rewriting the rule, we can put F directly into our diagram as one of the technicians.

5) You will want to make a note reminding yourself that G must supervise two employees, but once again, first

stop and think about what this tells us. We can put G right into our diagram by noting that she must either be the president or at least a manager (since technicians do not supervise anyone).

Key Deductions/Final Visualization

We've already jumped the gun and made a few deductions from the opening paragraph and the rules (it's okay to deduce as you go along; we usually discuss deduction in a separate paragraph in these written explanations for the sake of clarity. But there's more to think about before moving on to the questions. With only five entities and one (F) solidly fixed to a group (technician), you can bet that it would be worth our time to consider the numbers game and drive it to something concrete. Five entities and exactly one of them is president. What could be the numbers breakdown of president, managers, and technicians, respectively? **The only possibilities are 1, 1, 3 and 1, 2, 2**; we inferred from Rule 3 that the number of managers can't be greater than the number of technicians.

We could even take this thinking one step further by combining it with Rule 5. **If G is a manager, then the setup has to be 1, 1, 3**. Do you see why? If G's a manager, the requirement that she supervises at least two employees (technicians in this case), wouldn't leave any technicians for the other manager to supervise in the 1, 2, 2 setup.

Going another step further, **what if we know that there are two managers? Well, that means that the setup is 1, 2, 2, and G must be the president**. G can only be the president or a manager, and we just showed that G can't be a manager unless she's the only one.

This is quite a bit of deducing to do up front; don't get the idea that you couldn't have handled this game without working all of this out up front. But if you're able to deduce this far, it saves you a tremendous amount of time in the long run.

7.   B

We love these acceptability questions. Just check each rule against each choice. Rule 1 downs (D). Rule 3 cuts (A) and (E). Rule 4 (among others) takes care of (C), which leaves us with our answer.

8.   A

Here's where they test our deduction. This we already know: exactly one president (Rule 1), at least one manager (Rule 2), so a maximum of three technicians.

9.   E

We can cross off (A) and (B), thanks to our *first* deduction that F is a technician. We also deduced that if there are two managers, then the president must be G. Since G can't be one of two managers, we can cross off (C) and (D), leaving (E). If you hadn't made that second deduction, no problem; you're simply forced to make it now: If G is one of two managers, then there needs to be three technicians: Two for G to supervise (Rule 5) and one for the other manager to supervise. This is no good, because it leaves no one to be president.

10.   B

(A) No way. From the beginning we've said that there has to be at least two technicians.

(B) Yes. We also deduced at the start that this is indeed possible (as long as G is our president). On test day, mark (B) and go on, but to get some practice at spotting wrong choices, we'll continue.

(C) No. The only employee who isn't supervised is the president, and there's only one president, so only one employee will go unsupervised.

(D) No. We know that the only two possibilities are 1, 1, 3 and 1, 2, 2. There can't be more managers than technicians, thanks to Rule 3.

(E) Rule 2 said that at least one of the employees that the president supervises is a manager. Rule 3 says that every manager supervises at least one employee. Since every employee is only supervised by one employee, (E) is not possible.

11.   D

Start by working with the new information. F (a technician) is supervised by the president, and we know (Rule 2) that the president also supervises at least one manager, so the president supervises at least two employees. But since F is supervised by the president, the manager whom the president is supervising needs another technician to supervise (Rule 3). So now we have one president, one manager, and two technicians with only one more employee to place. Learn to ask yourself the relevant questions. Could it be a manager? No, all of the technicians are already being supervised, which would not leave anyone for a new manager to supervise. We therefore must be dealing with the 1, 1, 3 setup, which gives us our answer.

(A) No, G could indeed be that one manager supervising two of the three technicians.

(B) No, G could be the president. H could either be the one manager or even one of the technicians.

(C) No, L could be the president or the manager.

(E) No; as we've figured out, there are exactly *three* technicians.

12. C

So now K as well as G both supervise two employees. Since the maximum number of technicians (as we deduced) is three, either K or G must be president while the other is a manager (if they were both managers, they'd need *four* technicians to supervise). Where to now? Well, one of the two people supervised by the president can be K or G (whoever isn't the president), but whoever isn't president is going to need two technicians to supervise. The president is also going to need another employee to supervise. Can it be a manager? No, because, just as in question 5, there is only one employee left, and if that person was a manager, there would be no one left for him or her to supervise. So K and G must be president and manager, in either order, and all of the other employees, including L, must be supervised technicians.

(A) Rule 4 makes this impossible.

(B) only could be true. G could just as easily be president.

(D) is wrong. We deduced that there can be only one manager (G or K).

(E) Actually, we figured out that there are (once again) exactly three technicians.

Set Two

Quesions 1–5

The Action

We're asked to order the appointments for seven patients— P, Q, R, S, T, U, and W. These appointments have been chronologically numbered, 1 through 7, by the test makers. This should give you a big clue as to what your setup should look like. The **key issues** will be:

1) What patient has what appointment?

2) What patient's appointment can, must, or cannot be consecutive with what other patient's appointment?

The Initial Setup

Keep this simple. The appointments are numbered 1 to 7, so the intuitive way to represent this is to write the 1 through 7 across the page from left to right. Remember to keep a roster of the patients somewhere:

$$P \; Q \; R \; S \; T \; U \; W$$
$$1 \quad 2 \quad 3 \quad 4 \quad 5 \quad 6 \quad 7$$

The Rules

1) This rule does not mean that Q must have the appointment immediately before W (although she could). It just says that Q's appointment must come *sometime* before W's. Be sure you get the order right. Shorthand this by drawing a Q, a few dots to the right of it, and then a W.

2) Second rule, same as the first. Again, be sure you have the correct order. Draw a U, a few dots following it, and then a P.

3) Build this directly into your sketch. Either R or T will always have appointment number 3. Under the 3 in your sketch, draw "R or T."

4) At first this rule may have looked complex, but all it's saying is that R and S must have consecutive appointments. The specific order of their appointments is up for grabs, however. Draw "RS or SR" to give yourself a reminder.

Key Deductions

There's not a lot more to deduce, because the rules have little in common. Just be sure you understand the workings of each rule. In a game as straightforward as this, if you mess up a rule, you can lose quite a few easy points.

It's a good idea to try to identify the most important entity or entities—the ones that promise the most help. Normally, that's the one or two entities mentioned multiple times in the rules. However, in games like this, where no entity is mentioned twice, also pay special attention to the *most concrete* rules. Here, only R and T are tied to an appointment. Rule 3 told us that either R or T must go in slot 3. This is a big hint that R and T are going to be the most important entities. In other words, throughout the game you will be dealing with whether R or T will be the one to go in appointment 3, so that promises to be a good jumping-off-point and head start in the questions to follow.

The Final Visualization

Here's what you have as you go on to the questions:

P Q R S T U W

1   2   3   4   5   6   7
         R or T

Q...W   U...P   SR or RS

1. E

Use this acceptability question to test your grasp of the game's inner workings. Compare each rule against each choice, eliminating all the choices that violate a rule. (A) has P before U, which is the opposite of Rule 2. (B) has someone other than R or T in appointment 3. That's a no-no according to Rule 3. (C) separates R and S, which we know is not allowed according to Rule 4. (D) has W before Q, which is verboten according to Rule 1. We're left with our answer, choice (E).

2. E

The stem puts W in appointment 2 and P in appointment 5. It also tells you that you're looking for the choice that must be true, so the four wrong answers either could be true or cannot be true. What rule has W in it? Rule 1 says that Q has an earlier appointment than W. The only appointment before W, who takes appointment 2, is 1. Which rule contains P? Rule 2 says that U must precede P. P is in 5, Rule 3 tells us that either R or T is in 3, so the only place for U is in appointment 4. Scan the choices. Is "Q in 1" or "U in 4" a choice? Sure it is. U is in 4, choice (E).

If you didn't stop to check the choices at that point, you probably continued on, and recognized that assigning R to appointment 3 won't fly—that would separate R from S (Rule 4). So T will take appointment 3, leaving R and S to slots 6 and 7, in either order. Now that everything's done, it's clear that (E) must be true and that (B) and (D) are both false, while (A) and (C) are only *possibly* true.

3. B

In this "must be true" question, the four wrong choices either could be true or absolutely must be false. Don't just stare at this stem, your eyes glazing over; get the new information down in your test booklet. Be sure you get the order right. You should have written "TUR." In what rules have you seen these entities before? They're in plenty of them; let's start with Rule 4. S has to be next to R, and since U is on one side of R, S must be on the other. Now we have a group of 4 entities, "TURS."

Where else are these entities mentioned? Rule 3 told us that either T or R must take appointment 3. Both R and T are in the group of four. This has "limited option" written all over it. Whenever you can narrow things down to two or three possibilities, it's almost always worth it to go ahead and work them out. With R is 3: T will have to take appointment 1, U in 2, R in 3, and S in 4. We're left with P, Q, and W. As long as Q is before W (as Rule 1 mandates), these three will fill out the 5, 6, 7 slots. "Option 1," as it were, looks like this:

1   2   3   4   5   6   7
T   U   R   S   (P)(Q...W)

For the second possibility, T in slot 3, just move the "TURS" foursome over and get T in 3, U in 4, R in 5, and S in 6. Go back to the rules. Rule 2 says that P must follow U, and the only appointment left after U is 7. Q and W are left to take appointments 1 and 2. Rule 1 says that Q goes before W, so Q gets appointment 1 and W appointment 2. Everything is set in this "Option 2." Here's what it looks like:

1   2   3   4   5   6   7
Q   W   T   U   R   S   P

With both of these options fully fleshed out, it should be a simple (and quick) matter of checking each choice.
(A) In the first option, P could be in 5, Q in 6, and W in 7. (A) doesn't have to be true and is not the answer.

(B) In the first option, S is in 4 and P must be in 5, 6, or 7. In the second option, S is in 6 and P is in 7. S must precede P. Either way, choice (B) is true, and on test day you'd choose it and move on. For the record, we'll go through why the remaining choices needn't be true.

(C) In the second option, we see that not only is S not *immediately* before Q, S is actually *after* Q.

(D) Stay in the second option, where W (in appointment 2) doesn't immediately precede P (which takes appointment 7), and you see why (D) needn't be true.

(E) Back to the first option; S is in 4 and W is in 6 or 7 (Q must be before it, so W can't be in 5). W needn't precede S.

4.   B

In this "could be true EXCEPT" question, four of the choices could be true or must be true; the choice we're looking for will be the one that is *false*. The question stem tells us that P immediately precedes S. Where else have we seen P and S? Rule 4 demands that R be next to S. P is on one side of S, so R must be on the other. Rule 2 says that U must be before P (maybe right before P, maybe not). So that gives us "U . . . PSR."

We're used to deciding whether R or T goes in the 3 slot, so let's look there next. Can R go in 3? Nope. At least U, P, and S are before R. No way to put R in the 3 slot, so T must go there. Now, where can we put the "U . . . PSR" block? PSR are all together, so they can't take the 1, 2 slots. These three will have to follow T in the 4, 5, 6 or 5, 6, 7 slots. U can go anywhere as long as it precedes P. Q and W will fill in the leftovers as long as Q precedes W as Rule 1 requires. Now let's check out the choices.

(A) The ordering U, Q, T, P, S, R, W works and shows that R can immediately precede W. Since (A) can be true, it's not the answer.

(B) If T immediately precedes Q, then T is in 3, Q is in 4, and our PSR block must occupy 5, 6, and 7, respectively. But Rule 1 says that W comes after Q, and we have no slots left after Q. (B) is impossible and is the answer. Quickly, here are the orderings that show that the remaining choices all could be true.

(C) and (E) are both true in: Q, W, T, U, P, S, R.

(D) is true in: U, Q, T, W, P, S, R.

5.   D

This is another "must be true" question, so the wrong choices will be things that could be true or must be false. From the stem we get (make sure you get the order right) "PTW." In what rules have we seen these entities? Rules 1 and 2 mean that Q and U must go somewhere before our "PTW" block. Now, as usual, who will take slot 3, R or T? Here we have Q, U, and P who must all precede T. T can't

be in 3, so R must take that appointment. The "PTW" block must follow R in either 4, 5, 6 or 5, 6, 7. But remember Rule 4. S must take the 2 or 4 slot in order to be next to R. Q and U have to precede "PTW," so S, Q, and U will fill in the 1, 2, 4 slots. The only possibility for our "PTW" block is in slots 5, 6, and 7.

(A) R is in 3 and W is in 7. W comes *after* R, not before.

(B) U could take slot 4. U needn't precede R.

(C) U in 2 and S in 4 fulfill all the requirements and show that S does not have to come before U.

(D) R is in 3 and P is in 5. Indeed, R must precede P. (D) must be true and is the answer.

(E) S in 2 and Q in 4 shows that (E) doesn't have to be true.

Questions 6–12

The Action

We're called on to distribute six employees among three committees—Policy, Quality, and Sales. Each committee has three employees per committee for a total of nine. The six employees are divided up into officers—F, G, and H—and supervisors—k, l, and m (we'll use CAPS for the officers and lowercase for the supervisors to keep them separate). The **key issues** will deal with:

1) What employee is on what committee?
2) What employee can, must, or cannot be on the same committee as what other employee?
3) What employee can, must, or cannot be on more than one committee?

Key issue 3) comes about because we have six employees filling nine committee slots. This is the first thing you had to recognize: There are more slots to fill than people to fill 'em, so some employees must sit on more than one committee.

The Initial Setup

Keep this setup simple. Get the committees down and the number of employees in each. That and making a note of the employees is all that's needed at this stage:

OFFICERS	Supervisors
F G H	k l m

Policy	Quality	Sales

__ __ __   __ __ __   __ __ __

The Rules:

1) Each of the three committees must contain at least one of our officers. Make a note of this under each committee in your sketch.

2) Basically a loophole-closer, but very necessary. No employee will be left out of the game.

3) Huh? You probably blinked on this one. Can it possibly be that helpful? Yep: All three officers fill out the Policy committee, so go ahead and write them in. One-third of the game's work is over. Just be sure that you remember that the officers aren't done: They can still go on other committees (and, in fact, we need at least one officer per committee, as per Rule 1).

4) G, an officer, can't be on the same committee as l, a supervisor. Write "No Gl" as a reminder. Saying it to yourself (silently) a couple of times may cement it. Wherever we place G, l must go elsewhere, and vice versa.

5) A good, solid, concrete rule; we can go ahead and write k into the Sales Committee. Remind yourself that k can still go on the Quality Committee if need be.

Key Deductions

What originally looked like a grouping game with three groups turns out to be a game with only two groups: The Policy committee is filled. The main thing to keep in mind is the flexibility in this game. Just because one of the employees is assigned to a committee doesn't mean that she or he can't join an additional committee.

You may or may not have picked up on one additional bit of deductive thinking: Every entity must join at least one committee (thanks to Rule 2). The only entities not placed in a committee by the rules are l and m, and of course, as supervisors, they are closed out of the Policy Committee. Of the three slots in the Sales Committee, k takes one and an officer takes another, so at most, one slot in Sales is available for l and m. Meanwhile, on the Quality Committee, one slot is occupied by an officer; therefore, at most two slots are available for l and m. When all is said and done: *Where are l and m serving?* There are only three possibilities: l in Quality, m in Sales; m in Quality, l in Sales; or both l and m in Quality. In all of these possibilities, we see that either l or m (or both) must join the Quality Committee. So we can enter "l or m" over one of our Quality Committee spaces: At least one of that pair must be

in the Quality Committee. This is tricky thinking, but it proves very useful with question 10 in particular, and throughout the game.

The Final Visualization

Here's what we have going into the questions:

$$\underline{\text{OFFICERS}} \qquad \underline{\text{Supervisors}}$$
$$\text{F G H} \qquad\qquad \text{k l m}$$

Policy	Quality	Sales
F G H __	__ l/m __ __	__ k __
Off.	Off.	Off.

$$\text{Never G l}$$

6.   D

The word "acceptability" isn't used in this stem, but it's an acceptability question all the same. "Can be assigned together" is the big tip-off. We're dealing with the Sales Committee, so take what we know about that committee and look at each choice. Rule 5 told us that k must go on the Sales committee, so axe (A) and (B), which don't include her. Rule 4 prohibits G and l from being on the same committee, and down goes (C). Rule 1 requires at least one officer on each committee, so (E), which tries to get away with three supervisors, can be crossed off. We're left with (D), the answer.

7.   C

In a "must be true" question, the four wrong choices either could be true or must be false. We're given two pieces of information, so start with the one that's more concrete, and here it's that H is on only one committee. H is already on the Policy Committee, so that's it for H—it'll be left to G and F to take care of the other two committees. The second piece of info is that F and m must be separated; m has to be somewhere, so whatever committee m is on, the only officer left to join m is G. Rule 4 says that G and l can't be on the same committee, so l will have to be on the other committee with F.

Who can fill in the remaining slot in each committee? H is out of the running, according to the stem. F can't join the Gm committee (the stem says no Fm), and neither can l (Rule 4, again). The only employee who can join Gm is k. What about the Fl committee? Again, the stem rules out m (no Fm), and Rule 4 says no G. So only k can join Fl. The Policy Committee is F, G, H (as always). We don't know exactly which threesome is on which of the two remaining committees, but one will be G, m, k, and the other will be F, l, k. We see that (C) must be true, k is on exactly two committees.

(A) No. G, m, k could be on the Sales Committee.

(B) No. F, l, k could be on the Quality Committee.

(D) No. l is on exactly *one* committee, either Sales or Quality.

(E) No. m is on exactly *one* committee, either Sales or Quality.

8. B

In this "CANNOT be true" question, we're looking for the choice that must be false. The wrong choices either must be true or could be true. In questions like this with no new information, it's worth the time to scan the answer choices, keeping the rules in mind. (B) and (C) should spring out as likely candidates, since assigning anyone to all three committees radically restricts the other assignments— perhaps fatally. Can G or H sit on all three committees? What rules mention G or H? Rule 1 mentions H, but only to include H on the Policy Committee. G, on the other hand, is part of Rule 1 and Rule 4. Rule 4 says that G and l must be separated—and there you have it. Every employee (l included) must sit on at least one committee. Since l and G can't sit on the same committee, whatever committee l is on cannot also include G. G cannot sit on all three committees; (B) must be false and is the answer. Here are the committee groups that show that each wrong choice *could* be true:

(A) Policy: F, G, H; Quality: G, m, k; Sales: H, l, k

(C) Policy: F, G, H; Quality: H, m, k; Sales: H, l, k

(D) and (E) Policy: F, G, H; Quality: F, l, m; Sales: F, l, k

9. E

Another "must be true" question; the four wrong choices either could be true or must be false. Another stem with two pieces of information: Starting with the more concrete, F sits on three committees. So beyond just Policy, F also sits on Quality, and on Sales with k. As for G sitting on two committees, that would be Policy (as always) plus either Quality or Sales—leave it at that for the moment. Recognize that l and m are the only ones not yet assigned to a committee. Rule 4 dictates that whatever committee G sits on, l must sit on the other. So we're down to two "limited

options." If G is on Quality, then l must fill out Sales with F and k. That leaves m to fill out Quality with G and F. Option 1 looks like this:

Policy: F, G, H; Quality: F, G, m; Sales: F, k, l

Alternatively, we could put G on Sales. l must go on Quality, and m is left to fill out Quality. Option 2 looks like this:

Policy: F, G, H; Quality: F, l, m; Sales: F, G, k

Now, just check the choices against these two options, and we see that no matter what, m sits on the Quality Committee. (E) must be true and is the answer.

(A) In the second option, we see that G needn't be on the Quality Committee.

(B) In the first option, we see that G needn't be on the Sales Committee.

(C) Actually in both options, k can only be on the Sales Committee.

(D) In the second option, we see that l needn't be on the Sales Committee.

10. E

Another "acceptability" question; this time we're looking for an acceptable Quality Committee. Here's where the extra thinking up front pays off. We've already deduced that either l or m must be on the Quality Committee. (If you don't remember how, look back at Key Deductions.) The right answer must include either l or m or both, so right away cross off (A), (B), and (C). None of them include the needed l or m. From there treat this like a normal "acceptability" question. Compare each rule against each choice. (D) tries to put G and l together, which is a violation of Rule 4. (E) is all that's left and is the answer.

11. E

Another "must be true" question, and again the four wrong choices either could be true or must be false. The stem says that l is on two committees. The only two open to l are Quality and Sales (Policy is full of officers). Rule 4 rules out G from being the officer in either of these committees, so either F or H will fill those slots. k is still on Sales, so that committee is full with l, k, and either F or H. Meanwhile, m has yet to be assigned a committee, so it must be Quality. Quality is now full with l, m, and either F or H. Scan the choices. We see that m must sit on the Quality Committee, and (E) is the answer.

(A) It could be H that is on the Sales Committee.

(B) Absolutely not. Since l is on Sales, no way that G could be, too.

(C) It could be F that is on the Quality Committee.

(D) Nope. k is on Sales. The Quality Committee is F or H, l, and m.

12. B

In this "CANNOT be true" question, the four wrong choices either could be true or must be true. To prove a choice wrong, we just have to find an instance that shows that the choice can be true.

(A) Question 11 showed that the following grouping was possible: Policy: F, G, H; Quality: H, l, m; Sales: H, l, k. In this setup, F and G sat on exactly one committee. It could be true then, and it can be true now. Cross off (A).

(B) If F and H are on exactly one committee, then that committee must be Policy (Rule 3 has already placed them there). Rule 1 says that each committee must have at least one officer, and the only officer left is G. G goes on both Quality and Sales. But l must join at least one of these two committees (everyone must be used), yet Rule 4 prohibits putting G and l together. Answer choice (B) cannot be true and is the answer. For the record, here are why the remaining choices don't measure up:

(C) Back to question 11 where we saw the following grouping: Policy: F, G, H; Quality: F, l, m; Sales: F, l, k. There, we saw G and H sitting on exactly one committee. It could be true then, and it can be true now. Eliminate (C).

(D) The following grouping shows that F and m can be on the Sales Committee: Policy: F, G, H; Quality: H, l, k; Sales: F, k, m.

(E) The following grouping shows that G and k can be on the Quality Committee: Policy: F, G, H; Quality: G, k, m; Policy: F, k, l.

Set Three

Quesions 1–5

The Action

In this straightforward game, we're called on to match up two people, Vladimir and Wendy, with the food—fish, hot cakes, macaroni, poached eggs, or omelet—that each eats during one day's four meals: breakfast, lunch, dinner, and snack. The **key issues** will, predictably, be:

1) What foods can Vladimir and Wendy eat for each meal?

2) What foods can't Vladimir and Wendy eat for each meal?

The Initial Setup

Set up a little schedule:

	Brkfst	Lunch	Dinner	Snack
Vlad				
Wendy				

The Rules

Start with the most concrete rule. You'll find it way down there at the bottom.

7) For lunch, Wendy eats an omelet. Great, build it right into the schedule.

1) This rule is huge because it greatly restricts the possibilities in this game. For each meal, Vladimir and Wendy will eat different foods. This is why it's best to start with the most concrete rule. We just placed a big "O" for omelet in Wendy's lunch slot with Rule 7 (what Wendy, no hamburger?). Now we can put Rule 1 into effect. Vladimir cannot have an omelet for his lunch food. He must choose between fish, hot cakes, and macaroni. As far as the rest of the game goes, this is a rule that will have to be uppermost in your consciousness, along with:

2) Not only do Wendy and Vladimir not duplicate each other's food in a meal—the better to share and sample, I guess—but neither person eats the same thing twice. Again—nothing much to draw here; it's a fact that has to stay alive in your brain throughout.

3) The only foods that Vladimir and Wendy can eat for breakfast are hot cakes, poached eggs, and omelet. Note that since Wendy eats an omelet for lunch, Rule 2 means that she can't eat an omelet for breakfast. Enter her remaining possibilities into the schedule.

4) The only foods available for lunch are fish, hot cakes, macaroni, and omelet. We know Wendy eats an omelet here, so Rule 1 prohibits Vladimir from having an omelet as well. List his remaining possibilities on the schedule.

5) For dinner, the two must choose among fish, hot cakes, macaroni, and omelet. Rule 2 is still in effect—Wendy has had her omelet for the day—so list each person's remaining possibilities.

6) Only fish and omelet may be eaten for the snack. This is big. Having gotten an omelet for lunch, Wendy is left to have fish here. Rule 1 demands that Vladimir have something different from Wendy, so Vladimir's snack is omelet. Enter both facts on the schedule.

Key Deductions

By dealing with the most concrete rule (Rule 7) first, we were able to do most of our deducing as we went along. We've done some excellent thinking and should be prepared to blow through the questions. Before hitting the questions though, you can and should narrow things down a bit further. We deduced both snack orders: Wendy eats fish and Vladimir eats an omelet. Remember Rule 2: Wendy eats fish for her snack, so fish is unavailable for her throughout the rest of the day. Vladimir eats an omelet, so that's out for him. Omelet is already out for Wendy since she eats one for her lunch. This means that omelet can be crossed off for both people throughout the day.

The Final Visualization

Here is our extremely useful master sketch:

	Brkfst	Lunch	Dinner	Snack
Vlad	H/P	F, H, M	F, H, M	O
Wendy	H/P	O	H/M	F

1. E

A "must be true" question with no new information is almost always testing a big deduction. We made the extra deductions that Wendy eats fish for her snack and Vladimir eats an omelet for his (look above if you need a reminder of the work). The test makers spell out the former in choice (E).

2. D

What must Vladimir eat? Again, this question is most likely testing our big deduction about Vladimir. The only thing

we know for certain about his daily diet is that he eats an omelet for his snack, choice (D).

3. D

In this "could be true" question, the four wrong choices must be false. This question benefits from a quick redrawing of the master sketch. Looking at the sketch, we see that the only meal during which Wendy can eat macaroni is dinner. Write an "M" in her dinner square. Rule 1 means that macaroni is out for Vladimir's dinner. The only other meal where Vlad can eat the needed macaroni is lunch. Write an "M" in his lunch square. Back to Rule 2, which dictates that macaroni is now off-limits for both people in all of the other meals. Note the possibilities, and here's our new sketch:

	Brkfst	Lunch	Dinner	Snack
Vlad	H/P	M	F/H	O
Wendy	H/P	O	M	F

Now, it's a simple matter to check each choice against our new sketch and find the one that can be true. We see that Wendy could indeed eat hot cakes for breakfast. Choice (D) could be true and is the credited answer.

(A), (B), and (C) Vladimir eats macaroni for lunch, only.

(E) Wendy eats macaroni for dinner.

4. B

Another "could be true" question, so the four wrong choices must be false. Follow this chain of reasoning carefully: If Wendy doesn't eat macaroni, then the only food left for her dinner is hot cakes. Since she eats hot cakes for dinner, she can't eat them for her breakfast. The only food left for her breakfast is poached eggs. Wendy eats poached eggs for breakfast, so Vlad can't eat them. The only food left for Vlad's breakfast is hot cakes. Vlad eats hot cakes for breakfast, so he can't eat them for any other meal. Here's what this incarnation of the master sketch looks like:

	Brkfst	Lunch	Dinner	Snack
Vlad	H	F/M	F/M	O
Wendy	P	O	H	F

Once again, it's a simple matter to check the choices and find the one that could be true. Vladimir could eat fish for lunch, and (B) is the answer.

(A) and (D) No, Vladimir eats hot cakes for breakfast; Wendy eats the poached eggs.

(C) No, since Vladimir eats hot cakes for breakfast, the only foods open to him for lunch are fish and macaroni.

(E) No, Wendy eats hot cakes for dinner.

5. B

In a "cannot be true" question, the four wrong answers are either possibly true or definitely so. Wendy eats poached eggs for breakfast, so Vladimir can't eat them. The only other option for his breakfast is hot cakes. Now hot cakes are unavailable for the rest of his day. Scan the choices and (B) should leap out at you. We just said that Vladimir has hot cakes for breakfast. Rule 2 is still alive and strong, so he can't eat hot cakes at any other meal. (B) cannot be true and is the answer. All of the other choices are quite possible in this situation.

Questions 6–11

The Action

This fairly complex game involves matching cars with three different characteristics (family or sports car, new or used, and production models or research models) and then with a fourth characteristic, the floor they're displayed on. Important to note that each floor contains all cars of one of each of the three different characteristics, i.e., there will not be both new and used cars on a single floor. There's only one major **key issue** that every question will involve:

1) What characteristics are exhibited by the cars on each floor?

The Initial Setup

Since we're dealing with three floors each containing three characteristics, one possible way to visualize this is to draw a three-by-three table. We can label the vertical side of the box 3, 2, and 1, from top to bottom, and each box across horizontally would represent one of the three characteristics: style, age, and type. This way we can picture each floor and it's relevant traits:

	F/S	N/U	P/R
3			
2			
1			

The Rules

Where to start? As usual, with the concrete rules.

4) The cars on floor 1 are new. An "N" in the appropriate grid box will remind us that ALL of the cars on floor 1 are new.

5) The cars on floor 3 are used. A "U" in the appropriate floor 3 grid box means that all the cars exhibited there are used.

1) This rule is fairly lengthy, so take your time and be sure that you fully understand it. IF (that's a big if) there are both family and sports cars, then all of the family cars will be on lower floors than any of the sports cars. So if there are both kinds, floor 1 must be family cars and floor 3 must be sports cars. Understanding this rule is far more important than exactly how you choose to represent it on the page.

2) There are NO cars that are both used and research models. What does this tell us? If a car is used, then it must also be a production model. If a car is a research model, then it must be new. If a car is new . . . nothing. Be careful, a new car can either be a research model or a production model. "If U, then P" and "if R, then N" should help us remember this.

3) None of the cars in the exhibition are both research models and sports cars. Again, be careful when considering what this means. If a car is a research model, then it must be a family car. If a car is a sports car, then it must be a production model. If a car is a family car or a production model, then we know *nothing* (or at least nothing new). "If R, then F" and "if S, then P" will aid in sorting it out.

Key Deductions

The results of our work with Rules 2 and 3 certainly qualify as Key Deductions. However, there's even more to piece together. Rule 2 yielded "if Research, then New," and Rule 3 yielded "if Research, then Family." To make it easier we can combine those to get "**if Research, then New and Family.**" Also, don't neglect your grid. Rule 5 resulted in a big "U" under floor 3, and thanks to Rule 2, we know that "if Used, then Production." Therefore, **the floor 3 cars must be production models**. Two of the three characteristics are taken care of for that floor.

The Final Visualization

Here's what we have just before facing off with the questions:

If F + S, then $\frac{S}{F}$		F/S	N/U	P/R
If U, then P	3		U	P
If R, then N + F	2			
If S, then P	1		N	

6. A

If sports cars are on *exactly* two floors, then family cars must be on *exactly* one floor, and Rule 1 applies: Sports cars must be on floors 2 and 3, which eliminates (C) and (E), and family cars must be on floor 1, which contradicts choice (B). Floors 2 and 3 contain sports cars which are production models (Rule 3). Choice (D) is therefore out. Only choice (A), research models on floor 1, is possible.

7. D

No new information here, so move right on to the choices. Rule 2 kills choices (B), and (C), and (E) is also wrong, since we know that at least one floor has used cars. Rule 3 axes choice (A). We're left with choice (D), and it is indeed possible that exactly one floor has research models (as long as that floor is floor 1, since it would have to contain new research model family cars).

8. D

This is a "must be true" question with no new information. A quick scan through the choices in search of one of our earlier deductions turns up choice (D)—production models on floor 3. (A), (B), and (C) are possible only, while (E) is totally impossible.

9. E

Since we deduced that floor 3 contains production models, the 2 floors with research models must be floors 1 and

2. A quick glance at your scratchwork tells you that these research cars must be new family cars (Rules 2 and 3). Notice that this takes care of eight out of the nine possible boxes in our table. Also notice that the question is a "can be false" question. Here's where the on-the-ball test taker realizes that it's a good bet that the answer to the question will almost certainly deal with the one box that's still unresolved, which deals with the family/sports issue on floor 3 (everything else is determined, and therefore must be true). Choice (E), family cars on 3, could be false and therefore does the trick. Choices (A) through (D) correspond perfectly to the situation, so naturally they all must be true.

10. D

Rule 3: All research cars are family cars. Stem: All new cars are research cars. Therefore: All new cars are family cars, which happens to be choice (D).

Family cars need not be anything in particular, so choices (A) through (C) are out.

Similarly, in (E), a production model car could be a sports car.

11. A

If all production models are used, then a car that is not used (new), must not be production (research). So floor 1's new cars must be of the research variety, which means that floor 1's cars must also be family cars (Rule 3). We get this in choice (A). (B) through (E) could all be true, but also could be false.

Chapter 5: **Reading Comprehension**

- The 6 Basic Principles of Reading Comp
- The 4 Reading Comp Question Types
- Kaplan's 5-Step Method for Reading Comp

When preparing students for most tests, Kaplan emphasizes that reading for Reading Comp is not like any other reading they'll do. But that isn't as true in the case of the LSAT. Most legal careers will at times involve the selective, methodical approach to reading matter that this test section requires, and it's a skill you'll rely on heavily during law school as well.

The topics for LSAT Reading Comp passages are taken from four areas: social sciences, natural sciences, the humanities, and law. The passages are long, dense, and difficult—like at least some of the material you'll face in law school and your careers. So right now is a good time to start shoring up your reading skills.

Three of the passages will be approximately 450 words long and have five to eight questions associated with each. The fourth passage—which may fall anywhere in the section—will be a pair of shorter, related passages. The five to eight questions associated with that passage set will focus primarily on the relationship between the passages.

 GO ONLINE

How did you do in Reading Comp on your Diagnostic Quiz? Most test takers find the section harder than expected.

THE 6 BASIC PRINCIPLES OF READING COMP

Improvement in Reading Comp requires patience. You may not see dramatic improvement after taking only one section. But with steady practice, the principles and strategies below will increase your skill and confidence on this section.

KAPLAN EXCLUSIVE

Mark the passage as you read. Circle names, box dates, underline key sentences—whatever helps you navigate.

Read Critically

The single most important factor in Reading Comp is the basic skill that's relevant on all sections of the test: critical reading. Critical reading involves perspective—the ability to step back from a piece of prose and carefully evaluate it. You get no points for just "getting through" the passage. You must attack—not simply read—passages and questions. If you think in terms of attack, you're less likely to be distracted or to let the densely worded prose confuse you.

The following are some concrete ways to improve the specific critical reading skills necessary for Reading Comp:

- Paraphrase key ideas: Put the author's important concepts into your own words.
- Connect abstract ideas to your own experience: Visualize the subject matter if you can.
- Anticipate where the author is going: Each step of the way, ask: "What could or must follow?"
- Don't let complex words and sentences scare you: You don't have to become expert on the topic.
- Remember that authors are repetitious: Not every sentence adds a new idea.

Use Keywords

Like Logical Reasoning arguments, Reading Comp passages are full of structural signals—words or phrases that help the author string ideas together logically. They allow you to infer a great deal about content, even if that content is obscure or difficult. Conclusion signals (*therefore, consequently, thus*) and evidence signals (*because, since*) are extremely helpful, as are contrast signals (*but, however, although, by contrast*), which indicate an opposition or shift in ideas.

A Word About Outside Knowledge

On the LSAT, no outside knowledge is necessary. In Reading Comp, it's not necessary—or even helpful—to know anything about the topics covered in the passages. Everything you'll need to answer every question is included in the passage. This, too, is consistent with legal practice. When you read case law or a statute, it's irrelevant what you believe should be true, or what you read in an article on the way to work. What counts is what the case or statute says. In Reading Comp, correct answers must reflect only what the passage says or implies.

However, the passages are always logical, and always reflect ideas that you can understand. Don't read in a vacuum—relate what you read to your world, and recognize the common sense of the text. So use your own knowledge to help you understand the passages, but be careful not to let it interfere with answering questions correctly.

Read for the Topic, Scope, Purpose, and Main Idea

The first third of any passage usually introduces the topic, scope, main idea, and purpose and the author's attitude. Let's take a closer look at these crucial elements of a Reading Comp passage.

Topic, Scope, and Purpose

Topic and scope are both **objective**, meaning they include no reference to the author's point of view. The difference between them is that the **topic** is broader; the **scope** narrows the topic. Scope is particularly important because of the many answer choices that will be wrong because they fall outside the scope, even though they're within the broader topic.

The topic/scope distinction ties into the all-important author's **purpose**. The author deliberately narrows the scope by including certain aspects of the broader topic and excluding others. Those choices have to do with why the passage is being written in the first place. We can say that the topic is broadly stated (for instance, a passage's topic might be "solving world hunger"). Scope is narrower (a new technology for solving world hunger) and leads rather quickly to the author's subjective purpose (the author wrote in order to describe a new technology and its promising uses). The idea that the author sets out to convey is the main idea.

Main Idea

Almost every passage boils down to one **main idea**. The primary purpose and main idea are intertwined. Take, for example, the hypothetical passage described above, in which the author had the following purpose:

> To describe a new technology and its promising uses.

The main idea is simply a more detailed restatement of this without the active verb:

> Biochemical engineering (or whatever new technology is discussed) can help solve world hunger.

Most often, the main idea will be presented early in the passage, but sometimes the author will build up to it more gradually; you may not see the author's purpose or main idea until the very end.

In any case, the main idea appears somewhere in the passage, and when it does, take conscious note of it. For one thing, the purpose of everything else in the passage will be to support this idea. Furthermore, knowing the main idea will directly answer some of your questions and will make it easier to focus in on the right answer in others.

Get the Gist of Each Paragraph

The paragraph is the main structural unit of any passage. Find the **gist**, or purpose, of each succeeding paragraph, and attempt to relate it back to the passage as a whole. To do this, ask yourself:

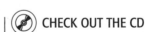 **CHECK OUT THE CD**

Practice finding the easiest questions in your CD Companion Reading Comp quizzes.

- Why did the author include this paragraph?
- What shift did the author have in mind when moving on to this paragraph?
- What bearing does this paragraph have on the author's main idea?

Use this process to create a roadmap of the passage, tying each paragraph to the structure and main idea. When a question requires you to look back into the passage, this roadmap will help you locate the answer.

Notice Structure and Tone

In a quest to master the content of a passage, test takers are notorious for ignoring the **structure**—how the author says it. One of the keys to success on this section is to understand not only the purpose, but also the structure of each passage, because the questions ask not only about the content of the passage, but about *how* the author advances his purpose and makes his point.

The following is a list of some of the classic LSAT passage structures:

- Passages based on differing opinions
- Passages based on a serious problem or situation
- Passages based on a strong opinion
- Passages based on significant new findings (common in science passages)

Many LSAT passages are based on variations of one of these classic structures. Your task is to seek them out actively. Knowing these classic structures can "jump start" your search.

And notice the author's position within these structures—the **tone**. Within the first classic structure, the author may simply relate the two sides of the story, or may at some point jump in and take a side, or even reject the conflicting opinions in favor of a third opinion. Within the second or third structure, the author may strongly advocate for or against a particular view. On the other hand, the author could simply describe the strongly held opinions of someone else. This author's writing style would be more descriptive, factual, and even, handed.

Notice the difference in tone between the two types of authors. Correct answer choices for a primary purpose question in the former case would use terms like *argue for, propose,* and *demonstrate,* whereas correct choices in the latter case would use terms like *describe* and *discuss.*

Don't Obsess over Details

In school, you probably read to memorize information for an exam. This is not the type of reading that's good for getting points on LSAT Reading Comp. You're reading for points, not retention, and the only thing that matters is that you're able to use the groundwork you've laid to answer the questions correctly.

What's more, it's an open-book test. If you've mapped the passage as you've read, you'll be able to quickly locate any details necessary to answer a question.

Do the Questions in the Order Best for You

Just as you skip any passage that slows you down too much, get the easy questions before tackling hard ones. After finishing a passage, quickly scan for global questions, especially main idea or primary purpose questions. Doing these first generally helps you solidify your grasp of these concepts, and you should already have answered these questions mentally as you read.

Then do any other global types—questions about the author's overall tone or the organization of the passage. Detail questions, especially those with line references, are good candidates to tackle next. Many test takers benefit from leaving the more difficult Logic or Inference questions for last.

This, of course, is only a rough suggested order. With practice, you may want to revise it to account for your own strengths and the difficulty level of each question. Some Inference questions may be easier than some Detail questions. So, for each question, ask yourself: "Can I answer this question quickly?"

Eliminate Wrong Choices First if You Have to Guess

One or more of the wrong answer choices on any Reading Comp question will fall into patterns you'll learn to recognize. Any wrong choice you can eliminate improves your chance of choosing the correct answer. The common wrong answer types in Reading Comp are:

- **180:** Choices that are exactly the opposite of the correct choice, which are especially common on "EXCEPT" or Strengthen/Weaken questions
- **Outside Scope:** Choices that go beyond the scope of the passage or the particular argument being focused on
- **Faulty Use of Detail:** Choices that use language or ideas from the stimulus, but misapply them conspicuously
- **Extreme:** Choices using words like *always, never, none, all,* and *every*, which are most likely wrong unless the language of the argument is extreme
- **Half Right, Half Wrong:** Choices that join a correct statement with an incorrect one; don't be hasty and choose your answer without reading the entire choice.

In addition, when you see that any two or more answer choices are very similar, that's a strong signal that they are wrong—only one choice can be correct.

 KAPLAN STRATEGY

The basic principles for Reading Comp success are:
- Read critically.
- Read for topic, scope, purpose, and main idea.
- Get the gist of each paragraph.
- Note structure and tone.
- Do the questions in the order that's best for you.
- Eliminate wrong choices first if you have to guess.

THE 4 CRUCIAL READING COMP QUESTION TYPES

While it might be convenient to cover the Reading Comp section in terms of the types of passages that typically appear on it, Kaplan has found that that's not the best way to master the section. In Logic Games, categorizing the games is helpful because grouping, sequencing, and matching games have their own sets of issues.

Such differences don't separate a humanities passage from one on social science, or a natural science passage from one on law; you read them in the same way. The only real variation you'll see in tackling the passages comes when you confront the comparative reading passage set, and even there the differences are minor. You'll employ an abbreviated version of the regular approach, identifying topic, scope, purpose, and main idea. You won't map the passages out paragraph by paragraph

 GO ONLINE

As you read through the question types, pay close attention to those you missed on the Diagnostic Quiz to see why you missed them.

because they're so much shorter, and you'll have to keep your eye on who said what and compare the scopes and tones of the passages, but the basic principles are just the same.

Global Questions

Global questions, which account for about 20–25 percent of all Reading Comp questions, ask you to sum up the author's overall intentions, ideas, or passage structure. In general, a Global question choice that zeros in on a detail or the content of one paragraph will be wrong. You'll often find Global questions at the beginning of question sets, and often one of the wrong choices will be a side issue discussed at the tail end of the passage. Scanning the verbs in the answer choices is a good way to take a first cut at the question: The verb in the correct choice must agree with the author's tone.

KAPLAN) EXCLUSIVE

Keep the main idea in mind, even when answering questions that don't ask for it. Even in the Detail questions, correct answers generally echo the main idea in one way or another.

Main Idea and Primary Purpose

The formats for these questions are pretty self-evident:

- Which one of following best expresses the main idea of the passage?
- The author's primary purpose is to . . .

Structure

Another type of Global question asks about the structure of a passage or an argument. The question might read: "Which of the following best describes the organization of the passage?"

Answer choices are usually worded very generally; they focus on the broad layout of the passage as opposed to the specific content. Here are a few possible ways that a passage could be organized:

- A hypothesis is stated and then analyzed.
- A proposal is evaluated, and alternatives are explored.
- A viewpoint is set forth and then subsequently defended.

When choosing among these choices, ask yourself: "Was there a hypothesis here? Was there an evaluation of a proposal or a defense of a viewpoint?" Make yourself identify where the hypothesis or evaluation is—don't think in generalities. These terms may all seem similar, but in fact, they're very different. If the answer choice includes a component you can't identify in the passage, it's wrong.

Author's Attitude

The tone question asks you to evaluate the author's attitude. Is the author passionate, fiery, neutral, angry, hostile, opinionated, low-key? Here's an example: "The author's tone in the passage can best be characterized as . . . " Don't confuse the nature of the content with the author's tone—a social science passage based on this century's grisliest murders may be presented in a cool, detached, and strictly informative way.

Logic Questions

Logic questions come in two distinct forms: function questions and reasoning questions.

Function Questions

These questions ask why the author included certain information—what role did it play in the author's overall argument. Answer choices that focus on *what* rather than *why* will be wrong for these Logic questions.

Reasoning Questions

These are similar to Logical Reasoning questions; treat them exactly as you would the same type of question in the Logical Reasoning section.

Inference Questions

Inference questions make up 55–60 percent of the Reading Comp section and are similar to Logical Reasoning questions. As you've seen in Logical Reasoning, an **inference** is a statement that must be true based on the passage, but that is contained "between the lines." The answer is strongly implied or hinted at but not stated directly.

So in that respect, Logical Reasoning and Reading Comp inferences are similar. The difference?

- Reading Comp text is tougher to get through than Logical Reasoning prose.

The same rules that apply to inferences in Logical Reasoning also apply to inferences in Reading Comp, and the skills learned there will serve you well here.

 MOBILE PREP

Keep practicing your other test skills. While you learn Reading Comp strategies, try some mobile Logical Reasoning.

Extracting valid inferences from Reading Comp passages often requires recognizing that information can be expressed in different ways. In fact, Inference questions often boil down to an exercise in translation.

Inference questions appear in a variety of different forms:

- It can be inferred from the passage that . . .
- The passage/author suggests/implies that . . .
- The author would probably agree that . . .
- The passage supports which one of the following statements . . .

Usually, some specific information will complete these questions, providing clues as to where in the passage the key to the answer will be. Occasionally, the stem won't contain specific information, in which case you simply have to work your way through the choices until you find the one that's supported by the text. When evaluating the answer choices, keep the relevant ideas firmly in mind. The farther you stray from them to endorse a choice, the more likely it is that this choice will be wrong.

KAPLAN STRATEGY

A good inference:

- Stays in line with the author's (or proponent's) tone.
- Stays within the scope of the passage.
- Is neither denied by, nor irrelevant to, the ideas stated in the passage.

Detail Questions

Detail questions, which make up roughly 10–20 percent of section, are directly answered in the text. Most students find these the easiest Reading Comp questions, since they're the most concrete. It's fairly simple to identify a Detail question from its stem:

- According to the passage/author . . .
- The author states that . . .
- The author mentions which one of the following as . . .

Sometimes the question provides a line reference, text quoted from the passage, or other clues to where the answer is located. (Just be careful with line references—they'll bring you to the right area, but usually the answer will be found in the lines before or after the referenced line.)

If you've created a good roadmap, it shouldn't take long to locate the relevant detail. And if that fails, you can put that question aside and return to it later. You may find the answer while you are working on other questions, and if not, you can return to it if and when you have the time to search through the passage.

Now that you have the basics of LSAT Reading Comp under your belt, learn the method that combines them all into a single *modus operandi*.

KAPLAN'S 5-STEP METHOD FOR READING COMP

1. Read the Passage Critically.

As outlined in the basic principles, read to identify the topic, scope, main idea, and purpose, paying close attention to structure and tone. Paraphrase ideas, and build your roadmap by noting the gist of each paragraph. For comparative reading passages, also note the common ground and the differences in scope and tone.

2. Read the Question Stem.

Identify exactly what the question asks. Mark keywords in the question (like *not* and *implies)*, if it helps you to keep focused on what's required. Look for clues—like proper nouns and names, line or paragraph references, or direct quotes—that will lead you to the answer.

3. Research the Relevant Text.

Using your roadmap, look back at any relevant language. Taking the time to locate the information can help you focus your mind and recall the details as precisely as the question demands. Sometimes just establishing that information appears in a particular paragraph will be enough to answer the question, but many answer choices are traps for those who try to rely on memory.

4. Make a Prediction.

Without wasting much time on it, a prediction of the expected answer (or at least a prephrase, whether in fine detail or the merest hint) will lead you to the correct choice and prevent you from falling for distracters.

5. Go to the Choices.

The preparation you've done will help you zero in on the right choice. Simply finding the choice that matches your prediction is the surest and most efficient approach, but you can eliminate wrong answer choices, if necessary.

Now let's try the 5-Step Method on an actual LSAT Reading Comp single passage.

For the time being, we've just included the question stems of the questions attached to this passage, since you don't want to get into answer choices until later. Remember that on test day, you don't have to do the passages in order, either—pick your best shots.

> Modern architecture has been criticized for emphasizing practical
> and technical issues at the expense of aesthetic concerns. The high-
> rise buildings constructed throughout the industrialized world in
> the 1960s and 1970s provide ample evidence that cost-efficiency and
> (5) utility have become the overriding concerns of the modern architect.
> However, Otto Wagner's seminal text on modern architecture, first
> published in Germany in 1896, indicates that the failures of modern
> architecture cannot be blamed on the ideals of its founders.
> Wagner's *Modern Architecture* called for a new style based on mod-
> (10) ern technologies and modes of construction. He insisted that there
> could be no return to traditional, preindustrial models; only by accept-
> ing wholeheartedly the political and technological revolutions of the
> nineteenth century could the architect establish the forms appropriate
> to a modern, urban society. "All modern creations," Wagner wrote,
> (15) "must correspond to the new materials and demands of the pres-
> ent...must illustrate our own better, democratic, self-confident, ideal

nature," and must incorporate the new "colossal technical and scientific achievements" of the age. This would indeed seem to be the basis of a purely materialist definition of architecture, a prototype for the

(20) simplistic form-follows-function dogma that opponents have identified as the intellectual basis of modern architecture.

But the picture was more complex, for Wagner was always careful to distinguish between art and engineering. Ultimately, he envisaged the architect developing the skills of the engineer without losing the

(25) powers of aesthetic judgment that Wagner felt were unique to the artist. "Since the engineer is seldom a born artist and the architect must learn as a rule to be an engineer, architects will in time succeed in extending their influence into the realm occupied by the engineers, so that legitimate aesthetic demands can be met in a satisfactory way." In

(30) this symbiotic relationship essential to modernism, art was to exercise the controlling influence.

No other prospect was imaginable for Wagner, who was firmly rooted as a designer and, indeed, as a teacher in the classical tradition. The apparent inconsistency of a confessed classicist advising against the

(35) mechanical imitation of historical models and arguing for new forms appropriate to the modern age created exactly the tension that made Wagner's writings and buildings so interesting. While he justified, for example, the choice of a circular ground plan for churches in terms of optimal sight lines and the technology of the gasometer, the true

(40) inspiration was derived from the centralized churches of the Italian Renaissance. He acknowledged as a rationalist that there was no way back to the social and technological conditions that had produced the work of Michelangelo or Fischer von Erlach, but he recognized his emotional attachment to the great works of the Italian Renaissance and

(45) Austrian baroque.

1. Which one of the following best expresses the main idea of the passage?

2. According to the passage, Wagner asserts which one of the following about the roles of architect and engineer?

3. The passage suggests that Wagner would be LEAST likely to agree with which one of the following statements about classical architecture and the modern architect?

4. The passage suggests which one of the following about the quotations from *Modern Architecture* cited in the second paragraph?

5. The author of the passage states which one of the following about the concerns of modern architecture?

6. The author mentions Wagner's choice of a "circular ground plan for churches" (line 38) most likely in order to

7. The passage is primarily concerned with

1. Read the Passage Critically.

The topic, modern architecture, is announced immediately, but it takes the rest of the first paragraph to narrow down the scope: how Wagner's book demonstrates that today's architects have strayed from the original ideals. The keyword *However* that opens the last sentence of the paragraph signals that departure; always pay attention to keywords like *but*, *however*, and *nevertheless* because they signal that the author is changing direction.

As you move through the rest of the passage, take care not to get bogged down in the details. Remember that your primary goal is to map, not to learn the passage in detail.

The second paragraph concedes that Wagner did advocate incorporation of modern science and technology into architecture. However, the third paragraph begins with another contrast keyword, *But*, and the author goes on to qualify that Wagner was careful to distinguish art from engineering. In fact, art was to "exercise the controlling influence." Finally, in the last paragraph, the author points to Wagner's classical roots.

The author's purpose and main idea were clear in the first paragraph, though it's always wise to keep reading with an open mind. He wants to demonstrate that today's architecture deviates significantly from the original aesthetic ideals of its founders.

2. Read the Question Stem.

Don't forget to select the order in which you'll do the questions. Be clear about what each question asks. Look at the question stems for this passage scanning for Global questions—especially *main idea* or *primary purpose*. If you come across the following question, you should attempt it with the passage fresh in your mind:

> 1. Which one of the following best expresses the main idea of the passage?

3. Research the Relevant Text.

In this case, and for most Global questions, your roadmap or a quick review of the gist of each paragraph will suffice.

4. Make a Prediction.

If you read critically, you will have already identified the main idea of the passage.

5. Go to the Choices.

Here are the answer choices for question 1:

> (A) Modern architecture has been criticized for emphasizing practical and technical issues and for failing to focus on aesthetic concerns.

(B) Critics have failed to take into account the technological innovations and aesthetic features that architects have incorporated into modern buildings.

(C) Wagner's *Modern Architecture* provides architects with a chronicle of the origins of modern architecture.

(D) Wagner's *Modern Architecture* indicates that the founders of modern architecture did not believe that practical issues should supersede the aesthetic concerns of the past.

(E) Wagner's seminal text, *Modern Architecture*, provides the intellectual basis for the purely materialistic definition of modern architecture.

 READ MORE

There's plenty of practice with challenging Reading Comp sets in Kaplan's *LSAT 180*.

Choice (D) has the right elements: the idea that the original ideals of modern architecture didn't support today's focus on the practical, and Wagner's book as evidence. Choice (A) is supported by the passage, but too narrow to be the main idea—it leaves out the whole issue of today's architecture deviating from the original ideals of modern architecture (let alone Wagner's book). (B) contradicts the passage, which indicates that most modern architects overlook the aesthetic. (C) is too narrow; it's true, but it leaves out the author's key point about today's architects having deviated from those origins. (E) focuses in on a detail at the end of paragraph 2—it might be tempting because the language is familiar, but that's a common trap.

Question 7 is another Global question that you may wish to answer early on. Continuing to scan the questions, the one with the line reference, question 6, may have caught your eye. Logic questions often take a bit more work, though, and it will probably be more efficient to attack Detail questions 2 and 5 next. The Inference questions, 3 and 4, are good to save for last.

Let's try one Detail question and one Inference question, repeating steps 2–5 of Kaplan's Method.

2. Read the Question Stem.

Here's the complete form (with answer choices) of question 2:

2. According to the passage, Wagner asserts which one of the following about the roles of architect and engineer?

(A) The architect should make decisions about aesthetic issues and leave decisions about technical matters to the engineer.

(B) The engineer has often developed the powers of aesthetic judgment previously thought to be unique to the architect.

(C) The judgment of the engineer should be as important as the judgment of the architect when decisions are made about aesthetic issues.

(D) The technical judgment of the engineer should prevail over the aesthetic judgment of the architect in the design of modern buildings.

(E) The architect should acquire the knowledge of technical matters typically held by the engineer.

 CHECK OUT THE CD

When you master the methods and strategies, you're ready for a full-length practice test.

Use the information in the stem to direct your search. Look for clues—like proper nouns and names, line or paragraph references, or direct quotes—that will lead you to the answer.

3. Research the Relevant Text.

The author talks about engineers in the third paragraph, so begin there.

4. Make a Prediction.

The author tells us only a couple of things about engineers: They're rarely born artists, and architects should extend their knowledge into the engineers' realm.

5. Go to the Choices.

Correct answer choice (E) is a paraphrase of the above: Architects should learn the technical aspects usually handled by engineers.

(A) contradicts the passage—the third paragraph says directly that the architect should involve himself in the technical aspects. (B) also contradicts paragraph 3, which says the engineer is "seldom a born artist," and so the burden falls to the architect to blend the technical with the aesthetic. (C) contradicts the last line of paragraph 3, where the author reminds us that in Wagner's vision, "art was to exercise the controlling influence." (D) also contradicts the last line of paragraph 3.

2. Read the Question Stem.

4. The passage suggests which one of the following about the quotations from *Modern Architecture* cited in the second paragraph?

(A) They represent the part of Wagner's work that has had the least influence on the architects who designed the high-rise buildings of the 1960s and 1970s.

(B) They describe the part of Wagner's work that is most often evoked by proponents of Wagner's ideas on the use of modern technology in architecture.

(C) They do not adequately reflect the complexity of Wagner's ideas on the use of modern technology in architecture.

(D) They reflect Wagner's active participation in the political revolutions of the nineteenth century.

(E) They provide an overview of Wagner's ideas on the relationship between art and technology.

The word "suggests" tips you off that this is an Inference question, but not all Inference questions are created equal. This one is a good choice to be first among Inference questions because it directs you to the second paragraph—some Inference questions leave it wide open as to where you might find the answer

3. Research the Relevant Text.

Use your clues from the stem: The right answer will tell you something about the quotations from Wagner's book referenced in the second paragraph. The first step, of course, is to see what paragraph 2 said about those quotations. But beware! Many questions (especially Inference and Logic questions) rely on the larger context.

4. Make a Prediction.

In paragraph 2 we learn that Wagner encouraged the incorporation of the technical into modern architecture and that this seems to be the basis for the current "form-follows-function dogma." That word "seems" is a clue, and the first sentence of paragraph 3 clinches it: It's really much more complex than that.

5. Go to the Choices.

That's correct answer choice (C) exactly. Such quotes might seem to advocate function over form, but the author tells us explicitly in the next paragraph that his analysis was more complicated.

Choice (A) is a 180: The quotations emphasize function, which the author says has become the dominant factor for today's architects. (B) also contradicts the passage; Wagner's followers would certainly point to his emphasis on aesthetics. (D) is outside the scope. (E) is inaccurate—an overview of Wagner's ideas would include his focus on aesthetics.

SUMMARY

The basic principles of Reading Comp are:

- Read critically.
- Read for topic, scope, purpose, and main idea.
- Note structure and tone.
- Get the gist of each paragraph.
- Do the questions in the order that's best for you.
- Eliminate wrong choices if you have to guess.

The Reading Comp question types are:

- Global questions ask the reader to sum up the author's overall ideas, attitudes, or structure.
- Logic questions include function and reasoning questions.
- Inference questions ask what is implied.
- Detail questions ask what is expressly stated.

Kaplan's 5-Step Method for Reading Comp

1. Read the passage critically.
2. Read the question stem.
3. Research the relevant text.
4. Make a prediction.
5. Go to the choices.

READING COMP PRACTICE

Set One

<u>Directions:</u> Each passage set in this test is followed by several questions. After reading the passage set, choose the best answer to each question. Your replies are to be based on what is stated or implied in the selection.

<u>Passage for Questions 1–7</u>

Innovations in language are never completely new. When the words used for familiar things change, or words for new things enter the language, they are usually borrowed or adapted from
(5) stock. Assuming new roles, they drag their old meanings along behind them like flickering shadows. This seems especially true of the language of the contemporary school of literary criticism that now prefers to describe its work simply and rather
(10) presumptuously as "theory," but is still popularly referred to as post-structuralism or deconstruction.

The first neologisms adopted by this movement were *signifier* and *signified*, employed to distinguish words from their referents and to illustrate
(15) the arbitrariness of the terms we choose. The use of these particular terms (rather than, respectively, *word* and *thing*) underlined the seriousness of the naming process and its claim on our attention. Since in English "to signify" can also mean "to
(20) portend," these terms also suggest that words predict coming events.

With the use of the term *deconstruction*, we move into another and more complex realm of meaning. The most common use of the terms
(25) *construction* and *deconstruction* is in the building trades, and their borrowing by literary theorists for a new type of criticism cannot help but have certain overtones to the outsider. First, the usage suggests that the creation and critical interpreta-
(30) tion of literature are not organic but mechanical processes; that the author of any piece of writing is not an inspired, intuitive artist, but merely a laborer who cobbles existing materials (words) into more or less conventional structures. The
(35) term *deconstruction* implies that the text has been put together like a building or a piece of machinery, and that it is in need of being taken apart, not so much in order to repair it as to demonstrate

underlying inadequacies, false assumptions, and
(40) inherent contradictions. This process can supposedly be repeated many times and by many literary hard hats; it is expected that each deconstruction will reveal additional flaws and expose the illusions or bad faith of the builder. The fact
(45) that deconstructionists prefer to describe their activities as *deconstruction* rather than *criticism* is also revealing. *Criticism* and *critic* derive from the Greek *kritikos*, "skillful in judging, decisive." *Deconstruction*, on the other hand, has no over-
(50) tones of skill or wisdom; it merely suggests demolition of an existing building. In popular usage *criticism* suggests censure but not change. If we find fault with a building, we may condemn it, but we do not carry out the demolition ourselves. The
(55) deconstructionist, by implication, is both judge and executioner who leaves a text totally dismantled, if not reduced to a pile of rubble.

1. Which one of the following best expresses the main idea of the passage?

   (A) Implicit in the terminology of the school of criticism known as deconstruction are meanings that reveal the true nature of the deconstructionist's endeavor.

   (B) The appearance of the terms *signifier* and *signified* in the field of literary theory anticipated the appearance of an even more radical idea known as deconstruction.

   (C) Innovations in language and the relations between old and new meanings of terms are a special concern of the new school of criticism known as deconstruction.

   (D) Deconstructionists maintain that it is insufficient merely to judge a work; the critic must actively dismantle it.

   (E) Progress in the field of literary theory is best achieved by looking for new terms like *signifier* and *deconstruction* that might suggest new critical approaches to a work.

2. Which one of the following is a claim that the author makes about deconstructionists?

(A) Deconstructionists would not have been able to formulate their views adequately without the terms *signifier* and *signified*.
(B) Deconstructionists had no particular purpose in mind in choosing to use neologisms.
(C) Deconstructionists do not recognize that their own theory contains inherent contradictions.
(D) Deconstructionists find little interest in the relationship between words and their referents.
(E) Deconstructionists use the terms *signifier* and *signified* to stress the importance of the process of naming.

3. Which one of the following generalizations about inventions is most analogous to the author's point about innovation in language?

(A) A new invention usually consists of components that are specifically manufactured for the new invention.
(B) A new invention is usually behind the times, never making as much use of all the available modern technology as it could.
(C) A new invention usually consists of components that are already available but are made to function in new ways.
(D) A new invention is most useful when it is created with attention to the historical tradition established by implements previously used to do the same job.
(E) A new invention is rarely used to its full potential because it is surrounded by out of date technology that hinders its application.

4. The author of the passage uses the word *criticism* in lines 44–47 primarily in order to

(A) give an example
(B) introduce a contrast
(C) undermine an argument
(D) codify a system
(E) dismiss an objection

5. Which one of the following best describes the function of the second paragraph within the passage as a whole?

(A) It introduces a hypothesis that the author later expands upon.
(B) It qualifies a claim made earlier by the author.
(C) It develops an initial example of the author's general thesis.
(D) It predicts a development.
(E) It presents a contrasting view.

6. The passage suggests that the author most probably holds the view that an important characteristic of literary criticism is that it

(A) demonstrates false assumptions and inherent contradictions
(B) employs skill and insight
(C) be carried out by one critic rather than many
(D) reveals how a text is put together like a building
(E) points out the superiority of conventional text structures

7. The passage suggests that which one of the following most accurately describes the author's view of deconstructionist thought?

(A) The author is guardedly optimistic about the ability of deconstruction to reveal the intentions and biases of a writer.
(B) The author endorses the utility of deconstruction for revealing the role of older meanings of words.
(C) The author is enthusiastic about the significant neologisms that deconstruction has introduced into literary criticism.
(D) The author regards deconstruction's tendency to focus only on the problems and faults of literary texts as too mechanical.
(E) The author condemns deconstruction's attempts to define literary criticism as a creative act.

Passage for Questions 8–13

Some meteorologists have insisted that the severity of the drought in sub-Saharan West Africa and its long duration (nearly 40 years to date) must be a sign of a long-term alteration in cli-
(5) mate. Among the theories proposed to explain this change, one hypothesis that has gained widespread attention attributes the drought to a cooling of the Northern Hemisphere. This hypothesis is based on the fact that, between 1945 and the early 1970s,
(10) the average annual air temperatures over the land-masses of the Northern Hemisphere decreased by about half a degree Fahrenheit (approximately one quarter of a degree Celsius—a small but signifi-cant amount). Several meteorologists have sug-
(15) gested that this cooling was caused by an increase in atmospheric dust emanating from volcanic eruptions and from urban and industrial pollu-tion; the dust reflected incoming sunlight, causing the ground to receive less solar radiation and to
(20) transfer less heat to the atmosphere. The cooling seemed to be more pronounced in the middle and high latitudes than in the tropics, an observation that is consistent with the fact that the sun's rays enter the atmosphere at a greater angle farther
(25) north, and so have to pass through more dust-laden atmosphere on the way to the earth.

Since winds are set in motion by differences in air pressure caused by unequal heating of the atmosphere, supporters of the cooling hypothesis
(30) have argued that a growing temperature dif-ferential between the unusually cool middle and high latitudes and the warm tropical latitudes is causing a southward expansion of the circum-polar vortex—the high-altitude westerly winds
(35) that circle the Northern Hemisphere at middle latitudes. According to this hypothesis, as the cir-cumpolar vortex expands, it forces south other components of large-scale atmospheric circulation and, in effect, displaces the northward-moving
(40) monsoon that ordinarily brings sub-Saharan rain. Proponents have further argued that this change in atmospheric circulation might be long-term since cooling in the Northern Hemisphere could be perpetuated by increases in ice and snow cover-
(45) age there, which would lead to reflection of more sunlight away from the earth, to further cooling,

and, indirectly, to further drought in sub-Saharan West Africa.

Despite these dire predictions, and even
(50) though the current African drought has lasted longer than any other in this century, the notion that the drought is caused by cooling of the Northern Hemisphere is, in fact, not well sup-ported. Contrary to the predictions of the cooling
(55) hypothesis, during one period of rapid Northern Hemisphere cooling in the early 1950s, the sub-Sahara was unusually rainy. Moreover, in the early 1980s, when the drought was particularly severe, Northern Hemisphere lands actually warmed
(60) slightly. And further doubt has been cast on the hypothesis by recent analyses suggesting that, when surface temperatures of water as well as land are taken into account, the Northern Hemisphere may not have cooled at all.
(65)

8. Which one of the following best expresses the main idea of the passage?

    (A) There is strong evidence to support the the-ory that an increase in atmospheric dust has contributed to the severity of the drought in sub-Saharan West Africa.
    (B) The suggestion that Northern Hemisphere cooling is contributing to a decline of rain-fall in sub-Saharan West Africa is open to question.
    (C) The expansion of the circumpolar vortex has caused a dramatic shift in the atmospheric circulation patterns above sub-Saharan West Africa.
    (D) The drought in sub-Saharan West Africa rep-resents a long-term, permanent alteration in global climate patterns.
    (E) Meteorologists cannot determine when the drought in sub-Saharan West Africa is likely to end.

9. The author's attitude toward the cooling hypothesis is best described as one of

(A) vehement opposition
(B) cautious skepticism
(C) growing ambivalence
(D) guarded enthusiasm
(E) strong support

10. According to the passage, proponents of the cooling hypothesis suggested that the circumpolar vortex is likely to expand when which one of the following occurs?

(A) The average annual atmospheric temperature of the tropics is significantly higher than normal for an extended period of time.
(B) The average annual snowfall in the Northern Hemisphere is lower than normal for an extended period of time.
(C) The average annual surface temperature of Northern Hemisphere waters is higher than the average annual surface temperature of Northern Hemisphere landmasses.
(D) There is a significant increase in the difference between the average annual atmospheric temperature of the tropics and that of the more northern latitudes.
(E) There is a significant increase in the difference between the average annual atmospheric temperatures of the middle and the high latitudes in the Northern Hemisphere.

11. Which one of the following can be inferred from the passage about the average annual temperature of the air over Northern Hemisphere landmasses before 1945?

(A) It was higher than it was between 1945 and the early 1970s.
(B) It was lower than it was during the early 1980s.
(C) It was the same as it was between 1945 and the early 1970s.
(D) It was the same as the annual average surface temperature of Northern Hemisphere landmasses and bodies of water between 1945 and the early 1970s.
(E) It was higher than the annual average surface temperature of Northern Hemisphere landmasses and bodies of water between 1945 and the early 1970s.

12. Which one of the following best describes the organization of the passage?

(A) Opposing points of view are presented, evidence supporting each point of view is discussed, and then one point of view is developed into a formal hypothesis.
(B) A theory is discussed and different points of view about the theory are discussed, supported, and then reconciled.
(C) A hypothesis is proposed, contradictory evidence is discussed, and then the hypothesis is amended.
(D) A theory explaining a phenomenon is proposed, supporting evidence is considered, and then the theory is disputed.
(E) A point of view is presented, a theory supporting the view is proposed, contradictory evidence is presented, and then a different theory is proposed.

13. A proponent of the cooling hypothesis would most likely argue that the return of the monsoon rains to sub-Saharan West Africa would indicate that which one of the following has also occurred?

(A) The amount of ice and snow coverage over the landmasses of the Northern Hemisphere has increased.
(B) The average annual temperature of the atmosphere over the middle and high latitudes of the Northern Hemisphere has decreased.
(C) The average annual temperature of the atmosphere over the tropics in the Northern Hemisphere has increased.
(D) Other components of large-scale atmospheric circulation, besides the circumpolar vortex, have expanded and moved southward.
(E) The atmospheric circulation pattern of the high-altitude westerly winds has resumed its normal pattern.

Set Two

Directions: Each passage set in this test is followed by several questions. After reading the passage set, choose the best answer to each question. Your replies are to be based on what is stated or implied in the selection.

Passage for Questions 1–8

Passage A

The best way to address the high numbers of consumer bankruptcy filings, especially Chapter 7 bankruptcy filings, was debated for more than a decade before the Bankruptcy Abuse Prevention
(5) and Consumer Protection Act (BAPCPA) was passed in 2005. Congress had previously passed significant reforms, but those reforms were vetoed by President Clinton in 2000. The current administration gained support from certain factions and
(10) presented the passage of "bankruptcy reform" as a victory, but in fact the law falls short of achieving its stated goals and is unlikely to have a long-term impact on consumer bankruptcy filing rates because:

(15) • It does nothing to alleviate the economic stresses at the root of the bankruptcy problem, such as uninsured medical expenses, that are most likely to trigger bankruptcy filings. Although recent studies indicate that lost
(20) work time, medical expenses, and other costs associated with illness and injury are responsible for approximately half of all consumer bankruptcy cases, BAPCPA is aimed almost exclusively at reducing "abusive" filings.

(25) • The pre-filing credit counseling requirement is too little, too late; U.S. Trustee-approved credit counseling agencies report that by the time potential bankruptcy petitioners reach them, fewer than five percent have any other
(30) viable option.

• The Chapter 7 means test and the schedules of allowable expenses applied in Chapter 13 calculations apply artificial figures or actual figures which may be outdated and irrelevant,
(35) resulting in payment obligations which may have little or no relationship to the debtor's actual ability to pay.

Passage B

With consumer bankruptcy filings well in excess of one million per year, it was clear to nearly everyone that reform was necessary. The beleaguered consumer credit industry appealed to
(5) Congress for help, and despite obstacles—including the veto of significant reforms in 2000—lawmakers passed the Bankruptcy Abuse Prevention and Consumer Protection Act (BAPCPA) in 2005. The goal was to tighten up consumer bankruptcy
(10) filing requirements and discourage the practice of running up credit card and other debt in anticipation of defaulting on accounts and discharging obligations in bankruptcy.

Under the new law, debtors must complete an
(15) approved credit counseling briefing before even filing a bankruptcy petition. Then, if the consumer still wants to file for Chapter 7 bankruptcy, he must qualify under a means test that first compares his income to the median income in his
(20) state and then, if his income exceeds the median, applies Internal Revenue Service figures to determine whether or not he has sufficient income to make partial payment to creditors.

The new provisions have been extraordinarily
(25) successful solving the bankruptcy problem. The law took effect in October of 2005. In the first quarter of 2006, there were only 65,397 consumer Chapter 7 bankruptcy cases filed, compared with 289,239 during the same period a year earlier.

1. Which of the following most accurately expresses the main point of passage A?

   (A) Most consumer bankruptcy cases are not the result of abuse, but are filed by people who have suffered setbacks due to medical problems.

   (B) Weaknesses in the 2005 bankruptcy reforms will likely limit the effectiveness of the new law in reducing consumer bankruptcy filings.

   (C) BAPCPA has been very successful in reducing the number of consumer bankruptcy filings in the United States.

   (D) The passage of the 2005 bankruptcy reforms was intended more for political gain and to build support for the current administration than to address an actual problem in the U.S. economy.

   (E) The 2005 bankruptcy reforms are unlikely to have a significant long-term impact on consumer bankruptcy filing rates because they do not go far enough in cracking down on fraudulent claims.

2. Which of the following is identified in passage A, but not in passage B, as an issue key to the development of successful bankruptcy reform?

   (A) A requirement that bankruptcy petitioners explore other options with a qualified professional before filing a bankruptcy petition

   (B) Screening of income and expenses to determine which consumers really need to file for bankruptcy protection and which can afford to pay back some or all of their debts

   (C) Addressing the financial and life issues that cause people to file for bankruptcy protection

   (D) Cutting down on fraudulent filings by more thoroughly investigating the income and assets of people filing bankruptcy petitions

   (E) Eliminating the political incentive for the passage of laws so that lawmakers can focus on the actual issues at hand rather than currying favor with interest groups

3. Which one of the following most accurately describes the relationship between the use of the phrase "bankruptcy problem" in passage A (lines 16–17) and the use of the same phrase in passage B (line 25)?

   (A) In both passages, the phrase refers to the unnecessarily high rate of bankruptcy filings in the U.S. in recent years.

   (B) In passage A, it refers to the failure of bankruptcy reform to address the core underlying issues, while in passage B, it is used to describe high filing rates.

   (C) In both passage A and passage B, it refers to the economic stresses that contribute to the high bankruptcy filing rates.

   (D) The reference in passage B is strictly to high bankruptcy filing rates, while the author of passage A uses the term more broadly.

   (E) In both passages A and B, the phrase refers to the difficulty of and delays involved in passing bankruptcy reform provisions.

4. If the author of passage A were to read passage B, which of the following objections would he or she be likely to raise regarding the analysis in passage B?

   (A) It is unfair to require consumers to explore other options before allowing them to file for bankruptcy protection.

   (B) The reforms vetoed by President Clinton in 2000 would have been no more or less successful than the statute enacted in 2005.

   (C) The bankruptcy filing statistics for the first quarter of 2006 are too low to be accurate.

   (D) The Internal Revenue Service figures used in the means test calculations do not always yield accurate information about the amount of income available to pay creditors.

   (E) Discouraging consumers from filing for bankruptcy protection after running up credit card and other debts is not a valid objective.

5. Passage A differs from passage B in that its tone is more

   (A) positive
   (B) critical
   (C) political
   (D) objective
   (E) unbiased

6. It can be inferred from the passages that the authors of both passages would agree that

   (A) the reason so many people have been filing bankruptcy in recent years is that economic stresses and personal crises like medical problems have left them little option
   (B) the bankruptcy reforms enacted in 2005 have already demonstrated their effectiveness in curbing excessive bankruptcy filings
   (C) in the early 2000s, the rate of bankruptcy filings in the United States was too high
   (D) President Clinton should not have vetoed the bankruptcy reforms passed by Congress in 2000
   (E) the credit counseling requirement in the new bankruptcy law does little to address the bankruptcy problem

7. Which of the following best describes a way in which the two passages are related to one another?

   (A) The two passages present conflicting statistics in support of their conclusions.
   (B) The authors reach differing conclusions, but do so without presenting contradictory evidence.
   (C) Passage B presents statistics that, if accurate, disprove the predictions made in passage A.
   (D) Each passage uses identical data to project very different outcomes.
   (E) Passage B provides a point-by-point rebuttal of the weaknesses alleged in passage A.

8. Based on their titles, which of the following pairs of documents relates in a manner most analogous to the relationship between passage A and passage B?

   (A) "Homeowners Association Policy Falls Short of Addressing Key Issues"; "New Homeowners Association Policy Already Making a Difference in the Neighborhood"
   (B) "Questionable Motivation in the City Council's Recent Actions"; "City Council Scores a Resounding Victory with New Ordinance"
   (C) "Why We Need an Antismoking Ordinance"; "Antismoking Ordinances and the Downfall of Freedom in the United States"
   (D) "Proposed Alternatives to the Current Expense Reporting System"; "How to Make the Most of Our Expense Reporting System"
   (E) "Mortgage Foreclosure Rates Skyrocketing Across the U.S."; "Mortgage Foreclosure 'Crisis' Blown Out of Proportion by Media"

Passage for Questions 9–15

Legal cases can be termed "hard" cases if they raise issues that are highly controversial, issues about which people with legal training disagree. The ongoing debate over the completeness of the
(5) law usually concerns the extent to which such hard cases are legally determinate, or decidable according to existing law.

H. L. A. Hart's *The Concept of Law* is still the clearest and most persuasive statement of both the
(10) standard theory of hard cases and the standard theory of law on which it rests. For Hart, the law consists of legal rules formulated in general terms; these terms he calls "open textured," which means that they contain a "core" of settled meaning and
(15) a "penumbra" or "periphery" where their meaning is not determinate. For example, suppose an ordinance prohibits the use of vehicles in a park. "Vehicle" has a core of meaning which includes cars and motorcycles. But, Hart claims, other
(20) vehicles, such as bicycles, fall within the peripheral meaning of vehicle, so that the law does not establish whether they are prohibited. There will always be cases not covered by the core meaning of legal terms within existing laws; Hart considers these
(25) cases to be legally indeterminate. Since courts cannot decide such cases on legal grounds, they must consider nonlegal (for example, moral and political) grounds, and thereby exercise judicial discretion to make, rather than apply, law.

(30) In Ronald Dworkin's view, the law is richer than Hart would grant; he denies that the law consists solely of explicit rules. The law also includes principles that do not depend for their legal status on any prior official recognition or enactment.
(35) Dworkin claims that many cases illustrate the existence of legal principles that are different from legal rules and that Hart's "model of rules" cannot accommodate. For Dworkin, legal rules apply in an all-or-nothing fashion, whereas legal principles
(40) do not: they provide the rationale for applying legal rules. Thus, because Dworkin thinks there is law in addition to legal rules, he thinks that legal indeterminacy and the need for judicial discretion do not follow from the existence of open texture
(45) in legal rules.

It would be a mistake, though, to dispute Hart's theory of hard cases on this basis alone. If Hart's claim about the open texture of general terms is true, then we should expect to find legal inde-
(50) terminacies even if the law consists of principles in addition to rules. Legal principles, as well as legal rules, contain general terms that have open texture. And it would be absurd to suppose that wherever the meaning of a legal rule is unclear,
(55) there is a legal principle with a clear meaning. Most interesting and controversial cases will occur in the penumbra of both rules and principles.

9. Which one of the following best expresses the main idea of the passage?

(A) The law will never be complete because new situations will always arise which will require new laws to resolve them.

(B) The most difficult legal cases are those concerning controversial issues about which trained legal minds have differing opinions.

(C) The concept of legal principles does not diminish the usefulness of the concept of the open texture of general terms in deciding whether hard cases are legally determinate.

(D) The concept of legal principles is a deleterious addition to the theory of law since any flaws exhibited by legal rules could also be shared by legal principles.

(E) The inherent inconsistency of terms used in laws provides a continuing opportunity for judges to exercise their discretion to correct defects and gaps in the law.

10. According to the passage, the term "legal principles," as used by Dworkin, refers to

    (A) a comprehensive code of ethics that governs the behavior of professionals in the legal system
    (B) explicit analyses of the terms used in legal rules, indicating what meanings the terms do and do not cover
    (C) legal doctrines that underlie and guide the use of accepted legal rules
    (D) legal rules that have not yet passed through the entire legislative procedure necessary for them to become law
    (E) the body of legal decisions regarding cases that required judicial discretion for their resolution

11. Which one of the following expresses a view that the author of the passage would most probably hold concerning legal principles and legal rules?

    (A) Legal rules are applied more often than legal principles when a case involves issues about which legal professionals disagree.
    (B) Both legal rules and legal principles are officially recognized as valid parts of the law.
    (C) Hart's "model of rules" has been superseded by a "model of principles" that sheds light on legal determinacy.
    (D) Legal principles are just as likely as legal rules to have terms that have both core and peripheral meanings.
    (E) Legal principles eliminate the need for judicial discretion in resolving the problems generated by the open texture of legal rules.

12. In the passage, the author uses the example of the word "vehicle" to

    (A) illustrate a legal rule that necessarily has exceptions
    (B) show how legal principles are applied in the construction of legal rules
    (C) represent the core of settled meaning of a legal term
    (D) serve as an example of a legal term with both a core and a periphery of meaning
    (E) provide a counterexample to Hart's concept of the open texture of legal terms

13. It can be inferred that the author of the passage regards Hart's theory of hard cases and the theory of standard law as

    (A) exhaustive
    (B) worthy of respect
    (C) interesting but impractical
    (D) plausible but unwieldy
    (E) hopelessly outmoded

14. Which one of the following is true of the term "legally determinate" (line 6) as it is used in the passage?

    (A) It represents the idea that every crime should have a fixed penalty rather than a range of penalties within which a judge can make an arbitrary choice.
    (B) It refers to a legal case that can be definitively resolved in favor of one side or the other according to the law in effect at the time.
    (C) It describes a legal rule that requires judges to limit their actions to applying written law when deciding cases over which people with legal training disagree.
    (D) It refers to any legal case that involves terms with imprecise meanings and thus relies for its resolution only on the determination of judges.
    (E) It refers to codified procedures for determining the legal outcome of complex issues in difficult cases.

15. In the passage, the author is primarily concerned with

    (A) outlining the problems that might be faced by a legislature attempting to create a complete body of law that would prevent judges from making rather than applying the law
    (B) justifying the idea that hard cases will always exist in the practice of law, no matter what laws are written or how they are applied
    (C) presenting evidence to support Dworkin's idea that legal rules apply in an all-or-nothing fashion, whereas legal principles apply in more sophisticated ways
    (D) critiquing the concept of the open texture of legal terms as a conceptual flaw in Hart's otherwise well-regarded book
    (E) demonstrating that Dworkin's concept of legal principles does not form the basis for a successful attack on Hart's theory of legally indeterminate cases

Set Three

Directions: Each passage set in this test is followed by several questions. After reading the passage set, choose the best answer to each question. Your replies are to be based on what is stated or implied in the selection.

Passage for Questions 1–8

Many literary scholars believe that Zora Neale Hurston's *Their Eyes Were Watching God* (1937) has been the primary influence on some of the most accomplished black women writing in the United
(5) States today. Indeed, Alice Walker, the author of the prize-winning novel *The Color Purple*, has said of *Their Eyes*: "There is no book more important to me than this one." Thus, it seems necessary to ask why *Their Eyes*, a work now viewed by a multitude
(10) of readers as remarkably successful in its complex depiction of a black woman's search for self and community, was ever relegated to the margins of the literary canon.

The details of the novel's initial reception help
(15) answer this question. Unlike the recently redis-covered and reexamined work of Harriet Wilson, *Their Eyes* was not totally ignored by book review-ers upon its publication. In fact, it received a mix-ture of positive and negative reviews both from
(20) white book reviewers working for prominent peri-odicals and from important figures within black literary circles. In the *Saturday Review of Literature*, George Stevens wrote that "the narration is exactly right, because most of it is dialogue and the dia-
(25) logue gives us a constant sense of character in action." The negative criticism was partially a result of Hurston's ideological differences with other members of the black literary community about the depiction of black Americans in literature.
(30) black writers of the 1940s believed that the black artist's primary responsibility was to create protest fiction that explored the negative effects of racism in the United States. For example, Richard Wright, the author of the much acclaimed *Native Son*
(35) (1940), wrote that *Their Eyes* had "no theme" and "no message." Most critics' and readers' expecta-tions of black literature rendered them unable to appreciate Hurston's subtle delineation of the life of an ordinary black woman in a black community,
(40) and the novel went quietly out of print.

Recent acclaim for *Their Eyes* results from the emergence of feminist literary criticism and the development of standards of evaluation specific to the work of black writers; these kinds of criti-
(45) cism changed readers' expectations of art and enabled them to appreciate Hurston's novel. The emergence of feminist literary criticism was cru-cial because such criticism brought new attention to neglected works such as Hurston's and alerted
(50) readers to Hurston's exploration of women's issues in her fiction. The Afrocentric standards of evalu-ation were equally important to the rediscovery of *Their Eyes*, for such standards provided read-ers with the tools to recognize and appreciate
(55) the black folklore and oral storytelling traditions Hurston incorporated within her work. In one of the most illuminating discussions of the novel to date, Henry Louis Gates, Jr., states that "Hurston's strategy seems to concern itself with the possibili-
(60) ties of representation of the speaking black voice in writing."

1. The passage suggests which one of the following about Harriet Wilson's novel?

   (A) It was written at the same time as *Their Eyes Were Watching God*, but it did not receive as much critical attention.
   (B) It greatly influenced black women writing after the 1940s.
   (C) It was widely read when it was published, but it has not received attention from liter-ary critics until recently.
   (D) It was not formally published, and the manu-script has only recently been discovered by literary critics.
   (E) It did not receive critical attention when it was published, but it has recently become the subject of critical study.

2. The passage offers support for which one of the following statements about literary reviewers and *Their Eyes Were Watching God*?

    (A) *Their Eyes* was widely acclaimed by reviewers upon its publication, even though it eventually went out of print.
    (B) The eventual obscurity of *Their Eyes* was not the result of complete neglect by reviewers.
    (C) Some early reviewers of *Their Eyes* interpreted the novel from a point of view that later became known as Afrocentric.
    (D) *Their Eyes* was more typical of the protest fiction of the 1940s than reviewers realized.
    (E) Most early reviewers of *Their Eyes* did not respond positively to the book.

3. Which one of the following best states the main idea of the passage?

    (A) Hurston's *Their Eyes Were Watching God* had little in common with novels written by black authors during the 1940s.
    (B) Feminist critics and authors such as Alice Walker were instrumental in establishing Hurston's *Their Eyes Were Watching God* as an important part of the American literary canon.
    (C) Critics and readers were unable to appreciate fully Hurston's *Their Eyes Were Watching God* until critics applied new standards of evaluation to the novel.
    (D) Hurston's *Their Eyes Were Watching God* was an important influence on the protest fiction written by black writers in the mid-20 century.
    (E) Afrocentric strategies of analysis have brought attention to the use of oral storytelling traditions in novels written by black Americans, such as Hurston's *Their Eyes Were Watching God*.

4. According to the passage, which one of the following is true of black folklore traditions as used in literature written in the United States?

    (A) They are an aspect of black American literature first recognized and written about by Henry Louis Gates, Jr.
    (B) They were not widely incorporated into novels written by black Americans until after the 1940s.
    (C) They were first used by a novelist in Zora Neale Hurston's *Their Eyes Were Watching God*.
    (D) They were not incorporated into novels published by black Americans in the 1940s.
    (E) They are an aspect of black literature that some readers did not fully appreciate until relatively recently.

5. The passage suggests that *Native Son* differs from *Their Eyes Were Watching God* in which one of the following ways?

    (A) It received fewer positive reviews at the time of its publication than did *Their Eyes*.
    (B) It is less typical of literature written by black Americans during the 1940s than is *Their Eyes*.
    (C) It is less focused on an ordinary individual's search for self within a black community than is *Their Eyes*.
    (D) It depicts more aspects of black American folklore than does *Their Eyes*.
    (E) It has received more attention from feminist and Afrocentric literary critics than has *Their Eyes*.

6. Which one of the following provides the clearest
    example of the kind of fiction that many black
    writers of the 1940s, as their views are described in
    the passage, believed should be written?

    (A) a novel that focuses on the interrelationships
        among four generations of black women
    (B) a historical novel that recreates actual events
        that occurred as black people suffered from
        oppression and racial injustice in a small
        town
    (C) a novel, based on biographical stories orally
        relayed to the author as a child, that
        describes the development of traditions in a
        black family
    (D) a novel that explores the psychological
        aspects of a relationship between a white
        man and a black man as they work together
        to organize protests against unjust working
        conditions
    (E) a novel that examines the different ways in
        which three black children experience their
        first day of school in a rural community

7. The author would be most likely to agree with
    which one of the following statements about the
    relationship between art and literary criticism?

    (A) The long-term reputation of a work of art
        is less dependent on the response of literary
        critics than on the response of readers and
        authors.
    (B) Experimental works of fiction are usually
        poorly received and misunderstood by liter-
        ary critics when they are first published.
    (C) The response of literary critics to a work of
        art can be determined by certain ideologi-
        cal perspectives and assumptions about the
        purpose of art.
    (D) Literary critics do not significantly affect the
        way most people interpret and appreciate
        literature.
    (E) The ideological bases of a work of art are the
        first consideration of most literary critics.

8. The primary purpose of the passage is to

    (A) correct a misconception
    (B) explain a reassessment
    (C) reconcile two points of view
    (D) criticize a conventional approach
    (E) announce a new discovery

Passage for Questions 9–14

In order to explain the socioeconomic achievement, in the face of disadvantages due to racial
discrimination, of Chinese and Japanese immigrants to the United States and their descendants,
(5) sociologists have typically applied either culturally
based or structurally based theories—but never
both together. To use an economic metaphor,
culturally based explanations assert the importance of the supply side of the labor market,
(10) emphasizing the qualities immigrant groups bring
with them for competition in the United States
labor market. Such explanations reflect a human
capital perspective in which status attainment is
seen as a result of individuals' ability to generate
(15) resources. Structurally based explanations, on the
other hand, examine the market condition of the
immigrants' host society, particularly its discriminatory practices and their impact on the status
attainment process of immigrant groups. In the
(20) economic metaphor, structural explanations assert
the importance of the demand side of the labor
market.

In order to understand the socioeconomic
mobility of Chinese and Japanese immigrants and
(25) their descendants, only an analysis of supply-side
and demand-side factors together, in the context
of historical events, will suffice. On the cultural
or supply side, differences in immigration pattern and family formation resulted in different
(30) rates of socioeconomic achievement for Chinese
and Japanese immigrants. For various reasons,
Chinese immigrants remained sojourners and did
not (except for urban merchants) establish families. They were also hampered by ethnic conflicts
(35) in the labor market. Japanese immigrants, on the
other hand, were less constrained, made the tran
sition from sojourner to settler within the first two
decades of immigration, and left low-wage labor
to establish small businesses based on a household
(40) mode of production. Chinese sojourners without
families were more vulnerable to demoraliza-
tion, whereas Japanese immigrants faced societal
hostility with the emotional resources provided
by a stable family life. Once Chinese immigrants
(45) began to establish nuclear families and produce
a second generation, instituting household pro-

duction similar to that established by Japanese
immigrants, their socioeconomic attainment soon
paralleled that of Japanese immigrants and their
(50) descendants.

On the structural or demand side, changes in
institutional constraints, immigration laws, labor
markets, and societal hostility were rooted in the
dynamics of capitalist economic development.
(55) Early capitalist development generated a demand
for low-wage labor that could not be fulfilled.
Early Chinese and Japanese immigration was a
response to this demand. In an advanced capitalist economy, the demand for immigrant labor is
(60) more differentiated: skilled professional and technical labor fills empty positions in the primary
labor market and, with the traditional unskilled
low-wage labor, creates two immigrant streams.
The high levels of education attained by the
(65) descendants of Chinese and Japanese immigrants
and their concentration in strategic states such as
California paved the way for the movement of the
second generation into the expanding primary
labor market in the advanced capitalist economy
(70) that existed after the Second World War.

9. Which one of the following best expresses the main idea of the passage?

    (A) The socioeconomic achievement of Chinese and Japanese immigrants and their descendants is best explained by a historical examination of the economic structures prevalent in the United States when such immigrant groups arrived.

    (B) The socioeconomic achievement of Chinese and Japanese immigrants and their descendants is best explained by an examination of their cultural backgrounds, in particular their levels of educational attainment.

    (C) The socioeconomic achievement of Chinese and Japanese immigrants and their descendants has taken place in the context of a culturally based emphasis on the economic welfare of the nuclear family.

    (D) Only the market structure of the capitalist economy of the United States, in which supply has historically been regulated by demand, can account for the socioeconomic achievement of Chinese and Japanese immigrants and their descendants.

    (E) Only an analysis that combines an examination of the cultures of Chinese and Japanese immigrant groups and the socioeconomic structure of the host country can adequately explain the socioeconomic achievement of Chinese and Japanese immigrants and their descendants.

10. Which one of the following can best be described as a supply-side element in the labor market, as such elements are explained in the passage?

    (A) concentration of small businesses in a given geographical area
    (B) need for workers with varying degrees of skill
    (C) high value placed by immigrants on work
    (D) expansion of the primary labor market
    (E) development of an advanced capitalist economy

11. Which one of the following best states the function of the author's mention of "two immigrant streams" (line 63)?

    (A) It demonstrates the effects of changes in human capital.
    (B) It illustrates the operation of the primary labor market.
    (C) It explains the nature of early Chinese and Japanese immigration.
    (D) It characterizes the result of changing demand-side factors.
    (E) It underscores an influence on the labor market.

12. It can be inferred that the author's analysis of the socioeconomic achievement of Chinese and Japanese immigrants and their descendants differs from that of most sociologists primarily in that most sociologists

    (A) address the effects of the interaction of causal factors
    (B) exclude the factor of a developing capitalist economy
    (C) do not apply an economic metaphor
    (D) emphasize the disadvantageous effects of racial discrimination
    (E) focus on a single type of theoretical explanation

13. It can be inferred that which one of the following was an element of the experiences of both Chinese and Japanese immigrants in the United States?

    (A) initial status as sojourners
    (B) slow accumulation of capital
    (C) quick transition from laborer to manager
    (D) rapid establishment of nuclear families
    (E) rapid acquisition of technical skills

14. The author is primarily concerned with

    (A) advancing a synthesis of approaches to an issue
    (B) challenging a tentative answer to a question
    (C) evaluating the soundness of theories
    (D) resolving the differences between schools of thought
    (E) outlining the achievements of a group

ANSWERS AND EXPLANATIONS

Set One	Set Two	Set Three
1. A	1. B	1. E
2. E	2. C	2. B
3. C	3. D	3. C
4. B	4. D	4. E
5. C	5. B	5. C
6. B	6. C	6. B
7. D	7. B	7. C
8. B	8. A	8. B
9. B	9. C	9. E
10. D	10. C	10. C
11. A	11. D	11. D
12. D	12. D	12. E
13. E	13. B	13. A
	14. B	14. A
	15. E	

Diagnostic Tool

Tally up your score and write down your results below.

Total Correct: _____ out of 42

Percentage Correct: # you got right x 100 ÷ 42: _____

Diagnose Your Results

Look back at the questions you got wrong and think back on your experience answering them.

Step 1: Find the Road Blocks

Some questions you struggled to answer. To improve your score, you need to pinpoint exactly what element of these "road blocks" tripped you up. To do that, ask yourself these two questions:

Am I weak in the skills being tested?

Reading Comprehension questions test critical reading skills, such as whether you can summarize the main idea of a passage, differentiate between ideas explicitly stated in a text and those implied by the author, make inferences based on information in a text, analyze the logical structure of a passage, or deduce the author's attitude about a topic

from the text. The Kaplan Reading Comp principles and methods in this book can help you focus on and develop the specific reading skills you need for better efficiency and comprehension on Test Day.

Was it the question type that threw me off?

Then you need to become more comfortable with it! Go back to the beginning of this chapter and review the Kaplan principles and methods. Make sure you understand them, and know how to apply them. You also need to be very familiar with the four Reading Comp question types. This will improve your speed and efficiency on Test Day. Finally, get as much practice as you can so you grow more at ease with this question type.

Step 2: Find the Blind Spots

Some questions you answered quickly and confidently, but got them wrong anyway! When you come across wrong answers like these, you need to figure out what you thought you were doing right, what it turns out you were doing wrong, and why that happened! The best way to do that is to **read the answer explanations!**

They give you a detailed breakdown of why the correct answer is correct, and why all the other answer choices are wrong. This helps to reinforce the Kaplan principles and methods for each question type, and helps you figure out what blindsided you so it doesn't happen again. Also, just like with your Road Blocks, try to get in as much practice as you can.

Step 3: Reinforce Your Strengths

Read through all the answer explanations for the ones you got right. Again, this helps to reinforce the Kaplan principles and methods for each question type, which in turn helps you work more efficiently so you can get the score you want. Now keep your skills sharp with more practice.

As soon as you are comfortable with all the LSAT question types and Kaplan methods, complete a full-length practice test under timed conditions. In this way, practice tests serve as milestones; they help you to chart your progress! So don't save them all for the final weeks.

If you are aiming for that top score, TRY OUT *LSAT 180*, Kaplan's advanced workbook that includes only the toughest LSAT questions and most focused strategies.

You can also visit Kaptest.com/LSAT for more details on Kaplan's online and classroom-based options, like LSAT Advanced, LSAT Extreme, and LSAT Crash courses.

Kaplan uses real LSAT questions, so you get the most comprehensive, test-like experience.

Set One

Questions 1–7

Topic and Scope: the literary philosophy of deconstruction; specifically, the connection between its terminology and its methods.

Purpose and Main Idea: The author's purpose is to demonstrate that links exist between deconstruction's terminology and its methods; the author argues that deconstructionist terminology provides clear insights into deconstruction's methods.

Paragraph Structure: Paragraphs 1 and 2 essentially point out that deconstructionist terminology reflects the philosophy's methods. The words—along with their prior meanings—that deconstructionists have "borrowed or adapted from stock" to define their philosophy imply certain things about that philosophy.

Paragraph three is the heart of the text. This paragraph discusses the specific ways in which the term *deconstruction* sheds light on deconstructionist methods. Basically, this term, which is taken from the construction industry, highlights deconstructionist efforts to demolish, rather than simply criticize, literary works.

1. A

(A) nicely captures the topic, scope, and purpose of the passage. With (B), these literary terms didn't predate deconstruction; rather, deconstructionists turned these words into literary terms. Besides, this is a mere detail in paragraph two; it's certainly not the text's main idea. (C) also plays on a detail in paragraph 2. (D) focuses on a detail in paragraph three. Moreover, this choice reflects the author's opinion of deconstruction, which isn't necessarily what deconstructionists think of deconstruction. (E) contradicts the author's critical attitude toward evaluating literature in light of "borrowed or adapted" terminology.

2. E

(E) is a good paraphrase of lines 15–18. (A) The author never claims that deconstruction would have been impossible without the use of these terms. He refers to them simply to highlight an aspect of deconstructionist philosophy. (B) is an *au contraire* choice. Lines 12–15 indicate that deconstructionists have chosen neologisms

for very specific reasons. (C) The author never says that deconstruction "contains inherent contradictions." What he says is that deconstructionists are on the lookout for contradictions in the work of others. (D) is another *au contraire* choice. Deconstructionists are interested enough "in the relationship between words and their referents" that they've developed terminology to illustrate this relationship.

3. C

The author's belief about innovation in language is that it consists of giving new meanings to existing words. (C) expresses precisely the same relationship—existing components "are made to function in new ways." None of the other choices reflects the author's fundamental idea about "borrowing or adapting" something that already exists to serve a new end.

4. B

In lines 44–46, the author sets up a contrast between *deconstruction* and *criticism*. Then he fleshes out this contrast by defining *criticism* and showing how it differs from *deconstruction*. With (A), lines 46–57 do contain an example of sorts—the example of the building. This example, however, is in the text because it *supports* the contrast that the author makes. (C), (D), and (E) are beyond the scope of the text. If anything, the author makes an argument in lines 46–56; he doesn't undermine one (C). Nor does he "codify a system" (D) or "dismiss an objection" (E): What system? What objection?

5. C

In paragraph 1, the author argues that the old meaning of words doesn't disappear when people use these words in new ways. In paragraph 2, the author provides an example of this phenomenon by showing that the word *signify* conjures up a certain idea, even though deconstructionists don't have this idea in mind when they use this word. Paragraph 2 neither "introduces a hypothesis" (A) nor "qualifies a claim" (B). It simply backs up an abstract argument made in paragraph 1 with a concrete example. (D) distorts a detail in the last sentence of paragraph 2. Paragraph 3 "presents a contrasting view" (E)—a view that takes issue with deconstruction.

6. B

In paragraph 3, the author's disapproval of deconstruction, which he thinks "has no overtones of skill or wisdom," is evident. Equally apparent is his approval of criticism, which he says is based on skill and insight. (A) is wrong because deconstructionists—not the author—think that it's important to "demonstrate false assumptions and inherent contradictions." With (C), the author has problems with deconstructionist philosophy, not with the *number* of deconstructionists (or, for that matter, other critics) who may analyze a work. (D) is a metaphor for an analytic process favored by deconstructionists. The author is critical of this analytic process. (E) distorts a detail. The author doesn't make any judgments about text structures; he makes a judgment about differing modes of literary criticism.

7.   D

(D) reflects the author's generally negative attitude toward deconstruction. The author isn't "guardedly optimistic" (A) or "enthusiastic" (C) about deconstruction. Nor does he "endorse" it in any respect (B). Indeed, he's critical of deconstruction's search for authorial bias, as well as the way it uses words and neologisms. (E) is too strongly negative. Besides, according to the author, deconstructionists don't think of literary criticism as a "creative act." Just the opposite; it's a repetitive, "mechanical" process.

Questions 8–13

Topic and Scope

Sub-Saharan West Africa's drought; specifically, a hypothesis that explains why sub-Saharan West Africa has been caught up in a long and severe drought.

Purpose and Main Idea

The author's purpose is to describe and assess a widespread hypothesis (the "cooling" theory) about the cause of sub-Saharan West Africa's drought; the author's main idea is that this hypothesis is unconvincing.

Paragraph Structure

Paragraph 1 sets out the basic hypothesis: A cooling of the Northern Hemisphere has caused the drought. Paragraphs 1 and 2 explain the reasoning behind this hypothesis. Essentially, atmospheric dust has reflected sunlight away from the ground, lowering the Northern Hemisphere's air temperature, which, in turn, has affected wind patterns, ultimately leading to less rainfall in sub-Saharan West Africa. Moreover, this detrimental development, proponents of the hypothesis believe, might be long term.

Paragraph 3 shifts gears from description to opinion. In this paragraph, the author basically says that the hypothesis is refuted by the meteorological facts.

8.   B

(B) encompasses the passage's topic (African drought) scope (a widespread hypothesis about the cause of the drought) and purpose (to describe and take issue with this hypothesis). (A) is *au contraire*. The author says that the "cooling hypothesis," which is based on the role of atmospheric dust, is "not well supported" by the meteorological facts. (C) focuses on a detail in paragraph 2, not the passage as a whole. (D), like (C), focuses on a detail in paragraph 2. Besides, this view is held by proponents of the "cooling hypothesis." It's not the author's view. (E) is beyond the scope of the passage, which offers no information about when the African drought is likely to end.

9.   B

In paragraph 3, the author says that the "cooling hypothesis" is "not well supported"; and he offers a number of meteorological facts that appear to undermine it. But he knocks the hypothesis in a very restrained tone. That's why "cautious skepticism" is a better description of his attitude than "vehement opposition" (A). With (C), the author's not "ambivalent" about the hypothesis. Lines 21–27 suggest that he gave it some credence at some point, but that's only the slightest of suggestions. (D) and (E) suggest that the author's a proponent of the hypothesis. That clearly isn't the case.

10.   D

Lines 34–35 is where this "circumpolar vortex," so called, is first mentioned; and what is causing it? Lines 31–34 tell us. Expansion of the circumpolar vortex, according to those who endorse the "cooling hypothesis," occurs when there's a growth in the temperature differential between the tropical latitudes and more northerly latitudes. (A) focuses on the tropics exclusively—no can do. (B) distorts a detail in paragraph 2. If anything, the circumpolar vortex might expand if there's *heavier* than normal snowfall for an extended period. (C) is beyond the scope of the passage, which doesn't mention temperature differentials between water and land. (E) is wrong: The significant difference is between the tropical latitudes, on the one hand, and the middle and high latitudes, on the other.

11. A

This question is very difficult; it's a good candidate to tackle after you've completed the other questions. Remember, since it isn't worth more than other easy questions, don't waste a lot of time on it if you don't see a quick path to the answer. You're asked here specifically about the air over Northern Hemisphere landmasses, not about the Northern Hemisphere in general. That makes the information in lines 8–12 relevant here, and clearly those temperatures declined after 1945. (A) just describes that the other way round: Temps were *higher, before*. Incidentally, information in lines 58–65 isn't relevant because it refers to the Northern Hemisphere water and land. With (B), since we're not given actual figures, we have no way to compare the pre-1945 period to the 1980s. All we know is that temperatures were warmer in both eras than they were between 1945 and the early 1970s. With (C), lines 8–12 state otherwise. With (D) and (E), we aren't given the actual data that would permit either comparison.

12. D

Paragraph 1 sets out the "cooling hypothesis," which addresses the cause of the African drought; the rest of paragraph 1—as well as all of paragraph 2—describe the hypothesis and its supporting evidence, and paragraph 3 disputes the hypothesis.

(A) An opposing point of view—the author's—isn't presented until the end of the passage. The formal hypothesis comes first.

(B) The author's view and that of proponents of the "cooling hypothesis" aren't reconciled; they're simply discussed.

(C) The author questions the "cooling hypothesis," but he never "amends" it. As far as we know, he simply rejects it.

(E) What different theory? The author doesn't offer one of his own.

13. E

Lines 37–41 indicate that those who endorse the "cooling hypothesis" believe that the sub-Saharan drought has been caused by a shift in normal wind patterns. This shift, they contend, has kept monsoon rains from reaching the sub-Saharan region. Thus, they would probably say that the return of such rains means that wind patterns have returned to normal.

(A) is *au contraire*: According to supporters of the "cooling hypothesis," an increase in ice and snow coverage would be likely to keep the rains at bay. (B) is also *au contraire*. According to hypothesis advocates, such a development would likely perpetuate the sub-Saharan drought. With (C), hypothesis advocates never directly link conditions in the tropics with sub-Saharan rain. (D) is another *au contraire* choice: Lines 37-42 identify this development as part of the causal chain of sub-Saharan drought.

Set Two

Questions 1–8

Topic and Scope

Like all comparative reading passages, these two have the same topic: the 2005 bankruptcy reforms. They also share a scope: the efficacy of those reforms.

Purpose and Main Idea

Next, we have to identify the purpose and main idea for each passage independently.

Passage A: The author's main idea is that the bankruptcy reforms enacted in 2005 aren't likely to be effective in the long run due to various flaws. His purpose is simply to argue or advance that point.

Passage B: The main idea in passage B is that the reforms have been a resounding success. Again, the author's purpose is simply to demonstrate that that's the case.

Relationship Between the Passages

Having assessed topic, scope, purpose, and main idea just as we do in regular passages (except that we have two purposes/main ideas), we move on to the one step that differs in comparative reading passages: Before moving on to the questions, we need to get a handle on the relationship between the passages.

The best starting point for that is to examine each passage's purpose/main idea. Passage A points out flaws in the bankruptcy reforms and predicts its failure, while passage B presents evidence to support the idea that it's already a success. But each author writes as though unaware of the other—one passage isn't responsive to the other or a direct rebuttal.

Since comparative passages are so short, we won't need roadmaps. Once we have topic, scope, purpose, and main idea and the relationship between the passages in hand, we can jump into the questions.

1.   B

This is a global (main point) question, and it relates only to one passage, so we have every reason to attack it first. And, just like in a single reading passage, we've already identified the main idea and should be able to simply refer to our groundwork and match up our prediction with the answer choices. We said the bankruptcy reforms aren't likely to be effective in the long term because of certain flaws. That's answer choice (B).

(A) is a distortion—we do hear about medical problems triggering bankruptcies, but not that they're "most" of the cases; further, it's only a detail, one of multiple flaws listed, not the main idea.

(C) is a 180. The author doesn't directly address the success of BAPCPA thus far, but his focus is on its failings.

(D) Another distortion—the author says that the current administration *gained* favor, but not that currying favor was its motivation; like (A), this is also too narrow to be the main idea.

(E) The first half of this answer choice looks like a clear winner, but it falls apart after "because." The author listed three reasons that the current reforms probably wouldn't work, and none of them had anything to do with fraud.

2.   C

This is just a twist on the old "EXCEPT" Detail question format. Here, however, we're going to have to check both passages and it may be time-consuming. The fact that the question relates to both passages is reason enough to leave it for later; the fact that it requires us to check every answer choice strongly reinforces that idea.

(A) The requirement that bankruptcy petitioners explore other options with a qualified professional is mentioned in both passages; it's part of the new bankruptcy law. But neither presents it as a key issue. The author of passage A presents it as a measure in the new bankruptcy law that isn't likely to have the intended impact.

(B) Again, neither author actually says this is a key feature. The author of passage B presents it in a positive light, but the author of passage A only says that it's not being done very effectively—he doesn't make any suggestion that it must be or even should be done at all.

(C) Bingo! The first reason author A offers for the projected failure of bankruptcy reform is the failure to address those issues (such as medical crisis).

(D) Passage A never mentions fraud.

(E) Distortion; beware of familiar language that's not responsive to the question.

3.   D

Again, the question requires reference to both passages, so it shouldn't be one of the first ones you attack. However, once you've finished the single-passage and Global questions, the line references make this one fairly inviting. You'll definitely want to go back to each passage and explicitly determine how the phrase is used in each passage independently before trying to determine the relationship, just like we did with the purpose and main idea before determining the relationship between the passages as a whole. In passage A, the author refers to the "bankruptcy problem" as having roots in socioeconomic problems. Clearly, this relates to the high number of bankruptcy filings, but author A has tied it in to the larger issue. Author B, on the other hand, tells us the "bankruptcy problem" has largely been solved. The evidence for this is strictly limited to a reduced number of filings, so this author is using the term much more narrowly: The "bankruptcy problem" was that too many people were filing.

That's a match for answer choice (D)

(A) While the phrase does refer to the high number of bankruptcy filings in both passages, the word "unnecessarily" here should be a red flag. We have no reason to believe that author A thinks the high number of bankruptcy filings were unnecessary. In fact, he's used the phrase in a paragraph citing a legitimate and largely unavoidable bankruptcy trigger.

(B) This one might be tempting; it illustrates the importance of the work we did on this question BEFORE looking at the answer choices. Passage A surely refers to the failure of bankruptcy reform to address the core underlying issues, but we're asked about something much more narrow: how this particular phrase is used.

(C) Passage B makes no mention of economic stresses as a contributing factor to bankruptcy.

(E) Both passages mentioned the difficulties and delays in passing the new bankruptcy laws, but neither used the phrase "bankruptcy problem" in that context. And context is everything when it comes to this question; there are several points and issues that could be classified as "bankruptcy problems," but we have to find the one that each author attached to that term.

4. D

Again, this question involves both passages, so it should be left for later. We're really looking for a point of disagreement, even if author A hasn't explicitly addressed the issue.

(A) Distortion—the author of passage A says the pre-filing credit counseling requirement doesn't help, but he doesn't say that it's unfair, only that it's ineffective.

(B) We don't have enough information to know either author's position on this issue; since author B didn't make any statements about it, there's no basis to invoke objections from author A.

(C) This one might have given you pause, since author A says the reforms won't work, and the statistics presented in passage B seem to indicate that they are working. But the author of passage A actually said that the reforms wouldn't work *long term*, and the statistics offered are from a time period ending less than six months after the law took effect; author A can accept these statistics without contradicting his doubts about the long-term impact.

(D) This is it—both authors talk about the calculations to determine whether or not a debtor can afford to pay back his creditors. However, the author of passage B touts this practice, while author A suggests that the numbers employed lead to inaccurate conclusions.

(E) We have no information about what author A would consider a valid objective; passage A only addresses the likelihood of effectiveness.

5. B

Another comparative question, but this one is global in nature, so it might be one of the first questions you attack when you run out of single-passage questions. Let's look back briefly at each passage. What is author A's attitude? Skepticism and fault-finding. He's taking apart the new law, listing its flaws, and predicting failure.

The author of passage B, on the other hand, is very positive. His discussion of the law is less analytical and more focused on his assessment of its success.

That means (A) is a 180: Author B is much more positive

(B) is correct: Author A is deconstructing the statute and listing its flaws—a "critical" approach in both senses of the word.

(C) Both passages make brief reference to political issues, but the focus of each is on the success/failure of the law.

(D) and (E) mean the same thing—always a bonus for you, since it clearly means neither one can be the right answer. Without that to guide us, though, either could be eliminated simply because the author in passage A takes a clear and strong position. This analysis is closely related to assessing purpose in any Reading Comp passage.

6. C

We're looking for common ground between the passages, but since this is an Inference question, it may not be explicitly stated (or at least, not in both passages). Can we predict an area of agreement between our authors? The only thing they seem to agree on is that there's a "bankruptcy problem." That's enough to identify correct answer choice (C), but if you didn't have a prediction at hand:

(A) The author of passage A certainly told us that a large number of bankruptcy filings were attributable to such crises, but author B gives no indication that he's on board with that idea. He implies that he thinks the problem is irresponsibility.

(B) So author B tells us, but this directly contradicts the main point of passage A.

(C) Author A clearly believes that there's a problem with the high number of bankruptcy filings; he thinks we haven't adequately addressed the underlying causes. Author B explicitly tells us there was a problem and it has been solved. Don't be fooled by the fact that author A thinks there's still a problem—the answer choice doesn't *limit* the problem to the early 2000s, making it the right answer.

(D) Neither author takes a clear position on this, although both mention the 2000 veto.

(E) We know that author A believes this, but author B doesn't talk about the efficacy of the provision directly. He lists it as a positive development, and so we can infer that he doesn't think it's largely useless, but we don't even have to go that far—simply note that he didn't say anything to indicate that he thought it did little to address the problem.

7. B

We've already determined that the two passages have the same topic and scope, but differing purposes and main ideas. In fact, their purposes/main ideas and the conclusions they draw are virtually contradictory: Author A wants us to know that bankruptcy reform in its current form won't work; author B wants to demonstrate that it's *already* working.

The answer choices here are phrased generally, so it may take a little more work to find what we're looking for. Let's generalize the relationship we've already determined—they reach opposite conclusions.

(A) Conflicting statistics? Like what? Didn't see any of those, only differing key points and predictions for the future.

(B) Correct! We already identified the different conclusions, but the authors don't dispute each other's facts.

(C) When in doubt, fill in the specifics that match each piece of the general statement. What is the prediction in passage A? *This new bankruptcy law won't work to reduce filings in the long run*. The language in this choice is strong: We're not looking for evidence that weakens the prediction, but that disproves it. Did author B give us any statistics that would *prove* this new law was going to keep filings down in the long term? Nope. Toss it out.

(D) Close, but the passages, though they don't contradict each other factually, don't actually employ "identical" data. (Note: when you see two answer choices as similar as this one and correct answer choice (B), look at the difference between them. Here, it's the suggestion that the authors use "identical" data—an extreme-sounding term that should set off alarm bells.)

(E) We established at the outset that passage B wasn't directly responsive to A, but if you have any doubt here, just check. Where did passage B take on the issue of underlying economic causes like medical problems? That's right—it didn't. Eliminate this.

8. A

We already determined that the relationship between passages A and B was that they reached differing conclusions about the effectiveness of the law, though they didn't directly contradict one another's evidence.

(A) A perfect match! Both titles relate to the same policy; one says it's flawed and the other says it's working already.

(B) The first part talks about motivation, the second about success. Those aren't conflicting positions on the same issue, as our authors took.

(C) Contradictory positions about the need for a law, which is entirely different from assessment/prediction of success or failure. Eliminate.

(D) Although both of these titles are on the same topic, there doesn't appear to be any direct relationship between them, particularly not a contradictory one; one could advocate an alternative and still be looking to maximize the effectiveness of the current system in the interim.

(E) These two titles do take contradictory positions as our authors do, but there is a subtle difference: These documents are addressing the problem (or lack thereof) itself, whereas our authors (and the authors in answer choice (A)) are assessing the effectiveness of a solution and coming to opposite conclusions.

Questions 9 –15

Topic and Scope

The concept of "hard" (tough, controversial) legal cases; specifically, to what extent such cases are "legally determinate," defined by the author as "decidable according to existing law."

Purpose and Main Idea

The author's purpose is to compare two legal thinkers' views of the law as a means of evaluating when and how controversial cases can be decided under existing law. By the end, we see that the author finds merit in both views but, in the main, finds Hart's conception of the open-endedness of legal terminology to be both persuasive and useful.

Paragraph Structure

Paragraph 1 presents some fundamental terminology and definitions—"hard" cases and "determinate"—as it lays out the passage's fundamental issue: How can hard cases be decided? Paragraph 2 belongs to Hart: his conception of law as legal rules with "open-textured" general terminology. It also includes an extended example and the suggestion that some cases need to be decided on moral or political, rather than strictly legal, grounds because their terminology isn't specific or determinate enough. Dworkin is the focus of paragraph 3: To him the law isn't just Hart's rules, but it also includes principles, and the two work in tandem to render "legal indeterminacy"—the deciding of cases on other than legal grounds—a nonissue. Paragraph 4, as noted above, is comfortable with both concepts—rules and principles—as the author forges a middle ground, deciding finally that there are difficult cases and a branch of law where things are simply not cut-and-dried, and judges must exercise some discretion.

9. C

Dworkin's concept is legal principles; Hart's is open-textured legal rules; paragraph 4 indicates the author's level of comfort with both; and (C) sums it all up and gets the topic and scope right, to boot. As long as you recognize the middle ground between Hart and Dworkin that the author is trying to forge in paragraph 4, you should be able to reject the four uncredited choices without straining for full comprehension of the text.

(A) begs the question of the topic and scope—the determinacy of hard cases—and comes down squarely on the side of the need for resolving all cases through law alone, something the author rejects. (B) is the choice for those who grab paragraph 1 and not much else. The definition of hard cases is a jumping-off point for the real issue of how such cases are to be decided, and (B) mentions none of that. (D)'s negative judgment of Dworkin's concept of legal principles is not supported by the author—indeed, the author embraces the concept in paragraph 4. (E) is a pretty radical distortion of this passage's content and tone. Hart's definition of legal terminology as "open textured" implies (quite sensibly) that language has some inherent flexibility of meaning—even legal language—and that judges need to exercise some judgment as a result; but all of that is a far cry from accusations of "inherent inconsistency" and "defects and gaps in the law."

10. C

This choice nicely paraphrases lines 40–41. (A) sounds like a plausible definition of the term "legal principles" on its face, but it has nothing to do with Dworkin or, indeed, with anything else in the passage. (B) Legal principles, as defined by Dworkin, don't explain legal rules: They coexist with them, within the body of established law (see lines 35–37). With (D), Dworkin believes that law exists outside of legal rules. With (E), Dworkin seems to be opposed to the notion that some cases need judicial discretion (lines

42–45), so he would not coin the term "legal principles" to mean cases that required same.

11. D

The answer comes from the final sentence—as well as the realization that rules are Hart's concept, principles are Dworkin's, and the author is trying to effect a synthesis of the two in the final paragraph. The "penumbra of both rules and principles," of course, is the place where things are not cut-and-dried and determinate (lines 15–16).

As for (A), the author never posits which—rules or principles—is appealed to more often in hard cases. (B) Official recognition, whatever that means, has nothing to do with this think piece on legal determinacy, or the author's effort to work out a theory of one part of the law.

(C) is wrong: Far from arguing that rules have been superseded by principles, the author believes that both exist in the law. (E) is wrong: The author hints strongly that those cases "in the penumbra of both rules and principles" will, in fact, require judges' discretion for their decidability.

12. D

Choice (D) sums up lines 18–22. (A) and (B) are off because the word "vehicle" is a term, not a rule or principle in and of itself.

13. B

This answer comes directly out of lines 8-11, which tie Hart's concept to the standard law and describe Hart's ideas as "clear" and "persuasive." (A) "Clear" and "persuasive" don't imply that a work or theory covers a topic "exhaustively." No evidence for this one. (C) and (D) are each half-right, half-wrong. "Interesting," sure; "plausible," okay; but "impractical" or "unwieldy"? It's unlikely that a theoretical think piece like this one would traffic much in practicality anyway; but if anything, the author does seem to see practical and workable (as opposed to "unwieldy") value in Hart's concept (see paragraph 4). (E) is hopelessly wrong. No matter how far back in history Hart's work dates—and of course we get no info to that effect—the author seems to find it relevant and well worth studying.

14. B

Some examinees, thrown by all of the heavy-duty terminology in paragraph 1, failed to see that "determinate" is clearly defined by lines 6–7 and paraphrased in (B).

Very straightforward. A demonstration of how one's frame of mind can make or break a particular LSAT question. (A) Penalties—sentences, punishments, etc.—are way beyond the scope of this investigation. (C) is wrong: The concept of judicial discretion doesn't come into the passage until much later, and then only in passing. This choice picks up on some terminology from the passage (lines 1–3) but is otherwise incoherent. (D) defines *"indeterminate"* pretty well. With (E), no reference to codified procedures can be found anywhere near line 6.

15. E

This choice, as written, basically just sums up lines 46–47, but that fact shouldn't unduly trouble you: After all, paragraph 4 is where the individual discussions of Hart and Dworkin are—it is, therefore, the most important paragraph—and lines 46–47 do encapsulate paragraph 4. So despite (E)'s evocation of only two lines, they *are* the most important lines and can stand acceptably as the author's purpose.

(A) is nonsense. The in-practice role of the legislative branch is about as far removed from this passage's concerns as can be. (B) is an issue that was raised and disposed of in paragraph 1. The topic may be hard cases, but the scope moves away from their definition to their determinacy, something that (B) ignores and (E) exploits. (C) paraphrases lines 38–41, but these lines aren't nearly as all-encompassing as lines 46–47. And in terms of the author's main purpose, Dworkin certainly doesn't deserve the pride of place that (C) assigns him. As for (D), if anyone is in the "critiquing Hart" business, it's Dworkin and not our author, who is trying to synthesize the views of the two thinkers.

Set Three

Questions 1–8

Topic and Scope

Zora Neale Hurston; specifically, different assessments of her novel, *Their Eyes Were Watching God*.

Purpose and Main Idea

The author's purpose is to explain why Hurston's novel has only recently received widespread praise, her main idea being simply that the development of new strands of literary criticism accounts for this turnaround.

Paragraph Structure

Paragraph 1 introduces the passage's basic question: Why was such an important and eventually influential novel dismissed when it first appeared? Paragraph 2 says that the novel was misunderstood and condemned, especially in the black literary community, because it was out of step with the black "protest fiction" of the time. Paragraph 3 explains that the rise of feminist and Afrocentric literary criticism has been behind the new appreciation of Hurston's novel.

1. E

Lines 15–18 say that Wilson's work, unlike Hurston's, was totally ignored upon its publication. But, like Hurston's work, it has recently been the object of literary inquiry. Harriet Wilson is mentioned only once (in line 16). Read the lines around such a reference carefully, for that's where you'll most likely find the answer.

(A) The passage doesn't say when Wilson's book was published, so we can't conclude that it was written at the same time as Hurston's novel. Moreover, Wilson's work didn't receive *any* critical attention.

(B) According to the passage (lines 1–5), it's *Hurston's* novel that has heavily influenced the writing of later black women.

(C) This passage mentions with the literary establishment's tardy appreciation of Wilson's novel, but does not say how widely read it was.

(D) Lines 15–18 make it clear that Wilson's novel *was* published.

2. B

Paragraph 2 mentions that Hurston's book went out of print because it wasn't understood by much of the black literary establishment and readership. (It was Harriet Wilson's novel, not Hurston's, that was relegated to obscurity because of critical neglect.) So (B) is correct.

(A) *Au contraire.* Hurston's novel received a lot of flak from reviewers when it appeared.

(C) Afrocentric interpretations of Hurston's novel, paragraph 3 reveals, are a more recent development.

(D) Paragraphs 2 and 3 make it clear that Hurston's work doesn't belong to the genre known as protest fiction.

(E) The passage says that the book received mixed reviews from white and black critics. There's not enough information to conclude that "most" reviewers gave it a less than positive reception.

3.   C

Choice (C) captures the author's topic (Hurston's novel), scope (earlier versus later assessments of her novel), and purpose (to explain why Hurston's novel has recently won acclaim).

(A) focuses on a detail in paragraph 2.

(B) According to the author, Afrocentric literary critics have *also* helped to bring Hurston's novel to prominence. Besides, this passage also discusses why Hurston's novel wasn't well-received initially—an aspect that (B) doesn't address.

(D) Hurston's novel was trashed by some early literary critics precisely because it wasn't protest fiction.

(E) focuses on a detail in paragraph 3.

4.   E

According to lines 52–56, the recent rise of Afrocentric literary analysis has brought to light black folklore traditions as represented in literature. During your work on the questions, remember the purpose of each paragraph. Here, paragraph 3's scope of recent developments should frame your consideration of what's going on in lines 52–56.

(A) distorts a detail in paragraph 3. Indeed, the only thing we're told about Gates is that he has written perceptively about Hurston's novel. (B) and (D) are beyond the scope of the passage, which is about literary criticism of Hurston's novel. We aren't told much about black novelists as a group. For all we know, black novelists writing before or during the 1940s *did* use folklore in their works. With (C), again, we don't know what other black authors were doing; so we can't conclude that Hurston was the first to incorporate black folklore into a novel.

5.   C

Paragraph 2 strongly implies that Wright's *Native Son* fell into the genre of protest fiction, which explored the issue of racism in the United States. In other words, whereas Hurston's novel concentrated on the life of one individual in the black community (lines 39–40), Wright's novel focused on the entire community, choice (C).

(A) is out: Since Wright's book fit into the dominant genre of the era, it's highly unlikely that it got a worse reception than

Hurston's novel, especially since we're told that Wright's novel was "much acclaimed." (B) is *au contraire*: Wright's novel is far *more* typical of mid-century black writing than Hurston's. With (D), we can't say that Wright's book has got more folklore in it than Hurston's, because the passage doesn't tell us exactly what's *in* his book. Except for the one reference, *Native Son* is outside the scope of the passage. With (E), no comparison is possible between Wright's book and Hurston's on the issue of feminist and Afrocentric attention, because the passage doesn't provide us with feminist and Afrocentric comments on Wright's novel.

6.   B

Lines 30–33 say that black writers of the 1940s believed that black literature should fall into the protest fiction genre—that is, they believed that it should tackle the issue of racism against blacks. The novel outlined in (B) has just such a focus. The novels in the other answer choices don't focus on racial discrimination. (D)'s "unjust working conditions" is not the same as racial discrimination.

7.   C

In paragraph 2, the author notes that some mid-century reviewers dismissed Hurston's book because it doesn't deal with racism, the issue that interested them. In paragraph 3, the author notes that later reviewers, influenced by feminism or Afrocentrism, applauded the book because it deals with issues of concern to feminists and blacks. Hence, the author is likely to agree with the notion that literary critics' "ideological perspectives and assumptions about the purpose of art" affect their analysis of art, choice (C).

The author would probably disagree with the statements in (A) and (D). After all, she largely attributes the early demise, as well as the later revival, of Hurston's novel to the efforts of literary critics. With (B), the author doesn't discuss any "experimental" works of fiction, whatever that term means. Thus, there's no telling what she'd have to say about how literary critics initially view them. (E) is too strong. True, the author notes that literary critics make much of the ideological premises of a book; but there's nothing in the passage to indicate that she thinks that they hone in on this aspect of a work above all else.

8.   B

The passage is mainly about the reassessment of Hurston's novel that grew out of new forms of literary criticism, or choice (B). (A) is out: What misconception? (C) distorts the contents of the passage. True, the author discusses early and more recent critiques of Hurston's novel, but she doesn't attempt to "reconcile" them. (D) are (E) are out: What conventional approach and what new discovery?

Questions 9–14

Topic and Scope

The socioeconomic success of Chinese and Japanese immigrants and their descendants; specifically, theories about how these groups coped with daunting conditions in the U.S.

Purpose and Main Idea

The author seeks to combine two distinct and commonly used sociological theories. The main idea—the idea that links the entire passage together—comes at the beginning of paragraph 2: The mobility of Chinese and Japanese immigrants is best understood by considering both supply-side (cultural) and demand-side (structural) analyses together.

Paragraph Structure

Paragraph 1 defines the two theories. Culturally based (supply side) explanations emphasize the cultural resources that immigrants bring with them to the U.S. Structurally based (demand side) explanations stress the market conditions in the U.S. that the immigrants must respond to.

Paragraph 2 starts with the main idea—both analyses are necessary—and then discusses the supply-side analysis, basically comparing the Chinese and Japanese experiences and taking up such issues as how each group immigrated and what happened subsequently. The gist of it is that the Japanese moved ahead a bit faster than the Chinese, but the situation more or less evened out in time.

Paragraph 3, predictably, focuses on the structural (demand side) explanation, which stresses economic conditions in the host country. The paragraph basically compares the demand for immigrant labor in early capitalist and advanced capitalist economies.

9.   E

The lengths of these choices is truly absurd (more LSAT antics)! But note: The first line or two of (E) gives it away. The other choices are traps. Prephrasing helps: "The proper analysis combines supply-side and demand-side theories."

It also helps if you push aside any choices that don't start to work in the first line or so. (E), unlike all the others, pulls us in from its first five words: "Only an analysis that combines . . ." (E) alone echoes the opening sentence of paragraph 2 and encompasses all paragraphs.

(A) is too narrow; it refers to the second theory, the structurally based explanation. (B) has the same problem, in reverse: It focuses on the culturally based explanation. (C) focuses narrowly on the nuclear family, a supporting detail in paragraph 2. (D), like (A), focuses on the structural explanation.

10. C

If you correctly associate supply side with the immigrant point of view—with, as paragraph 1 says, the "qualities immigrant groups bring with them [to the host] market"—then choice (C) *must* stand out. All the others refer to demand-side elements: economic realities in the host country.

11. D

The cited sentence—actually the first 4 sentences of paragraph 3—are talking about changes in demand-side factors: the evolution in the host country from an early capitalist economy to an advanced capitalist economy, which eventually creates the demand for both skilled and unskilled labor ("two immigrant streams").

(A) "Human capital" is a jargon term that's irrelevant to paragraph 3. It came up in paragraph 1, in relation to the cultural or supply-side perspective. (B) is confusing; it may be tempting but is inaccurate. The cited sentence mentions the primary labor market, but seemingly in relation to skilled labor only. The stem asks about "two immigrant streams"—about both skilled and unskilled labor. (C) focuses wrongly on early immigration. The "two immigrant streams" is a later response to an advanced capitalist economy. (E) is as imprecise as (B). The passage says nothing about the two immigrant streams having any *influence* on the labor market.

12. E

The answer echoes the gist of paragraph 1. The author describes the two sociological treatments as typically applied separately. She then asserts at the beginning of paragraph 2 that both should be used together.

(A) is illogical and never implied. No doubt everybody—the author and all sociologists—would be interested in the interaction of causal factors. (B) is *au contraire*: The structuralists focus on conditions in the host country, very much including "early capitalist development." Moreover, nothing implies that more sociologists ascribe to the cultural perspective than to the structural. With (C), true, the author uses the economic metaphors of supply side and demand side to describe the two theories, but there's no sense that the majority of sociologists would disavow those metaphors. (D) is another distortion. Issues of racial discrimination against immigrants (says paragraph 1) are integral to both sociological theories, which the author embraces.

13. A

This is inferable from paragraph 2. Chinese immigrants can only be said to have "remained sojourners" (line 32) if they had *been* such; likewise, if the Japanese "made the transition from sojourner" (lines 36-37), they must have *been* sojourners at some point. The stem clearly refers to info in paragraph 2, which compares the mobility of Chinese and Japanese immigrants. The gist is that the two groups assimilated at different rates, which eliminates all the wrong choices, leaving (A).

(B) is apparently true of Chinese but not of Japanese immigrants. (C) and (D) are both true of the Japanese, who quickly established small businesses, but less so of Chinese, who took longer to establish roots. With (E), technical skills are never mentioned, but are inferably more true of the Japanese, who initially advanced faster than the Chinese.

14. A

(A) says it all. The author's purpose is to combine the two sociological perspectives. Only considering them together, she says at the start of paragraph 2, "will suffice." With (B), the verb "challenging" doesn't work. The author doesn't challenge either of the two theories; she wants to *use* them. Nor is there any reference to a "tentative answer to a question." (C) distorts the author's approach. She doesn't evaluate the theories; she makes use of them. (D) also distorts: No "differences" are resolved. The two approaches involve distinct perspectives, but they're not opposed to each other. (E) is way off: The only mention of "group achievement" comes in paragraph 2, and the focus there is on *two* immigrant groups, not one. The bigger concern, in any case, is to apply the sociological theories.

Chapter 6: **Writing Sample**

- Sample essay topics and responses
- The 8 basic Writing Sample principles
- Kaplan's 4-Step Method for the Writing Sample

The Writing Sample comes at the end of your LSAT day. It consists of a scenario followed by two possible courses of action. You'll have 35 minutes to make a written case for your position.

This section tests your ability to write a clean, consise, and persuasive argument. No outside knowledge whatsoever is required.

You will need to have a pencil to write the essay, as well as scrap paper to plan out your response before you actually write it. Your essay must be confined to the space provided, which is roughly the equivalent of two sheets of standard lined paper. You won't be given additional paper, so you'll have to keep your argument concise. Usually, two or three paragraphs will be enough. Note that there's really no time or space to change your mind or radically alter your essay once you've begun writing, so *plan your argument out carefully before beginning to write*. Make sure to write as legibly as you can.

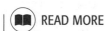 READ MORE

The Writing Sample may be crucial in some admissions decisions. Take it seriously and read on.

The Writing Sample is ungraded, but it is sent to law schools along with your LSAT score. Many law schools use the Writing Sample to help make decisions on borderline cases or to decide between applicants with otherwise comparable credentials. Granted, it may not carry the same weight as the scored sections of the test, but since it can impact on your admission chances, your best bet is to take it seriously.

Sample Essay Topic

The following is an example of a Writing Sample topic:

> The program director of a television station must select the guest for the first edition of *Timewaves*, a new talk show. Write an argument in favor of selecting one of the guests over the other, with the following considerations in mind:
>
> - *Timewaves* must have enough mass appeal to attract a significant viewing audience in a competitive time slot.
> - *Timewaves* must continue the company's tradition of providing serious commentary on current topics.
>
> Jeanne Josephs—a popular writer—is known for her sharp analysis of national issues. Her most recent article, published in a widely read news magazine, was entitled "Success: Who's Got It and Why." In the article, Josephs interviews celebrities in various fields, including sports, business, and the arts, about their views on success and how they achieved it. Josephs has not appeared on a television talk show in several years. Last year, however, she won a prestigious journalism award for "The Private Pain of Politics," a series of articles on the toll public office has taken on the family lives of prominent politicians. At that time reports about Josephs and her work appeared in many major newspapers.
>
> Dr. Kingston Evans—a prominent psychologist—recently led an expert panel in a study of drug use in several affluent suburban communities. The panel's controversial final report, "Drugs in Suburbia," is to be published as a book soon after the first edition of *Timewaves* is shown. The report is said to expose establishment figures, including public officials, as narcotics suppliers to the suburban market. The study received some media attention after the panel's conclusion—that drugs are more prevalent though less visible in the suburbs than in the inner city—was inadvertently revealed. At the same time, there have been accusations that the study is an inaccurate, sensationalized account of a serious issue. Dr. Evans, however, is a distinguished professor with a well-respected body of academic research to his credit.

READ MORE

LSAC offers a wide sampling of other essay topics with their practice tests. The more of them you examine, the more likely that you'll have relevant ideas prepared for test day.

THE 8 BASIC WRITING SAMPLE PRINCIPLES

Here are the most important rules of thumb to remember when attacking the Writing Sample.

Use Scrap Paper to Plan Your Essay

The proctors give you scrap paper for a reason—so use it. Make yourself a rudimentary outline, listing the points you want to make in each paragraph. Ideally, you should know what you want to say and how you want to say it before putting pencil to paper.

Don't Obsess Over Your Position

Nobody really cares whether you consider the argument strong or which choice you make (there are valid arguments to be made in support of both Josephs and Evans). What's important is how well you support your position. Generally, the Decision alternatives are written to be pretty evenly matched, so there's no right or wrong answer, just a well-supported or ill-supported position.

Get Right to the Point

The first sentence should immediately offer a statement of your position. Assume that the reader is already familiar with the situation; there's no need to waste time describing the scenario.

Use a Clear, Simple Essay Format

Since you already know the structure of your essay topic, you can decide in advance how you will structure your response. One possibility is the "winner/loser" format, in which the first body paragraph begins with an assessment of the option you've chosen in light of each of the two criteria in the prompt. The second body paragraph explains why the loser doesn't fulfill the criteria as well.

Another possibility is to organize the essay by criteria. For instance, in the prompt you just read, the first body paragraph would address the ability of each of the possible guests to attract a large audience, and the second would address how each would fit the station's goal of providing serious commentary on current topics.

Regardless of which format you use—or whether you create a format of your own—it's important to begin the essay with a clear statement of your choice and to end with an affirmation of your decision. It's also critical that your essay is coherent in its reasoning and that your decision is clearly supported in view of the criteria given.

Whether you adopt one of these formats or use one of your own, the most important thing is that your essay be coherent in its reasoning. The more organized your essay is, the more persuasive it will be.

Mention, But Downplay, the Opposing View

There's no denying that the other option has some positive points or that your choice has a weakness. Failure to acknowledge that there's another viable position can create the impression that you haven't fully analyzed the issue. So you'll want to acknowledge the other side, but do so in a way that downplays its importance. Well-thought-out sentence structure will help you do so. For instance, you might write, "Although Jeanne Josephs recently won a prestigious journalism award, her subject matter . . ." or "Despite Dr. Evans's professional reputation . . . " Acknowledging these points demonstrates that you see the big picture, and anticipating and dealing with likely counterarguments strengthens your argument.

Don't Simply Repeat Facts From the Prompt

Try instead to offer an *interpretation of the facts in light of the stated criteria*. Your readers already know all the same facts you do. Your job is to interpret and present those facts in light of the stated criteria. For instance, it's not enough to simply point out that Jeanne Josephs won a prestigious journalism award—you must tie that to one or both of the criteria. For instance, you might point out that the publicity surrounding this award will help draw viewers, or that the award enhances her credibility and thus makes her a good choice to maintain the station's history of providing serious commentary. Merely parroting what's written in the topic won't win you any points with the law schools.

KAPLAN) EXCLUSIVE

Readers will be prejudiced against your Writing Sample if it's hard to decipher. If your writing is bad, print.

Write Well

It sounds obvious, of course, but you should try to make your prose as clean and flawless as you can. Some people get so entangled in content that they neglect the mechanics of essay writing. But spelling, grammar, and writing mechanics are important. Use structural signals to keep your writing fluid and clear, and use transitions between paragraphs to keep the entire essay unified. Above all, write or print legibly.

Budget Your Time Wisely

We suggest spending roughly five to seven minutes reading the topic and planning out your essay. Use the scrap paper provided to jot down a quick outline of the points you intend to make. Then spend about 25 minutes writing the essay. This should be plenty of time; remember, you're only looking at three or four paragraphs at the most. This schedule will leave about three to five minutes at the end to proofread your essay for spelling and grammar.

KAPLAN'S 4-STEP METHOD FOR THE WRITING SAMPLE

1. Prompt.

Before you start to write, be sure you understand the prompt and the scenario it presents. Writing off-topic suggests that you are unable to focus your ideas, or that you don't care.

2. Plan.

Decide which alternative you will support based on the number and quality of your supporting examples. *It doesn't have to be your real opinion*, but you must express a clear opinion and support it with the types of reasoning you learned in Logical Reasoning.

Always plan your approach thoroughly before you start to write. Essays that wander aimlessly, or start with one opinion but change to another halfway through, are unpleasant to read and make an overall bad impression.

3. Produce.

Use most of your time to write the essay. Think through each sentence before starting to write it. Start a new paragraph for each new idea. Stick to your plan.

4. Proofread.

Don't skip this step. Save a couple of minutes to make sure you haven't left out words (or even sentences) that are necessary for the reader to follow your reasoning. Planning to proofread also helps ensure that you will complete the essay.

 GO ONLINE

Your downloadable study sheet summarizes these strategies.

SAMPLE ESSAY

Using the sample prompt (repeated below) write an essay, using the next two lined pages, and observing the 35-minute time limit. Then check your essay, making sure it observes the basic principles outlined above.

KAPLAN) EXCLUSIVE

In your essay, it's OK to bring up factors that aren't listed, but that you think are relevant to the decision maker's choice—just be sure to cover the listed criteria as well.

> The program director of a television station must select the guest for the first edition of *Timewaves*, a new talk show. Write an argument in favor of selecting one of the guests over the other, with the following considerations in mind:
> - *Timewaves* must have enough mass appeal to attract a significant viewing audience in a competitive time slot.
> - *Timewaves* must continue the company's tradition of providing serious commentary on current topics.
>
> Jeanne Josephs—a popular writer—is known for her sharp analysis of national issues. Her most recent article, published in a widely read news magazine, was entitled "Success: Who's Got It and Why." In the article, Josephs interviews celebrities in various fields, including sports, business, and the arts, about their views on success and how they achieved it. Josephs has not appeared on a television talk show in several years. Last year, however, she won a prestigious journalism award for "The Private Pain of Politics," a series of articles on the toll public office has taken on the family lives of prominent politicians. At that time reports about Josephs and her work appeared in many major newspapers.
>
> Dr. Kingston Evans—a prominent psychologist—recently led an expert panel in a study of drug use in several affluent suburban communities. The panel's controversial final report, "Drugs in Suburbia," is to be published as a book soon after the first edition of *Timewaves* is shown. The report is said to expose establishment figures, including public officials, as narcotics suppliers to the suburban market. The study received some media attention after the panel's conclusion—that drugs are more prevalent though less visible in the suburbs than in the inner city—was inadvertently revealed. At the same time, there have been accusations that the study is an inaccurate, sensationalized account of a serious issue. Dr. Evans, however, is a distinguished professor with a well-respected body of academic research to his credit.

 KAPLAN)

Sample Response

Compare your answer to the following sample response:

The program director should choose Jeanne Josephs as the first guest on Timewaves.

As a popular author, Josephs will be able to attract a significant audience. The fact that Josephs has not appeared on a television talk show for several years could be viewed as a negative, but it could also provide an excellent marketing point for the show. Some viewers will undoubtedly make a special point of tuning in because it is the writer's first appearance in so many years. And, while even the press she got upon receiving her award last year is a bit stale, the prominence of the celebrities, sports figures, and politicians she wrote about will be an added draw.

Dr. Evans is not likely to draw as broad an audience. In addition to his topic being narrower, his publicity has thus far been limited, and his book will not yet have been released when the show airs. While the controversy surrounding the study might attract some viewers, it is also a significant negative factor in view of the station's second goal.

Jeanne Josephs has established a reputation as a sharp political commentator and won a prestigious journalism award just last year. Although the fact that much of her work has centered around celebrities may create something of a lightweight impression at first glance, her focus on the element of success and her recent accolades are in keeping with the station's effort to continue to provide serious commentary on current topics. Despite the academic reputation enjoyed by Dr. Evans, his current work is surrounded by controversy. Additionally, although the topic is certainly current, Evans can hardly be considered an objective commentator.

While there are potential benefits to choosing each guest, Josephs's unsullied reputation in her field, popularity, and broader subject matter make her the better choice to fulfill the station's stated goals.

 EXCLUSIVE

It's a big mistake to leave the Writing Sample unfinished. Also be strict with yourself, so that you'll have at least a few minutes left at the end to read over what you've written.

The argument in this essay is clearly structured and supported with the facts provided in the prompt; this is what makes it successful. Always keep in mind that there is no right or wrong answer in the Writing Sample section.

Note the writer even concedes the fact that Evans may be considered more serious than Josephs, but goes on to diminish this argument, using the facts. This shows that the writer has considered the strengths of the other candidate. Remember to think like a lawyer! Again, recognizing and dealing with possible objections to your argument makes your argument stronger.

In addition, notice that the essay is concise and well written. It starts and ends strong, with a clear statement of the writer's choice. Also, grammar, punctuation, and word choice are effective. The reader (including admissions officers!) will be looking for that, too.

Do the practice essay provided in the following pages. You'll find additional prompts and sample responses in your Online Companion.

SUMMARY

The basic Writing Sample principles are:

- Use scrap paper to plan your essay.

- Don't obsess over your position.

- Get right to the point.

- Use a clear, simple essay format.

- Mention but downplay the opposing view.

- Don't simply repeat facts from the prompt.

- Write carefully.

- Budget your time wisely.

Kaplan's 4-Step Method for the Writing Sample

1. Prompt.

2. Plan.

3. Produce.

4. Proofread.

WRITING SAMPLE PRACTICE

Essay One

Green Earth, an organization devoted to preserving the environment, has decided to expand its activities into the field of publishing. Write an argument in favor of selecting one or the other of the following manuscripts as the organization's inaugural publication. Consider the following when making your decision:

- Green Earth wishes to develop a reputation as a publishing house for scholarly and influential works on the environment.
- Green Earth is financially dependent on the voluntary contributions of its supporters and hopes to raise significant funds through proceeds from the book.

John Dailey, a journalist who has spent most of his career traveling the world in order to gain firsthand knowledge of environmental issues, has submitted a collection of essays discussing both his experiences and a variety of environmental problems. Dailey's work has always been extremely popular, and his book would likely prove one of the few accessible texts addressing the difficult scientific issues underlying many of today's environmental problems. Despite his extensive experience and careful research, several scholars have recently expressed concern about the scientific accuracy of some of Dailey's reports. Dailey, currently researching a new article on herbal medicines obtained from endangered plant species in the Amazon rain forest, has not yet had time to prepare a response.

Ginny Fredericks, a professor and author of several well-known scientific studies of environmental issues, has submitted a manuscript proposing a sweeping plan of action for preserving the environment. Dr. Fredericks's reputation as a scientist guarantees that the book, the crowning achievement of her long and distinguished career, will receive a significant amount of media attention. However, those accustomed to her impartial approach to environmental questions may be taken aback and perhaps outraged by her impassioned argument for a very radical program of action. Dr. Fredericks has volunteered to donate a percentage of the proceeds from a lecture tour she plans in conjunction with her book to the book's publisher. But William Stone, a noted philanthropist and longtime supporter of Green Earth, has expressed concern over the organization's support of such a potentially controversial figure.

Sample Response

Green Earth should make Dr. Fredericks's book its inaugural publishing project. Dr. Fredericks's professional background will help to achieve Green Earth's goal of developing a reputation as a publishing house for scholarly and influential works on the environment. While Dr. Fredericks has departed from her usual objective approach, her history of factual presentation only enhances the credibility of her proposal, increasing the likelihood that the book will be taken seriously and will impact the perception of environmental issues. John Dailey, although an expert in a sense, is a journalist and not a scientist. His scientific information has already been called into question, and if it turns out that the challenge is valid, the reputation of the publisher would undoubtedly suffer. In addition, Dailey's book is geared toward a consumer audience, intentionally "accessible," and as such might not be regarded as a scholarly work at all, despite the possible value and accuracy of his information.

Green Earth also hopes to raise funds through the publication of the book. Dr. Fredericks will enjoy significant media attention, which will undoubtedly fuel sales of the book. Additionally, the controversy surrounding her departure from her usually objective perspective is likely to enhance sales rather than harm them. Any loss of funding from the one philanthropist who has expressed concern will likely be more than offset by the potential profits from the book—and Mr. Stone has only expressed concern, not indicated directly that his contributions will be affected if Green Earth goes ahead with the Fredericks book. While Dailey's book will probably have popular appeal based on his past popularity and the accessibility of his material, the risk of sales being completely undermined by the challenges to his scientific data cannot be adequately assessed at this point.

The manuscript submitted by Dr. Fredericks will better ensure that Green Earth achieves its financial goals, while building the reputation it desires.

Chapter 7: **The Final Week**

Is it starting to feel like your whole life is a buildup to the LSAT? You've known about it for years, worried about it for months, and now spent weeks in solid preparation for it. As the test gets closer, you may find your anxiety is on the rise.

You shouldn't worry. After the preparation you've received from the Kaplan's LSAT Comprehensive Program, you're in good shape for the test. To calm any pretest jitters you may have, though, let's go over a few strategies for the days before the test.

THE WEEK BEFORE THE TEST

The week or so leading up to the test should be all about keeping up your skills but avoiding burnout and anxiety. You should do the following:

- Recheck your admission ticket for accuracy; if corrections are necessary, they must be made in writing.
- Practice getting up as early as you'll have to on test day and review test material, preferably your most recent Practice Tests.
- Visit the testing center if you haven't already. This is a good way to ensure that you don't get lost on the day of the test and know where to park. See the actual room where your test will be administered and take notice of little things—like the kind of desk you'll be working on, whether the room is likely to be hot or cold. Remember, you must be on time—the proctors won't wait for you and you won't be allowed in after testing has begun.

 CHECK OUT THE CD

Try brief practice sessions in the final week using targeted quizzes.

Practice Timing

Most test centers have a clock on the wall that the proctor will use to time the test, but don't take anything for granted—your test center may not (stranger things have been known to happen). You should definitely bring along your own timing device, such as a watch or a stopwatch, so long as it doesn't make any noise (devices that beep on the hour or sound an alarm at specified times are prohibited from the testing site). The LSAC specifically prohibits timing devices that have functions other than strictly telling time, so you should be careful in your selection.

GO ONLINE

Print a copy of your downloadable Study Sheet to take with you on test day.

It's also best to practice using a timing routine that you'll follow during the real test. Some students find it helpful to set their watches at 25 past the hour for the scored sections, such as 11:25. This way, they know that the section will end exactly when their watch says 12:00. Others reset their watches exactly on the hour at the beginning of each section, and know that every section will end 35 minutes later. Still others synchronize their watches with the room clock and follow the proctor's timing guidelines. It doesn't matter which procedure you adopt, or even if you come up with one of your own, just as long as you use it consistently, so that keeping track of time on test day is second nature.

THE DAY BEFORE THE TEST: AN LSAT SURVIVAL KIT

Avoid doing intensive studying the day before the test. There's little you can do to help yourself at this late date, and you may exhaust yourself and burn out.

Put together an "LSAT survival kit" containing the following items:

- Your admission ticket
- Appropriate photo ID
- A non-beeping timepiece
- Copy of a logic game you've already done (look it over to warm you up and boost confidence)
- A few No. 2 pencils (slightly dull points fill the ovals best)
- Pencil sharpener
- Eraser
- Aspirin, antacid, and tissues
- CD player or iPod
- Some water and high-energy, natural sugar snacks (apples, bananas, nuts, trail mix) for the break

Take the night off entirely. Go to see a movie or watch some TV. Try not to think about the test. Get to bed early.

THE DAY OF THE TEST

Get up early, leaving yourself plenty of time.

Read something to warm up your brain—you don't want the LSAT to be the first written material your brain tries to assimilate that day.

Dress in layers for maximum comfort; you'll be able to adjust to the testing room's temperature.

In traveling to the test center, leave yourself enough time for traffic and mass transit delays.

Be ready for a long day. Total testing time, remember, is three hours and 30 minutes. When you add the administrative paperwork before and after, and the 10- to 15-minute break in the middle, you're looking at an experience of four and a half to six hours.

Test Center Procedures

Don't get flustered when they fingerprint you and check your ID as you enter the testing room—this is standard operating procedure. The test administrators do this because occasionally they have reason to believe that some test takers are not exactly who they say they are. If you're on the up and up, you'll have nothing to worry about.

After the test booklets are handed out, and you've filled out all of the required information, the test will begin. Your proctor should write the starting and ending time of each section on a blackboard in front of the room, and will usually announce the time remaining at specified intervals, such as when there's 10 minutes remaining, 5 minutes remaining, and 1 minute remaining.

Taking the Test

Here are some last-minute reminders to help guide your work on the test:

> **KAPLAN EXCLUSIVE**
>
> Don't forget your stress-management techniques during the test. Breathe deeply, stretch, and relax as needed. Imagine yourself succeeding.

- Confidence is key. Accentuate the positives, and don't dwell on the negatives!
- Remember you can get a lot of questions wrong and still score high—so don't panic when faced with difficult material.
- Don't get bogged down in the middle of any section. At the end of every section are questions that may be really easy—get to them!
- Transfer your answers methodically; don't leave any answers blank. To ensure accuracy, say the question number and choice to yourself (silently, of course) as you grid.
- Give all five choices a fair shot in Logical Reasoning and Reading Comp, time permitting. For Logic Games, go with the objectively correct answer as soon as you find it.
- Don't be alarmed by extra-tough questions at the beginning, especially in Logical Reasoning. It happens. Skip past tough ones and come back to them later, making sure to circle them in the test booklet.
- Preview the Logic Games before you launch into them. The third or fourth game could be the easiest one. Skip over any Reading Comp passage that slows you down too much, and come back to it later.
- Don't try to figure out which section is unscored. It can't help you, and you may be wrong.

Test Rhythm

Between sections 1 and 2, 2 and 3, and 4 and 5, the proctor will say only: "Time's up on this section. Go on to the next section."

Notice that there's no break here—you must go immediately from one section to the next. Also, if you finish a section early, you're not allowed to move on to another section. They're pretty strict about this one, so watch your step. If you have extra time, spend it looking back over your work on that section alone.

After section 3, you'll be instructed to close your test booklets and take a 10- to 15-minute break. Pay no attention to people's nervous chatter during the break. Some will say it's the hardest test since the dawn of time; others will say it's so easy they can't believe it. Either kind of comment can rattle you. Instead, put on your headphones and tune into your iPod's LSAT playlist or a favorite CD.

KAPLAN⟩ EXCLUSIVE

During the break, avoid nervous chatter about how hard the test is or which section was experimental. Have a snack and listen to your CD player or iPod.

After the break, you'll return to the testing room for the remaining sections. Then, after section 5, your test materials will be collected, and the Writing Sample materials will be handed out.

After the Writing Sample is collected, the test ends and you're free to get on with your life. For most of you, this means getting back to the rest of the application and admission process we will talk about in the section titled, "Getting into Law School." In the short term, however, this signals the beginning of a well-deserved night out to unwind.

AFTER THE TEST

Cancellation and Multiple Scores Policy

Unlike many things in life, the LSAT allows you a second chance. If you end the test feeling that you've really not done as well as you could have, you have the option of canceling your score. Canceling a test means that it won't be scored. It will just appear on your score report as a cancelled test. No one will know how well or poorly you really did—not even you.

How to Cancel

There are two ways you can cancel your score:

1. You can cancel your score immediately after the test, by blackening both bubbles on the Score Cancellation Section and signing your name to cerify the statement.
2. You can mail or fax the signed cancellation form to Law Services within nine calendar days of the test.

Kaplan strongly advises against cancelling your score immediately. There's no reason to rush this important decision. Moreover, answer-sheet cancellations are processed with the tests, so confirmation won't be received for four to five weeks; if the cancellation was not properly completed, you won't have any chance to correct the error.

When Should You Cancel

When deciding whether to cancel your score, a good rule of thumb is to make an honest assessment of whether you'll do better on the next test. Wishful thinking doesn't count; you need to have a valid reason to believe that the next time would be different. Remember, no test experience is going to be perfect. If you were distracted by the proctor's hacking cough this time around, next time you may be even more distracted by construction noise, or a cold, or the hideous lime-green sweater of the person sitting in front of you.

Two legitimate reasons to cancel your test are illness and personal circumstances that cause you to perform poorly on that particular day. Also, if you feel that you didn't prepare sufficiently, then it may be advisable to cancel your score and approach your test preparation a little more seriously the next time.

But keep in mind that test takers historically underestimate their performance, especially immediately following the test. They tend to forget about all of the things that went right and focus on everything that went wrong. So unless your performance is terribly marred by unforeseen circumstances, don't cancel your test immediately—at least sleep on the decision for one or two nights, and if you still feel you want to do it again, then send in the form. Just remember, cancellations are permanent. Once the form is sent, you can't change your mind.

What the Schools Will See

If you do cancel your test and then take it again for a score, your score report will indicate that you've canceled a previous score. Since it won't be scored, you don't have to worry about this score showing up on any subsequent score report. If you take more than one test without canceling, then all the scores will show up on each score report, so the law schools will see them all. Most law schools average LSAT scores, although there are a few exceptions. Check with individual schools for their policy on multiple scores.

Post-LSAT Festivities

After all the hard work you've done preparing for and taking the LSAT, you want to make sure you take time to celebrate afterwards. Plan to get together with friends the evening after the test. Relax, have fun, let loose. After all, you've got a lot to celebrate. You prepared for the test ahead of time. You did your best. You're going to get a good score.

So start thinking about all of the great parties you'll be attending at the law school of your choice.

 GO ONLINE

Take the online survey to let us know how you did (and how well we prepared you)!

PART THREE

Real LSAT Practice Tests and Explanations

How to Calculate Your Score

Step 1

For each practice test add together your total number correct for all four sections. This is your raw score.

Section I (# correct)   _____

Section II (# correct)   _____

Section III (# correct)   _____

Section IV (# correct)   _____
_____

Total Correct (raw score)   _____

Step 2

Find your raw score on the table below and read across to find your scaled score and your percentile.

Raw Score	Scaled Score	Percentile Rank	Raw Score	Scaled Score	Percentile Rank	Raw Score	Scaled Score	Percentile Rank
0	120	0	34	138	9	68	157	70
1	120	0	35	138	9	69	158	70
2	120	0	36	139	10	70	158	74
3	120	0	37	140	13	71	159	77
4	120	0	38	140	13	72	160	77
5	120	0	39	140	13	73	160	80
6	120	0	40	141	15	74	161	80
7	120	0	41	142	17	75	162	83
8	121	0	42	142	17	76	162	83
9	122	0	43	143	20	77	163	86
10	122	0	44	144	23	78	164	88
11	123	0	45	144	23	79	164	88
12	124	0	46	144	23	80	165	88
13	124	0	47	145	26	81	166	90
14	125	0	48	146	29	82	166	92
15	126	1	49	146	29	83	167	92
16	126	1	50	147	33	84	168	93
17	127	1	51	147	33	85	168	95
18	128	1	52	148	37	86	169	95
19	129	1	53	148	37	87	170	96
20	130	2	54	149	41	88	171	96
21	130	2	55	150	45	89	172	97
22	130	2	56	150	45	90	173	97
23	131	2	57	150	45	91	174	98
24	132	3	58	151	50	92	174	98
25	133	3	59	151	50	93	175	98
26	133	3	60	152	54	94	176	99
27	133	3	61	153	58	95	177	99
28	134	4	62	154	58	96	178	99
29	135	5	63	154	58	97	179	99
30	136	6	64	155	62	98	180	99
31	136	6	65	155	66	99	180	99
32	137	8	66	156	66	100	180	99
33	137	8	67	157	70	101	180	99

Practice Test 1

LSAT PRACTICE TEST 1 ANSWER SHEET

Remove (or photocopy) the answer sheet and use it to complete the practice test.

How to Take the Practice Tests

Before taking each test, find a quiet place where you can work uninterrupted for about two and a half hours. Make sure you have a comfortable desk and several No. 2 pencils.

Each Practice Test includes four scored multiple-choice sections. Keep in mind that on the actual LSAT, there will be an additional multiple-choice section—the experimental section—that will not contribute to your score, plus an unscored Writing Sample.

Once you start a Practice Test, don't stop (except for a 5- to 10-minute break after the second section) until you've gone through all four sections. Remember, you can review any questions within a section, but you may not go back or forward a section.

Good luck!

Start with number 1 for each section. If a section has fewer questions than answer spaces, leave the extra spaces blank.

Section I

1. Ⓐ Ⓑ Ⓒ Ⓓ Ⓔ	9. Ⓐ Ⓑ Ⓒ Ⓓ Ⓔ	17. Ⓐ Ⓑ Ⓒ Ⓓ Ⓔ	25. Ⓐ Ⓑ Ⓒ Ⓓ Ⓔ
2. Ⓐ Ⓑ Ⓒ Ⓓ Ⓔ	10. Ⓐ Ⓑ Ⓒ Ⓓ Ⓔ	18. Ⓐ Ⓑ Ⓒ Ⓓ Ⓔ	26. Ⓐ Ⓑ Ⓒ Ⓓ Ⓔ
3. Ⓐ Ⓑ Ⓒ Ⓓ Ⓔ	11. Ⓐ Ⓑ Ⓒ Ⓓ Ⓔ	19. Ⓐ Ⓑ Ⓒ Ⓓ Ⓔ	27. Ⓐ Ⓑ Ⓒ Ⓓ Ⓔ
4. Ⓐ Ⓑ Ⓒ Ⓓ Ⓔ	12. Ⓐ Ⓑ Ⓒ Ⓓ Ⓔ	20. Ⓐ Ⓑ Ⓒ Ⓓ Ⓔ	28. Ⓐ Ⓑ Ⓒ Ⓓ Ⓔ
5. Ⓐ Ⓑ Ⓒ Ⓓ Ⓔ	13. Ⓐ Ⓑ Ⓒ Ⓓ Ⓔ	21. Ⓐ Ⓑ Ⓒ Ⓓ Ⓔ	29. Ⓐ Ⓑ Ⓒ Ⓓ Ⓔ
6. Ⓐ Ⓑ Ⓒ Ⓓ Ⓔ	14. Ⓐ Ⓑ Ⓒ Ⓓ Ⓔ	22. Ⓐ Ⓑ Ⓒ Ⓓ Ⓔ	30. Ⓐ Ⓑ Ⓒ Ⓓ Ⓔ
7. Ⓐ Ⓑ Ⓒ Ⓓ Ⓔ	15. Ⓐ Ⓑ Ⓒ Ⓓ Ⓔ	23. Ⓐ Ⓑ Ⓒ Ⓓ Ⓔ	
8. Ⓐ Ⓑ Ⓒ Ⓓ Ⓔ	16. Ⓐ Ⓑ Ⓒ Ⓓ Ⓔ	24. Ⓐ Ⓑ Ⓒ Ⓓ Ⓔ	

right in Section I

wrong in Section I

Section II

1. Ⓐ Ⓑ Ⓒ Ⓓ Ⓔ	9. Ⓐ Ⓑ Ⓒ Ⓓ Ⓔ	17. Ⓐ Ⓑ Ⓒ Ⓓ Ⓔ	25. Ⓐ Ⓑ Ⓒ Ⓓ Ⓔ
2. Ⓐ Ⓑ Ⓒ Ⓓ Ⓔ	10. Ⓐ Ⓑ Ⓒ Ⓓ Ⓔ	18. Ⓐ Ⓑ Ⓒ Ⓓ Ⓔ	26. Ⓐ Ⓑ Ⓒ Ⓓ Ⓔ
3. Ⓐ Ⓑ Ⓒ Ⓓ Ⓔ	11. Ⓐ Ⓑ Ⓒ Ⓓ Ⓔ	19. Ⓐ Ⓑ Ⓒ Ⓓ Ⓔ	27. Ⓐ Ⓑ Ⓒ Ⓓ Ⓔ
4. Ⓐ Ⓑ Ⓒ Ⓓ Ⓔ	12. Ⓐ Ⓑ Ⓒ Ⓓ Ⓔ	20. Ⓐ Ⓑ Ⓒ Ⓓ Ⓔ	28. Ⓐ Ⓑ Ⓒ Ⓓ Ⓔ
5. Ⓐ Ⓑ Ⓒ Ⓓ Ⓔ	13. Ⓐ Ⓑ Ⓒ Ⓓ Ⓔ	21. Ⓐ Ⓑ Ⓒ Ⓓ Ⓔ	29. Ⓐ Ⓑ Ⓒ Ⓓ Ⓔ
6. Ⓐ Ⓑ Ⓒ Ⓓ Ⓔ	14. Ⓐ Ⓑ Ⓒ Ⓓ Ⓔ	22. Ⓐ Ⓑ Ⓒ Ⓓ Ⓔ	30. Ⓐ Ⓑ Ⓒ Ⓓ Ⓔ
7. Ⓐ Ⓑ Ⓒ Ⓓ Ⓔ	15. Ⓐ Ⓑ Ⓒ Ⓓ Ⓔ	23. Ⓐ Ⓑ Ⓒ Ⓓ Ⓔ	
8. Ⓐ Ⓑ Ⓒ Ⓓ Ⓔ	16. Ⓐ Ⓑ Ⓒ Ⓓ Ⓔ	24. Ⓐ Ⓑ Ⓒ Ⓓ Ⓔ	

right in Section II

wrong in Section II

Section III

1. Ⓐ Ⓑ Ⓒ Ⓓ Ⓔ	9. Ⓐ Ⓑ Ⓒ Ⓓ Ⓔ	17. Ⓐ Ⓑ Ⓒ Ⓓ Ⓔ	25. Ⓐ Ⓑ Ⓒ Ⓓ Ⓔ
2. Ⓐ Ⓑ Ⓒ Ⓓ Ⓔ	10. Ⓐ Ⓑ Ⓒ Ⓓ Ⓔ	18. Ⓐ Ⓑ Ⓒ Ⓓ Ⓔ	26. Ⓐ Ⓑ Ⓒ Ⓓ Ⓔ
3. Ⓐ Ⓑ Ⓒ Ⓓ Ⓔ	11. Ⓐ Ⓑ Ⓒ Ⓓ Ⓔ	19. Ⓐ Ⓑ Ⓒ Ⓓ Ⓔ	27. Ⓐ Ⓑ Ⓒ Ⓓ Ⓔ
4. Ⓐ Ⓑ Ⓒ Ⓓ Ⓔ	12. Ⓐ Ⓑ Ⓒ Ⓓ Ⓔ	20. Ⓐ Ⓑ Ⓒ Ⓓ Ⓔ	28. Ⓐ Ⓑ Ⓒ Ⓓ Ⓔ
5. Ⓐ Ⓑ Ⓒ Ⓓ Ⓔ	13. Ⓐ Ⓑ Ⓒ Ⓓ Ⓔ	21. Ⓐ Ⓑ Ⓒ Ⓓ Ⓔ	29. Ⓐ Ⓑ Ⓒ Ⓓ Ⓔ
6. Ⓐ Ⓑ Ⓒ Ⓓ Ⓔ	14. Ⓐ Ⓑ Ⓒ Ⓓ Ⓔ	22. Ⓐ Ⓑ Ⓒ Ⓓ Ⓔ	30. Ⓐ Ⓑ Ⓒ Ⓓ Ⓔ
7. Ⓐ Ⓑ Ⓒ Ⓓ Ⓔ	15. Ⓐ Ⓑ Ⓒ Ⓓ Ⓔ	23. Ⓐ Ⓑ Ⓒ Ⓓ Ⓔ	
8. Ⓐ Ⓑ Ⓒ Ⓓ Ⓔ	16. Ⓐ Ⓑ Ⓒ Ⓓ Ⓔ	24. Ⓐ Ⓑ Ⓒ Ⓓ Ⓔ	

right in Section III

wrong in Section III

Section IV

1. Ⓐ Ⓑ Ⓒ Ⓓ Ⓔ	9. Ⓐ Ⓑ Ⓒ Ⓓ Ⓔ	17. Ⓐ Ⓑ Ⓒ Ⓓ Ⓔ	25. Ⓐ Ⓑ Ⓒ Ⓓ Ⓔ
2. Ⓐ Ⓑ Ⓒ Ⓓ Ⓔ	10. Ⓐ Ⓑ Ⓒ Ⓓ Ⓔ	18. Ⓐ Ⓑ Ⓒ Ⓓ Ⓔ	26. Ⓐ Ⓑ Ⓒ Ⓓ Ⓔ
3. Ⓐ Ⓑ Ⓒ Ⓓ Ⓔ	11. Ⓐ Ⓑ Ⓒ Ⓓ Ⓔ	19. Ⓐ Ⓑ Ⓒ Ⓓ Ⓔ	27. Ⓐ Ⓑ Ⓒ Ⓓ Ⓔ
4. Ⓐ Ⓑ Ⓒ Ⓓ Ⓔ	12. Ⓐ Ⓑ Ⓒ Ⓓ Ⓔ	20. Ⓐ Ⓑ Ⓒ Ⓓ Ⓔ	28. Ⓐ Ⓑ Ⓒ Ⓓ Ⓔ
5. Ⓐ Ⓑ Ⓒ Ⓓ Ⓔ	13. Ⓐ Ⓑ Ⓒ Ⓓ Ⓔ	21. Ⓐ Ⓑ Ⓒ Ⓓ Ⓔ	29. Ⓐ Ⓑ Ⓒ Ⓓ Ⓔ
6. Ⓐ Ⓑ Ⓒ Ⓓ Ⓔ	14. Ⓐ Ⓑ Ⓒ Ⓓ Ⓔ	22. Ⓐ Ⓑ Ⓒ Ⓓ Ⓔ	30. Ⓐ Ⓑ Ⓒ Ⓓ Ⓔ
7. Ⓐ Ⓑ Ⓒ Ⓓ Ⓔ	15. Ⓐ Ⓑ Ⓒ Ⓓ Ⓔ	23. Ⓐ Ⓑ Ⓒ Ⓓ Ⓔ	
8. Ⓐ Ⓑ Ⓒ Ⓓ Ⓔ	16. Ⓐ Ⓑ Ⓒ Ⓓ Ⓔ	24. Ⓐ Ⓑ Ⓒ Ⓓ Ⓔ	

right in
Section IV

wrong in
Section IV

 GO ONLINE

Be sure to add your scores to your
syllabus.

Practice Test 1

Section I: **Logical Reasoning**

Directions: The questions in this section are based on the reasoning contained in brief statements or passages. For some questions, more than one of the choices could conceivably answer the question. However, you are to choose the <u>best</u> answer; that is, the response that most accurately and completely answers the question. You should not make assumptions that are by commonsense standards implausible, superfluous, or incompatible with the passage. After you have chosen the best answer, blacken the corresponding space on your answer sheet.

1. Before the printing press, books could be purchased only in expensive manuscript copies. The printing press produced books that were significantly less expensive than the manuscript editions. The public's demand for printed books in the first years after the invention of the printing press was many times greater than demand had been for manuscript copies. This increase demonstrates that there was a dramatic jump in the number of people who learned how to read in the years after publishers first started producing books on the printing press.

Which one of the following statements, if true, casts doubt on the argument?

(A) During the first years after the invention of the printing press, letter writing by people who wrote without the assistance of scribes or clerks exhibited a dramatic increase.
(B) Books produced on the printing press are often found with written comments in the margins in the handwriting of the people who owned the books.
(C) In the first years after the printing press was invented, printed books were purchased primarily by people who had always bought and read expensive manuscripts but could afford a greater number of printed books for the same money.
(D) Books that were printed on the printing press in the first years after its invention often circulated among friends in informal reading clubs or libraries.
(E) The first printed books published after the invention of the printing press would have been useless to illiterate people, since the books had virtually no illustrations.

2. Bevex, an artificial sweetener used only in soft drinks, is carcinogenic for mice, but only when it is consumed in very large quantities. To ingest an amount of Bevex equivalent to the amount fed to the mice in the relevant studies, a person would have to drink 25 cans of Bevex-sweetened soft drinks per day. For that reason, Bevex is in fact safe for people.

In order for the conclusion that Bevex is safe for people to be properly drawn, which one of the following must be true?

(A) Cancer from carcinogenic substances develops more slowly in mice than it does in people.
(B) If all food additives that are currently used in foods were tested, some would be found to be carcinogenic for mice.
(C) People drink fewer than 25 cans of Bevex-sweetened soda per day.
(D) People can obtain important health benefits by controlling their weight through the use of artificially sweetened soft drinks.
(E) Some of the studies done on Bevex were not relevant to the question of whether or not Bevex is carcinogenic for people.

3. Harry: Airlines have made it possible for anyone to travel around the world in much less time than was formerly possible.

Judith: That is not true. Many flights are too expensive for all but the rich.

Judith's response shows that she interprets Harry's statement to imply that

(A) the majority of people are rich
(B) everyone has an equal right to experience world travel
(C) world travel is only possible via routes serviced by airlines
(D) most forms of world travel are not affordable for most people
(E) anyone can afford to travel long distances by air

GO ON TO THE NEXT PAGE.

KAPLAN

4. Nutritionists have recommended that people eat more fiber. Advertisements for a new fiber-supplement pill state only that it contains "44 percent fiber."

The advertising claim is misleading in its selection of information on which to focus if which one of the following is true?

(A) There are other products on the market that are advertised as providing fiber as a dietary supplement.
(B) Nutritionists base their recommendation on medical findings that dietary fiber protects against some kinds of cancer.
(C) It is possible to become addicted to some kinds of advertised pills, such as sleeping pills and painkillers.
(D) The label of the advertised product recommends taking three pills every day.
(E) The recommended daily intake of fiber is 20 to 30 grams, and the pill contains one-third gram.

5. Many environmentalists have urged environmental awareness on consumers, saying that if we accept moral responsibility for our effects on the environment, then products that directly or indirectly harm the environment ought to be avoided. Unfortunately it is usually impossible for consumers to assess the environmental impact of a product, and thus impossible for them to consciously restrict their purchases to environmentally benign products. Because of this impossibility there can be no moral duty to choose products in the way these environmentalists urge, since _____.

Which one of the following principles provides the most appropriate completion for the argument?

(A) a moral duty to perform an action is never based solely on the effects the action will have on other people
(B) a person cannot possibly have a moral duty to do what he or she is unable to do
(C) moral considerations should not be the sole determinants of what products are made available to consumers
(D) the morally right action is always the one whose effects produce the least total harm
(E) where a moral duty exists, it supersedes any legal duty and any other kind of duty

6. Advertisement: Anyone who exercises knows from firsthand experience that exercise leads to better performance of such physical organs as the heart and the lungs, as well as to improvement in muscle tone. And since your brain is a physical organ, your actions can improve its performance, too. Act now. Subscribe to *Stimulus*: read the magazine that exercises your brain.

The advertisement employs which one of the following argumentative strategies?

(A) It cites experimental evidence that subscribing to the product being advertised has desirable consequences.
(B) It ridicules people who do not subscribe to *Stimulus* by suggesting that they do not believe that exercise will improve brain capacity.
(C) It explains the process by which the product being advertised brings about the result claimed for its use.
(D) It supports its recommendation by a careful analysis of the concept of exercise.
(E) It implies that brains and muscle are similar in one respect because they are similar in another respect.

GO ON TO THE NEXT PAGE.

KAPLAN

Questions 7–8

Coherent solutions for the problem of reducing health-care costs cannot be found within the current piecemeal system of paying these costs. The reason is that this system gives health-care providers and insurers every incentive to shift, wherever possible, the costs of treating illness onto each other or any other party, including the patient. That clearly is the lesson of the various reforms of the 1980s: push in on one part of this pliable spending balloon and an equally expensive bulge pops up elsewhere. For example, when the government health-care insurance program for the poor cut costs by disallowing payments for some visits to physicians, patients with advanced illness later presented themselves at hospital emergency rooms in increased numbers.

7. The argument proceeds by

(A) showing that shifting costs onto the patient contradicts the premise of health-care reimbursement

(B) attributing without justification fraudulent intent to people

(C) employing an analogy to characterize interrelationships

(D) denying the possibility of a solution by disparaging each possible alternative system

(E) demonstrating that cooperation is feasible by citing an instance

8. The argument provides the most support for which one of the following?

(A) Under the conditions in which the current system operates, the overall volume of health-care costs could be shrunk, if at all, only by a comprehensive approach.

(B) Relative to the resources available for health-care funding, the income of the higher-paid health-care professionals is too high.

(C) Health-care costs are expanding to meet additional funds that have been made available for them.

(D) Advances in medical technology have raised the expected standards of medical care but have proved expensive.

(E) Since unfilled hospital beds contribute to overhead charges on each patient's bill, it would be unwise to hold unused hospital capacity in reserve for large-scale emergencies.

9. The commercial news media emphasize exceptional events such as airplane crashes at the expense of those such as automobile accidents, which occur far more frequently and represent a far greater risk to the public. Yet the public tends to interpret the degree of emphasis the news media give to these occurrences as indicating the degree of risk they represent.

If the statements above are true, which one of the following conclusions is most strongly supported by them?

(A) Print media, such as newspapers and magazines, are a better source of information than are broadcast media.

(B) The emphasis given in the commercial news media to major catastrophes is dictated by the public's taste for the extraordinary.

(C) Events over which people feel they have no control are generally perceived as more dangerous than those which people feel they can avert or avoid.

(D) Where commercial news media constitute the dominant source of information, public perception of risk does not reflect actual risk.

(E) A massive outbreak of cholera will be covered more extensively by the news media than will the occurrence of a rarer but less serious disease.

10. A large group of hyperactive children whose regular diets included food containing large amounts of additives was observed by researchers trained to assess the presence or absence of behavior problems. The children were then placed on a low-additive diet for several weeks, after which they were observed again. Originally nearly 60 percent of the children exhibited behavior problems; after the change in diet, only 30 percent did so. On the basis of these data, it can be concluded that food additives can contribute to behavior problems in hyperactive children.

The evidence cited fails to establish the conclusion because

(A) there is no evidence that the reduction in behavior problems was proportionate to the reduction in food-additive intake

(B) there is no way to know what changes would have occurred without the change of diet, since only children who changed to a low-additive diet were studied

(C) exactly how many children exhibited behavior problems after the change in diet cannot be determined, since the size of the group studied is not precisely given

(D) there is no evidence that the behavior of some of the children was unaffected by additives

(E) the evidence is consistent with the claim that some children exhibit more frequent behavior problems after being on the low-additive diet than they had exhibited when first observed

GO ON TO THE NEXT PAGE.

11. In 1990 major engine repairs were performed on 10 percent of the cars that had been built by the National Motor Company in the 1970s and that were still registered. However, the corresponding figure for the cars that the National Motor Company had manufactured in the 1960s was only five percent.

Which one of the following, if true, most helps to explain the discrepancy?

(A) Government motor vehicle regulations generally require all cars, whether old or new, to be inspected for emission levels prior to registration.

(B) Owners of new cars tend to drive their cars more carefully than do owners of old cars.

(C) The older a car is, the more likely it is to be discarded for scrap rather than repaired when major engine work is needed to keep the car in operation.

(D) The cars that the National Motor Company built in the 1970s incorporated simplified engine designs that made the engines less complicated than those of earlier models.

(E) Many of the repairs that were performed on the cars that the National Motor Company built in the 1960s could have been avoided if periodic routine maintenance had been performed.

12. No mathematician today would flatly refuse to accept the results of an enormous computation as an adequate demonstration of the truth of a theorem. In 1976, however, this was not the case. Some mathematicians at that time refused to accept the results of a complex computer demonstration of a very simple mapping theorem. Although some mathematicians still hold a strong belief that a simple theorem ought to have a short, simple proof, in fact, some simple theorems have required enormous proofs.

If all of the statements in the passage are true, which one of the following must also be true?

(A) Today, some mathematicians who believe that a simple theorem ought to have a simple proof would consider accepting the results of an enormous computation as a demonstration of the truth of a theorem.

(B) Some individuals who believe that a simple theorem ought to have a simple proof are not mathematicians.

(C) Today, some individuals who refuse to accept the results of an enormous computation as a demonstration of the truth of a theorem believe that a simple theorem ought to have a simple proof.

(D) Some individuals who do not believe that a simple theorem ought to have a simple proof would not be willing to accept the results of an enormous computation as proof of a complex theorem.

(E) Some nonmathematicians do not believe that a simple theorem ought to have a simple proof.

13. If you climb mountains, you will not live to a ripe old age. But you will be bored unless you climb mountains. Therefore, if you live to a ripe old age, you will have been bored.

Which one of the following most closely parallels the reasoning in the argument above?

(A) If you do not try to swim, you will not learn how to swim. But you will not be safe in boats if you do not learn how to swim. Therefore, you must try to swim.

(B) If you do not play golf, you will not enjoy the weekend. But you will be tired next week unless you relax during the weekend. Therefore, to enjoy the weekend, you will have to relax by playing golf.

(C) If you work for your candidate, you will not improve your guitar playing. But you will neglect your civic duty unless you work for your candidate. Therefore, if you improve your guitar playing, you will have neglected your civic duty.

(D) If you do not train, you will not be a good athlete. But you will become exhausted easily unless you train. Therefore, if you train, you will not have become exhausted easily.

(E) If you spend all of your money, you will not become wealthy. But you will become hungry unless you spend all of your money. Therefore, if you become wealthy, you will not become hungry.

14. Marine biologists had hypothesized that lobsters kept together in lobster traps eat one another in response to hunger. Periodic checking of lobster traps, however, has revealed instances of lobsters sharing traps together for weeks. Eight lobsters even shared one trap together for two months without eating one another. The marine biologists' hypothesis, therefore, is clearly wrong.

The argument against the marine biologists' hypothesis is based on which one of the following assumptions?

(A) Lobsters not caught in lobster traps have been observed eating one another.

(B) Two months is the longest known period during which eight or more lobsters have been trapped together.

(C) It is unusual to find as many as eight lobsters caught together in one single trap.

(D) Members of other marine species sometimes eat their own kind when no other food sources are available.

(E) Any food that the eight lobsters in the trap might have obtained was not enough to ward off hunger.

GO ON TO THE NEXT PAGE.

15. Eight years ago hunting was banned in Greenfield County on the grounds that hunting endangers public safety. Now the deer population in the county is six times what it was before the ban. Deer are invading residential areas, damaging property, and causing motor vehicle accidents that result in serious injury to motorists. Since there were never any hunting-related injuries in the county, clearly the ban was not only unnecessary but has created a danger to public safety that would not otherwise exist.

Which one of the following, if true, provides the strongest additional support for the conclusion above?

(A) In surrounding counties, where hunting is permitted, the size of the deer population has not increased in the last eight years.

(B) Motor vehicle accidents involving deer often result in damage to the vehicle, injury to the motorist, or both.

(C) When deer populations increase beyond optimal size, disease and malnutrition become more widespread among the deer herds.

(D) In residential areas in the county, many residents provide food and salt for deer.

(E) Deer can cause extensive damage to ornamental shrubs and trees by chewing on twigs and saplings.

16. Comets do not give off their own light but reflect light from other sources, such as the Sun. Scientists estimate the mass of comets by their brightness: the greater a comet's mass, the more light that comet will reflect. A satellite probe, however, has revealed that the material of which Halley's comet is composed reflects 60 times less light per unit of mass than had been previously thought.

The statements above, if true, give the most support to which one of the following?

(A) Some comets are composed of material that reflects 60 times more light per unit of mass than the material of which Halley's comet is composed.

(B) Previous estimates of the mass of Halley's comet which were based on its brightness were too low.

(C) The total amount of light reflected from Halley's comet is less than scientists had previously thought.

(D) The reflective properties of the material of which comets are composed vary considerably from comet to comet.

(E) Scientists need more information before they can make a good estimate of the mass of Halley's comet.

17. Office manager: I will not order recycled paper for this office. Our letters to clients must make a good impression, so we cannot print them on inferior paper.

Stationery supplier: Recycled paper is not necessarily inferior. In fact, from the beginning, the finest paper has been made of recycled material. It was only in the 1850s that paper began to be made from wood fiber, and then only because there were no longer enough rags to meet the demand for paper.

In which one of the following ways does the stationer's response fail to address the office manager's objection to recycled paper?

(A) It does not recognize that the office manager's prejudice against recycled paper stems from ignorance.

(B) It uses irrelevant facts to justify a claim about the quality of the disputed product.

(C) It assumes that the office manager is concerned about environmental issues.

(D) It presupposes that the office manager understands the basic technology of paper manufacturing.

(E) It ignores the office manager's legitimate concern about quality.

GO ON TO THE NEXT PAGE.

Questions 18–19

When Alicia Green borrowed a neighbor's car without permission, the police merely gave her a warning. However, when Peter Foster did the same thing, he was charged with automobile theft. Peter came to the attention of the police because the car he was driving was hit by a speeding taxi. Alicia was stopped because the car she was driving had defective taillights. It is true that the car Peter took got damaged and the car Alicia took did not, but since it was the taxi that caused the damage this difference was not due to any difference in the blameworthiness of their behavior. Therefore Alicia should also have been charged with automobile theft.

18. The statement that the car Peter took got damaged and the car Alicia took did not plays which one of the following roles in the argument?

   (A) It presents a reason that directly supports the conclusion.
   (B) It justifies the difference in the actual outcome in the two cases.
   (C) It demonstrates awareness of a fact on which a possible objection might be based.
   (D) It illustrates a general principle on which the argument relies.
   (E) It summarizes a position against which the argument is directed.

19. If all of the claims offered in support of the conclusion are accurate, each of the following could be true EXCEPT:

   (A) The interests of justice would have been better served if the police had released Peter Foster with a warning.
   (B) Alicia Green had never before driven a car belonging to someone else without first securing the owner's permission.
   (C) Peter Foster was hit by the taxi while he was running a red light, whereas Alicia Green drove with extra care to avoid drawing the attention of the police to the car she had taken.
   (D) Alicia Green barely missed hitting a pedestrian when she sped through a red light ten minutes before she was stopped by the police for driving a car that had defective taillights.
   (E) Peter Foster had been cited for speeding twice in the preceding month, whereas Alicia Green had never been cited for a traffic violation.

20. According to sources who can be expected to know, Dr. Maria Esposito is going to run in the mayoral election. But if Dr. Esposito runs, Jerome Krasman will certainly not run against her. Therefore Dr. Esposito will be the only candidate in the election.

The flawed reasoning in the argument above most closely parallels that in which one of the following?

   (A) According to its management, Brown's Stores will move next year. Without Brown's being present, no new large store can be attracted to the downtown area. Therefore the downtown area will no longer be viable as a shopping district.
   (B) The press release says that the rock group Rollercoaster is playing a concert on Saturday. It won't be playing on Friday if it plays on Saturday. So Saturday will be the only day this week on which Rollercoaster will perform.
   (C) Joshua says the interviewing panel was impressed by Marilyn. But if they were impressed by Marilyn, they probably thought less of Sven. Joshua is probably right, and so Sven will probably not get the job.
   (D) An informant says that Rustimann was involved in the bank robbery. If Rustimann was involved, Jones was certainly not involved. Since these two are the only people who could have been involved, Rustimann is the only person the police need to arrest.
   (E) The review said that this book is the best one for beginners at programming. If this book is the best, that other one can't be as good. So this one is the book we should buy.

21. The initial causes of serious accidents at nuclear power plants have not so far been flaws in the advanced-technology portion of the plants. Rather, the initial causes have been attributed to human error, as when a worker at the Browns Mills reactor in the United States dropped a candle and started a fire, or to flaws in the plumbing, exemplified in a recent incident in Japan. Such everyday events cannot be thought unlikely to occur over the long run.

Which one of the following is most strongly supported by the statements above?

(A) Now that nuclear power generation has become a part of everyday life, an ever-increasing yearly incidence of serious accidents at the plants can be expected.

(B) If nuclear power plants continue in operation, a serious accident at such a plant is not improbable.

(C) The likelihood of human error at the operating consoles of nuclear power generators cannot be lessened by thoughtful design of dials, switches, and displays.

(D) The design of nuclear power plants attempts to compensate for possible failures of the materials used in their construction.

(E) No serious accident will be caused in the future by some flaw in the advanced-technology portion of a nuclear power plant.

22. There is a widespread belief that people can predict impending earthquakes from unusual animal behavior. Skeptics claim that this belief is based on selective coincidence: people whose dogs behaved oddly just before an earthquake will be especially likely to remember that fact. At any given time, the skeptics say, some of the world's dogs will be behaving oddly.

Clarification of which one of the following issues would be most important to an evaluation of the skeptics' position?

(A) Which is larger, the number of skeptics or the number of people who believe that animal behavior can foreshadow earthquakes?

(B) Are there means other than the observation of animal behavior that nonscientists can use to predict earthquakes?

(C) Are there animals about whose behavior people know too little to be able to distinguish unusual from everyday behavior?

(D) Are the sorts of behavior supposedly predictive of earthquakes as pronounced in dogs as they are in other animals?

(E) Is the animal behavior supposedly predictive of earthquakes specific to impending earthquakes or can it be any kind of unusual behavior?

23. Defendants who can afford expensive private defense lawyers have a lower conviction rate than those who rely on court-appointed public defenders. This explains why criminals who commit lucrative crimes like embezzlement or insider trading are more successful at avoiding conviction than are street criminals.

The explanation offered above would be more persuasive if which one of the following were true?

(A) Many street crimes, such as drug dealing, are extremely lucrative and those committing them can afford expensive private lawyers.

(B) Most prosecutors are not competent to handle cases involving highly technical financial evidence and have more success in prosecuting cases of robbery or simple assault.

(C) The number of criminals convicted of street crimes is far greater than the number of criminals convicted of embezzlement or insider trading.

(D) The percentage of defendants who actually committed the crimes of which they are accused is no greater for publicly defended than for privately defended defendants.

(E) Juries, out of sympathy for the victims of crimes, are much more likely to convict defendants accused of violent crimes than they are to convict defendants accused of "victimless" crimes or crimes against property.

GO ON TO THE NEXT PAGE.

24. Many major scientific discoveries of the past were the product of serendipity, the chance discovery of valuable findings that investigators had not purposely sought. Now, however, scientific research tends to be so costly that investigators are heavily dependent on large grants to fund their research. Because such grants require investigators to provide the grant sponsors with clear projections of the outcome of the proposed research, investigators ignore anything that does not directly bear on the funded research. Therefore, under the prevailing circumstances, serendipity can no longer play a role in scientific discovery.

Which one of the following is an assumption on which the argument depends?

(A) Only findings that an investigator purposely seeks can directly bear on that investigator's research.

(B) In the past few scientific investigators attempted to make clear predictions of the outcome of their research.

(C) Dependence on large grants is preventing investigators from conducting the type of scientific research that those investigators would personally prefer.

(D) All scientific investigators who provide grant sponsors with clear projections of the outcome of their research receive at least some of the grants for which they apply.

(E) In general the most valuable scientific discoveries are the product of serendipity.

25. Police statistics have shown that automobile antitheft devices reduce the risk of car theft, but a statistical study of automobile theft by the automobile insurance industry claims that cars equipped with antitheft devices are, paradoxically, more likely to be stolen than cars that are not so equipped.

Which one of the following, if true, does the most to resolve the apparent paradox?

(A) Owners of stolen cars almost invariably report the theft immediately to the police but tend to delay notifying their insurance company, in the hope that the vehicle will be recovered.

(B) Most cars that are stolen are not equipped with antitheft devices, and most cars that are equipped with antitheft devices are not stolen.

(C) The most common automobile antitheft devices are audible alarms, which typically produce ten false alarms for every actual attempted theft.

(D) Automobile owners who have particularly theft-prone cars and live in areas of greatest incidence of car theft are those who are most likely to have antitheft devices installed.

(E) Most automobile thefts are the work of professional thieves against whose efforts antitheft devices offer scant protection.

STOP

IF YOU FINISH BEFORE TIME IS CALLED, YOU MAY CHECK YOUR WORK ON THIS SECTION ONLY.
DO NOT WORK ON ANY OTHER SECTION IN THE TEST.

KAPLAN

Practice Test 1

Section II: **Analytical Reasoning**

Time—35 minutes
24 questions

Directions: Each group of questions in this section is based on a set of conditions. In answering some of the questions, it may be useful to draw a rough diagram. Choose the response that most accurately and completely answers each question and blacken the corresponding space on your answer sheet.

Questions 1–7

Seven consecutive time slots for a broadcast, numbered in chronological order 1 through 7, will be filled by six song tapes—G, H, L, O, P, S—and exactly one news tape. Each tape is to be assigned to a different time slot, and no tape is longer than any other tape. The broadcast is subject to the following restrictions:

L must be played immediately before O.
The news tape must be played at some time after L.
There must be exactly two time slots between G and P, regardless of whether G comes before P or whether G comes after P.

1. If G is played second, which one of the following tapes must be played third?

   (A) the news
   (B) H
   (C) L
   (D) O
   (E) S

2. The news tape can be played in any one of the following time slots EXCEPT the

   (A) second
   (B) third
   (C) fourth
   (D) fifth
   (E) sixth

3. If H and S are to be scheduled as far from each other as possible, then the first, the second, and the third time slots could be filled, respectively, by

   (A) G, H, and L
   (B) S, G, and the news
   (C) H, G, and L
   (D) H, L, and O
   (E) L, O, and S

4. If P is played fifth, L must be played

   (A) first
   (B) second
   (C) third
   (D) fourth
   (E) sixth

5. What is the maximum number of tapes that can separate S from the news?

   (A) 1
   (B) 2
   (C) 3
   (D) 4
   (E) 5

6. Which one of the following is the latest time slot in which L can be played?

   (A) the third
   (B) the fourth
   (C) the fifth
   (D) the sixth
   (E) the seventh

7. The time slot in which O must be played is completely determined if G is assigned to which one of the following time slots?

   (A) the first
   (B) the third
   (C) the fourth
   (D) the fifth
   (E) the sixth

GO ON TO THE NEXT PAGE.

Questions 8–12

Doctor Yamata works only on Mondays, Tuesdays, Wednesdays, Fridays, and Saturdays. She performs four different activities—lecturing, operating, treating patients, and conducting research. Each working day she performs exactly one activity in the morning and exactly one activity in the afternoon. During each week her work schedule must satisfy the following restrictions:

She performs operations on exactly three mornings.
If she operates on Monday, she does not operate on Tuesday.
She lectures in the afternoon on exactly two consecutive calendar days.
She treats patients on exactly one morning and exactly three afternoons.
She conducts research on exactly one morning.
On Saturday she neither lectures nor performs operations.

8. Which one of the following must be a day on which Doctor Yamata lectures?

(A) Monday
(B) Tuesday
(C) Wednesday
(D) Friday
(E) Saturday

9. On Wednesday Doctor Yamata could be scheduled to

(A) conduct research in the morning and operate in the afternoon
(B) lecture in the morning and treat patients in the afternoon
(C) operate in the morning and lecture in the afternoon
(D) operate in the morning and conduct research in the afternoon
(E) treat patients in the morning and treat patients in the afternoon

10. Which one of the following statements must be true?

(A) There is one day on which the doctor treats patients both in the morning and in the afternoon.
(B) The doctor conducts research on one of the days on which she lectures.
(C) The doctor conducts research on one of the days on which she treats patients.
(D) The doctor lectures on one of the days on which she treats patients.
(E) The doctor lectures on one of the days on which she operates.

11. If Doctor Yamata operates on Tuesday, then her schedule for treating patients could be

(A) Monday morning, Monday afternoon, Friday morning, Friday afternoon
(B) Monday morning, Friday afternoon, Saturday morning, Saturday afternoon
(C) Monday afternoon, Wednesday morning, Wednesday afternoon, Saturday afternoon
(D) Wednesday morning, Wednesday afternoon, Friday afternoon, Saturday afternoon
(E) Wednesday afternoon, Friday afternoon, Saturday morning, Saturday afternoon

12. Which one of the following is a pair of days on both of which Doctor Yamata must treat patients?

(A) Monday and Tuesday
(B) Monday and Saturday
(C) Tuesday and Friday
(D) Tuesday and Saturday
(E) Friday and Saturday

Questions 13–18

Each of seven judges voted for or else against granting Datalog Corporation's petition. Each judge is categorized as conservative, moderate, or liberal, and no judge is assigned more than one of those labels. Two judges are conservatives, two are moderates, and three are liberals. The following is known about how the judges voted:

> If the two conservatives and at least one liberal voted the same way as each other, then both moderates voted that way.
> If the three liberals voted the same way as each other, then no conservative voted that way.
> At least two of the judges voted for Datalog, and at least two voted against Datalog.
> At least one conservative voted against Datalog.

13. If the two moderates did not vote the same way as each other, then which one of the following could be true?

   (A) No conservative and exactly two liberals voted for Datalog.
   (B) Exactly one conservative and exactly one liberal voted for Datalog.
   (C) Exactly one conservative and all three liberals voted for Datalog.
   (D) Exactly two conservatives and exactly one liberal voted for Datalog.
   (E) Exactly two conservatives and exactly two liberals voted for Datalog.

14. Which one of the following must be true?

   (A) At least one conservative voted for Datalog.
   (B) At least one liberal voted against Datalog.
   (C) At least one liberal voted for Datalog.
   (D) At least one moderate voted against Datalog.
   (E) At least one moderate voted for Datalog.

15. If the three liberals all voted the same way as each other, which one of the following must be true?

   (A) Both moderates voted for Datalog.
   (B) Both moderates voted against Datalog.
   (C) One conservative voted for Datalog and one conservative voted against Datalog.
   (D) One moderate voted for Datalog and one moderate voted against Datalog.
   (E) All three liberals voted for Datalog.

16. If exactly two judges voted against Datalog, then which one of the following must be true?

   (A) Both moderates voted for Datalog.
   (B) Exactly one conservative voted for Datalog.
   (C) No conservative voted for Datalog.
   (D) Exactly two liberals voted for Datalog.
   (E) Exactly three liberals voted for Datalog.

17. Each of the following could be a complete and accurate list of those judges who voted for Datalog EXCEPT:

   (A) two liberals
   (B) one conservative, one liberal
   (C) two moderates, three liberals
   (D) one conservative, two moderates, two liberals
   (E) one conservative, two moderates, three liberals

18. If the two conservatives voted the same way as each other, but the liberals did not all vote the same way as each other, then each of the following must be true EXCEPT:

   (A) Both conservatives voted against Datalog.
   (B) Both moderates voted for Datalog.
   (C) At least one liberal voted against Datalog.
   (D) Exactly two liberals voted for Datalog.
   (E) Exactly five of the judges voted against Datalog.

GO ON TO THE NEXT PAGE.

Questions 19–24

An official is assigning five runners—Larry, Ned, Olivia, Patricia, and Sonja—to parallel lanes numbered consecutively 1 through 5. The official will also assign each runner to represent a different charity—F, G, H, J, and K—not necessarily in order of the runner's names as given. The following ordering restrictions apply:

The runner representing K is assigned to lane 4.
Patricia is assigned to the only lane between the lanes of the runners representing F and G.
There are exactly two lanes between Olivia's lane and the lane of the runner representing G.
Sonja is assigned to a higher-numbered lane than the lane to which Ned is assigned.

19. Which one of the following is a possible assignment of runners to lanes by the charity they represent?

	1	2	3	4	5
(A)	F	G	H	K	J
(B)	G	H	J	K	F
(C)	G	K	F	J	H
(D)	H	J	G	K	F
(E)	J	H	F	K	G

20. The lane to which Patricia is assigned must be a lane that is

(A) next to the lane to which Larry is assigned
(B) next to the lane to which Ned is assigned
(C) separated by exactly one lane from the lane to which Ned is assigned
(D) separated by exactly one lane from the lane to which Olivia is assigned
(E) separated by exactly one lane from the lane to which Sonja is assigned

21. If Olivia is assigned to lane 2, which one of the following assignments must be made?

	Charity	Lane
(A)	F	1
(B)	G	5
(C)	H	1
(D)	H	3
(E)	J	5

22. Which one of the following is a complete and accurate list of runners each of whom could be the runner representing F?

(A) Larry, Ned
(B) Patricia, Sonja
(C) Larry, Ned, Olivia
(D) Larry, Ned, Sonja
(E) Ned, Patricia, Sonja

23. If Ned is the runner representing J, then it must be true that

(A) the runner representing G is assigned to lane 1
(B) the runner representing H is assigned to lane 2
(C) Larry is the runner representing K
(D) Olivia is the runner representing F
(E) Patricia is the runner representing H

24. If Larry represents J, which one of the following could be the assignment of runners to lanes?

	1	2	3	4	5
(A)	Larry	Olivia	Ned	Patricia	Sonja
(B)	Larry	Ned	Olivia	Sonja	Patricia
(C)	Larry	Sonja	Patricia	Ned	Olivia
(D)	Ned	Olivia	Larry	Patricia	Sonja
(E)	Ned	Sonja	Olivia	Patricia	Larry

STOP

IF YOU FINISH BEFORE TIME IS CALLED, YOU MAY CHECK YOUR WORK ON THIS SECTION ONLY.
DO NOT WORK ON ANY OTHER SECTION IN THE TEST.

KAPLAN

Practice Test 1
Section III: Reading Comprehension

Time—35 minutes
27 Questions

Directions: Each passage in this section is followed by a group of questions to be answered on the basis of what is stated or implied in the passage. For some of the questions, more than one of the choices could conceivably answer the question. However, you are to choose the best answer; that is, the response that most accurately and completely answers the question, and blacken the corresponding space on your answer sheet.

The labor force is often organized as if workers had no family responsibilities. Preschool-age children need full-time care; children in primary school need care after school and during school (5) vacations. Although day-care services can resolve some scheduling conflicts between home and office, workers cannot always find or afford suitable care. Even when they obtain such care, parents must still cope with emergencies, such as (10) illnesses, that keep children at home. Moreover, children need more than tending; they also need meaningful time with their parents. Conventional full-time workdays, especially when combined with unavoidable household duties, are too inflexible (15) for parents with primary child-care responsibility.

Although a small but increasing number of working men are single parents, those barriers against successful participation in the labor market that are related to primary child-care respon- (20) sibilities mainly disadvantage women. Even in families where both parents work, cultural pressures are traditionally much greater on mothers than on fathers to bear the primary child-rearing responsibilities.

(25) In reconciling child-rearing responsibilities with participation in the labor market, many working mothers are forced to make compromises. For example, approximately one-third of all working mothers are employed only part-time, even (30) though part-time jobs are dramatically underpaid and often less desirable in comparison to full-time employment. Even though part-time work is usually available only in occupations offering minimal employee responsibility and little opportunity for (35) advancement or self-enrichment, such employment does allow many women the time and flexibility to fulfill their family duties, but only at the expense of the advantages associated with full-time employment.

(40) Moreover, even mothers with full-time employment must compromise opportunities in order to adjust to barriers against parents in the labor market. Many choose jobs entailing little challenge or responsibility or those offering flexible scheduling, (45) often available only in poorly paid positions, while other working mothers, although willing and able to assume as much responsibility as people without

children, find that their need to spend regular and predictable time with their children inevitably (50) causes them to lose career opportunities to those without such demands. Thus, women in education are more likely to become teachers than school administrators, whose more conventional full-time work schedules do not correspond to the schedules (55) of school-age children, while female lawyers are more likely to practice law in trusts and estates, where they can control their work schedules, than in litigation, where they cannot. Nonprofessional women are concentrated in secretarial work and (60) department store sales, where their absences can be covered easily by substitutes and where they can enter and leave the work force with little loss, since the jobs offer so little personal gain. Indeed, as long as the labor market remains hostile to parents, and (65) family roles continue to be allocated on the basis of gender, women will be seriously disadvantaged in that labor market.

1. Which one of the following best summarizes the main idea of the passage?
   (A) Current trends in the labor force indicate that working parents, especially women, may not always need to choose between occupational and child-care responsibilities.
   (B) In order for mothers to have an equal opportunity for advancement in the labor force, traditional family roles have to be reexamined and revised.
   (C) Although single parents who work have to balance parental and career demands, single mothers suffer resulting employment disadvantages that single fathers can almost always avoid.
   (D) Although child-care responsibilities disadvantage many women in the labor force, professional women (such as teachers and lawyers) are better able to overcome this problem than are nonprofessional women.
   (E) Traditional work schedules are too inflexible to accommodate the child-care responsibilities of many parents, a fact that severely disadvantages women in the labor force.

GO ON TO THE NEXT PAGE.

2. Which one of the following statements about part-time work can be inferred from the information presented in the passage?

   (A) One-third of all part-time workers are working mothers.

   (B) Part-time work generally offers fewer opportunities for advancement to working mothers than to women generally.

   (C) Part-time work, in addition to having relatively poor wages, often requires that employees work during holidays, when their children are out of school.

   (D) Part-time employment, despite its disadvantages, provides working mothers with an opportunity to address some of the demands of caring for children.

   (E) Many mothers with primary child-care responsibility choose part-time jobs in order to better exploit full-time career opportunities after their children are grown.

3. It can be inferred from the passage that the author would be most likely to agree with which one of the following statements about working fathers in two-parent families?

   (A) They are equally burdened by the employment disadvantages placed upon all parents—male and female—in the labor market.

   (B) They are so absorbed in their jobs that they often do not see the injustice going on around them.

   (C) They are shielded by the traditional allocation of family roles from many of the pressures associated with child-rearing responsibilities.

   (D) They help compound the inequities in the labor market by keeping women from competing with men for career opportunities.

   (E) They are responsible for many of the problems of working mothers because of their insistence on traditional roles in the family.

4. Of the following, which one would the author most likely say is the most troublesome barrier facing working parents with primary child-care responsibility?

   (A) the lack of full-time jobs open to women

   (B) the inflexibility of work schedules

   (C) the low wages of part-time employment

   (D) the limited advancement opportunities for nonprofessional employees

   (E) the practice of allocating responsibilities in the workplace on the basis of gender

5. The passage suggests that day care is at best a limited solution to the pressures associated with child rearing for all of the following reasons EXCEPT:

   (A) Even the best day care available cannot guarantee that children will have meaningful time with their parents.

   (B) Some parents cannot afford day-care services.

   (C) Working parents sometimes have difficulty finding suitable day care for their children.

   (D) Parents who send their children to day care still need to provide care for their children during vacations.

   (E) Even children who are in day care may have to stay home when they are sick.

6. According to the passage, many working parents may be forced to make any of the following types of career decisions EXCEPT:

   (A) declining professional positions for nonprofessional ones, which typically have less conventional work schedules

   (B) accepting part-time employment rather than full-time employment

   (C) taking jobs with limited responsibility, and thus more limited career opportunities, in order to have a more flexible schedule

   (D) pursuing career specializations that allow them to control their work schedules instead of pursuing a more desirable specialization in the same field

   (E) limiting the career potential of one parent, often the mother, who assumes greater child-care responsibility

7. Which one of the following statements would most appropriately continue the discussion at the end of the passage?

   (A) At the same time, most men will remain better able to enjoy the career and salary opportunities offered by the labor market.

   (B) Of course, men who are married to working mothers know of these employment barriers but seem unwilling to do anything about them.

   (C) On the other hand, salary levels may become more equitable between men and women even if the other career opportunities remain more accessible to men than to women.

   (D) On the contrary, men with primary child-rearing responsibilities will continue to enjoy more advantages in the workplace than their female counterparts.

   (E) Thus, institutions in society that favor men over women will continue to widen the gap between the career opportunities available for men and for women.

GO ON TO THE NEXT PAGE.

KAPLAN

Critics have long been puzzled by the inner contradictions of major characters in John Webster's tragedies. In his *The Duchess of Malfi*, for instance, the Duchess is "good" in demonstrating the obvious
(5) tenderness and sincerity of her love for Antonio, but "bad" in ignoring the wishes and welfare of her family and in making religion a "cloak" hiding worldly self-indulgence. Bosola is "bad" in serving Ferdinand, "good" in turning the Duchess's thoughts toward
(10) heaven and in planning to avenge her murder. The ancient Greek philosopher Aristotle implied that such contradictions are virtually essential to the tragic personality, and yet critics keep coming back to this element of inconsistency as though it were an
(15) eccentric feature of Webster's own tragic vision.

The problem is that, as an Elizabethan playwright, Webster has become a prisoner of our critical presuppositions. We have, in recent years, been dazzled by the way the earlier Renaissance and medieval
(20) theater, particularly the morality play, illuminates Elizabethan drama. We now understand how the habit of mind that saw the world as a battleground between good and evil produced the morality play. Morality plays allegorized that conflict by present-
(25) ing characters whose actions were defined as the embodiment of good or evil. This model of reality lived on, overlaid by different conventions, in the more sophisticated Elizabethan works of the following age. Yet Webster seems not to have been as heav-
(30) ily influenced by the morality play's model of reality as were his Elizabethan contemporaries; he was apparently more sensitive to the more morally complicated Italian drama than to these English sources. Consequently, his characters cannot be evaluated
(35) according to reductive formulas of good and evil, which is precisely what modern critics have tried to do. They choose what seem to be the most promising of the contradictory values that are dramatized in the play, and treat those values as if they were the
(40) only basis for analyzing the moral development of the play's major characters, attributing the inconsistencies in a character's behavior to artistic incompetence on Webster's part. The lack of consistency in
(45) Webster's characters can be better understood if we recognize that the ambiguity at the heart of his tragic vision lies not in the external world but in the duality of human nature. Webster establishes tension in his plays by setting up conflicting systems of value
(50) that appear immoral only when one value system is viewed exclusively from the perspective of the other. He presents us not only with characters that we condemn intellectually or ethically and at the same time impulsively approve of, but also with judgments we
(55) must accept as logically sound and yet find emotionally repulsive. The dilemma is not only dramatic: it is tragic, because the conflict is irreconcilable, and because it is ours as much as that of the characters.

8. The primary purpose of the passage is to
(A) clarify an ambiguous assertion
(B) provide evidence in support of a commonly held view
(C) analyze an unresolved question and propose an answer
(D) offer an alternative to a flawed interpretation
(E) describe and categorize opposing viewpoints

9. The author suggests which one of the following about the dramatic works that most influenced Webster's tragedies?
(A) They were not concerned with dramatizing the conflict between good and evil that was presented in morality plays.
(B) They were not as sophisticated as the Italian sources from which other Elizabethan tragedies were derived.
(C) They have never been adequately understood by critics.
(D) They have only recently been used to illuminate the conventions of Elizabethan drama.
(E) They have been considered by many critics to be the reason for Webster's apparent artistic incompetence.

10. The author's allusion to Aristotle's view of tragedy in lines 11–13 serves which one of the following functions in the passage?
(A) It introduces a commonly held view of Webster's tragedies that the author plans to defend.
(B) It supports the author's suggestion that Webster's conception of tragedy is not idiosyncratic.
(C) It provides an example of an approach to Webster's tragedies that the author criticizes.
(D) It establishes the similarity between classical and modern approaches to tragedy.
(E) It supports the author's assertion that Elizabethan tragedy cannot be fully understood without the help of recent scholarship.

11. It can be inferred from the passage that modern critics' interpretations of Webster's tragedies would be more valid if
(A) the ambiguity inherent in Webster's tragic vision resulted from the duality of human nature
(B) Webster's conception of the tragic personality were similar to that of Aristotle
(C) Webster had been heavily influenced by the morality play
(D) Elizabethan dramatists had been more sensitive to Italian sources of influence
(E) the inner conflicts exhibited by Webster's characters were similar to those of modern audiences

GO ON TO THE NEXT PAGE.

12. With which one of the following statements regarding Elizabethan drama would the author be most likely to agree?

   (A) The skill of Elizabethan dramatists has in recent years been overestimated.
   (B) The conventions that shaped Elizabethan drama are best exemplified by Webster's drama.
   (C) Elizabethan drama, for the most part, can be viewed as being heavily influenced by the morality play.
   (D) Only by carefully examining the work of his Elizabethan contemporaries can Webster's achievement as a dramatist be accurately measured.
   (E) Elizabethan drama can best be described as influenced by a composite of Italian and classical sources.

13. It can be inferred from the passage that most modern critics assume which one of the following in their interpretation of Webster's tragedies?

   (A) Webster's plays tended to allegorize the conflict between good and evil more than did those of his contemporaries.
   (B) Webster's plays were derived more from Italian than from English sources.
   (C) The artistic flaws in Webster's tragedies were largely the result of his ignorance of the classical definition of tragedy.
   (D) Webster's tragedies provide no relevant basis for analyzing the moral development of their characters.
   (E) In writing his tragedies, Webster was influenced by the same sources as his contemporaries.

14. The author implies that Webster's conception of tragedy was

   (A) artistically flawed
   (B) highly conventional
   (C) largely derived from the morality play
   (D) somewhat different from the conventional Elizabethan conception of tragedy
   (E) uninfluenced by the classical conception of tragedy

GO ON TO THE NEXT PAGE.

Cultivation of a single crop on a given tract of land leads eventually to decreased yields. One reason for this is that harmful bacterial phytopathogens, organisms parasitic on plant hosts, increase in the soil surrounding
(5) plant roots. The problem can be cured by crop rotation, denying the pathogens a suitable host for a period of time. However, even if crops are not rotated, the severity of diseases brought on by such phytopathogens often decreases after a number of years as the microbial
(10) population of the soil changes and the soil becomes "suppressive" to those diseases. While there may be many reasons for this phenomenon, it is clear that levels of certain bacteria, such as *Pseudomonas fluorescens*, a bacterium antagonistic to a number of harm-
(15) ful phytopathogens, are greater in suppressive than in nonsuppressive soil. This suggests that the presence of such bacteria suppresses phytopathogens. There is now considerable experimental support for this view. Wheat yield increases of 27 percent have been obtained in
(20) field trials by treatment of wheat seeds with fluorescent pseudomonads. Similar treatment of sugar beets, cotton, and potatoes has had similar results.

These improvements in crop yields through the application of *Pseudomonas fluorescens* suggest that
(25) agriculture could benefit from the use of bacteria genetically altered for specific purposes. For example, a form of phytopathogen altered to remove its harmful properties could be released into the environment in quantities favorable to its competing with and
(30) eventually excluding the harmful normal strain. Some experiments suggest that deliberately releasing altered nonpathogenic *Pseudomonas syringae* could crowd out the nonaltered variety that causes frost damage. Opponents of such research have objected that the
(35) deliberate and large-scale release of genetically altered bacteria might have deleterious results. Proponents, on the other hand, argue that this particular strain is altered only by the removal of the gene responsible for the strain's propensity to cause frost damage, thereby
(40) rendering it safer than the phytopathogen from which it was derived.

Some proponents have gone further and suggest that genetic alteration techniques could create organisms with totally new combinations of desirable traits
(45) not found in nature. For example, genes responsible for production of insecticidal compounds have been transposed from other bacteria into pseudomonads that colonize corn roots. Experiments of this kind are
(50) difficult and require great care: such bacteria are developed in highly artificial environments and may not compete well with natural soil bacteria. Nevertheless, proponents contend that the prospects for improved agriculture through such methods seem excellent.
(55) These prospects lead many to hope that current efforts to assess the risks of deliberate release of altered microorganisms will successfully answer the concerns of opponents and create a climate in which such research can go forward without undue impediment.

15. Which one of the following best summarizes the main idea of the passage?

(A) Recent field experiments with genetically altered *Pseudomonas* bacteria have shown that releasing genetically altered bacteria into the environment would not involve any significant danger.

(B) Encouraged by current research, advocates of agricultural use of genetically altered bacteria are optimistic that such use will eventually result in improved agriculture, though opponents remain wary.

(C) Current research indicates that adding genetically altered *Pseudomonas syringae* bacteria to the soil surrounding crop plant roots will have many beneficial effects, such as the prevention of frost damage in certain crops.

(D) Genetic alteration of a number of harmful phytopathogens has been advocated by many researchers who contend that these techniques will eventually replace such outdated methods as crop rotation.

(E) Genetic alteration of bacteria has been successful in highly artificial laboratory conditions, but opponents of such research have argued that these techniques are unlikely to produce organisms that are able to survive in natural environments.

16. The author discusses naturally occurring *Pseudomonas fluorescens* bacteria in the first paragraph primarily in order to do which one of the following?

(A) prove that increases in the level of such bacteria in the soil are the sole cause of soil suppressivity

(B) explain why yields increased after wheat fields were sprayed with altered *Pseudomonas fluorescens* bacteria

(C) detail the chemical processes that such bacteria use to suppress organisms parasitic to crop plants, such as wheat, sugar beets, and potatoes

(D) provide background information to support the argument that research into the agricultural use of genetically altered bacteria would be fruitful

(E) argue that crop rotation is unnecessary, since diseases brought on by phytopathogens diminish in severity and eventually disappear on their own

GO ON TO THE NEXT PAGE.

17. It can be inferred from the author's discussion of *Pseudomonas fluorescens* bacteria that which one of the following would be true of crops impervious to parasitical organisms?
    (A) *Pseudomonas fluorescens* bacteria would be absent from the soil surrounding their roots.
    (B) They would crowd out and eventually exclude other crop plants if their growth were not carefully regulated.
    (C) Their yield would not be likely to be improved by adding *Pseudomonas fluorescens* bacteria to the soil.
    (D) They would mature more quickly than crop plants that were susceptible to parasitical organisms.
    (E) Levels of phytopathogenic bacteria in the soil surrounding their roots would be higher compared with other crop plants.

18. It can be inferred from the passage that crop rotation can increase yields in part because
    (A) moving crop plants around makes them hardier and more resistant to disease
    (B) the number of *Pseudomonas fluorescens* bacteria in the soil usually increases when crops are rotated
    (C) the roots of many crop plants produce compounds that are antagonistic to phytopathogens harmful to other crop plants
    (D) the presence of phytopathogenic bacteria is responsible for the majority of plant diseases
    (E) phytopathogens typically attack some plant species but find other species to be unsuitable hosts

19. According to the passage, proponents of the use of genetically altered bacteria in agriculture argue that which one of the following is true of the altered bacteria used in the frost-damage experiments?
    (A) The altered bacteria had a genetic constitution differing from that of the normal strain only in that the altered variety had one less gene.
    (B) Although the altered bacteria competed effectively with the nonaltered strain in the laboratory, they were not as viable in natural environments.
    (C) The altered bacteria were much safer and more effective than the naturally occurring *Pseudomonas fluorescens* bacteria used in earlier experiments.
    (D) The altered bacteria were antagonistic to several types of naturally occurring phytopathogens in the soil surrounding the roots of frost-damaged crops.
    (E) The altered bacteria were released into the environment in numbers sufficient to guarantee the validity of experimental results.

20. Which one of the following, if true, would most seriously weaken the proponents' argument regarding the safety of using altered *Pseudomonas syringae* bacteria to control frost damage?
    (A) *Pseudomonas syringae* bacteria are primitive and have a simple genetic constitution.
    (B) The altered bacteria are derived from a strain that is parasitic to plants and can cause damage to crops.
    (C) Current genetic-engineering techniques permit the large-scale commercial production of such bacteria.
    (D) Often genes whose presence is responsible for one harmful characteristic must be present in order to prevent other harmful characteristics.
    (E) The frost-damage experiments with *Pseudomonas syringae* bacteria indicate that the altered variety would only replace the normal strain if released in sufficient numbers.

GO ON TO THE NEXT PAGE.

In 1887 the Dawes Act legislated wide-scale private ownership of reservation lands in the United States for Native Americans. The act allotted plots of 80 acres to each Native American adult. However, the Native
(5) Americans were not granted outright title to their lands. The act defined each grant as a "trust patent," meaning that the Bureau of Indian Affairs (BIA), the governmental agency in charge of administering policy regarding Native Americans, would hold the allotted
(10) land in trust for 25 years, during which time the Native American owners could use, but not alienate (sell) the land. After the 25-year period, the Native American allottee would receive a "fee patent" awarding full legal ownership of the land.
(15) Two main reasons were advanced for the restriction on the Native Americans' ability to sell their lands. First, it was claimed that free alienability would lead to immediate transfer of large amounts of former reservation land to non-Native Americans, consequently
(20) threatening the traditional way of life on those reservations. A second objection to free alienation was that Native Americans were unaccustomed to, and did not desire, a system of private landownership. Their custom, it was said, favored communal use of land.
(25) However, both of these arguments bear only on the transfer of Native American lands to non-Native Americans; neither offers a reason for prohibiting Native Americans from transferring land among themselves. Selling land to each other would not threaten the
(30) Native American culture. Additionally, if communal land use remained preferable to Native Americans after allotment, free alienability would have allowed allottees to sell their lands back to the tribe.
When stated rationales for government policies
(35) prove empty, using an interest-group model often provides an explanation. While neither Native Americans nor the potential non-Native American purchasers benefited from the restraint on alienation contained in the Dawes Act, one clearly defined group did ben-
(40) efit: the BIA bureaucrats. It has been convincingly demonstrated that bureaucrats seek to maximize the size of their staffs and their budgets in order to compensate for the lack of other sources of fulfillment, such as power and prestige. Additionally, politicians
(45) tend to favor the growth of governmental bureaucracy because such growth provides increased opportunity for the exercise of political patronage. The restraint on alienation vastly increased the amount of work, and hence the budgets, necessary to implement the statute.
Until allotment was ended in 1934, granting fee patents
(50) and leasing Native American lands were among the principal activities of the United States government. One hypothesis, then, for the temporary restriction on alienation in the Dawes Act is that it reflected a compromise between non-Native Americans favor-
(55) ing immediate alienability so they could purchase land and the BIA bureaucrats who administered the privatization system.

KAPLAN

21. Which one of the following best summarizes the main idea of the passage?

(A) United States government policy toward Native Americans has tended to disregard their needs and consider instead the needs of non-Native American purchasers of land.

(B) In order to preserve the unique way of life on Native American reservations, use of Native American lands must be communal rather than individual.

(C) The Dawes Act's restriction on the right of Native Americans to sell their land may have been implemented primarily to serve the interests of politicians and bureaucrats.

(D) The clause restricting free alienability in the Dawes Act greatly expanded United States governmental activity in the area of land administration.

(E) Since passage of the Dawes Act in 1887, Native Americans have not been able to sell or transfer their former reservation land freely.

22. Which one of the following statements concerning the reason for the end of allotment, if true, would provide the most support for the author's view of politicians?

(A) Politicians realized that allotment was damaging the Native American way of life.

(B) Politicians decided that allotment would be more congruent with the Native American custom of communal land use.

(C) Politicians believed that allotment's continuation would not enhance their opportunities to exercise patronage.

(D) Politicians felt that the staff and budgets of the BIA had grown too large.

(E) Politicians were concerned that too much Native American land was falling into the hands of non-Native Americans.

GO ON TO THE NEXT PAGE.

23. Which one of the following best describes the organization of the passage?

    (A) The passage of a law is analyzed in detail, the benefits and drawbacks of one of its clauses are studied, and a final assessment of the law is offered.
    (B) The history of a law is narrated, the effects of one of its clauses on various populations are studied, and repeal of the law is advocated.
    (C) A law is examined, the political and social backgrounds of one of its clauses are characterized, and the permanent effects of the law are studied.
    (D) A law is described, the rationale put forward for one of its clauses is outlined and dismissed, and a different rationale for the clause is presented.
    (E) The legal status of an ethnic group is examined with respect to issues of landownership and commercial autonomy, and the benefits to rival groups due to that status are explained.

24. The author's attitude toward the reasons advanced for the restriction on alienability in the Dawes Act at the time of its passage can best be described as

    (A) completely credulous
    (B) partially approving
    (C) basically indecisive
    (D) mildly questioning
    (E) highly skeptical

25. It can be inferred from the passage that which one of the following was true of Native American life immediately before passage of the Dawes Act?

    (A) Most Native Americans supported themselves through farming.
    (B) Not many Native Americans personally owned the land on which they lived.
    (C) The land on which most Native Americans lived had been bought from their tribes.
    (D) Few Native Americans had much contact with their non-Native American neighbors.
    (E) Few Native Americans were willing to sell their land to non-Native Americans.

26. According to the passage, the type of landownership initially obtainable by Native Americans under the Dawes Act differed from the type of ownership obtainable after a 25-year period in that only the latter allowed

    (A) owners of land to farm it
    (B) owners of land to sell it
    (C) government some control over how owners disposed of land
    (D) owners of land to build on it with relatively minor governmental restrictions
    (E) government to charge owners a fee for developing their land

27. Which one of the following, if true, would most strengthen the author's argument regarding the true motivation for the passage of the Dawes Act?

    (A) The legislators who voted in favor of the Dawes Act owned land adjacent to Native American reservations.
    (B) The majority of Native Americans who were granted fee patents did not sell their land back to their tribes.
    (C) Native Americans managed to preserve their traditional culture even when they were geographically dispersed.
    (D) The legislators who voted in favor of the Dawes Act were heavily influenced by BIA bureaucrats.
    (E) Non-Native Americans who purchased the majority of Native American lands consolidated them into larger farm holdings.

STOP

IF YOU FINISH BEFORE TIME IS CALLED, YOU MAY CHECK YOUR WORK ON THIS SECTION ONLY.
DO NOT WORK ON ANY OTHER SECTION IN THE TEST.

Practice Test 1

Section IV: **Logical Reasoning**

Time—35 minutes
25 questions

Directions: The questions in this section are based on the reasoning contained in brief statements or passages. For some questions, more than one of the choices could conceivably answer the question. However, you are to choose the best answer; that is, the response that most accurately and completely answers the question. You should not make assumptions that are by commonsense standards implausible, superfluous, or incompatible with the passage. After you have chosen the best answer, blacken the corresponding space on your answer sheet.

1. In 1974 the speed limit on highways in the United States was reduced to 55 miles per hour in order to save fuel. In the first 12 months after the change, the rate of highway fatalities dropped 15 percent, the sharpest one-year drop in history. Over the next 10 years, the fatality rate declined by another 25 percent. It follows that the 1974 reduction in the speed limit saved many lives.

   Which one of the following, if true, most strengthens the argument?

   (A) The 1974 fuel shortage cut driving sharply for more than a year.
   (B) There was no decline in the rate of highway fatalities during the twelfth year following the reduction in the speed limit.
   (C) Since 1974 automobile manufacturers have been required by law to install lifesaving equipment, such as seat belts, in all new cars.
   (D) The fatality rate in highway accidents involving motorists driving faster than 55 miles per hour is much higher than in highway accidents that do not involve motorists driving at such speeds.
   (E) Motorists are more likely to avoid accidents by matching their speed to that of the surrounding highway traffic than by driving at faster or slower speeds.

2. Some legislators refuse to commit public funds for new scientific research if they cannot be assured that the research will contribute to the public welfare. Such a position ignores the lessons of experience. Many important contributions to the public welfare that resulted from scientific research were never predicted as potential outcomes of that research. Suppose that a scientist in the early twentieth century had applied for public funds to study molds: who would have predicted that such research would lead to the discovery of antibiotics—one of the greatest contributions ever made to the public welfare?

   Which one of the following most accurately expresses the main point of the argument?

   (A) The committal of public funds for new scientific research will ensure that the public welfare will be enhanced.
   (B) If it were possible to predict the general outcome of a new scientific research effort, then legislators would not refuse to commit public funds for that effort.
   (C) Scientific discoveries that have contributed to the public welfare would have occurred sooner if public funds had been committed to the research that generated those discoveries.
   (D) In order to ensure that scientific research is directed toward contributing to the public welfare, legislators must commit public funds to new scientific research.
   (E) Lack of guarantees that new scientific research will contribute to the public welfare is not sufficient reason for legislators to refuse to commit public funds to new scientific research.

GO ON TO THE NEXT PAGE.

3. When workers do not find their assignments challenging, they become bored and so achieve less than their abilities would allow. On the other hand, when workers find their assignments too difficult, they give up and so again achieve less than what they are capable of achieving. It is, therefore, clear that no worker's full potential will ever be realized.

Which one of the following is an error of reasoning contained in the argument?

(A) mistakenly equating what is actual and what is merely possible
(B) assuming without warrant that a situation allows only two possibilities
(C) relying on subjective rather than objective evidence
(D) confusing the coincidence of two events with a causal relation between the two
(E) depending on the ambiguous use of a key term

4. Our tomato soup provides good nutrition: for instance, a warm bowl of it contains more units of vitamin C than does a serving of apricots or fresh carrots!

The advertisement is misleading if which one of the following is true?

(A) Few people depend exclusively on apricots and carrots to supply vitamin C to their diets.
(B) A liquid can lose vitamins if it stands in contact with the air for a protracted period of time.
(C) Tomato soup contains important nutrients other than vitamin C.
(D) The amount of vitamin C provided by a serving of the advertised soup is less than the amount furnished by a serving of fresh strawberries.
(E) Apricots and fresh carrots are widely known to be nutritious, but their contribution consists primarily in providing a large amount of vitamin A, not a large amount of vitamin C.

Questions 5–6

The government provides insurance for individuals' bank deposits, but requires the banks to pay the premiums for this insurance. Since it is depositors who primarily benefit from the security this insurance provides, the government should take steps to ensure that depositors who want this security bear the cost of it and thus should make depositors pay the premiums for insuring their own accounts.

5. Which one of the following principles, if established, would do most to justify drawing the conclusion of the argument on the basis of the reasons offered in its support?

(A) The people who stand to benefit from an economic service should always be made to bear the costs of that service.
(B) Any rational system of insurance must base the size of premiums on the degree of risk involved.
(C) Government-backed security for investors, such as bank depositors, should be provided only when it does not reduce incentives for investors to make responsible investments.
(D) The choice of not accepting an offered service should always be available, even if there is no charge for the service.
(E) The government should avoid any actions that might alter the behavior of corporations and individuals in the market.

6. Which one of the following is assumed by the argument?

(A) Banks are not insured by the government against default on the loans the banks make.
(B) Private insurance companies do not have the resources to provide banks or individuals with deposit insurance.
(C) Banks do not always cover the cost of the deposit-insurance premiums by paying depositors lower interest rates on insured deposits than the banks would on uninsured deposits.
(D) The government limits the insurance protection it provides by insuring accounts up to a certain legally defined amount only.
(E) The government does not allow banks to offer some kinds of accounts in which deposits are not insured.

GO ON TO THE NEXT PAGE.

7. When individual students are all treated equally in that they have identical exposure to curriculum material, the rate, quality, and quantity of learning will vary from student to student. If all students are to master a given curriculum, some of them need different types of help than others, as any experienced teacher knows.

If the statements above are both true, which one of the following conclusions can be drawn on the basis of them?

(A) Unequal treatment, in a sense, of individual students is required in order to ensure equality with respect to the educational tasks they master.

(B) The rate and quality of learning, with learning understood as the acquiring of the ability to solve problems within a given curriculum area, depend on the quantity of teaching an individual student receives in any given curriculum.

(C) The more experienced the teacher is, the more the students will learn.

(D) All students should have identical exposure to learn the material being taught in any given curriculum.

(E) Teachers should help each of their students to learn as much as possible.

8. George: Some scientists say that global warming will occur because people are releasing large amounts of carbon dioxide into the atmosphere by burning trees and fossil fuels. We can see, though, that the predicted warming is occurring already. In the middle of last winter, we had a month of springlike weather in our area, and this fall, because of unusually mild temperatures, the leaves on our town's trees were three weeks late in turning color.

Which one of the following would it be most relevant to investigate in evaluating the conclusion of George's argument?

(A) whether carbon dioxide is the only cause of global warming

(B) when leaves on the trees in the town usually change color

(C) what proportion of global emissions of carbon dioxide is due to the burning of trees by humans

(D) whether air pollution is causing some trees in the area to lose their leaves

(E) whether unusually warm weather is occurring elsewhere on the globe more frequently than before

9. Student representative: Our university, in expelling a student who verbally harassed his roommate, has erred by penalizing the student for doing what he surely has a right to do: speak his mind!

Dean of students: But what you're saying is that our university should endorse verbal harassment. Yet surely if we did that, we would threaten the free flow of ideas that is the essence of university life.

Which one of the following is a questionable technique that the dean of students uses in attempting to refute the student representative?

(A) challenging the student representative's knowledge of the process by which the student was expelled

(B) invoking a fallacious distinction between speech and other sorts of behavior

(C) misdescribing the student representative's position, thereby making it easier to challenge

(D) questioning the motives of the student representative rather than offering reasons for the conclusion defended

(E) relying on a position of power to silence the opposing viewpoint with a threat

10. Famous personalities found guilty of many types of crimes in well-publicized trials are increasingly sentenced to the performance of community service, though unknown defendants convicted of similar crimes almost always serve prison sentences. However, the principle of equality before the law rules out using fame and publicity as relevant considerations in the sentencing of convicted criminals.

The statements above, if true, most strongly support which one of the following conclusions?

(A) The principle of equality before the law is rigorously applied in only a few types of criminal trials.

(B) The number of convicted celebrities sentenced to community service should equal the number of convicted unknown defendants sentenced to community service.

(C) The principle of equality before the law can properly be overridden by other principles in some cases.

(D) The sentencing of celebrities to community service instead of prison constitutes a violation of the principle of equality before the law in many cases.

(E) The principle of equality before the law does not allow for leniency in sentencing.

GO ON TO THE NEXT PAGE.

11. Scientific research at a certain university was supported in part by an annual grant from a major foundation. When the university's physics department embarked on weapons-related research, the foundation, which has a purely humanitarian mission, threatened to cancel its grant. The university then promised that none of the foundation's money would be used for the weapons research, whereupon the foundation withdrew its threat, concluding that the weapons research would not benefit from the foundation's grant.

Which one of the following describes a flaw in the reasoning underlying the foundation's conclusion?

(A) It overlooks the possibility that the availability of the foundation's money for humanitarian uses will allow the university to redirect other funds from humanitarian uses to weapons research.

(B) It overlooks the possibility that the physics department's weapons research is not the only one of the university's research activities with other than purely humanitarian purposes.

(C) It overlooks the possibility that the university made its promise specifically in order to induce the foundation to withdraw its threat.

(D) It confuses the intention of not using a sum of money for a particular purpose with the intention of not using that sum of money at all.

(E) It assumes that if the means to achieve an objective are humanitarian in character, then the objective is also humanitarian in character.

12. To suit the needs of corporate clients, advertising agencies have successfully modified a strategy originally developed for political campaigns. This strategy aims to provide clients with free publicity and air time by designing an advertising campaign that is controversial, thus drawing prime-time media coverage and evoking public comment by officials.

The statements above, if true, most seriously undermine which one of the following assertions?

(A) The usefulness of an advertising campaign is based solely on the degree to which the campaign's advertisements persuade their audiences.

(B) Only a small percentage of eligible voters admit to being influenced by advertising campaigns in deciding how to vote.

(C) Campaign managers have transformed political campaigns by making increasing use of strategies borrowed from corporate advertising campaigns.

(D) Corporations are typically more concerned with maintaining public recognition of the corporate name than with enhancing goodwill toward the corporation.

(E) Advertising agencies that specialize in campaigns for corporate clients are not usually chosen for political campaigns.

13. The National Association of Fire Fighters says that 45 percent of homes now have smoke detectors, whereas only 30 percent of homes had them 10 years ago. This makes early detection of house fires no more likely, however, because over half of the domestic smoke detectors are either without batteries or else inoperative for some other reason.

In order for the conclusion above to be properly drawn, which one of the following assumptions would have to be made?

(A) Fifteen percent of domestic smoke detectors were installed less than 10 years ago.

(B) The number of fires per year in homes with smoke detectors has increased.

(C) Not all of the smoke detectors in homes are battery operated.

(D) The proportion of domestic smoke detectors that are inoperative has increased in the past 10 years.

(E) Unlike automatic water sprinklers, a properly functioning smoke detector cannot by itself increase fire safety in a home.

GO ON TO THE NEXT PAGE.

KAPLAN

14. Advertisement: HomeGlo Paints, Inc., has won the prestigious Golden Paintbrush Award given to the one paint manufacturer in the country that has increased the environmental safety of its product most over the past three years for HomeGlo Exterior Enamel. The Golden Paintbrush is awarded only on the basis of thorough tests by independent testing laboratories. So when you choose HomeGlo Exterior Enamel, you will know that you have chosen the most environmentally safe brand of paint manufactured in this country today.

The flawed reasoning in the advertisement most closely parallels that in which one of the following?

(A) The ZXC audio system received the overall top ranking for looks, performance, durability, and value in *Listeners' Report* magazine's ratings of currently produced systems. Therefore, the ZXC must have better sound quality than any other currently produced sound system.

(B) Morning Sunshine breakfast cereal contains, ounce for ounce, more of the nutrients needed for a healthy diet than any other breakfast cereal on the market today. Thus, when you eat Morning Sunshine, you will know you are eating the most nutritious food now on the market.

(C) The number of consumer visits increased more at Countryside Market last year than at any other market in the region. Therefore, Countryside's profits must also have increased more last year than those of any other market in the region.

(D) Jerrold's teachers recognize him as the student who has shown more academic improvement than any other student in the junior class this year. Therefore, if Jerrold and his classmates are ranked according to their current academic performance, Jerrold must hold the highest ranking.

(E) Margaret Durring's short story "The Power Lunch" won three separate awards for best short fiction of the year. Therefore, any of Margaret Durring's earlier stories certainly has enough literary merit to be included in an anthology of the best recent short fiction.

15. The consistency of ice cream is adversely affected by even slight temperature changes in the freezer. To counteract this problem, manufacturers add stabilizers to ice cream. Unfortunately, stabilizers, though inexpensive, adversely affect flavor. Stabilizers are less needed if storage temperatures are very low. However, since energy costs are constantly going up, those costs constitute a strong incentive in favor of relatively high storage temperatures.

Which one of the following can be properly inferred from the passage?

(A) Even slight deviations from the proper consistency for ice cream sharply impair its flavor.

(B) Cost considerations favor sacrificing consistency over sacrificing flavor.

(C) It would not be cost-effective to develop a new device to maintain the constancy of freezer temperatures.

(D) Stabilizers function well only at very low freezer temperatures.

(E) Very low, stable freezer temperatures allow for the best possible consistency and flavor of ice cream.

16. Edwina: True appreciation of Mozart's music demands that you hear it exactly as he intended it to be heard; that is, exactly as he heard it. Since he heard it on eighteenth-century instruments, it follows that so should we.

Alberto: But what makes you think that Mozart ever heard his music played as he had intended it to be played? After all, Mozart was writing at a time when the performer was expected, as a matter of course, not just to interpret but to modify the written score.

Alberto adopts which one of the following strategies in criticizing Edwina's position?

(A) He appeals to an academic authority in order to challenge the factual basis of her conclusion.

(B) He attacks her judgment by suggesting that she does not recognize the importance of the performer's creativity to the audience's appreciation of a musical composition.

(C) He defends a competing view of musical authenticity.

(D) He attacks the logic of her argument by suggesting that the conclusion she draws does not follow from the premises she sets forth.

(E) He offers a reason to believe that one of the premises of her argument is false.

GO ON TO THE NEXT PAGE.

17. Since the introduction of the Impanian National Health scheme, Impanians (or their private insurance companies) have had to pay only for the more unusual and sophisticated medical procedures. When the scheme was introduced, it was hoped that private insurance to pay for these procedures would be available at modest cost, since the insurers would no longer be paying for the bulk of health care costs, as they had done previously. Paradoxically, however, the cost of private health insurance did not decrease but has instead increased dramatically in the years since the scheme's introduction.

Which one of the following, if true, does most to explain the apparently paradoxical outcome?

(A) The National Health scheme has greatly reduced the number of medical claims handled annually by Impania's private insurers, enabling these firms to reduce overhead costs substantially.

(B) Before the National Health scheme was introduced, more than 80 percent of all Impanian medical costs were associated with procedures that are now covered by the scheme.

(C) Impanians who previously were unable to afford regular medical treatment now use the National Health scheme, but the number of Impanians with private health insurance has not increased.

(D) Impanians now buy private medical insurance only at times when they expect that they will need care of kinds not available in the National Health scheme.

(E) The proportion of total expenditures within Impania that is spent on health care has declined since the introduction of the National Health scheme.

18. In clinical trials of new medicines, half of the subjects receive the drug being tested and half receive a physiologically inert substance—a placebo. Trials are designed with the intention that neither subjects nor experimenters will find out which subjects are actually being given the drug being tested. However, this intention is frequently frustrated because_____.

Which one of the following, if true, most appropriately completes the explanation?

(A) often, the subjects who receive the drug being tested develop symptoms that the experimenters recognize as side effects of the physiologically active drug

(B) subjects who believe they are receiving the drug being tested often display improvements in their conditions regardless of whether what is administered to them is physiologically active or not

(C) in general, when the trial is intended to establish the experimental drug's safety rather than its effectiveness, all of the subjects are healthy volunteers

(D) when a trial runs a long time, few of the experimenters will work on it from inception to conclusion

(E) the people who are subjects for clinical trials must, by law, be volunteers and must be informed of the possibility that they will receive a placebo

19. It takes 365.25 days for the Earth to make one complete revolution around the Sun. Long-standing convention makes a year 365 days long, with an extra day added every fourth year, and the year is divided into 52 seven-day weeks. But since 52 times 7 is only 364, anniversaries do not fall on the same day of the week each year. Many scheduling problems could be avoided if the last day of each year and an additional day every fourth year belonged to no week, so that January 1 would be a Sunday every year.

The proposal above, once put into effect, would be most likely to result in continued scheduling conflicts for which one of the following groups?

(A) people who have birthdays or other anniversaries on December 30 or 31

(B) employed people whose strict religious observances require that they refrain from working every seventh day

(C) school systems that require students to attend classes a specific number of days each year

(D) employed people who have three-day breaks from work when holidays are celebrated on Mondays or Fridays

(E) people who have to plan events several years before those events occur

GO ON TO THE NEXT PAGE.

KAPLAN

20. Graphologists claim that it is possible to detect permanent character traits by examining people's handwriting. For example, a strong cross on the "t" is supposed to denote enthusiasm. Obviously, however, with practice and perseverance people can alter their handwriting to include this feature. So it seems that graphologists must hold that permanent character traits can be changed.

The argument against graphology proceeds by

(A) citing apparently incontestable evidence that leads to absurd consequences when conjoined with the view in question
(B) demonstrating that an apparently controversial and interesting claim is really just a platitude
(C) arguing that a particular technique of analysis can never be effective when the people analyzed know that it is being used
(D) showing that proponents of the view have no theoretical justification for the view
(E) attacking a technique by arguing that what the technique is supposed to detect can be detected quite readily without it

Questions 21–22

Historian: There is no direct evidence that timber was traded between the ancient nations of Poran and Nayal, but the fact that a law setting tariffs on timber imports from Poran was enacted during the third Nayalese dynasty does suggest that during that period a timber trade was conducted.

Critic: Your reasoning is flawed. During its third dynasty, Nayal may well have imported timber from Poran, but certainly on today's statute books there remain many laws regulating activities that were once common but in which people no longer engage.

21. The critic's response to the historian's reasoning does which one of the following?

(A) It implies an analogy between the present and the past.
(B) It identifies a general principle that the historian's reasoning violates.
(C) It distinguishes between what has been established as a certainty and what has been established as a possibility.
(D) It establishes explicit criteria that must be used in evaluating indirect evidence.
(E) It points out the dissimilar roles that law plays in societies that are distinct from one another.

22. The critic's response to the historian is flawed because it

(A) produces evidence that is consistent with there not having been any timber trade between Poran and Nayal during the third Nayalese dynasty
(B) cites current laws without indicating whether the laws cited are relevant to the timber trade
(C) fails to recognize that the historian's conclusion was based on indirect evidence rather than direct evidence
(D) takes no account of the difference between a law's enactment at a particular time and a law's existence as part of a legal code at a particular time
(E) accepts without question the assumption about the purpose of laws that underlies the historian's argument

GO ON TO THE NEXT PAGE.

23. The workers at Bell Manufacturing will shortly go on strike unless the management increases their wages. As Bell's president is well aware, however, in order to increase the workers' wages, Bell would have to sell off some of its subsidiaries. So, some of Bell's subsidiaries will be sold.

   The conclusion above is properly drawn if which one of the following is assumed?

   (A) Bell Manufacturing will begin to suffer increased losses.
   (B) Bell's management will refuse to increase its workers' wages.
   (C) The workers at Bell Manufacturing will not be going on strike.
   (D) Bell's president has the authority to offer the workers their desired wage increase.
   (E) Bell's workers will not accept a package of improved benefits in place of their desired wage increase.

24. One sure way you can tell how quickly a new idea—for example, the idea of "privatization"—is taking hold among the population is to monitor how fast the word or words expressing that particular idea are passing into common usage. Professional opinions of whether or not words can indeed be said to have passed into common usage are available from dictionary editors, who are vitally concerned with this question.

   The method described above for determining how quickly a new idea is taking hold relies on which one of the following assumptions?

   (A) Dictionary editors are not professionally interested in words that are only rarely used.
   (B) Dictionary editors have exact numerical criteria for telling when a word has passed into common usage.
   (C) For a new idea to take hold, dictionary editors have to include the relevant word or words in their dictionaries.
   (D) As a word passes into common usage, its meaning does not undergo any severe distortions in the process.
   (E) Words denoting new ideas tend to be used before the ideas denoted are understood.

25. Because migrant workers are typically not hired by any one employer for longer than a single season, migrant workers can legally be paid less than the minimum hourly wage that the government requires employers to pay all their permanent employees. Yet most migrant workers work long hours each day for 11 or 12 months a year and thus are as much full-time workers as are people hired on a year-round basis. Therefore, the law should require that migrant workers be paid the same minimum hourly wage that other full-time workers must be paid.

   The pattern of reasoning displayed above most closely parallels that displayed in which one of the following arguments?

   (A) Because day-care facilities are now regulated at the local level, the quality of care available to children in two different cities can differ widely. Since such differences in treatment clearly are unfair, day care should be federally rather than locally regulated.
   (B) Because many rural areas have few restrictions on development, housing estates in such areas have been built where no adequate supply of safe drinking water could be ensured. Thus, rural areas should adopt building codes more like those large cities have.
   (C) Because some countries regulate gun sales more strictly than do other countries, some people can readily purchase a gun, whereas others cannot. Therefore, all countries should cooperate in developing a uniform international policy regarding gun sales.
   (D) Because it is a democratic principle that laws should have the consent of those affected by them, liquor laws should be formulated not by politicians but by club and restaurant owners, since such laws directly affect the profitability of their businesses.
   (E) Because food additives are not considered drugs, they have not had to meet the safety standards the government applies to drugs. But food additives can be as dangerous as drugs. Therefore, food additives should also be subject to safety regulations as stringent as those covering drugs.

STOP

IF YOU FINISH BEFORE TIME IS CALLED, YOU MAY CHECK YOUR WORK ON THIS SECTION ONLY.
DO NOT WORK ON ANY OTHER SECTION IN THE TEST.

KAPLAN

Practice Test 1
Writing Sample

LSAT WRITING SAMPLE TOPIC

The city of Stockton must choose an event to inaugurate its new auditorium, an open-air stage with seats for about 15,000 people and a surrounding lawn with room for 30,000 more. Write an argument in favor of hiring either of the following performers with these considerations in mind:

- The city hopes the inaugural performance will raise as much money as possible to pay off the auditorium's construction loans.
- The city wants to obtain considerable positive publicity for the new auditorium.

Astrani, one of the legends of popular music, is giving a farewell concert tour before retiring. He has proposed holding the final three concerts in Stockton; because of his elaborate sets and costumes, tickets would be sold only for the auditorium's seats, and no lawn seating would be available. Astrani never allows souvenirs to be sold at his concerts, but the city will receive 20 percent of the proceeds from ticket sales. If the tour ends in Stockton, a well-known director will film the historic event and plans to release a full-length feature which will share the final shows with fans around the world.

A number of prominent bands have organized "Animal-Aid" to raise money for endangered species. The concert has already generated significant attention in the press, and a number of important arenas competed for the privilege of hosting the event. Stockton's new auditorium is the organizer's first choice as the site for the all-day concert, and the city would be allowed to design and sell souvenirs commemorating the event. While tickets would be available for both the seats and surrounding lawn, all of the proceeds from ticket sales would go to Animal-Aid. The auditorium's security expert is concerned that the facility's novice staff may not yet have the experience to handle a large crowd during an all-day event.

_____

_____

_____

_____

_____

_____

_____

_____

_____

_____

_____

_____

GO ON TO THE NEXT PAGE.

KAPLAN

STOP

IF YOU FINISH BEFORE TIME IS CALLED, YOU MAY CHECK YOUR WORK ON THIS SECTION ONLY.
DO NOT WORK ON ANY OTHER SECTION IN THE TEST.

Practice Test 1: **Answer Key**

Section I Logical Reasoning	Section II Analytical Reasoning	Section III Reading Comprehension	Section IV Logical Reasoning
1. C	1. C	1. E	1. D
2. C	2. A	2. D	2. E
3. E	3. C	3. C	3. B
4. E	4. C	4. B	4. E
5. B	5. E	5. D	5. A
6. E	6. C	6. A	6. C
7. C	7. D	7. A	7. A
8. A	8. B	8. D	8. E
9. D	9. C	9. A	9. C
10. B	10. E	10. B	10. D
11. C	11. E	11. C	11. A
12. A	12. E	12. C	12. A
13. C	13. B	13. E	13. D
14. E	14. C	14. D	14. D
15. A	15. E	15. B	15. E
16. B	16. A	16. D	16. E
17. B	17. E	17. C	17. D
18. C	18. B	18. E	18. A
19. C	19. E	19. A	19. B
20. B	20. D	20. D	20. A
21. B	21. B	21. C	21. A
22. E	22. D	22. C	22. D
23. D	23. B	23. D	23. C
24. A	24. A	24. E	24. D
25. D		25. B	25. E
		26. B	
		27. D	

Answers and Explanations

SECTION I: LOGICAL REASONING

1. C

The author concludes in the last sentence that more people were able to read directly after the invention of the printing press. The evidence provided is the greater demand for the new printing press books relative to the demand for expensive manuscript copies. In short, the argument is: More books were bought, therefore more people could read. In making this argument, the author assumes that the number of books sold is directly related to the number of people who can read, but maybe existing readers simply bought more books when the press made them cheaper. (C) breaks down the assumption by implying that the same number of people were buying a greater number of books.

(A) shifts the scope from reading to writing. You can infer no relevant connection between letter writing and *learning* to read, and even if you could (A) would strengthen the argument rather than weaken it.

(B) basically says that people who can read can also write. Like (A), it has no bearing on the relative number of *readers* before the press and after.

(D) and (E) give information about the post-printing press world only, so they are irrelevant. You have no way of knowing whether *earlier* manuscript copies circulated in a manner similar to that described in (D), or whether the manuscript copies *before* the press were also useless to illiterate people (E). Further, even if a comparison to the previous era had been made, neither (D) nor (E) would weaken the argument. If anything, more frequent book lending and decreased utility to the illiterate would strengthen the notion that more books sold implies that more people learned how to read.

- The main issue here is one of *comparison*. You're not concerned simply with determining that there were lots of readers after the invention of the printing press, which (D) and (E) seem to suggest. Rather, you need to know whether there were *more* readers after the invention of the press than before, so (D) and (E) are irrelevant.

- Watch those scope shifts! Reading and writing may conjure up similar images in your mind, but are certainly two different things. You should cross off choices like (A) and (B) quickly.

- Read critically! The phrase "this demonstrates that . . ." strongly suggests that what comes next (i.e., what is *being* demonstrated) is the conclusion, while what comes before (what *does* the demonstrating) is the evidence for this conclusion.

2. C

The author here concludes that Bevex is safe for people based on the evidence that a person would need to drink 25 cans of Bevex-sweetened drinks a day for it to be harmful. Although it may seem unlikely, nothing in the stimulus prevents a person from drinking 25 cans of Bevex drinks a day. Thus, the author must be assuming that people don't drink that many cans of Bevex-sweetened drinks, (C).

(A) offers an irrelevant comparison. What does the developmental time for mice cancer relative to that of human cancer have to do with Bevex? There's also a scope shift here: The issue is whether or not Bevex, which causes cancer in mice, *can* cause cancer in people, not *how long* such a cancer would take to develop.

(B) Other food additives are also bad for mice? This has nothing to do with the safety of Bevex for humans, and so is outside the scope—not a necessary element of the argument.

(D) The health benefits of weight control are outside the scope.

(E) refers to non-relevant studies on Bevex which, basically, is a flat-out announcement that this choice is beyond the scope and not necessary to the argument.

- A stem that asks "what must be true in order to draw this conclusion?" is indirectly asking, "What is the central assumption?" Treat it like any other assumption question.

- An assumption is a piece of information that is *necessary* to an argument. An outside-the-scope statement is a statement that is *irrelevant* to an argument. Therefore, if a choice is outside the scope of the argument, it need not be assumed.

- The phrase "For that reason . . ." tells you that what's coming up is the conclusion.

3. E

Here you get a little communication breakdown between Harry and Judith. The stem alerts you right away that you're concerned with Judith's response, so begin there. Paraphrasing, Judith essentially says, "Not true. Lots of people can't afford to fly." So she must have thought she heard, "Most people (or anyone) can afford to fly." Scanning the choices, you find this in (E).

The other choices provide various opportunities to misinterpret Harry's statement, but you only want *Judith's* misinterpretation.

(A) addresses the wealth of people in general, while Judith is only responding to the affordability of flight.

(B) introduces the *right* to experience travel, which is far removed from the financial ability of people to do so, the only issue involved in Judith's response.

(C) Judith's response addresses only the affordability of flight, so you have no reason to think that Harry's statement implies (C).

(D) shifts the scope away from airlines to other forms of travel, which are not addressed by Judith or by Harry.

- Always read the question stem first in Logical Reasoning. Here, you're asked to determine how Judith interprets Harry's statement, which means that the focus is truly on Judith. Often, the simplest approach to a "crossed-wires" question like this is to read the second person's statement first in order to prephrase what that person must have thought she heard.

- Go where the points are! The stem strongly suggests that what Harry actually says is of little importance, and that Judith's statement is paramount here. And this example provides a great reminder for your LSAT prep in general: Your job is not to master every line of printed material on the test, but rather to rack up points. If you can get this point by blowing past Harry, do it.

4. E

The ads for the new pill state only that it contains 44 percent fiber. Based on the nutritionists' recommendation, it is fair to assume that the ads mean to imply that people will get lots of fiber by taking these pills; after all, it is a fiber supplement. But you should always be suspicious when an argument (especially an advertisement!) employs percentages. Could it be that the ads are trying to suggest

that by taking these pills, one would receive 44 percent of the fiber she needs? The more likely interpretation (the one the advertisers don't want people to see) is that the pill *itself* may be made up of 44 percent fiber, which doesn't mean that it contains a lot of fiber *relative to the amount of fiber one needs*. If (E) is true, these pills actually contain very little fiber—only 1/60 to 1/90 of the recommended daily intake. If this is the case, that 44 percent number is misleading; such a minuscule amount would hardly count as a supplement at all. If (E) is true, the ads should focus on the actual amount of fiber these pills add to one's diet, not on the irrelevant statistic offered, namely, how much of each pill is made up of fiber. (It is clear why the ads don't focus on the correct info; no one who knew the truth would buy such a useless product.)

(A) brings up other products, while the focus here is on these fiber pills only.

(B) addresses the basis of the nutritionists' recommendation, which isn't part of the advertisement itself.

(C) What does addiction to other types of pills have to do with the validity of these fiber ads?

(D) offers a classic example of a scope shift by referring to the *label* on the actual product while you're interested specifically in the product's *advertisement*.

- You may have found this stem a bit complex. Feel free to skip a question like this temporarily and return to it later if time permits. It's better to move on than to allow any one question to sap your confidence or your time, especially at the beginning of a section.

- If you understand how percentages differ from raw numbers, you won't mistake one for the other. A large percentage of something little is often, in actual terms, little. Here, the 44 percent figure is meant to sound impressive, but in actual terms it may amount to very little fiber. If (E) is true, the impression given by the 44 percent figure is misleading.

5. B

Essentially, the author says that it is impossible for consumers to avoid environmentally harmful products and that, therefore, consumers can't be held morally accountable for not avoiding them. Stated in more general terms, the author grants moral exemption for things beyond one's control. An appropriate concluding principle to the paragraph must be, at the very least, highly consistent with this general theme, and the completion must also be completely consistent with the statement "because of this impossibility there can be no moral duty." Perhaps you were able to prephrase the kind of principle the test makers are after: "One can't be held morally accountable for actions that are impossible to avoid." This is what you get in (B).

If you had trouble prephrasing an answer here, you could still get the point by eliminating the wrong choices. Each wrong choice fails either because it shifts the scope, or doesn't provide the proper follow-up to the first part of the final sentence; that is, it ignores the notion of the impossible situation consumers face in following the environmentalists' recommendation.

(A) It is the unavoidable nature of an action that is in question here, not its effects.

(C) The stimulus focuses on the morality of consumption, not production, so (C) goes astray and cannot logically complete the argument.

(D) brings up the new concept of "least total harm," and ignores the issue of the conundrum faced by consumers trying to act in the way the environmentalists urge. This impossibility to act in this way is the central theme of the passage, and the principle in (D) has nothing to do with it at all.

(E) brings up other kinds of duty, but the author speaks only of moral duty, so this choice goes beyond the scope of the argument.

- Anticipating where the author is going is always a helpful strategy for dealing with Logical Reasoning stimuli and Reading Comp passages. However, a fill-in-the-blank question rewards you *directly* for your ability to predict where the author is going.

6. E

Here you get another advertisement, and it's easy to pick out the main point—"Subscribe to this magazine." The rest of the ad tells you *why* you should subscribe: The brain is a physical organ and since physical organs benefit from exercise, it follows that the brain will benefit from exercise. This magazine will exercise the brain, therefore this magazine will benefit the brain. What's the method? The ad compares the brain and muscles in the sense that they are both physical organs, and then reasons that since exercise helps one (muscles) it will also help the other (the brain). With all the comparisons being made here, the word "similar" in choice (E) should jump out. The ad implies that brains and muscles must be similar in one respect (they

will both benefit from exercise) because they are similar in another (they are both physical organs).

(A) What experimental evidence?

(B) The ad may begin rather brusquely by stating that "anyone who exercises knows . . ." but it certainly does not ridicule anyone, so choice (B) will not do.

(C) The ad never explains how the magazine "exercises your brain"—it simply employs an analogy to attempt to demonstrate *that* it does. The "process" itself is never explained.

(D) Most ads, this one included, don't offer a careful analysis of anything. They offer sound bites, and sometimes, as in this case, a comparison. When you look closely, you see that there is no "careful analysis."

- The LSAT uses words very precisely. A "careful analysis" (D) is just that: something a scientist, scholar, or researcher might provide, not what you get in this light sales pitch. "Experimental evidence" in (A) is simply off the mark too. Put each choice through its paces, and if what it offers is not in the stimulus, cross it off.

7. C

Here's a second Method of Argument question in a row, so once again, you should pay attention to the logical structure as you read. First comes the claim that a reduction in health care costs won't happen within the current "piecemeal payment" system. Why? Because in this system there's an incentive to shift the financial burden to someone else. This is illustrated by the notion of a "pliable spending balloon"—push in on one part and an equally expensive bulge pops up in another. It's likely you've seen this argumentative technique before: When an author says that a health-care system, for example, *is like a balloon*, she is making an analogy. A suitable prephrase for this author's method would be "a claim is made, explained, and illustrated by analogy." Choice (C) gets the point.

(A) Shifting of cost to the patient is mentioned as a minor detail, but the "premise" of health-care reimbursement is not mentioned at all.

(B) is excessively negative in tone; the author speaks of flaws in the system, not of fraud by the people involved.

(D) No alternatives are mentioned, much less disparaged.

(E) goes against the passage: The instance cited in the last sentence is an example of a previous *failure* of an analogous system, not a demonstration of the feasibility of cooperation.

- The wrong choices in a Method of Argument question all fail to address the central structure of the argument. Try each choice out rigorously. Ask yourself: "Is this in here? Is this the way the argument proceeds?" You may have skimmed past the balloon analogy in your initial reading of the stimulus, but a thorough test of (C) would force you to ask "Is there an analogy here?" Actively searching the stimulus for an analogy, the balloon should then jump off the page, so to speak.

8.   A

Now you're asked for an inference, and there's really no way to proceed here except by testing out the choices. Luckily, the first one fits the bill, and you can derive this inference from an interpretation of the first sentence. As you'll recall, the claim was that within the current "piecemeal" system, the problem of reducing health-care costs cannot be solved. What this means is that *if* a solution is to be found, it must come from something other than a "piecemeal" system, and (A)'s "comprehensive approach" is just the ticket. Translate "non-piecemeal" as "comprehensive," and you have choice (A).

Each of the other choices goes beyond the scope, and here you also find a few unjustified value assessments.

(B) You can't infer anything about the income of health-care professionals relative to available funding. The system's out of whack, for sure, but how the income of health-care professionals fits into the equation is never addressed.

(C) attempts to explain the rise in health care costs in a manner inconsistent with the author's explanation. Additional funds are not the problem; shift of burden is.

(D) The passage concerns the cost, not the quality of medical care. Furthermore, the issue of medical "technology" is so far from the scope that you can cut this choice for this word alone.

(E) goes way beyond the scope, dealing with the wisdom (a value assessment) of hospital capacity utilization and the issue of "large-scale emergencies."

- Some Inference questions are vulnerable to prephrasing; namely, questions with stimuli involving formal logic. If you see two or more statements that can be combined, go ahead and combine them and then scan the choices for the result. This is just like the process of making deductions in Logic Games. But in a stimulus like this one, the statements don't link up as easily, and the test makers are most likely looking for an interpretation or paraphrase of one particular part of the passage. In this case, it's best to move right on to evaluating the choices.

9.   D

Here's another Inference question, and a perfect place to enact the advice in the bullet point immediately above. It's possible to prephrase an answer, but it's still closer to the open-ended type of passage than the formal logic type, so simply evaluating the choices will be the best way to go unless a prephrase comes to mind. The statements in the stimulus center on the emphasis of the news media on spectacular events and the public's interpretation of this emphasis. The public links the amount of media attention to the actual risk of the events described, even though this may lead to a discrepancy between the perceived risk and the actual risk of certain events. The media gives more attention to more dramatic but statistically less risky accidents, and so if the public depends on the news media, the public will have a skewed idea of these risks. Taken together, this is precisely what the conclusion in choice (D) states.

(A) offers an irrelevant comparison. "Commercial media" includes both print and broadcast media, and the author draws no distinction between them.

(B) The author addresses the *results* of the media's behavior, not the *cause* of it. Whether the media pander to the "public's taste" is not a concern of the author.

(C) The passage gives you no basis on which to assess or infer anything about this issue of "control." You can assume that of the examples listed, planes and cars, many people would feel that they have more control driving than flying. But, first of all, this is an opinion that is not supported one way or the other by the passage. Secondly, these are just two examples that illustrate the author's overall point. For all you know, other "spectacular" events that are perceived as dangerous may be events over which people feel they have more control.

(E) attempts to make a specific prediction based on the statements given. However, it's hard to tell from the information given which would be the more "exceptional event," and so you cannot infer which event would receive more extensive coverage.

- Inferring a conclusion is different from forming a general inference. The latter could come as a result, interpretation, or combination of any part of the stimulus. It's not unusual for a general inference to be derived from a single sentence of a long stimulus. An example of this is question 8 above, in which (A) is simply an interpretation of the first sentence. An inferred *conclusion*, however, must take account of the overall movement of the passage; it must reflect where the author is going with the argument.

10. B

A large group was studied and a percentage of members exhibited behavioral problems. A dietary change was made and a decrease in this percentage was observed. Therefore, the author concludes, the change in diet caused the behavioral change. Such an argument necessarily assumes that no other factors may have influenced this behavioral change. The fact that no control group was used in the study to see if any other factors might be contributing to the behavioral change is a flaw in the study and in its interpretation by the author. The observed changes might have occurred in a control group as well, perhaps due to the extra attention the children received while involved in the study, or to other factors that may have been present. Choice (B) describes this flaw.

(A) is a true statement—no evidence is given relating the quantity of additives to the quantity of behavioral problems, but then again, no claims are made regarding this relationship, either. So the argument doesn't logically require such support.

(C) is also a true statement, but it's not a flaw since the percentage, not the actual *number* of problem children, is the issue here.

(D) is irrelevant, since the children who were *unaffected* by the dietary change are outside the scope of the argument.

(E) offers an alternative interpretation of the study, but goes beyond the scope by mentioning the *frequency* of behavioral problems. The author is concerned only with the percentage of children exhibiting behavioral problems, not with the specific *frequency* of those problems.

- In a Flaw question, steer clear of choices that fault the author for failing to provide information that the author has no obligation to provide. Evidence of a "proportionate reduction" (A), the exact number

of problem children (C), and evidence regarding children unaffected by additives (D) are all irrelevant to the argument at hand. It is true that the author doesn't supply these pieces of evidence, but don't let that fool you: They are beyond the scope of her specific argument, so she doesn't have to address them.

11. C

When asked to explain a discrepancy in the stimulus, the first step is to locate the discrepancy. The unusual thing in the situation described is that a smaller percentage of the *older* cars had engine work done. One might think that a greater percentage of older cars would need repairs, but notice that the stimulus refers to which automobiles *had* repairs, not which *needed* them. If the cars from the 1960s are probably in more need of repair, why have a greater percentage of 1970s cars received repairs? Maybe you tried to prephrase an answer. You're dealing with percentages again, not raw numbers, so fewer older cars on the road wouldn't make for a good answer. Maybe you considered the economics associated with repairs: If a car is worth $500, and engine repairs cost $1,000, it probably doesn't make much financial sense to get the car repaired. This is the idea that gets the point: If older cars are not worth the expense, and are scrapped instead of repaired, then the statistics described in the stimulus are understandable. (C) nicely clears up the discrepancy.

(A) Inspection for emission levels probably would turn up more problems in older cars, which suggests that the older cars would have a greater percentage of repairs, so (A) only deepens the mystery.

(B) New cars are out of the scope based on the dates provided in the passage. Even if you considered the 1970s cars "new" (at least, newer than cars from the 1960s), this choice would, like (A), make the facts even less understandable.

(D) Whether or not simplified car engines result in fewer repairs is pretty shaky, but even if they did, (D) would also suggest that the 60's models would need more repairs.

(E) chastises those negligent 60's car owners for not maintaining their cars, but it doesn't mention 1970s cars, and thus does nothing to explain the discrepancy.

- When attempting to resolve a discrepancy, be wary of choices that further confound the odd result or finding found in the stimulus.

- When the discrepancy revolves around two groups or things (which is usually the case), quickly eliminate any choice, like (E) here, that offers information that relates to only one of them. A true resolution to such a discrepancy must be based on a fact that in some way relates to both groups.

12. A

Here you have an example of the type of formal logic inference question alluded to in the bullet point of question 8. How do you know formal logic is involved? There are three sentences. The first begins with "*no* mathematicians," the second with "*some* mathematicians," and the third with "*some* mathematicians." And in fact, despite the seemingly technical nature of the stimulus, the correct inference can be derived directly from a combination of the first and third sentences: No current mathematician would flatly refuse to accept a lengthy proof. But some mathematicians (that means current ones) still believe that simple theorems should have simple proofs. Since both of these statements are about the same group, current mathematicians, you can combine them: Some mathematicians (current ones) who believe proofs should be simple would not flatly refuse to accept a lengthy one—again, because of the first sentence: No current mathematician would reject a lengthy proof.

(B) and (E) The statements in the stimulus don't say anything about *non*mathematicians, so these two choices are outside the scope.

(C) and (D) both discuss "individuals" and not specifically "mathematicians." While it may be true that the term "individuals" includes mathematicians, it also includes everyone else, and that's too general for this argument.

- It's crucial to translate statements correctly: " some mathematicians *still* hold a strong belief . . ." means that these are *current* mathematicians, the same ones that appear in sentence 1, but not the same as the 1976 mathematicians in the second sentence. This is how you know to combine the first and third sentences; they both speak of a common group.
- The beauty of formal arguments is that they usually operate within strictly defined parameters. Therefore, when a choice offers a term that isn't perfectly within this boundary, such as "nonmathematician" or "individual," you can be reasonably sure that that choice is beyond the scope.

13. C

In question 13 you get more practice with formal logic in the form of a Parallel Reasoning question. Since it's just a straight parallel question (and not parallel flaw), characterize the conclusion. The conclusion is conditional—if one thing occurs, then another will occur. Now check the conclusions for each of the answer choices. In this question (like many parallel questions), you won't have to go any further than that to find the correct answer.

(A) concludes definitely—"you must try to." Eliminate it.

(B) has a conditional conclusion, but the format doesn't match—it isn't "if one thing occurs, another will," but "if you *want* one thing to occur, then you must do another." A little tougher to recognize, but definitely not a match. Eliminate it.

(C) A perfect match. If one thing, then another—the conclusion is a match, so hold on to this for now. You could check the evidence and confirm, but it won't be necessary for this question, since a quick check of all five choices will show that this is the only matching conclusion.

(D) Close, but this says "If one thing then *not* another. That's not a match and can be eliminated.

(E) Same pattern as (D). Eliminate it.

- The amount of formal logic on the LSAT varies from test to test, and from section to section. Formal logic is all over Logic Games, and it shows up in Logical Reasoning mainly in Inference and Parallel Reasoning questions like this one.

14. E

Here's a pleasant topic: lobster cannibalism. The argument is short, to the point, and missing a major chunk (so to speak), which is good because you're asked to find the author's assumption. Marine biologists theorize that trapped lobsters eat one another in response to hunger. The author refutes this claim by pointing out cases in which several lobsters trapped together for weeks or months did *not* eat one another. Notice, however, that there's nothing in the author's evidence that gives you an idea of how hungry the lobsters were, or how much food they had at the time they were trapped. For all you know, these lobsters could make do for much more than two months before getting hungry enough to eat one another. The author assumes that the lobsters she cites in her evidence were hungry lobsters. If they weren't hungry, then she has no business trampling on the marine biologists' theory.

(A) Lobsters that *aren't* in traps? They are outside the trap *and* outside the scope.

(B) and (C) are irrelevant. Neither affects the validity of the biologists' hypothesis (or, more to the point, the author's claim that the hypothesis is wrong).

(D) Other species of marine life are outside the scope; nothing about them can help fill the void in this argument about lobsters.

- Strong unqualified conclusions such as "the hypothesis is clearly wrong" are much more difficult to defend than qualified conclusions such as "the theory is *probably* wrong" or "the evidence *seems to show* the hypothesis is *unlikely.*" Often, the assumption in arguments containing strong unqualified conclusions involves an alternative explanation or possibility—that is, a factor that the author has overlooked.

- Some question stems are a little wordy and introduce characters with whom you're not yet familiar. Don't let this throw you. Use that information to direct your reading of the stimulus and focus in on the pieces that will help you to answer the question.

15. A

The author is not happy about the ban on hunting: the deer population has multiplied by six, and the large deer population has caused property damage and accidents. Therefore, the author feels that the ban on hunting was unnecessary and has created safety hazards "that would not otherwise exist." But do you know for sure that the increase in the deer population was caused by the ban on hunting? The author assumes that the population explosion was *caused* by the ban on hunting because the increase came *after* the ban on hunting. Implicit in this assumption is the belief that the deer population would not have grown if the ban *weren't* enacted. Granted, there does seem to be a rational connection between fewer deer being shot and more deer being alive, but the author hasn't ruled out other factors. Choice (A) compensates for this weakness by showing how the deer population has *not* grown in nearby locales where hunting is allowed, suggesting that the deer population would not have grown in Greenfield if hunting had not been banned; (A) bolsters the author's assumption, and in so doing strengthens the argument.

(B) lends support only to evidence already given—that deer are often the unwitting cause of injury and accidents. It's

not necessarily true that this is a direct result of the ban on hunting, however, since deer could probably wander on to the street whether or not hunting kept their population in check.

(C) is concerned with the welfare of the deer. While this might strengthen one type of argument against the ban on hunting, it doesn't strengthen the author's point that the increase in the number of deer is bad for *people*.

(D) doesn't do much either way. It may bring up a possible alternative explanation for the growth in the deer population, but it doesn't even do that well since you don't know whether the residents provided sustenance for the deer before the ban or only since it was enacted.

(E) provides more evidence for the statement that deer cause damage, but the author's conclusion isn't merely that damage occurs—it's that the damage is a result of the ban on hunting.

- One of the surest ways to strengthen an argument is to shore up a central assumption.

- Make sure you strengthen the right argument, that is, the one that's on the page. As shown above, many of the wrong choices lend support to arguments other than the one the author is making. This is why it's important to keep the author's conclusion firmly in mind while you evaluate the choices.

- Strengthening an argument is not the same as proving it. Correct choice (A) doesn't objectively *prove* that the ban was unnecessary and has created new risks to the public, as the author maintains, but it does increase the likelihood that the author is on target.

- Learn to recognize the kind of "after, therefore caused by" style of reasoning demonstrated in this argument. An author can't say that X causes Y based on evidence that Y came after X. Such an argument assumes that no other factor is responsible for Y.

16. B

The stem tells you to look for a valid inference. Scientists estimate the mass of comets by their brightness. It was recently discovered that the material in Halley's comet is less reflective than was once thought—that is, it reflects less light per unit of mass. Well, then, it follows that the comet must be bigger, or, rather, more massive than previously thought. With this thought in mind, (B) shines—the previous estimates based on its brightness were too low.

The key here (and this may have been tricky to some) is to understand that the total amount of light given off is constant. So if it is discovered that much less light is reflected *per unit* of mass, yet the overall light reflected is the same, then it must be true that the comet is larger than previously thought. While scientists thought Halley's comet was a smaller comet shining very brightly, it is in fact a larger comet that gives out much less light per unit of mass.

(A) could be true based on the statements in the stimulus, but then again it could also be false. Maybe all comets are made of the same material; who knows? While this statement is not inconsistent with the stimulus, neither is it supported by the stimulus.

(C) claims that the total amount of light is less than previously thought, but this seems rather unlikely. Total amount of light is what the scientists have been using to make their estimates, and, as mentioned above, in this case you need to take this to be constant. The *interpretation* of the total amount of reflected light is what has come into question, not the amount itself.

(D) As in (A), you can't infer anything about the properties of other comets. This statement may or may not be true; you have no way of knowing from this passage.

(E) Brightness is still an effective way to estimate the mass of comets, which means that the newly received information can lead to a good estimate of the mass of Halley's comet. You therefore can't infer that more info is necessary.

- If you notice a pattern in the kinds of questions that give you trouble, make a habit of skipping those questions during your first run through the section. Some students shy away from numerical Logical Reasoning questions, and that's okay. If you had trouble interpreting what "60 times less light per unit of mass" meant, then this question may have been a good one to put off until later.

17. B

Next is an argument over paper. Previewing the stem, as always, you see that you're asked to critique the stationer's response to the office manager's comment. The office manager strongly implies that recycled paper is inferior. An appropriate response would address this concern, perhaps by stating that "recycled paper is not inferior," and then backing up that claim with good, solid evidence. The stationer does indeed address the issue, saying that recycled paper is not necessarily inferior, but then goes off on a tangent discussing the history of recycling in the production of paper. Now really, who cares about paper from the beginning of time? The stationer's evidence is irrelevant to the issue at hand: whether the recycled paper of today, the kind the office manager would use, is inferior. This is the stationer's major flaw—he fails to provide relevant evidence to support his claim in the defense of recycled paper, (B).

(A) If anything, the little history lesson indicates the stationery supplier *assumes* the office manager's ignorance on the topic.

(C) and (D) The environmental aspect of paper recycling and the basic technology of paper manufacturing aren't addressed in either side of the dialogue, so these choices can be eliminated.

(E) The stationer *does* explicitly address the manager's concern about quality by saying that recycled paper is not necessarily inferior, and then attempts to present evidence to back this up. The failure is in the *nature* of the evidence (it's irrelevant to current quality), not that he doesn't address the issue.

- It often helps to imagine how you would react to the various scenarios presented in Logical Reasoning. Since you know from the stem that you're to critique the second person's response, you can put yourself in the place of the first person, who would likely respond to the stationer: "Thanks for the history lesson, Jack, but I don't see what that has to do with the paper for our letters." When you put yourself in the place of the office manager, it's easier to see how the stationer's response is irrelevant.

18. C

The stem alerts you to the important statement: Peter's car got damaged, but Alicia's did not. You're asked to determine the purpose of this statement, so you'll need to examine the context in which it appears. Alicia and Peter committed the same offense—they borrowed cars without permission. Both were caught, but only Peter was punished. The author feels that Peter was punished only because the car he was driving was damaged while in his possession, although not by him. And here's the purpose of the statement mentioned in the stem: The author implies that equal crimes deserve equal punishment and, acknowledging the difference in the two situations, argues that this difference really shouldn't affect the magnitude of the offense since Peter didn't cause the damage. The author *acknowledges but downplays* the difference in situations. Someone might object to his argument by pointing out that Peter's car was damaged while Alicia's was not. Realizing this, the author mentions the damage done to the car to illustrate his awareness of the situation and to head off possible objections to the argument based on this fact—a preemptive strike, if you will.

Wrong choices (A), (B), and (D) all contradict the general gist of the argument:

(A) The different outcomes highlighted in the stem wouldn't support the conclusion that equal crimes deserve equal punishment, since the crimes would not then be equal after all. The author argues that this difference in results isn't relevant; she certainly doesn't use the difference to support her argument.

(B) It is clear from the conclusion and the overall tone of the passage that the author doesn't feel that the difference in outcomes is justified.

(D) The statement in question is not used to directly support the argument—it's meant to address a thorny issue in advance in order to get it out of the way. Furthermore, the statement concerns a specific difference in the results of this particular situation; it therefore is not even a "general principle."

(E) The statement in question is a minor detail the author counterargued, not a summary of anything, and certainly not a central focus of the argument.

- Use sentence structure to help you understand Logical Reasoning stimuli. The structure "It is true that . . ., *but* . . ." strongly suggests that the author is admitting a fact, but attempting to downplay or dismiss it. This kind of prephrased notion accords nicely with correct choice (C).

- Use the skills you develop on other LSAT sections wherever they may apply. This variation of a Logical Reasoning Method of Argument question is very similar to the popular Reading Comp "purpose of detail" question.

19. C

No use rehashing the argument; it's all analyzed in question 18. You're looking for a statement that cannot be true, so simply try out the choices.

(A) Would justice have been better served if Peter had received only a warning? It's possible; it's certainly not inconsistent with the idea of equal punishment, since Peter and Alicia committed the same crime and Alicia got off with just a warning. Since (A) could be true, it can't be the answer, and you should move on.

(B) Is it possible that this is Alicia's first offense of this nature? Sure. If Peter is a first offender too, then you still have the possibility of equal crimes.

(C) essentially says that Peter was engaged in unsafe and illegal behavior when he hit the cab, while Alicia was well behaved. Can this be true? No: This choice contradicts the author's notion that the difference in the two cases was not due to any difference in the culpability of the two offenders. For that matter, it also directly contradicts the statement that the cab driver was at fault for Peter's accident. (C) can't be true, and is the answer. For the record:

(D) tells you that Alicia wasn't all that well behaved even before she was caught for the busted taillights. This is possible; this transgression is said to have occurred at an earlier time and thus is not connected to her apprehension. Since this information doesn't provide a major difference in the relevant circumstances of the respective cases, (D) could be true and is not the answer.

(E) offers up another historical difference between the offenders, not a difference between the offenses, so like all of the other wrong choices it's not inconsistent with the author's argument.

- A statement that "could be true" is any statement that does not flatly contradict the stimulus. Such a statement need not be inferable, probable, or even likely; as long as it doesn't go directly against anything in the stimulus, it theoretically could be true. In a "could be true EXCEPT" question, the correct choice will be the one that truly conflicts with the information in the stimulus; that is, the choice that cannot be true.

20. B

This is a parallel Flaw question, so our approach is a little different—you want to characterize the flaw in the stimulus and then check the answer choices for the corresponding flaw. The evidence in the argument states that if one particular candidate runs, another will not. The conclusion, though, says that *no one* else will run. So the argument makes a general conclusion (no one will run against Esposito) from specific evidence (Krasman will not run against Esposito). It overlooks the possibility that someone else might run against Esposito. You need to find the answer choice that is flawed in the same way.

(A) The problem here is a scope shift—the evidence is about not being able to attract large stores, but the conclusion is about not being "viable as a shopping district."

It's similar in spirit to the stimulus, and a tempting wrong answer choice for the test taker who doesn't know to characterize the flaw specifically, but it's not a match for the flaw you identified.

(B) A perfect match. The evidence says the group won't play on a specific day, and the conclusion says it won't play on *any* day but Saturday. Just like the stimulus, this argument bases a broad conclusion on very narrow evidence—and overlooks the possibility that the band will play on any of the days not mentioned.

(C) The conclusion here is a very specific prediction, which is all you need to recognize in order to know that this argument doesn't match the "specific evidence/general conclusion" pattern of the stimulus.

(D) There's no flaw here. That's all you need to know, since you're looking to match the flaw that appeared in the stimulus. Eliminate.

(E) Another scope shift, from "the best one for a specific group" to "the one you should buy." That's a flaw, but not the same one you saw in the stimulus. Eliminate.

- Notice how the second sentence of correct choice (B) is written in reverse order compared with its counterpart in the original. The original was of the form "If X, then not Y." In (B), the second sentence reads "Not Y, if X." Logically, this is the same thing: "If it is raining, the car will not be dry" is equivalent to "The car will not be dry if it is raining." The correct choice is allowed to reverse a term, as long as it remains logically parallel to the original.

21. B

You're told in this Inference question that all nuclear accidents thus far have been caused by human error. Now jump to the last sentence, which requires a bit of a translation because of the double negative employed. "*Cannot* be thought *unlikely*" means "it is thought likely." So the author essentially says in the last sentence that such everyday events of human error are likely to continue into the future. If human error won't end, and human error is the cause of nuclear accidents, you can infer that nuclear accidents are likely to occur again. Aside from the double negatives, it's a fairly straightforward inference. (B)'s "not improbable" means "probable, likely," so (B) is a close paraphrase of the inference.

(A) is a bit excessive; an "ever-increasing incidence of accidents" is a major exaggeration of "not unlikely." You can't infer that there will be more incidents every succeeding year from evidence that merely suggests that these incidents will probably happen.

(C) also goes overboard by suggesting that nothing can be done about the likelihood of human error.

(D) refers to nuclear power plant design, while the argument focuses on human error. The construction material for plants is outside the scope, and there's no way you can infer anything about them.

(E) attempts to make an absolute prediction about the technology side of the issue, but this prediction is not inferable: Just because an accident caused by a flaw in technology has never happened doesn't mean it never will.

- This question provides a good example of the way the test makers test your ability to translate tricky phrases. The passage and the correct choice both contain double negatives, and it's up to you to translate them into a more manageable form. "NOT UNlikely" means "likely." "NOT IMprobable" means "probable." Correctly translating complex phrases into simpler ones is not unimportant for LSAT success.

22. E

This question stem is somewhat unusual and complex: It asks you which question would elicit answers that would be relevant to evaluating a part of the stimulus, namely, the skeptics' position. That's a good place to start: The skeptics' position is that unusual animal behavior doesn't really predict earthquakes. It is a coincidence, they say, since unusual behavior is not really unusual; at any given time, some dogs will be behaving oddly. It may be hard to prephrase an answer here—your best bet is to evaluate each choice in light of each one's possible relevance to this issue. Choice (E) raises the most relevant question: How unusual is the unusual behavior anyway? If the so-called "unusual behavior" can be anything from barking to running in circles, then the skeptics may have a point, and the behavior may only be remembered because it came just before an earthquake. If, however, a dog stands up on its hind legs and does a jig immediately preceding an earthquake *and at no other time*, the skeptics' argument is weakened. The answer to the question posed in (E) would allow you to better evaluate the skeptics' position, which is why (E) gets the point.

The wrong choices, predictably, go outside of the scope, since anything that's relevant to the argument is necessarily *within* the scope.

(A) offers an irrelevant comparison. Who cares which group is more numerous? The issue is which group is *correct*.

(B) asks if there are other ways to predict earthquakes, but the issue in the stimulus is whether or not this one particular method, observing animal behavior, is reliable.

(C) asks about other animals, but the skeptics have focused their skepticism on dogs. Besides, even the non-skeptics in our stimulus wouldn't be likely to base their belief on behavior that is indistinguishable from normal behaviors.

(D) also focuses on other animals and thus strays from the apparent focus of the skeptics. Also, how *pronounced* the behavior is *isn't* the point—the point is how *unusual* the behavior is.

- "Relevant data" questions are fairly rare on the LSAT, but when they do appear they can be challenging since there will often be a variety of things that might be helpful in evaluating the argument. This makes it difficult to prephrase an answer to the question. Two thoughts that should help you test the choices in such a question: First, consider the various possible answers to each question (most can be answered with a yes or a no) and then see whether the different answers would lead to a different evaluation of the issue in question. Secondly, pay close attention to the scope of the argument; the wrong choices will be irrelevant and can therefore be eliminated.

23. D

The argument boils down to this: White-collar criminals are less likely to be convicted because they can afford expensive defense lawyers. A common assumption central to many such arguments of causality is that there are no other reasons for the stated result, in this case the lower conviction rate. If there is a greater percentage of the falsely accused in white collar crimes, these alleged criminals would be less likely to be convicted for reasons other than their expensive defense lawyers—it's simply a case that a greater percentage of them are innocent. This alternative explanation of the facts damages the argument that the smaller percentage of convictions for white-collar crimes *is due to the efforts of expensive lawyers*. Choice (D) supports the stimulus by ruling out this possible alternative explanation: By saying that the percentage of truly guilty defendants represented by public lawyers is no greater than the percentage guilty represented by private lawyers, (D) lends support to the idea that it *is* the attorney who makes the difference in the outcome of the case.

(A) is inconsistent with the notion that there is a higher conviction rate among street criminals. If street criminals can afford expensive lawyers, then, according to the argument,

you would expect little difference in the conviction rate of white-collar and street criminals.

(B) The relative skill level of *most* prosecutors has no effect on this argument. The prosecutors that *actually* handle white-collar cases could still be those few prosecutors that have the required skills.

(C) You are interested in the conviction *rate*, a percentage, not in the absolute number of convictions.

(E) weakens the argument by suggesting that there is a reason *other than* the effects of high-priced lawyers that impacts on the cited difference in conviction rates: Juries are simply more comfortable convicting street criminals as opposed to white-collar criminals.

- In many arguments that assert causality (expensive lawyers *cause* fewer convictions), the author ignores possible alternative explanations. In other words, the author assumes that nothing else but the factor she cites could have led to the result. A choice that offers such an alternative weakens the argument by breaking down that central assumption. Conversely, a choice that eliminates from consideration a likely alternative—as (D) does here—strengthens the argument by shoring up the central assumption that nothing *else* led to the stated result.

24. A

Due to funding restrictions, scientists are bound to ignore findings that are not directly related to the goals of the funded research. Therefore, according to the author, serendipity (a kind of luck that yields unexpected happy results) can no longer play a role in discovery. In other words, since all findings must be directly related to goals, serendipity can't play a role in research. The author assumes that anything that researchers are not purposely looking for can't be directly related. It certainly seems possible, after all, that research might bring unexpected findings that *are* related, that *can* be used because, although unexpected, they do bear on the stated goals of the research. This assumption is described in (A).

(B) contradicts the stimulus's assertion that serendipity, and not clear predictions, played a major role in past scientific discovery.

(C) The author does not venture into the territory of the personal preference of the scientists. Nothing, therefore, need be assumed about this in order for the conclusion regarding the death of scientific serendipity to stand.

(D) gets things backwards: Those who receive grants must provide clear projections, which does not necessarily mean that those who provide clear projections must get grants.

Even if the opposite of (D) is true, if some scientists who provide clear projections don't get grants, the argument remains unaffected because it's structured around those scientists who *do* receive their grants.

(E) brings up the concept of "value," which is outside the scope of this argument. The value of a finding isn't necessarily related to the way in which it was found. Nothing regarding "value" need be assumed.

- In order for a statement to meet the definition of an assumption, it must be both missing, meaning *unstated*, and required, meaning *necessary* for the argument to work.

- All assumptions stay within the scope of the argument. Notice how "findings purposely sought" in correct choice (A) is right in line with the major theme of the passage, whereas scientists' *preferences* (C) and the *value* of findings (E) are outside the scope.

25. D

The first step in resolving an apparent paradox is to locate it. Police statistics show that antitheft devices reduce the risk of car theft. However, insurance companies claim that cars with such devices are *more likely* to be stolen. And therein lies the apparent paradox: Cars with antitheft devices appear to be both more likely *and* less likely to be stolen. Resolution of this inconsistency lies in the fact that the groups in the two statistical claims are not identical. The police statistics refer to a reduction in risk: One car with the device is less likely to be stolen than is *the same car* without the device. The insurance industry stats, however, compare different groups of cars—those with the devices to those without. So it is possible for the antitheft devices to both reduce the overall risk of car theft for a single car and increase the likelihood of theft for that car *in comparison to cars without the device*. If (D) is true, the scenario makes sense: It allows for the police statistics to be true—the same car is less likely to be stolen with an antitheft device than without it—while still allowing for the insurance industry claims to be true, since these are the cars that are both most likely to be stolen and, perhaps because they are so attractive to thieves, most likely to have an antitheft device.

(A) Time is not in question in the argument. Whenever the theft *is* reported, it will find its way into the statistics, and the apparent paradox will still exist.

(B) approaches the issue from the wrong perspective. In both the police and the insurance industry claims, the

issue is the change in the risk percentage from one level to another depending on the installation of the device. (B) offers general information that does not impact on the issue of the *increase* or *reduction* of risk associated with the device. (B) can be a true statement and still offer no help in resolving the paradox.

(C) doesn't help to explain either claim, much less how they could be true together. If certain antitheft devices tend to produce many false alarms for every actual attempted theft (C), then the devices seem *less* valuable as crime prevention devices, since people presumably won't pay attention to alarms that almost always "cry wolf." But this still wouldn't explain why cars equipped with these devices are *more* likely to be stolen, and it seems inconsistent with the notion that these devices are effective in preventing car thefts.

(E) undermines in the same way as (C) the claim that the devices are effective in preventing thefts, but still wouldn't explain why cars equipped with the devices are more likely to be stolen than their unequipped counterparts. So (E) does nothing to solve the mystery.

- Often, LSAT "apparent paradoxes" are based on subtle scope shifts. Once you pick out the shift in scope, you're better able to debunk the paradox—that is, show that the situation is not paradoxical at all. In this case, the key was noticing the difference between the statistical claims: The police stats speak of one car's comparative risk with and without the device. The insurance industry's claims, on the other hand, speak of the likelihood that a car that will be stolen comes from the group of cars with the device or the group of cars without it.

SECTION II: ANALYTICAL REASONING

GAME 1—Broadcast News

The Action

"Seven consecutive time slots" immediately suggests a sequencing game, and that's exactly what you get in Game 1. A slight oddity is introduced, but it turns out to be inconsequential: Six of the seven entities are song tapes with letter names, while the last entity is referred to as a "news tape." Usually such a differentiation between entities means something, but here it doesn't—if you call the news tape N, you simply have seven lettered entities to fit into seven time slots, which is as familiar a game action as any you'll see on the Logic Games section. You're told that no tapes share a time slot, and no tape is longer than any other, which are just loophole closers. So far then, any tape can be slotted anywhere.

The Initial Setup

A roster of the entities and seven dashes on your page should do it for an initial setup—there's no need to get any fancier than that. You can include the news tape, N, alphabetically between L and O, or keep N separate for now, just in case this tape takes on some special significance in the game. (As you'll see, it doesn't—N will be regarded as just another entity.)

G H L O P S and N

— — — — — — —

The Rules

1) Rule 1 is a traditional sequencing rule that pairs up a couple of entities in a specific order. The upshot is that you'll always have LO somewhere in the list, and you can simply denote this as ALWAYS LO.

2) Rule 2 links up nicely with Rule 1, and you probably didn't have to wait until you got to Step 4 of the Kaplan Method to combine these rules to create an even bigger cluster: LO . . . N. Song tape O comes immediately after L, and then N must come some time after that. The dots remind you that it's okay for other tapes to come between O and N; the rule is satisfied as long as N is anywhere to the right of LO.

3) Don't let the wordiness of Rule 3 intimidate you: All it says is that two tapes must come between G and P, but G and P can appear in either order. This allows for two possibilities: G _ _ P or P _ _ G.

Deductions

In a game so basic, there's often not much in the way of deductions. However, there are usually some implications of the rules that are worth noting. Take, for example, our main LO . . . N bloc. What does this tell you about L? **L can't be played in slots six or seven, right?** If it were, there wouldn't be enough room for N at the end, and possibly O as well. Similarly, **N can't be played in slots one or two,** because that would shove L, O, or both off the map at the beginning of the sequence. These may not seem like major deductions, but these limitations directly help you bag a few questions, notably questions 2 and 6.

The Final Visualization

Here's what you have to work with heading into the questions:

G H L O P S and N

— — — — — — —

Always LO . . . N

G _ _ P or P _ _ G

The Big Picture

- Shorthanding a rule on the page will help you to solidify the rule in your mind and to convince yourself that you've interpreted the rule correctly. The wordiness of Rule 3 can be reduced to the convenient shorthand indicated above, and if you had any doubt as to the correct interpretation of that rule, working out the two concrete possibilities on your page should have helped to ease such doubt.

- The purpose of shorthand is to relieve you of the burden of returning to the written rules on the page. Rereading the text of Rules 1 and 2 takes longer than eyeballing the LO . . . N bloc created by those rules.

- Not all entities fulfill the same roles within a game. Some entities, like L, O, and N here, are major players: They form blocs that practically scream for attention in many questions. Blocs are important in that they often offer a starting point in the questions—something to immediately focus on when you don't know where to begin.

- On the other side of the spectrum from the major players are the "floaters." These entities are by no means unimportant. While you may begin your work in many of the questions with your blocs and high-profile entities, you'll often be called upon to fill in the ordering with the more unrestricted entities. That's why it's a good idea to at least take notice of the entities bound by few, or even no, restrictions. Here, H and S are not mentioned at all in the rules, and both are completely free to roam throughout the schedule to fill in the gaps left by the others.

- A familiar game type with seven questions is a great place to begin work on the Logic Games section. Here, the test makers were kind and put this game right up front. But sometimes they hide these easier games later on in the section. Preview the section quickly before jumping into the first game. Hopefully, you'll find the one that's easiest for you, and there's nothing better for your confidence (and your score) than to get off to a fast start on the easiest game on the section.

The Questions

1. C

Whenever you see a new "if" in the question stem, get the information into a new sketch and see where it leads. Placing G into the second slot kicks Rule 3 into effect, forcing P into slot 5; that's the only way that exactly two time slots will fit between G and P as mandated by Rule 3. That leaves the LO . . . N bloc as your next major concern. The LO pair physically fits into slots 3 and 4 or slots 6 and 7, but the latter case leaves no room for N. So L must be played third, and O fourth. The stem asks which tape must be third, and there you have it: L, choice (C).

- Usually a sequencing game will begin with an acceptability question, giving you the opportunity to try out the rules and pick up an easy point. But even though this game lacks a standard

acceptability question, a question like this one is a nice substitute—you get to try your hand at the rules and "get acquainted" with the game. Use the first few questions to reinforce your understanding of the game.

- Don't let slightly odd conventions throw you off. It's obvious from this first question that "the news" tape will be referred to as such throughout the game, but to you it's plain old "N."

2. A

You've already given N all the consideration that question 2 requires. Recall N's limitations, discussed in the Deductions section above: N cannot be played first, because then there would be no room for the LO pair before it, and N can't be played second, because even if you squeeze O into slot 1, L would be left out in the cold. You're looking for the time slot that N can't take, so it's either 1 or 2. The test makers chose "second" for (A).

- You need not draw something new for every question. Non-"if" questions, especially, are sometimes answerable based on your knowledge of the game and the sketching you did up front.

- Don't waste time on additional choices after you've found a choice that works. N *cannot* be second, so that's all you need to know to select (A). You don't have to *also* prove that slots 3, 4, 5, and 6 are okay for N; they *must* be, since there can be only one correct answer. It doesn't hurt to notice that you're implicitly told that N can take any slot from 3 to 6; for all you know, this information may come in handy later. If you noticed this, great. But if you spent time *checking* (B) through (E) "just for good measure," you need to work on how you prioritize your time.

3. C

Here, the two free agents, H and S, are to be slotted as far from each other as possible. "How far is that?" is the question that should come to mind. You may as well try placing them on opposite sides of the ordering, that is, in slots 1 and 7. And it doesn't matter which is on which side, since neither H nor S has any relationship to any other entity, thus making them functionally identical. Trying it out, you find that it is possible to place H and S on opposite ends of the ordering, as long as L and O take slots 3 and

4, respectively. If this pair is in any other consecutive slots between 2 and 6, there's no way to satisfy Rule 3. A little trial and error shows that L and O must be in slots 3 and 4, surrounded by G and P, in either order, in 2 and 5. N is left for slot 6.

Now, you're asked about the first three slots, and while there's some variability in slots 1 and 2 (slot 1 can be H or S, and slot 2 can be G or P), slot 3 is definitely reserved for L, so our best bet is to check the choices for that. This narrows the possibilities down to (A) and (C), and (A) is out for two reasons: First, G H L is an impossible way to start the sequence under any circumstances: Rule 1 would force O into slot 4, while Rule 3 would have it going to P. That's enough to eliminate (A). The other problem with (A) is that it doesn't fulfill the requirement in the stem: H, in slot two, is not the furthest it could be from S. That leaves (C): H G L is a possible beginning for the ordering under these circumstances, as long as you flesh it out with O P N S, in that order.

- Don't be afraid of a little trial and error—taking a few extra seconds to test out various arrangements before hitting the choices often pays off in a big way. Shrewd test takers look for ways to eliminate choices in bunches. Here, playing with the possibilities until noting that L is a definite for slot three is the way to kill (B), (D), and (E) in one fell swoop. Remember, though, that you have to make good judgments about the use of your time—a question that requires playing out different scenarios may be best left until the end of the game, not just to save time but because you may do some directed work on other questions that will help you find the answer.

4. C

What happens when P is fifth? G is second, and you're right back at question 1 again. Lucky for us, since you've already worked through this scenario: As you saw there, when G is second and P is fifth, L must be third, (C).

- "Too easy," you're thinking? Every Logic Games section has its share of low, medium, and high difficulty points, and the way to master the timing of the section and finish in 35 minutes is to snap up the easy points quickly, leaving extra time for the more difficult games and questions.
- Don't be surprised to see the same question asked in different forms. As you get on in a game,

strive to use previous work whenever possible to help answer questions, or at least eliminate a few choices. And in fact, you get another opportunity to apply this strategy in question 5.

5. E

What's the greatest number of tapes you can get between S and N? As mentioned just above, you can use our previous orderings to help you out here. You've seen the same partial ordering in questions 1 and 4:

$$\text{\_\_} \quad G\ L\ O\ P\ \text{\_\_}\ \text{\_\_}$$

Can you get all the tapes between S and N? Sure; if the familiar GLOP sequence occupies slots 2 through 5, you can place S into slot 1 and N into slot 1 (which leaves H for slot 6), and you're done. It is possible to fit all five of the other tapes between S and N, (E).

- When asked for a maximum in any situation, start with the greatest number possible. It makes no sense to test whether three time slots can come between S and N; even if the answer is yes, you'd still have to test four, and then five. Start at the highest number and work your way down. The same principle applies to handling the stem in question 3 here, in which you're asked to put as much distance as possible between H and S. Conversely, when asked for a *minimum*, start testing the smallest possible number and work your way up.
- The ordering above is not the only one that proves that S and N can be separated by all of the other tapes; S H P L O G N is another example. You could have gotten the point by constructing any one of a number of acceptable orderings that place S first and N last. But you're interested in *saving time*, and it's fastest to use previous work that's already down on the page.

6. C

Another quick point for work already done: You thought through L's limitations up front, so this one shouldn't take much more than a few seconds. Since both O and N must come after L, L cannot be played sixth or seventh, which means the latest slot possible for L is fifth, (C). And placing L fifth causes no other violations, as the ordering G H S P L O N readily proves.

- Don't be surprised to find a "gimme" late in the game. The questions are not presented in order of difficulty, and sometimes the test makers reward those who reach the end of games with a quick and easy point.

7.   D

You're looking for a time slot for G that will decisively fix the time slot for O, and once again previous work in questions 1 and 4 can help you out. In both of those questions, G was second, which forced L to be third and O to be fourth. "Second," which would therefore be a viable answer, is conspicuously absent; notice how the choices jump right from "first" to "third." This is not a problem, though, once you remember that G and P are interchangeable in this game. You can switch

$$\_\ G\ L\ O\ P\ \_\ \_$$

from questions 1 and 4 to

$$\_\ P\ L\ O\ G\ \_\ \_$$

without altering the logic in any way. P in 2 and G in 5 would thus force the same situation you've seen a number of times—L in 3 and O in 4. So placing G in slot 5 fixes O in slot 4, and (D) is correct for the final question of this first game.

For the record:

(A) If G is first, then P is fourth, and O can be slotted third or sixth.

(B) If G is third, then P is sixth, and O can be slotted second or fifth.

(C) If G is fourth, then P could be first, in which case O can be slotted third or sixth.

(E) If G is sixth, then P is third, and O can be slotted second or fifth.

- Again, it's fastest to rely on previous work, but it's not the only way to get the answer. You may have resorted to trying out the choices, in which case the method would be to put G first, then third, then fourth, and so on, each time testing for whether O can be fit into more than one possible slot. When you try G fifth, you'll find O is limited to slot 4, confirming (D) as the correct answer. This is a valid method, and *will* get the point. But since you've

seen a situation very much like this before, the better and *faster* way is to consult earlier work.

GAME 2—Doctor's Activities

The Action

Next you come face to face with the hectic world of one Doctor Yamata, who performs various activities during the course of a week. Scheduling events or activities during days of a week, mornings and afternoons, isn't too unusual—this common everyday scenario is the foundation of a number of games you'll encounter in a Kaplan course. One odd feature of this one, though, is the actual days of the week; notice that Thursday is missing (probably golf day). Hopefully you didn't breeze by this little wrinkle. The action mainly involves distributing four activities over the course of a week, which places the game in the grouping camp. Most schedule games have a heavy sequencing element, but here there's really only one true sequencing rule, Rule 3. And the questions don't really hinge on normal sequencing aspects, such as "before" and "after." So call this a grouping game of distribution with a slight sequencing element attached. You're asked to distribute activities over the course of a slightly irregular workweek.

The Initial Setup

A chart indicating the mornings and afternoons of Yamata's workdays (don't forget, no Thursday!) is in order here, with the activities listed underneath. There are numerous ways to shorthand the activities: For convenience, use L for lecturing, O for operating, T for treating patients, and C for conducting research.

	M	T	W	Th	F	S
AM				X		
PM				X		

L O T C

Note that the intro paragraph specifies that exactly one activity will be performed during each morning and afternoon shift, which eliminates the possibility of placing multiple letters in a single box. Our job, then, is to fill each box (time slot) with exactly one letter (activity) as directed by the rules and questions.

The Rules

1) Rule 1 narrows things down nicely—three of the five boxes in our top morning row will be filled with O's. You're not sure which yet, but it's a start. Sketch in "OOO" to the right of the morning row.

2) Rule 2 is an if-then rule, common to grouping games of distribution. If O Mon, no O Tues. Naturally, you want to think through the contrapositive, and get that down on the page as well: If O Tues, no O Mon. It's possible at this point to combine this with Rule 1, since both deal with operating. But hold off for now and wait until Step 4 of the Kaplan Method; you'll piece it all together below in the Deductions section.

3) Here's the sequencing rule alluded to: you need to place L's in the afternoon row on "exactly two *consecutive* calendar days." This raises the question "what *are* "consecutive calendar days" in this setup?" Here's where the missing Thursday comes into play. In Yamata's schedule, consecutive calendar days are Monday and Tuesday, Tuesday and Wednesday, and Friday and Saturday—*not Wednesday and Friday*. Wednesday and Friday are not "consecutive calendar days." For now, indicate the consecutive L's on the page, and move on.

4) Rule 4 tells you that you'll need to fit exactly one T in the morning row and exactly three T's in the afternoon row—another significant fact that you'll come back to in a jiffy.

5) Conducting research, C, gets into the act, or at least into the top morning row, exactly once. Indicate that near your other morning notes.

6) No L's or O's on Saturday, which turns out to be a key piece of information that allows you to blow this game wide open.

Deductions

Before reading these deductions, go back over the game and the rules and try to piece the puzzle together yourself. If you had no trouble the first time, and feel you got most or all of the deductions, that's great; you probably breezed through the questions, and you need not repeat this exercise. If you had trouble with this game, Step 4 of the Kaplan Method is the skill you need to work on, and this is a great game on which to practice making deductions.

Here's the objective: **It may take a few minutes, but it's possible to deduce a full 5 of the 10 calendar slots, and to narrow the other five down to a few possible activities.** When you've gone as far as you can go, check your work against the following Deductions.

Begin with the afternoon lectures. You need to place two L's on consecutive calendar days, and you know two major things: There can be no lecture on Saturday (Rule 6), so Friday-Saturday is impossible for the two consecutive L's; and, as discussed above, *Wednesday and Friday are not consecutive calendar days*. That means that the two afternoon lectures must be on Monday-Tuesday or on Tuesday-Wednesday. Either way, then, **Tuesday afternoon is devoted to lecturing, and the other afternoon lecture must be on Monday or Wednesday.** You also know that you must place exactly three T's in the afternoon slots (Rule 4), which along with the two L's completes the afternoon roster. Well, what slots are available? You just deduced that one L is on Tuesday afternoon. If the other afternoon L is scheduled for Monday, then treating patients would fall on Wednesday, Friday, and Saturday afternoons. If, however, the other afternoon L is on Wednesday, then treating patients would take place on Monday, Friday, and Saturday afternoons. Either way, **the good doctor must treat patients on Friday and Saturday afternoons. The other afternoon T will fall on Monday or Wednesday, whichever is not taken up by the remaining afternoon lecture.**

What about the morning time slots? The entities are set; you're to distribute 3 O's, 1 T, and 1 C into the five morning slots (Rules 1, 4, and 5). There's lots of information regarding the operating days, and operating takes up three of the five morning slots, so begin there. No O on Saturday—Rule 6 forbids it. That makes it easier: **Saturday morning will be devoted to treating patients or conducting research,** and you can focus on distributing 3 O's into the first four days—Monday, Tuesday, Wednesday, and Friday. And Rule 2 narrows down the possibilities even further: If she operates on Monday, then she doesn't operate on Tuesday, which means she must operate on Wednesday and Friday. Similarly, if she operates on Tuesday, then she doesn't operate on Monday (the contrapositive of Rule 2), and must again operate on Wednesday and Friday to satisfy Rule 1. Either way, **Yamata must operate on Wednesday and Friday mornings, and the third operating morning will be on Monday or Tuesday. Whichever activity is not on Saturday morning, T or C, will fall on Monday or Tuesday morning, the slot not taken by the final O.**

The Final Visualization

Whew! It may seem like a lot of time to spend up front, but as you'll see, compiling this great information into one sketch makes for quick, stress-free questions later on. Here's the load of deductions you have to work with heading into the questions:

	M	T	W	Th	F	S	
AM	O	X	O	X	O	T/C	OOO C T
PM	L/T	L	L/T	X	T	T	LL TTT

O
(with two arrows pointing down to M and W)

If O Mon, then no O Tues
If O Tues, then no O Mon

The Big Picture

- Some games have no significant Deductions. Others are *entirely based* on Deductions. The rest fall somewhere in the middle, containing one or two major deductions that make the questions more manageable. Granted, you can get points in this game without working through the steps described above, but this will probably take you much longer; you may be forced to reinvent the wheel for every question, and that involves time and stress. The most efficient and timely way to handle a game is to piece as much together as possible before hitting the questions. The point of your Logic Games practice is to hone and reinforce this skill. If you got most or all of the deductions on your own the first time around, great! Keep doing what you're doing. If not, use games like this as an opportunity to get to that level. That's what practice is for.

- Critical reading is essential for success on every section of the LSAT. Just because there's much less text in the Logic Games section than in the others doesn't mean you can read less carefully. In fact, just the opposite is the case: The relative brevity of the games makes every rule, every line, even every *word* that much more important—just think of the difference between "exactly" and "at least." And speaking of reading critically . . .

- When a rule like Rule 3 here uses a phrase like "consecutive calendar days," stop to make sure you know what that means *in the context of the game.* Here, Wednesday and Friday are not "consecutive calendar days." Those who overlooked this fact were in for a rough time of it.

The Questions

8. B

Tuesday afternoon is a definite lecture. Armed with our Deductions, question 8 is a definite five-second point.

(A), (C), (D) and (E) As you've seen, the second afternoon lecture must be on either Monday or Wednesday, so (A) and (C) are possible only, while (D) and (E) are flat out impossible.

9. C

As you deduced, operating is a must for Wednesday morning, which narrows the choices down to (C) and (D). The Wednesday afternoon activity must be either lecturing or treating patients, which confirms (C) and eliminates (D) as the possible schedule for Wednesday.

Questions 10 and 11 follow question 12.

12. E

Right off the sketch: Treating patients is the activity for Friday and Saturday afternoon, (E).

- Like many battles, this game is won or lost in the planning stage, that is, in the setup. Proper work up front saves time, cuts down on stress, and boosts confidence during Step 5 of the Kaplan Method, answering the questions. If you've put in the work, this is the reward.

- While questions 10 and 11 require a little more thought, the answers to questions 8, 9, and 12 can be simply read off the final sketch, which is why you should do them together. If you've started honing your time management skills, you may have even done the questions in this order. When so much has been deduced, try scanning the questions for things that have already been determined (non-"ifs" are a good bet).

- In Logic Games, confidence is key—don't second-guess yourself. If you've made deductions up front, *use them.* Trust your Final Visualization: It's based on your understanding of the game, and if you took your time and were careful, there's no reason to doubt your work now. The questions *should* largely be falling into your lap—that's your reward for all your great thinking up front.

10. E

Another non-"if," but this one's a little more involved. Still, all you need to do is check the choices against the sketch.

(A) Must Yamata treat patients on both shifts of a single day? She treats patients in the afternoon on Saturday, but could conduct research Saturday morning. Friday has T in the afternoon and O in the morning. And the final afternoon T could be on Wednesday, a day on which she operates in the morning. So (A) need not be true.

(B) Must she conduct research and lecture on the same day? No—the two afternoon L's could be scheduled for Tuesday and Wednesday, both days on which Yamata can perform operations in the morning.

(C) Must she conduct research and treat patients on the same day? No—Yamata could treat patients on Wednesday, Friday, and Saturday afternoons, while conducting research only on Monday morning.

(D) Must she lecture and treat patients on the same day? No—the one morning T can be placed on Saturday, far away from the two afternoon L's.

(E) must be correct. And in fact, there's no way to avoid having at least one day containing a lecture and operation. One lecture is always Tuesday, and the other is Monday or Wednesday. If it's on Monday, then you have L's Monday and Tuesday, and exactly one operation must fall on either Monday or Tuesday morning. If, however, the second afternoon lecture is on Wednesday, then that's all you need to know: Yamata must operate on Wednesday morning, so no matter how you space out the afternoon lectures, there will always be at least one day containing both a lecture and operation.

- The more writing you do up front—that is, the more deductions you make—the less writing you'll need to do during the questions stage. In most cases, you won't need to lift your pencil for a non-"if" question; just follow the directions in the stem and look for the answer in your master sketch, or check each choice against the sketch, as the case may be.

- Here's another way to save time: When trying out choices, if you've eliminated four, choose the other by process of elimination without checking it. This goes back to the point made above regarding confidence: If you have it, you trust your work, and are comfortable penciling in (E) without bothering to check it, because you know that (A) through (D) are wrong, and there has to be *some* answer. Less confident gamesters, on the other hand, think "Oh

no, I may have done something wrong. Better work out (E) . . ." Try to get out of this habit; work through a remaining choice only if you're *really* unsure of your work on the others.

- In a "must be true" question, the correct answer often involves one or more of the most restricted entities. If you need to try out the choices, you can possibly save some time by trying these choices first.

11. E

Here's our first "if" question—suppose that Yamata operates on Tuesday. No problem; that means that the days for operations are set at Tuesday, Wednesday, and Friday, and you're interested in when she can possibly treat patients. According to Rule 4, she must treat patients on exactly three afternoons; that alone eliminates (A) and (B), which include only two afternoons. Furthermore, you know from our work up front that she must treat patients Friday and Saturday afternoons; in fact, that's the answer to question 12, and allows you to delete (C), which leaves out Friday afternoon. (D) falls by the wayside, because operating is scheduled for Wednesday morning. (E) is all that remains, and represents a perfectly valid schedule for treating patients.

- Notice how the if-clause in the stem was unnecessary, as you were able to eliminate all of the wrong choices straight from the rules and deductions. Occasionally the test makers will throw in a superfluous "if"—but it doesn't happen often. In any case, don't worry if you think you can answer the question without enacting the if-clause; this situation is not without precedent.

GAME 3—Conservatives, Moderates, and Liberals

The Action

You're presented with seven judges, each of whom voted either for or against a petition. One way to look at this is that each entity is either in or out, which strongly suggests grouping—specifically a grouping game of selection. The entities are two conservatives, two moderates, and three liberals.

The Initial Setup

First, get the basics down on the page. Since it's a Selection game, start with a list of the entities; as you work through the rules, circle the fors and cross out the againsts.

C C M M L L L

The Rules

4) A quick scan of the rules tells you that Rule 4 is the most concrete, and you can put this information right into the sketch: At least one conservative votes against Datalog, which means that you can cross out one C.

3) While you're at it, you may as well take care of Rule 3, and save the two conditional rules for last. Rule 3 tells you that at least two judges vote for Datalog, and at least two against. Take a moment to give some thought to what this rule means. There are seven judges, and they all vote. That means that a requirement for at least two fors and at least two againsts strictly limits our possible breakdowns—you could have a 2-5 split or a 3-4 split. Those are the only possibilities that comply with this rule.

1) Now the if-thens: If both conservatives and at least one liberal voted the same way, then both moderates voted that way as well. Thanks to Rule 4, you can take this one step further (although if this didn't jump out at you, you'd save this for the Deduction step). You know from that rule that at least one conservative said nay. Thus, if both conservatives and at least one liberal voted the same way, then that way must be against. The rule then tells you that under these circumstances, the two moderates will vote against as well:

C̶ C̶ M̶ M̶ L̶ L L

Now you may have taken this rule even further, or you may have waited until Step 4 of the Kaplan Method. If you handled the rules in order from 1 to 4, that's probably what you did, but since you've already incorporated Rules 3 and 4, continue. Since you still need two votes in favor of the petition (Rule 3), in this situation the two remaining liberals must have voted for it. So Rule 1, if enacted, really boils down to this:

If both Cs vote against and one L votes against, then:

C̶ C̶ M̶ M̶ L̶ L̇ L̇

Remember, though, that this rule is conditional—what you just played out happens only **if** two conservatives and one liberal vote the same. This doesn't, therefore, go in your master sketch—if you thought this through in advance, a little sketch off to the side to reflect the implications of this rule is in order.

2) If the three liberals voted the same, then neither conservative voted that way, which is to say that both conservatives voted the other way. You can shorthand this any way that makes sense to you. Here's one possibility:

If Ls the same, then Cs opposite

Now take a further look at the implications of this rule in "Deductions."

Deductions

You've already worked through a few implications of the rules by combining the more concrete Rules 3 and 4 with the first two if-then rules. But a little extra thought will reveal one more major thing—did you see it? It's derived by combining Rules 2 and 4.

If the three liberals voted the same, then both conservatives voted the opposite, and you know from Rule 4 that at least one conservative voted against. So the situation works if all three liberals voted *for* the petition, in which case both conservatives must have voted against. But the other option is impossible: If all the liberals voted *against* the petition, then Rule 2 would require that both conservatives vote *for* it. But that would violate Rule 4, so it's impossible for all three liberals to vote against the petition. Which means, driving this thought to completion, that **at least one liberal must have voted for the petition.** This insight bags questions 14 and 15 directly, and is just useful knowledge throughout. Circle an L (and you can make your shorthand for Rule 2 more specific thanks to this deduction). Now you're ready to attack the questions.

The Final Visualization

Here's what a good final sketch might look like:

C C M M L Ⓛ L

at least 2 FOR
at least 2 AGAINST
if both Cs AGAINST and 1 L AGAINST, then both Ms
AGAINST and 2 Ls FOR
if all Ls FOR, then both Cs AGAINST

The Big Picture

- Use your experience on previous games to help you grasp the action of each game you face. While the games each have different characters and settings, their logical structures repeat over and over again. Here, voting for or against a petition is the same as any other yes/no decision for an entity—deciding whether an entity goes on a boat trip or not, sits on a committee or not, is selected as a book for a course or not, and so on. In each case, each entity is either in or out. Seen in this light, this game is nothing more than a standard grouping game of selection, and should be treated as such.

- You need not tackle the rules in the order given on the page. A concrete rule like Rule 4 here is a good rule to begin with because it allows you to add information directly into the sketch, which often makes it easier to assimilate the other rules. Getting something definite on the page gives you some substance around which the more abstract rules can be worked out.

- Always drive information toward the concrete. "If the two conservatives voted the same way . . ." in Rule 1 means something very definite in light of Rule 4. It means "if both conservatives voted *against* . . ." Always translate statements in light of the other information at your disposal. Here's a tangible example of how handling the concrete Rule 4 first pays off when dealing with the more abstract Rule 1.

The Questions

13. B

If the moderates split their votes, then one voted for and the other voted against. Quickly jot this down in a new sketch:

C C M Ⓜ Ⓛ L L

The contrapositive of Rule 1, which you should have noted earlier in the setup stage, is that if the moderates split their votes, then it cannot be true that both conservatives and at least one liberal voted the same way. But following this train of thought gets a little messy, because there are a few different ways to ensure this doesn't happen. The better method here, since you're dealing with a "could be true" question, is to test the choices against the sketch just created and eliminate those that contradict the information.

(A) The voting arrangement that would result from (A) would violate Rule 1: you would have both conservatives and one liberal voting against the petition, which, according to Rule 1, would force both moderates to vote against as well. But the stem has it otherwise.

(B) works. It looks like this:

C Ⓒ M Ⓜ Ⓛ L̸ L̸

However, don't play it out until you consider whether the remaining choices can be quickly eliminated—what *can't* happen is far more concrete than what *might* happen.

(C) violates Rule 2—if all three liberals voted for the petition, then both conservatives would have to vote against, but (C) has one of the conservatives voting in favor of the petition.

(D) and (E) both violate Rule 4, which requires at least one "nay" among the conservatives.

- Don't hesitate to redraw a master sketch when new information is given; it takes very little time to jot down a few Cs, Ms, and Ls on the page. Plus, you'll then have representative scenarios to look back on later.

14. C

Here's the reward for the deduction described above—you deduced that at least one liberal must have voted for the petition. That's because if all the liberals voted no, Rule 2 would have both conservatives voting yes. But Rule 4 disallows that, which means that it cannot be true that all the liberals voted against, which in turn means that at least one liberal must have voted in favor of the petition, (C).

(A) and (B) No, all the liberals could vote in favor of the petition, in which case both conservatives would vote against.

(D) and (E) The moderates can swing all possible ways; as you saw in question 13, they can split their votes. On the other hand, both can vote for, or both can vote against, so (D) and (E) both *could* be true, but need not be.

- If you didn't make the "liberal" deduction early on, you're forced to work it out here. That's not the end of the world—the game is not all lost. The important thing is to realize that the answer here is something that must be true without any conditional circumstances—that is, without being derived from a hypothetical—which means that it must be true for the *entire game*, not just for this question. If it's not already in your master sketch, build it in as if it were a given rule.

- If you must resort to testing the choices in a "must be true" question, try to *prove the exception*. For example, in (A), to test whether at least one conservative must have voted for the petition, see if it's possible that *no* conservatives voted for it. Since this *is* possible, you've proven an exception to (A), which shows that (A) need not be true and should be crossed off. However, this is a time-consuming process compared to the direct approach, and when it's necessary you should consider leaving that question until the end of the game.

15. E

Now, whether you made the deduction regarding the liberals early on, or just now in the previous question, you can and should use this information to bag question 15. If all three liberals voted the same way . . . yup, that's right, they must all vote *for*, because it's impossible for all of them to vote against, for reasons elaborated just above and in the "Deductions" section. And there's the point in (E).

With the liberals all voting for the petition, Rule 2 mandates that both conservatives vote against. So here's what you know of the voting so far:

$$\ell \; \ell \quad M \; M \quad Ⓛ Ⓛ Ⓛ$$

(A), (B) and (D) As Rule 1 is not in effect here, the moderates are totally free to vote any old way: both for, both against, or one each way. So these three choices all *could* be true, but need not be.

(C) is impossible—as shown above, both conservatives have to vote "nay" in this situation.

- Use your work on the first few questions to pick up insights you may have missed during the setup stage. If you made the deductions you discussed earlier, then questions 14 and 15 should have been a breeze. This is why you should strive to make deductions up front. But if you didn't see these things, then at least you could have picked up these points now, and in the process seen that at least one liberal must always vote yes, and that Rule 2 is only applicable in one direction—if the three liberals vote together, it must be for, not against.

16. A

Your job in this one is to figure out how you can fit exactly two no votes (which means five votes for) into the sketch. You already know one definite no, a conservative thanks to Rule 4. And you've seen, most recently in question 15, the case in which both conservatives vote against the petition. Filling out the rest in line with the stem's mandate results in this arrangement:

$$\ell \; \ell \quad Ⓜ Ⓜ \quad Ⓛ Ⓛ Ⓛ$$

No problems there; but is this the only way to get a 2-5 breakdown of "nays" to "yeas"? Giving the second *against* to one of the moderates doesn't work—then all three liberals vote *for*, which according to Rule 2 means that both conservatives would have to vote *against*. But if the second (and therefore last) against goes to a moderate, the other conservative would have to vote in favor, which cannot be. So it's impossible for a moderate here to cast the second against vote, which means both moderates must vote for the petition, (A).

You may have waited until you worked out the other possible scenario before moving to the choices, in which case you would have worked out this arrangement:

This is the only other way to satisfy the stem, which again confirms that (A) must be true. As for the wrong choices, they all *could* be true, but need not be: (C) and (E) are true in the first possible scenario but not in the second. (B) and (D) are true in the second but not in the first.

- Some "if" questions specify an exact occurrence, and others, like this one, are more vague. You're told that exactly two judges voted against, but you're not told *which*—that would give it all away. So you must make it concrete. Ask yourself "How can this happen?"—and the first thing to do is to see if it's happened before in earlier questions. That gets you halfway there, but you still have to inquire if there are *other* possible ways to place exactly two votes against, and in this case, there is one more possible scenario. Armed with the only two possible voting schemes, you can answer any question thrown your way.

- In a "must be true" question, scan the choices whenever you discover something new. Here, you could have picked up the point as soon as you noticed that the second against couldn't go to a moderate.

17. E

We're looking for the choice that contains the list of judges that cannot be a complete and accurate list of judges in favor of the petition. Before jumping into complicated scenarios, see if you can derive the answer by checking the choices against the concrete rules, Rules 3 and 4. Rule 4 is easy—there must always be at least one conservative voting against the petition, so if any choice contains two conservatives, that must be the answer (remember, the entities in the choices represent judges voting *for* the petition). No luck. But Rule 3 does the trick. Are there any choices that would result in a lack of two judges on either side? Yes: (E) uses every judge but one conservative, which would result in six "yeas" and only one "nay." Just add 'em up—six judges voting in favor of the proposal is a direct violation of Rule 3.

- Translate complex-sounding stems into a workable framework—something that will inform your attack on the question. When asking if certain judges can constitute a "complete and accurate list of those judges who voted for Datalog," the test makers are really asking whether you can circle those judges and cross out the rest. Translated this way, the test for each choice is fairly straightforward.

- Always keep the numbers aspect of the game in the forefront of your mind—sometimes, as here, working out the numbers will lead to a shortcut. All you had to do was add up the number of judges in (E) to see that it's impossible for all the members in that group of judges to vote yes to the petition.

- All rules are *not* created equal: Concrete rules like Rules 3 and 4 are usually easier to work with than conditional rules like Rules 1 and 2, so gravitate toward the concrete whenever you have a choice of rules with which to begin your attack on a question.

18. B

Take it one step at a time: The conservatives voted the same way, which means (thanks to Rule 4) that they both voted no. Next you're told that the liberals didn't all vote the same way. You deduced (and saw later in question 14) that at least one liberal must vote for the petition, so now you know that at least one must vote against. So far then, this is how the votes went:

$$\mathcal{C}\ \mathcal{C}\ M\ M\ L\ \textcircled{L}\ \mathcal{L}$$

This situation triggers Rule 1—both conservatives and at least one liberal voted the same way, against—which means that both moderates must vote against as well. But wait—you may as well complete the voting: With only one *for* vote out of six so far, Rule 3 requires that the remaining liberal vote for the petition, resulting in:

$$\mathcal{C}\ \mathcal{C}\ M\ M\ \textcircled{L}\ \mathcal{L}\ \textcircled{L}$$

Every choice conforms to this arrangement except (B), which is impossible (and therefore correct): Under these circumstances, both moderates must have voted against, not for the petition.

- Take complicated stems apart. When a stem contains more than one new "if" incorporate one at a time into a new sketch, and then see how the resulting situation is affected by the rules.

- Read the stems carefully, and don't overlook the word EXCEPT. It's capitalized to make it stand out on the page, but in the heat of the moment some test takers do all the right work but then miss this word, and answer the wrong question. It's a shame to miss a point for this reason, and since the Logic Games section contains such a variety of stems (*must be true, could be true, must be false, could be false, is impossible, cannot be true,* and so on), it's not a bad idea to double-check each stem just before moving to the choices, just to make sure you're answering the question that was asked.

GAME 4—Runners and Charities

The Action

Next up you have runners in five consecutively numbered lanes, which immediately suggests sequencing, and indeed, you will be concerned with the order of the runners in the five lanes. But you have another concern as well—the runners are also matched up with charities, so in fact the game is a sequencing/matching hybrid.

The Initial Setup

Since there are two levels to this sequence, put the lane numbers on the page with the runners and charities listed off to the side, like so:

	1	2	3	4	5
LNOPS					
fghjk					

With this setup, you have space in your sketch to insert the line of runners, as well as space for the charities the runners represent. As this also makes the matchups of runners to charities readily apparent, both game actions can be accommodated within this one simple sketch.

The Rules

1) Nice and concrete: You can insert k right into lane 4 in the lower line of our sketch. And, since each runner represents a different charity, cross k off your list.

2) This is slightly complex in that it posits a relationship between runner P and charities f and g. The use of the word "only" in this rule tells you that no other runner besides P comes between charities f and g, so whether it's fPg or gPf, this trio will form a solid bloc somewhere in the sketch. Jot this down off to the side for now, and come back to analyze its implications during Step 4 of the Kaplan Method. Keep your notations in a structure consistent with your sketch.

$$\begin{array}{ccc} P & & P \\ f \_\_ g & or & g \_\_ f \end{array}$$

3) Rule 3 also deals with both a runner and charity, in this case runner O and charity g:

$$O \_\_ \underset{g \;\; or \;\; g}{\_\_\_\_\_} O$$

4) Here's a straightforward sequencing rule involving only runners:

$$N \ldots S$$

is a perfect reminder of this, and you're ready to combine the rules and see what you can deduce.

Deductions

Now, remember what you said back in Game 2 (and applied in Game 3): One of the best ways to find deductions is to focus on duplications—entities that appear in more than one rule, and here, that entity is charity g. So investigate the possible lanes for charity g. Rule 1 places charity k in lane 4, which severely restricts g's position: In order to satisfy Rule 2 (that is, to get P between g's lane and f's lane), g's lane can only be lanes 1, 3, or 5—that k in 4 prevents any other possibility. But lane 3 is impossible for g because of Rule 3: If g is in 3, there's no way to get exactly two lanes between g and runner O. Therefore, you have limited options. **Charity g must be in either lane 1 or lane 5**, so it's worth investigating what happens in both cases. And, in either case, f must be in Lane 3.

OPTION 1:

If g is in lane 1, then runner P is in lane 2, followed by charity f in lane 3 (Rule 2). Rule 3 kicks in, forcing runner O to lane 4, along with charity k, which is always in that lane. That leaves charities h and j to float between lanes 2 and 5, and runners N, S, and free agent L to fill in remaining lanes 1, 3, and 5, so long as N precedes S (Rule 4). This first option, therefore, boils down to this:

	1	2	3	4	5
NSL		P		O	
	g	h/j	f	k	h/j

You may note that in this option lane 5 must go to runner S or L, as N can't be in 5. You can write this in if you like, or simply deal with the remaining runners accordingly in each question.

OPTION 2:

If g is in lane 5, then runner P is in lane 4 (along with k), and charity f takes lane 3, again thanks to Rule 2. Rule 3 forces O into lane 2. Again, charities h and j will float, this time between lanes 1 and 2. And again, runners N, S, and L will take lanes 1, 3 and 5, with N before S in 1 or 3 and S or L in 5. Here's this second option:

	1	2	3	4	5
N...S L		O		P	
	h/j	h/j	f	k	g

Notice that **charity f is in lane 3** in both options, which means that this is another solid deduction that must hold for the entire game.

The Final Visualization

This now consists of the two options on the page. Every acceptable ordering and matchup will have to correspond to one of these two options, which will lighten our workload considerably when it comes to answering the questions.

The Big Picture

- When a major entity in the game is limited to one of two positions, it's usually worth working out what happens in each case. The resulting scenarios are "limited options," and when you can reduce the possibilities down to a pair of options, your work in the questions will be greatly reduced.

- Once again, it may seem like a lot of work up front, but working out limited option scenarios actually goes faster than you might imagine if you work methodically and keep your cool. The opportunity for some quick and easy points should be incentive enough to take the little bit of extra time.

- Don't be intimidated by a game that has more than one game action; if you can handle a basic sequencing game, and are comfortable with matching games, then a hybrid of the two need not be unusually difficult. If you use your experience from past games to help you handle each game action, you shouldn't have unusual difficulty with a game that combines those actions.

- In games that contain more than one group of entities, it's imperative that you keep them straight. Here, some rules are about the runners, some about the charities, and some about both. As you'll see below, the same goes for the questions. Pay careful attention to the information thrown your way, and continually ask yourself which group is the relevant one for the task at hand. Use different notation for each group, like the capital and lower-case letters you've used above.

The Questions

19. E

This Acceptability question is your first opportunity to use the options you created—note that you're concerned only with charities here. You deduced that in both options, charity f must be in lane 3, which allows you to quickly eliminate (A), (B), and (D). Of the remaining choices, (C) violates Rule 1—k must be in lane 4—which is why the ordering in (C) doesn't jibe with either of the options listed on the page. (E) remains and gets the point.

- Acceptability questions aren't just quick points— they're useful tools, providing you with a first-hand opportunity to see how the rules and entities interrelate, and to test out any deductions or limited option scenarios you may have come upon in the setup stage.
- Even if you hadn't worked out the two options above, an acceptability question is always eminently doable using the Kaplan method—just take each rule in turn and check each choice against it until only one choice remains.

20. D

In Option 1, P is in lane 2 and O is in lane 4. In Option 2, they're reversed: O is in 2 and P is in 4. Either way, (D) has it right: P and O must be separated by exactly one lane.

(A) In Option 1, P is in lane 2 and L can take lane 5.

(B) and (C) In Option 2, P is in lane 4 and N can be in lane 1. So contrary to both (B) and (C), it's possible to have exactly two lanes between the lanes of P and N.

(E) is impossible: In Option 1, S is either right next to P or separated by two lanes from P; in Option 2, S, in lanes 3 or 5, is always right next to P.

- The beauty of limited options is that the full range of possibilities for each entity is pretty much established on the page. So when a question asks about a specific entity, you need only to find that entity in each option and note how it behaves.

21. B

Here's your first "if" question, and it steers you clearly toward Option 2, the only option in which O is in lane 2. All you need to do is check the choices against Option 2, looking for the assignment that must be made. Charity g in lane 5 is the one the test makers chose, (B).

(A) and (D) are impossible—charity f must always be in lane 3.

(C) is only possible; in Option 2, h *could* be in lane 1, but could also be in lane 2, with j in 1.

(E) No—in Option 2, charity j must be in either lane 1 or 2.

- In a game in which you're able to create limited options, use the if-clauses in the question stems to direct you to the option that's in effect. Very often, the new "if" will lead to one and only one of the options, which narrows down the possible arrangements even further and makes your work that much easier.

22. D

Rule 2 directly rules out Patricia as f's representative, as Patricia must run in the lane *between* the lanes of charities f and g. That eliminates (B) and (E). Both Larry and Ned appear in all of the remaining choices, so those runners must be part of the correct list, and you need not bother with them. The question then boils down to Olivia and Sonja. If neither can represent f, then (A) is it. If only O can, then you choose (C), and if Sonja can, (D) is the winner. A glance at either option on the page confirms that Sonja can represent f, a charity that you know is always in lane 3.

- Look for shortcuts when putting together a "complete and accurate list." If you've eliminated some choices, and the remaining ones all have certain entities in common, then those entities must be part of the list, and need not be checked. Zero in on the *differences* between the remaining choices, and look for the simplest test that will allow you to single out the winner.

23. B

For the sake of comparison, approach this question without the benefit of the limited options worked out above. Ned is to represent charity j, and you need to determine what must be true. For all you know, there are lots of ways this can happen, and as there's not much information on Ned (only Rule 4, which doesn't narrow things down much) and *no* information on charity j (a "free agent"), you have no choice but to pop N and j into lanes and see how they fare.

What about lane 1? If N represents j in lane 1, nothing is triggered directly, so you'd better consider the large bloc of entities, the fPg bloc. With charity k always in lane 4, and j now in lane 1, the only way to space charities f and g with exactly one lane between them for P would be to place them in lanes 3 and 5, with P in lane 4. But f and g could theoretically go in either order, so which is in 3 and which is in 5? You just have to try it out, in which case you find that g in 3 is impossible, because there would be no way to satisfy Rule 3. (More perceptive test takers might realize at this point that g can *never* be in 3, but others who proceed piecemeal like this may not realize this and think that this observation only applies to this question, thereby diminishing the value of this important insight.) So in this case, with N representing j in lane 1, charity f must be in 3 and charity g in 5, which forces runner O and the one remaining charity, h, into lane 2.

Whew! Are you done? No; all you've done is prove that N *can* represent j in lane 1, which would help you in a "could be true question," but is only part of the battle in a "must be true" question. For all you know, N and j can occupy other lanes, so you now have to test out other scenarios. What about N and j in lane 2? The only way to place the fPg bloc would be to place them again in lanes 3, 4, and 5, respectively, but this leads to a violation: Rule 3 would then force O into lane 2, but you've just placed N there.

Moving along, could N and j take lane 3? No, because there's no way to then place the fPg bloc at all. Lane 4 is off limits, because charity k already occupies that space, and lane 5 is no good, because N can never be in lane 5, lest it violate Rule 4.

So after this somewhat lengthy analysis, you've proven that there's only one lane in which N can represent charity j, and it leads to this scenario:

	1	2	3	4	5
N...S L	N	O	S/L	P	S/L
	j	H	f	k	g

Now you're in a position to recognize for sure what must be true—charity h's runner is assigned to lane 2, (B). All of the other choices here must be false:

(A) No, charity g's runner is assigned to lane 5.

(C) No, Patricia represents charity k here.

(D) and (E) No, Olivia represents charity h here.

- It's hard to backtrack to this piecemeal approach once you've worked out the two possible scenarios, the limited options. But the exercise makes a point: If you take the rules at face value, and don't look for implications, deductions, or limited options up front, many Logic Games questions will require the kind of extensive work described here. You can eventually arrive at the right answers, but the section would probably take longer than 35 minutes. This "brute force" approach to Logic Games is like coming at a wooden door with a hammer rather than a key. You may get in eventually, but at what cost? In Logic Games, the cost of a plodding approach is *time*. It does no good to get every question you attempt right, if you only get to half the questions. Incidentally . . .

- With the benefit of using our limited options, question 23 would go something like this: In Option 1, j is either in lane 2, represented by P, or lane 5, a lane off limits to N (Rule 4). This means that Option 2 must be in effect here, the option in which j is either in lanes 1 or 2. If j is to be matched up with N, it must be in lane 1, because O takes lane 2 in this option. That leaves charity h for lane 2, (B). Limited options allow you to see quickly what must happen when N and j pair up.

24. A

Finally, you're looking for an acceptable ordering of runners if Larry is matched with charity j. Your options help you immediately: No matter what, O and P must take lanes 2 and 4, in either order. But three of the five choices—(B), (C), and (E)—don't conform to this, and can be axed on this basis alone. That leaves (A) and (D), both acceptable orderings in general, but obviously one will not accord with the mandate in the stem. Both have O in lane 2 and P in lane 4, which places this scenario squarely in Option 2. In that Option, charity j is either in lane 1 or lane 2, and if L is to be matched with j, it must be in lane 1, leaving N and S to lanes 3 and 5, respectively (Rule 4). L O N P S works, and therefore could be the assignment of runners to lanes under these conditions.

- It's important to know how to look for and work out limited options within games, but it's also vital to know how to *use* them to answer questions. Just because you generate the options doesn't necessarily guarantee success on the game. Go back, if necessary, and review how the options on the page were best used to generate quick points, and resolve to investigate limited option scenarios whenever the opportunity arises.

SECTION III: READING COMPREHENSION

Passage 1—Working Women

Topic and Scope

Working parents in the labor force; specifically, the problems that working mothers face in a world that seems hostile to their goals and responsibilities

Purpose and Main Idea

The author's purpose is to describe the conditions in the workplace that disadvantage working parents, especially women. The main idea surfaces in its full form at the end: If the job market continues to be inflexible, and thus hostile toward parents, and if women still have to bear most of the burden of child care, then women will continue to be disadvantaged in the labor market.

Paragraph Structure

Paragraph 1 describes how the labor force is structured in such a way that workers' family responsibilities are ignored. Examples are given that demonstrate how regular full-time workdays, combined with everyday chores, don't allow the flexibility needed by parents who are responsible for child care. The topic is evident, but the specific focus on women's difficulties is yet to come.

Paragraph 2 introduces the notion that among working parents, women suffer the disadvantages of the workplace more than men. There's also a second point made here that further complicates the plight of the working mother—women are under greater cultural pressure to take responsibility for child care than men.

Paragraphs 3 and 4 spell out in greater detail the specific problems of working mothers. Paragraph 3 focuses on the disadvantages of part-time work, while paragraph four outlines the problems of mothers who work full-time. The final sentence of the passage is a reflection of the first sentence, but with a particular emphasis on the problems of women. If workplace conditions and cultural standards don't change, women will continue to be seriously disadvantaged in the labor market.

The Big Picture

- Always keep your eye out for the author's main idea, no matter where in the passage it may appear. Don't always expect the main idea to jump out of the first paragraph; in some passages, the main idea doesn't fully emerge until the end. This is the case here: The first three paragraphs establish the topic and scope, and offer many examples that support the author's own skepticism that emerges fully in the last sentence.

- Very often, the scope of the passage will be clearly defined by the end of the first paragraph, but that's not always the case. Remain open to slight shifts, particularly, a narrowing of the scope as the passage develops. In paragraph 1, the scope seems to include "working parents," but paragraph two suggests that the author is concerned mainly with the case of women. The examples presented in the last two paragraphs bear this out.

The Questions

1. E

This Global question asks about the passage's big idea, which is developed throughout but emphasized in the last sentence. You should be able to prephrase this answer: you're looking for a statement to the effect that women have great difficulty pursuing a career while raising children. (E) tells you that traditional workplace organization is too rigid, which makes it difficult for working parents to both work and care for their children. Furthermore, this especially disadvantages working mothers, which is precisely the author's message.

(A) Nothing in the passage suggests that the author believes that life will get easier for working parents, or that there is a trend toward flexibility in the working world, so this isn't the main idea.

(B) captures some of the flavor of the author's feelings, but the author's criticism is directed more toward the inflexibility of the working world than toward traditional family roles. Sure, the author feels that cultural pressures on women to care for children exacerbate the problem, but this isn't the main message. In any case, you cannot infer that changes in traditional family roles are *necessary* for equal opportunity.

(C) is beyond the scope of the passage, since you have hardly any information about single parents and their work life and none about a comparison between single mothers and single fathers.

(D) centers on a comparison that the author never makes. The author makes a point of saying in the last paragraph that *both* professional and nonprofessional working mothers are disadvantaged by inflexible work schedules, but never indicates which group is better at dealing with the situation. (Even if this comparison were indicated, it still wouldn't be the main idea of the passage.)

- In Global questions, beware of choices like (B) that capture only part of the author's true intent. (B) correctly notes the author's skepticism, but directs it toward the wrong target.

2.   D

Part-time work is the subject of paragraph 3. The last sentence of this paragraph tells you that although part-time work isn't personally enriching, it does allow women "flexibility to fulfill their family duties" (line 37). In the context of this passage, women's family duties include primary child-rearing responsibilities. Choice (D) connects the phrase "family duties" to its meaning in the context of the passage, and that's why (D) is inferable.

(A) erroneously reverses the statistic in the second sentence of the third paragraph, so look back there. One-third of working mothers work part-time; but you certainly can't conclude from this that one-third of part-time workers are working mothers. Familiar language in answer choices can mislead you if you attempt to rely on memory rather than the text.

(B) According to the passage, part-time work is intrinsically flawed because it offers little opportunity for challenge or advancement. But there's no basis for comparing working mothers to *women in general* in this respect. You can't infer that part-time work is more limiting for working mothers than it is for women in general.

(C) is not inferable because the passage doesn't indicate anything about part-time employees working during holidays. The closest the passage comes to "holidays" is the talk about "vacations" in paragraph 1, but this has no relation to the discussion of part-time work in paragraph 3.

(E) attempts to combine two unrelated elements. The passage discusses part-time work and full-time work, but does not discuss the possibility of part-time work *leading to* full-time careers. Again, this is a connection you cannot make.

- For many Reading Comp Inference questions, you'll need to translate a word or phrase into its meaning within the larger context of the passage.

- Beware of choices that attempt to combine two or more elements of the passage in a way that the author never intends. Many wrong choices, like (C) and (E) here, use the passage's language but distort its ideas.

3.   C

You're looking for another inference: something left unsaid that's nonetheless strongly supported. Working fathers in two-parent families are discussed in paragraph 2: When both parents work, cultural pressures put the primary responsibility for child rearing on women. If women in two-parent families have primary child-rearing responsibilities, you can infer that working fathers, thanks to these cultural traditions, have secondary, or lesser, child-rearing responsibilities.

(A) contradicts the theme of the passage. The author makes it clear that women bear the greater brunt of the labor market disadvantages in the two-parent working couple.

(B) is outside the scope; you know nothing about the possible workaholic tendencies of husbands that might lead them to ignore injustice.

(D) and (E) both heap blame on men themselves for women's problems in the labor force, but the issue of who is to blame is never really addressed in the passage. You're told that the labor market works against the priorities of parents, but you can't infer from this that working fathers in two-parent families compound the problem (D), or are the ones responsible for the "traditional roles" (E)—the author simply cites cultural pressures as the cause for this. Blame, if anywhere, must go to the system and society itself; ascribing it to this specific group, "working fathers in two-parent families," is unwarranted.

- Read critically! There's a big difference between saying "this system is terrible" and saying "here's who to blame." The author does a lot of the former, and little if any of the latter. Recognizing this allows you to axe (D) and (E) quickly.

4. B

We've seen that the author believes that inflexible work schedules and gender-based allocation of family roles are the reasons why working mothers occupy a disadvantaged place in the work force. But this question asks for the most troublesome barrier for working parents, not just mothers, so the answer must have something to do with the rigidity of work schedules. This is supported in lines 12–15 ("Conventional workdays . . . are too inflexible for parents"); paragraph 3 (working mothers are forced to take part-time work for the flexibility, but at the expense of the benefits of full-time work); and paragraph 4 (professionals and nonprofessionals alike have to sacrifice in all kinds of ways in order to secure the flexibility needed to raise children).

(A) is barking up the wrong tree: The author says nothing about a lack of full-time jobs available to women; rather, full-time work is not practically feasible for many working mothers, which is not the same as saying that it's not *available*.

(C) and (D) focus on details about part-time work and nonprofessional employees, but neither is important enough to be cited as the "most troublesome barrier" facing working parents. Both of these details are part of the larger problem, which is that the inflexible structure of the workplace forces some parents to even consider such positions in the first place.

(E) The allocation of workplace responsibilities based on gender is outside the scope. The author doesn't deal with gender-based issues in the workplace, but rather with the factors that determine whether certain kinds of people (working parents) can even take certain jobs in the first place.

- Prephrase answers to the fullest extent possible. This may seem like a detail-oriented question, but in truth it's really asking you what the author thinks is the biggest problem with the system, and that question is answered throughout the passage: Inflexible schedules create all kinds of problems for working parents.

- Expect at least two (and sometimes even three) questions in a Reading Comp set to be very similar. The reason for this is that the test makers like to test the main idea in different ways. Despite their differences, questions 1 and 4 in this set test the same basic thing, and notice the similarity in the wording of their respective correct choices: 1(E): "Traditional work schedules are too inflexible . . .," 4(B): "the inflexibility of work schedules." Don't be scared off if the answers you chose for two different questions seem too much alike.

5. D

The focus is on day care here, and your knowledge of the passage structure should help you to quickly focus in on lines 5–12 of paragraph 1 where the inadequacies of day care are addressed. You're asked for the exception; which reason wasn't addressed?

Check off the answer choices that you find in the text. All of the points raised in the choices are mentioned in this paragraph except for the point brought up in (D). Although school vacations are mentioned in the second sentence, this topic is used to illustrate the notion that school-age children need care when school is not in session. It has no connection to the issue of day care; the author never says or implies that day care for preschool children is interrupted during vacations.

(A) Day care's inability to guarantee parent-child quality time comes up in lines 10–12.

(B) and (C) Affording and finding suitable day care, (B) and (C) respectively, are issues discussed in the third sentence.

(E) The problem of sick children comes up in the fourth sentence.

- If you make a good mental roadmap of the passage as you read through, you won't have to waste time finding the relevant area of the passage for each particular question. Here, the mention of the limitations of day care should have directed you right to paragraph 1.

6. A

In this EXCEPT question you're asked to locate a type of career decision working parents might face that's *not* discussed by the author. Refer back to the passage to eliminate those the author does mention. The specific issue and conflicts are addressed in the last two paragraphs, so start there. In the end, you should have found that the decision in (A) is the odd one out: Although the author mentions both professional and nonprofessional jobs and the circumstances that both entail, the author never states or implies that working parents are forced to decline professional jobs for nonprofessional ones.

(B) Taking part-time over full-time work appears in paragraph 3, where the author writes about compromises that working mothers make.

(C) and (D) Taking jobs with less responsibility and pursuing less desirable specializations both appear in paragraph 4. If you caught the basic gist of that paragraph, you probably were able to axe these choices without having to refer back to the passage.

(E) is another choice that may not have required a glance back to the passage; it's a main focus of the whole passage, and is suggested throughout, but most particularly at the beginning of the third paragraph.

- In Reading Comp, be on the lookout for choices that mention things stated in the passage, but relate them to one another in ways the author didn't. The author does deal with professional and nonprofessional positions, but not in the way presented in (A). Because this is an EXCEPT question, (A) is our answer. In creating a choice like this, the test makers are trying to separate careful from careless readers.

7. A

The final question of this passage asks for the choice containing the sentence that would best follow the concluding sentence. The best place to start is by taking another look at that concluding sentence: Women will continue to be disadvantaged in the labor market as long as the market is hostile toward parents and as long as family roles are based on gender. Well, if women continue to be disadvantaged, it makes sense to say that men will continue to be advantaged; that is, they will do better in the labor market. (A) logically follows from the argument. This is not to say that this is the direction the author has to go if she decides to continue the passage, but it does make for an appropriate and logical continuation.

(B) is unwarranted. You have no reason to believe that men are unwilling to do anything about employment barriers. In addition, it changes the subject from the matter at hand— the current and future state of parents in the job market.

(C) is also an unlikely continuation because it discusses "salaries," an issue barely touched on in the passage.

(D) refers to men with primary child-raising responsibilities, but the passage presents no information about their role in the workplace.

(E) tries to relate gender-related societal traditions to gender differences in career opportunities, but there's no indication that this is where the author is going with all this. (E) makes it sound as if the first thing causes the other, whereas the author discusses societal institutions only as a part of a larger problem.

- Note how closely related (A) is to the author's message throughout the passage; it is a logical corollary to the theme "working women are *especially* disadvantaged in the labor force." The point is, even when you're asked to go beyond the passage, the correct answer will be based strongly on what the author has actually said.

Passage 2—John Webster

Topic and Scope

Elizabethan playwright John Webster and how critics misinterpret his work

Purpose and Main Idea

The author's purpose is to describe how the criticism of the contradictions in the characters of Webster's tragedies is misdirected. The main idea is that critics have been confused by the contradictory nature of Webster's characters because of certain mistaken assumptions they have made about the playwright himself.

Paragraph Structure

Paragraph 1 sets up the main idea but doesn't quite get there. First you're told that the critics are confused by the contradictory nature of Webster's characters. Then the author provides examples of the contradictory nature of Webster's characters. Aristotle is cited as believing that contradiction is necessary for tragedy, and the paragraph ends with another hint that the critics are off base.

The author delivers her main point in the first sentence of paragraph 2. Critics have been confused by the contradictory nature of Webster's characters because of certain mistaken assumptions they have made about the playwright himself. According to the author, critics have assumed that Webster was a typical Elizabethan playwright, and as such intended to create characters who were meant to be either good or evil, but not both. Thus, when Webster's characters exhibit both good and evil tendencies, critics have ascribed this to incompetence on the part of the playwright, rather than to deliberate design on his part. The author takes exception to this view, saying that Webster intentionally created characters that were grey rather than black and white, characters that were both good and evil. According to the author, Webster was not a typical Elizabethan playwright. This is what has led to confusion and, ultimately, to mistaken judgments about his competence.

The Big Picture

- A passage like this one is a good place to begin your work on the Reading Comp section because the purpose and structure are fairly easy to grasp.

After some brief background facts are presented in the first paragraph, the author's message appears at the beginning of the second paragraph, while the rest of the passage just fleshes out that message.

- Always take note of the author's allegiances. Here, they are hinted at in the beginning paragraph, and then fully expounded in the rest of the passage: The author is pro-Webster and against the critics' judgments.

- Don't be intimidated by the length of the second paragraph. A paragraph like this is not broken up because it essentially harps on the same point throughout—it provides support for the author's position that the critics have misinterpreted Webster's work. With only two paragraphs, the passage's structure is not difficult to discern.

The Questions

8. D

The most straightforward kind of Global question simply asks about the author's purpose in writing the passage: The author wrote this passage in order to take issue with critics over their interpretation of Webster's characters. In the second paragraph, the author explains how critics have misunderstood Webster's characters and provides a more plausible interpretation of those characters' inconsistencies. Put another way, then, the author's purpose in writing this passage is to offer a more convincing alternative explanation, (D).

(A) There is no ambiguity requiring clarification here. The critics' position is clear; the author simply disagrees with it and offers her own take on the matter.

(B) The author doesn't support the mainstream view of Webster's work, but rather tears it down and supplies what she considers to be a more plausible explanation.

(C) has some truth to it—the author *does* propose an answer to the problem of the contradictory nature of Webster's characters, but there's no unresolved question at issue in the passage. As mentioned in the explanation to (A) above, the critics have a definite point of view about Webster's work and the author has simply taken issue with this view.

(E) is perhaps trickier than the rest. The author's purpose isn't to describe two opposing viewpoints; she offers an opposing viewpoint to counter that of the critics.

Furthermore, the author doesn't categorize viewpoints—she simply rejects one in favor of another.

- You've already done the work for Global questions as you read, so prephrase and stay focused. If you do, you'll be less likely to be swayed by the wrong choices, which often *sound impressive*, even when they're not on target.

- If you're forced to eliminate, be strategic. Understanding the structure of the passage allows you to eliminate many wrong choices in a "purpose" question. Here, there's no ambiguous assertion (A) or unresolved question (C) built into the structure of this passage. Understanding the general thrust of the argument—here's what the critics say, here's how the author counters—should be enough to allow you to axe these choices.

9. A

Here's an Inference question about the works that most influenced Webster's own tragedies. The best way to approach this question is to quickly reread the section that deals with influences on Webster's plays, namely lines 29–37. Here you're told that Webster was influenced by earlier Italian dramas, whose characters, unlike those in the morality play, are not black and white, but rather morally complex, both good and evil. That's essentially what (A) says in a slightly different way.

(B) is wrong on two counts: For one thing, Webster *was* influenced by Italian sources. For another, the other Elizabethan tragedies referred to in (B) were based on earlier morality plays that were English, not Italian.

(C) you can't conclude that critics don't adequately *understand* Italian drama just because they have failed to evaluate Webster's tragedies in light of this genre. All you know from the passage is that critics apparently feel that this genre is not relevant to understanding Webster's work, a different point entirely.

(D) Italian dramas, according to the passage, have *not* been used as a basis for interpreting Elizabethan drama. Rather, Elizabethan works have been interpreted as an outgrowth of earlier morality plays, a non-Italian genre. (The lone exception to this rule that you're aware of is the author's use of Italian drama to understand the work of John Webster, a single, nontraditional Elizabethan playwright.)

(E) contradicts the passage. Critics have considered Webster's work to be incompetent because they have always evaluated it in light of earlier morality plays, rather than Italian drama. Indeed, the author attacks critics precisely for failing to examine Webster's work in light of Italian drama.

- Make sure you're familiar with the various kinds of wrong answer types. In Inference questions, a common wrong choice is the one that brings up an irrelevant issue, such "critics' *understanding* of Italian dramas" in (C). Nothing can be inferred about this. However, the other wrong choices, (B), (D), and (E), fall into another category; they all contradict information in the passage. If a choice is the least bit inconsistent with the passage, it can't be the valid inference you seek.

10. B

Why did the author mention Aristotle's view of tragedy? In lines 11–14 you see that Aristotle implied that character inconsistencies are a *natural* part of tragedies, *and yet* Webster's critics still view these inconsistencies as eccentric. The keywords "and yet" are extremely helpful. Aristotle is cited as an authority supporting the notion that character inconsistency is essential to tragedy, *and yet* the critics ignore this evidence and still believe that Webster's vision is eccentric. So the author cites Aristotle to bolster her own argument that Webster's conception was not eccentric. Translate "not eccentric" as "not idiosyncratic" and you have (B).

(A) and (C) both contradict the thrust of the passage. Aristotle's view is introduced in order to bolster the author's *dissenting* view of Webster's work, not the mainstream view of critics, with which the author does not agree. So (A) is out. (C) is out for much the same reason; the author approves of Aristotle's view of tragedy, which is precisely why she cites it. She criticizes the critics' view, not the doctrines of Aristotle.

(D) For one thing, the author is not out to establish the similarity between classical and modern approaches to tragedy—that's beyond the more narrow purpose of this passage. Furthermore, since Aristotle and most modern critics seem to *disagree* on the nature of tragedy, how could introducing Aristotle's view establish a similarity between classical and modern approaches?

(E) starts off pretty well: "supports the author's assertion . . ." but is all downhill from there. This passage is about one Elizabethan playwright, John Webster; it's not about Elizabethan tragedy in general. Like (D), this choice is much too broad in scope. Not only that, but the author doesn't seem to be particularly fond of recent scholarship, so (E) also goes against the thrust of the passage.

- When a question asks for the function of a detail, consider purpose and how the detail fits into that purpose. Is the detail an opposing point of view that the author will try to discredit? Is it there to provide a contrast to the author's opinion? Is it there to support the author's opinion? In this case, if you were able to recognize the Aristotle reference as support for the author's view, you'd be able to narrow the choices down to (B) and (E).

11. C

What piece of information would make the critics' interpretations of Webster's tragedies more valid? Well, a good place to start would be with a reminder of what, according to the author, makes those interpretations *invalid*. It's the same idea you've been harping on thus far: The author believes that the critics mistakenly assume that Webster based his tragedies on earlier morality plays. So, if Webster *had* actually based his tragedies on earlier morality plays, with their black and white characters, yet his own tragedies still featured morally ambiguous characters, you could safely conclude that he was, as the critics contend, incompetent.

(A) Webster's tragic vision would seem more competent, not less, if it were based on the duality of human nature.

(B) Aristotle was mentioned to uphold the validity of employing contradiction in tragedy, so again, the fact that Webster's vision conforms to Aristotle's would only *support* the author's argument, rather than increase the validity of the critics' interpretation.

(D) According to the author, the critics' position is based on the assumption that Elizabethan dramatists, including Webster, were primarily influenced by the English morality play, not by the Italian dramatists. It's hard to see how disputing this assumption would bolster the critics' position.

(E) The modern audience is outside the scope; it could have no bearing on how and why Webster created his characters, and thus no bearing on the critics' interpretation of them.

- Interpret the wording in the stem in order to determine your task for each question. Most stems are self-explanatory, but others, like this one, are more complex and tricky. Essentially, this is a Strengthen question disguised as an Inference question.

- Be on the lookout for that common wrong-answer type, the *180* choice—a choice that provides the opposite of what you're looking for. Here, (A) and (B) support the notion that Webster *was* on target with his tragic vision, that his characters' duality was *not* due to his own artistic incompetence. This is the opposite of something that would strengthen the critics' interpretation.

12. C

You're looking for a statement about Elizabethan drama with which the author would agree. By now, you know that the author thinks that Webster was an exception to the rule that Elizabethan drama in general was heavily influenced by the morality play, which points you directly to choice (C).

(A) comes from out of the blue; nowhere in the passage does the author state or imply that the skill of Elizabethan dramatists has been overestimated recently. The author only argues that Webster's work should not be evaluated according to the same criterion used to judge the work of other Elizabethan dramatists.

(B), (D), and (E) all go against the author's point of view. Contrary to (B), the author doesn't think that Webster's works are typical of Elizabethan drama, just the opposite. (D) is out for the same reason: Since Webster's works were different, it's wrong to evaluate them in light of mainstream Elizabethan drama. As for (E), the author flatly says that mainstream Elizabethan drama was influenced by the morality play, not by Italian and classical sources.

- Don't be surprised when some questions merely ask you for what you've known all along. Don't look for a trick or think to yourself "it can't be this simple." Expect that some questions will revolve around the clear themes from the passage—these are the points that you need to rack up confidently and quickly in order to buy time for the more difficult ones.

13. E

Question 13 is very similar to question 11, and both are tied closely to the passage's main idea: how critics have wrongly assessed Webster's works. In question 11, you reiterated the main point that critics have assumed (wrongly) that Webster was influenced by earlier morality plays. They have done so because *most* Elizabethan dramatists were influenced by morality plays. Choice (E) says this, only substituting "same sources as his contemporaries" for "morality plays."

(A) Critics have found Webster's characters, in contrast to those of other Elizabethan dramatists, morally ambiguous, not black and white.

(B) 180. As you've seen over and over, the author's point is that critics have assumed (albeit incorrectly) that Webster's works derived from morality plays, which were English, not Italian.

(C) Critics have attributed Webster's alleged artistic flaws to his supposed inability to copy the style of the earlier morality play, rather than to ignorance of the classical definition of tragedy.

(D) Lines 37–43 tell you that critics have found that Webster's tragedies provide at least some basis for character analysis.

- Often two or more questions in a Reading Comp set will test the same concept. Use your work on earlier questions to help you answer later questions whenever possible. (And in this case, there's a good reason for the similarity: Both questions are tied to the author's main idea.)

14. D

The last question in this set asks about the author's view of Webster's conception of tragedies. All along you've seen that the author feels that Webster was not an incompetent Elizabethan playwright, but rather simply had a *different conception* of tragedy than most Elizabethan playwrights—a conception based on Italian drama rather than the English morality play. Lines 30–35, in fact, make this very point; (D) is the answer.

All four wrong choices contradict the author's point of view:

(A) Critics, not the author, consider Webster's conception of tragedy to be flawed.

(B) The author thinks Webster's conception of tragedy was unusual for, not typical of, an Elizabethan playwright.

(C) The author argues that Webster's tragedies derived from Italian drama, not the morality play.

(E) The author thinks that the morally complex nature of the characters in Webster's tragedies is fully consistent with Aristotle's classical conception of tragedy.

- The word "implies" in a question stem suggests an Inference question, but some inferences are so close to the actual text that they seem almost like explicit details. All along you've discussed how the author believes Webster's vision of tragedy was different and unique among his Elizabethan contemporaries. (D) simply reiterates this point.

- For the third question in a row, most of the wrong choices are inconsistent with the information in the passage. When there are two or more points of view in a passage (here you have the author vs. the critics), make sure you keep them straight in your mind. Know at all times who is arguing *what*. Then you'll be less likely to attribute a point of view to the wrong group and to fall for a 180 choice.

Passage 3—Phytopathogens

Topic and Scope

Agriculture; specifically, the effects of using genetically altered bacteria for specific agricultural purposes

Purpose and Main Idea

The author's purpose is to describe a debate over the agricultural benefits of using genetically altered bacteria on crops. The main idea, not fully evident until the second and third paragraphs, is that some are encouraged by the research in this field, while others still remain skeptical.

Paragraph Structure

Paragraph 1 essentially establishes the lingo for the passage. It begins with some brief background information (the impact of phytopathogens, crop rotation, and "suppressive soil" on agricultural yields), and then moves on to the topic at hand: Phytopathogens, or "bad" bacteria— "bad" because they're harmful to crops—may be suppressed by putting "good" bacteria such as *Pseudomonas fluorescens* into the soil. The rest of the first paragraph simply provides some evidence in support of this point by citing increased crop yields.

In paragraph 2 you learn that increased crop yields suggest that putting genetically altered "good" bacteria into the soil might be beneficial to agriculture in general. A few examples are given, and you find out that there are both proponents and opponents of such a course of action.

Paragraph 3 simply takes the debate a step further by giving you additional information about the work being done by the proponents—those who want to use genetically altered bacteria on the soil.

The Big Picture

- Although some test takers get flustered by natural science passages, they're really not much different from social science or humanities passages. Sure, they often contain some technical words or phrases, but these will be defined and explained in the passage. And they often compensate for the technical language with a very clear passage structure. As with all passages, nail down the author's purpose,

structure, and main idea, and you'll be in a position to answer most if not all of the questions.

- Never try to memorize details—many of them will not be tested. Instead, keep in mind the big idea, in this case that there is a debate over whether releasing genetically altered bacteria into the soil is a good idea. *That such a debate is taking place* is the message the author wants to convey.

- Strive to understand the author's place in the argument. This author's tone, despite the seemingly rosy ending, can only be described as neutral and objective. He cites examples as well as the proponents' case and the opponents' reservations about bacterial use in agriculture. And in the end, it is "many" (not necessarily including the author) who are encouraged by the prospects for the procedure. Detached, objective, informative; not at all unusual for a natural science passage.

The Questions

15. B

As is often the case, the first question in the set is a standard Global question asking the main idea. As discussed, the author is interested in conveying the notion that some people out there favor the use of genetically altered bacteria as a means for improving agricultural yields, while others oppose this course of action. (B) captures the spirit of this precisely.

(A), (C), and (E) are all too narrow in scope to qualify as the main idea. The passage's main message is that there's a *debate* going on in the scientific community about whether genetically altered bacteria will improve agriculture. The author discusses recent research and experiments because they support this message, which means that they're nothing more than supporting details. Moreover, (A) and (C) can also be thrown out on the grounds that they're unequivocally positive in tone—they completely ignore the concerns of the opponents of genetically altered bacteria.

(D) Crop rotation is never characterized as "outdated," nor is there any suggestion of getting rid of it. It is merely mentioned in the beginning as background information. This passage isn't about the possible effects of genetic research on crop rotation; it's about a debate over the efficacy of using genetic engineering to boost agriculture, a different issue.

KAPLAN

- Don't lose sight of the forest for the trees! In a passage like this some test takers will focus exclusively on the scientific jargon and lose sight of the fact that the author's real purpose is to alert the reader to the existence of a *debate* over the cited procedure. If you came out of the passage with that notion intact, you should have had no problems with this question.

- Once again, watch out for choices like (D) that combine elements from the passage in ways the passage did not. Choices that use the passage's language but distort its ideas are common in both Global and Inference questions.

16. D

Next up is another "function of a detail" question. This is just like question 10 in the previous passage, which asked you why Aristotle was mentioned by the author. The same procedure applies: Locate the detail and try to understand the role it plays in context. The stem directs you to the first paragraph, where *Pseudomonas fluorescens* appears. Here you find out that this bacterium seems to suppress harmful phytopathogens, thereby contributing to improved crop yields. In the first sentence of the second paragraph, the author cites this fact—"These improvements in crop yields. . ."—in support of the belief that putting genetically altered bacteria into the soil might be a good thing for agriculture. In other words, the author uses this example to show how the position advocated by the proponents regarding genetically altered bacteria might have evolved. Choice (D) makes this point, employing slightly different language.

(A) contradicts information in the passage. In lines 11–12, the author specifically says that there may be a number of reasons, not just one, for soil suppressivity.

(B) Even if the "treatment of wheat seeds" is the same thing as "spraying wheat fields," there's still no explanation as to *why* the yields increased, only that they did increase.

(C) The passage never details any "chemical processes." Even if it had, that's not *why* the author discussed *Pseudomonas fluorescens*.

(E) The author never says or implies that crop rotation is unnecessary (see first bullet point below). Moreover, the author never says or implies that phytopathogens "eventually disappear on their own"; this is an exaggeration.

- Choice (E) here is the second choice so far that is wrong because it distorts the example of crop

rotation mentioned in the first paragraph (choice (D) in question 15 is the other). The "distortion" is a common wrong answer type, and if you're hazy on what is meant by this, simply compare these two choices to what is actually said about crop rotation in the passage. Hopefully you'll see how these choices distort the example, and you'll be able to recognize similar kinds of distortions in other wrong choices.

- If you find yourself stumbling over the lingo in the passage, feel free to abbreviate, just as you do in Logic Games. There's no reason to mentally stumble over the term "harmful phytopathogens" again and again; you can just as easily think of them as the "bad p-things."

17. C

According to line 4, "phytopathogens" are parasitic. So crops "impervious" to parasites cannot be harmed by phytopathogens. Such crops will therefore not be helped by the addition of *Pseudomonas fluorescens* to the soil around them; after all, the reason for adding this bacterium to the soil in the first place is to protect crops from harmful phytopathogens. This benefit would be absent for crops that are impervious to parasites, which points to (C).

(A) Nothing in the passage says or suggests that the presence or absence of *Pseudomonas fluorescens* in the soil around crops is in any way connected to the susceptibility of crops to phytopathogens. In other words, *Pseudomonas fluorescens* may be present whether or not there are parasites for it to act against.

(B) and (D) The passage doesn't provide you with any facts about these crops mentioned in the stem—those that are resistant to phytopathogens—so you can't infer anything about their growth patterns or their effects on other crops.

(E) is out for much the same reason as (A): All you know about "impervious" crops is that they're immune to phytopathogenic bacteria. You can't infer from this how much of such bacteria surrounds these plants in comparison to other crops. There may be a lot, there may be a little; all you know for sure is that no matter how much surrounds the roots of these plants, it has no detrimental effect.

- Since you know nothing of these new plants mentioned in the stem, any valid inference must relate back to something you know about from the passage. This is why any choice that discusses only elements related to the new topic (impervious plants) must be wrong. How could you know anything about their growth patterns, (B) and (D)? This strongly suggests that the answer will in some way have to relate back to *Pseudomonas fluorescens*, which narrows the choices down to (A) or (C).

18. E

As you know by now, crop rotation is discussed at the beginning of the passage, so look there. The author says that crop rotation cuts down on the problem posed by phytopathogens by denying them a "suitable host." This is how crop rotation can cure the problem of decreased yield. Working straight from the language, plants that "deny phytopathogens a suitable host" must be *unsuitable* hosts. This suggests that not every phytopathogen can attach to every host, which in turn means that specific phytopathogens must attack specific kinds of plants. All of this points directly to (E).

(A) According to the passage, crop rotation seems to help crops not by making *them* stronger, but rather by making their environment less harmful.

(B) If anything, lines 7–17 seem to suggest that the number of *Pseudomonas fluorescens* bacteria in the soil increases when crops are *not* rotated. What happens to their number when crops *are* rotated is anyone's guess.

(C) Compounds produced by the roots of crop plants are outside the scope of the passage. Nothing allows you to infer what kind of compounds such roots might produce, let alone what connection this might have to the benefits of crop rotation.

(D) Although you know that phytopathogenic bacteria cause crop disease, there's no information in the passage that would indicate that they're responsible for *most* crop diseases. More importantly, as in (C), even if you could agree to this, what connection does this have to the way in which crop rotation increases yield?

- Make sure you answer the actual question that is asked. The question here isn't "what can be generally inferred from the passage?" The question is "what can be inferred regarding the way in which crop rotation increases yield?" That's a big difference. Critical reading is rewarded not just in the passage but also in the stems and answer

choices. Just like a Detail stem, this kind of specific inference stem will direct you to the right place to research the answer in the passage.

19. A

In this one, you're interested in what proponents of genetic engineering think about the altered bacteria used in the frost-damage experiments, and that's outlined in lines 36–41. Line 36, specifically ("Proponents, on the other hand, argue that . . ."), announces that this is where the answer is likely to be found. The proponents assert that genetically altered bacteria used in these experiments differ from the naturally occurring bacteria *only* in that one gene—the one that causes frost damage—has been removed from the altered bacteria, which brings you to (A).

(B) distorts a detail brought up in lines 54–56, which, in any case, has nothing to do with the frost-damage experiments.

(C) Those who favor the use of altered bacteria never make any comparison between the safety and effectiveness of the altered bacteria used in the frost-damage experiments and naturally occurring *Pseudomonas fluorescens.* They merely claim that the altered bacteria in these experiments are safer than the phytopathogenic bacterium from which it was derived, *Pseudomonas syringae.*

(D) Proponents claim that the altered bacteria will attack one type of phytopathogen, the one that causes frost damage to crops; nowhere do they say or imply that the altered bacteria fought against "several types of naturally occurring phytopathogens."

(E) This claim is never made by the supporters of genetic engineering; in fact, they never discuss anything regarding the number of bacteria released. If anything, it is the *opponents* who speak of "large-scale release" of genetically altered bacteria, and not in the specific context of the frost-damage experiments at that.

- Formal logic terms have the same meaning on all three sections of the LSAT. While you encounter formal logic most often in Logic Games, and then in Logical Reasoning, formal logic terms do pop up in Reading Comp passages as well. Here, the proponents assert that the bacteria in question is altered "only" by the removal of the responsible gene; a correct translation of this is that this bacteria differs from the original only in that it has one fewer gene, (A).

- Detail questions that ask what is stated or argued will be answerable straight from the passage, so your main job is to locate the relevant text. Correct choice (A) here is simply a slight rewording of lines 37–39.

20. D

Again you're concerned with the frost-damage issue, but this time you're asked what, if true, would weaken the proponents' argument. You just reviewed their argument for the sake of the previous question, so it should be fresh in our minds: These proponents claim that the new bacteria, which is the old minus the one harmful gene, limits frost damage without causing any harmful effects. Well, if it were true that the deletion of one gene could indeed cause harmful effects, this argument would be weakened. (D) leads you in that direction: If the gene removed from the original pathogenic bacteria may very well be responsible for protecting the crop in other ways, then removing this gene may thus endanger the crop and therefore warrant the opponents' fear of "deleterious results."

(A) Primitive and simple? So what? This has no bearing on the argument that the altered bacteria are safer because it doesn't contain the gene that causes frost damage.

(B) is entirely consistent with the proponents' argument, so it obviously doesn't weaken their argument. They never claimed that the altered bacteria derived from anything *but* a harmful phytopathogen. Indeed, their claim is that they're turning a harmful bacterium into a beneficial one by altering its genetic structure.

(C) Commercial production of genetically altered bacteria is irrelevant to the issue of the safety of such bacteria, which is after all the cornerstone of the proponents' argument.

(E) The info in (E)—how the altered variety works most efficiently—doesn't address the safety issue. Instead, it speaks to the effectiveness of the altered bacteria, a different issue entirely.

- When you see a Weaken question in Reading Comp, use the same strategies you use in Logical Reasoning. Remember, an argument can only be weakened on its own terms, which in this case is safety and harm to crops. Choice (D) addresses this issue. Wrong choices (A), (C), and (E) do not, and must be eliminated. Choice (B) is within the scope, as it deals with the "harmful to crops" issue, but as you saw, (B) is perfectly consistent with the proponents' argument and is therefore not a weakener.

- Use your work on one question to help you answer related questions. Question 19 forced you to review the argument of the proponents of the use of genetically altered bacteria in frost-damage experiments. Question 20 asks you to weaken this same argument, so you need waste no time in familiarizing yourself with the issue at hand, and you can jump right into attacking this argument.

Passage 4—The Dawes Act

Topic and Scope

Legislation regulating the private ownership of reservation lands for Native Americans—specifically, the stated and actual intentions of the legislators behind the Dawes Act

Purpose and Main Idea

The author's purpose is to describe the Dawes Act and the reasons advanced for a particular restriction in the act, and then to discredit these reasons and argue that another factor may have influenced this legislation. The main idea doesn't become evident until the final paragraph, but it's not a difficult one to grasp: The author thinks that the clause in the Dawes Act restricting land sales for 25 years had nothing to do with protecting the interests of Native Americans, but rather was intended to serve the interests of government bureaucrats and, by extension, politicians.

Paragraph Structure

Paragraph 1 introduces the Dawes Act, a piece of legislation that dealt with land ownership by Native Americans. This paragraph simply provides you with some facts about the act: Under its terms, each Native American adult was granted limited ownership of 80 acres of land, which they could use but not sell for 25 years.

In paragraph 2 you find out two reasons *why* Native Americans were restricted from selling their land: This would prevent the sale of Native American land to non-Native Americans and thus preserve the Native American way of life; secondly, Native Americans were not really ready for, or interested in, full private ownership because of their tradition of communal land use.

Paragraph 3 questions the validity of this rationale on the grounds that it doesn't explain why Native Americans were prohibited from selling land to each other, or to the tribe.

This leads directly into paragraph 4, in which the author's purpose in writing the passage becomes clear. As stated above, the author feels that the real motivation for the "restriction on alienation" clause was self-interest on the part of government bureaucrats and politicians, not the wellbeing of Native Americans, as originally stated. That's the author's message, and it's spelled out in a bit more detail in the remainder of this paragraph.

The Big Picture

- As you read, continually ask "why is the author telling me this?" Why are you told the specifics of the Dawes Act in paragraph 1? You don't know by the end of that paragraph—which is a good clue that the purpose and main idea are yet to come. Paragraph 2 offers two reasons for the "restriction of sale" clause in the act. Why are you told this? Still not sure; this *could* be a purely descriptive passage, but there are still two paragraphs to go. In paragraph 3, things really heat up; the author objects to the reasons cited in the previous paragraph, and this objection sets up the crucial paragraph 4, in which an entirely new interpretation of the true intentions of the "restriction on alienation" clause is put forth. A careful reader, asking the right questions along the way, can discern not only the main idea wherever it appears, but also the *structure* of the passage: paragraphs 1 and 2 supply background; paragraph 3 questions a previous account of the facts; and paragraph 4 provides the author's hypothesis and main idea.

- Use the definitions provided in the passage, and substitute simpler words for complex ones whenever possible. In the first paragraph, "alienate" is defined in parentheses as "sell." Forms of the more complicated term appear throughout the rest of the passage—"alienability" and "alienation," for example. In paraphrasing the passage as you read, simply substitute the easier word "sell" whenever these words appear. The more you translate and simplify the author's ideas, the better you'll understand the passage.

The Questions

21. C

You start off with another standard Global question asking about the main idea of the passage. Well, as just mentioned, the author's main message appears at the end of the passage; she disagrees with the stated reasons for the restriction on Native American land sales contained in the Dawes Act, and instead posits her own theory that this restriction was meant to serve the interests of bureaucrats and politicians, not Native Americans. The first three paragraphs of the passage lay the foundation for this message, and the last paragraph delivers it. Whenever you're dealing with a Global question, you should already have determined the answer during your reading of the passage, so don't get distracted—use the work you've already done to pick up quick points.

(A) is way too broad in scope: This passage is specifically about the Dawes Act, not about general U.S. government policy toward Native Americans. Secondly, as far as the Dawes Act was concerned, it was intended to serve the interests of bureaucrats and politicians, not non-Native Americans, who were specifically precluded by the act from purchasing Native American land.

(B) can also be eliminated for a couple of reasons. For one thing, it's much too narrow in scope: Communal land use is discussed only briefly in the second and third paragraphs. More importantly, the author never makes the claim that communal land use is necessary if Native Americans are to preserve their way of life; all you know is that they favored this form.

(D) is a true statement—the Dawes Act *did* expand U.S. government activity in the area of land administration. But is that why the author wrote the passage, to point this out? Or does this fact lead somewhere bigger? Indeed it does; it acts as support for the notion that bureaucrats and politicians, not Native Americans, benefited from the clause in the Dawes Act restricting land sales. Anything that supports a larger point can't be the main idea (see bullet point below).

(E) twists a detail in the passage. According to the Dawes Act, Native Americans could not sell their land for 25 years. After that period of time was up, they were free to sell, and presumably some did so. In any case, the author's interest in the Dawes Act lies elsewhere.

- A choice may contain true information based on the passage and yet still not be the main idea. Take (D), for instance: Even if you had trouble recognizing the author's main idea, the fact that the true statement in (D) is used in the passage to lead somewhere else, to something bigger, is enough to tell you that (D) itself isn't the main idea. Anything that supports a *larger* point can't be the main idea of the passage.

22. C

This question asks which reason for the end of land allotment best supports the author's conception of politicians. The best place to start is with a consideration of the author's opinion of politicians, which should be at the forefront of your mind because it ties directly in with the main idea. In lines 40–47, the author makes politicians out to be totally self-interested individuals who support

policies that tend to increase their own political influence. If the reason for the end of land allotment was that it failed to serve political interests, as (C) has it, then you would be more likely to believe that the author's characterization of politicians is correct.

(A) is out because the author doesn't believe that politicians are motivated by concern for the welfare of others; they're out for their own, not the Native Americans', interests.

(B) would provide evidence of a certain kind of mean-spiritedness or anti-Native American stance on the part of the politicians, but the author doesn't suggest this at all; she simply says that politicians are motivated by self-interest in this matter, not that they have any particular problem with the Native Americans' conception of land use.

(D) The author says that politicians *favor* the growth of government bureaucracy because this enhances prospects "for the exercise of political patronage." Politicians therefore wouldn't push for an end to allotment on the grounds that the BIA, a part of the government's bureaucracy, had become too big; according to the author, this is what politicians want.

(E) Again, the author is convinced that politicians would never push for an end to a policy solely on the basis of that policy's effect on others. If (E) is the true reason for the end of allotment, then the author hasn't portrayed the politicians very well.

- Treat a Strengthen question in Reading Comp the same as you would in Logical Reasoning: Focus in on the relevant argument, and see what effect, if any, each choice has on it. The only difference here is that the stem directs you right to the relevant material (in this case, the author's view of politicians), whereas in Logical Reasoning you often have to first pinpoint the author's conclusion yourself.

23. D

This Global question deals specifically with the organization of the passage, which provides for a quick and easy point for those test takers who pay careful attention to the passage structure as they read. You discussed above how the first paragraph describes the Dawes Act, the second paragraph discusses the official explanation behind one of its clauses (restriction on selling land), the third paragraph takes issue with the official explanation, and the last paragraph sets out an entirely different rationale for the clause (political self-interest). (D) contains all of these elements, and is correct.

(A) immediately goes off track; the legislative *process* leading to the enactment of the Dawes Act is never mentioned, much less analyzed in detail. Moreover, no final assessment of the law itself is given—all you get is an analysis of the rationale behind one of its clauses.

(B) You're never told about the history of the Dawes Act, and the author never advocates its repeal. After all, line 49 tells you that "the allotment was ended in 1934."

(C) is a bit more plausible than (A) or (B), especially up until the end of the choice, but it goes wrong when it speaks of studying the lasting effects of the Dawes Act. That's simply not what the author does. Again, the author is interested in explaining the "real" (as opposed to the official) rationale behind one of its clauses, the land sales clause.

(E) This passage is about the political overtones of *one particular clause of one particular law*; it's not about the overall legal status of Native Americans in matters of land ownership and commercial autonomy, although it does touch on these issues.

- An "organization of the passage" question in RC is similar to a Method of Argument question in LR. In both cases, test every element of the choice to see whether that element is indeed part of the passage or argumentative structure. If even one thing in the choice doesn't match, then throw that choice out.

- Notice how many of the wrong choices can be eliminated for the same reason: They deal with the Dawes Act in general while the author is primarily concerned with only one of its clauses.

24. E

Next up is a question that asks about the author's attitude toward the official explanation behind the land sales clause of the Dawes Act. This answer can definitely be predicted, and you quite possibly were able to answer this one without a look back to the passage; the whole main idea of the passage revolves around this very attitude. The only reason the author offers her own interpretation of the motivations behind the land sales clause is because she is very dissatisfied with the "official" explanation. That immediately rules out any choice with a positive sentiment, such as (A)'s "credulous" and (B)'s "approving." It also rules out neutrality, (C)'s "indecisive."

No, the author's attitude is *negative*, and so the question boils down to *how* negative: Is she "mildly questioning," (D), or "highly skeptical," (E)? You may have needed to return to the text to select between these two remaining choices, but you shouldn't have had any trouble finding clues in the third paragraph and the beginning of the fourth. In particular, notice how the author calls the official explanation "empty." This is enough to confirm the author's attitude as highly skeptical; "mildly questioning" is too weak. If the author only "mildly" questioned the official rationale for the clause, the opposition in the third paragraph wouldn't be so strongly stated, and the author may not have seen the need to provide her own hypothesis. And she wouldn't have used the word "empty" to describe the official explanation.

- When asked to describe the author's attitude toward something, first break it down to positive, negative, or indifferent. This should help you eliminate between two and four wrong choices. Then, if necessary, look for clues in the passage to narrow your choice down to the winner.

- Critical readers understand how even small words can provide a world of meaning. Think about it: If you were arguing a point with a friend, and your friend said your argument was "empty," you would not get the impression that he was "mildly questioning" your notion, so "highly skeptical" is a better description of his opinion. And the same is true here. That one little word in line 35 confirms (E) as the correct choice.

25. B

In this question, you're asked to infer something about Native American life before the Dawes Act, so it makes sense to review what the Dawes Act was all about. It was intended to give ownership of land to Native Americans (albeit with the proviso that they couldn't sell it for 25 years). This strongly suggests that before the Dawes Act, Native Americans didn't own land, doesn't it? Why else would the government adopt a law to give ownership to them? It doesn't make sense to give land to someone who already owns that land. (B) is inferable, and it's nicely qualified too; notice how it says "not many" rather than "no." You may not be able to infer that "no" Native Americans owned their own land; there may have been a few exceptions. But from the way the law is described, you *can* infer that few Native Americans owned their own land immediately before the passage of the Dawes Act.

(A) The way in which Native Americans supported themselves is not tied to the issue of land ownership. You don't have enough information to infer that most Native Americans supported themselves through farming.

(C) goes against the grain of the passage. If Native Americans had bought land from their tribes before the Dawes Act, why would there be any need for this act? Native Americans, after all, would already have owned their own land.

(D) doesn't make much sense at all: There's no necessary connection between the degree of contact between Native and non-Native Americans and the issue of land ownership.

(E) If anything, the opposite is suggested: The government might have had the impression that many Native Americans *would* sell their land to non-Native Americans; this was one of the reasons advanced for the restriction. But you say *might* because the author argues that this was not the *true* reason for the land sales restriction. In any case, you can't draw the inference in (E) based on the information contained in the passage.

- Don't read extra facts or interpretations into the passage: Under the sway of (A), you may have reasoned that the government enacted the Dawes Act because most Native Americans were farmers without title to the land which they worked. But while there may be some logic in this line of thought, nothing in the passage supports this notion. Don't take a logical leap simply because it leads to a credible-sounding idea; stay within the framework of the passage.

26. B

Here's a Detail question regarding, not surprisingly, the author's main area of concern, the land sales clause of the Dawes Act. And hopefully you didn't let the long stem confuse you; it simply asks how land ownership for the first 25 years differed from land ownership thereafter. And you know this; it's all part of the background information of the first paragraph. Lines 5–15 tell you that during the first 25 years of ownership, a Native American landowner could not sell his land; he had only limited title. After 25 years of ownership, however, the Native American landowner was granted full title to the land, giving the landowner the right to sell the land.

(A) and (D) As far as you know, the government never placed any sort of conditions on how Native Americans could use their land.

(C) has the facts backward. The government had control over land sales during the *first* 25 years, but no control after that.

(E) There's no mention of the government asking Native Americans to pay a fee to develop their land.

- Don't be intimidated by the length or wordiness of a question stem. This stem is basically a long-winded way of asking about what you already know and have known since paragraph one: According to the clause, after 25 years, the Native Americans could freely sell their land. Before that, they couldn't.

27. D

Lastly, you're asked to determine which of five possible facts would strengthen the author's argument regarding the motivation for the Dawes Act. This takes you right back to the author's main idea, which is that the restriction on selling was included to benefit burcaucrats, which, in turn, benefited politicians. All of this is made clear in the middle of the last paragraph. Choice (D) underscores the influence of BIA bureaucrats on the legislators who enacted the act, and therefore supports the author's argument and gets the point.

(A) would, if anything, tend to weaken, rather than strengthen, the author's argument. The author views politicians as self-interested individuals, but non-Native Americans who owned land next to Native American land were inferably hurt by the Dawes Act to the extent that they were unable to purchase land from Native American landowners for 25 years. Thus, if politicians who owned land next to Native American land had voted for such a piece of legislation, this could not be considered self-interested behavior.

(B), (C), and (E) The "facts" brought up in these remaining choices are all outside the scope of the author's main argument. Remember, the argument is based on the behavior and motivations of *bureaucrats* and *politicians*, not on the behavior of Native Americans or non-Native American land purchasers. How these groups behave may be of some interest to us, but does not affect the gist of the author's argument because that argument centers on other groups.

- When asked to strengthen or weaken an argument, immediately eliminate choices that fall outside the scope. Since this author's main idea focuses on the true motivations of politicians and bureaucrats, you can immediately narrow the choices in this question down to (A) and (D).

- Main idea, purpose, and structure, taken together, form the cornerstone of every LSAT RC passage. If you can nail these down, you'll be ready for the questions. You've seen this before, of course, in this program, or in a class or workshop, perhaps. Look back over the correct answers to questions 21–27 and notice how almost every question in this set revolved in some way around these elements. Resolve now to continually improve your ability to pick out the main idea, purpose, and structure of every RC passage you read, and when test day arrives, you'll be able to make your way through this section with confidence.

SECTION IV: LOGICAL REASONING

1. D

You're asked to strengthen the argument, which centers around two specific events: reduction in the speed limit and the marked decrease in the rate of highway fatalities over the next ten years. At this point you can probably guess what the author's conclusion will be: that the first event (the change in speed limit) caused the second event (the steady decrease in the rate of highway fatalities). Sure enough, the author concludes in the last sentence that the reduced speed limit saved lives. A reduction in the speed limit followed by a decline in the fatality rate *suggests* that there may be cause and effect at work, but it doesn't *prove* it. What this argument needs is more evidence that, in fact, there *is* a causal relationship between speed limits and highway fatalities. Choice (D) provides this: If drivers driving over 55 mph are more likely to suffer or cause fatalities, then you have greater reason to believe that the author's argument—lowering the speed limit to 55 mph reduced the fatality rate—is on target.

(A) The stimulus discusses fatality *rates*, that is, fatalities per some given number of drivers. Having fewer people driving due to the fuel shortage has no bearing on the argument, because the author is concerned with the fatality *rate*, and not the sheer number of drivers.

(B) The 12th year? First of all, year 12 is outside the scope; the argument is nicely contained in years 1 through 11 after the reduction in the speed limit. Secondly, the fact that the rate didn't continue downward indicates nothing; perhaps the life-saving potential of the 55 mph speed limit was fully realized after 11 years.

(C) actually weakens the argument by providing an alternative explanation for the reduction in the fatality rate. Contrary to the author's assertion, it could have been the seat belts, rather than the speed limit, that saved lives during the period mentioned.

(E) If (E) is true, then it's possible that driving *faster* may save more lives in those cases where many people are speeding. Therefore, (E) may weaken the argument by suggesting that a reduction in speed didn't save lives after all.

- Anticipate as you read; this keeps you one step ahead of the game. Many Logical Reasoning arguments are structurally similar, so you're likely to come upon the same kinds of arguments again and again. Here, once you're told about a reduction in the speed limit and then a decline in the fatality rate, it's almost a lock that the author is going to conclude that the first caused the second. And speaking of causality . . .

- No doubt you've seen the "X happened, then Y happened, therefore X caused Y" form of argument before (or if you're at the beginning of your preparation, you certainly will see it in the future). Even in cases like this one, where a causal relationship seems plausible, the author still must provide substantive proof of causality, and here, (D) adds the kind of solid evidence the argument is lacking.

2. E

The author's point of view jumps forcefully off the page from the second sentence: "Such a position ignores the lessons of experience." So you know right away that the author is arguing against the "position" in the first sentence: the refusal of some legislators to commit public money to research lacking a clearly defined public benefit. Predictably, the author's rationale for arguing against this position comes next: Many unexpected, yet socially beneficial discoveries have emerged from just such research. Antibiotics are offered as an example of a hugely beneficial discovery that was accidentally born out of the seemingly unrelated study of molds. Where is the author going with all this? You may have been able to prephrase, at least in spirit, if not word for word, the point the author is leading toward: The legislators are wrong—specifically, they are wrong to refuse to fund research solely because that research isn't *guaranteed* to benefit the public welfare. (E) is a close paraphrase of this idea.

(A) is overly optimistic: The author's notion that you can't know for sure whether a given research program will benefit society is a far cry from arguing that *any* public funding for scientific research will *necessarily* enhance the public good.

(B) is too broad, for it necessarily leads to an absurd result: Suppose the predicted "general outcome" of a new research effort was utter failure, something with no public use, or something that would even harm the public? Would legislators *really* be willing to fund such research? According to (B), simply knowing the outcome would result in funding, but this is far from the point the author is trying to make.

(C) While the author may possibly agree with (C), still, this isn't the main point she's trying to make. The author's evidence is not presented in order to lament what could have been the case for past discoveries, but rather to show what the unexpected results of past research can tell you about the shortsightedness of the legislators' current position.

(D) The author believes that legislators should fund research, but not, as (D) has it, because this would ensure that the research is *directed* toward the public good. Rather, she promotes funding because you can't be sure what research, regardless of its direction, will ultimately increase the public good.

- Use your critical reading skills in the Logical Reasoning section, where applicable. The second sentence highlighted above is a clear indicator of authorial purpose, much like the kind of statements you're trained to look for in RC passages. Such a sentence is of the utmost importance: This one tells you that this author thinks the legislators' view is wrong, and the rest of the stimulus exists as evidence for this notion. That alone is almost enough to get the point, or at least narrow the choices down considerably.

- Don't confuse a statement with which the author might agree, like (C) here, with the author's main point. It's very possible for a statement to be consistent with the author's argument without it being the main point she's trying to make.

3.   B

The stem tells you you're looking for a Flaw. First you get evidence: Workers who aren't challenged become bored and achieve less than they're capable of. As if that weren't bad enough, employers face another risk: Workers who find their jobs *too* challenging get discouraged, and they, too, achieve less than they are capable of. The last sentence is the conclusion, indicated clearly by the keyword "therefore." Workers, the author concludes, cannot possibly realize their full potential. This is only true if there is no middle ground—a healthy amount of challenge: not too much, not too little. The conclusion is therefore based on the assumption that the two extremes mentioned in the evidence are the only possibilities. But nothing in the evidence precludes the existence of just the right amount of challenge, which would allow for full realization of a worker's potential. (B) describes this flaw. As *Goldilocks* teaches us, this porridge is too hot, this porridge is too cold, but this porridge is *just right*.

(A) The whole argument aims to show that what is actual—workers' actual achievements—never matches what

is possible—their potential achievements—so the author *isn't* falsely equating the actual and the possible.

(C) The author reasons from general principles of cause and effect: "If a worker isn't challenged (or is *too* challenged), then . . ." But no clue is given as to whether these are, or are intended to be "objective" or "subjective." The principles themselves aren't the problem; the logic bogs down in the author's failure to consider that these principles don't describe all possible levels of challenge in the workplace.

(D) accuses the author of confusing correlation (coincidence of two events) with causation. But the author *does* provide evidence for causality in the form of a middle term for both cases. Unchallenging work leads to *boredom* and too-difficult work leads to *discouragement*, so the problem with this argument is not the confusion of coincidence and causality.

(E) Only a few key terms are included in the argument: assignments, challenging, achieve, and potential. None of these, however, is hard to understand or decipher. There is no such ambiguity here; each of these terms is clear.

- Read critically, especially when the stem tells you there is a problem with the argumentation. In such cases, always keep an eye out for alternative possibilities or explanations that the author ignores. When an author assumes without evidence that no such alternative exists, then the omission of this alternative possibility is usually the source of the Flaw.

- Look at the Kaplan process at work. Here's the optimal chain of events in getting this point: Previewing the stem tells you to break the argument into evidence and conclusion and look for the gap; prephrasing leads you to question "What if the challenge is just right?"; and scanning the choices with this thought in mind leads to correct choice (B). Your preparation task is to continually hone this process so it will be as close to automatic as possible by test day.

4.   E

Another misleading ad; you'll recall you saw one back in section 1, question 4, and now you get one in this section, question 4. You're asked to find the statement that, if true, would make the ad misleading. The claim is that the soup provides good nutrition. The evidence for this claim is signaled by the keyword phrase "for instance," which turns out to be one example of the soup's nutritional value—a warm bowl of this tomato soup provides more units of vitamin C than does a serving of carrots or apricots. Presumably, this comparison is intended to astound us, as the exclamation mark makes clear.

But there are a lot of holes to be punched in this argument, and hopefully you were able to prephrase at least one or two. First off, vitamin C is only one nutrient. If the soup has nothing else to offer, then the ad is a bit misleading because consumers might reasonably expect a food to provide more than one type of nutrient. Secondly, you don't know that the comparison is fair: Just how much vitamin C do apricots or carrots have? To get even pickier, just how big is the soup bowl, and how many carrots or apricots make "a serving"? The test makers chose to exploit the second ambiguity in (E): If carrots and apricots aren't particularly good sources of vitamin C, then the fact that the soup provides *more* vitamin C isn't as impressive as it's meant to sound. And since that's the only support offered for the claim, the ad would be misleading if (E) were true.

(A) Carrots and apricots don't have to provide all the vitamin C a person needs in order for them to be rich in vitamin C. Even if most people get their vitamin C elsewhere, carrots and apricots might still be excellent sources of vitamin C, in which case the validity of the ad is not undermined.

(B) The ad hypes a cup of *warm* soup, not room temperature soup that's been lying around for a long time, so this fact doesn't affect the advertisement's claim.

(C) Bully for the soup; let the company use this information in its next ad. Tomato soup's strengths in other respects wouldn't make this ad misleading.

(D) Strawberries and their vitamin C content are irrelevant. The ad stands or falls on the relevance of the comparison of the soup's vitamin C content with that of apricots and carrots. As long as the soup is nutritious, it doesn't matter how the soup compares to other foods.

- Always focus on the scope of the argument presented. Here, the argument is not simply that the soup is nutritious, but rather that it's nutritious *for a specific reason*—more vitamin C than apricots and carrots. If the ad is misleading, there must be some breakdown between this evidence and the claim, which means that the right answer will almost surely contain info about apricots and carrots. This alone narrows the choices down to (A) and (E). You won't always be able to prephrase a Strengthen or Weaken question directly, because there's almost

always more than one possible way to affect the argument—but keeping your eye on the hole is the trick. You're looking for an answer a choice that says "just because the soup has more Vitamin C than carrots and apricots doesn't necessarily mean it's nutritious."

5.   A

You're looking for the principle that best supports the argument's conclusion. The argument begins with a statement of contrast, signaled by the keyword "but": Deposit insurance is *provided* to individuals, but *paid for* by banks. Since (here's evidence) depositors are the primary beneficiaries of deposit insurance, those depositors who want the insurance (here's the conclusion) should pay for it—not a very complicated argument. Depositors should pay for deposit insurance because it's designed to benefit them, not the banks. The author is appealing to the more general principle that those who benefit from something should be those who pay for that something. Replace "something" with the more specific "economic service," and you have correct choice (A).

(B) The argument centers on who benefits and who pays. Risk and the *level* of payments have nothing to do with the argument, so the principle in (B) is of no help.

(C) The economic rationale for when to provide deposit insurance doesn't help this argument at all. The issue is who should *pay* for deposit insurance, not *whether* it should be offered.

(D) The argument is about what should happen in the case of "depositors who want this security." The right to refuse a service that one *doesn't* pay for is an entirely separate issue that's outside the scope.

(E) is such a broad principle that you can't be sure how it relates to the author's argument. It's quite possible that relieving banks of the burden of paying deposit insurance premiums, and forcing depositors to do so, *would* alter the behavior of corporations and individuals in the marketplace. In that case, the principle in (E) would stand in opposition to the argument, which posits that the government *should* step in to change the current practice.

- Often, the principle that supports an argument is nothing more than a slightly more general restatement of the argument itself. Here, if you substitute "deposit insurance" for "economic service" in (A), it's easy to see how the principle in (A) and the author's main point are nearly identical.

6.   C

The assumption here is tough to prephrase. The argument, you'll recall, is that since depositors benefit from deposit insurance, they should pay the premiums. At present, the banks pay. But what if, in fact, the banks simply pass this cost on to the depositors? This is not an unusual business practice; a store with property taxes to pay on a new parking lot, for example, may increase its prices to cover the cost, and the same may be true here. The author must believe that the banks do not defer the cost in this way, because if they did, then the argument that the government should make depositors pay these premiums directly would make no sense because they'd *already* be paying them. If, contrary to (C), banks *always* pass the cost of the premiums along to the depositors, then the depositors are really paying the premiums and there is no injustice in the situation, and therefore no need for the government to step in.

(A) Insuring loans made by banks? This is outside the scope of the argument, which concerns *deposit* insurance, so (A) isn't a necessary part of this argument.

(B) The argument centers on government-provided deposit insurance; private insurance of deposits is a different issue. Whether other types of deposit insurance can exist is irrelevant and therefore need not be assumed.

(D) *How much* protection the government provides is one step removed from the focus of the argument, which is about who should *bear the cost*. The author's argument that the burden of cost should be shifted is in no way dependent on the existence of any such insurance protection limit.

(E) seems to contradict the argument: The statement "depositors who *want* this security" strongly implies that depositors have the choice of insured or uninsured accounts. This suggests, contrary to (E), that the government *does* allow banks to offer some uninsured accounts.

- The wrong choices in Assumption questions are often outside the scope like (A) and (B), or run contrary to the argument, as in the case of (E) here. Notice how "in the scope" correct choice (C) is—the

argument is specifically about who pays the cost of deposit insurance, and this is exactly the issue addressed in (C).

7.   A

Here's a stimulus about education, and you're asked to infer a conclusion. Take inventory of the information in the stimulus: First you learn that exposure to identical curriculum results in unequal learning by students—specifically, some students will learn more, better, and faster than others. If more equal results are to be achieved (if you want all the students to master the material), some will require different types of teaching from others. In the first sentence, the author defines equal treatment as identical exposure to curriculum; you can infer from this that she considers *different* exposure to curriculum to be "unequal" treatment. In this context, the last sentence means that equal results—i.e., the equal mastery of the curriculum—requires *unequal* treatment, (A). The author is leading toward the main point that unequal treatment is necessary for equal educational results.

(B) The word "quantity" comes up only in the context of learning—in (B), the notion of the quantity of *teaching* appears. The author argues that different students may need different *types* of help; but that's not enough to infer how the "quantity of teaching" may affect the rate and quality of learning.

(C) All you can infer from the reference to experienced teachers is that the author believes that these teachers agree with her premise stated in the second sentence. This doesn't, however, allow you to infer any kind of connection between experienced teachers and successful students; more information is necessary for this.

(D) A 180 answer choice—identical exposure leads to variances in learning. (D) is the exact opposite of the author's call for "different types of help" that's necessary for all students to master the material..

(E) seems like a nice sentiment, and the author may well agree with it. It isn't, however, inferable from these statements. The "different types of help" necessary for mastery is a vague and undefined notion; it doesn't mandate that teachers teach as much as they can to every student. After all, this intensive attention may not be the kind of help some students need.

- Beware of red herrings. The closing remark "as any experienced teacher knows. . ." may be a secondary piece of support—an appeal to authority. But in relation to the main argument, it's just a flourish, and is not really required in a logical sense. Such references are often used to generate wrong choices like (C).

8.   E

Talk about a scope shift! George supports a conclusion about global warming with evidence from his town. George says that global warming *is* occurring because his town has recently exhibited an unusual warming trend, but you know that that could be a coincidence. What you really need to know in evaluating George's argument is whether the trends cited in his town are truly global trends—is the rest of the world getting warmer too? If so, his conclusion may hold up. If not, you have no reason to believe that George's experience is an indicator of a global trend.

(A) Whether there are other causes of global warming is irrelevant. George merely argues that global warming *is occurring* on the basis of recent weather in *his* area.

(B) you know as much about the leaves as you need to know: they're three weeks late in changing color. Whether they're three weeks late from September 1 or some other date doesn't matter. What *is* relevant is whether the rest of the world's leaves also turned later than usual.

(C) How the carbon dioxide gets into the atmosphere is irrelevant; the fact is that it's there, scientists predict global warming because of it, and George agrees. Why George agrees forms the basis of his argument—it is around this issue that our inquiry into his argument must occur.

(D) distorts the leaves example: Leaves are important only insofar as they've turned color late. Trees *losing* leaves, and possible causes for this, have no relation to George's theory, and thus are also irrelevant.

- When an author employs such a large shift in scope, any one of a number of questions could be asked regarding the argument, but recognizing the assumption will open the door to all of them. Here, George assumed that the experience in his town was representative of a global trend. Recognizing that disparity between the scope of the evidence (here, local weather) and the scope of the conclusion (global warming) will lead to the answer in all evidence/conclusion based question types.

- Information that is not relevant to an argument is often irrelevant because it is outside the scope.

Your reaction to the wrong choices in a question like this should be "who cares?" When that reaction strikes you, it's usually a sign to cross that choice off quickly.

9.   C

The student rep argues that the university has wrongly punished a student who was expelled for verbally harassing his roommate. The dean's response begins "But what you're saying is that our university should endorse verbal harassment"—to which the student rep would probably respond "No, I'm not saying that at all; all I'm saying is that the punishment is wrong." The dean mischaracterizes the representative's position as an argument that the university should *endorse* verbal harassment, probably because that position is much easier to attack, (C). Upon careful inspection, you see that the student rep may defend the right to free speech, but never says the university should endorse harassment. The student rep has a perfect right to believe in a middle ground: a position from which the university neither endorses verbal harassment nor tramples on free speech.

(A) The conflict centers on the reasons for the expulsion; no one mentions the *process* by which the student was expelled (was it done by mail, in person, etc.).

(B) The rep argues about verbal harassment and free speech, and the dean argues about the same. The dean distorts the rep's argument, but does not point out a distinction between speech and other sorts of behavior.

(D) is wrong on both counts. The dean doesn't question the student representative's motives; if she did, she would say something about the rep's intentions, something she never does. Moreover, she *does* offer reasons for the expulsion, just not good reasons in the context of this debate.

(E) There's no threat made by the dean. The dean's argument rests on the claim that endorsing verbal harassment would be a threat to the *university*. So although she mentions a threat, she doesn't make one.

- In dialogue questions, you're often asked to critique the second speaker's response. Sometimes the second speaker misinterprets the first speaker's remarks; other times he or she attempts to cleverly argue around them. In either case, it's often helpful to put yourself in the place of the first speaker, and imagine how you might respond to the second person's comeback. Here, when the dean says "you say that . . .", the first speaker would likely retort "I said no such thing." This notion, or prephrase, leads nicely to (C)'s "misdescribes the representative's position."

- Offering bad reasons is not the same as offering no reasons at all. Some choices in Flaw questions accuse the author of presenting no evidence to back up a conclusion. If you're going to select a choice like this, make sure that in fact there *is no* evidence presented (which is fairly rare on the LSAT), as opposed to the case in which evidence, albeit faulty, *is* offered.

10. D

When you need to infer a conclusion from the stimulus, it's best to think about where the argument is leading. It pays to be famous: According to the first sentence, celebrities convicted of crimes are increasingly being sentenced to community service, whereas unknown convicts almost always get locked up for the same crimes. Doesn't sound very fair, does it?

Next, you find out that the principle of equality before the law does not permit celebrity status to affect the sentencing of criminals. This principle seems to directly conflict with the example in the first sentence. If, in fact, celebrities are getting off easier because of their celebrity status, then some judges out there aren't paying much attention to the principle of equality before the law. That's the one solid conclusion that's inferable from the passage. Some of the punishments described in the first sentence *conflict* with the principle described in the second, and it seems as though the author stopped just short of presenting the conclusion contained in (D).

(A) points out that the principle of equality is getting sidestepped, but it does so too strongly. The stimulus implies only that the principle is getting sidestepped in *some cases* dealing with celebrities, and you can't therefore infer that the principle is overlooked in *most types* of criminal trials.

(B) The passage compares the punishments of unknown and famous defendants who have committed similar crimes. (B) ignores the "similar crimes" feature of the argument and broadly suggests that equal numbers of both groups be sentenced to community service. This is not where the author is going, as the types of crimes committed by these groups and the relative number of criminals in each group may be very different. Furthermore, (B) is a strongly prescriptive statement; it out-and-out says what *should* be done. While this passage *could* have a

recommendation appended to it, the author has given no indication that he's headed in that direction.

(C) It's not at all clear that sentencing celebrities to community service is in line with "another principle," as (C) has it, nor is it clear that this overriding of the principle of equality before the law is "proper," as is also implied by (C).

(E) Leniency is a new and ambiguous term, which is a good reason to kill this choice right away. For all you know, the principle of equality before the law is compatible with leniency; nothing forbids this, so (E) isn't the conclusion you seek.

- When asked to infer a conclusion, think to yourself: "Where is the author going with all this?" The answer must be more than just a statement with which the author would likely agree; it must encompass the overarching idea the author set out to express when he or she sat down to write.

- A prephrase of an answer need not be eloquent or pretty to be effective. "Hey, these ideas conflict . . ." is a valid way of thinking about the notions presented in the first and second sentences. From there, it's a short jump to (D), which states that the example in sentence one violates the principle in sentence two.

11. A

The stem tells you that there's a flaw in the foundation's conclusion, so you need to find the disconnect between the evidence and the conclusion. The humanitarian-minded foundation gives a certain university an annual grant for scientific research, but hesitated when it discovered that the physics department began to work on weapons-related research. The foundation, feeling, no doubt, that weapons research would be incompatible with its humanitarian mission, threatened to cancel the grant. In response, the university assured the foundation that none of the foundation's money would fund the weapons research, whereupon the foundation went ahead and bestowed the grant because it concluded that the money wouldn't benefit the weapons research.

The foundation's reasoning boils down to this: Since our money won't be *spent on* weapons research, our providing money won't *benefit* the weapons research. That's a little optimistic, isn't it? The university could, after all, take the foundation's money, use it to fund only humanitarian research, and then divert *other* funding from the humanitarian projects to the weapons research. Maybe you were able to prephrase (A): Just because the weapons research won't receive the foundation's money doesn't assure that the foundation's money won't *indirectly* aid the weapons research.

(B) Overlooking the possibility in (B) isn't a logical problem. The question is whether the grant will benefit the weapons research in the physics department. If other departments are up to no good, then those bad departments might benefit from money diverted from the physics department, but the weapons research in the physics department would still be unaffected, and that's the point at issue.

(C) It's fairly obvious that the university did make its promise in order to retain the grant, and it's unlikely anyone at the foundation missed this point. Understanding the motivation of the university isn't relevant to the issue of whether the weapons research will benefit from the grant.

(D) Neither the foundation nor the university expects that the grant money won't be used, so (D) is not a proper criticism of the foundation's logic.

(E) Discussion of means and ends is simply confusing; no such distinction is raised in the stimulus between an objective and the means to that objective. The only "objective" that can be discerned here is the university's desire to conduct research to build weapons, and the foundation folks certainly don't believe anything about that objective is humanitarian in character.

- Some choices will evoke an immediate response of "huh?" True, if you misunderstand the argument or overlook something important in the stimulus, a choice that appears utterly baffling can turn out to be the correct answer. But if you've understood the argument fairly well, and come upon a choice that just seems out of left field, even difficult to understand, chances are it's wrong.

- Always keep your eyes peeled for alternative possibilities. In this one, a valid possibility (that the funding may indirectly benefit weapons research) is overlooked by one party, and that forms the basis of its faulty reasoning.

12. A

This question presents an interesting twist: It's a "weaken the argument" question, but the argument to be weakened is in the answer choices, and the weakener is the stimulus. This means a greater time investment and an adaptation of your process, which may mean this is a good question to skip and come back to at the end.

In the stimulus you find that an advertising strategy developed for and used by political campaigns has now successfully been applied to corporate accounts. The strategy is to design controversial ads that will become news, generate media attention, and evoke public responses from officials. Thus, the companies get a lot more exposure than they pay for. You don't have to look very far for the choice that's incompatible with this notion; (A) directly violates the "get something for nothing" principle behind the strategy. This strategy flies in the face of the assertion in (A), which says that the usefulness of an ad campaign is based *solely* on the degree to which the ads themselves persuade people. (A) does not consider extra media coverage or public comment by officials to be relevant to an ad's effectiveness. If the statements in the stimulus are true, then (A) is seriously weakened by the fact that some ads are successful thanks to a factor besides persuading the public—namely because they make the news and generate free publicity for the client.

(B) makes too much of the mention of political campaigns: Even though the strategy was originally developed for political campaigns, this is just a little side note—the stimulus focuses on corporate ads, not political ads, so (B) is unaffected by the stimulus.

(C) The assertion that political campaigns have borrowed strategies from corporate advertising is unaffected by the fact that corporate advertising has returned the compliment.

(D) This assertion is actually *strengthened* by the stimulus argument. If, as the stimulus says, ads are now designed to be controversial for maximum exposure value, then it makes sense that name recognition is a bigger priority than the generation of goodwill.

(E) No contradiction here: It's possible for one realm of advertising to borrow strategies from another without the same agencies handling both kinds of campaigns. The stimulus talks about a borrowing of ad strategy, not ad agencies, so the stimulus in no way weakens the assertion in (E).

- Considering the hundreds, and possibly thousands of Logical Reasoning questions you will do for practice before your test, it is highly unlikely that you will come across a question type that's entirely different from anything you've seen. You may, however, find a question that differs slightly from its usual appearance. Don't panic! Simply relate the question to the kinds you're familiar with, and proceed from there.

13. D

Here's the basic argument in which you need to locate an assumption: The likelihood of the early detection of fires hasn't risen even though the percentage of homes with smoke detectors has. This is because over half of these smoke detectors don't work. But what if, 10 years ago, the same problem existed? If, ten years ago, over half of the smoke detectors didn't work, then early detection of fires should be more, not less common now. If the same percentages of detectors were inoperative then as now, then the sheer increase in the percentage of homes with detectors would make early detection more likely now than 10 years ago. Therefore, in order for the conclusion to stand, this must not be the case—the percentage of inoperative detectors must be *higher* now; otherwise, the author's argument gets smoked out. Adding (D) to the scenario, the conclusion can be properly drawn. If you deny (D), the argument falls apart.

(A) is unnecessary. In fact, it's quite possible that no new smoke detectors have been installed in the last 10 years. How can this be? If there are far fewer houses than there were ten years ago, and the ones that no longer exist are ones that didn't have smoke detectors (maybe they burned down...), then the percentage of homes with smoke detectors would have risen, exactly as the stimulus says, yet *no* smoke detectors need have been installed in the last 10 years. This is an extreme case, but the fact that it's logically possible proves that (A) is not a necessary part of this argument.

(B) and (E) The number of fires (B) and the putting out of fires (E) are both issues one step removed from the crux of the argument, which is the likelihood of *early detection* of fires. Smoke detectors don't prevent or put out fires, after all, they just report them—which means that these two choices are outside the scope of the argument, and as such are not necessary assumptions.

(C) Why couldn't *all* smoke detectors be battery operated? Nothing in the argument requires that some smoke detectors aren't battery-operated, as (C) claims. Everything the author says could be true even if every smoke detector ran on batteries—the "other" malfunctions that aren't battery-related could simply be caused by a different part of battery-operated detectors.

- Always be aware of the raw numbers that lurk behind every percentage. The percentage of homes that have smoke detectors is affected by both the number of homes with detectors *and* the total number of homes. If the percentage of houses with smoke detectors has risen, you can't necessarily conclude that *more* detectors were installed, because the other side of the equation might have changed: As you saw in (A), there could instead be *fewer* total houses.

- Always pay attention to the scope of the argument. Here, (B) and (E) are smoke from other fires.

14. D

The first Parallel Reasoning question in the section is based on an ad for HomeGlo Paints, and the stem alerts you to the fact that the reasoning is flawed. Your task, then, is to characterize the flaw, and here it's a scope shift. The award is given to the product that has most *increased* its environmental safety over the last three years, yet the argument concludes that HomeGlo is the *most* environmentally safe brand of paint in the country today. "Most improved" is not necessarily synonymous with "most environmentally safe." You need to find the choice that commits the same error. Check the choices, bearing in mind that you can use the Kaplan technique of comparing conclusions to quickly eliminate a few.

(A) Also contains a scope shift, but it's a different one—you're looking for an answer choice that confuses improvement with overall quality.

(B) The "*most* nutritious food" seems to match the conclusion of the original. However, like (A), there's no element of improvement here. The cereal is allegedly the healthiest cereal on the market. From this, the conclusion generalizes the cereal's top health ranking to *all* foods, which is a fallacy, but not the one found in the stimulus.

(C) again, this argument is flawed by a scope shift (from visits to profits), but there's no question of improvement vs. overall quality.

KAPLAN

(E) Likewise, the scope shift here is between one particular story and the same author's earlier stories—a flaw, but not the one you're looking for.

(D) Contains the same flaw as the stimulus—most improved performance isn't the same thing as "best" performance.

15. E

There are so many different elements to this Inference question that a prephrase is not likely to jump to mind here—the best you can do is follow the logic, making sure you understand exactly what information you are (and are not) given, and eliminate the choices that attempt to combine the statements in ways not supported by the stimulus.

Slight changes in freezer temperature are bad for the consistency of ice cream. The ill effects of these changes can be minimized through the use of stabilizers, but that has its own drawback: Stabilizers detract from the ice cream's flavor. So at this point it looks like a trade-off: In order to prevent a possible consistency problem resulting from temperature change, a small loss in flavor may have to be tolerated. Stabilizers, however, are less necessary (a good thing) if really low storage temperatures are maintained. But even that's a problem. Very low storage temperatures are expensive. So again you've got a trade-off. Consistency is at risk—it can be preserved by using stabilizers or very low storage temperatures, but neither of these is a perfect solution, because stabilizers detract from flavor and low storage temperatures are expensive. As mentioned above, there's a lot swirling around in this one, so the best thing to do is keep the trade-offs in mind and move on to carefully evaluate each choice.

(A) posits an unsupported connection between consistency and flavor. No such connection is stated or implied in the passage. Deviations in storage temperature affect ice cream's consistency, and stabilizers affect its flavor, but (A) mistakenly has deviations in consistency affecting flavor.

(B) 180. As stated in the last sentence, cost considerations favor high storage temperatures due to the increasing cost of energy, and high temperatures require the use of stabilizers, which maintain consistency but adversely affect flavor. So cost considerations favor sacrificing flavor for consistency, not the other way around.

(C) is way off the mark: Nothing in the passage allows you to infer that new technologies would be too costly to develop.

(D) goes against the grain of the passage. You're told that at low temperatures stabilizers are less necessary, which strongly implies that stabilizers are used mainly to maintain the consistency of ice cream stored at relatively high temperatures. Consequently, to say that these stabilizers function well *only* at low temperatures seems to contradict the evidence.

(E) must be inferable, by process of elimination. To preserve consistency it is necessary to have either very low storage temperatures or stabilizers. If you want the best taste, however, you have to avoid the stabilizers. So, to produce the best consistency *and* the best taste in ice cream, you need low, stable freezer temperatures.

- A common wrong answer type in Inference questions is the unwarranted comparison or connection, illustrated nicely in (A) here. It appears often when the stimulus contains two or more groups or elements, such as this argument's "consistency" and "flavor." If there's no stated or implied connection between the two, cross off any choices that attempt to assert that there is.

16. E

As is often the case in a dialogue question, you're asked about how the second person responds to the first, so first get a grip on Edwina's argument so you can see how Alberto's response proceeds. Edwina's conclusion, signaled by the keywords "it follows that," is that you should hear Mozart's music on eighteenth-century instruments. Her evidence for this is that "true appreciation" requires hearing it the way Mozart intended, but this is precisely the point at which Alberto strikes: He questions whether the manner in which Mozart *intended* his music to be heard is in fact the manner in which he actually heard it. What makes you think this is so?— he asks Edwina. It's possible that there's a difference in how Mozart heard his music performed and how he intended it to be played; as evidence, Alberto presents the fact that eighteenth-century performers were expected to *modify* the scores they were given. Essentially then, Alberto presents a reason to believe that Edwina's argument relies upon a false premise, (E).

(A) Alberto appeals to an historical fact, yes, but not to an academic authority (see the second bullet point below).

(B) Alberto attempts to show that the creative license of the eighteenth-century performer extended even to changing the written score. This is not intended to make Edwina more appreciative of performers, though. Rather, it's intended to smash the important connection she draws between what an eighteenth-century performer delivered and what Mozart intended to hear.

(C) "Musical authenticity" is certainly an ambiguous term in this context, but Alberto doesn't attack any view about what is authentic music. Rather, he confines his attack to Edwina's assertion that Mozart heard his music as he intended it to be played. There is no other "competing view" of musical authenticity presented here.

(D) confuses Alberto's point of contention. He doesn't attack the logic that binds Edwina's conclusion to her premises. Instead, he attacks one of the premises itself, the one that says that Mozart heard his music as he intended it to sound.

- It's important in every Logical Reasoning question to understand the author's or speaker's conclusion, and what evidence is used to back it up. But in some questions, like question 16, correctly making this distinction leads directly to the answer. Alberto, in his first sentence, directly attacks part of Edwina's argument. If you recognized that the part under attack is her evidence, you should have gravitated toward (E). Remember, on the LSAT, the word "premise" is simply another word for "evidence."

- An "appeal to authority" is a very specific thing; citing facts by themselves does not constitute an appeal to authority. "The venerable Professor So-and-So" or "The Prestigious Committee on Such-and-Such" are examples of an academic authority. If you chose (A), look back until you convince yourself that no such authority figure appears in this debate.

- Take a look back at (E), and make sure you understand the difference between an attack on an author's *overall* logic—that is, the relationship between evidence and conclusion—and an attack on the evidence itself.

17. D

The stem alerts you to the existence of a paradox in the stimulus—an apparent conflict that you'll be called upon to resolve. So what's strange or unusual about the information in the passage? The mystery appears to be that the cost of private health insurance rose dramatically at a time when it was expected to fall. Due to the new health scheme, the only medical costs that Impanians must pay are those for unusual and sophisticated treatments; it was hoped these procedures could be covered by inexpensive, private

insurance. Since the private insurance companies would only rarely have to pay off on such claims (because the policies would cover only *unusual* treatments), it was expected that such insurance would be affordable. Not so—the cost of these policies soared. It's our job to find the choice that could explain this unexpected result.

In a Paradox question, you may not prephrase exactly, but you need to focus in on the *kind* of evidence you're looking for. The expectation that private policies would be modestly priced was based on the notion that the companies wouldn't have to pay off on them often—unusual treatments are supposedly rare. The fact that the cost of these policies *has* increased dramatically strongly suggests that the companies *are* incurring more medical costs than expected, and anything that leads you in that direction will help solve the mystery. (D) gets you there: If the shrewd Impanians buy these policies only when they know they'll need the kind of care these policies cover, then it's easier to understand why, despite the original expectations, the cost of these policies has increased.

(A) deepens the mystery: If insurers' overhead costs have been substantially reduced, you'd have even more reason to expect them to offer cheaper policies.

(B) is also of no help. If 80 percent of all costs are now footed by the National Health scheme, private insurers should have much less to pay, and the expectation of modest costs still seems reasonable.

(C) suggests that while the poorer Impanians use the National Health Scheme, most, if not all of them, haven't bought private health insurance. Yet, since these people *never* had private health insurance, their failure to purchase it now doesn't explain why policy costs have risen.

(E) The slice of the expenditure pie occupied by health care in the overall Impanian economy isn't relevant here—the apparent discrepancy concerns an unexpected change *within* the health care system, not health care's relative place in the economy as a whole. (If you could conclude from (E) that insurers' costs have risen, then it might explain the paradox. But you can't, so it doesn't.)

- The first step in a Paradox question is to understand the nature of the surprising event, finding, situation, or discrepancy. Only then will you be able to confidently settle on the choice that does away with the apparent conflict.

- It's not unusual in Paradox questions to find choices that deepen the mystery rather than solve it. Make sure you don't accidentally choose one of these choices simply because it has *some* effect on the situation—the effect you're looking for here is resolution.

18. A

Next you need to fill in the blank, which in this case represents an explanation, signaled by the word "because." The situation is fairly straightforward: Half the test subjects in clinical trials for new medicines receive the actual drug, while the others get a placebo, a substance that has no physiological effect. Neither experimenters nor patients are supposed to know who gets what, but alas, this intention is often frustrated because . . . and that's all you get; you have to fill in the remaining piece of the argument.

It's not difficult to prephrase a general explanation: There must be something about the drug or placebo that makes it possible to tell who got which. The placebo, by definition, should have no noticeable effects. Therefore, if one of the two substances produces marked effects on the subjects who receive it, that substance should be the drug. This is the general idea behind correct choice (A), which says that the drug may have side effects that the experimenters recognize. For example, if half the subjects lose their hair within days of taking the medication, this would be a pretty strong indication that those subjects were in fact getting a drug and not a placebo. (A) provides a plausible explanation for why it's not always possible to keep the recipients of the drug and the placebo a secret.

(B) would, if true, most likely *confuse* the experimenters. If subjects getting the placebo often display physical changes, they should be harder to differentiate from those getting the real drug (assuming that those getting the drug will also display some improvement or at least some change).

(C) and (E) merely tell you what kind of subjects are chosen for certain drug trials, which does nothing to explain how experimenters would come to realize which of these subjects are receiving the drug. Neither choice contains any information about what happens during the experiment; the particulars of the selection procedure are therefore irrelevant to the explanation you seek.

(D) would, if anything, make it tougher for the experimenters to determine who's getting the real drug. If experimenters can't observe the experiment for its entire run, then it's less likely they'll notice something that tips them off.

- Fill-in-the-blank questions are fairly rare on the LSAT, but they do appear from time to time. They're not,

however, an entirely different breed of question; often, they work just like Inference questions, or in a case like this, like a Paradox question: Why, if the trials are designed with a particular intention in mind, is this intention often frustrated? If a fill-in-the-blank question appears on your test, try to nail down its "action," and use your knowledge from other question types, where applicable, to solve it.

19. B

Ever wonder what day of the week your birthday (or an anniversary or holiday) will fall on during any given year? You'll never need to wonder again, according to this author, if her plan is enacted. Simply place the last day of each year, and that pesky extra day added every four years, into "limbo," and January 1 will fall on a Sunday every year. This is because 52 weeks times seven days a week equals 364, not 365, the number of days in the current calendar. Get rid of that last day (well, you can't get rid of it altogether, but you *can* call it something different, like "Extra Day," or "blue" for that matter), and the year would divide up perfectly into weeks, and the beginning of every year would fall on the same day of the week. In fact, *every* date on the calendar would always fall on the same day of the week. Then, according to the author, scheduling conflicts will be resolved, because everyone will always know on which day of the week the important events of their lives fall.

If you got the gist of the stem, however, you'd know in advance that this proposal will not clear up conflicts in every possible situation, and you're looking for that situation that would continue to result in the kind of scheduling conflicts the new plan is intended to eliminate. It's not easy to prephrase an answer here, so the best approach is probably to evaluate the situations in each choice, asking yourself "will the new method work here?"

(B) contains the situation that throws the system off kilter, because it contains a stipulation based not on dates, or days of the week—which will all be constant under the new plan—but rather on *an interval* containing a *raw number* of days. This will be fine until the end of the year (or until the designated special time in a leap year) when the extra day is added in. The extra day counts as a day to the religious observers of (B), even though it's not referred to as one of the normal days of the week. If religious workers have to refrain from work every seventh day, their day of rest will vary from year to year (see the bullet point below).

(A) points out dates that might fall outside of a week. This might seem distressing to you, assuming you had an anniversary on one of these dates, but it wouldn't force a conflict. Why not? The "extra" days are not part of any week, and so they won't *change* days of the week from year to year. The anniversaries would be scheduled for these "non-week" dates just as though they fell regularly in a week.

(C) just requires that a certain number of days be devoted to school. This isn't a problem, because there would still be plenty of days for school. Remember, all that would change under the author's proposal is the day of the week upon which a calendar day would fall, not the number of days in a year.

(D) is no problem, either. Since every calendar day would fall on the same day of the week, the new system would merely standardize three-day weekends. So if July 4th (or whatever) formed a three-day weekend one year, then it would form a three-day weekend next year, and so on, forever. Eerie, perhaps, but not a conflict.

(E) These people would benefit from the new calendar. As long as the events they're planning don't occur at the very end of the year, they'll know exactly what day of the week the event will fall on simply by consulting the current year's calendar.

- In questions involving numerical elements, it sometimes helps to formulate a quick example in order to test a choice. If you work out the situation in (B), you see that it *will* cause scheduling conflicts from year to year: Suppose on a non–leap year (to make it easier) such an employee designates the first Sunday of the year as the day of rest. For the next 52 weeks, every Sunday will be the day of rest. But then the next Sunday will be postponed until the beginning of the next year and there will be an extra day between week 52 and the first week of the next year, which means that the day off at the end of the year will fall on the makeup day, and seven days from then will be the following Saturday. For these people, the system doesn't work—their day of rest will vary from year to year.

20. A

The stem here announces a Method of Argument question, and also tells you that the argument is directed against graphology. The graphologists' claim comes in the first sentence: Handwriting can reveal permanent character traits. But the author is skeptical: People who want to be deemed "enthusiastic" can simply work on crossing their "t"s in a stronger fashion. And then comes the final sentence, which may have sounded bizarre if you didn't

recognize its tone. How can graphologists believe that "permanent" character traits can be changed? They can't: "Permanent" means unchangeable, and the author knows this. The author, in this final sentence, is being sarcastic, in order to make the point that the graphologists' view, when confronted by his evidence, leads to an absurd result. The author prefaces his evidence with the word "obviously," which is meant to show, as correct choice (A) has it, that this evidence is "incontestable"—and it does indeed sound reasonable that people could alter their handwriting to include the features that denote good character traits, as the author proposes. This evidence, when combined with the graphologists' view, leads to an absurd result, the impossible changing-permanent character trait. (A) cites the correct method here.

(B) A platitude is a commonplace or banal remark. The author doesn't dismiss the claim that handwriting reveals permanent character traits as being a platitude. He implies that the claim is *absurd*, not commonplace.

(C) The author presents evidence to suggest the incoherence of graphology theory in general, not to say that it can never work when people are aware that this kind of analysis is being used. The author intends to show, by implication, that the entire theory is flawed. He *doesn't* set out specifically to show that the method will be ineffectual in one particular circumstance, that is, when people are aware of its use.

(D) is subtle, but wrong. The author doesn't dismiss graphology's claims as "unjustified"—that would entail saying that the claim is simply not backed up by sufficient evidence. This is not the author's approach; rather, he works to show that the claim is absurd because it implies a contradiction, namely, changeable permanent characteristics.

(E) The author never says that permanent character traits can be detected without graphology—he doesn't criticize graphology for being *unnecessary*.

- Every element in the correct answer to a Method of Argument question must match the structural elements of the argument. Nothing in the correct choice can be superfluous. So, in (A), the apparently incontestable evidence is the idea that people can change their handwriting, the absurd consequence is the idea that permanent character traits can be altered, and the view in question is the idea that graphology can identify permanent character traits. If any piece doesn't match, the answer can't be correct.

21. A

Two points hinge on a dispute between an historian and a critic, and the first point is awarded for correctly characterizing the critic's method of argument. First the historian's argument: During the third Nayalese dynasty, a law taxing timber imports from Poran was enacted. So, although you have no actual evidence of the timber trade, you do have evidence that a law concerning timber trade was put into effect, which *suggests* the existence of a timber trade. The critic finds this reasoning flawed. She grants that the historian's conclusion may well be true—Nayal may indeed have imported timber from Poran—but this conclusion isn't supported by the evidence: It ignores the fact that many laws now exist governing activities that people no longer engage in. Her point, then, is that the historian's argument is flawed because it overlooks the possibility that any given law (specifically, the ancient Nayalese law) may be out of date and thus not truly reflect the activity of a particular era. In suggesting that evidence regarding today's statute books is relevant to the argument concerning ancient Poran and Nayal, the author is, as (A) has it, implying an analogy between present and past. Specifically, she implies that modern day laws and ancient laws are alike in that both can outlive their usefulness.

(B) The critic doesn't identify any principles at all, preferring to point to the specific example of a few outdated laws.

(C) is actually a better description of the *historian's* argument. He's the one who explains that the timber trade is established as a possibility, but not a certainty. The critic's response merely *recognizes* that this trade is a possibility and then goes on to attack the significance that the historian attaches to the Nayalese law.

(D) The critic attacks the historian's "indirect" evidence by implying that similar evidence in the modern period wouldn't necessarily support the same kind of conclusion. But she never offers a list of things that such indirect evidence could be checked against in order to prove its validity. In short, the critic never mentions any specific criteria.

(E) The critic uses an example of modern law to make a point about the old Nayalese law; thus, she isn't pointing out dissimilarities in laws—in fact, just the opposite.

- Some choices in Method of Argument questions are wrong because what the choice posits is "just not there." There's no better way to eliminate such

choices than to simply recognize that what they say is going on in the argument is "just not there." Choices (B) and (D) are particularly good examples of this: General principle? Explicit criteria? They're "just not there."

22. D

Now to pick up the second point related to this debate; you're asked for the flaw in the critic's response. The historian's argument rests on the evidence that the Nayalese law was *enacted* in the third dynasty. So he's banking on the notion that a law regulating a non-existent trade wouldn't be enacted, which seems to make sense. The critic shifts the scope away from "enacted" to "exists"—she argues that just because a law is on the books doesn't mean that it's up-to-date. But this is an unfair response, because "enacted," a word that the critic evidently missed, rules out this possible objection. It's highly unlikely that a law would be out of date at the time it was enacted. In order to truly weaken the historian's argument, the critic would need to offer examples of laws that were irrelevant when they were first put into effect. Her mistake is therefore to overlook the fact that the historian's evidence concerns the *enactment* of a law, not its mere *existence*, (D).

(A) The critic's evidence *doesn't* contradict the possibility of no timber trade between the ancient nations, and thus she *does* provide evidence consistent with this possibility. Remember than in logical terms, "consistent" means nothing more than "not contradictory." However, this is not a flaw in her reasoning. It's perfectly acceptable for this to be the case; you would almost expect her evidence to lean in that direction. Moreover, the critic's response attacks the historian's reasoning, not his conclusion that timber was probably traded.

(B) The current laws cited are intended to illustrate outdated laws, not outdated *timber* laws. They need not have anything to do with the timber trade because the author is citing these laws only to show that laws in general (and that would include ancient Nayalese tariffs) can be outdated.

(C) The distinction between direct and indirect evidence is not lost on the critic. She attacks the historian's reference to the Nayalese tariff, which is pretty clearly stated as indirect evidence. The critic's flaw is that she misses or misinterprets a concept *contained* in this indirect evidence ("enactment"), not that she fails to recognize the evidence as indirect.

(E) The critic doesn't accept the historian's assumption, but rather misunderstands it. The critic thinks the historian is assuming that the existence of a law at a particular time indicates that the activity it regulates also exists at that time. As you've seen, however, the historian is assuming only that the *enactment* of a law at some time indicates the existence of the activity it regulates at that time.

- In two-question stimuli, you can attack the questions in any order you like. If you immediately noticed the scope shift and hence the flaw in the critic's response, you may have jumped right to Flaw question 22 while the flaw was fresh in your mind. Section management techniques are crucial because they offer you yet another way to take control of the test.

- This dialogue offers a nice example of how most scope shifts are born: A word or phrase is either ignored, or subtly changed into something else. The historian said "enacted," but a careful reading of the critic's response reveals that the critic heard "existed." Why is the LSAT this picky? Because the practice of law itself is about the interpretation of laws and statutes, whose meanings hinge on the precise definitions of the words used.

23. C

The argument is missing a large chunk, as you may have noticed from the abrupt conclusion at the end (and also from the stem which tells you that there's a necessary assumption to be filled in here). The author concludes that some subsidiaries will be sold. Why? Because that's the only way to raise wages and avoid a strike. The author must be assuming that there will be no strike, (C). Then and only then does it make sense to say for sure that subsidiaries will be sold, specifically to raise the money to increase the workers' wages.

(A) forecasts increased losses. This is a completely new concept, and you can't conclude anything from it, including the conclusion here that subsidiaries will be sold.

(B) Selling the subsidiaries has been presented as a requirement for raising workers' wages. If, as (B) says, workers' wages *aren't* going to go up, then the author's conclusion becomes truly mystifying, rather than necessary.

(D) Suppose that the president doesn't have the power to authorize the pay increase. Does that contradict the conclusion? No. You don't care who can or will authorize the pay increase, only whether or not the workers are going to get it.

(E) just reinforces one of the premises, namely, the one saying that the workers insist on increased wages. Because this adds nothing new to the argument, it can't justify the conclusion.

- Formal logic is often hidden within seemingly casual arguments. The stimulus argument has a casual tone, but it's actually a formal argument comprised of two conditional statements. First, you get the word "unless" in the first sentence, a word which is used in a very precise way on the LSAT. The correct interpretation of this statement is: *If the workers don't get more money, then they'll strike.* Sentence two can be translated into a common if-then statement: *If workers' wages are to increase, then some subsidiaries have to go.* If you recognized and understood the precise meanings of these formal logic statements, you may have had an easier time with the question.

24. D

This stem offers two important pieces of information. First, you're looking for an assumption, and second, you're told what the argument entails: a "method . . . for determining how quickly a new idea is taking hold." As you read through the stimulus, you need to focus on this method and determine what assumption it relies on.

The method is presented right off the bat. One way to find out how quickly a new idea is taking hold among people is to see how fast the words that describe the new idea pass into everyday language. The second sentence elaborates on this notion: You can tell when a word has passed into everyday usage by consulting experts, namely dictionary editors.

So the notion underlying the method is this: If the vocabulary associated with a new idea has found acceptance, then so has the idea itself. That's true *if* the words, as they pass into common usage, continue to refer to the idea. If the words have passed into usage with altered meanings, then the connection between the words and the idea is severed and you cannot infer the popularity of the latter from the popularity of the former. In order for the method described to work, it must be assumed that no such distortion occurs along the way, as (D) points out.

(A) Just because the author describes dictionary editors as being vitally concerned with words that enter common usage, he needn't assume that they *aren't* professionally interested in lots of other things, such as (A)'s rarely used words.

(B) demands too much of the editors. They need only have an informed opinion about when new words have been accepted into everyday speech. They don't have to have "exact numerical criteria."

(C) The causality expressed in (C) runs counter to the proposed method. Dictionary editors follow new words to see if they become popular enough to be included in a dictionary. The method proposed by the author involves consulting dictionary editors to see if a new idea *has* taken hold, not using editors to *help* ideas take hold by including certain words in their dictionary.

(E) Far from helping the argument, (E) would sink it. If the words tend to be used before the ideas they represent are understood, then a word's passing into everyday speech wouldn't allow you to infer that the idea it represents has been embraced.

25. E

Last up is a Parallel Reasoning question, so you'll begin by characterizing the conclusion. It's a recommendation—specifically, that one thing should be brought more in line with another.

(A) The conclusion is a recommendation, but not that one thing should be made more comparable to another. Eliminate it.

(B) does tell you that one thing should be made more like another. Keep it for now. However, on your second pass through, you'll compare the evidence. The stimulus evidence says that one thing is like another (migrant workers put in similar work schedules to those of full-time workers). There's no such comparison in (B), so it will be eliminated as well.

(C) Another recommendation, but this one relates to the development of a uniform policy, not bringing one specific thing in line with another. Eliminate.

(D) Recommendation relates to who should make a decision, not the substance of the treatment of two particular groups. Eliminate.

(E) Conclusion first—standards applied to one category should be the same as standards applied to another. That's a match. Now look at the evidence. It points to a common element between the two groups, just like the stimulus. It's a match!

- This question contains a lot of text, and it may have been wise to skip it in order to return to any others you left behind during the section. There is no one right order in which to attack the questions, but if you continuously decide the order that's best for you, including which ones to skip and hold off until later and when it's appropriate to return to them, then you're taking matters into your own hands, and you're on the right track.

Practice Test 2

LSAT PRACTICE TEST 2 ANSWER SHEET

Remove (or photocopy) the answer sheet and use it to complete the practice test.

How to Take the Practice Tests

Before taking each test, find a quiet place where you can work uninterrupted for about two and a half hours. Make sure you have a comfortable desk and several No. 2 pencils.

Each Practice Test includes four scored multiple-choice sections. Keep in mind that on the actual LSAT, there will be an additional multiple-choice section—the experimental section—that will not contribute to your score, plus an unscored Writing Sample.

Once you start a Practice Test, don't stop (except for a 5- to 10-minute break after the second section) until you've gone through all four sections. Remember, you can review any questions within a section, but you may not go back or forward a section.

Good luck!

Start with number 1 for each section. If a section has fewer questions than answer spaces, leave the extra spaces blank.

Section I

1. Ⓐ Ⓑ Ⓒ Ⓓ Ⓔ   9. Ⓐ Ⓑ Ⓒ Ⓓ Ⓔ   17. Ⓐ Ⓑ Ⓒ Ⓓ Ⓔ   25. Ⓐ Ⓑ Ⓒ Ⓓ Ⓔ
2. Ⓐ Ⓑ Ⓒ Ⓓ Ⓔ   10. Ⓐ Ⓑ Ⓒ Ⓓ Ⓔ   18. Ⓐ Ⓑ Ⓒ Ⓓ Ⓔ   26. Ⓐ Ⓑ Ⓒ Ⓓ Ⓔ
3. Ⓐ Ⓑ Ⓒ Ⓓ Ⓔ   11. Ⓐ Ⓑ Ⓒ Ⓓ Ⓔ   19. Ⓐ Ⓑ Ⓒ Ⓓ Ⓔ   27. Ⓐ Ⓑ Ⓒ Ⓓ Ⓔ   # right in Section I
4. Ⓐ Ⓑ Ⓒ Ⓓ Ⓔ   12. Ⓐ Ⓑ Ⓒ Ⓓ Ⓔ   20. Ⓐ Ⓑ Ⓒ Ⓓ Ⓔ   28. Ⓐ Ⓑ Ⓒ Ⓓ Ⓔ
5. Ⓐ Ⓑ Ⓒ Ⓓ Ⓔ   13. Ⓐ Ⓑ Ⓒ Ⓓ Ⓔ   21. Ⓐ Ⓑ Ⓒ Ⓓ Ⓔ   29. Ⓐ Ⓑ Ⓒ Ⓓ Ⓔ
6. Ⓐ Ⓑ Ⓒ Ⓓ Ⓔ   14. Ⓐ Ⓑ Ⓒ Ⓓ Ⓔ   22. Ⓐ Ⓑ Ⓒ Ⓓ Ⓔ   30. Ⓐ Ⓑ Ⓒ Ⓓ Ⓔ
7. Ⓐ Ⓑ Ⓒ Ⓓ Ⓔ   15. Ⓐ Ⓑ Ⓒ Ⓓ Ⓔ   23. Ⓐ Ⓑ Ⓒ Ⓓ Ⓔ   # wrong in Section I
8. Ⓐ Ⓑ Ⓒ Ⓓ Ⓔ   16. Ⓐ Ⓑ Ⓒ Ⓓ Ⓔ   24. Ⓐ Ⓑ Ⓒ Ⓓ Ⓔ

Section II

1. Ⓐ Ⓑ Ⓒ Ⓓ Ⓔ   9. Ⓐ Ⓑ Ⓒ Ⓓ Ⓔ   17. Ⓐ Ⓑ Ⓒ Ⓓ Ⓔ   25. Ⓐ Ⓑ Ⓒ Ⓓ Ⓔ
2. Ⓐ Ⓑ Ⓒ Ⓓ Ⓔ   10. Ⓐ Ⓑ Ⓒ Ⓓ Ⓔ   18. Ⓐ Ⓑ Ⓒ Ⓓ Ⓔ   26. Ⓐ Ⓑ Ⓒ Ⓓ Ⓔ
3. Ⓐ Ⓑ Ⓒ Ⓓ Ⓔ   11. Ⓐ Ⓑ Ⓒ Ⓓ Ⓔ   19. Ⓐ Ⓑ Ⓒ Ⓓ Ⓔ   27. Ⓐ Ⓑ Ⓒ Ⓓ Ⓔ   # right in Section II
4. Ⓐ Ⓑ Ⓒ Ⓓ Ⓔ   12. Ⓐ Ⓑ Ⓒ Ⓓ Ⓔ   20. Ⓐ Ⓑ Ⓒ Ⓓ Ⓔ   28. Ⓐ Ⓑ Ⓒ Ⓓ Ⓔ
5. Ⓐ Ⓑ Ⓒ Ⓓ Ⓔ   13. Ⓐ Ⓑ Ⓒ Ⓓ Ⓔ   21. Ⓐ Ⓑ Ⓒ Ⓓ Ⓔ   29. Ⓐ Ⓑ Ⓒ Ⓓ Ⓔ
6. Ⓐ Ⓑ Ⓒ Ⓓ Ⓔ   14. Ⓐ Ⓑ Ⓒ Ⓓ Ⓔ   22. Ⓐ Ⓑ Ⓒ Ⓓ Ⓔ   30. Ⓐ Ⓑ Ⓒ Ⓓ Ⓔ
7. Ⓐ Ⓑ Ⓒ Ⓓ Ⓔ   15. Ⓐ Ⓑ Ⓒ Ⓓ Ⓔ   23. Ⓐ Ⓑ Ⓒ Ⓓ Ⓔ   # wrong in Section II
8. Ⓐ Ⓑ Ⓒ Ⓓ Ⓔ   16. Ⓐ Ⓑ Ⓒ Ⓓ Ⓔ   24. Ⓐ Ⓑ Ⓒ Ⓓ Ⓔ

Section III

1. Ⓐ Ⓑ Ⓒ Ⓓ Ⓔ   9. Ⓐ Ⓑ Ⓒ Ⓓ Ⓔ   17. Ⓐ Ⓑ Ⓒ Ⓓ Ⓔ   25. Ⓐ Ⓑ Ⓒ Ⓓ Ⓔ
2. Ⓐ Ⓑ Ⓒ Ⓓ Ⓔ   10. Ⓐ Ⓑ Ⓒ Ⓓ Ⓔ   18. Ⓐ Ⓑ Ⓒ Ⓓ Ⓔ   26. Ⓐ Ⓑ Ⓒ Ⓓ Ⓔ
3. Ⓐ Ⓑ Ⓒ Ⓓ Ⓔ   11. Ⓐ Ⓑ Ⓒ Ⓓ Ⓔ   19. Ⓐ Ⓑ Ⓒ Ⓓ Ⓔ   27. Ⓐ Ⓑ Ⓒ Ⓓ Ⓔ   # right in Section III
4. Ⓐ Ⓑ Ⓒ Ⓓ Ⓔ   12. Ⓐ Ⓑ Ⓒ Ⓓ Ⓔ   20. Ⓐ Ⓑ Ⓒ Ⓓ Ⓔ   28. Ⓐ Ⓑ Ⓒ Ⓓ Ⓔ
5. Ⓐ Ⓑ Ⓒ Ⓓ Ⓔ   13. Ⓐ Ⓑ Ⓒ Ⓓ Ⓔ   21. Ⓐ Ⓑ Ⓒ Ⓓ Ⓔ   29. Ⓐ Ⓑ Ⓒ Ⓓ Ⓔ
6. Ⓐ Ⓑ Ⓒ Ⓓ Ⓔ   14. Ⓐ Ⓑ Ⓒ Ⓓ Ⓔ   22. Ⓐ Ⓑ Ⓒ Ⓓ Ⓔ   30. Ⓐ Ⓑ Ⓒ Ⓓ Ⓔ
7. Ⓐ Ⓑ Ⓒ Ⓓ Ⓔ   15. Ⓐ Ⓑ Ⓒ Ⓓ Ⓔ   23. Ⓐ Ⓑ Ⓒ Ⓓ Ⓔ   # wrong in Section III
8. Ⓐ Ⓑ Ⓒ Ⓓ Ⓔ   16. Ⓐ Ⓑ Ⓒ Ⓓ Ⓔ   24. Ⓐ Ⓑ Ⓒ Ⓓ Ⓔ

Section IV

1. Ⓐ Ⓑ Ⓒ Ⓓ Ⓔ	9. Ⓐ Ⓑ Ⓒ Ⓓ Ⓔ	17. Ⓐ Ⓑ Ⓒ Ⓓ Ⓔ	25. Ⓐ Ⓑ Ⓒ Ⓓ Ⓔ
2. Ⓐ Ⓑ Ⓒ Ⓓ Ⓔ	10. Ⓐ Ⓑ Ⓒ Ⓓ Ⓔ	18. Ⓐ Ⓑ Ⓒ Ⓓ Ⓔ	26. Ⓐ Ⓑ Ⓒ Ⓓ Ⓔ
3. Ⓐ Ⓑ Ⓒ Ⓓ Ⓔ	11. Ⓐ Ⓑ Ⓒ Ⓓ Ⓔ	19. Ⓐ Ⓑ Ⓒ Ⓓ Ⓔ	27. Ⓐ Ⓑ Ⓒ Ⓓ Ⓔ
4. Ⓐ Ⓑ Ⓒ Ⓓ Ⓔ	12. Ⓐ Ⓑ Ⓒ Ⓓ Ⓔ	20. Ⓐ Ⓑ Ⓒ Ⓓ Ⓔ	28. Ⓐ Ⓑ Ⓒ Ⓓ Ⓔ
5. Ⓐ Ⓑ Ⓒ Ⓓ Ⓔ	13. Ⓐ Ⓑ Ⓒ Ⓓ Ⓔ	21. Ⓐ Ⓑ Ⓒ Ⓓ Ⓔ	29. Ⓐ Ⓑ Ⓒ Ⓓ Ⓔ
6. Ⓐ Ⓑ Ⓒ Ⓓ Ⓔ	14. Ⓐ Ⓑ Ⓒ Ⓓ Ⓔ	22. Ⓐ Ⓑ Ⓒ Ⓓ Ⓔ	30. Ⓐ Ⓑ Ⓒ Ⓓ Ⓔ
7. Ⓐ Ⓑ Ⓒ Ⓓ Ⓔ	15. Ⓐ Ⓑ Ⓒ Ⓓ Ⓔ	23. Ⓐ Ⓑ Ⓒ Ⓓ Ⓔ	
8. Ⓐ Ⓑ Ⓒ Ⓓ Ⓔ	16. Ⓐ Ⓑ Ⓒ Ⓓ Ⓔ	24. Ⓐ Ⓑ Ⓒ Ⓓ Ⓔ	

☐ # right in Section IV

☐ # wrong in Section IV

 GO ONLINE

Be sure to add your scores to your syllabus.

Practice Test 2
Section I: Logical Reasoning

Time—35 minutes
25 questions

<u>Directions:</u> The questions in this section are based on the reasoning contained in brief statements or passages. For some questions, more than one of the choices could conceivably answer the question. However, you are to choose the <u>best</u> answer; that is, the response that most accurately and completely answers the question. You should not make assumptions that are by commonsense standards implausible, superfluous, or incompatible with the passage. After you have chosen the best answer, blacken the corresponding space on your answer sheet.

1. Of all the surgeons practicing at the city hospital, the chief surgeon has the worst record in terms of the percentage of his patients who die either during or immediately following an operation performed by him. Paradoxically, the hospital's administrators claim that he is the best surgeon currently working at the hospital.

Which one of the following, if true, goes farthest toward showing that the administrators' claim and the statistic cited might both be correct?

(A) Since the hospital administrators appoint the chief surgeon, the administrators are strongly motivated to depict the chief surgeon they have chosen as a wise choice.

(B) In appointing the current chief surgeon, the hospital administrators followed the practice, well established at the city hospital, of promoting one of the surgeons already on staff.

(C) Some of the younger surgeons on the city hospital's staff received part of their training from the current chief surgeon.

(D) At the city hospital those operations that inherently entail the greatest risk to the life of the patient are generally performed by the chief surgeon.

(E) The current chief surgeon has a better record of patients' surviving surgery than did his immediate predecessor.

2. Between 1971 and 1975, the government office that monitors drug companies issued an average of 60 citations a year for serious violations of drug-promotion laws. Between 1976 and 1980, the annual average for issuance of such citations was only 5. This decrease indicates that the government office was, on average, considerably more lax in enforcing drug-promotion laws between 1976 and 1980 than it was between 1971 and 1975.

The argument assumes which one of the following?

(A) The decrease in the number of citations was not caused by a decrease in drug companies' violations of drug-promotion laws.

(B) A change in enforcement of drug-promotion laws did not apply to minor violations.

(C) The enforcement of drug-promotion laws changed in response to political pressure.

(D) The government office should not issue more than an average of 5 citations a year to drug companies for serious violations of drug-promotion laws.

(E) Before 1971 the government office issued more than 60 citations a year to drug companies for serious violations of drug-promotion laws.

GO ON TO THE NEXT PAGE.

3. Sheila: Health experts generally agree that smoking a tobacco product for many years is very likely to be harmful to the smoker's health.

Tim: On the contrary, smoking has no effect on health at all: although my grandfather smoked three cigars a day from the age of 14, he died at age 96.

A major weakness of Tim's counterargument is that his counterargument

(A) attempts to refute a probabilistic conclusion by claiming the existence of a single counterexample

(B) challenges expert opinion on the basis of specific information unavailable to experts in the field

(C) describes an individual case that is explicitly discounted as an exception to the experts' conclusion

(D) presupposes that longevity and health status are unrelated to each other in the general population

(E) tacitly assumes that those health experts who are in agreement on this issue arrived at that agreement independently of one another

4. The case of the French Revolution is typically regarded as the best evidence for the claim that societies can reap more benefit than harm from a revolution. But even the French Revolution serves this role poorly, since France at the time of the Revolution had a unique advantage. Despite the Revolution, the same civil servants and functionaries remained in office, carrying on the day-to-day work of government, and thus many of the disruptions that revolutions normally bring were avoided.

Which one of the following most accurately characterizes the argumentative strategy used in the passage?

(A) demonstrating that the claim argued against is internally inconsistent

(B) supporting a particular position on the basis of general principles

(C) opposing a claim by undermining evidence offered in support of that claim

(D) justifying a view through the use of a series of persuasive examples

(E) comparing two positions in order to illustrate their relative strengths and weaknesses

5. A person can develop or outgrow asthma at any age. In children under 10, asthma is twice as likely to develop in boys. Boys are less likely than girls to outgrow asthma, yet by adolescence the percentage of boys with asthma is about the same as the percentage of girls with asthma because a large number of girls develop asthma in early adolescence.

Assuming the truth of the passage, one can conclude from it that the number of adolescent boys with asthma is approximately equal to the number of adolescent girls with asthma, if one also knows that

(A) a tendency toward asthma is often inherited

(B) children who develop asthma before two years of age are unlikely to outgrow it

(C) there are approximately equal numbers of adolescent boys and adolescent girls in the population

(D) the development of asthma in childhood is not closely related to climate or environment

(E) the percentage of adults with asthma is lower than the percentage of adolescents with asthma

6. Harry Trevalga: You and your publication have unfairly discriminated against my poems. I have submitted 30 poems in the last two years and you have not published any of them! It is all because I won the Fenner Poetry Award two years ago and your poetry editor thought she deserved it.

Publisher: Ridiculous! Our editorial policy and practice is perfectly fair, since our poetry editor judges all submissions for publication without ever seeing the names of the poets, and hence cannot possibly have known who wrote your poems.

The publisher makes which one of the following assumptions in replying to Trevalga's charges of unfair discrimination?

(A) The poetry editor does not bear a grudge against Harry Trevalga for his winning the Fenner Poetry Award.

(B) It is not unusual for poets to contribute many poems to the publisher's publication without ever having any accepted for publication.

(C) The poetry editor cannot recognize the poems submitted by Harry Trevalga as his unless Trevalga's name is attached to them.

(D) The poetry editor's decisions on which poems to publish are not based strictly on judgments of intrinsic merit.

(E) Harry Trevalga submitted his poems to the publisher's publication under his pen name.

GO ON TO THE NEXT PAGE.

KAPLAN

7. In a study of the effect of radiation from nuclear weapons plants on people living in areas near them, researchers compared death rates in the areas near the plants with death rates in areas that had no such plants. Finding no difference in these rates, the researchers concluded that radiation from the nuclear weapons plants poses no health hazards to people living near them.

Which one of the following, if true, most seriously weakens the researchers' argument?

(A) Nuclear power plants were not included in the study.
(B) The areas studied had similar death rates before and after the nuclear weapons plants were built.
(C) Exposure to nuclear radiation can cause many serious diseases that do not necessarily result in death.
(D) Only a small number of areas have nuclear weapons plants.
(E) The researchers did not study the possible health hazards of radiation on people who were employed at the nuclear weapons plants if those employees did not live in the study areas.

8. It was once believed that cells grown in laboratory tissue cultures were essentially immortal. That is, as long as all of their needs were met, they would continue dividing forever. However, it has been shown that normal cells have a finite reproductive limit. A human liver cell, for example, divides 60 times and then stops. If such a cell divides 30 times and then is put into a deep freeze for months or even years, it "remembers" where it stopped dividing. After thawing, it divides another 30 times—but no more.

If the information above is accurate, a liver cell in which more than 60 divisions took place in a tissue culture CANNOT be which one of the following?

(A) an abnormal human liver cell
(B) a normal human liver cell that had been frozen after its first division and afterward thawed
(C) a normal cell that came from the liver of an individual of a nonhuman species and had never been frozen
(D) a normal liver cell that came from an individual of a nonhuman species and had been frozen after its first division and afterward thawed
(E) an abnormal cell from the liver of an individual of a nonhuman species

9. Complaints that milk bottlers take enormous markups on the bottled milk sold to consumers are most likely to arise when least warranted by the actual spread between the price that bottlers pay for raw milk and the price at which they sell bottled milk. The complaints occur when the bottled-milk price rises, yet these price increases most often merely reflect the rising price of the raw milk that bottlers buy from dairy farmers. When the raw-milk price is rising, the bottlers' markups are actually smallest proportionate to the retail price. When the raw-milk price is falling, however, the markups are greatest.

If all of the statements above are true, which one of the following must also be true on the basis of them?

(A) Consumers pay more for bottled milk when raw-milk prices are falling than when these prices are rising.
(B) Increases in dairy farmers' cost of producing milk are generally not passed on to consumers.
(C) Milk bottlers take substantially greater markups on bottled milk when its price is low for an extended period than when it is high for an extended period.
(D) Milk bottlers generally do not respond to a decrease in raw-milk prices by straightaway proportionately lowering the price of the bottled milk they sell.
(E) Consumers tend to complain more about the price they pay for bottled milk when dairy farmers are earning their smallest profits.

GO ON TO THE NEXT PAGE.

Questions 10–11

If the public library shared by the adjacent towns of Redville and Glenwood were relocated from the library's current, overcrowded building in central Redville to a larger, available building in central Glenwood, the library would then be within walking distance of a larger number of library users. That is because there are many more people living in central Glenwood than in central Redville, and people generally will walk to the library only if it is located close to their homes.

10. Which one of the following, if true, most strengthens the argument?

(A) The public library was located between Glenwood and Redville before being moved to its current location in central Redville.

(B) The area covered by central Glenwood is approximately the same size as that covered by central Redville.

(C) The building that is available in Glenwood is smaller than an alternative building that is available in Redville.

(D) Many of the people who use the public library do not live in either Glenwood or Redville.

(E) The distance that people currently walk to get to the library is farther than what is generally considered walking distance.

11. Which one of the following, if true, most seriously weakens the argument?

(A) Many more people who currently walk to the library live in central Redville than in central Glenwood.

(B) The number of people living in central Glenwood who would use the library if it were located there is smaller than the number of people living in central Redville who currently use the library.

(C) The number of people using the public library would continue to increase steadily if the library were moved to Glenwood.

(D) Most of the people who currently either drive to the library or take public transportation to reach it would continue to do so if the library were moved to central Glenwood.

(E) Most of the people who currently walk to the library would remain library users if the library were relocated to central Glenwood.

12. Light utility trucks have become popular among consumers who buy them primarily for the trucks' rugged appearance. Yet although these trucks are tough-looking, they are exempt from the government's car-safety standards that dictate minimum roof strength and minimum resistance to impact. Therefore, if involved in a serious high-impact accident, a driver of one of these trucks is more likely to be injured than is a driver of a car that is subject to these government standards.

The argument depends on the assumption that

(A) the government has established safety standards for the construction of light utility trucks

(B) people who buy automobiles solely for their appearance are more likely than other people to drive recklessly

(C) light utility trucks are more likely than other kinds of vehicles to be involved in accidents that result in injuries

(D) the trucks' rugged appearance is deceptive in that their engines are not especially powerful

(E) light utility trucks are less likely to meet the car-safety standards than are cars that are subject to the standards

13. Five years ago, during the first North American outbreak of the cattle disease CXC, the death rate from the disease was 5 percent of all reported cases, whereas today the corresponding figure is over 18 percent. It is clear, therefore, that during these past 5 years, CXC has increased in virulence.

Which one of the following, if true, most substantially weakens the argument?

(A) Many recent cattle deaths that have actually been caused by CXC have been mistakenly attributed to another disease that mimics the symptoms of CXC.

(B) During the first North American outbreak of the disease, many of the deaths reported to have been caused by CXC were actually due to other causes.

(C) An inoculation program against CXC was recently begun after controlled studies showed inoculation to be 70 percent effective in preventing serious cases of the illness.

(D) Since the first outbreak, farmers have learned to treat mild cases of CXC and no longer report them to veterinarians or authorities.

(E) Cattle that have contracted and survived CXC rarely contract the disease a second time.

GO ON TO THE NEXT PAGE.

Questions 14–15

Economist: Some policymakers believe that our country's continued economic growth requires a higher level of personal savings than we currently have. A recent legislative proposal would allow individuals to set up savings accounts in which interest earned would be exempt from taxes until money is withdrawn from the account. Backers of this proposal claim that its implementation would increase the amount of money available for banks to loan at a relatively small cost to the government in lost tax revenues. Yet, when similar tax-incentive programs were tried in the past, virtually all of the money invested through them was diverted from other personal savings, and the overall level of personal savings was unchanged.

14. The passage as a whole provides the most support for which one of the following conclusions?

   (A) Backers of the tax-incentive proposal undoubtedly have some motive other than their expressed aim of increasing the amount of money available for banks to loan.
   (B) The proposed tax incentive is unlikely to attract enough additional money into personal savings accounts to make up for the attendant loss in tax revenues.
   (C) A tax-incentive program that resulted in substantial loss of tax revenues would be likely to generate a large increase in personal savings.
   (D) The economy will be in danger unless some alternative to increased personal savings can be found to stimulate growth.
   (E) The government has no effective means of influencing the amount of money that people are willing to put into savings accounts.

15. The author criticizes the proposed tax-incentive program by

   (A) challenging a premise on which the proposal is based
   (B) pointing out a disagreement among policymakers
   (C) demonstrating that the proposal's implementation is not feasible
   (D) questioning the judgment of the proposal's backers by citing past cases in which they had advocated programs that have proved ineffective
   (E) disputing the assumption that a program to encourage personal savings is needed

16. Although all birds have feathers and all birds have wings, some birds do not fly. For example, penguins and ostriches use their wings to move in a different way from other birds. Penguins use their wings only to swim under water at high speeds. Ostriches use their wings only to run with the wind by lifting them as if they were sails.

Which one of the following is most parallel in its reasoning to the argument above?

   (A) Ancient philosophers tried to explain not how the world functions but why it functions. In contrast, most contemporary biologists seek comprehensive theories of how organisms function, but many refuse to speculate about purpose.
   (B) Some chairs are used only as decorations, and other chairs are used only to tame lions. Therefore, not all chairs are used for sitting in despite the fact that all chairs have a seat and some support such as legs.
   (C) Some musicians in a symphony orchestra play the violin, and others play the viola, but these are both in the same category of musical instruments, namely string instruments.
   (D) All cars have similar drive mechanisms, but some cars derive their power from solar energy, whereas others burn gasoline. Thus, solar-powered cars are less efficient than gasoline-powered ones.
   (E) Sailing ships move in a different way from steamships. Both sailing ships and steamships navigate over water, but only sailing ships use sails to move over the surface.

GO ON TO THE NEXT PAGE.

Questions 17–18

Jones: Prehistoric wooden tools found in South America have been dated to 13,000 years ago. Although scientists attribute these tools to peoples whose ancestors first crossed into the Americas from Siberia to Alaska, this cannot be correct. In order to have reached a site so far south, these peoples must have been migrating southward well before 13,000 years ago. However, no such tools dating to before 13,000 years ago have been found anywhere between Alaska and South America.

Smith: Your evidence is inconclusive. Those tools were found in peat bogs, which are rare in the Americas. Wooden tools in soils other than peat bogs usually decompose within only a few years.

17. The point at issue between Jones and Smith is

   (A) whether all prehistoric tools that are 13,000 years or older were made of wood
   (B) whether the scientists' attribution of tools could be correct in light of Jones's evidence
   (C) whether the dating of the wooden tools by the scientists could be correct
   (D) how long ago the peoples who crossed into the Americas from Siberia to Alaska first did so
   (E) whether Smith's evidence entails that the wooden tools have been dated correctly

18. Smith responds to Jones by

   (A) citing several studies that invalidate Jones's conclusion
   (B) accusing Jones of distorting the scientists' position
   (C) disputing the accuracy of the supporting evidence cited by Jones
   (D) showing that Jones's evidence actually supports the denial of Jones's conclusion
   (E) challenging an implicit assumption in Jones's argument

19. Editorial: It is clear that if this country's universities were living up to both their moral and their intellectual responsibilities, the best-selling publications in most university bookstores would not be frivolous ones like *TV Today* and *Gossip Review*. However, in most university bookstores the only publication that sells better than *Gossip Review* is *TV Today*.

If the statements in the editorial are true, which one of the following must also be true on the basis of them?

   (A) People who purchase publications that are devoted primarily to gossip or to television programming are intellectually irresponsible.
   (B) It is irresponsible for university bookstores to carry publications such as *Gossip Review* and *TV Today*.
   (C) Most people who purchase publications at university bookstores purchase either *TV Today* or *Gossip Review*.
   (D) Many people who attend this country's universities fail to live up to both their moral and their intellectual responsibilities.
   (E) At least some of this country's universities are not meeting their moral responsibilities or their intellectual responsibilities or both.

Questions 20–21

Saunders: Everyone at last week's neighborhood association meeting agreed that the row of abandoned and vandalized houses on Carlton Street posed a threat to the safety of our neighborhood. Moreover, no one now disputes that getting the houses torn down eliminated that threat. Some people tried to argue that it was unnecessary to demolish what they claimed were basically sound buildings, since the city had established a fund to help people in need of housing buy and rehabilitate such buildings. The overwhelming success of the demolition strategy, however, proves that the majority, who favored demolition, were right and that those who claimed that the problem could and should be solved by rehabilitating the houses were wrong.

20. Which one of the following principles, if established, would determine that demolishing the houses was the right decision or instead would determine that the proposal advocated by the opponents of demolition should have been adopted?

(A) When what to do about an abandoned neighborhood building is in dispute, the course of action that would result in the most housing for people who need it should be the one adopted unless the building is believed to pose a threat to neighborhood safety.

(B) When there are two proposals for solving a neighborhood problem, and only one of them would preclude the possibility of trying the other approach if the first proves unsatisfactory, then the approach that does not foreclose the other possibility should be the one adopted.

(C) If one of two proposals for renovating vacant neighborhood buildings requires government funding whereas the second does not, the second proposal should be the one adopted unless the necessary government funds have already been secured.

(D) No plan for eliminating a neighborhood problem that requires demolishing basically sound houses should be carried out until all other possible alternatives have been thoroughly investigated.

(E) No proposal for dealing with a threat to a neighborhood's safety should be adopted merely because a majority of the residents of that neighborhood prefer that proposal to a particular counterproposal.

21. Saunders's reasoning is flawed because it

(A) relies on fear rather than on argument to persuade the neighborhood association to reject the policy advocated by Saunders's opponents

(B) fails to establish that there is anyone who could qualify for city funds who would be interested in buying and rehabilitating the houses

(C) mistakenly equates an absence of vocal public dissent with the presence of universal public support

(D) offers no evidence that the policy advocated by Saunders's opponents would not have succeeded if it had been given the chance

(E) does not specify the precise nature of the threat to neighborhood safety supposedly posed by the vandalized houses

22. For the writers who first gave feudalism its name, the existence of feudalism presupposed the existence of a noble class. Yet there cannot be a noble class, properly speaking, unless both the titles that indicate superior, noble status and the inheritance of such titles are sanctioned by law. Although feudalism existed in Europe as early as the eighth century, it was not until the twelfth century, when many feudal institutions were in decline, that the hereditary transfer of legally recognized titles of nobility first appeared.

The statements above, if true, most strongly support which one of the following claims?

(A) To say that feudalism by definition requires the existence of a nobility is to employ a definition that distorts history.

(B) Prior to the twelfth century, the institution of European feudalism functioned without the presence of a dominant class.

(C) The fact that a societal group has a distinct legal status is not in itself sufficient to allow that group to be properly considered a social class.

(D) The decline of feudalism in Europe was the only cause of the rise of a European nobility.

(E) The prior existence of feudal institutions is a prerequisite for the emergence of a nobility, as defined in the strictest sense of the term.

GO ON TO THE NEXT PAGE.

23. Mayor Smith, one of our few government officials with a record of outspoken, informed, and consistent opposition to nuclear power plant construction projects, has now declared herself in favor of building the nuclear power plant at Littletown. If someone with her past antinuclear record now favors building this power plant, then there is good reason to believe that it will be safe and therefore should be built.

The argument is vulnerable to criticism on which one of the following grounds?

(A) It overlooks the possibility that not all those who fail to speak out on issues of nuclear power are necessarily opposed to it.

(B) It assumes without warrant that the qualities enabling a person to be elected to public office confer on that person a grasp of the scientific principles on which technical decisions are based.

(C) It fails to establish that a consistent and outspoken opposition is necessarily an informed opposition.

(D) It leads to the further but unacceptable conclusion that any project favored by Mayor Smith should be sanctioned simply on the basis of her having spoken out in favor of it.

(E) It gives no indication of either the basis of Mayor Smith's former opposition to nuclear power plant construction or the reasons for her support for the Littletown project.

24. Advertisement: In today's world, you make a statement about the person you are by the car you own. The message of the SKX Mach-5 is unambiguous: Its owner is Dynamic, Aggressive, and Successful. Shouldn't you own an SKX Mach-5?

If the claims made in the advertisement are true, which one of the following must also be true on the basis of them?

(A) Anyone who is dynamic and aggressive is also successful.

(B) Anyone who is not both dynamic and successful would misrepresent himself or herself by being the owner of an SKX Mach-5.

(C) People who buy the SKX Mach-5 are usually more aggressive than people who buy other cars.

(D) No car other than the SKX Mach-5 announces that its owner is successful.

(E) Almost no one would fail to recognize the kind of person who would choose to own an SKX Mach-5.

25. The great medieval universities had no administrators, yet they endured for centuries. Our university has a huge administrative staff, and we are in serious financial difficulties. Therefore, we should abolish the positions and salaries of the administrators to ensure the longevity of the university.

Which one of the following arguments contains flawed reasoning that most closely parallels the flawed reasoning in the argument above?

(A) No airplane had jet engines before 1940, yet airplanes had been flying since 1903. Therefore, jet engines are not necessary for the operation of airplanes.

(B) The novelist's stories began to be accepted for publication soon after she started using a computer to write them. You have been having trouble getting your stories accepted for publication, and you do not use a computer. To make sure your stories are accepted for publication, then, you should write them with the aid of a computer.

(C) After doctors began using antibiotics, the number of infections among patients dropped drastically. Now, however, resistant strains of bacteria cannot be controlled by standard antibiotics. Therefore, new methods of control are needed.

(D) A bicycle should not be ridden without a helmet. Since a good helmet can save the rider's life, a helmet should be considered the most important piece of bicycling equipment.

(E) The great cities of the ancient world were mostly built along waterways. Archaeologists searching for the remains of such cities should therefore try to determine where major rivers used to run.

STOP

IF YOU FINISH BEFORE TIME IS CALLED, YOU MAY CHECK YOUR WORK ON THIS SECTION ONLY.
DO NOT WORK ON ANY OTHER SECTION IN THE TEST.

KAPLAN

Practice Test 2

Section II: **Analytical Reasoning**

Time—35 minutes
24 questions

<u>Directions:</u> Each group of questions in this section is based on a set of conditions. In answering some of the questions, it may be useful to draw a rough diagram. Choose the response that most accurately and completely answers each question and blacken the corresponding space on your answer sheet.

Questions 1–5

A gymnastics instructor is planning a weekly schedule, Monday through Friday, of individual coaching sessions for each of six students—H, I, K, O, U, and Z. The instructor will coach exactly one student each day, except for one day when the instructor will coach two students in separate but consecutive sessions. The following restrictions apply:

    H's session must take place at some time before Z's session.

    I's session is on Thursday.

    K's session is always scheduled for the day immediately before or the day immediately after the day for which O's session is scheduled.

    Neither Monday nor Wednesday can be a day for which two students are scheduled.

1. Which one of the following is a pair of students whose sessions can both be scheduled for Tuesday, not necessarily in the order given?

    (A) H and U
    (B) H and Z
    (C) K and O
    (D) O and U
    (E) U and Z

2. If K's session is scheduled for Tuesday, then which one of the following is the earliest day for which Z's session can be scheduled?

    (A) Monday
    (B) Tuesday
    (C) Wednesday
    (D) Thursday
    (E) Friday

3. Which one of the following must be true?

    (A) If U's session is scheduled for Monday, H's session is scheduled for Tuesday.
    (B) If U's session is scheduled for Tuesday, O's session is scheduled for Wednesday.
    (C) If U's session is scheduled for Wednesday, Z's session is scheduled for Tuesday.
    (D) If U's session is scheduled for Thursday, Z's session is scheduled for Friday.
    (E) If U's session is scheduled for Friday, Z's session is scheduled for Thursday.

4. Scheduling Z's session for which one of the following days determines the day for which U's session must be scheduled?

    (A) Monday
    (B) Tuesday
    (C) Wednesday
    (D) Thursday
    (E) Friday

5. If H's session is scheduled as the next session after U's session, which one of the following could be true about H's session and U's session?

    (A) U's session is scheduled for Monday, and H's session is scheduled for Tuesday.
    (B) U's session is scheduled for Thursday, and H's session is scheduled for Friday.
    (C) They are both scheduled for Tuesday.
    (D) They are both scheduled for Thursday.
    (E) They are both scheduled for Friday.

GO ON TO THE NEXT PAGE.

Questions 6–12

A square parking lot has exactly eight lights—numbered 1 through 8—situated along its perimeter as diagramed below.

The lot must always be illuminated in such a way that the following specifications are met:

At least one of any three consecutively numbered lights is off.
Light 8 is on.
Neither light 2 nor light 7 is on when light 1 is on.
At least one of the three lights on each side is on.
If any side has exactly one of its three lights on, then that light is its center light.
Two of the lights on the north side are on.

6. Which one of the following could be a complete and accurate list of lights that are on together?

(A) 1, 3, 5, 7
(B) 2, 4, 6, 8
(C) 2, 3, 5, 6, 8
(D) 3, 4, 6, 7, 8
(E) 1, 2, 4, 5, 6, 8

7. Which one of the following lights must be on?

(A) light 2
(B) light 3
(C) light 4
(D) light 5
(E) light 6

8. If light 1 is off, which one of the following is a light that must also be off?

(A) light 3
(B) light 4
(C) light 5
(D) light 6
(E) light 7

9. Which one of the following statements must be true?

(A) If light 2 is on, then light 6 is off.
(B) If light 3 is on, then light 2 is on.
(C) If light 4 is on, then light 3 is off.
(D) If light 5 is off, then light 4 is on.
(E) If light 6 is off, then light 1 is on.

10. If light 5 is on, which one of the following could be true?

(A) Light 1 is off and light 6 is off.
(B) Light 1 is on and light 7 is on.
(C) Light 2 is off and light 4 is on.
(D) Light 2 is off and light 6 is off.
(E) Light 6 is on and light 7 is on.

11. If light 4 is on, each of the following statements must be true EXCEPT:

(A) Light 1 is on.
(B) Light 2 is on.
(C) Light 5 is off.
(D) Light 6 is on.
(E) Light 7 is off.

12. Suppose that it is no longer part of the specifications that two lights on the north side be on. If all of the other original specifications remain the same, and if exactly one light on the north side is on, which one of the following statements could be false?

(A) Light 1 is off.
(B) Light 2 is on.
(C) Light 3 is off.
(D) Light 4 is on.
(E) Light 5 is on.

GO ON TO THE NEXT PAGE.

Questions 13–17

Seven children are to be seated in seven chairs arranged in a row that runs from west to east. All seven children will face north. Four of the children are boys: Frank, Harry, Ivan, and Joel. Three are girls: Ruby, Sylvia, and Thelma. The children are assigned to chairs according to the following conditions:

Exactly one child sits in each chair.

No boy sits next to another boy.

Ivan sits next to and east of the fourth child in the row.

Sylvia sits east of Ivan.

Frank sits next to Ruby.

13. What is the maximum possible number of different pairs of chairs in which Frank and Ruby could sit?

(A) one
(B) two
(C) three
(D) four
(E) five

14. Which one of the following statements must be false?

(A) Both Harry and Joel sit east of Frank.
(B) Both Harry and Ruby sit east of Frank.
(C) Both Harry and Joel sit west of Frank.
(D) Both Harry and Ruby sit west of Frank.
(E) Both Joel and Ruby sit east of Frank.

15. If Thelma sits next to Ivan, and if Frank sits next to Thelma, which one of the following statements could be false?

(A) Both Frank and Ivan sit east of Ruby.
(B) Both Frank and Ruby sit west of Thelma.
(C) Both Frank and Sylvia sit east of Ruby.
(D) Both Frank and Thelma sit west of Sylvia.
(E) Both Frank and Ruby sit west of Joel.

16. If Frank does not sit next to any child who sits next to Ivan, which one of the following statements could be true?

(A) Harry sits west of Frank.
(B) Joel sits west of Ivan.
(C) Ruby sits west of Frank.
(D) Thelma sits west of Frank.
(E) Thelma sits west of Ruby.

17. If Frank sits east of Ruby, which one of the following pairs of children CANNOT sit next to each other?

(A) Frank and Thelma
(B) Harry and Ruby
(C) Harry and Sylvia
(D) Ivan and Ruby
(E) Joel and Ruby

GO ON TO THE NEXT PAGE.

Questions 18–24

The organisms W, X, Y, and Z respond to the antibiotics ferromycin, ganocyclene, and heptocillin in a manner consistent with the following:

Each of the organisms responds to at least one of the antibiotics.

No organism responds to all three antibiotics.

At least two but not all four or the organisms respond to ferromycin.

If W responds to any antibiotic, then X responds to that antibiotic.

If an organism responds to ferromycin, then it responds to ganocyclene.

Y responds to ferromycin.

18. Each of the following can be true EXCEPT:

   (A) W responds to heptocillin.
   (B) X responds to ganocyclene.
   (C) X responds to heptocillin.
   (D) Y responds to heptocillin.
   (E) Z responds to ganocyclene.

19. Which one of the following could be true?

   (A) W, X, and Z all respond to ferromycin.
   (B) W, X, and Z all respond to ganocyclene.
   (C) W and exactly one other organism respond to ganocyclene.
   (D) W responds to more of the antibiotics than X does.
   (E) More of the organisms respond to ferromycin than to ganocyclene.

20. Which one of the following could be true?

   (A) Exactly one of the organisms responds to ferromycin.
   (B) All four of the organisms respond to heptocillin.
   (C) At least one of the organisms responds both to ferromycin and to heptocillin.
   (D) At least one of the organisms responds neither to ganocyclene nor to heptocillin.
   (E) At least one of the organisms responds to ganocyclene but does not respond to ferromycin.

21. If X does not respond to ferromycin, then which one of the following must be true?

   (A) W responds to ganocyclene.
   (B) X responds to ganocyclene.
   (C) X responds to heptocillin.
   (D) Z responds to ferromycin.
   (E) Z responds to heptocillin.

22. If any of the organisms responds to two of the antibiotics, then which one of the following is true about such an organism?

   (A) It must respond to ferromycin.
   (B) It must respond to ganocyclene.
   (C) It must respond to heptocillin.
   (D) It cannot respond to ferromycin.
   (E) It cannot respond to ganocyclene.

23. If none of the organisms responds to heptocillin, then which one of the following must be true?

   (A) W responds to ferromycin.
   (B) X responds to ferromycin.
   (C) Z responds to ferromycin.
   (D) Exactly three of the organisms respond to ganocyclene.
   (E) Exactly four of the organisms respond to ganocyclene.

24. If three of the organisms respond to exactly the same set of antibiotics as each other, and if Z does not respond to ferromycin, then each of the following must be true EXCEPT:

   (A) W responds to ferromycin.
   (B) X responds to ganocyclene.
   (C) Z responds to ganocyclene.
   (D) W responds to exactly the same set of antibiotics as Y.
   (E) X responds to exactly the same set of antibiotics as Y.

STOP

IF YOU FINISH BEFORE TIME IS CALLED, YOU MAY CHECK YOUR WORK ON THIS SECTION ONLY.
DO NOT WORK ON ANY OTHER SECTION IN THE TEST.

Practice Test 2
Section III: Reading Comprehension

Time—35 minutes
27 Questions

<u>Directions:</u> Each passage in this section is followed by a group of questions to be answered on the basis of what is <u>stated</u> or <u>implied</u> in the passage. For some of the questions, more than one of the choices could conceivably answer the question. However, you are to choose the <u>best</u> answer; that is, the response that most accurately and completely answers the question, and blacken the corresponding space on your answer sheet.

After thirty years of investigation into cell genetics, researchers made startling discoveries in the 1960s and early 1970s which culminated in the development of processes, collectively known as recombinant
(5) deoxyribonucleic acid (rDNA) technology, for the active manipulation of a cell's genetic code. The technology has created excitement and controversy because it involves altering DNA—which contains the building blocks of the genetic code.
(10)   Using rDNA technology, scientists can transfer a portion of the DNA from one organism to a single living cell of another. The scientist chemically "snips" the DNA chain of the host cell at a predetermined point and attaches another piece of DNA
(15) from a donor cell at that place, creating a completely new organism.
     Proponents of rDNA research and development claim that it will allow scientists to find cures for disease and to better understand how genetic informa-
(20) tion controls an organism's development. They also see many other potentially practical benefits, especially in the pharmaceutical industry. Some corporations employing the new technology even claim that by the end of the century all major diseases will be treated
(25) with drugs derived from microorganisms created through rDNA technology. Pharmaceutical products already developed, but not yet marketed, indicate that these predictions may be realized.
     Proponents also cite nonmedical applications
(30) for this technology. Energy production and waste disposal may benefit: genetically altered organisms could convert sewage and other organic material into methane fuel. Agriculture might also take advantage of rDNA technology to produce new
(35) varieties of crops that resist foul weather, pests, and the effects of poor soil.
     A major concern of the critics of rDNA research is that genetically altered microorganisms might escape from the laboratory. Because these microorganisms
(40) are laboratory creations that, in all probability, do not occur in nature, their interaction with the natural world cannot be predicted with certainty. It is possible that they could cause previously unknown perhaps incurable diseases. The effect of genetically
(45) altered microorganisms on the world's microbiological predator-prey relationships is another potentially

serious problem pointed out by the opponents of rDNA research. Introducing a new species may disrupt or even destroy the existing ecosystem. The col-
(50) lapse of interdependent relationships among species, extrapolated to its extreme, could eventually result in the destruction of humanity.
     Opponents of rDNA technology also cite ethical problems with it. For example, it gives scientists the
(55) power to instantly cross evolutionary and species boundaries that nature took millennia to establish. The implications of such power would become particularly profound if genetic engineers were to tinker with human genes, a practice that would bring us one
(60) step closer to Aldous Huxley's grim vision in *Brave New World* of a totalitarian society that engineers human beings to fulfill specific roles.

1. In the passage, the author is primarily concerned with doing which one of the following?

    (A) explaining the process and applications of rDNA technology
    (B) advocating continued rDNA research and development
    (C) providing evidence indicating the need for regulation of rDNA research and development
    (D) summarizing the controversy surrounding rDNA research and development
    (E) arguing that the environmental risks of rDNA technology may outweigh its medical benefits

2. According to the passage, which one of the following is an accurate statement about research into the genetic code of cells?

    (A) It led to the development of processes for the manipulation of DNA.
    (B) It was initiated by the discovery of rDNA technology.
    (C) It led to the use of new treatments for major diseases.
    (D) It was universally heralded as a great benefit to humanity.
    (E) It was motivated by a desire to create new organisms.

GO ON TO THE NEXT PAGE.

3. The potential benefits of rDNA technology referred to in the passage include all of the following EXCEPT:

   (A) new methods of waste treatment
   (B) new biological knowledge
   (C) enhanced food production
   (D) development of less expensive drugs
   (E) increased energy production

4. Which one of the following, if true, would most weaken an argument of opponents of rDNA technology?

   (A) New safety procedures developed by rDNA researchers make it impossible for genetically altered microorganisms to escape from laboratories.
   (B) A genetically altered microorganism accidentally released from a laboratory is successfully contained.
   (C) A particular rDNA-engineered microorganism introduced into an ecosystem attracts predators that keep its population down.
   (D) Genetically altered organisms designed to process sewage into methane cannot survive outside the waste treatment plant.
   (E) A specific hereditary disease that has plagued humankind for generations is successfully eradicated.

5. The author's reference in the last sentence of the passage to a society that engineers human beings to fulfill specific roles serves to

   (A) emphasize the potential medical dangers of rDNA technology
   (B) advocate research on the use of rDNA technology in human genetics
   (C) warn of the possible disasters that could result from upsetting the balance of nature
   (D) present *Brave New World* as an example of a work of fiction that accurately predicted technological developments
   (E) illustrate the sociopolitical ramifications of applying genetic engineering to humans

6. Which one of the following, if true, would most strengthen an argument of the opponents of rDNA technology?

   (A) Agricultural products developed through rDNA technology are no more attractive to consumers than are traditional crops.
   (B) Genetically altered microorganisms have no natural predators but can prey on a wide variety of other microorganisms.
   (C) Drugs produced using rDNA technology cost more to manufacture than drugs produced with traditional technologies.
   (D) Ecosystems are impermanent systems that are often liable to collapse, and occasionally do so.
   (E) Genetically altered microorganisms generally cannot survive for more than a few hours in the natural environment.

Acknowledgment is made to the following sources from which material has been adapted for use in this test:

From "Stopping a 'Gruesome Parade of Horribles': Criminal Sanctions to Deter Corporate Misuse of Recombinant DNA Technology" by Richard Kevin Zepfel, Southern California Law Review, Volume 59, pages 641–665. © 1986 by the University of Southern California. Used by permission.

GO ON TO THE NEXT PAGE.

KAPLAN

Gray marketing, the selling of trademarked products through channels of distribution not authorized by the trademark holder, can involve distribution of goods either within a market region or across market (5) boundaries. Gray marketing within a market region ("channel flow diversion") occurs when manufacturer-authorized distributors sell trademarked goods to unauthorized distributors who then sell the goods to consumers within the same region. For example, (10) quantity discounts from manufacturers may motivate authorized dealers to enter the gray market because they can purchase larger quantities of a product than they themselves intend to stock if they can sell the extra units through gray market channels.

(15) When gray marketing occurs across market boundaries, it is typically in an international setting and may be called "parallel importing." Manufacturers often produce and sell products in more than one country and establish a network of authorized dealers in each (20) country. Parallel importing occurs when trademarked goods intended for one country are diverted from proper channels (channel flow diversion) and then exported to unauthorized distributors in another country.

(25) Trademark owners justifiably argue against gray marketing practices since such practices clearly jeopardize the goodwill established by trademark owners: consumers who purchase trademarked goods in the gray market do not get the same "extended product," (30) which typically includes pre- and postsale service. Equally important, authorized distributors may cease to promote the product if it becomes available for much lower prices through unauthorized channels.

Current debate over regulation of gray marketing (35) focuses on three disparate theories in trademark law that have been variously and confusingly applied to parallel importation cases: universality, exhaustion, and territoriality. The theory of universality holds that a trademark is only an indication of the source or (40) origin of the product. This theory does not recognize the goodwill functions of a trademark. When the courts apply this theory, gray marketing practices are allowed to continue because the origin of the product remains the same regardless of the specific route (45) of the product through the channel of distribution. The exhaustion theory holds that a trademark owner relinquishes all rights once a product has been sold. When this theory is applied, gray marketing practices are allowed to continue because the trademark own- (50) ers' rights cease as soon as their products are sold to a distributor. The theory of territoriality holds that a trademark is effective in the country in which it is registered. Under the theory of territoriality, trademark owners can stop gray marketing practices in (55) the registering countries on products bearing

their trademarks. Since only the territoriality theory affords trademark owners any real legal protection against gray marketing practices, I believe it is inevitable as well as desirable that it will come to be consis- (60) tently applied in gray marketing cases.

7. Which one of the following best expresses the main point of the passage?
    (A) Gray marketing is unfair to trademark owners and should be legally controlled.
    (B) Gray marketing is practiced in many different forms and places, and legislators should recognize the futility of trying to regulate it.
    (C) The mechanisms used to control gray marketing across markets are different from those most effective in controlling gray marketing within markets.
    (D) The three trademark law theories that have been applied in gray marketing cases lead to different case outcomes.
    (E) Current theories used to interpret trademark laws have resulted in increased gray marketing activity.

8. The function of the passage as a whole is to
    (A) criticize the motives and methods of those who practice gray marketing
    (B) evaluate the effects of both channel flow diversion and parallel importation
    (C) discuss the methods that have been used to regulate gray marketing and evaluate such methods' degrees of success
    (D) describe a controversial marketing practice and evaluate several legal views regarding it
    (E) discuss situations in which certain marketing practices are common and analyze the economic factors responsible for their development

9. Which one of the following does the author offer as an argument against gray marketing?
    (A) Manufacturers find it difficult to monitor the effectiveness of promotional efforts made on behalf of products that are gray marketed.
    (B) Gray marketing can discourage product promotion by authorized distributors.
    (C) Gray marketing forces manufacturers to accept the low profit margins that result from quantity discounting.
    (D) Gray marketing discourages competition among unauthorized dealers.
    (E) Quality standards in the manufacture of products likely to be gray marketed may decline.

GO ON TO THE NEXT PAGE.

10. The information in the passage suggests that proponents of the theory of territoriality would probably differ from proponents of the theory of exhaustion on which one of the following issues?

(A) the right of trademark owners to enforce, in countries in which the trademarks are registered, distribution agreements intended to restrict distribution to authorized channels

(B) the right of trademark owners to sell trademarked goods only to those distributors who agree to abide by distribution agreements

(C) the legality of channel flow diversion that occurs in a country other than the one in which a trademark is registered

(D) the significance consumers attach to a trademark

(E) the usefulness of trademarks as marketing tools

11. The author discusses the impact of gray marketing on goodwill in order to

(A) fault trademark owners for their unwillingness to offer a solution to a major consumer complaint against gray marketing

(B) indicate a way in which manufacturers sustain damage against which they ought to be protected

(C) highlight one way in which gray marketing across markets is more problematic than gray marketing within a market

(D) demonstrate that gray marketing does not always benefit the interests of unauthorized distributors

(E) argue that consumers are unwilling to accept a reduction in price in exchange for elimination of service

12. The author's attitude toward the possibility that the courts will come to exercise consistent control over gray marketing practices can best be characterized as one of

(A) resigned tolerance
(B) utter dismay
(C) reasoned optimism
(D) unbridled fervor
(E) cynical indifference

13. It can be inferred from the passage that some channel flow diversion might be eliminated if

(A) profit margins on authorized distribution of goods were less than those on goods marketed through parallel importing

(B) manufacturers relieved authorized channels of all responsibility for product promotion

(C) manufacturers charged all authorized distributors the same unit price for products regardless of quantity purchased

(D) the postsale service policies of authorized channels were controlled by manufacturers

(E) manufacturers refused to provide the "extended product" to consumers who purchase goods in the gray market

GO ON TO THE NEXT PAGE.

Any study of autobiographical narratives that appeared under the ostensible authorship of African American writers between 1760 and 1865 inevitably raises concerns about authenticity and inter-
(5) pretation. Should an autobiography whose written composition was literally out of the hands of its narrator be considered as the literary equivalent of those autobiographies that were authored independently by their subjects?
(10)   In many cases, the so-called edited narrative of an ex-slave ought to be treated as a ghostwritten account insofar as literary analysis is concerned, especially when it was composed by its editor from "a statement of facts" provided by an African American subject.
(15) Blassingame has taken pains to show that the editors of several of the more famous antebellum slave narratives were "noted for their integrity" and thus were unlikely to distort the facts given them by slave narrators. From a literary standpoint, however, it is not
(20) the moral integrity of these editors that is at issue but the linguistic, structural, and tonal integrity of the narratives they produced. Even if an editor faithfully reproduced the facts of a narrator's life, it was still the editor who decided what to make of these facts,
(25) how they should be emphasized, in what order they ought to be presented, and what was extraneous or germane. Readers of African American autobiography then and now have too readily accepted the presumption of these eighteenth- and nineteenth-century
(30) editors that experiential facts recounted orally could be recorded and sorted by an amanuensis-editor, taken out of their original contexts, and then published with editorial prefaces, footnotes, and appended commentary, all without compromising the validity
(35) of the narrative as a product of an African American consciousness.
    Transcribed narratives in which an editor explicitly delimits his or her role undoubtedly may be regarded as more authentic and reflective of the narrator's
(40) thought in action than those edited works that flesh out a statement of facts in ways unaccounted for. Still, it would be naive to accord dictated oral narratives the same status as autobiographies composed and written by the subjects of the stories themselves. This
(45) point is illustrated by an analysis of Works Progress Administration interviews with ex-slaves in the 1930s that suggests that narrators often told interviewers what they seemed to want to hear. If it seemed
(50) impolitic for former slaves to tell all they knew and thought about the past to interviewers in the 1930s, the same could be said of escaped slaves on the run in the antebellum era. Dictated narratives, therefore, are literary texts whose authenticity is difficult to determine.
(55) Analysts should reserve close analytic readings for independently authored texts. Discussion of collaborative texts should take into account the conditions that governed their production.

14. Which one of the following best summarizes the main point of the passage?
(A) The personal integrity of an autobiography's editor has little relevance to its value as a literary work.
(B) Autobiographies dictated to editors are less valuable as literature than are autobiographies authored by their subjects.
(C) The facts that are recorded in an autobiography are less important than the personal impressions of its author.
(D) The circumstances under which an autobiography was written should affect the way it is interpreted as literature.
(E) The autobiographies of African Americans written between 1760 and 1865 deserve more careful study than they have so far received.

15. The information in the passage suggests that the role of the "editor" (lines 22–24) is most like that of
(A) an artist who wishes to invent a unique method of conveying the emotional impact of a scene in a painting
(B) a worker who must interpret the instructions of an employer
(C) a critic who must provide evidence to support opinions about a play being reviewed
(D) an architect who must make the best use of a natural setting in designing a public building
(E) a historian who must decide how to direct the reenactment of a historical event

16. Which one of the following best describes the author's opinion about applying literary analysis to edited autobiographies?
(A) The author is adamantly opposed to the application of literary analysis to edited autobiographies.
(B) The author is skeptical of the value of close analytical reading in the case of edited autobiographies.
(C) The author believes that literary analysis of the prefaces, footnotes, and commentaries that accompany edited autobiographies would be more useful than an analysis of the text of the autobiographies.
(D) The author believes that an exclusively literary analysis of edited autobiographies is more valuable than a reading that emphasizes their historical import.
(E) The author believes that the literary analysis of edited autobiographies would enhance their linguistic, structural, and tonal integrity.

GO ON TO THE NEXT PAGE.

17. The passage supports which one of the following statements about the readers of autobiographies of African Americans that were published between 1760 and 1865?
    (A) They were more concerned with the personal details in the autobiographies than with their historical significance.
    (B) They were unable to distinguish between ghostwritten and edited autobiographies.
    (C) They were less naive about the facts of slave life than are readers today.
    (D) They presumed that the editing of the autobiographies did not affect their authenticity.
    (E) They had little interest in the moral integrity of the editors of the autobiographies.

18. Which one of the following words, as it is used in the passage, best serves to underscore the author's concerns about the authenticity of the autobiographies discussed?
    (A) "ostensible" (line 2)
    (B) "integrity" (line 17)
    (C) "extraneous" (line 26)
    (D) "delimits" (line 38)
    (E) "impolitic" (line 50)

19. According to the passage, close analytic reading of an autobiography is appropriate only when the
    (A) autobiography has been dictated to an experienced amanuensis-editor
    (B) autobiography attempts to reflect the narrator's thought in action
    (C) autobiography was authored independently by its subject
    (D) moral integrity of the autobiography's editor is well established
    (E) editor of the autobiography collaborated closely with its subject in its editing

20. It can be inferred that the discussion in the passage of Blassingame's work primarily serves which one of the following purposes?
    (A) It adds an authority's endorsement to the author's view that edited narratives ought to be treated as ghostwritten accounts.
    (B) It provides an example of a mistaken emphasis in the study of autobiography.
    (C) It presents an account of a new method of literary analysis to be applied to autobiography.
    (D) It illustrates the inadequacy of traditional approaches to the analysis of autobiography.
    (E) It emphasizes the importance of the relationship between editor and narrator.

GO ON TO THE NEXT PAGE.

A conventional view of nineteenth-century Britain holds that iron manufacturers and textile manufacturers from the north of England became the wealthiest and most powerful people in society after about
(5) 1832. According to Marxist historians, these industrialists were the target of the working class in its struggle for power. A new study by Rubinstein, however, suggests that the real wealth lay with the bankers and merchants of London. Rubinstein does not deny
(10) that a northern industrial elite existed but argues that it was consistently outnumbered and outdone by a London-based commercial elite. His claims are provocative and deserve consideration.

Rubinstein's claim about the location of wealth
(15) comes from his investigation of probate records. These indicate the value of personal property, excluding real property (buildings and land), left by individuals at death. It does seem as if large fortunes were more frequently made in commerce than in industry
(20) and, within industry, more frequently from alcohol or tobacco than from textiles or metal. However, such records do not unequivocally make Rubinstein's case. Uncertainties abound about how the probate rules for valuing assets were actually applied. Mills
(25) and factories, being real property, were clearly excluded; machinery may also have been, for the same reason. What the valuation conventions were for stock-in-trade (goods for sale) is also uncertain. It is possible that their probate values were much lower
(30) than their actual market values; cash or near-cash, such as bank balances or stocks, were, on the other hand, invariably considered at full face value. A further complication is that probate valuations probably took no notice of a business's goodwill (favor with the
(35) public) which, since it represents expectations about future profit-making, would today very often be a large fraction of market value. Whether factors like these introduced systematic biases into the probate valuations of individuals with different types of busi-
(40) nesses would be worth investigating.

The orthodox view that the wealthiest individuals were the most powerful is also questioned by Rubinstein's study. The problem for this orthodox view is that Rubinstein finds many millionaires who
(45) are totally unknown to nineteenth-century historians; the reason for their obscurity could be that they were not powerful. Indeed, Rubinstein dismisses any notion that great wealth had anything to do
(50) with entry into the governing elite, as represented by bishops, higher civil servants, and chairmen of manufacturing companies. The only requirements were university attendance and a father with a middle-class income.
(55) Rubinstein, in another study, has begun to buttress his findings about the location of wealth by analyzing

income tax returns, which reveal a geographical distribution of middle-class incomes similar to that of wealthy incomes revealed by probate records. But
(60) until further confirmatory investigation is done, his claims can only be considered partially convincing.

21. The main idea of the passage is that

(A) the Marxist interpretation of the relationship between class and power in nineteenth-century Britain is no longer viable
(B) a simple equation between wealth and power is unlikely to be supported by new data from nineteenth-century British archives
(C) a recent historical investigation has challenged but not disproved the orthodox view of the distribution of wealth and the relationship of wealth to power in nineteenth-century Britain
(D) probate records provide the historian with a revealing but incomplete glimpse of the extent and location of wealth in nineteenth-century Britain
(E) an attempt has been made to confirm the findings of a new historical study of nineteenth-century Britain, but complete confirmation is likely to remain elusive

22. The author of the passage implies that probate records as a source of information about wealth in nineteenth-century Britain are

(A) self-contradictory and misleading
(B) ambiguous and outdated
(C) controversial but readily available
(D) revealing but difficult to interpret
(E) widely used by historians but fully understandable only by specialists

23. The author suggests that the total probate valuations of the personal property of individuals holding goods for sale in nineteenth-century Britain may have been

(A) affected by the valuation conventions for such goods
(B) less accurate than the valuations for such goods provided by income tax returns
(C) less, on average, if such goods were tobacco-related than if they were alcohol-related
(D) greater, on average, than the total probate valuations of those individuals who held bank balances
(E) dependent on whether such goods were held by industrialists or by merchants or bankers

GO ON TO THE NEXT PAGE.

24. According to the passage, Rubinstein has provided evidence that challenges which one of the following claims about nineteenth-century Britain?
    (A) The distribution of great wealth between commerce and industry was not equal.
    (B) Large incomes were typically made in alcohol and tobacco rather than in textiles and metal.
    (C) A London-based commercial elite can be identified.
    (D) An official governing elite can be identified.
    (E) There was a necessary relationship between great wealth and power.

25. The author mentions that goodwill was probably excluded from the probate valuation of a business in nineteenth-century Britain most likely in order to

    (A) give an example of a business asset about which little was known in the nineteenth century
    (B) suggest that the probate valuations of certain businesses may have been significant underestimations of their true market value
    (C) make the point that this exclusion probably had an equal impact on the probate valuations of all nineteenth-century British businesses
    (D) indicate that expectations about future profit-making is the single most important factor in determining the market value of certain businesses
    (E) argue that the twentieth-century method of determining probate valuations of a business may be consistently superior to the nineteenth-century method

26. Which one of the following studies would provide support for Rubinstein's claims?

    (A) a study that indicated that many members of the commercial elite in nineteenth-century London had insignificant holdings of real property
    (B) a study that indicated that, in the nineteenth century, industrialists from the north of England were in fact a target for working-class people
    (C) a study that indicated that, in nineteenth-century Britain, probate values of goods for sale were not as high as probate values of cash assets
    (D) a study that indicated that the wealth of nineteenth-century British industrialists did not appear to be significantly greater when the full value of their real property holdings was actually considered
    (E) a study that indicated that at least some members of the official governing elite in nineteenth-century Britain owned more real property than had previously been thought to be the case

27. Which one of the following, if true, would cast the most doubt on Rubinstein's argument concerning wealth and the official governing elite in nineteenth-century Britain?

    (A) Entry into this elite was more dependent on university attendance than on religious background.
    (B) Attendance at a prestigious university was probably more crucial than a certain minimum family income in gaining entry into this elite.
    (C) Bishops as a group were somewhat wealthier, at the point of entry into this elite, than were higher civil servants or chairmen of manufacturing companies.
    (D) The families of many members of this elite owned few, if any, shares in iron industries and textile industries in the north of England.
    (E) The composition or this elite included vice-chancellors, many of whom held office because of their wealth.

STOP

IF YOU FINISH BEFORE TIME IS CALLED, YOU MAY CHECK YOUR WORK ON THIS SECTION ONLY.
DO NOT WORK ON ANY OTHER SECTION IN THE TEST.

Practice Test 2

Section IV: **Logical Reasoning**

Time—35 minutes
25 questions

Directions: The questions in this section are based on the reasoning contained in brief statements or passages. For some questions, more than one of the choices could conceivably answer the question. However, you are to choose the best answer; that is, the response that most accurately and completely answers the question. You should not make assumptions that are by commonsense standards implausible, superfluous, or incompatible with the passage. After you have chosen the best answer, blacken the corresponding space on your answer sheet.

1. The cafeteria at Acme Company can offer only four main dishes at lunchtime, and the same four choices have been offered for years. Recently mushroom casserole was offered in place of one of the other main dishes for two days, during which more people chose mushroom casserole than any other main dish. Clearly, if the cafeteria wants to please its customers, mushroom casserole should replace one of the regular dishes as a permanent part of the menu.
The argument is most vulnerable to criticism on the grounds that it fails to consider

(A) the proportion of Acme Company employees who regularly eat lunch in the company cafeteria

(B) whether any of the ingredients used in the cafeteria's recipe for mushroom casserole are included in any of the regular main dishes

(C) a desire for variety as a reason for people's choice of mushroom casserole during the days it was offered

(D) what foods other than main dishes are regularly offered at lunchtime by the cafeteria

(E) whether other meals besides lunch are served in the Acme Company cafeteria

2. When old-growth forests are cleared of tall trees, more sunlight reaches the forest floor. This results in a sharp increase in the population of leafy shrubs on which the mule deer depend for food. Yet mule deer herds that inhabit cleared forests are less well-nourished than are herds living in old-growth forests.
Which one of the following, if true, most helps to resolve the apparent paradox?

(A) Mule deer have enzyme-rich saliva and specialized digestive organs that enable the deer to digest tough plants inedible to other deer species.

(B) Mule deer herds that inhabit cleared forests tend to have more females with young offspring and fewer adult males than do other mule deer populations.

(C) Mule deer populations are spread throughout western North America and inhabit hot, sunny climates as well as cool, wet climates.

(D) As plants receive more sunlight, they produce higher amounts of tannins, compounds that inhibit digestion of the plants' proteins.

(E) Insect parasites, such as certain species of ticks, that feed primarily on mule deer often dwell in trees, from which they drop onto passing deer.

3. Genevieve: Increasing costs have led commercial airlines to cut back on airplane maintenance. Also, reductions in public spending have led to air traffic control centers being underfunded and understaffed. For these and other reasons it is becoming quite unsafe to fly, and so one should avoid doing it.

Harold: Your reasoning may be sound, but I can hardly accept your conclusion when you yourself have recently been flying on commercial airlines even more than before.

Which one of the following relies on a questionable technique most similar to that used in Harold's reply to Genevieve?

(A) David says that the new film is not very good, but he has not seen it himself, so I don't accept his opinion.

(B) A long time ago Maria showed me a great way to cook lamb, but for medical reasons she no longer eats red meat, so I'll cook something else for dinner tonight.

(C) Susan has been trying to persuade me to go rock climbing with her, claiming that it's quite safe, but last week she fell and broke her collarbone, so I don't believe her.

(D) Pat has shown me research that proves that eating raw green vegetables is very beneficial and that one should eat them daily, but I don't believe it, since she hardly ever eats raw green vegetables.

(E) Gabriel has all the qualifications we have specified for the job and has much relevant work experience, but I don't believe we should hire him, because when he worked in a similar position before his performance was mediocre.

GO ON TO THE NEXT PAGE.

KAPLAN

4. All people residing in the country of Gradara approve of legislation requiring that certain hazardous wastes be disposed of by being burned in modern high-temperature incinerators. However, waste disposal companies planning to build such incinerators encounter fierce resistance to their applications for building permits from the residents of every Gradaran community that those companies propose as an incinerator site.

Which one of the following, if true, most helps to explain the residents' simultaneously holding both of the positions ascribed to them?

(A) High-temperature incineration minimizes the overall risk to the human population of the country from the wastes being disposed of, but it concentrates the remaining risk in a small number of incineration sites.

(B) High-temperature incineration is more expensive than any of the available alternatives would be, and the higher costs would be recovered through higher product prices.

(C) High-temperature incineration will be carried out by private companies rather than by a government agency so that the government will not be required to police itself.

(D) The toxic fumes generated within a high-temperature incinerator can be further treated so that all toxic residues from a properly operating incinerator are solids.

(E) The substantial cost of high-temperature incineration can be partially offset by revenue from sales of electric energy generated as a by-product of incineration.

5. Elena: While I was at the dog show, every dog that growled at me was a white poodle, and every white poodle I saw growled at me.

Which one of the following can be properly inferred from Elena's statement?

(A) The only white dogs that Elena saw at the dog show were poodles.

(B) There were no gray poodles at the dog show.

(C) At the dog show, no gray dogs growled at Elena.

(D) All the white dogs that Elena saw growled at her.

(E) Elena did not see any gray poodles at the dog show.

Questions 6–7

Derek: We must exploit available resources in developing effective anticancer drugs such as the one made from mature Pacific yew trees. Although the yew population might be threatened, the trees should be harvested now, since an effective synthetic version of the yew's anticancer chemical could take years to develop.

Lola: Not only are mature yews very rare, but most are located in areas where logging is prohibited to protect the habitat of the endangered spotted owl. Despite our eagerness to take advantage or a new medical breakthrough, we should wait for a synthetic drug rather than threaten the survival of both the yew and the owl, which could have far-reaching consequences for an entire ecosystem.

6. Which one of the following is the main point at issue between Lola and Derek?

(A) whether the harvesting of available Pacific yews would have far-reaching environmental repercussions

(B) whether the drugs that are effective against potentially deadly diseases should be based on synthetic rather than naturally occurring chemicals

(C) whether it is justifiable to wait until a synthetic drug can be developed when the capacity for producing the yew-derived drug already exists

(D) the extent of the environmental disaster that would result if both the Pacific yew and the spotted owl were to become extinct

(E) whether environmental considerations should ever have any weight when human lives are at stake

7. Lola's position most closely conforms to which one of the following principles?

(A) Unless people's well-being is threatened, there should be no higher priority than preserving endangered plant and animal populations.

(B) Medical researchers should work with environmentalists to come to an agreement about the rate of the Pacific yew and the spotted owl.

(C) Environmental concerns should play a role in decisions concerning medical research only if human lives are not at stake.

(D) Only medical breakthroughs that could save human lives would justify threatening the environment.

(E) Avoiding actions that threaten an entire ecosystem takes precedence over immediately providing advantage to a restricted group of people.

GO ON TO THE NEXT PAGE.

KAPLAN

8. The director of a secondary school where many students were having severe academic problems impaneled a committee to study the matter. The committee reported that these students were having academic problems because they spent large amounts of time on school sports and too little time studying. The director then prohibited all students who were having academic problems from taking part in sports in which they were active. He stated that this would ensure that such students would do well academically.

The reasoning on which the director bases his statement is not sound because he fails to establish that

(A) some students who spend time on sports do not have academic problems
(B) all students who do well academically do so because of time saved by not participating in sports
(C) at least some of the time the students will save by not participating in sports will be spent on solving their academic problems
(D) no students who do well academically spend time on sports
(E) the quality of the school's sports program would not suffer as a result of the ban

9. It can safely be concluded that there are at least as many trees in Seclee as there are in Martown.

From which one of the following does the conclusion logically follow?

(A) More trees were planted in Seclee in the past two years than in Martown.
(B) Seclee is the region within which Martown is located.
(C) Martown is suffering from an epidemic of tree-virus infection.
(D) The average annual rainfall for Seclee is greater than the average annual rainfall for Martown.
(E) The average number of trees cut down annually in Martown is higher than in Seclee.

Questions 10–11

A distemper virus has caused two-thirds of the seal population in the North Sea to die since May 1988. The explanation for the deaths cannot rest here, however. There must be a reason the normally latent virus could prevail so suddenly: clearly the severe pollution of the North Sea waters must have weakened the immune system of the seals so that they could no longer withstand the virus.

10. The argument concerning the immune system of the seals presupposes which one of the following?

(A) There has been a gradual decline in the seal population of the North Sea during the past two centuries.
(B) No further sources of pollution have been added since May 1988 to the already existing sources of pollution in the North Sea.
(C) There was no sudden mutation in the distemper virus which would have allowed the virus successfully to attack healthy North Sea seals by May 1988.
(D) Pollution in the North Sea is no greater than pollution in the Mediterranean Sea, off the coast of North America, or in the Sea of Japan.
(E) Some species that provide food for the seals have nearly become extinct as a result of the pollution.

11. Which one of the following, if true, most strongly supports the explanation given in the argument?

(A) At various times during the last ten years, several species of shellfish and seabirds in the North Sea have experienced unprecedentedly steep drops in population.
(B) By reducing pollution at its source, Northern Europe and Scandinavia have been taking the lead in preventing pollution from reaching the waters of the North Sea.
(C) For many years, fish for human consumption have been taken from the waters of the North Sea.
(D) There are two species of seal found throughout the North Sea area, the common seal and the gray seal.
(E) The distemper caused by the virus was a disease that was new to the population of North Sea seals in May 1988, and so the seals' immune systems were unprepared to counter it.

GO ON TO THE NEXT PAGE.

KAPLAN

12. It is clear that none of the volleyball players at yesterday's office beach party came to work today since everyone who played volleyball at that party got badly sunburned and no one at work today is even slightly sunburned.

Which one of the following exhibits a pattern of reasoning that most closely parallels that in the argument above?

(A) Since everyone employed by TRF who was given the opportunity to purchase dental insurance did so and everyone who purchased dental insurance saw a dentist, it is clear that no one who failed to see a dentist is employed by TRF.

(B) Since no one who was promoted during the past year failed to attend the awards banquet, evidently none of the office managers attended the banquet this year since they were all denied promotion.

(C) Since the Donnely report was not finished on time, no one in John's group could have been assigned to contribute to that report since everyone in John's group has a reputation for getting assignments in on time.

(D) Everyone with an office on the second floor works directly for the president and, as a result, no one with a second floor office will take a July vacation because no one who works for the president will be able to take time off during July.

(E) Since all of the people who are now on the MXM Corporation payroll have been employed in the same job for the past five years, it is clear that no one who frequently changes jobs is likely to be hired by MXM.

Questions 13–14

The dean of computing must be respected by the academic staff and be competent to oversee the use of computers on campus. The only deans whom academics respect are those who hold doctoral degrees, and only someone who really knows about computers can competently oversee the use of computers on campus. Furthermore, the board of trustees has decided that the dean of computing must be selected from among this university's staff. Therefore, the dean of computing must be a professor from this university's computer science department.

13. Which one of the following is an assumption on which the argument depends?

(A) Academics respect only people who hold doctoral degrees.

(B) All of this university's professors have obtained doctoral degrees.

(C) At this university, every professor who holds a doctoral degree in computer science really knows about computers.

(D) All academics who hold doctoral degrees are respected by their academic colleagues.

(E) Among this university's staff members with doctoral degrees, only those in the computer science department really know about computers.

14. Which one of the following statements, if true, would weaken the argument?

(A) There are members of this university's staff who hold doctoral degrees and who are not professors but who really know about computers.

(B) There are members of this university's philosophy department who do not hold doctoral degrees but who really know about computers.

(C) Computer science professors who hold doctoral degrees but who are not members of this university's staff have applied for the position of dean of computing.

(D) Several members of the board of trustees of this university do not hold doctoral degrees.

(E) Some members of the computer science department at this university are not respected by academics in other departments.

GO ON TO THE NEXT PAGE.

Questions 15–16

Consumer advocate: Under the current absence of government standards for food product labeling, manufacturers are misleading or deceiving consumers by their product labeling. For example, a certain brand of juice is labeled "fresh orange juice," yet the product is made from water, concentrate, and flavor enhancers. Since "fresh" as applied to food products is commonly understood to mean pure and unprocessed, labeling that orange juice "fresh" is unquestionably deceptive.

Manufacturer: Using words somewhat differently than they are commonly used is not deceptive. After all, "fresh" can also mean never frozen. We cannot be faulted for failing to comply with standards that have not been officially formulated. When the government sets clear standards pertaining to product labeling, we will certainly comply with them.

15. On the basis of their statements above, the consumer advocate and the manufacturer are committed to disagreeing about the truth of which one of the following statements?
    (A) In the absence of government standards, common understanding is the arbiter of deceptive labeling practices.
    (B) Truthful labeling practices that reflect common standards of usage can be established by the government.
    (C) The term "fresh" when it is applied to food products is commonly understood to mean pure and unprocessed.
    (D) Terms that apply to natural foods can be truthfully applied to packaged foods.
    (E) Clear government standards for labeling food products will ensure truthful labeling practices.

16. Which one of the following principles, if established, would contribute most to a defense of the manufacturer's position against that of the consumer advocate?
    (A) In the absence of government definitions for terms used in product labeling, common standards of understanding alone should apply.
    (B) Government standards for truthful labeling should always be designed to reflect common standards of understanding.
    (C) People should be free, to the extent that it is legal to do so, to exploit to their advantages the inherent ambiguity and vagueness in language.
    (D) When government standards and common standards for truthful labeling are incompatible with each other, the government standards should always take precedence.
    (E) In their interpretation of language, consumers should never presume that vagueness indicates an attempt to deceive on the part of manufacturers unless those manufacturers would reap large benefits from successful deception.

17. Certain items—those with that hard-to-define quality called exclusivity—have the odd property, when they become available for sale, of selling rapidly even though they are extremely expensive. In fact, trying to sell such an item fast by asking too low a price is a serious error, since it calls into question the very thing—exclusivity—that is supposed to be the item's chief appeal. Therefore, given that a price that will prove to be right is virtually impossible for the seller to gauge in advance, the seller should make sure that any error in the initial asking price is in the direction of setting the price too high.

The argument recommends a certain pricing strategy on the grounds that
    (A) this strategy lacks a counterproductive feature of the rejected alternative
    (B) this strategy has all of the advantages of the rejected alternative, but fewer of its disadvantages
    (C) experience has proven this strategy to be superior, even though the reasons for this superiority elude analysis
    (D) this strategy does not rely on prospective buyers' estimates of value
    (E) the error associated with this strategy, unlike the error associated with the rejected alternative, is likely to go unnoticed

GO ON TO THE NEXT PAGE.

18. In order to control the deer population, a biologist has proposed injecting female deer during breeding season with 10 milligrams of a hormone that would suppress fertility. Critics have charged that the proposal poses health risks to people who might eat the meat of treated deer and thereby ingest unsafe quantities of the hormone. The biologist has responded to these critics by pointing out that humans can ingest up to 10 milligrams of the hormone a day without any adverse effects, and since no one would eat even one entire deer a day, the treatment would be safe.

The biologist's response to critics of the proposal is based on which one of the following assumptions?

(A) People would be notified of the time when deer in their area were to be treated with the hormone.

(B) The hormone that would be injected into the deer is chemically similar to hormones used in human contraceptives.

(C) Hunting season for deer could be scheduled so that it would not coincide with breeding season.

(D) The hormone in question does not occur naturally in the female deer that would be injected.

(E) Most people do not consider deer meat to be part of their daily diet and eat it only on rare occasions.

19. A recent survey conducted in one North American city revealed widespread concern about the problems faced by teenagers today. Seventy percent of the adults surveyed said they would pay higher taxes for drug treatment programs, and 60 percent said they were willing to pay higher taxes to improve the city's schools. Yet in a vote in that same city, a proposition to increase funding for schools by raising taxes failed by a narrow margin to win majority approval.

Which one of the following factors, if true, would LEAST contribute to an explanation of the discrepancy described above?

(A) The survey sample was not representative of the voters who voted on the proposition.

(B) Many of the people who were surveyed did not respond truthfully to all of the questions put to them.

(C) The proposition was only part of a more expensive community improvement program that voters had to accept or reject in total.

(D) A proposition for increasing funds for local drug treatment centers also failed to win approval.

(E) The proposition to raise taxes for schools was couched in terminology that many of the voters found confusing.

Questions 20–21

So-called environmentalists have argued that the proposed Golden Lake Development would interfere with bird-migration patterns. However, the fact that these same people have raised environmental objections to virtually every development proposal brought before the council in recent years indicates that their expressed concern for bird-migration patterns is nothing but a mask for their antidevelopment, antiprogress agenda. Their claim, therefore, should be dismissed without further consideration.

20. Which one of the following questionable argumentative techniques is employed in the passage?

(A) taking the failure of a given argument to establish its conclusion as the basis for claiming that the view expressed by that conclusion is false

(B) rejecting the conclusion of an argument on the basis of a claim about the motives of those advancing the argument

(C) using a few exceptional cases as the basis for a claim about what is true in general

(D) misrepresenting evidence that supports the position the argument is intended to refute

(E) assuming that what is true of a group as a whole is necessarily true of each member of that group

21. For the claim that the concern expressed by the so-called environmentalists is not their real concern to be properly drawn on the basis of the evidence cited, which one of the following must be assumed?

(A) Not every development proposal opposed in recent years by these so-called environmentalists was opposed because they believed it to pose a threat to the environment.

(B) People whose real agenda is to block development wherever it is proposed always try to disguise their true motives.

(C) Anyone who opposes unrestricted development is an opponent of progress.

(D) The council has no reason to object to the proposed Golden Lake Development other than concern about the development's effect on bird-migration patterns.

(E) When people say that they oppose a development project solely on environmental grounds, their real concern almost always lies elsewhere.

GO ON TO THE NEXT PAGE.

22. Psychologists today recognize childhood as a separate stage of life which can only be understood in its own terms, and they wonder why the Western world took so long to see the folly of regarding children simply as small, inadequately socialized adults. Most psychologists, however, persist in regarding people 70 to 90 years old as though they were 35 year olds who just happen to have white hair and extra leisure time. But old age is as fundamentally different from young adulthood and middle age as childhood is—a fact attested to by the organization of modern social and economic life. Surely it is time, therefore, to acknowledge that serious research into the unique psychology of advanced age has become indispensable.

Which one of the following principles, if established, would provide the strongest backing for the argument?

(A) Whenever current psychological practice conflicts with traditional attitudes toward people, those traditional attitudes should be changed to bring them in line with current psychological practice.

(B) Whenever two groups of people are so related to each other that any member of the second group must previously have been a member of the first, people in the first group should not be regarded simply as deviant members of the second group.

(C) Whenever most practitioners of a given discipline approach a particular problem in the same way, that uniformity is good evidence that all similar problems should also be approached in that way.

(D) Whenever a society's economic life is so organized that two distinct times of life are treated as being fundamentally different from one another, each time of life can be understood only in terms of its own distinct psychology.

(E) Whenever psychologists agree that a single psychology is inadequate for two distinct age groups, they should be prepared to show that there are greater differences between the two age groups than there are between individuals in the same age group.

23. Sabina: The words used in expressing facts affect neither the facts nor the conclusions those facts will support. Moreover, if the words are clearly defined and consistently used, the actual words chosen make no difference to an argument's soundness. Thus, how an argument is expressed can have no bearing on whether it is a good argument.

Emile: Badly chosen words can make even the soundest argument a poor one. After all, many words have social and political connotations that influence people's response to claims expressed in those words, regardless of how carefully and explicitly those words are defined. Since whether people will acknowledge a fact is affected by how the fact is expressed, the conclusions they actually draw are also affected.

The point at issue between Emile and Sabina is whether

(A) defining words in one way rather than another can alter either the facts or the conclusions the facts will justify

(B) a word can be defined without taking into account its social and political connotations

(C) a sound argument in support of a given conclusion is a better argument than any unsound argument for that same conclusion

(D) it would be a good policy to avoid using words that are likely to lead people either to misunderstand the claims being made or to reason badly about those claims

(E) a factor that affects neither the truth of an argument's premises nor the logical relation between its premises and its conclusion can cause an argument to be a bad one

GO ON TO THE NEXT PAGE.

24. Most disposable plastic containers are now labeled with a code number (from 1 to 9) indicating the type or quality of the plastic. Plastics with the lowest code numbers are the easiest for recycling plants to recycle and are thus the most likely to be recycled after use rather than dumped in landfills. Plastics labeled with the highest numbers are only rarely recycled. Consumers can make a significant long-term reduction in the amount of waste that goes unrecycled, therefore, by refusing to purchase those products packaged in plastic containers labeled with the highest code numbers.

Which one of the following, if true, most seriously undermines the conclusion above?

(A) The cost of collecting, sorting, and recycling discarded plastics is currently higher than the cost of manufacturing new plastics from virgin materials.

(B) Many consumers are unaware of the codes that are stamped on the plastic containers.

(C) A plastic container almost always has a higher code number after it is recycled than it had before recycling because the recycling process causes a degradation of the quality of the plastic.

(D) Products packaged in plastics with the lowest code numbers are often more expensive than those packaged in the higher-numbered plastics.

(E) Communities that collect all discarded plastic containers for potential recycling later dump in landfills plastics with higher-numbered codes only when it is clear that no recycler will take them.

25. Despite a steady decrease in the average number of hours worked per person per week, the share of the population that reads a daily newspaper has declined greatly in the past 20 years. But the percentage of the population that watches television daily has shown a similarly dramatic increase over the same period. Clearly, increased television viewing has caused a simultaneous decline in newspaper reading.

Which one of the following, if true, would be most damaging to the explanation given above for the decline in newspaper reading?

(A) There has been a dramatic increase over the past 20 years in the percentage of people who tell polltakers that television is their primary source of information about current events.

(B) Of those members of the population who do not watch television, the percentage who read a newspaper every day has also shown a dramatic decrease.

(C) The time people spend with the books and newspapers they read has increased, on average, from one to three hours per week in the past 20 years.

(D) People who spend large amounts of time each day watching television are less able to process and remember printed information than are those who do not watch television.

(E) A typical television set is on six hours a day, down from an average of six and a half hours a day five years ago.

STOP

IF YOU FINISH BEFORE TIME IS CALLED, YOU MAY CHECK YOUR WORK ON THIS SECTION ONLY.
DO NOT WORK ON ANY OTHER SECTION IN THE TEST.

Practice Test 2
Writing Sample

SIGNATURE _____ / ___ /

LSAT WRITING SAMPLE TOPIC

The English department at Corbett University must choose a text for the college's first-year composition course. Write an argument in favor of selecting either of the following texts with these considerations in mind:

- The department has a strong commitment to teaching basic writing skills, such as grammar and essay organization.
- The department wants to increase the students' enthusiasm for and interest in writing.

During the three years that the department has used The Standard Textbook of English, instructors in other departments have reported significant improvement in students' writing skills. Nicknamed "The Best and the Dullest," the text contains classic essays from both ancient and modern authors and is organized to illustrate the various forms of the essay—such as narration, exposition and persuasion. The essays average more than 10 pages, and almost all are written in a formal style. While students find some of the subjects foreign, they feel the materials covered are often useful in their other course work.

A new text, *The Modern Writer*, contains both an introduction describing the basics of grammar and a number of journalistic essays by contemporary authors. The pieces are typically short (only two to three pages) and explore topics of interest to most college students, such as popular music and career planning. The style of the essays tends to be informal, even colloquial. Each chapter contains several essays on a given topic and exercises designed to aid students in developing essays of their own. Although the introduction provides an adequate overview of basic grammar, the text does not discuss the essay form.

GO ON TO THE NEXT PAGE.

STOP

IF YOU FINISH BEFORE TIME IS CALLED, YOU MAY CHECK YOUR WORK ON THIS SECTION ONLY.
DO NOT WORK ON ANY OTHER SECTION IN THE TEST.

Practice Test 2: **Answer Key**

Section I Logical Reasoning	Section II Analytical Reasoning	Section III Reading Comprehension	Section IV Logical Reasoning
1. D	1. D	1. D	1. C
2. A	2. B	2. A	2. D
3. A	3. D	3. D	3. D
4. C	4. D	4. A	4. A
5. C	5. A	5. E	5. C
6. C	6. C	6. B	6. C
7. C	7. B	7. A	7. E
8. B	8. B	8. D	8. C
9. D	9. D	9. B	9. B
10. B	10. A	10. A	10. C
11. B	11. B	11. B	11. A
12. E	12. E	12. C	12. D
13. D	13. C	13. C	13. E
14. B	14. C	14. D	14. A
15. A	15. E	15. E	15. A
16. B	16. B	16. B	16. C
17. B	17. D	17. D	17. A
18. E	18. D	18. A	18. D
19. E	19. B	19. C	19. D
20. B	20. E	20. B	20. B
21. D	21. D	21. C	21. A
22. A	22. B	22. D	22. D
23. E	23. E	23. A	23. E
24. B	24. C	24. E	24. C
25. B		25. B	25. B
		26. D	
		27. E	

Answers and Explanations

SECTION I: LOGICAL REASONING

1. D

Sounds like a paradox to be reconciled—the language is a bit unusual, but the task is the same as in any other Paradox question. The first thing you need to do is identify what seems to be wrong, and the language of the stimulus makes that easy—the word "Paradoxically" in the final sentence points to the apparent contradiction. The best surgeon has the worst fatality record. Why might that be?

Perhaps you were able to prephrase a specific answer here; if not, you at least should have gone into the choices with a clear idea of the seeming inconsistency, along with a general notion of what would clear it up: something that makes it understandable that the surgeon considered the best can also be the one who loses the most patients. (D) serves this purpose: The fact that the chief surgeon gets the hardest cases, the ones that entail "the greatest risk to life," explains why he may lose the most patients without suffering damage to his reputation.

(A) would explain why the administrators would praise the chief surgeon to the heavens even if he were a bumbling fool, but that's not what you're looking for. You need to show how the administrators' claim could be *correct*—that the chief surgeon is the best they've got, despite the fact that he loses the most patients.

(B) provides info on how the chief became the chief, but doesn't touch on the mystery at hand.

(C) Training in what—how to kill people? There's nothing about the chief's training activities that lends a clue as to why so many of his patients don't pull through despite his great skill.

(E) The hospital is looking up! Still, this doesn't solve the paradox, which has nothing to do with any comparison between this chief and the last one. The fact that you don't know the perceived skill level of the previous chief surgeon doesn't help matters either.

- Try to stay one step ahead of the game. The question stem doesn't confirm that you're dealing with a Paradox question, but strongly suggests it. Reconciling things or disposing of an "apparent

discrepancy" is the action of the typical Paradox question. Approach the stimulus as you would any other paradoxical situation; see what's the big surprise, and consider ways in which it may not be so odd after all.

- It helps to restate the paradox to yourself as a means of testing the choices. Ask yourself "if he's the best, why does he lose the most patients?" Follow that up with "because he trained some younger surgeons on the staff," (C), or "hey, you should have seen the *last* guy," (E). Huh? Viewed in this context, these choices are clearly irrelevant. They don't answer the question at hand.

2. A

What's assumed? Find the evidence and the conclusion, and think about what's necessary to connect them. You can dispose of all the numbers and figures as you reduce the argument down to its basics: Because the average number of citations is down in a later period as compared to an earlier period, the agency that issues the citations must be easing up. Does something seem odd about that? Aren't there other possibilities? Maybe the companies are simply cleaning up their act and not engaging as much in the activities that would warrant citations? The author, though, assumes that there are no other possible explanations. Otherwise, how would she jump to the conclusion that the government office is more lax in enforcing the laws based simply on the decrease of citations? This argument works only if the decrease in citations was not caused by something else. That's what you get in (A).

(B) The issue of minor violations is outside the scope of this argument, which deals with a change in the number of citations for *serious* violations.

(C) Why the government office is supposedly more lax regarding this matter is never explored; you're told only that it is. Like (B), the issue dealt with here (reasons for the change in policy) is outside the scope—you're only concerned with *whether* enforcement policies have become more lax.

(D) This choice is prescriptive, which rules it out as a possible assumption. The author merely states a fact (the decrease) and infers a conclusion based on that fact. Nothing about what the office should or should not do plays into the argument. The argument is not lacking a mandate regarding the maximum number of citations the office should issue.

(E) is outside the scope. What happened *before* 1971 takes you beyond the relevant time frame here.

- The key to successful paraphrasing is getting rid of as much wording as you can. Boil the argument down to its essence. The fact that the author is talking about citations for violations of drug promotion laws issued by a government agency is largely ornamental; the same logic could have appeared in a stimulus about a decrease in failing grades issued by a teacher. Zero in on the logic of the various stimuli, and you'll begin to recognize logical patterns that will be of great help on test day.

- If you can determine that a choice is outside the scope of the argument, you can be sure that that choice need not be assumed in order for the argument to work.

3. A

Tim's argument is a counterargument—a response to Sheila's statement—and you're asked to spot where Tim goes wrong. Sheila cites an argument that's familiar to you all from the sides of cigarette boxes: Smoking over time may be dangerous to one's health. Tim begs to differ, and you wait with bated breath to see how Tim can make such a sweeping statement as "smoking has no effect on health at all."

Enter Grandpa who, according to Tim, smoked like a fiend since an early age but died at the ripe old age of 96. There's plenty to prephrase here: Maybe Tim's grandfather was severely ill his whole life as a result of smoking; the evidence Sheila cites doesn't say smoking will kill people at an early age, only that it will make them unhealthy. More blatantly, however, you may have noticed how Tim overlooks the qualified nature of Sheila's statement—long-term smoking is "very likely" to cause health problems, which doesn't mean that every single person who smokes for years will become ill. Surely, the single case of Tim's grandfather cannot counter the reasonably qualified position of the experts; even a few thousand such exceptions among the millions who smoke are not inconsistent with their view. Using bigger words, (A) describes the failure of Tim's counterargument. "Very likely" from the stimulus matches up with "probabilistic," while grandpa is the "single counterexample."

(B) It doesn't matter that the experts don't know about the specific good fortune of Tim's grandfather; they're probably aware themselves of smokers who don't follow the pattern they outline. But even if they're not, the real problem is that Tim's evidence is simply not sufficient to counter the experts' general proposition, not that the experts are unaware of the example he uses.

(C) is just not there: In neither argument do you hear of any exceptions to the experts' position that would possibly discount Tim's evidence in advance.

(D) If anything, Tim assumes that there *is* a connection between longevity and health. By citing the case of his grandfather, he's implying that grandpa's ripe old age indicates that he was a healthy long-term smoker. This implication is a large part of his attempt to rebut the experts' claim.

(E) Tim never addresses the method by which the experts achieved consensus on this issue. His argument deals only with their specific claim, and in no way assumes anything about how they came to settle on that claim. For all it matters to Tim's argument, the experts may have formulated their opinion as a group.

- Prephrase answers whenever you can—and in argument-based questions that should be most of the time. Evaluating each answer choice should be a last resort.

4. C

Next you're asked to recognize how the author makes her point—a Method of Argument question. An example (the French Revolution) is cited as evidence for a claim (the positives of revolutions outweigh the negatives). "*But . . .*" —and you know enough of this contrast keyword to anticipate where things are going from here—the example isn't a good one: Other circumstances made it easy for France to avoid the disruptions typical of revolutions. What these other circumstances are you really needn't worry about at this point, because you know from reading the stem that answering the question may not require this specific information. In fact, all you need to grasp is the general structure just mentioned above to at least eliminate a handful of choices and zero in on the winner. Take the choices in order and match each one to the structure you've discerned thus far:

(A) The claim that societies get more good than bad out of revolutions is merely supported by one example that the author believes doesn't make the case. The author says that the evidence doesn't adequately support the conclusion; she doesn't argue or demonstrate that the argument is internally inconsistent. (B) The first half is believable, if you take "a particular position" to mean the notion that the claim cited in the first sentence may not be true. But are "general principles" used to support this position? No. Very specific evidence regarding societal realities of the French Revolution are presented to refute what is "typically regarded as the best evidence" for the claim.

(C) Is the author opposed to the claim? She certainly seems to be, although she may not state her opposition outright. But she does go to great lengths to knock out the evidence by arguing that using the case of the French Revolution to support the claim is misguided. France's "unique advantage," bureaucratic stability, is her evidence that Revolutionary France is not a good example with which to support the claim. If you knock out the best evidence for a claim, you undermine the claim as well. All of which matches the strategy in (C).

(D) There is no "series" of persuasive examples used to make the author's case. Dismissing the main example in support of the claim argued against is more like it.

(E) What two positions? There's only one claim here, there's no comparison per se, and there's nothing pertaining to strengths and weaknesses (the "strengths" part may be a distortion of the notion of France's "unique advantage"). (E) is far from the method employed here.

- In Method of Argument questions, you must switch gears and concern yourself less with the specifics and more with the mechanics of the argument. Try to paraphrase the argument in general terms as you go along; that will make it easier to deal with the kind of abstract answer choices that often accompany MOA questions.

- "Internally inconsistent" doesn't simply mean "bad"—it means that the argument contains contradictory premises. The author doesn't make that case here, even though she does strongly suggest that the claim doesn't hold water.

5. C

Although the format of the question is a little odd, you're just looking for a missing piece of evidence. The stem tells you that the conclusion you're looking to support is that the number of adolescent boys with asthma is approximately equal to the number of adolescent girls with asthma. What evidence do you already have to support that idea? Asthma is twice as likely to strike boys than girls in kids under 10, and boys are less likely to outgrow it. Yet the percentages of boys and girls with asthma equal up around adolescence, because that's when a lot of girls develop the disease.

Now, you're looking for a piece of information that would allow you to conclude that the *number* of cases of asthma of adolescent boys and girls is roughly the same. Notice how you're jumping from evidence regarding percentages to a conclusion regarding raw numbers. To argue that the fact that the same percentage of two groups share a characteristic means that the same *number* in each group share that characteristic, it must be assumed that the number of people in each group is roughly identical.

Try some numbers: Say that 50% of the adolescent boys and 50% of the adolescent girls have asthma. But if there are 50 million girls in this group and only 20 million boys, then it can't be claimed that the actual number of cases in each group is equal too. If (C) is true—if the number of adolescent boys is roughly the same as the number of adolescent girls in the population—then and *only* then would it be valid to conclude that the number of adolescent boys and girls with asthma is roughly equal, based on the fact that their *percentages* are equal.

(A) and (D) How people *get* asthma is irrelevant to the numbers/percentages issue. You're concerned here with the issue of how many people in a certain age group have asthma, not with how people get or don't get the disease, so these choices don't help you form the conclusion called for in the stem.

(B) You're concerned with the tally of *adolescents* with asthma. The info in (B) is far removed from this.

(E) offers an irrelevant comparison between asthmatic adults and adolescents. But again, the argument specifically centers on a comparison between two groups of adolescents, and adults have nothing to do with this.

- Use the stem to direct your attack on the question—which includes the decision to put it off until later if you so choose. It's obvious from the stem that this is another question involving numbers, and if you've determined that these aren't your strong suit, don't hesitate to put it off based on the stem alone.

- The jump from percentages to numbers always entails the danger of distortion; take special care to think about the raw numbers that determined the percentages in the first place. Percentage info may be totally misleading, depending on the numbers that make them up—and the test makers often take advantage of that fact. Take, for example, the cited fact that boys under 10 are twice as likely as girls under ten to get asthma. But what if there are ten times more girls than boys in this age group? Even though boys are more *likely* victims, the raw numbers would strongly suggest that there are actually more girls in this age group with asthma than boys.

6.   C

A rare full-named character makes an appearance in this one: Poet Harry Trevalga claims that none of the poems he submitted was published due to a vengeful editor's jealousy over Harry's winning a prize she thought she deserved. "No way!" says the publisher: All the submissions are anonymous to the editor, so she couldn't have even known which poems were his. You're looking for an assumption underlying the publisher's response, and again, you may have been able to prephrase something here. What if there's some other way the editor could have known which poems were his? Certainly some poets have distinctive styles, right? This would surely sink his rebuttal, so he must be assuming that there is no other way she could possibly recognize his work. (C) states this assumption.

(A) Grudge or no grudge, the basis of the publisher's response is that the editor couldn't have unfairly dismissed Trevalga's work even if she tried. She can despise him for winning the award for all the publisher cares; his defense lies in another arena.

(B) Whether or not Trevalga's case is *typical* is beside the point, since the point at issue is the possibility of discrimination against his work.

(D) weakens the publisher's argument by suggesting that other factors (e.g., the "I hate you because you won the award that should have been mine!" factor) besides merit may come into play. It would be better for the publisher's argument to reassure Harry that merit, and only merit, is the deciding factor in choosing poems to publish.

(E) Since the poems are judged without names, nothing need be assumed about what name Trevalga may have used. The publisher's whole point is that names are irrelevant, implying that Harry got dinged simply because his poems don't make the grade.

7.   C

The stem tells you you're looking for a weakener, so you can attack the stimulus looking for gaps between the evidence and the conclusion. First the study itself (evidence): Researchers compared the death rates of people who live near nuclear weapons plants with the death rates of people who live in areas without these plants. The researchers concluded that, because there was no difference in *death rates*, radiation from nuclear weapons plants poses no *health hazards* to people who live near them. (C) explains

that exposure to radiation can cause health problems that won't necessarily kill you, which weakens the argument by demonstrating that equal death rates don't mean equal health.

(A) talks about nuclear power plants, which are beyond the scope. This study is only concerned with nuclear *weapons* plants.

(B) raises the issue of death rates, information that might even *strengthen* this specious argument by giving more information to imply that nukes don't cause deaths.

(D) The number of areas with nuclear weapons plants is pretty much outside the scope, and only serves to strengthen the idea that you shouldn't worry about these plants. (D) is no weakener.

(E) goes beyond the scope as well. The researchers' conclusion is only pertinent to people living near nuclear weapons plants, and so (E)'s reference to an additional study can't weaken the self-contained conclusion of this argument.

- Always pay attention to the scope of the conclusion, and note when the author makes extreme claims like "nuclear weapons plants pose no health hazards at all." Such conclusions are hard to support and easy to weaken. In this stimulus—and in many stimuli—the scope of the evidence is much narrower than what's claimed in the conclusion.

8.   B

The question stem tells you you're looking for an inference about a particular kind of liver cell. People used to think that cells would divide forever, on into infinity, but it's been discovered that normal cells have a limit on the number of times they can divide. The author then brings up the example of a normal human liver cell, which divides 60 times, before stopping forever. Even if this kind of cell is frozen, you're told, it will pick up where it left off if thawed, and, no matter what, it will only divide 60 times. You're asked about a hypothetical liver cell that divides *more* than 60 times. What do you know? Normal human liver cells only divide 60 times, so this cell can't be both normal and human. And thus (B) leaps up and begs to be chosen as the choice that this cell can't be.

(A), (C), (D), and (E) are all outside the scope. You only know about normal human cells. But (A) refers to an abnormal cell, and (C), (D) and (E) refer to nonhuman cells. Since such cells don't fall under the limitations posed by the stimulus, any of them could have divided over 60 times.

- The whole question is largely a matter of scope. The scope of the author's inquiry is normal human liver cells, only; notice how all of the other choices are outside this scope.

9. D

The stem says you need to make an inference, but tells you nothing more. Keep that in mind as you go through the stimulus. Hmm, milk trends. The LSAT occasionally has these "as one goes up, the other goes down" questions, and if you have trouble following upward and downward trends you should skip such questions at first, and come back if you have time. That said, the only logical attack is to plunge in with care—breaking it down into manageable chunks.

First of all, people complain that milk bottlers take huge markups on the bottled milk they sell to consumers. According to the author, these complaints are most likely to arise when they are least warranted (or deserved) considering the spread between the price bottlers pay for raw milk and the price they charge the consumer for the bottled milk. Well, when do these complaints occur? When the bottled-milk price rises. That makes sense, right? The consumer sees the expensive milk on the shelf, and complains.

But according to the author, these increases just reflect the rise in the price of raw milk. At this point, the time of the most complaints, the spread between the raw-milk price and the bottled-milk price is actually the smallest. So the bottlers are making less money on the deal, even though the consumers are complaining the most. Yet when the raw-milk price is falling, the bottlers make the most money, since the spread is greater. What can you infer from all of this? If the bottlers make more money, and have a greater spread, or markup, when the raw-milk price is down, then you must infer that milk bottlers don't immediately lower the price of bottled milk in a corresponding amount when the raw-milk price goes down. This is what (D) says.

(A) It needn't be true that consumers are actually paying more for milk when raw-milk prices fall. All you know is that bottlers don't lower the price to reflect the drop in raw-milk price—the price could stay the same, or even be lowered slightly but not proportionately to the drop in raw-milk prices.

(B) brings in dairy farmers, who are way beyond the scope, so you needn't assume anything about how their costs might affect the price of tea in China, or milk in Kansas, or whatever.

(C) Since you're only given information about circumstances when prices rise and fall, you can't make any inferences about extended periods of time.

(E) again goes outside the scope with dairy farmers, about whom nothing can be inferred.

- An inference must be true based on the stimulus. Don't pick a choice like (A) that is merely plausible or even probable. If it *could* be false, it's wrong.

10. B

The author claims that *if* the library shared by Redville and Glenwood were relocated from central Redville to central Glenwood, *then* a larger number of library users would be within walking distance of the library. Well, first of all, realize that, although the two buildings are described by terms such as "overcrowded" and "larger," the conclusion is not based on these characteristics—it's only based on the number of people who will be within walking distance of the building.

Moving on, the evidence provided is that there are many more people living in central Glenwood than in central Redville, and most people will walk to the library only if it's near their house. To strengthen the argument, you need to fill in a missing piece. There are more people living in central Glenwood than in central Redville, but you don't know anything about the area of either city. If Glenwood has more people but they're spread out over a larger area, then maybe moving the library won't place it within walking distance for more people. So it would be to the argument's advantage to show that the two areas are around the same size. (B) says just this, supporting the argument by making its evidence even more relevant.

(A) Where the library *was* doesn't help convince you that the library should either move or stay where it is. The library's previous location is outside the scope.

(C) You're only concerned with how accessible the library will be for walkers, so the size of the building is outside the scope. This could be a tempting choice for the test taker who didn't clearly break down evidence and conclusion, since size and overcrowding is mentioned in the stimulus.

(D) Since you're concerned with people who can walk to the library, (D)'s mention of people who don't live in either town can neither strengthen nor weaken this argument.

(E) If people currently walk farther than standard walking distance, then perhaps the new library will cater to these people more readily. But you can't assume that, because you don't know where they're walking *from*; (E) is too vague to have any effect on the argument.

- To strengthen an argument, look to bolster an assumption in that argument. If you can fill in a missing piece, you've made the argument stronger.

11. B

Now you must weaken the same argument, which, you'll recall, says that if the library were moved to Glenwood, it would be within walking distance of a larger number of library users. But what the evidence actually told you was that it would be in walking distance of more *people.* That doesn't mean that all, or even most, of these people are library users. If (B) were true—if there are fewer potential library users in central Glenwood than there are now in central Redville, then the claim that moving the library would put it within walking distance of more library users would be substantially weakened. Its main assumption would be torn down. So (B) is correct.

(A) It makes sense that, since the library's now in Redville, more Redvillians than Glenwoodians are walking there. The choice doesn't say anything about the *potential* number of walking users if the library were moved, so it's no weakener.

(C) has it backward. The prediction that library use would grow after the Glenwood move tends to strengthen, not weaken the argument.

(D) mentions non-walking library users, which is outside the scope of the argument. Knowing that some people drive or ride to the library has no impact on the different potential for *walking* library users after a change in library location.

(E) doesn't affect the numbers you're concerned with— those library users who will be able to walk to the library before and after the proposed move.

- Some LSAT arguments contain more than one weakness. Here, for example, the strengthener and weakener picked up on different assumptions. So it's not always possible to precisely prephrase a strengthener or weakener. But you can still spot either one by analyzing the connection between evidence and conclusion.

12. E

As should be clear from the question stem, you're looking for an assumption. The author tells you that light utility trucks are now popular, and that consumers like their rugged looks. The trucks, however, are exempt from safety standards for roof strength and resistance to impact. That's the evidence, and the conclusion is that, in a serious, high-impact crash, a driver of a light utility truck is more likely to be hurt than is a driver of a car that must meet the government safety standards.

So what's the author assuming? Well, for the likelihood of injury to be higher, the actual roof strength and resistance to impact for the trucks would have to be lower than that of cars that fall under government regulation. In order to draw her conclusion, then, the author would have to assume that the trucks wouldn't meet the standards required of those cars. This is what (E) tells you.

(A) is clever but outside the scope. You needn't assume that there *are* any safety standards for light utility trucks—all you know is that the trucks are exempt from certain standards that apply to cars. Whether these trucks have any safety standards besides the ones mentioned doesn't play into the argument.

(B) goes way too far. The author doesn't talk at all about the likelihood of accidents, which is implied here by the idea of reckless driving. She only discusses the likelihood of injuries *if* an accident happens to occur.

(C) makes the same insinuations as (B), but again you have no reason to believe that the trucks have more accidents than do cars or other kinds of vehicles. Even if that's false, the argument could *still* be viable—it's all about what will happen *if* accidents occur.

(D) mentions the power of the trucks' engines, which is beyond the scope here. There's absolutely no reference to engine power, stated or implied. Remember, an assumption is something that the author must be taking for granted as true. No way is the author counting on the trucks' being "deceptively rugged."

13. D

A Weaken question, so you have to identify evidence and conclusion. The keywords, "It is clear, therefore" point you right to the conclusion—CXC has increased in virulence over the past five years. What's the evidence? Five years ago, during the first outbreak of a cattle disease called CXC in North America, the death rate was 5 percent of all reported cases. Today though, the death rate of all reported cases is over 18 percent. The author attributes this increase in death rate to increased virulence, but is it the only possible explanation?

No...the author assumes that increased virulence is the cause, and overlooks the possibility that there's some other reason the numbers are increasing. (D) explains that farmers can now treat mild cases of CXC but don't bother reporting them. If this were true, then there would be fewer mild cases in the pool, and so it would be more likely that a reported case would be a fatal one. That's another explanation for the increased reported death rate, and thus weakens the author's conclusion that CXC became more virulent in the last five years.

(A) If it were true that many recent CXC deaths were attributed to another disease, then there would be *even more* recent fatalities from CXC than the author assumes. This would be a strengthener, not a weakener!

(B) also tends to strengthen the argument, by claiming that many deaths reported to be CXC five years ago were actually caused by something else. Again, that would imply that the fatality group five years ago was even smaller.

(C) The question is whether you can conclude based on these statistics that CXC has become more virulent over the past five years. The inoculation program has nothing to do with the strength of the disease, and so can't weaken (or in any way impact) the argument.

(E) is outside the scope, since information about survivors won't affect the disease pool. There's no way to tell how and if these survivors would have any impact on the data here.

- Many LSAT questions concern percents, but don't get caught up in the numbers. Many are more manageable when you consider alternative possibilities.

14. B

Questions 14 and 15, an Inference and a Method of Argument respectively, have the same stimulus. And for all its length and variety of jargon, this one is really not so tough if you break it down. Some people, namely policymakers, think that the country needs a higher level of personal savings if continued economic growth is to be assured. And a certain plan would let people have savings accounts in which the interest would be tax-exempt until money is withdrawn from the account.

The people who support that proposal claim that it would increase personal savings, giving banks more money to loan, and not costing the government much in lost taxes. The down side, the author explains, is that when this kind of plan was tried in the past, almost all the money that went into these tax-deferred accounts came out of other kinds of accounts. Do you see that? People just *moved* their money—they didn't put *more* money in.

For question 14, you have to draw a conclusion from all this. The author presents a plan to make personal savings more desirable and thus stimulate growth, but then explains that, when similar programs were tried in the past, they were unsuccessful. What's the next step? That this program probably won't be successful either! Since no distinction is

made between this program and those that took place in the past, why should this one succeed? Choice (B) outlines this conclusion quite nicely. The proposed plan, just like the others, probably won't attract enough savings to make up for the loss in taxes.

(A) brings up the backers' motives—you don't have any information about their motives in the stimulus, and so can't draw any conclusions about them.

(C) distorts the terms in the passage, trying to link lost taxes to increased savings in a way that the author never does. The plan calls for increasing savings while not losing much in taxes. The author believes this won't work, period—there's no way to conclude that a *different* program, one that resulted in lots of lost taxes, would result in higher savings.

(D) you have no reason to believe that the economy is on the verge of disaster. The only thing you know is that some policymakers think that, for continued growth, more savings are needed. If anything, the allusion to "continued" economic growth indicates that the economy is *not* currently in trouble.

(E) is out in left field as well, since you can't conclude that there's *no* effective way that the government can influence savings. You just know that *this* plan probably won't work. Other plans that might be more effective go unmentioned.

- Choices that question arguers' motives are almost never correct on the LSAT.
- Beware of answer choices that are too extreme. The author here merely suggests that this plan won't work because similar programs didn't achieve the desired result. (B)'s "is *unlikely* to attract . . ." fits this tone perfectly. (A)'s "undoubtedly," (D)'s "*will* be in danger," and (E)'s "*no* effective means . . ." are all too extreme.

15. A

You're not done—you still have a Method question to dispose of. How does the author criticize the program? Well, she shows that the overall level of personal savings probably won't change, considering past programs' rate of success. If the level won't change, then the loss in taxes won't be compensated for. Since the planners are counting on a rise in savings, you can say that the author shoots down the main support for the plan. Phrased a little differently, (A) says just this: She challenges the premise—the idea of a rise in savings—on which the plan is based.

(B) There's no disagreement expressed here, since you only know about the plan of certain policymakers. The author doesn't point out any opposing views among this group, so (B) is out.

(C) is tempting because it reflects the tone of the author's pessimism, but it's not the *implementation* that she sees as impossible, but the possible inefficacy of a plan based on a shaky premise.

(D) also tries to lead you into temptation by mentioning "past cases." But it's not that the backers approved the plans that didn't work—there's no evidence that these particular folks were involved with those plans at all. Although the author uses the unsuccessful programs to point out the potential failure of the program in question, no one is questioning the judgment of the proposal's backers.

(E) is way off: The author only has a problem with this particular program, since she believes that it won't be successful. The author never disputes the *necessity* of a program to boost personal savings.

- Stick to the basic facts in a Method of Argument question. Here, some people believe something is necessary. The author never disputes this—goodbye (E). They propose a plan, but similar plans didn't work in the past. Did *these* particular people advocate these past plans? No way to tell: goodbye (D). Nowhere is any disagreement among the policymakers brought up, so (B) is out as well. So three of the five choices simply conflict with the basic structure of the passage. The good critical reader should be able to narrow this one down to (A) and (C) fairly readily.

16. B

Find the conclusion, then search for the argument with a parallel conclusion. It's also possible to begin with the evidence, but in this and many similar questions, the conclusion is the simplest piece, so it's the easiest to match up.

Looking at the stimulus, you see that the conclusion is "some birds do not fly." Pretty clear. All the rest of the information is just backing this up by explaining that, though all birds have feathers and wings, some birds use them for different purposes. Find the parallel.

(A) compares ancient philosophers with modern biologists, discussing their goals for study. There's no comparison in the stimulus conclusion, so you can eliminate this one.

(B) The word "therefore" is a great structural signal telling you that a conclusion is coming. There you find "not all chairs are used for sitting in." This could be rephrased as

"some chairs are not used for sitting in" and that's parallel to "some birds do not fly." Keep it and check the remaining conclusions—if you're left with more than one answer choice, you can check the evidence and find that this argument has the same kinds of evidence, giving examples of chairs that aren't used for sitting. Furthermore, "seat" and "support" match up perfectly with "feathers" and "wings" as two characteristics of the respective categories (chairs and birds). (B) is parallel and correct.

(C) Two things are in the same category—no "some are not." Eliminate.

(D) A comparison between two things—eliminate.

(E) A distinction between two things—not a match. That eliminates all but (B), and you'll never even have to look at the evidence.

- Parallel Reasoning questions can be time consuming, but a methodical, piece-by-piece approach will increase your speed and your accuracy.

17. B

The next two questions share a dialogue stimulus. The first is a Point at Issue question, and in order to answer it, you have to find the answer choice that is addressed by both speakers and about which their positions conflict.

(A) There's no discussion whatsoever of rock, iron, bronze, etcetera—neither speaker takes a position, so this one's out.

(C) There's no debate at all about the dating of the tools—it's the attribution of the tools to a certain group of people that's in question. Eliminate.

(D) Jones talks about when these peoples must have migrated, but Smith doesn't mention it at all—eliminate.

(E) brings up Smith's evidence. Well, all Smith says is that the tools in question were found in peat bogs where wood doesn't decompose as fast as in regular soils. Neither one raises the question about whether the tools are dated correctly in the first place.

- In Point at Issue questions, the correct answer will be 1) an issue that both speakers address; and 2) an issue on which they have *different* opinions. Take this methodical approach to the answer choices.

18. E

You need to find Smith's method of argument—the way in which she responds to Jones. She says that Jones' evidence is unconvincing, and points out that Jones has based his argument on the lack of wooden tools dating before 13,000 years ago. Jones has assumed that, because these tools weren't found, they never existed. Smith blows this apart by pointing out the soil problem, thus attacking Jones' major assumption. This is best expressed in (E).

(A) Smith doesn't cite any studies at all in her retort.

(B) Smith doesn't think that Jones is misrepresenting the scientists' position; she's just unconvinced by Jones' argument.

(C) is a little tricky, because Smith does dispute the accuracy of Jones' argument, but it's not the supporting evidence that's in question—it's the validity of Jones' assumption that the tools in question didn't exist.

(D) says that Smith accuses Jones of a self-contradiction, but if that were the case you'd hear Smith say, "Your evidence proves just the opposite point."

- Many Method of Argument choices provoke the "huh?" response. If you see a choice that seems out of left field, just cross it off with confidence. Don't waste time rereading the stimulus and never bend over backward for an answer choice. Look for the one that is unquestionably correct.

19. E

Next up is a classic Inference question—"if this is true, then what else must be true?"—and the stimulus is set up in standard if/then format: *If* universities were living up to their moral and intellectual responsibilities, *then* the bestsellers in college bookstores wouldn't be fluff like *TV Today* and *Gossip Review*. The contrapositive is: If the best-selling publications in most university bookstores ARE *TV Today* and *Gossip Review*, then some of this country's universities **must not be** fulfilling their moral or intellectual responsibilities.

With that in mind, you can move to the second sentence of the editorial, and look!—that's just the first part of the contrapositive you just created. Well, if all this must be true, then you need the choice that completes that contrapositive, (E)—some of the universities aren't meeting their moral responsibilities or their intellectual responsibilities.

(A) talks about individuals who read these publications, while the stimulus focuses on universities, so (A) needn't be true.

(B) goes too far, because the author is concerned that these publications are *best-sellers*, not that they are stocked in the first place.

(C) would like to fool you into thinking that, because in most university bookstores *Gossip Review* and *TV Today* sell better than any other publication, most purchasers in all university bookstores must buy one of those two. Not necessarily! It's possible that most people who buy books at university bookstores purchase *neither* of the two, while the number of people who *do* buy these is large enough to make these the bes-tsellers.

(D) is hopelessly vague—you don't even know for sure that the people who are buying this trash from university bookstores are people who attend these schools. Also, (D) is much like (A) in that it focuses on individuals rather than on universities, and nothing about individuals need be true in this context.

- When confronted with an if/then statement, stop to think through the contrapositive, and you'll be well on your way to answering the question.

20. B

It's another two-question stimulus for questions 20 and 21, the fourth one in this section, and for this one you have two very different question stems. The former is a tangled and wordy one, asking you to find the principle involved, while the latter is a straightforward Flaw stem.

Speaker Saunders starts by telling you about last week's neighborhood meeting, at which everyone agreed about a certain problem—a row of abandoned houses was a threat to the safety of the community. Saunders goes on to say that no one disputes that the problem has now gone away: Since the houses have been torn down, there's no more problem. The stimulus gets a little thornier here, as Saunders goes on to explain that *some* people thought that the buildings, which were in pretty good shape, shouldn't be demolished, since the city had a fund that would help people who need housing to buy and fix up buildings like the ones in question. Saunders then concludes that, since the demolition was so successful in eradicating the problem, those who favored it must be right, and those who opposed it must be wrong.

Question 20 is a somewhat unusual Principle question— you're asked for a principle that would resolve the issue either way, not simply support one conclusion or outcome. That means detailed prephrasing isn't realistic—you'll probably have to check each answer choice. Carefully compare the actual facts as laid out by Saunders to the wording in each choice:

(A) explains that, in this kind of dispute, the plan that results in the most housing for people should be adopted. Okay, that means the opponents' proposal, right? But wait, there's more. (A) goes on to say that this is true *unless* the building is a threat to safety. Well, these buildings were a threat!—and you have no way of knowing whether they would continue to be a threat after the renovation; (A) thus gives you no clear option as to what should be done in this circumstance, so it can't be the principle you seek.

(B) says that when there are two proposals to solve a community problem, and when only one of them would preclude trying the other, then the one that doesn't close off the other possibility should be adopted. This seems like the perfect choice. You know that demolishing the buildings precluded trying the other plan—rehabilitating the buildings. So, according to this principle, the neighborhood should have adopted the opponents' plan and tried to rehabilitate the buildings—if that had failed, *then* the wrecking ball could be called in. (B) provides a coherent plan that allows you to resolve the conflict, and so it's correct.

(C) leaves you hanging, as (A) did. Yes, the opponents' plan calls for government funding, so by that token the demolition plan should be chosen. Yet you know that the government funds for these projects *have* been secured. So, again, the evil "unless" eliminates this choice.

(D) tells you that the neighborhood can't choose demolition until all other possibilities have been investigated. Well, you don't know if *all* other plans were looked into, so (D) won't let you choose demolition, yet it also doesn't give you any clue about whether the opponents' plan should have been adopted or not. Too vague.

(E) says that no proposal should be chosen merely because of a majority opinion favoring that proposal. Well, the majority favored demolition, and so this principle tells you that the buildings shouldn't be demolished on this ground alone. You don't know anything about how a decision *can* be made from this principle—just how it *can't* be.

- Section management strategies are crucial on the LSAT. Look at the length of this one: Between the stimulus, the long and complicated stem, and the lengthy choices, it takes up an entire side of the page! Skip it temporarily if it intimidates you—some test takers preferred to tackle the shorter and simpler question 21 first. Look to take control of the test in every possible way you can.

21. D

So what's the flaw? Saunders claims that, since the demolition strategy worked, those who favored it must be right and those who opposed it must be wrong. But he doesn't consider the idea that the opposing plan might *also* have worked—maybe it would even have worked *better* given a chance. He doesn't even try to show that the demolition plan was the only alternative; he neglects the possibility that the opposing plan, if adopted, might have also solved the safety problem. Saunders supplies no evidence against the opposing plan, as (D) correctly points out, so it's premature for him to declare the rehab proponents wrong.

(A) You don't know what kind of scare tactics Saunders and his buddies may have used in the actual meeting, but these aren't a factor in this argument, which comes after the fact.

(B) has more to do with the opposing side. In order for the rehab folks to fully make their case, *they* would eventually have to establish that there were eligible people interested in participating in the program. Saunders, however, certainly doesn't need to furnish this kind of information.

(C) You know that there *was* some vocal public dissent, and Saunders doesn't try to pretend that there wasn't. He makes no claim of "universal public support."

(E) Everyone agreed that the houses were a safety threat, and the specific nature of the danger isn't part of the dispute between the demolition supporters and the opposing faction. Saunders need not elaborate on this.

- Don't fault the author for not supplying info that's not directly relevant to the issue at hand. The flaw must relate to something that's central to the argument.

- When an author or speaker claims "these people are wrong," he or she must supply evidence for this assertion. Here, Saunders pronounces the rehab supporters wrong simply based on the success of the demolition plan. He needs more ammo than that, as (D) rightfully points out.

22. A

The stem asks for the claim most strongly supported by the stimulus. The author begins by explaining that, for the creators of the name "feudalism," the existence of a noble class was essential for the very existence of feudalism. The author goes on to explain that there can't be a noble class unless the titles that indicate superior status as a noble and the inheritance of those titles are both sanctioned by law. Next you're told that feudalism existed in Europe as early as the eighth century, even though it wasn't until the twelfth century that the inheritance of noble titles was recognized by the law.

This is pretty bizarre: Feudalism apparently existed in the eighth century even though legal recognition of title inheritance—one of the conditions of a noble class, and by extension feudalism—didn't happen until the twelfth century. Something doesn't match up, but it's not easy to prephrase a proper inference here. You have to go to the choices.

(A) is a valid inference; it plays off of the discrepancy in the dates cited in the stimulus. If feudalism requires the existence of a noble class, then history is distorted, since feudalism did exist before the twelfth century, but not in the terms of the definition given. The definition must therefore be inappropriate, which is essentially what (A) says.

(B) There *was* a dominant class before the twelfth century under some definitions, even though the class in question doesn't live up to the nobility definition.

(C) confuses the idea of legal status—it's not that these "nobles" were legally but not socially noble; it's that they couldn't live up to the definition posed by those who invented the name "feudalism."

(D) There's no causation implied in the relationship between the decline of feudalism and the rise of nobility. The author mentions the correlation only to point out the gap in the definition of feudalism from an historical perspective.

(E) has it all backward: The definition in the stimulus says that nobility must exist before feudalism can exist, while (E) says the opposite.

- Pay attention when the author defines terms. When that happens, the definition will usually be the key to the question.

23. E

You're asked to find the flaw, so begin with evidence and conclusion. Mayor Smith, in the past, has opposed nuclear power plant projects, and the record shows that her decisions have been informed and consistent. The mayor has now shown support for building a nuclear power plant in Littletown. According to the author, if someone like Mayor Smith with a past anti-nuke record now thinks that a nuclear power plant is okay, you should believe that the plant will be safe and should be built. But where's the evidence? There are no studies to show that it'll be safe, or even profitable, or efficient, or anything. All you know is that, if Mayor Smith thinks it's okay, then it's okay with the author. (E) picks up on the lack of relevant evidence, so it's correct.

(A) You know that Mayor Smith, the subject of the argument, spoke out against nukes in the past, and so you needn't consider a lack of information about people

who don't speak out to be a flaw in this argument—they're outside the scope of the stimulus.

(B) implies that the author is assuming that Mayor Smith must know everything about the technical details of the power plant for her to make decisions about it. You have no reason to believe that the author thinks this—she could have well-informed advisors, or this could simply be an uninformed decision. It's all based on the mayor's reputation, so (B) is not a good critique.

(C) The author claims that Smith's opposition in the past was outspoken, consistent, and informed, and that's all she needs to say on the matter. She need not establish that consistent and outspoken opposition *always* leads to informed opposition.

(D) goes too far, since the author doesn't bring up any other issues—her argument is confined to the power plant. Although this choice does touch on the idea of an appeal to authority, it pushes the idea too far.

- Your practice with LR questions should make you pretty sensitive to the kinds of evidence that authors put forth, as well as when evidence is faulty and when no evidence is given at all. The fact that someone favors a position does not, by itself, constitute evidence. Why does the good mayor here favor the plants now when she was vehemently opposed to them in the past? A good question—and one the author conveniently sidesteps.

24. B

Next up is an advertisement-type stimulus that appears occasionally on the LSAT—this one for a car, the impressive-sounding SKX Mach-5. According to the ad, you are defined by your car in today's society. The message sent by this car—call it the Mach for short—is that its owner is Dynamic, Aggressive, and Successful. That's the main premise here, and the ad concludes with a typical Madison Avenue tagline: "Shouldn't you own one?"

This is essentially a formal logic statement hidden in casual language: If one owns a Mach, then one declares oneself dynamic, aggressive, and successful. What must be true based on this information? Choice (B), which tells you that a person who is *not* dynamic and successful would be misrepresenting himself or herself by owning a Mach. To own a Mach-5 when you're a sluggish, passive flop would *certainly* be misrepresentation, according to the logic of the ad.

(A) *could* be true, but it needn't be so. If one owns a Mach, then one must be pronouncing oneself dynamic, aggressive, and successful. Whether one actually *is* these things or is misrepresenting oneself, as (B) suggests, is another story. But of course there are all the non–Mach owners, who could easily pronounce themselves, and actually be, any combination of those adjectives, or none of the above. So (A) is far from inferable.

(C) Mach owners must be stating that they're "Aggressive," with a Capital A, but are not necessarily more aggressive than owners of other cars.

(D) is like (C)—you don't know about any other cars; as far as you know, other cars announce the success of their owners too.

(E) is concerned with most people recognizing that Mach owners are dynamic, aggressive, and successful, but you can't infer this from the ad. Just because Mach owners announce their traits through their car doesn't mean they actually possess those traits or, if they do, that they're apparent to almost everyone.

- If the statements in the stimulus can be translated into if/then format, inference questions become more manageable. Then the contrapositive can yield the answer, or at least get you one step closer.

25. B

For this Parallel Reasoning question, apply the Kaplan "compare the conclusions" strategy. First of all, you're told that the great universities in medieval times endured for centuries, and they had no administrators. The university in question has tons of administrators, and the university's in bad financial shape. So, concludes the author, you should get rid of the administrators to ensure that the university will endure.

Hmm. Sounds like correlation mistaken for causation. Who's to say that a lack of administrators was the *reason* that the great medieval universities endured? The best way to start to seek a parallel to this flawed argument is to look for a parallel to the conclusion, in the form of "You should (strong recommendation)."

If you eliminate choices with this in mind, only (B), (D), and (E) are possible. Choice (A) concludes with "Jet engines aren't necessary," and (C) concludes with "new methods of control are needed." Both of these are ruled out by their conclusions, which are more statements of fact than strong recommendations. And actually, (D) isn't so great either—while it does include the word "should," determining how something should be considered is more of a value judgment than the kind of direct recommendation found in the original. So you're down to (B) and (E) without even considering the evidence.

(B) commits the same correlation-causation flaw as the original argument. The author of (B) makes it seem as if the computer is the magic element in the novelist's success, just as the lack of administration "caused" the medieval universities to endure. In both cases, it's argued that mimicking the successful element will lead to success in a different case, but both ignore the fact that these elements may not in fact *cause* these successes. (B) it is.

(E) doesn't contain the correlation-causation idea, since there's no plan to change a bad situation by copying a different situation. The recommendation in (E) is actually a reasonable one, given the evidence in the first sentence.

- The correlation/causation flaw shows up in many question types. Be dubious of all claims of causation, or situations in which a belief in causation is clearly implied. When the author concludes or implies that A caused B, consider the possibility that B caused A, that some other factor caused both, or that they're simply correlated with no causal relationship at all.

SECTION II: ANALYTICAL REASONING

Game 1—Gymnastic Schedule

The Action

"Weekly schedule" is a sure sign of sequencing, and indeed, you are mainly concerned with ordering students throughout a five-day period from Monday through Friday. One small wrinkle, though: There are six students for the five days, so exactly one day will get two students, whose sessions will be "separate but consecutive." This two-student day lends a very small grouping element to the game, but so small in fact that we'll just consider this to be a standard sequence with a minor twist. If you took a peek at the rules, you'd notice that all but the last deal with typical sequencing concerns.

The Initial Setup

No great difficulty picturing this setup; simply get the days of the week and students down on the page and you're ready to see what the rules have in store for the aspiring gymnasts: ("No days free" is a good reminder of the stipulation in the intro paragraph that aside from the double-student day, the coach meets with exactly one student each day.)

H I K O U Z

$\overline{M}$ $\overline{T}$ $\overline{W}$ $\overline{Th}$ $\overline{F}$

NO DAYS FREE

The Rules

2) No reason not to jump right to the most concrete rule of the bunch: Student I is on Thursday, so build that right into the sketch.

1) Standard sequencing fare: H . . . Z should help you to remember this. You should make a mental note, however, that due to the slight wrinkle (the two-student day), this rule does not necessarily imply that H's session will be on an earlier day of the week than Z's. It must come "some time before," which leaves open the possibility that H can be the first student of the two-student day with Z's lesson later that day.

3) Here's the more standard adjacency type of sequencing rule that you're used to: K and O must fall on consecutive days of the week, in either order. KO or OK will remind you of this.

4) Monday and Wednesday will have one student, so the two-student day will be Tuesday, Thursday, or Friday.

Deductions

Not much to combine here, is there? Notice that no entity appears in more than one rule, a fact that makes it less likely that a big deduction will exist. Trying out a few scenarios leads to the conclusion that the possibilities are not very limited thus far, which means that the best bct is to move right on to the questions.

The Final Visualization

This contains all that we'll take with you into the questions:

H I K O U Z

$\overline{M}$ $\overline{T}$ $\overline{W}$ $\overset{1}{\overline{Th}}$ $\overline{F}$
(1)   (1)
H . . . Z
KO or OK
NO DAYS FREE

•   Before you jump into the rules in the order given on the page, scan them for something concrete to build into your sketch. Sometimes, having something definite down on the page will make the more abstract rules easier to handle.

•   The action of the game informs how the rules play out, which is why the first step in tackling a Logic Game is to determine the game action and note the limitations it implies. Rule 1 must be properly understood in the context of *this* game, which includes one two-person day; it would mean something else in a standard sequencing scenario in which this wrinkle didn't exist.

•   Critical reading is crucial in Logic Games. They may not sound much different, but the phrases "some time before" in Rule 1 and "the day immediately before or after" in Rule 3 mean very different things. As noted above, the former allows for sessions on the same day, while the latter does not.

•   Always turn negatives into positives. You're less interested in where things are *not* than where they *must* or *could* be.

•   It's worthwhile noticing which entities are unrestricted. Here, U has no limitations, and is therefore the "floater." Often, such an entity will be used to shore up an ordering while the other entities are behaving as prescribed.

The Questions

1. **D**

The game gets off to a nasty start with this "could be true" question—with no big deductions at your disposal, there's not much to do but try out the choices. You could postpone this one for later, hoping to see a pair among the choices show up together on Tuesday in another question, but that's not all that likely, so you may as well simply get to it. First, you can check to see if any choices directly violate a rule, and in fact (C) does—Rule 3: K and O, scheduled for immediately consecutive days, can never be on the same day. It would nice if a choice contained I who must be on Thursday, but no such luck, so from here you'll just have to test the remaining choices:

(A) Can H and U pair up on Tuesday? Nope—that leaves no room for the KO bloc. With H and U taking up the double day, there's no way to get K and O on consecutive days without doubling up somewhere else. And that means that *any* pair that doesn't include either K or O for Tuesday will result in the same violation. This insight effectively eliminates (B) and (E), and you've already axed (C) for the reason stated above, so (D) must be correct. If you test it out, you'll see that

$$K \; O H \quad I \, Z$$

$$\overline{M} \quad \overline{T} \quad \overline{W} \quad \overline{Th} \quad \overline{F}$$
$$\;\; U$$

is a valid ordering, confirming (D) as the pair that could be scheduled for Tuesday.

- You need to bring an arsenal of strategies to bear on the Logic Games section. You'll sometimes have to resort to your second or third preferred option in tackling a question (testing out choices is pretty low on the list because it can be time intensive), but even then a little thinking on your feet can go a long way. Here, you considered postponing the question, and decided against it. Then you tried to kill a few choices directly, but only eliminated one. Then you resigned yourself to simply testing out the remainders, but noticed something in the process of testing out (A) that allowed you to eliminate all the others as well. You may not have followed this exact path, but the point should be clear: Good LG test takers have, and employ, many weapons.

2. B

K is on Tuesday, so get that into a new sketch. Not much to work with, but the question's specificity tells you where to go next—find the earliest spot for Z. The earliest day is Monday, and while Rule 1 would allow H and Z on Monday (as long as H went first), Rule 4 forbids it—the double-student day can't be Monday. What about Tuesday for Z? No problem there:

$$\overline{M} \quad \overline{T} \quad \overline{W} \quad \overline{Th} \quad \overline{F}$$
$$H \quad K \quad O \quad I \quad U$$
$$\quad\;\, Z$$

This ordering takes care of the stem and satisfies all the rules, proving that Tuesday, (B), is the earliest day for Z under these circumstances.

- When asked for the earliest day for some event, start with the earliest day possible and work your way up. When asked for the latest, or biggest, or the maximum, etc. in any situation, start up top and work your way down. This approach saves time.

3. D

Ouch. A non-"if" "must be true" question is perfectly welcome when there's a big deduction up front, but what must be true here given no new information? Nothing, really, except maybe something negative like "Z cannot be scheduled for Monday"—but the choices here are all themselves hypotheticals.

This is a great question to leave for last, though the task is made a little easier by using work from the previous two questions. The schedule you formed in question 2 allows you to axe (E)—there you see that U can be on Friday while Z need not be on Thursday. And the schedule you created in question 1 shows that U and O could both be on Tuesday, effectively killing (B). The rest, however, you'll have to work out:

(A) If U is on Monday, does H have to be on Tuesday? The test is to see whether you can place H on some other day. And you can: If K and O are on Tuesday and Wednesday (in either order), then H can be on Thursday with Z on Friday. So (A) need not be true.

(C) With U on Wednesday, K and O can take Monday and Tuesday, leaving H and Z for Thursday and Friday, respectively. So U on Wednesday does not force Z into Tuesday, and you can cross off (C).

(D) is all that's left, so it must be correct. For the record: With U on Thursday, the KO pair must be scheduled during two consecutive days between Monday and Wednesday. To get H before Z, H must take the leftover day before Thursday while Z is slotted for Friday.

- Always refer back to your previous work when asked about what could be true. In this case, you may have even held off on question 3 until you got a few more orderings under your belt from questions 4 and 5. An excellent idea, which unfortunately wouldn't have helped in this case, as the orderings created in those questions don't allow you to eliminate any further choices here. But the thought is correct, and the goal of this kind of practice is to form good habits by test day.

4. D

This requires some trial and error, but a little cleverness makes the job easier. You're asked to find the day for Z that would fix U's position in the schedule. The shortcut here is to recognize that the end of the week will probably pose more restrictions given the fact that I is already placed on Thursday. Testing out Z on those days at the end, you'll find that Thursday, (D), is indeed the spot for Z that would fix U's time slot as well: If Z is on Thursday with I, then the double-student day is used up. The adjacent KO bloc will have to fall on consecutive days between Monday and Wednesday (in either order), and H's session must also be before Thursday to satisfy Rule 1.

Either way, U is the only student left for Friday. All of the other choices leave U an option of at least two days in the ordering. (Note: If you started testing from the beginning, you would have noticed, as you pointed out above in question 2, that Z can never be scheduled for Monday. If Z's on Monday, then H would have to come before Z on Monday (Rule 1), setting up a situation that would violate Rule 4.)

> • Remember your arsenal of strategies? Here's another example of good question strategy that the better LG test takers try to employ. If you have no other choice but to try out choices, see whether some choices are more likely candidates than others, and jump right to those first. It won't always work, but here that strategy is rewarded. You're looking for a situation that will fully restrict U's placement, so you may as well gravitate toward the part of the schedule that's most restricted *to begin with*; and that's the area around I.

5. A

You get some info to work with here, but once again you're faced with the prospect of testing out various scenarios. The schedule from question 1 applies, as H's session could be immediately after U's in that one, but unfortunately none of the choices conform to that schedule. And there's not even a likely candidate here as in the previous question, so you really have no choice but to try 'em out. Luckily, (A) comes through as the winner, as illustrated by the following schedule:

$$\overline{M} \quad \overline{T} \quad \overline{W} \quad \overline{Th} \quad \overline{F}$$
$$U \quad H \quad Z \quad I \quad O$$
$$K$$

There are other ways to space out Z, K, and O from the middle to end of the week, but all you need is one instance that works with respect to H and U to choose (A) for this "could be true" question. As for the rest:

(B) With U doubling up with I on Thursday, it's not possible to put H on Friday and still have H's session before Z's (Rule 1). Sure, you could put Z later on Friday, but then you'd have two two-student days, in violation of the numbers rule in the intro.

(C) Scheduling both H and U on Tuesday causes the same problem you saw back in question 1—there would be no way to place the consecutive KO pair without doubling up somewhere else.

(D) With I already on Thursday (Rule 2), placing this pair there would result in three Thursday students. No good.

(E) If H and U were on Friday, then Rule 1 would force Z onto Friday's roster as well, overburdening the poor coach with three Friday lessons. Again, no good.

> • In a "could be true" question, as soon as you've found a scenario that works, circle it and move on. But if you're not sure whether an option will work, don't waste time testing it out until you've checked to see which choices can be readily eliminated.

Game 2—Parking Lot Lights

The Action

Lighting the parking lot—that's your job here. A picture is provided, illustrating the location of eight lights around a square lot. And what exactly are you called on to do? It's nothing fancy; you're simply to decide whether each light is on or off. Some understood this game action to be similar to that of a grouping game of selection—each light being either in or out, on or off. If that conception helped you, great. You can just as easily group this one in the "oddball" category—a spatial arrangement game with a selection element.

The Initial Setup

There's nothing initially to draw; your best bet is to work off the picture on the page. There's plenty of room on the bottom of the page to recreate the square when necessary. But it's worth deciding at this point how you're going to indicate whether a light's on or off. A simple but effective solution is to circle a number whose light is on and put an X through a number whose light is off.

The Rules

2) No reason not to jump to the simplest and most concrete rule of the bunch: Light 8 is on. Circle it.

1) This one needs some interpretation. "At least one of any three consecutively numbered lights is off." First of all, what are consecutively numbered lights? Well, there's no special definition provided, so lights 1, 2, and 3, for example, or 6, 7, 8. All this rule tells you is

that if any consecutive trio of lights like these are all on, that's a violation. In other words, if lights 2 and 3 are on, then 1 and 4 must be off.

But wait a minute: What about the trio 7, 8, 1, or 8, 1, 2? The lights in each of these trios are physically adjacent to one another in the picture, but certainly wouldn't be considered "consecutively numbered." It's a good question, but this possible slight ambiguity is taken care of by Rule 3. In the meantime, your task is to represent the rule on the page. Perhaps you came up with "NO 3 CONSEC ON" or something to that effect that will enable to you to quickly access this restriction.

3) The safest way to handle Rule 3 is to first translate it into if/then form: "IF 1 ON, THEN 2 OFF AND 7 OFF." Did you work through the contrapositive? "IF 2 OR 7 OR BOTH ON, THEN 1 OFF." Get both down on your page.

As just mentioned, this rule turns the possible ambiguity alluded to above into a moot point: Since 1 and 2 can never be on at the same time, and 1 and 7 can never be on at the same time, you don't have to worry about the trios 8, 1, 2 and 7, 8, 1. The test makers probably didn't mean for these to qualify as "consecutively numbered" trios, but Rule 3 makes the issue irrelevant.

4) "AT LEAST ONE ON EACH SIDE" captures the gist, although as shorthand it's not much shorter than the original. You may have simply chosen to remember this rule, or circle it on the page. If you were unsure of the meaning, again, try out an example. Lights 5, 6, and 7, for example—the three south-side lights—cannot all be off. If two of them are off, then the other one must be on. The west side, of course, automatically satisfies this rule thanks to Rule 2's illumination of light 8.

5) This requires care as well: If a side has exactly one light on, then it has to be the middle light. Perhaps another quick example is in order to clarify this: Light 5 cannot be the only illuminated light on the south side; *that* would violate this rule. Again, the shorthand is a little problematic; there's just no really concise way to say this. Come up with some written way to express this, or commit it to memory, or circle it on the page. Here, just say "IF EX 1 ONE ON, THEN MIDDLE." As long as you know what the rule *means*, you'll be okay.

6) Finally, a rule that's a little more specific than some of the previous ones—two northern lights are on, which means two out of the trio 1, 2, 3. And that, thankfully, leads you right to a big deduction. Did you see it?

Deductions

Hopefully upon registering the final rule you asked yourself "which two can they be?" 1 and 2? Nope—Rule 3 forbids it. Which means you're talking either 1 and 3, or 2 and 3. One of those pairs of northern lights must be on to satisfy Rule 6. In either case, **light 3 must be on** and one of the questions, question 7, is answered already. Circle light 3 in your master sketch, and you're ready to roll.

The Final Visualization

You can redraw the sketch as needed, when new information arrives. But expect to be able to get some quick points simply by referring to the master sketch created around the picture on the page:

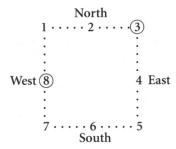

No 3 Consecutive On

If 1 On	2 off and 7 off
If 2 or 7 both On	1 off
At least one on each side	
If Ex 1 On	Middle

The Big Picture

- How do you know when to postpone a game for later in the section? Many factors play into this decision.

  - Certainly when the action is unfamiliar and seems unmanageable, that's a good reason to hold off. This game may be a little unusual, but the action is fairly straightforward—turning lights on or off.

  - Another factor in postponing is the nature of the rules: Are they complex or straightforward? Wordy or concise? Difficult or easy to shorthand? The rules in this game seem to fall more into the difficult category, although some test takers who handled them okay found the questions fairly manageable.

- In this section, most found Game 3 simpler than this one, but Game 4 more difficult. If you skipped this game to get to the basic sequencing Game 3 (or better yet, if you jumped right to Game 3 to lead off the section), then you're doing the right thing in taking control of the test.

- Sometimes, the easiest way to grasp an abstract rule is to think through examples that would violate it. This is a good way to come to terms with what a difficult rule really means.

- Some games contain rules that just aren't all that amenable to shorthand. Try your best to capture the gist of each such rule in some form, or, if need be, simply circle the rule on the page.

The Questions

6. C

Shouldn't have had much trouble here if you used the Kaplan Method for this Acceptability question. Rule 2 is the easiest to check—light 8 must be included in any "complete and accurate" list of illuminated lights, but (A) begs to differ, and must be axed. (A) also violates Rule 3 by having lights 1 and 7 on together, and (E) violates the same rule by lighting up both 1 and 2. No good. Rule 1 gets rid of (D); 6, 7, and 8 are consecutive and therefore can't all be on at the same time. (D) also violates Rule 6, a rule that is also not met by (B), which fails to light two lights on the north side. (You may have chucked (B) and (E) right away by noticing that they don't reflect the big deduction above—that 3 is always on.) The losers are chock full of violations here. (C) remains and gets the point.

- Move swiftly in Acceptability questions to apply the Kaplan technique of comparing what you know to the choices, and throwing out the violators. Also feel free to use any deductions you made up front to speed your work.

7. B

Here's the reward for those of you who worked out the implications of Rule 6 as you did above: Light 3 must be on because of a combination of Rules 3 and 6 (see "Deductions").

- If you miss a deduction up front, but are forced to make it in the course of answering a non-if "must be true" question, recognize that what you've discovered is not particular to that question but holds for the entire game. Build that information right into the sketch and use it the rest of the way.

8. B

If you're on top of the rules, a glance at the master sketch should be enough to answer this one. Light 1 is up north, and you know something special about the northern lights—two of them must be on. If 1 is off, then 2 and 3 are on, which has a direct implication for light 4: Rule 1 insists that under these conditions, light 4 must be off. Luckily, that's exactly what you're looking for. If 1 is off, then 4 must be off—(B).

- Don't jump into drawing a new sketch until you're sure that you need one. Many questions, like this one, are manageable by just consulting your master sketch.

9. D

No new info to add here, so you have a choice. You can either hold off on question 9 until you have more possible scenarios worked out in the final three questions (although question 12 doesn't help in this case because it involves a rule change), or you can just plow through the choices. If you were feeling good with the game to this point, and were having no problem using the sketch to eyeball the situations posed by the choices, then tackling this one now wouldn't be a terrible mistake. For the sake of continuity, you'll work through each choice here, but for the record, (A) can be eliminated from the correct answer to question 6 (which you should have noticed in either case); (B) can be axed thanks to the arrangement to be worked out in question 11, and (E) thanks to the correct choice of question 10. Choice (C) falls to the big deduction (a.k.a. the answer to question 7), as light 3 can never be off. So the method of using other work allows you to narrow the choices all the way down to (D). Here's how it would have gone if you handled the question in the order presented:

(A) Correct choice (C) in Acceptability question 6 offers you a valid collection of lights that are on: 2, 3, 5, 6, and 8. Clearly, since this is acceptable, (A) is not—if light 2 is on, light 6 can be on, too.

(D) If 3 is on (and you know by now it's *always* on), must 2 be on? No; you can satisfy Rule 6 by turning on light 1 instead, which is fine as long as 7 is off.

(C) Light 3 is never off. A quick elimination thanks to your big deduction.

(D) Yup: If 5 is off, then you're left with only light 3 blazing on the east side. That's a no-no according to Rule 5—better send some juice over to light 4, pronto. So (D) must be true. If 5 is off, then 4 must be on. For the record:

(E) is out-and-out false: If southern middle light 6 is off, then 5 and 7 must be on (Rules 4 and 5). And if 7 is on, then 1 is off, contrary to (E).

- Use your previous work to eliminate choices whenever possible. And in some cases, you may even wish to skip a question temporarily so that the ones that come after will in effect *become* "previous work" upon your return to the skipped question.

10. A

You certainly may have benefited from jotting down a new sketch to incorporate question 10's hypothetical—circle light 5 along with 8 and 3 and you're ready to go. The first thing to notice is that light 4 must be off; otherwise Rule 1 is violated with 3, 4, and 5 on simultaneously. You're looking for a choice that could be true under these circumstances, so it's on to the choices.

(A) And you don't have to look far: It's quite possible for lights 1 and 6 to be off here, provided that 2 and 7 are on. So (A) it is. (Note that this eliminates (E) in question 9.) On test day, you would circle (A) and move on, but for the record, here's how the others pan out:

(B) directly contradicts Rule 3—1 and 7 can never be on together.

(C) denies what you've just deduced—that 4 must be off any time 5 is on.

(D) is perhaps the trickiest one to eliminate, because it forces many rules into play. But ultimately it fails, too, and here's why: If both 2 and 6 are off, then 1 must be on (Rule 6), and 7 must be on (Rule 5). But firing up both 1 and 7 violates Rule 3, so (D) isn't possible.

(E) would create a consecutive 5, 6, 7 trio, not to mention a 6, 7, 8 trio, both of which are expressly forbidden by Rule 1.

- In Logic Games, when you find a choice early in the list of choices that works, take it and move on. This is one effective way to store up time that you may need at the end of the section.

11. B

You may or may not have created a new sketch for question 10, but it certainly helps here to plot out the chain of deductions. A circle around light 4 demands an X through lights 2 and 5 (lest you end up with three consecutive lights illuminated). Light 1 must therefore be the other light on up north (Rule 6). And with 1 on, 7 is off, thanks to Rule 3. That leaves 6 as the only light left to illuminate the south side, and Rule 4 tells you that the south side can't go dark. So there you have it, the entire lighting design, so to speak: 1, 3, 4, 6, and 8 on; 2, 5, and 7 off. Every choice matches up except (B).

- In a "must be true" question, it pays to scan the list of choices as soon as you make each deduction—no sense doing more work than you need to. But in a "must be true EXCEPT" question, you've got a lot of deductions to make simply because you have four choices containing true statements to rule out. Better in this case to just roll with the deductions and expect to fill in most, if not all, of the info possible. Then you can simply compare the choices to your sketch, looking for the odd man out.

12. E

Uh-oh, they're shaking things up. No sooner is the "two northern lights" rule lifted than you're told that exactly one light's on up there. No problem, you know which one it is—must be the middle one, light 2, because of Rule 5. For the first time, you get to go back on the big deduction and cross out light 3 along with light 1. You need at least one light on for the east side, and with 3 off, it's down to 4 and 5. You've seen this before: If only the end light, light 5, were on, then Rule 5 would be violated. So at least middle light 4 must be on, and light 5 could, but need not, be on as well. The choice that could be false, therefore, is (E); maybe yes, maybe no. All of the others are definite.

- In a "could be false" question, the wrong choices all must be true. (Note that this stem is essentially asking the same thing as the previous question.) Make sure you're adept at characterizing the right and wrong choices for every type of question they can throw at you; know in advance to testing the choices how the right and wrong ones will behave.

- Use your judgment as to whether or not to deal with a rule change question or put it off for later. In the worst-case scenario, such a question will require a lot of new work and just may not be worth the time and effort. But if you're in a groove on the game, you may wish to play right through. If not, it's certainly okay to have taken a stab at the first six questions, and the seventh rule-changer may be expendable. (Do try, of course, to return at the end to any questions you skip if there's time.) Whichever approach you take, be sure to remember that since they've removed a rule, the work you do for this question *can't* be used to answer any other.

Game 3—Seven Children in Chairs

The Action

Back to the basics here: "Seven chairs arranged in a row" immediately denotes sequencing as the game action. The entities, children, are split into boys and girls, but that's not so tough to incorporate. And that west to east business, with all children facing north?—simply a different way of describing the kids' relationships to one another. The reference to "facing north" suggests that there may be a left-right element to the game, which turns out not to be the case. So it simply boils down to seven chairs, seven kids, putting them in order—you've seen this (or will before we're through with you) dozens of times.

The Initial Setup

Since the east-west thing seems to play a big part in the questions, there's no harm in jotting down a W and E to remind yourself at a glance which children are east of and west of each other. Get the boys and girls down on the page, throw in seven chairs, and you're ready to see how the seating arrangement will be determined.

The Rules

1) Talk about strict. No fun for these kids; one kid per chair. Just a loophole-closer that you most likely assumed anyway.

2) It's hard to wait for Step 4 of the Kaplan Method to consider the implications of Rule 2: There are four boys, and none of them sits next to any other one. Well, that's not so easy to do in a sequence of only seven kids, is it? Your reaction to each rule is supposed to be "what does this mean" in the context of this game—and you needn't postpone a deduction until Step 4 if it jumps right out at you. Hopefully you saw that the only way to space out four nonadjacent entities in a sequence of seven is to place them in spots 1, 3, 5, and 7—there's simply no other way. At this point, just put a b for boy over those slots in your sketch, and a g for girl over the others. (Boy, girl, boy, girl . . . how quaint.)

3) Here's the most concrete rule of the bunch, one that you may have jumped to right away: It requires a touch

of interpretation, but essentially means that Ivan is fifth. Chairs 5, 6, and 7 are the chairs east of chair 4, and the only one of those next to 4 is 5.

4) "East of" in this game means to the right, so this boils down to the usual sequencing notation I . . . S. Perhaps you thought this through in accordance with the deduction stated above. Hold off until Step 4 and deal with it in "Deductions" below.

5) Fr or rF must appear somewhere in the ordering.

Deductions

You jumped all over Rule 2 above; it seemed natural to work through the implications of the rule at that point. If you didn't think it through then, you probably did so now. As you recall, you deduced that boys must sit in chairs 1, 3, 5, and 7, which leaves the girls in chairs 2, 4, and 6. Now you can combine that with Rules 3 and 4. Since Ivan is in chair 5, and Sylvia must be east of that, Sylvia must be in chair 6 or chair 7. But 7 is a boy's chair, so Sylvia must sit in chair 6. Is that it?

Don't stop there; what else can you deduce? With Sylvia in 6, the other girls, Ruby and Thelma, must split chairs 2 and 4. And Frank, who must sit next to Ruby, must therefore sit in either chair 1 or chair 3. This latter piece of information comes in especially handy throughout the questions. (You could take it one step further by noticing that either Harry or Joel must occupy chair 7, but the game isn't won or lost on this tidbit.)

The Final Visualization

This reflects the rules and all the deductions discussed above:

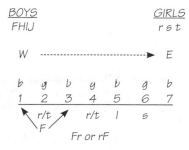

The Big Picture

- When the proctor says "turn the page and begin work on Section X" and you find yourself faced with Logic Games, quickly look through the section and determine the most efficient order in which to attack the games. In this section, many found this game to be a good place to start. It may not seem like a big deal, because you plan to get to every game anyway. But the psychological advantage of diffusing anxiety at the beginning of the section by totally crunching the first game you do is immense—and if you do end up running out of time, you don't want to miss easy points that you would have picked up quickly if only you'd gotten to those questions. A garden-variety Sequencing game like this may be just the ticket.

- Don't let a little wrinkle in a game fluster you; "west of" and "east of" are nothing more than "to the left of" and "to the right of."

- Deduce as much as you can up front. It's optimal to determine exactly where an entity must go: s in 6 is an example of that. The next best thing is to limit an entity's position to one of two spots, and here, r, t, and F all fall into that category. As mentioned above, knowing that F must be in 1 or 3 turns out to be especially helpful.

- Notice the entities that aren't restricted by any rules. Here, H and J are interchangeable "floaters" who will be used to fill in the gaps in the ordering. If you deduced that one of them must be in chair 7, even better.

- When the entities of a game fall into different categories (such as boys and girls here), you may wish to differentiate the groups on your page. Using uppercase and lowercase letters is a tried and true method. If that helps you, use it (though here, there didn't seem to be much chance of confusing the boys and girls).

The Questions

13. C

The major challenge of question 13 is figuring out exactly what they're looking for, so a careful reading is in order. First of all, what *is* a "pair of chairs in which Frank and Ruby can sit"? Check it out: You see from the sketch that Frank can be in chair 1 with Ruby in chair 2, so chairs 1 and 2 together count as one acceptable pair for this couple linked by Rule 5. Keeping Ruby in 2, Frank can move to 3 without a hitch, so there's a second pair, chairs 2 and 3. But Ruby can also be in chair 4 when Frank's in 3, so 3 and 4 together counts as the third pair. Any others? Nope, so three it is, (C).

- Read the stems carefully, and take as much time as you need to fully decipher the task at hand. There's

no way here to come up with an accurate number if you're hazy on what's being asked.

14. C

Next you're to find a statement that must be false, which means that each wrong choice will either be true or possibly true. Notice how all the choices involve Frank, which is nice because you know plenty about Frank's prospects. In fact, simply recognizing that Frank can be in the first chair gets rid of (A), (B), and (E), since if Frank were to take chair 1, *everyone* would be east of him. Upon analysis, you see that (C) is the impossibility you seek: you deduced up front that Frank must sit in 1 or 3. But even if you slide Frank down as far east as possible—that is, chair 3—there's no way to fit both free agents Harry and Joel west of him, because either Ruby or Thelma must take chair 2. (D) is possible: One of the boy floaters, in this case Harry, can hang out with Ruby on the west side of Frank—H in 1, R in 2, and F in 3 would do the trick. But you can't get both Harry and Joel west of Frank: one of those guys has to be in the easternmost chair 7.

- Use your deductions; this work is done to save you time in the questions.

- Don't immediately rush to use your pencil. Become adept at eyeballing your shorthand and master sketch to eliminate choices and pick up points in non-"if" questions like this one.

15. E

Good solid info is offered in this one, so get it all down in a new sketch.

Ivan's in chair 5, so if Thelma's next to him, she must be in chair 4, because you've already slotted Sylvia for chair 6. The stem also tells you that Frank is next to Thelma, so put F in chair 3, which leaves Ruby for chair 2. Free agents Harry and Joel will float between chairs 1 and 7. You're looking for something that could be false, and you can shorten your work by scanning the choices for Harry and Joel; after all, they're the only ones not fully restricted here. Only Joel appears, and way down in (E). Lo and behold, Joel's elusive nature does in fact make (E) the correct choice. (E) would be true if Joel's in chair 7, but would be false if Joel's in chair 1.

- If most entities are set in a particular question, and you're asked for something that could be *false*, you may be able to save a bit of time by scanning the choices for the one or two entities that still have some leeway; chances are the right answer will have something to do with them. The fact that Joel could be in chair 1 or chair 7 in this case means (E) could be false.

16. B

You already have Frank's location narrowed down to either 1 or 3, and the information in the stem allows you to deduce it must be 1. How? Because chair 3 is next to chair 4, which *does* seat a child sitting next to Ivan (who you know is in 5). The stem says Frank can't sit in such a seat, so Frank goes to 1, which forces Ruby into 2 (Rule 5) and Thelma into chair 4. Once again, you're left with the two free agents, H and J, this time floating between chairs 3 and 7. Checking the choices, you see that only (B) could be true—if Joel's in 3 and Harry's in 7, then Joel indeed would be sitting west of Ivan. All of the others are impossible. (You may have eliminated (A), (C), and (D) quickly on account of the fact that with Frank in chair 1, ain't nobody west of him.)

• Sometimes the test makers will use slightly obscure language to toughen up an otherwise simple game. Once you make the new information concrete, all that's left is to plug away. And if you've done good work up front, *that* should be the easy part.

17. D

If you're not yet convinced of the importance of the Frank deduction, here's another question that falls pretty easily thanks to the fact that Frank must be in 1 or 3. If Frank took chair 1, he wouldn't be east of Ruby as the stem demands; so Frank must sit in chair 3 with Ruby in chair 2. That again lands Thelma in chair 4, which again leaves 1 and 7 for Harry and Joel to fight over. Again, everyone's placed but those two. From this ordering, you can see quite readily that the only pair that cannot be next to each other is the duo of Ivan and Ruby—Frank and Thelma come between them. Choice (A) contains folks that *are* next to each other, while the others contain pairs that could be, depending on where Harry and Joel sit.

• Nothing says the last question of a game must be a killer, or even difficult. Question 17 posed the same basic challenge as the previous two: to digest the information in the stem and to use it to trigger deductions based on what you already know.

Game 4—Organisms and Antibiotics

The Action

The key verb phrase in the opening paragraph here is "respond to"; each organism responds to the three antibiotics in some manner, so you're dealing with a matching game. Does W get F, or G, or H—or some combination thereof? No doubt that's what the rules are going to help you to decide, and the same goes of course for the other three organisms. No tricks here.

The Initial Setup

The simplest way to match up the entities in two groups is to list the definite entities horizontally in columns across your page (here, the four organisms) and place the choices for those entities off to the side, to be filled in as needed. A simple list or grid like so will suffice, and certainly won't take long to draw or recopy when necessary:

	W	X	Y	Z
F G H				

The Rules

6) Keeping with the Kaplan strategy of beginning with the most concrete information, a quick scan of the rules reveals that Y responds to F, so draw it in. Having incorporated this, you may have been drawn to the other rules about F:

5) Anywhere you place an F, you'll also have to place a G, so you may as well place a G under organism Y since you just placed an F there from Rule 6. Off to the side, you'll want to indicate "If F, then G." The contrapositive should be readily apparent: "If no G, then no F."

3) Rule 3 is about F too, but this one you'll have to shorthand off to the side. Did you simply make the rule shorter, by writing something to the effect of "2 but not 4 Fs"? If you did, you need to remind yourself to ferret out the *implications* of the rules: that is, to turn negatives into positives and state the meaning of the rules as clearly as possible. "2 or 3 Fs" is much better. That's what the rule really *means* in the context of this game.

There's no indication that any of the remaining rules should be given priority at this point, so jump back to the beginning. As it turns out, Rules 1 and 2 can be combined on the fly:

1) and 2) Each organism responds to at least one antibiotic, but no organism responds to all three. You can and should perform the same simple arithmetic as above to deduce that each organism will respond to either one or two antibiotics. "Each gets one or two" is one of many ways to remind you of this.

4) Lastly, Rule 4: Whatever antibiotics W gets, X gets too. Take a few seconds to work out the implications of this. Whatever goes in the W column must also appear in the X column. But does it work the other way around? No. If W responds to two antibiotics, then X must have the same two. But if W gets only one—for example, G— then X must get G but can also get one more antibiotic, F or H.

Deductions

You've already begun your deductive work by piecing together the number information above. You saw that **each organism will respond to either one or two antibiotics**, and also that **exactly two or three organisms will respond to F**. You also went right ahead and put FG into the Y column, and now, factoring in Rule 2, you can safely conclude that **organism Y, responding to F and G, is done and fully accounted for**.

What else? You can combine Rules 2 and 5 to deduce that **no organism responds to both F and H**. F requires G, and adding H as well would violate Rule 2. And here's one more thing you may have noticed (but if you didn't, is not a huge drawback): What happens if W responds to F? Then so does X (Rule 4). And you know that Y responds to F (Rule 6), so Z cannot because then all four would be responding to F, in violation of Rule 3. Stated simply: **If W responds to F, then Z doesn't respond to F**. If you saw this, great, if not, no biggie; you probably had the opportunity to work through this at some point during the questions. You won't even bother including it in the master sketch. And speaking of which:

The Final Visualization

Here is all the information you have at your disposal to dispose of the seven questions hanging in the balance:

	W	X	Y	Z
F G H				
	1 or 2	1 or 2	done	1 or 2

2 or 3 Fs

If F, then G - - - If no G, then no F
Whatever W gets, X gets
Never FH

The Big Picture

- Don't let impressive-sounding terminology throw you off your rhythm in Logic Games. "Organisms" and "antibiotics" sound more complicated than, say, "boys" and "girls," but they stand for the same thing—two groups of entities that need to be matched up. Same goes for the lengthy names of the antibiotics themselves; treat these simply as any other entities F, G, and H.

- Don't make things hard on yourself! Some test takers make the game more complex than it really is. This is a straightforward matching scenario, no twists. So a simple list on the page of the entities to be linked up is the simplest and most effective way to go.

- Number information is crucial in grouping and matching games. Always take any info regarding numbers as far as you can, and always try to turn negative statements into positive ones. "Not all four respond to F" in this case *means* one, two, or three *do* respond to F. Combining that with "at least two," you can narrow it down to two or three.

The Questions

18. D

May as well begin by checking your deductions, looking for the odd man out here. And your previous work with Y takes you where you need to go. You saw that since Y gets F (Rule 6), and therefore gets G (Rule 5), it cannot get H also because that would violate Rule 2. (D) is the impossibility here; all the rest work just fine.

- In a "can be true EXCEPT" question, all four wrong answers present situations that are possible, so you can notice these things and build that information into your conception of the game, or at least remain aware that you can refer back to these choices to see a number of matchups that are possible.

19. B

You've most likely deduced enough up front to knock these choices out quickly, so take 'em one at a time. You're looking for something that's possible:

(A) Since Y already has F, linking W, X, and Z with F would result in four F's—a direct violation of Rule 3.

(B) No problem here: Nothing prohibits four Gs across the board. You need to get one more F in there to take care of Rule 3, but other than that, smooth sailing.

(C) If W responds to G, then so does X (Rule 4), and you already know that Y responds to G. So (C) is impossible: If W responds to G, then at least two more that you know of must respond to G as well.

(D) directly contradicts Rule 4: Whatever W gets, X gets, so there's no way W can respond to *more* antibiotics than X.

(E) Same thought as (D), only stemming from Rule 5: Whatever gets F, gets G; so there can't be more organisms with F than G.

- In Logic Games, when you're fully satisfied that a choice does the trick, circle it and move on, even if it appears early on in the list of choices. If you still feel the desire to check the other choices, you need to work up the extra confidence necessary to allow you to save time wherever you can.

20. E

Same drill as 19. You're looking for what could be true, so test the choices until something possible appears. Unfortunately, you have to wait until the bottom of the list in (E): Rule 5 states that wherever there's F, there's G. This doesn't work the other way around. While Y has both F and G, it's perfectly possible for at least one of the other organisms to have G without F. In fact, consulting the partial arrangement worked out for correct choice (B) in question 19 confirms this: It's possible that G is linked to all four while only two organisms respond to F. (E) could be true. As for the others:

(A) directly contradicts Rule 3—you need two or three F's here.

(B) As you saw earlier, Y cannot respond to H because it already responds to F and G and no organism is allowed to respond to all three.

(C) Here's another deduction you worked out above: Since whatever responds to F must also respond to G (Rule 5), no organism that responds to F may respond to H because that would lead to a prohibited threesome.

(D) is the trickiest of the bunch because it's stated in the negative. Is it possible for any organisms to be without G and H? Well, Rule 1 reminds you that each organism must match up with at least one antibiotic, and if G and H are out, then F is the only one left. But a solo F is against the rules—Rule 5 in particular, which states that wherever F appears, G appears.

- The corollary to the bullet point in question 19 is that if you've confidently eliminated four choices, the other one must be correct and *need not be checked*. The underlying element common to both pieces of advice is *confidence* in your work. When you've determined that (A) through (D) are impossible, you simply *know* that the answer must be (E). It may take only a few seconds to verify it, but those few seconds, and all those "few seconds" accumulated on similar examples throughout the section, add up to time you may sorely need by the end of the section.

21. D

The first new "if" of the game: No F for X. The contrapositive of Rule 4 tells you that whatever X doesn't get, W doesn't get, so no F for X also means no F for W. You still need another F to satisfy Rule 3, so Z must respond to F, as well as to G thanks to Rule 5. Do you have your answer yet? Yup—(D) must be true, and gets the point. (A), (B), and (C) can, but need not, be true, while (E) is flat-out impossible: If Z responds to H, then Z's got the trifecta, all three antibiotics—and you know of course that that's not allowed.

- In a "must be true" question, scan the choices as soon as you make a deduction or two. Here, there's no need to worry about the status of W and X after you've determined that they can't get F. Once you've figured out where F must be, you have enough info to nail the question. In a more difficult question, the test makers might force you to work out the remaining possibilities, and might state the choices more abstractly in accordance with this. But you never know how far they want you to go, so if you can take a quick shot, do it. If need be, you can always go further.

22. B

There are many ways to go about this one. One quick way is to plot out the possibilities and check them against the choices. The only pairs of antibiotics an organism can respond to are FG and GH. The only other pair that can be formed from the three antibiotics is FH, and you've seen a number of times why this pair doesn't work (where F goes, G goes, therefore no H—all that Rule 2 and Rule 5 business). So call FG option 1, and GH option 2. Checking the choices:

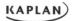

(A) Not in option 2 it doesn't.

(B) Yup. Either way, G is called into service. That's the answer, and naturally you'd move on immediately. But for the record:

(C) No H in option 1.

(D) Sure it can—right there in option 1.

(E) Such an organism *must* respond to G.

- There are often a number of routes into a question. Here, you may have noticed that you already have an example that matches the situation described in the stem—Y responds to two antibiotics, F and G. This alone gets rid of (C), (D), and (E), as it proves that an acceptable twosome *need not* include H and *could* include F and G. From here it's a hop, skip, and jump to concluding that G is the one that's required no matter what. Follow up on whatever seems the most practical approach. If you get the point quickly and confidently, you really can't argue with any approach you take.

23. E

H is off the market for the sake of this question, which means that this scenario is going to be dominated by Fs and Gs. But wait a minute: Wherever F is, G is. And wherever F *isn't*, G is going to have to be there, too, since H is temporarily out of the picture. Bottom line: G is ubiquitous; omnipresent so to speak. Or, another way to put it is (E). (D) is obviously wrong if (E) is right; there must be four Gs, not three. (A) and (B) bite the dust if you give an FG pair to Z and solo Gs to W and X. However, you can also place FG pairs under W and X, with a solo G in Z's slot, contrary to the assertion in (C).

- Even in more complicated questions, it may be possible to deduce the answer directly. If not, use your pencil and plot out arrangements in order to eliminate choices. Often, you'll be able to axe more than one choice with any particular arrangement.

24. C

The second if-clause is more concrete than the first, so it's wise to begin there. If Z doesn't get F, then Z gets G or H or both. So far so good. But that plays into the more abstract new information, which tells you that three of the four organisms respond to the same set of antibiotics. Since Y responds to F, and Z doesn't, and you still need at least two F's listed, Z must be the odd organism out: W, X, and Y

must therefore be the three identical ones. Each of those responds to both F and G, while Z responds to G or H or both, as noted above. That tells you almost everything you could possibly know about the situation, and all the choices match this scenario except for (C): It's possible that Z responds to only H.

- If a question has more than one new "if" added, work with the more concrete information first. That will make it easier to piece together the implications of the more abstract information in the stem.

SECTION III: READING COMPREHENSION

Passage 1—rDNA

Topic and Scope

Recombinant deoxyribonucleic acid—specifically, the controversy surrounding rDNA research's potential effects

Purpose and Main Idea

The author comes across as neither advocate nor critic of this technology, despite acknowledging both its potential benefits and hazards. The author's intent, it seems, is to set out both sides of a controversial issue.

Paragraph Structure

The first paragraph tells you that the development of rDNA technology "has created excitement and controversy" in the scientific world because it permits scientists to engage in genetic engineering.

Paragraph 2 gives you a bit of information about the technology itself.

The third and fourth paragraphs describe the potential benefits of this technology, while the fifth and sixth describe its potential hazards.

The Big Picture

- The information above is all you really need to take away from this passage. As usual, there are a lot of details. Note where they appear, but don't try to memorize them. Remember, always read for purpose and structure rather than for content. The former two will get you the points.

- When you see an unfamiliar scientific term like "recombinant deoxyribonucleic acid," how should you react? Should you freak out? Should you hyperventilate? Of course not! What you should do is come up with a simple reference for the term. Here, the passage does it for you by shortening recombinant deoxyribonucleic acid to just rDNA. But it won't always be that convenient; sometimes you're going to have to do the work yourself. If that's the case, treat these words as you would, say, strange names in a logic game.

- Science passages aren't more difficult than social science or humanities passages. In fact, if you don't let unfamiliar terms intimidate you, they're often quite straightforward. Don't try to deal with scientific terminology on the scientifically minded author's own terms: Reduce scientific terms to your own, simpler ones.

The Questions

1. D

First up is a Global question asking the author's purpose. The author's intent is to discuss the debate over rDNA technology, noting the arguments of both proponents and opponents of the technology, without taking sides on the matter. That points directly to (D).

(A) completely ignores the most important element of the passage, the controversy surrounding rDNA. (A) would be closer to correct if the passage consisted of only paragraphs two through four.

(B), (C), and (E) have the wrong tone. Phrases like "advocating continued . . . research" in (B), "providing evidence . . . for regulation of . . . research" in (C), and "arguing that the . . . risks . . . may outweigh its...benefits" in (E) are out of sync with the neutral tone of the passage. They suggest that the author takes some sort of stand on rDNA technology, which is simply not the case here. Additionally, none of these choices mentions the scientific controversy that's at the heart of the passage (the controversy between supporters and critics of rDNA technology).

- For Global questions, incorrect choices will always misrepresent either the tone or content of the passage; often they will misrepresent both.

2. A

Next up is a specific detail question about genetic codes. You should have noted that these codes are discussed in the first paragraph. In the first sentence, you're told outright that research into genetic codes led to the development of rDNA technology, which makes (A) the answer.

(B) has the causal relationship backward: Research into genetic codes paved the way for the discovery of rDNA technology.

(C), (D), and (E) can each be eliminated for a couple of reasons. For one thing, the issues raised in these choices apply to rDNA technology, not to research on genetic codes. Moreover, the third paragraph makes it clear that new medical treatments, (C), may become a reality in the future; they don't exist today. Likewise, the fifth and sixth paragraphs make it clear that praise for this technology, (D), has been far from universal. As for (E), the passage never says or implies that the development of rDNA technology was motivated by a desire to create new lifeforms; indeed, the passage tells you that many scientists oppose the technology because it gives humanity this capability.

- Construct a strong roadmap as you read so you won't waste precious time trying to relocate details later.

3. D

You're asked to identify something that isn't cited in the passage as a potential benefit of rDNA technology. Well, the best way to approach this all/EXCEPT question is to identify the potential benefits of rDNA technology, and eliminate the corresponding choices. That's because you know where to find the potential benefits: They're listed in the third and fourth paragraphs. Potential nonmedical benefits in the areas of waste treatment, (A), agriculture, (C), and energy production, (E), are noted in paragraph 4, while potential medical benefits, including new knowledge, (B), are brought up in paragraph 3. By process of elimination, then, you're left with (D). If you read the last half of the third paragraph carefully, you'll notice that a potential benefit of rDNA technology is the development of new drugs, not less expensive ones. So, (D) is correct.

- When you're asked about passage details, take the few extra seconds to look back at the appropriate text; you'll avoid costly mistakes. Don't base your answers on your memory of the passage; go back and check.

4.   A

This one allows you to use your Logical Reasoning skills as you weaken an argument put forward by opponents of rDNA technology: Which of five scenarios would most undercut their position? As in Logical Reasoning, attack this question by asking yourself what these folks say. The fifth paragraph tells you that they are extremely worried about laboratory safety: extremely worried that new organisms created there will escape into, and wreak havoc on, the environment. However, if some sort of unbreachable containment system were to be developed, laboratory safety would no longer be an issue, and critics of rDNA technology would have the wind taken right out of their sails, right? Choice (A) is thus the best weakener here.

(B) tends to bolster the argument that laboratories are unsafe and that the threat of escape is justified. In any case, that one bug might be successfully contained doesn't render less valid the fears that others might escape and cause trouble.

(C) The fact that an rDNA-produced microorganism has its number kept in check by predators doesn't counteract the opponents' claim that it may still cause damage to the ecosystem. The fact that it can survive at all in the world outside the laboratory suggests that the opponents' argument may still be justified.

(D) It sounds like this particular creation is in check, but what does this say about the general possibility that microorganisms will escape, which, is after all, the chief worry of opponents? This danger still looms, regardless of the seeming success of the organisms highlighted in (D).

(E) Opponents are worried about the potential for rDNA technology to *cause* disease. The notion of eradicating disease may bolster the supporters' argument, but that doesn't mean it necessarily weakens the opposing side.

- Strengthen/Weaken questions in Reading Comp function in the same way as Strengthen/Weaken questions in Logical Reasoning.

5.   E

You need to determine the role in the passage of a specific reference. To do this, you must understand the context in which it appears. That can be accomplished by reading the lines around the reference itself. In this particular case, then, you need to read and understand the last paragraph. So, what's being said? Simply put, opponents of rDNA technology fear that it could be misused to create some sort of nightmarish totalitarian society. That makes (E) the answer.

(A) is out because the critics' opposition to rDNA technology on medical grounds appears in lines 41–47— way earlier than the last sentence.

(B) Opponents, not supporters, of rDNA technology refer to the possibility of a grim future in which people are genetically engineered to serve a specific function. Also, remember that you're being asked why the *author* does something, and you decided above that this author is simply describing or summarizing an issue, not taking sides or "advocating" anything.

(C) True, critics of rDNA technology fear that its use could lead to a natural disaster, but the reference in the last sentence of the passage has nothing to do with this fear.

(D) Huxley's *Brave New World* (a fascinating book, for those of you who haven't already read it) is introduced as an example of how society *might* develop in the future if rDNA technology is misused. That's entirely different from saying that it "accurately predicted technological developments."

- Keep your eyes open for answer choices that speak of things that may be supported in the text yet are irrelevant to the question at hand. Somewhere, someone is worried about the type of disaster mentioned in (C), but that has nothing to do with the purpose of the author's reference in the final sentence.

6.   B

The final question in this set is exactly like question 4, except that you're asked to identify a scenario that would *strengthen*, rather than weaken, an argument made by opponents of rDNA technology. Once again, start by asking yourself about their arguments. By now, you know that they oppose this technology on medical, environmental and ethical grounds. As the fifth and sixth paragraphs tell you, they think that rDNA technology has the potential to cause great harm to both the natural environment and human society. So look for a situation in which rDNA technology causes this sort of harm. Such a scenario is outlined in (B): If invulnerable organisms were to get loose in nature, they could very well cause an ecological catastrophe similar to the one sketched in the fifth paragraph.

(A) and (C) After all, it's the supporters who claim that it will result in agricultural and medical benefits. The opponents don't address these issues, so (A) and (C) are irrelevant to their argument.

(D) and (E) would weaken, rather than strengthen, the critics' case. If as (D) says the environment is unstable to start with and prone to sudden collapse, then would releasing laboratory-created organisms into it be much of an additional risk? Maybe not. And if as (E) says, genetically altered organisms can't survive in nature for more than a few hours, then what damage could they do? Probably not too much, right?

- RC questions can be very closely related to each other. Use your work on the easier one to give you a head start on the harder one.

Passage 2—Gray Marketing

Topic and Scope

Gray marketing, a practice that involves the sale of trademarked products through unauthorized channels

Purpose and Main Idea

At first, the passage is merely descriptive, but the author reveals his true feelings in the third paragraph, setting forth an argument to establish that gray marketing should be curtailed.

Paragraph Structure

The first couple of paragraphs give some general background information on gray marketing, basically defining it and then telling you how it occurs within a specific region and across international boundaries.

Only in the third paragraph do you begin to get a sense of what the author thinks about gray marketing, when he or she argues that it's unfair to trademark owners, essentially by stating that their opposition to it is justified.

In paragraph 4, the author reviews three legal theories for regulating gray marketing activities, and concludes that only the last of them—territoriality—is both workable and just. The final sentence clearly reveals the author's position: He thinks it's "inevitable" that the territoriality interpretation will win the day.

The Big Picture

- Generally, passages in which the author's point of view isn't apparent early are harder to handle than passages that have a clear purpose in paragraph 1. Consider saving them for later in your section.

- This is a very dense passage, and it makes no sense to try to absorb all of the details as you read through it. But notice how neat its structure is. The first two paragraphs discuss how gray marketing works, the third describes why it's unfair, and the last evaluates proposed legal remedies. That's what you should be getting out of the text: full comprehension of the structure, not the content. If you identify and keep this structure in mind, you shouldn't have any trouble relocating details when necessary.

The Questions

7. A

The first one in the set is a Global question, so you should already have predicted this answer as you read the passage. Well, in the context of a general discussion of gray marketing—what it is, how it works, whom it injures, and how it is addressed by the legal system—the author denounces the practice as unfair to trademark owners and recommends a legal remedy for it. (A) catches all of this.

None of the incorrect choices really captures either the author's negative attitude toward gray marketing or optimistic outlook about placing legal controls on it. But they can all be eliminated for other reasons as well.

(B) and (D) are both too narrow in scope. The passage goes well beyond a mere description of how gray marketing works, (B), and "the futility of trying to regulate it" flies in the face of the author's prediction at the end. The passage also goes beyond a general description of legal decisions involving the practice, (D). Another problem with (D) is that, according to the author, two of the three theories result in the same legal outcome.

(C) and (E) are outside the scope of the passage. Nothing is ever said to the effect that putting a stop to gray marketing within markets is a different ball game than putting a stop to it across markets, (C). In fact, at the beginning of the last paragraph, the author makes a point of telling you that current legal theories for controlling gray market activities have thus far been applied only to cases across markets. As for (E), the passage never claims that current legal theories have increased the amount of gray marketing activity. True, two of them do nothing to curb it, but that's very different from saying that they encourage it.

- Wrong choices, especially in Global questions, will often be wrong for a couple of reasons. Demand a choice that does the job unequivocally.
- Some wrong choices bring up two things from the passage but compare or combine them in a way that the passage doesn't.

8. D

Next up is another Global question. Again, you're looking for the choice that accurately summarizes both the tone and content of the entire passage. That's (D). The author describes gray marketing in the first two paragraphs, denounces it in the third, and judges several legal theories for regulating it in the last paragraph.

(A) is outside the scope of the passage. The author really has nothing critical to say about gray marketers, but rather criticizes the practice itself.

(B) and (C) are, in contrast, too narrow in scope. While the first three paragraphs discuss channel flow diversion, parallel importation, and their harmful effects, (B) completely ignores the legal dimension of gray marketing. And while (C) addresses the legal dimension of gray marketing, it totally ignores all of the stuff in the first three paragraphs.

(E) is way too broad in scope. This passage is about one specific marketing practice: gray marketing.

- In Global questions, watch out for choices that mention a detail from the passage but blow it up into the main idea.

9. B

Now you need a specific argument against gray marketing. You should have gone directly to the third paragraph, since the author's arguments against the practice appear there—that's the benefit of mapping the passage as you read. In the last sentence of this paragraph, you're told that authorized dealers may not want to promote a product that is being sold for lower prices by gray marketers, (B).

(A), (C), and (E) The author never claims that gray marketing damages manufacturers by making it difficult to track sales efforts, (A), by lowering profit margins, (C), or by lowering product quality, (E).

(D) has it backward: The author's argument is that gray marketing hurts manufacturers, not unauthorized dealers, whom the author would clearly like to get rid of.

- Paying attention to the terms of the argument helps you eliminate "outside the scope" choices with confidence.

10. A

Legal matters, the theories of territoriality and exhaustion, should have pointed you to the last paragraph. Lines 46–58 reveal that these two theories differ on the rights of manufacturers: According to the exhaustion theory, manufacturers have no legal right to regulate the way in which distributors sell products to the public, while the territoriality theory holds that manufacturers do have such a right in countries where they have registered their trademarks. That's what (A) says in a slightly different way.

(B) is a bit trickier. Once again, territoriality and exhaustion differ only on the issue of whether manufacturers have the right to exercise control over the way in which distributors sell products to the public; these theories are not concerned with the issue of manufacturer sales to distributors.

(C) is out because territoriality turns a blind eye to gray marketing practices in countries where manufacturers have not registered their trademarks. So, in these cases, it's not different from exhaustion.

(D) and (E) The theories in question have nothing whatsoever to do with either consumer preferences, (D), or the marketing value of trademarks, (E); territoriality and exhaustion deal exclusively with the rights of manufacturers. So the issues in these two choices are outside the scope.

- Success in Reading Comp depends on knowing where to look up details. That's why your roadmap of the passage is so important.

11. B

The stem's reference to the effect of gray marketing on "goodwill" should send you to the third paragraph. The concept of goodwill is introduced as part of the author's argument against gray marketing, isn't it? Gray marketing, the author contends, is an unjust practice because it threatens the business reputations of manufacturers: reputations that they have built up by treating consumers properly. This points straight to (B).

(A) The author doesn't fault manufacturers (the trademark owners) for anything; and, indeed, is very sympathetic to their position. Perhaps you axed this one because of the phrase "consumer complaints," an issue that shows up nowhere in the passage.

(C) The difference between gray marketing within and across markets, which comes up in the first couple of paragraphs, is completely irrelevant to the issue of goodwill. Besides, the author never says that gray marketing across markets is a tougher problem than gray marketing within markets.

(D) can be tossed out for the simple reason that threats to goodwill injure manufacturers, not gray marketers.

(E) The fact that some consumers purchase gray market products indicates that they are willing to sacrifice service in order to get a reduced price. In any case, this isn't the reason the author talks about goodwill.

- When dealing with a Logic question about the role of a detail, it's important to understand the context in which that detail appears.

12. C

This question asks you to characterize the author's feelings about the possibility of legal action to control gray marketing. In the last sentence of the passage, the author says that legal protection is both "inevitable and desirable," and this conclusion is based on evidence beginning with the keyword "Since." The use of such words suggests that the author's attitude is one of measured confidence or "reasoned optimism," (C).

(A), (B) and (E) "Resigned tolerance," (A), "utter dismay," (B), and "cynical indifference," (E)—all negative or strongly negative in tone—are completely out of sync with the author's positive attitude.

(D) "Unbridled fervor," on the other hand, is far too exuberant a phrase to summarize the author's more low-key outlook.

- Many people have problems questions that ask about the author's attitude because they try to answer such questions on a "hunch." Don't rely on your own feelings to infer something about the author's—go to the text for support!

13. C

The topic is "channel flow diversion," which is also the topic of the first paragraph. By telling you that some authorized distributors take advantage of manufacturer quantity discounts to enter the gray market, lines 10–15 suggest how channel flow diversion, the term for gray marketing within a local market, might be lessened—get rid of quantity discounts. That's what (C) says, albeit in somewhat different language.

(A) Gray marketing is not going to be impeded as long as profit margins are lower on goods sold through authorized channels. Besides, the passage never says that parallel importing, the term for gray marketing across national boundaries, has any impact on channel flow diversion.

(B) The way to decrease channel flow diversion is to make it economically unattractive to potential gray marketers: It's difficult to see how relieving authorized distributors of advertising responsibilities, (B), would accomplish this.

(D) Manufacturers already determine post-sale service policies, yet this apparently hasn't cut into the amount of channel flow diversion taking place.

(E) Manufacturers have never provided an "extended product" to consumers who buy in the gray market, yet this hasn't impeded channel flow diversion either.

- Here's a prime example of an Inference question that doesn't require you to do much more than recognize that information in the passage can be expressed in different terms. As always on the LR and RC sections, the ability to paraphrase text is key.

Passage 3—African American Autobiographies

Topic and Scope

African American autobiographies—specifically, the difference in literary quality between autobiographies authored directly by their subjects as opposed to those composed by second hand editors

Purpose and Main Idea

The author writes to alert you to the literary difference between the two forms of narrative mentioned above. The main idea is that authentic narratives trump the edited versions; only the former warrant close analytic readings, while those compiled by editors should be recognized as such and viewed in light of their origin.

Paragraph Structure

The first paragraph lays out the main question of the passage: Are autobiographies written by editors equivalent to those actually written by their subjects? African American narratives between 1760 and 1865 are the autobiographies in question, and you have to wait for paragraph 2 for the author's answer to the question posed in the last sentence.

In paragraph 2, the author's message becomes quite clear: From the point of view of literary analysis, there's a big difference between these two forms of autobiography; only those actually written by the subjects themselves, it is argued, are authentic representations of the African American experience. This is essentially the passage's big idea.

Paragraph 3 simply refines and reinforces this message. Narratives in which editors make it a point to stay out the way, so to speak, are better than ones in which the editor's voice is obtrusive, but these are still not as good as the real thing—stories told directly by the subjects themselves. An example of this is given, and the author reinforces the main point by stating that close readings should be reserved for the authentic documents.

The Big Picture

- Like most passages, this one contains a lot of details. Again, don't waste time trying to memorize them; it's much more important to grasp *purpose* and *structure* than to assimilate details.

- Don't be put off by long paragraphs; even these can usually be broken down into fairly simple ideas. Follow the flow and try to summarize, as you did above, the most important thing to take out of such long blocks of text.

- Keywords are especially important, but sometimes they come packaged as phrases instead of single words. Nonetheless, keep your ear attuned to anything that announces authorial purpose, structure, or logic. Note the phrase "This point is illustrated by . . . " in paragraph 3—this tells you you're about to see an example. Use that information to keep ahead of the game.

The Questions

14. D

First up is a Global question looking for the author's main point. As you just got through saying, the big idea is that autobiographies put together by editors are fundamentally different from those untouched by any but the subject's hand. In a literary sense, the latter is an authentic representation of the African American experience; the former is not. All of this leads straight to (D). The phrase "circumstances under which" etc. adequately covers the ground covered by the passage, and nicely mirrors the wording of the last sentence of the passage.

(A) According to lines 19–27, (A) is a true statement: In the author's view, the integrity of editors has no bearing on the literary value of edited autobiographies. But this is nothing more than a detail in the second paragraph; it's way too narrow in scope to be considered the passage's main idea.

(B) is true as well: The author thinks that edited autobiographies are less valuable as literature than are "dictated" ones. But dictated autobiographies are mentioned only in the third paragraph. The passage revolves around the difference between edited and unedited autobiographies. Dictated autobiographies are just one type of edited autobiography.

(C) plays on a detail. The author never claims that personal impressions are more important than facts, but rather contends that personal impressions affect the way in which facts are set down. In any case, this certainly can't be considered the passage's main idea.

(E) The author *does* seem to believe that African American autobiographies need to be studied more carefully—that's apparent throughout the passage, especially at the end of the second and third paragraphs. But this choice doesn't mention the fundamental difference between edited and unedited autobiographies, the theme that's at the heart of this passage.

- Just because something may be true or is strongly supported by the information in the passage doesn't mean that it suffices as the passage's main idea. Be selective! Go with the one that encompasses the most essential elements of the passage.

15. E

You're asked to apply what you know of editors from the passage to an external situation, specifically looking for the one that exhibits the same type of role as editors as that role is portrayed in the passage. So begin by asking yourself what part editors played in molding collaborative autobiographies. According to lines 23–27, editors took the facts provided by the subject of the autobiography and presented those facts in the way they thought was most appropriate. Looking over the answer choices, this role is closest to that of historians whose job it is to reenact historical events. Like editors, these historians would take a bunch of facts and present them in the way they felt was proper. (E) gets the point.

The roles in the other choices don't involve the interpretation of historical facts. This is most obviously true of the artist in (A) and the architect in (D). The worker in (B) interprets instructions, not facts. And the critic in (C) deals with the strengths and weaknesses of a work of art, not with facts.

16. B

What does the author think about applying literary analysis to edited autobiographies? You already know the author's opinion of such works: They're inauthentic because they can distort the subject's life experiences and feelings. This attitude strongly suggests that the author has doubts about "close analytic readings" of these texts, right? What's the point of closely analyzing a work that's inauthentic? Indeed, in the penultimate sentence of the last paragraph, the author explicitly states that "analysts should reserve close analytic readings for independently authored (i.e., unedited) texts." (B) is the one that expresses this attitude.

(A) is too extreme. In the last sentence of the passage, the author says that literary analysis of edited autobiographies must come to grips with "the conditions that governed their production." In other words, the author's not "adamantly opposed" to all literary analysis of edited works; he or she just thinks that one particular type of literary analysis, the close analytic reading of texts, is inappropriate for edited works.

(C) and (E) twist details in paragraph two: Nowhere does the author advocate analyzing prefaces, footnotes, and commentaries (C); if anything, the author feels these have served as red herrings, masking the lack of authenticity of edited texts. As for (E), linguistic, structural, and tonal integrity are contrasted in the passage to the moral integrity

of editors. Nowhere does the author state or imply that analysis enhances these.

(D) raises an issue that the author never addresses—the historical reading of such narratives.

- Learn to recognize classic wrong answer types so that you can eliminate such choices quickly. Here you have a good mix: extreme (A), distortion (C) and (E), and outside the scope (D).

17. D

Next you're asked about past readers of African American autobiographies. These readers are mentioned only once, in lines 28–36. There, you're told that they, like the editors, believed that edited autobiographies were no less genuine a representation of the African American consciousness than unedited works. That makes (D) the answer.

(A), (C), and (E) You simply aren't told what aspect of the autobiographies most interested earlier readers (A), whether they were more knowledgeable about the facts of slave life than contemporary readers (C), or whether they were interested in the moral integrity of the editors (E). (A) and (C) present comparisons that are simply unwarranted; there's no support for them at all. (E), on the other hand, tries to connect the moral integrity issue in some way to these earlier readers, but there's no support for this connection anywhere.

(B) makes no sense at all, since "ghostwritten" autobiographies, according to the first sentence of the second paragraph, are edited autobiographies.

- Another wrong answer type, common in Logical Reasoning questions as well, is the unwarranted or irrelevant comparison. These can be tempting because they often involve recognizable elements or characters from the passage, but simply compare them in a way that's unsupported by the text.

18. A

The stem is a bit on the long side, but essentially you're after the word that reveals the author's skepticism about the authenticity of edited autobiographies. That's really what the question's asking, right? Choice (A)'s "ostensible" fits the bill. As it's used in the passage, ostensible means "supposed" or "presumed." Using the word "ostensible" to describe the authorship of the narratives is the author's way of saying right off the bat that he's doubtful of the authenticity of some of these works. Any study of these autobiographies supposedly ("ostensibly") written by the subjects themselves would, according to the author, raise concerns about authenticity.

If you didn't see this, you might still have gotten the correct answer through process of elimination. None of the other words refers to the author's feelings about edited autobiographies. In fact, each refers to ideas and issues discussed considerably later. "Integrity," (B), and "delimits," (D), relate to the editors of autobiographies, rather than to the author's attitude toward the works themselves. Similarly, "extraneous," (C), relates to the facts that appear in edited autobiographies, while "impolitic," (E), relates to people being interviewed in the 1930s.

- If you have trouble with a wordy or complicated question stem, you may wish to consider postponing the question for later. Remember, you need not work through every question to get a top score. Just remember to fill in a guess for any question you don't get to.

19. C

You can make quick work of question 19, dealing with "close analytic readings" of texts. As you mentioned back in question 16, the author thinks that close analytic readings are useful only in cases where autobiographies have been written by their subjects. Lines 55–56 explicitly make this point. (C), which says exactly the same thing, is one of the easier points on this section.

(A), (D), and (E) all mention an editor, so they can be eliminated right off the bat. It's edited collaborative texts that the author specifically says shouldn't receive close readings.

(B) raises an issue that's outside the scope of the passage (though it sounds good, doesn't it?).

- Not every question in a Reading Comp set tests a different concept. Often, the issues in various questions are related, so, just as in Logic Games, use your work and thinking from previous questions to help you with later ones when possible.

20. B

Why bring up Blassingame?—asks the final question of the set. To determine this, it's important to grasp the context in which he's discussed. The name isn't too hard to find; Blassingame is cited by the author in the beginning of

paragraph two as someone who believes that editors were honest, and therefore would not have played fast and loose with the facts. Directly after this point is made, the author goes on to say that personal integrity is *not* the issue (note the "however"); what *is* at issue, according to the author, is the "linguistic, structural, and tonal integrity" of autobiographies produced by editors. In other words, Blassingame is introduced as an example of a scholar with a misplaced emphasis when it comes to the study of African American autobiography. And that's (B).

(A) is out because Blassingame's point of view contradicts, rather than supports, the author's point of view.

(C) Blassingame's method of studying autobiographies is in line with the one that has traditionally been used by scholars. If anyone has a new idea about how to look at autobiographies, it's the author.

(D) is a bit tricky if you don't keep context in mind. Remember, what the author *really* objects to is Blassingame's assessment of the editor's role, not his adherence to the traditional approach to literary analysis of African American autobiography.

(E) distorts information in the passage: The author doesn't think the editor-narrator relationship is important; if anything, he or she thinks that it causes problems. In any case, this isn't the reason why Blassingame appears in the text.

- Logic function questions test whether you're up on what the author's up to, such as why he includes a word, an example, a paragraph, and so on. Keywords help the author to tell the story in a coherent manner, and by extension help you to keep tabs on the author. The contrast keyword "however" is the key to this question.

Passage 4—Rubinstein's Theory

Topic and Scope

Wealth in Britain; specifically, Rubinstein's theory of wealth and power in 19th-century Britain

Purpose and Main Idea

The author's purpose is to evaluate Rubinstein's work; his specific main idea is that Rubinstein has made a valuable contribution to the question, but hasn't entirely proven his case.

Paragraph Structure

In the first paragraph, the author tells you that Rubinstein's theory takes issue with the traditional, Marxist interpretation of 19th-century British history; in contrast to Marxist historians, Rubinstein argues that real wealth lay with a commercial elite in London, rather than with northern industrialists.

The second paragraph tells you about the evidence that Rubinstein uses to substantiate his view; specifically, investigations of probate records. Such records do seem to show more commercial fortunes than industrial ones, but the keyword "However" alerts you to a complication: These investigations don't fully make Rubinstein's case because of ambiguities inherent in the probate valuation process.

Paragraph 3 goes on to say that Rubinstein also disagrees with the Marxist interpretation of history with respect to the connection between wealth and power; according to him, the rich were not necessarily the most powerful people in society.

The final paragraph tells you that Rubinstein has begun to strengthen his views by collecting evidence from tax records. The last sentence, introduced with the contrast keyword "But," reinforces the author's point that you can't fully accept Rubinstein's theory without further proof.

The Big Picture

- Coming into the passage you don't need to know anything about Rubinstein or his theory. All the information you need to answer the questions is in the passage. So don't worry when a passage mentions a theory. You have everything you need.

- When a theory is presented, try to determine the author's position on the matter. The questions will test whether you've picked up on it. This author finds Rubinstein's theory "provocative," but only "partially convincing."

The Questions

21. C

First up is a typical Global question, so you've already done the work necessary to answer this question. Now, as you just finished saying, this passage is about Rubinstein's theory of the distribution of wealth and power in 19th-century Britain, a theory the author finds intriguing, but still

insufficiently documented to displace the traditional view of 19th-century Britain. (C) is the closest to this.

(A) contradicts the author's message: Rubinstein's theory, according to the author, is not strong enough to overturn the traditional, Marxist interpretation of history. Besides, this passage is primarily about Rubinstein's theory, not about the Marxist view of history.

(B) is out because the author never tells you what sort of relationship between wealth and power he or she expects to find in new data. Additionally, this choice completely misses the message of the passage, which (again) is that a new theory has emerged to challenge the orthodox view of 19th-century Britain.

(D) is a true statement: The passage says that probate records are indeed a revealing, though imperfect, source of information about the location of wealth in 19th-century Britain. The problem with (D) is that it's simply too narrow in scope to qualify as the big idea of the passage—a discussion of the benefits and drawbacks of examining probate records is limited to the second paragraph.

(E) is also too narrow. Furthermore, the author never says that confirmation of Rubinstein's theory "is likely to remain elusive"; to say that Rubinstein hasn't gotten it 100 percent right yet is not to predict that he won't someday.

- The correct answer to a Global question must reflect the scope of the entire passage.

22. D

In the first part of the second paragraph, the author notes that probate records provide interesting information about the distribution of wealth in 19th-century Britain. But in the remainder of the paragraph, he or she notes that there are a number of problems concerning the correct interpretation of these records. So choice (D) is the answer—it touches both bases.

(A), (B), and (C) Remember, the author thinks that probate records are eye opening, though hard to interpret. Of (A), (B), and (C), only (B)'s "ambiguous" and (C)'s "controversial" capture a sense of this feeling. But the second parts of these choices don't fit the bill: "Outdated" gets the time frame wrong, and "readily available" is outside the scope of the issue. (A), meanwhile, is way too critical.

(E) Rubinstein, as far as you know, is the only historian to have worked with these records. Moreover, the author never says or implies that only specialists are able to decipher them.

- Many Reading Comp choices can be eliminated because of a single word or phrase that conflicts with the author's tone or opinion on a certain matter.

23. A

You're interested in whether the author thinks that probate records accurately reflect the value of 19th-century "goods for sale." This issue comes up in lines 27–32, where the author more or less tells you that probate values for such goods may have been dependent upon valuation conventions. That's (A).

(B) is out for the simple reason that the author never draws a comparison between the accuracy of probate and income tax records.

(C) is out because the author never draws a comparison between tobacco- and alcohol-related goods. As a matter of fact, the only thing the author says about tobacco and alcohol is that people in these industries tended to make more money than people in textiles or metals.

(D) Lines 29–32 tell you that (D) is the opposite of what the author believes: Probate values for bank balances were higher.

(E) The author never implies that valuation conventions for goods for sale were dependent upon a person's occupation. Rather, the author says that general probate valuations, in contrast to goods for sale valuations, may have been affected by occupation, but that's a completely different story.

- Don't bend over backward for an answer choice. Look for the one choice that the test makers have set up to be excellent. Choices that require you to make up a story in order for them to work are always wrong.

24. E

Now you're asked specifically about Rubinstein's challenge to the orthodox view of 19th-century Britain. Rubinstein challenges the orthodox view on two points: (1) he claims that a London-based commercial elite, rather than a northern industrial elite, was the true center of wealth, and (2) he claims that there was no relationship between wealth and power. Either of these views would be satisfactory as the right answer; the test makers picked the second, (E).

(A) and (D) are too vague: Both Rubinstein and the traditionalists believe that the distribution of wealth between commerce and industry was unequal, (A), and that a governing elite can be identified, (D). It's the specifics of this economic inequality and the precise makeup of this elite that they disagree on. The claims in (A) and (D) don't reflect these nuances.

(B) The claim that the tobacco and alcohol industries were more lucrative than the textiles and metals industries, (B), is based on Rubinstein's research—it's not a point of contention between him and the traditionalists.

(C) If you stop reading too soon, desperate for an answer, you're tempted by poor choices like (C): The existence of a London-based commercial elite is actually a claim made by Rubinstein himself.

- Many LSAT Reading Comp passages present multiple views, and it's up to you to keep them straight. Use your roadmap to keep track of who says what.

25. B

This one asks why the author points out that "goodwill" was excluded from 19th-century probate valuations. Since you're being asked why a detail has been included in the passage, the context in which it appears is all-important. If you look back at lines 28–40, you'll find that the exclusion of goodwill is brought up in the midst of a general discussion about why many 19th-century British businesses were undervalued in probate records. That makes (B) the answer.

(A) and (E) are outside the scope: The author doesn't say that little was known about the concept of goodwill in the 19th century, (A); nor does the author ever make a comparison between 19th- and 20th-century probate valuation methods, (E).

(C) If anything, the author implies that the exclusion of goodwill may have had an unequal impact across different types of business.

(D) is wrong for a couple of reasons. First, the author's interested only in 19th-century British businesses, not businesses in general. Second, the author never says that goodwill is "the most important factor in determining the market value of certain businesses."

- If you keep your focus on the scope of the passage in your initial read, you won't be distracted by choices that violate it.

26. D

Now you need to determine which of five studies would support Rubinstein's claims. As mentioned in question 24, Rubinstein makes two basic claims: (1) True wealth was in the hands of a commercial elite in London, not in the hands of a northern industrial elite, and (2) there was no direct link between wealth and power. So, you're looking for a study that would support one or both of these claims. (D) fits the bill: Rubinstein's claim about the location of wealth, after all, rests on probate records, which don't include the value of real property. If it were to be discovered that real property did not, in fact, add to the riches of industrialists, this finding would tend to confirm Rubinstein's belief that true wealth lay in the hands of a London-based commercial elite.

(A) would tend to undermine Rubinstein's claim that real wealth in 19th-century Britain was in the hands of a London-based commercial elite.

(B) A study that indicated that working-class people targeted northern industrialists would support the traditional, Marxist view of 19th-century Britain. Rubinstein, as you know, opposes this view.

(C), too, would tend to undermine Rubinstein's claims: If the probate values of goods for sale in that era were found to be lower than probate values of cash assets, this would indicate that industrialists had more wealth in comparison to members of the commercial elite than Rubinstein seems to think. That is, this would tend to confirm one of the uncertainties that the author suggests could limit the value of Rubinstein's theory.

(E) would tend to undermine Rubinstein's claim that there was no connection between money and power.

- In Reading Comp and in Logical Reasoning, you have to be clear as to *which* argument you're strengthening or weakening. Expect a few 180 choices to tempt those that get this backward.

27. E

Now you're asked to pick the scenario that would cast the most doubt on Rubinstein's argument about the connection between wealth and power. Well, as paragraph 3 tells you, Rubinstein argues that there was no such connection in 19th-century Britain: Wealth, in other words, didn't automatically give one power, and lack of wealth

didn't automatically exclude one from power. So, if it was to be shown that there *was* indeed some sort of tangible connection between wealth and power—that possession of wealth *did* lead to power—this would certainly weaken Rubinstein's argument. (E) makes this connection, and therefore casts the most doubt on Rubinstein's wealth-power hypothesis.

(A) To enter the ruling elite, according to Rubinstein, one needed only two things: a university degree and a father with a middle-class income. (A), therefore, would tend to strengthen, rather than weaken, Rubinstein's argument.

(B) and (C) present irrelevant comparisons. (B) compares the relative importance of the two factors Rubinstein claims are prerequisites for power; but Rubinstein never compares them with *each other*, so nothing about this damages his claim. Maybe schooling is more crucial than income, maybe the other way around, who knows? As for (C), the wealth of powerful bishops compared with that of powerful civil servants and company bosses is also irrelevant. These powerful bishops may have had a little more dough than the other members of the elite, but that doesn't mean they were truly wealthy by societal standards. In other words, the fact that they were a little better off financially than the others doesn't weaken Rubinstein's opposition to the claim that power resides in the hands of society's wealthiest.

(D) tends to weaken the traditional Marxist claim, not Rubinstein's argument. The Marxists are the ones who saw the textile and iron barons of the north as the power elite, the ones against which the workers waged their battle.

- Strengthen and Weaken questions are mainstays of the Logical Reasoning section, but don't be surprised if a few pop up on your RC section as well.

- Make sure you focus on the right argument. There are three here: the traditional Marxist view, Rubinstein's view that this traditional view is incorrect, and the author's view that Rubinstein's critique is provocative but incomplete. If you keep them straight from the beginning, then Strengthen/ Weaken questions should be a whole lot easier.

SECTION IV: LOGICAL REASONING

1. C

If you read the question stem first, as the Kaplan LR Method requires, you know exactly what you're looking for: something the author fails to consider. That's a specific kind of logical flaw.

Paraphrase the argument: The Acme cafeteria can only offer four main dishes, and they've offered the same ones for years. When mushroom casserole was offered for two days in place of one of the other dishes, the masses went wild—they loved it. The author concludes that the only way to make these people happy is to now offer mushroom casserole in place of one of the other dishes. It's likely you were able to prephrase what's wrong with this picture: The author sees the mushroom casserole itself as being the catalyst for the seeming popularity of the dish, but while it *could* be true that most people are desperately enamored with mushroom casserole, it seems quite likely that people were simply starving for some variety. Choice (C) spells out this alternative explanation for the mushroom craze, and makes you wonder how many times a person can eat mushroom casserole before getting tired of it? Making this dish a permanent part of the menu, based merely on the evidence of two days, may not be such a great idea after all, if you consider that the need for variety may have driven people to it.

(A) The proportion of employees who eat at the cafeteria has nothing to do with the argument; it's not *who's* eating, but rather *what's being eaten* that matters.

(B) The ingredients of the dishes, and especially the possibility of overlap among the dishes, are outside the scope.

(D) and (E) Only "main dishes at lunchtime" are addressed, so other dishes and other meals are also outside the scope of the argument.

- Reading the question stem first tells you specifically what your focus should be when you read through the stimulus; in this case, what factor in the argument is going right over the author's head? (Of course, it must also be a factor that's *relevant* to the argument. The author also "fails to consider" why the sky is blue, but that's not part of the argument's scope.)

2. D

There's a paradox afoot in question 2, so the first step is to isolate the surprise. Reduced to its basics, the argument reads like this: Even though clearing forests of tall trees results in more sunlight and thus more leafy shrubs, upon which mule deer depend for food, mule deer that live in cleared forests aren't as well-nourished as are herds living in uncleared forests. So more leafy shrubs *should* mean well-nourished mule deer, but in fact lead to the opposite. What's going on?

Clearly, there's something you're not being told about the leafy shrubs or the greater quantity of sunlight that may explain away this surprising fact, but it's not easy to prephrase the exact resolution. Move to the choices, looking for an additional factor that will solve the mystery.

(A) doesn't address the paradox; it talks about differences between mule deer and other deer, an issue that's outside the scope.

(B) introduces a distinction within the mule deer population between those that live in cleared forests and those that don't, but it doesn't address the problem of less well-nourished deer. It would only be useful if you had some reason to think that females with young offspring are generally less well nourished than adult males—but you've no reason to believe this.

(C) Huh? You're not looking for trivia tidbits regarding the mule deer, fascinating as they may be. You're demanding specific information regarding why mule deer with supposedly more food are less well nourished—and this isn't it.

(D) is, finally, a satisfying answer, even though it fails to mention deer at all. It directly addresses the reason why sunny forests produce less well-nourished deer. If increased sunlight actually leads to the creation of food that is not digestible, as (D) says, the deer can eat to their little hearts' content and they won't reap any benefits. (D) is directly relevant to the mystery at hand, and offers the best resolution.

(E) might help explain why deer might become *better* nourished when the forest is cleared of tall trees, because the parasites wouldn't have a jumping-off point. In terms of resolving the paradox at hand, (E) is of no help at all.

- When you see the word "paradox" in a question stem, think "surprise." A situation that should appear a certain way or lead to a certain logical result instead leads somewhere totally different. Your job in resolving the paradox (or "seeming discrepancy") is to find the choice that explains the surprise.

3.   D

Your task in this Parallel Reasoning question is to find the argument that mimics Harold's response to Genevieve. Genevieve gives concrete reasons supporting her argument, and while acknowledging that her reasoning is sound, Harold dismisses it because she herself flies often. So locate the choice in which someone discounts a conclusion on the grounds that the person making a recommendation doesn't follow her own advice.

(A) doesn't include a person giving concrete reasons: It's simply a person saying "Thumbs down." Furthermore, the judgment regards something the person *hasn't* done, not something the person does despite his or her own judgment.

(B) isn't saying why a person should or shouldn't do anything. No judgment is offered at all. This person simply isn't cooking lamb tonight because her friend doesn't eat it. This may make sense if she's having Maria over for dinner, but it has no relation to Harold's logic.

(C) would be closer if Susan had given concrete, sound reasons why rock climbing is safe but nevertheless refused to do it herself. But no: Susan says it's safe, *does* go ahead and do it, and then breaks her collarbone. You can't exactly fault this person for doubting her safety claim.

(D) Bingo. Here you have a person who presents valid evidence to support a statement, but whose argument is dismissed since she doesn't practice what she preaches.

(E) isn't even a reply to someone else's argument, so you can cross it off right away.

- The best way to deal with most Parallel Reasoning questions is to characterize the conclusion. Then, if necessary after checking the conclusion against the answer choices, do the same with the evidence. The content won't lead you to the correct answer; accurately identifying its *structure* will.

4.   A

Next up you need to find an explanation for why certain residents seem to hold two contradictory opinions at once. On the one hand, all Gradarans want hazardous waste to be burned in high-temperature incinerators—they want laws to that effect to be passed. But companies that are trying to build the incinerators in question can't find any place to build them because people who live in Gradaran communities are protesting the building permit applications. What's the average Gradaran on the street saying?

The old NIMBY argument: "Not in *my* backyard! I want the incinerator to get rid of that waste, but I don't want to have to look at it, or smell it, or be potentially harmed by it." This is basically what (A) says. Incineration of this kind is great for the population at large, but it has risks for the people closest to the incineration sites. (A) explains how Gradarans can simultaneously hold both opinions cited; if (A) is true, these opinions don't really conflict at all.

(B) and (E) raise the issue of cost, but that's not a factor, as far as you know, in the people's decision making. So no appeal to cost will explain why the Gradarans hold seemingly opposing positions, or will help to resolve them.

(C) is off the subject too, since you don't know anything about how the use of private companies to carry out the incineration will influence public opinion. No help.

(D) seems to try to make the incinerators seem safe, if that's what turning toxic waste fumes into solids means. But that has nothing to do with the paradox at hand. The specifics of the process have no bearing on the seemingly conflicting positions.

- When seeking to resolve an apparent conflict, stick closely to the scope of the contradiction. Here there's an ambiguity regarding the residents' support for the overall plan. Issues such as cost or who will carry it out are beyond this scope.

5.   C

The stimulus is only one sentence; Elena doesn't have to say too much to reveal her deep-seated paranoia regarding white poodles. While the question stem should be, "Why didn't someone tell Elena not to attend dog shows?" it's not. So you mustn't spend precious time concerning yourself with Elena's fragile emotional state.

In this one sentence, Elena really makes two interdependent statements: Every dog that growled at her was a white poodle (all X were Y), and every white poodle she saw growled at her (all Y were X). So you know that if you don't have one, you can't have the other, right? It could never be true that, at the dog show, a white poodle looked at her and didn't growl. It could also never be true that a dog that growled at her wasn't a white poodle. There's no point in guessing what the correct inference will be, since it could be one of many, so look through the choices until you find the answer.

(A) You can't infer (A), because you don't know whether or not Elena saw any other dogs. She may have seen a hundred other white breeds—she may have seen none.

(B) is not inferable either. Remember, all you know about is Elena's bad karma with white poodles. There very well could have been lots of gray poodles at the show, or any other color, for that matter—you have no way of knowing. If there *were* dogs of other colors there, you know for sure that they didn't growl at Elena. Speaking of which . . .

(C) is the answer for just that reason. Because all dogs that aren't white poodles have been excluded from the growling category, (C) must be true.

(D) If you knew that the only type of white dog that Elena saw was a white poodle, then (D) would be true, but you can't know this for certain.

(E) Once again, you can't know anything about any type of dog that isn't a white poodle except that it didn't growl at her. Maybe she saw some gray poodles, maybe she didn't.

- Understanding and interpreting if/then statements is an absolute necessity in Logic Games, but it's important for Logical Reasoning, too.

6.   C

Questions 6 and 7 share the same stimulus, a conversation between Derek and Lola. Essentially, Derek argues that you need to harvest yew trees now to develop an anticancer drug, because an effective man-made drug would take too long to develop. Lola takes the "friend of nature" stance, arguing that it's more important to protect the rare yew trees and the endangered spotted owl, and therefore you should wait for a synthetic drug to be manufactured.

Skimming through Derek's argument, what stands out? How about "you must exploit . . . " and "the trees should be harvested now." If you can get an effective anticancer drug *now*, Derek says, why wait? Lola's key words, "Despite our eagerness . . . " and "you should wait rather than threaten . . . " shows that she believes there is a justifiable alternative to chopping down rare trees and killing off animals. These keywords clue you in on the main point at issue: to wait or not to wait. Only (C) deals with the delay issue, so it's the correct choice here.

(A) Derek doesn't argue that harvesting yews won't have repercussions—in fact, he allows that it may—so (A) is off base.

(B) Neither Derek nor Lola seems particularly concerned with whether drugs *in general* should be synthetic or natural, so (B) isn't a point of contention either. What worries them are the specific considerations that are entailed in this particular decision—namely, waiting a long time versus threatening the ecosystem.

(D) doesn't work because Derek doesn't quantify the environmental impact of harvesting yew trees, nor does he even mention the spotted owl.

(E) is too broad, specifically in its use of the word "ever": Derek and Lola are talking about a specific set of circumstances, not a plan of action in general. To blow this disagreement up into a general conflict between environmental and human needs is too extreme.

- In dialogue questions, try to boil down the speakers' key points and don't get bogged down in detail. If you do reduce the respective arguments to their most basic formulations, the point at issue should emerge fairly clearly—it's the one both parties address, and take different positions on.

- When prose is dense (and even when it isn't), look for the basic grammatical clues to help you get a handle on the argument.

7.   E

For the second question of this two-parter, you're asked to identify the principle to which Lola's position most closely conforms. In simpler terms, what general thing must Lola believe in order to argue as she does?

Recap Lola's argument: She believes that it's more important to protect the ecosystem from long-lasting damage than it is to provide a resource that would quickly enable a new medical breakthrough. In other words, weighing the pros and cons, Lola thinks the cancer cure can wait for a synthetic solution since adopting Derek's plan will damage the ecosystem. This notion of prioritizing is captured in every element of (E): The action that threatens an ecosystem and that should be avoided is harvesting the yews; avoiding this action is more important to Lola than immediately helping the restricted group, the cancer sufferers.

(A) If anything, the principle in (A) works against Lola's position. The well-being of cancer patients is certainly threatened, so one who subscribes to the principle in this one would ostensibly favor harvesting the yews to provide quicker relief to the sufferers.

(B) Neither medical researchers nor environmentalists are mentioned in Lola's argument, so it's extremely doubtful that this principle can form the bedrock of Lola's argument. Furthermore, the tone isn't right—nothing suggests that Lola would favor the kind of compromise indicated in (B).

(C) and (D) Neither of these principles can underlie Lola's position, as human lives *are* at stake and you *do* presumably have a situation in which human lives can be saved. Believers in these principles would in all likelihood sacrifice the environmental concerns and support Derek's call to harvest the yews. But Lola goes the other way.

- The wrong choices in Principle questions often present notions that support the opposite of the argument in question. Here, a number of wrong choices conform somewhat to *Derek's* position. This is a good reminder of the importance of keeping the various positions straight, which is of course a skill that holds you in good stead on Reading Comp as well.

8. C

From the question stem, you know that there's a flaw in the reasoning—specifically, something that's necessary to the argument isn't established. Your job is to figure out what that might be. A committee's study states that certain students weren't excelling academically because they spent too much time playing sports and too little time studying. Based on this finding, a school director decides to prohibit those students from playing sports. This, he thinks, will guarantee that they'll do well. Does this make any sense?

Evidently not, or else the test makers wouldn't have designated this a Flaw question. Picture the jock in your homeroom who goofed off during school and only cared about sports. If he suddenly wasn't allowed to play any sports, would he necessarily spend his newfound free time pursuing the academic life? What's the guarantee that schoolwork would suddenly become a priority? It's possible, but hardly a sure thing. This is the error in the director's reasoning—that time is all that's needed to turn these jocks into brains. (C) hits on the omission in the director's argument.

(A), (B), and (D) The scope of the argument is very specific—athletes with academic problems. Jocks who *don't* have trouble in school, (A), and academic stars in general, (B) and (D), are outside this scope. In other words, the director need not establish that some sporty students *don't* have academic problems (A), because he's only worried about the ones who do. Likewise, the director also needn't establish anything about students who *don't* have academic problems. The relationship between academic performance and sports participation is only described for bad students. The director need not prove that academic success is totally

incompatible with playing sports, as (B) and (D) would have it, in order to propose that the academically challenged athletes reprioritize their time.

(E) What would happen to the sports program as a result of the ban is outside the scope of the argument, which simply concerns the director's prohibition and his reason for it. Whether or not the teams decline has nothing to do with whether or not the banned students' schoolwork would improve.

- Don't fault an author, speaker, or in this case, character for not doing something he or she is not *logically obligated* to do. Sure, many of these choices describe things the director failed to establish, but that's only half the question. The other half, of course, is: was it necessary to establish these things? (C) is the only choice that contains an omission that the director absolutely needs to establish in defending his ban.

9. B

What fact could be provided that would lead you to conclude that there are at least as many trees in Seclee as there are in Martown? There has to be some sort of relationship between the two regions for this to be true.

(A) isn't much help. You don't know how many trees were in Seclee or Martown before the planting; for all you know, Seclee was totally treeless before the planting and Martown was a veritable rain forest.

(B) does provide that crucial relationship. If Martown is in Seclee, then every tree in Martown must be in Seclee, and so Seclee must have at least as many trees as Martown. So (B)'s the answer.

(C) doesn't tell you anything helpful. Martown could be choked with tree growth and Seclee could be a wasteland for all you know. They may not be healthy trees in Martown, but that doesn't matter.

(D) You'd need all sorts of additional information for (D) to help you reach any conclusion, so you know it's no good. Rainfall, indeed.

(E) Since you don't know how many trees both towns started out with, you can't know which has more now. Again, no help.

- This question wasn't your standard Inference question. Usually you reason from the stimulus to the correct answer, not the other way around. You

always need to be ready for the possibility that the test makers will put a different spin on a familiar question type.

10. C

Two more questions for the price of one; questions 10 and 11 deal with the seals of the North Sea. It appears that distemper is a virus that has caused two-thirds of the seals in the North Sea to die off since May 1988. The virus can't be totally to blame, however, since it's been there (albeit latent) for a while. The author concludes that it must be the severe pollution that has caused the seals to become vulnerable to the disease.

So essentially there's a cause and effect argument at work here. The first question asks you what the author is assuming in coming to this conclusion. Whenever you're faced with a causal argument, consider alternative possibilities. In concluding that the pollution is to blame, the author is assuming that no other possible cause is at work; (C) plays off this issue. If there was a sudden mutation in the distemper virus, there would be an alternate explanation for the death of the poor lovable seals, and the author's argument would be greatly weakened. Therefore, in implicating the pollution as the cause of death, the author *must* presuppose that no such mutation occurred.

(A) The author isn't claiming there has been such a decline over the last 200 years, nor is such a claim relevant to his argument.

(B) The argument would actually be stronger *without* (B), so it can't be the assumption. If further sources of pollution *have* been added since May 1988, it would only support the author's contention that pollution was the cause of the decline in seal population.

(D) too can only weaken the argument, as it suggests that pollution levels in the North Sea, at least relative to other bodies of water, is not that high. But since you have no way of knowing what the levels are at in these other seas, (D) offers nothing more than irrelevant comparisons that are far from necessary pieces of this argument.

(E) isn't necessary for the author's argument either. The author isn't arguing that the seals are dying because their food is gone, but because the seals themselves are becoming sick. The seals' food species can be surviving quite nicely in the polluted water of the North Sea, and the author's argument about the seals' immune systems would still hold.

- Keep your mind open to alternative explanations at all times, especially in arguments involving cause

and effect relationships. Recognizing possibilities that the author overlooks can assist you in a number of question types, including Assumption, Strengthen/Weaken, and Flaw.

11. A

Next you're asked to find the choice that supports the explanation for the drop in seal population, so find the choice that either discounts plausible alternative explanations or shores up the pollution account offered by the author.

(A) accomplishes the latter: It bolsters the idea that the North Sea pollution has weakened the seals' immune systems by making it likely that the same thing has happened to other North Sea species. (A) may not *prove* the author's case, but it doesn't have to: It makes you more likely to believe that pollution *is* the factor at work here, as the author contends. If you didn't think that (A) went far enough, you should at least have been able to eliminate the others for familiar reasons.

(B) and (E) both weaken the author's argument—(B) by suggesting that pollution in the North Sea isn't that severe, and (E) by suggesting an alternate explanation for the seals' sudden acquisition of distemper.

(C) is outside the scope: The fact that fish have been taken out of the water for human consumption doesn't tell you anything about the pollution level of the water or about the effect of pollution on seals.

(D) The author doesn't distinguish between different kinds of seals, so (D) has no effect on the argument either.

- The job of a strengthener is not to *prove* an argument, nor does a weakener have to *disprove* it. They simply make the argument more or less *likely*—and that's the test you should have in mind when evaluating choices in these kinds of questions.

- Choices that fall outside the scope of an argument can have no bearing on the argument's validity.

12. D

Most of the time, your best bet in Parallel Reasoning is to express the conclusion in abstract terms and throw out the choices that depart from that; then do the same for the pieces of evidence, until all you're left with is the credited choice.

Here, the conclusion says that it is clear that no one in a certain group did something. However, the conclusion isn't particularly helpful in making eliminations in this question, so you'll have to move on and characterize the evidence. Everyone in one group shares a characteristic, and no one in a second group has that characteristic.

(A) can be eliminated based on the conclusion—it interjects the negative "no one who *failed* to do something."

(B) Also fails to match up because of the negatives it introduces, but this time they're in the evidence.

(C) This evidence relates to having a "reputation" for doing something, not a direct statement (as you saw in the stem) that members of the group *had* done something. Eliminate.

(D) works on both counts, though it might be tough to recognize at first since the terms are reversed—make sure you take the time to break down each piece in *logical* terms.

(E) You can get rid of (E) just by looking at its conclusion, which refers to what is "likely" to happen. There's nothing that corresponds to this in the original.

- Pay no attention at all to the fact that in the original stimulus the conclusion is the first sentence, whereas in (D) the conclusion is placed in the middle. As a matter of fact, the test writers often deliberately mix up the order of the sentences in the correct answer to a Parallel Reasoning question to throw you off the track. Keep in mind that the decision of where to place the conclusion in the argument—beginning, middle or end—is a stylistic choice rather than a logical one.

- Remember, you can handle the questions in any order you want. A time-consuming question like this one may be well worth postponing.

13. E

The stimulus for questions 13 and 14 concerns a decision regarding the hiring of a dean of computing. There are several qualifications to be demonstrated. The dean must be: 1) respected by the academic staff, and 2) competent to oversee the use of computers on campus. In order for the dean to be respected, he must 3) hold a doctoral degree. In order to competently oversee the use of computers he must 4) really know about computers. Makes sense so far. Furthermore, he must 5) already be on the university staff. The conclusion is that the dean of computing must therefore be a professor from the computer science department.

Question 13 asks you for the assumption upon which this argument depends. Well, the author made a "logical leap" (or "illogical leap," as the case may be) from the idea that the dean must know a lot about computers,

to the conclusion that the dean will have to come from the computer science department. It makes sense that a professor from the computer science department would be *eligible* for the job, but it doesn't make sense to automatically rule out other departments' professors without supporting evidence. In doing so, the author assumes that no one outside the computer science department could fulfill all of the qualifications. (E) gets at this point: The author assumes that only those in the computer science department really know about computers.

(A) Replace the word "people" with "deans" and you'd have a restatement of the evidence in the second sentence. As written, what academics think about *people* in general is outside the scope, which means that nothing about this need be assumed.

(B) It's not necessary for all of the professors to have doctoral degrees, only the ones qualified for this position.

(C) Every professor? Again, you're not concerned with all of them, only the one who is to be chosen.

(D) takes the issue too far. When it comes to respect, all you care about is what kind of *dean* the academic staff respects. Whether *all* eggheads with doctorates are respected is another issue, and one that's not particularly relevant to the issue at hand.

- Read carefully! As far as respect is concerned, the author tells you only what kind of *dean* earns respect from academics. Respect for people in general (A) or for "all academics" (D) is a broader topic, and therefore nothing about these things need be assumed here. If you understood the limited scope of the "respect requirement," you should have been able to axe these two choices quickly.

14. A

Question 14 asks you to find the statement that would weaken the argument, and (A) challenges the author's conclusion that the dean must be a professor. The members of the university staff described in this choice fulfill all the requirements outlined by the author, yet they aren't professors. If they exist (and you are to assume they do from the "if true" clause in the stem), then one of them could be chosen, and the author's final pronouncement would be inaccurate; (A) thus weakens the argument.

(B) One of the main stipulations for candidacy is having a doctoral degree. The academics described in this choice do not challenge the author's conclusion in any way.

(C) What does it matter that these other professors applied? The author isn't making any claims about who will *apply* for the position. This choice is simply outside the scope of the argument.

(D) offers another peripheral tidbit of information that doesn't address the argument in the slightest. The board of trustees makes a cameo appearance by mandating the final requirement that the new dean must come from the university staff. What credentials the members of this board of trustees possess have no bearing on the author's conclusion—the doctoral requirement pertains only to candidates for the position.

(E) would weaken the argument if the author had claimed that *any one* of the members of the computer science department is qualified to be the dean of computing. But she didn't, so it doesn't.

15. A

Another double-question stimulus. And a wordy stimulus it is at that. As always, see if you can pare it down to a manageable amount of information.

The consumer advocate believes that manufacturers are misleading customers with their product labeling. The example used is the term "fresh." According to the advocate, the common understanding of the word "fresh" does not apply to the actual product. So, to sum up the advocate's position, not using words according to their commonly understood definition is a misleading act. The manufacturer, however, counterargues that such an act is not deceptive, since words can have other, equally valid meanings. If there are no rules with which to comply, there can't be anything deceptive about such labeling.

Question 15 asks what the two are disagreeing about. Recap the principle behind the dispute. The advocate argues that in the absence of laws governing labeling practices, common understanding should be used as a guideline. Under that interpretation, she considers the orange juice label deceptive. But the manufacturer says that in the absence of standards, other definitions could suffice, since "fresh" can also signify something besides the "common" meaning. Based on this reasoning, the manufacturer feels the label is *not* deceptive. They therefore disagree about (A)—whether, in the absence of standards, common meaning determines deception or not. The advocate thinks it does; the manufacturer thinks it does not.

(B) Neither party says or suggests the government *couldn't* institute truthful labeling requirements.

(C) The manufacturer doesn't dispute this point, raised by the consumer advocate, but only says the term can also have other meanings.

(D) The consumer advocate's argument doesn't target natural foods—and takes no position on what can be done truthfully—only on what's being done deceptively. Eliminate.

(E) The consumer advocate doesn't ever mention what could or should occur *after* government standards are created; she's only concerned with the here and now, which means the absence of government standards.

- The answer to a Point at Issue question must contain an issue that's addressed by both parties to the dispute. If either party has nothing to say on a particular issue addressed in a choice, cross that choice off.

16. C

Now for part two: "Which principle would strengthen the manufacturer's argument?" The manufacturer says, in short, that it's okay to play with the meaning of words so long as the government doesn't prohibit it. Look for a choice that provides that freedom.

(A) reiterates the advocate's stance; that's definitely not going to help the manufacturer's position in the least.

(B) would also work against the manufacturer: Sticking to common usages would preclude the fancy wordplay the manufacturer employs to condone what the advocate feels are deceptive labeling practices. The manufacturer would want the freedom to use alternative meanings. The creation of standards that reflect common understandings could only hurt his case.

(C) This principle is just what the manufacturer was trying to communicate, however crudely. There could be several meanings for any one word, so why can't I use them as long as there's no legal prohibition? If this principle were established, this point would be strengthened considerably, so (C) is correct. For the record:

(D) is nonsensical, because government standards don't exist in this scenario, so any judgment about them is beside the point.

(E) is beyond the scope, since the motivation behind the manufacturer's labeling practices isn't addressed, nor is the consumers' take on the issue a factor in this argument.

17. A

This is a quirky Method of Argument question, and a glance at the stem tells you that you need to find the grounds that the author uses to recommend a certain strategy. What's it all about?

First of all, items with the quality of exclusivity have an odd property: The items, when they become available, sell very quickly even though they're very expensive. You're then told that trying to sell an exclusive item cheaply is a mistake. Why? Because it makes people doubt its exclusivity. You then have the conclusion of the argument—signaled by "therefore." Given that it's almost impossible for a seller to gauge a correct price for an item in advance, the seller should be sure that any error is on the side of setting the price too high. That way, a seller won't price an exclusive item too low, and thus endanger the perception of its exclusivity, which is, after all, its chief appeal.

This is a Method of Argument question, so put the argument into more abstract terms. How does the author promote the strategy of setting prices too high? By explaining that setting prices too low will endanger the item's appeal, while setting the price too high doesn't entail this risk. So he recommends one strategy by pointing out a counterproductive feature of the alternative plan. That's (A).

(B) The author doesn't present any advantages of the alternate plan, so this can't be right.

(C) The author doesn't talk about past experience at all, and although the quality of exclusivity is "hard to define," the reasons that the strategy is superior are more concrete—it avoids a specific danger run by the alternative.

(D) Ah, but the strategy *does* rely on "buyers' estimates of value." Buyers presumably value exclusive items quite highly precisely *because* of their exclusivity, and the strategy is intended to preserve that perception of exclusivity and hence the value of such items in the minds of buyers.

(E) is a little tricky, but assume that setting the price of an exclusive item too high is what the test makers mean by "the error associated with this strategy." The point is not that no one will *notice* if the price is too high, but rather that an exorbitant price, while possibly unattainable, will not damage the item's key attribute—the perception of its exclusivity. So the author doesn't advocate the strategy for the reason cited in (E), but because the potential error associated with the strategy is much less damaging than erring on the other side.

- Don't bend over backward for an answer choice. If you have to make up a story to support a choice, or engage in extensive interpretation, you've found a wrong choice.

18. D

The biologist, in response to the problem of deer overpopulation, has proposed injecting female deer in breeding season with 10 milligrams of a fertility-suppressing hormone. Critics say that the biologist's idea would pose health risks to people who might eat the deer meat, and consume unsafe amounts of the hormone. The last sentence begins with "The biologist has responded . . . " and that should perk up your ears since the stem asks for the assumption underlying the biologist's response to the critics.

The biologist says that people can eat up to 10 milligrams of the hormone a day without any problems, and since no one would eat a whole deer a day, the plan is safe. What's the assumption? Well, if the deer are injected with 10 milligrams, and people can safely eat up to 10 milligrams a day, the assumption must be that there's no way that people would get *more* than 10 milligrams of the hormone from eating deer—that there's no way that there could be more of the hormone in a given deer.

This seems reasonable as long as the deer lack this hormone naturally; but if they don't, then adding another 10 milligrams may push the amount above the danger level for humans. Then, it would be conceivable that a consumable portion of deer *could* contain dangerous amounts of the hormone. (D) hits on this issue; the biologist assumes that the deer don't naturally have this hormone in them. If they did, then the deer would have more than 10 milligrams of the hormone after the injection, and the biologist's argument would be thrown into question.

(A) and (C) According to his plan, deer-eaters are safe anyway, so they needn't be warned, (A), and it wouldn't matter when the deer were killed, (C).

(B) is off the subject. "Chemically similar to human contraceptives?" That tells you nothing about whether it's harmful in the doses in question, so nothing about this need be assumed.

(E) The biologist needn't assume that most people don't eat deer often; in fact, it's made clear that even frequent deer-eaters will be safe.

- Not every statement that strengthens an argument is an assumption. Here, some wrong choices do something to allay fears about the deer meat, but that doesn't make them assumptions. The assumption will be not just something that helps the argument, but something the author relies on in drawing his conclusion.

19. D

This time you need to find the choice that would *least* contribute to an explanation of the paradox, or discrepancy, at hand. What's the problem?

The author begins by saying that a survey revealed that people are concerned about problems facing teenagers. The survey indicates that 70 percent of adult respondents said they would pay higher taxes for drug treatment programs and 60 percent said they would pay more taxes for better schools. Yet, the author says (and that's a paradox keyword), a proposition voted on in the same city, one that would fund schools by raising taxes, failed to get majority approval. Four of the choices will solve this mystery, while the correct choice will leave the mystery intact.

(A) would help resolve the puzzle by suggesting that the sample wasn't drawn in a representative, and therefore predictive, way: Maybe there were more parents or teachers or people concerned about education in the survey population than in the general voting population.

(B) readily explains the paradox, if true: If people lied on the survey, then it's no wonder that the attitudes expressed in the survey weren't reflected in the voting booth. A simple case of people not willing to "put their money where their mouth is."

(C) is pretty helpful too, since if the education plan were part of a bigger package, and people didn't like other parts of the package or thought it was too expensive, then they probably would have voted against the entire package, even though they favored one portion of it.

(D) is the answer. Just because funds for a drug treatment center weren't approved either, that doesn't help explain why the school proposition was voted down. The two are unrelated. (D) is no help, so it's correct here.

(E) is another good helper, introducing as it does the possibility that people may not have voted for the proposition simply because they didn't understand it.

- Whenever you see a survey on the LSAT, consider whether the survey is representative of the larger group. Here, the evidence concerned survey respondents, but the conclusion concerned voters.

Those groups are different, even though they might overlap, and so it shouldn't be surprising that views expressed by one aren't reflected in the actions of the other.

20. B

It's another two-question stimulus for questions 20 and 21; you need to find the author's questionable Method of Argument and the main assumption that would make the argument work.

The author begins with an attitude—these "so-called" environmentalists are messing things up by claiming that a proposed development would interfere with bird migration. She goes on to explain that this concern is just a mask for their anti-progress agenda and that the claim should be dismissed. What's the evidence? That these people have raised similar environmental objections to just about every development proposal in recent years. Sound fishy? It sure does: Who's to say that all of these claims weren't perfectly valid? Choice (B) says this: The author questions the environmentalists' motives, believing that they're just antiprogress, and she uses this prejudice to reject their argument.

(A) is kind of wordy, but all it says is that the conclusion is false because the argument doesn't prove it to be true. That's not what's happening here, since the author doesn't dispute the probability of the bird-migration problems on the basis of a lack of proof, but on the basis of her lack of confidence in those who support the position—the environmentalists.

(C) Are there any "exceptional cases" described here? No, the objections are described as the environmentalists' *standard* response, so (C) is out. If you can't match a piece of the description to something specific in the argument, it can't be the right answer in a method of argument question.

(D) The environmentalists don't provide any evidence, as far as you're told, for the assertion that the development will interfere with the migration patterns, so there's nothing for the author to "misrepresent."

(E) distinguishes between a group and a smaller segment of that group, but there's no flaw of this kind in the argument. The author refers to the same people throughout, so whether you view the environmentalists as individuals or as members of a unified group, there's nothing wrong with assuming consistency in their position.

- When an author argues against the motives of a group, check to see if there's any logical evidence supplied to support the author's opposition. Simply saying "these people have an agenda" isn't enough to damage their position.

21. A

Your work with question 20 should make this one quite manageable. For all the verbiage of the question stem, all you really need to do is to find the assumption that will make the author's argument valid, and you've already seen from the previous question what's missing from the argument: The author questions the environmentalists' argument against the development because they've objected to just about every other development plan in the past, but you don't know if these were *valid* objections or not because you don't know the circumstances of the objections.

The author believes these objections were based not on the facts but on the environmentalists' agenda. If, in fact, some or all of these objections are shown to be invalid, then she may have a legitimate point, and it would be more reasonable to believe that they really aren't all that concerned with the migration patterns. (A) works in this vein: It tells you that, indeed, not every proposal was challenged because it posed a threat to the environment. If you add the sentiment in (A) to the mix, then the author has good reason to doubt the validity of their claim.

(B) The assumption that development-blockers always disguise their motives is neither reasonable nor helpful in this context. It's not necessary to say that all development-blockers disguise their motives in order to argue that these people may be doing that.

(C) goes too far—you don't know anything about people who oppose "unrestricted development," so any assumptions about them won't help the author's argument.

(D) is out as well since *other* reasons for objecting to the development are beyond the scope. They won't help the author at all. In fact, if anything, (D) suggests that the environmentalists' professed concern for the birds is genuine.

(E) is too vague, since it talks about people who oppose development on environmental grounds in general, while you're concerned with this specific group. Furthermore, the explanation that their concern *almost always* lies elsewhere is too vague to pin this rap on the environmentalists in question.

- Notice that this is the last of five—count em', five!—double-question stimuli on this section. That's fairly high for an LSAT Logical Reasoning section. But remember that every double-question stimulus presents an opportunity to get two points for the price of one, so you should welcome these and look to use your work on the first question to help you work through the second.

22. D

Another Principle question is up next, and a long stimulus to tackle. It's not very dense, though. Psychologists now understand that childhood is different from adulthood, and they wonder why it took people so long to figure out how silly they were to see children as little, imperfectly socialized grownups. However, the author claims, most psychologists still see people between the ages of 70 and 90 as adults with the same needs as people 35 years of age—no distinction is made in their minds. Old age, according to the author, is as different from young- and middle-adulthood as childhood is. This is attested to, she claims, by the organization of social and economic life.

So the distinctions are social and economic; remember that. It's time, she concludes, for psychological research into old age, and you need a principle that will back up this assertion. A good way to support this argument would be to shore up the author's main points—namely that old age is different from middle age because of social and economic circumstances, and thus, it has a unique psychology. This is enough of a prephrase to take with you into the choices.

(A) brings up a conflict between current psychological practice and traditional attitudes, but you don't have that conflict here. Basically, both current practice and traditional attitudes seem to think that old age isn't so different from adulthood—it's only the author who's in conflict, and she's arguing *against* current psychological practice.

(B) is a little confusing, so try to fit the circumstances of the stimulus into the mold here. Two groups of people related to each other—okay, middle-age adults and people of advanced age. And any member of the second must have been a member of the first—well, that works, since older people must have been middle-age adults.

But wait, the last clause confuses things. People in the first group, middle-age adults, shouldn't be regarded as deviant members of the second group, older people. That's not the problem—the problem is that older people are being viewed as part of the same group as middle-age adults. So (B) doesn't hit the target.

(C) says that when most practitioners do one thing, then all similar problems should be approached the same way. But if this principle were adopted, then everyone should see old age as an extension of middle-adulthood, and that would contradict, not support, the author's argument.

(D) brings up economic life, which sounds good, if you think back to the stimulus. When a society's economics are organized so that two different times of life are treated very differently—and according to the author that's true about middle adulthood and old age—then each time can only be understood in terms of a unique psychology. Yup, that's what the author wants. If this principle were adopted, her argument would be greatly enhanced, making (D) correct here. For the record:

(E) Most psychologists *don't* believe that one psychology is inadequate for these two age groups, so (E) is shot down right off the bat.

- A Section Management tip: If you're running low on time at the end of an LR section, and you turn the page to the final four or five questions, eyeball them to see if you can tell which may be time-consuming and therefore good candidates to skip. Notice how much longer question 22 is than the remaining questions—and the fact that it's a Principle question isn't too inviting either, as these often tend to be abstract and difficult. When you make decisions about what questions to do *when*, you're taking control of the test as you should.

23. E

Next up is a Point at Issue question, asking you to find the crux of Emile and Sabina's argument. Sabina begins by explaining that words are not an important part of an argument: they don't affect the facts, evidence, or conclusion. In fact, she says, if the words are used clearly and consistently, with the same definitions throughout, the words have no influence on an argument's validity. So, she concludes, the expression of an argument can have no bearing on whether it's good or not. Emile has the opposite viewpoint: Poorly chosen words can make even the most valid argument into a poor argument, since many words have connotations that influence people's response to claims that utilize those words. According to Emile, since whether people will acknowledge a fact is influenced by the way in which it is expressed, the conclusions that listeners or readers draw are affected by the words used.

So what's the point at issue? They disagree about whether words can influence the validity of an argument: Sabina says no, Emile says yes. But they're not arguing about the actual facts contained in an argument, or the logical form thereof. It's all about the influence of language and expression, right? (E) says precisely this, that the two are arguing about whether a factor (in this case language or expression) that doesn't affect the truth of an argument's evidence or the logic of the premises' relationship can have an effect on an argument's validity. Yes, it's wordy, but it's correct.

(A) raises the issue of defining words in different ways. Both people bring up the definition of words, and Sabina stresses that if words are consistently defined, there's no problem. Emile doesn't dispute this—he just claims that people will respond to the connotations of words no matter how they're defined. How words are *defined* isn't the crux of the argument.

(B) is somewhat similar, since it brings up definitions again, and, again, the two don't dispute that words can be defined without connotation: The definition isn't the point. The question is whether or not factors besides the definitions matter.

(C) No one doubts that a sound argument is better than an unsound one—they're talking about whether language can cause an argument to be sound or unsound.

(D) talks about avoiding the use of misleading words, but no one is disputing the validity of this suggestion.

- While answering a Point at Issue question, if you notice that the speakers agree on some issues, remember them. They'll probably show up as wrong answer choices.

24. C

This is a straightforward weakener—you need to undermine the author's conclusion. You learn that most plastic containers are labeled with code numbers that indicate what kind of plastic they are made of. The lowest-numbered plastics are the easiest to recycle, and the highest numbered are rarely recycled, and probably wind up in landfill. The author concludes that consumers can make significant waste reductions by refusing to buy products packed in higher-numbered plastics.

The best way to weaken this is to weaken the main evidence that higher-numbered plastics are the worst for the environment. Choice (C) does so perfectly, by explaining that high-numbered plastics have almost always already been recycled. This choice points out that these plastics aren't as unfriendly as the author believes—they are the fruits of the recycling efforts that he's supporting. Refusing to use these containers would thwart the recycling effort.

(A) concerns the cost of recycling as opposed to the cost of manufacturing new plastics, but it's not this kind of cost that's the issue—it's the cost to the *environment*. This choice is beyond the scope, and therefore it's no weakener.

(B) There's an implied "if" in the author's argument: Consumers can make a long-term reduction *if* they refuse to buy the higher-numbered items. That's the argument. The fact that many consumers aren't *aware* of the codes doesn't affect this line of reasoning, because the author is arguing about what would happen if they *were* and if they acted as he suggests.

(D) may weaken the idea that consumers will go along with the plan, since the products he wants them to buy will be more expensive, but it doesn't affect the gist of the argument—that a reduction will occur *if* they boycott those higher-numbered containers.

(E) is a vague strengthener, shoring up the idea that higher-numbered plastics are difficult to recycle.

- Any time you can translate a conclusion into if/then format, do so—it will make the argument easier to understand. Speaking of which . . .

- In an argument that takes the form "if X, then Y," choices that deal with the *likelihood* or *feasibility* of X usually have no effect on the argument. Here, wrong choices (B) and (D) play off the idea that consumers may not be willing or able to follow the author's prescription—but that's irrelevant because the argument is about what will happen *if* they *do*.

25. B

According to the author, the share of the population that reads a daily paper has gone down appreciably in the last 20 years, even though the average number of hours that people work per week has also gone down. However, the percentage of people that watch TV every day has gone up about the same amount over the same period. From this, the author concludes that increased TV viewing has caused the decline in newspaper reading.

What's the best way to weaken this conclusion? Well, you could show that even among people who *don't* watch TV, the percentage that also don't read the paper has shown an appreciable decrease. That would strongly suggest that increased TV viewing isn't the cause of decreased paper

reading for these people, which would call the author's conclusion into question. That's (B).

(A) can't help you at all, since it talks about the *primary source* of current events: beyond the scope.

(C), (D), and (E) You don't know anything about the *amount of time* people spend reading—you're concerned with *whether* they read the paper every day or not. (C) is outside the scope, as are (D) and (E): (D) talks about the effect of TV on people's mental abilities, and (E) about the number of hours people have their TVs on. Scope violators every which way you turn.

- With a strong grasp of the scope of an argument, you can zero in on the correct answer and quickly eliminate many wrong answer choices.

Practice Test 3

LSAT PRACTICE TEST 3 ANSWER SHEET

Remove (or photocopy) the answer sheet and use it to complete the practice test.

How to Take the Practice Tests

Before taking each test, find a quiet place where you can work uninterrupted for about two and a half hours. Make sure you have a comfortable desk and several No. 2 pencils.

Each Practice Test includes four scored multiple-choice sections. Keep in mind that on the actual LSAT, there will be an additional multiple-choice section—the experimental section—that will not contribute to your score, plus an unscored Writing Sample.

Once you start a Practice Test, don't stop (except for a 5- to 10-minute break after the second section) until you've gone through all four sections. Remember, you can review any questions within a section, but you may not go back or forward a section.

Good luck!

Start with number 1 for each section. If a section has fewer questions than answer spaces, leave the extra spaces blank.

Section I

1. (A) (B) (C) (D) (E)   9. (A) (B) (C) (D) (E)   17. (A) (B) (C) (D) (E)   25. (A) (B) (C) (D) (E)
2. (A) (B) (C) (D) (E)   10. (A) (B) (C) (D) (E)   18. (A) (B) (C) (D) (E)   26. (A) (B) (C) (D) (E)
3. (A) (B) (C) (D) (E)   11. (A) (B) (C) (D) (E)   19. (A) (B) (C) (D) (E)   27. (A) (B) (C) (D) (E)   # right in Section I
4. (A) (B) (C) (D) (E)   12. (A) (B) (C) (D) (E)   20. (A) (B) (C) (D) (E)   28. (A) (B) (C) (D) (E)
5. (A) (B) (C) (D) (E)   13. (A) (B) (C) (D) (E)   21. (A) (B) (C) (D) (E)   29. (A) (B) (C) (D) (E)
6. (A) (B) (C) (D) (E)   14. (A) (B) (C) (D) (E)   22. (A) (B) (C) (D) (E)   30. (A) (B) (C) (D) (E)
7. (A) (B) (C) (D) (E)   15. (A) (B) (C) (D) (E)   23. (A) (B) (C) (D) (E)   # wrong in Section I
8. (A) (B) (C) (D) (E)   16. (A) (B) (C) (D) (E)   24. (A) (B) (C) (D) (E)

Section II

1. (A) (B) (C) (D) (E)   9. (A) (B) (C) (D) (E)   17. (A) (B) (C) (D) (E)   25. (A) (B) (C) (D) (E)
2. (A) (B) (C) (D) (E)   10. (A) (B) (C) (D) (E)   18. (A) (B) (C) (D) (E)   26. (A) (B) (C) (D) (E)
3. (A) (B) (C) (D) (E)   11. (A) (B) (C) (D) (E)   19. (A) (B) (C) (D) (E)   27. (A) (B) (C) (D) (E)   # right in Section II
4. (A) (B) (C) (D) (E)   12. (A) (B) (C) (D) (E)   20. (A) (B) (C) (D) (E)   28. (A) (B) (C) (D) (E)
5. (A) (B) (C) (D) (E)   13. (A) (B) (C) (D) (E)   21. (A) (B) (C) (D) (E)   29. (A) (B) (C) (D) (E)
6. (A) (B) (C) (D) (E)   14. (A) (B) (C) (D) (E)   22. (A) (B) (C) (D) (E)   30. (A) (B) (C) (D) (E)
7. (A) (B) (C) (D) (E)   15. (A) (B) (C) (D) (F)   23. (A) (B) (c) (D) (E)   # wrong in Section II
8. (A) (B) (C) (D) (E)   16. (A) (B) (C) (D) (E)   24. (A) (B) (C) (D) (E)

Section III

1. (A) (B) (C) (D) (E)   9. (A) (B) (C) (D) (E)   17. (A) (B) (C) (D) (E)   25. (A) (B) (C) (D) (E)
2. (A) (B) (C) (D) (E)   10. (A) (B) (C) (D) (E)   18. (A) (B) (C) (D) (E)   26. (A) (B) (C) (D) (E)
3. (A) (B) (C) (D) (E)   11. (A) (B) (C) (D) (E)   19. (A) (B) (C) (D) (E)   27. (A) (B) (C) (D) (E)   # right in Section III
4. (A) (B) (C) (D) (E)   12. (A) (B) (C) (D) (E)   20. (A) (B) (C) (D) (E)   28. (A) (B) (C) (D) (E)
5. (A) (B) (C) (D) (E)   13. (A) (B) (C) (D) (E)   21. (A) (B) (C) (D) (E)   29. (A) (B) (C) (D) (E)
6. (A) (B) (C) (D) (E)   14. (A) (B) (C) (D) (E)   22. (A) (B) (C) (D) (E)   30. (A) (B) (C) (D) (E)
7. (A) (B) (C) (D) (E)   15. (A) (B) (C) (D) (E)   23. (A) (B) (C) (D) (E)   # wrong in Section III
8. (A) (B) (C) (D) (E)   16. (A) (B) (C) (D) (E)   24. (A) (B) (C) (D) (E)

Section IV

1. Ⓐ Ⓑ Ⓒ Ⓓ Ⓔ	9. Ⓐ Ⓑ Ⓒ Ⓓ Ⓔ	17. Ⓐ Ⓑ Ⓒ Ⓓ Ⓔ	25. Ⓐ Ⓑ Ⓒ Ⓓ Ⓔ
2. Ⓐ Ⓑ Ⓒ Ⓓ Ⓔ	10. Ⓐ Ⓑ Ⓒ Ⓓ Ⓔ	18. Ⓐ Ⓑ Ⓒ Ⓓ Ⓔ	26. Ⓐ Ⓑ Ⓒ Ⓓ Ⓔ
3. Ⓐ Ⓑ Ⓒ Ⓓ Ⓔ	11. Ⓐ Ⓑ Ⓒ Ⓓ Ⓔ	19. Ⓐ Ⓑ Ⓒ Ⓓ Ⓔ	27. Ⓐ Ⓑ Ⓒ Ⓓ Ⓔ
4. Ⓐ Ⓑ Ⓒ Ⓓ Ⓔ	12. Ⓐ Ⓑ Ⓒ Ⓓ Ⓔ	20. Ⓐ Ⓑ Ⓒ Ⓓ Ⓔ	28. Ⓐ Ⓑ Ⓒ Ⓓ Ⓔ
5. Ⓐ Ⓑ Ⓒ Ⓓ Ⓔ	13. Ⓐ Ⓑ Ⓒ Ⓓ Ⓔ	21. Ⓐ Ⓑ Ⓒ Ⓓ Ⓔ	29. Ⓐ Ⓑ Ⓒ Ⓓ Ⓔ
6. Ⓐ Ⓑ Ⓒ Ⓓ Ⓔ	14. Ⓐ Ⓑ Ⓒ Ⓓ Ⓔ	22. Ⓐ Ⓑ Ⓒ Ⓓ Ⓔ	30. Ⓐ Ⓑ Ⓒ Ⓓ Ⓔ
7. Ⓐ Ⓑ Ⓒ Ⓓ Ⓔ	15. Ⓐ Ⓑ Ⓒ Ⓓ Ⓔ	23. Ⓐ Ⓑ Ⓒ Ⓓ Ⓔ	
8. Ⓐ Ⓑ Ⓒ Ⓓ Ⓔ	16. Ⓐ Ⓑ Ⓒ Ⓓ Ⓔ	24. Ⓐ Ⓑ Ⓒ Ⓓ Ⓔ	

right in
Section IV

wrong in
Section IV

 GO ONLINE

Be sure to add your scores to your syllabus.

Practice Test 3
Section I: Analytical Reasoning

Time—35 minutes
24 questions

<u>Directions:</u> Each group of questions in this section is based on a set of conditions. In answering some of the questions, it may be useful to draw a rough diagram. Choose the response that most accurately and completely answers each question and blacken the corresponding space on your answer sheet.

<u>Questions 1–6</u>

Exactly eight consumers—F, G, H, J, K, L, M, and N—will be interviewed by market researchers. The eight will be divided into exactly two 4-person groups—group 1 and group 2—before interviews begin. Each person is assigned to exactly one of the two groups according to the following conditions:

   F must be in the same group as J.
   G must be in a different group from M.
   If H is in group 1, then L must be in group 1.
   If N is in group 2, then G must be in group 1.

1. Group 1 could consist of

   (A) F, G, H, and J
   (B) F, H, L, and M
   (C) F, J, K, and L
   (D) G, H, L, and N
   (E) G, K, M, and N

2. If K is in the same group as N, which one of the following must be true?

   (A) G is in group 1.
   (B) H is in group 2.
   (C) J is in group 1.
   (D) K is in group 2.
   (E) M is in group 1.

3. If F is in the same group as H, which one of the following must be true?

   (A) G is in group 2.
   (B) J is in group 1.
   (C) K is in group 1.
   (D) L is in group 2.
   (E) M is in group 2.

4. If L and M are in group 2, then a person who could be assigned either to group 1 or, alternatively, to group 2 is

   (A) F
   (B) G
   (C) H
   (D) J
   (E) K

5. Each of the following is a pair of people who could be in group 1 together EXCEPT:

   (A) F and G
   (B) F and H
   (C) F and L
   (D) H and G
   (E) H and N

6. If L is in group 2, then each of the following is a pair of people who could be in group 1 together EXCEPT:

   (A) F and M
   (B) G and N
   (C) J and N
   (D) K and M
   (E) M and N

GO ON TO THE NEXT PAGE.

Questions 7–11

Five people—Harry, Iris, Kate, Nancy, and Victor—are to be scheduled as contestants on a television show, one contestant per day, for five consecutive days from Monday through Friday. The following restrictions governing the scheduling of contestants must be observed:

Nancy is not scheduled for Monday.

If Harry is scheduled for Monday, Nancy is scheduled for Friday.

If Nancy is scheduled for Tuesday, Iris is scheduled for Monday.

Kate is scheduled for the next day after the day for which Victor is scheduled.

7. Victor can be scheduled for any day EXCEPT:

   (A) Monday
   (B) Tuesday
   (C) Wednesday
   (D) Thursday
   (E) Friday

8. If Iris is scheduled for the next day after Harry, which one of the following lists all those days any one of which could be the day for which Harry is scheduled?

   (A) Monday, Tuesday
   (B) Monday, Wednesday
   (C) Monday, Thursday
   (D) Monday, Tuesday, Wednesday
   (E) Monday, Wednesday, Thursday

9. If Kate is scheduled for Wednesday, which one of the following could be true?

   (A) Iris is scheduled for Friday.
   (B) Nancy is scheduled for Tuesday.
   (C) Nancy is scheduled for an earlier day than the day for which Harry is scheduled.
   (D) Nancy is scheduled for an earlier day than the day for which Iris is scheduled.
   (E) Nancy is scheduled for an earlier day than the day for which Kate is scheduled.

10. If Kate is scheduled for Friday, which one of the following must be true?

   (A) Harry is scheduled for Tuesday.
   (B) Harry is scheduled for Wednesday.
   (C) Iris is scheduled for Monday.
   (D) Iris is scheduled for Wednesday.
   (E) Nancy is scheduled for Wednesday.

11. If Iris is scheduled for Wednesday, which one of the following must be true?

   (A) Harry is scheduled for an earlier day than the day for which Nancy is scheduled.
   (B) Harry is scheduled for an earlier day than the day for which Kate is scheduled.
   (C) Kate is scheduled for an earlier day than the day for which Harry is scheduled.
   (D) Nancy is scheduled for an earlier day than the day for which Kate is scheduled.
   (E) Nancy is scheduled for an earlier day than the day for which Iris is scheduled.

GO ON TO THE NEXT PAGE.

Questions 12–17

An art teacher will schedule exactly six of eight lectures—fresco, history, lithography, naturalism, oils, pastels, sculpture, and watercolors—for three days—1, 2, and 3. There will be exactly two lectures each day—morning and afternoon. Scheduling is governed by the following conditions:

Day 2 is the only day for which oils can be scheduled.

Neither sculpture nor watercolors can be scheduled for the afternoon.

Neither oils nor pastels can be scheduled for the same day as lithography.

If pastels is scheduled for day 1 or day 2, then the lectures scheduled for the day immediately following pastels must be fresco and history, not necessarily in that order.

12. Which one of the following is an acceptable schedule of lectures for days 1, 2, and 3, respectively?

   (A) Morning: lithography, history, sculpture
       Afternoon: pastels, fresco, naturalism
   (B) Morning: naturalism, oils, fresco
       Afternoon: lithography, pastels, history
   (C) Morning: oils, history, naturalism Afternoon: pastels, fresco, lithography
   (D) Morning: sculpture, lithography, naturalism
       Afternoon: watercolors, fresco, pastels
   (E) Morning: sculpture, pastels, fresco
       Afternoon: lithography, history, naturalism

13. If lithography and fresco are scheduled for the afternoons of day 2 and day 3, respectively, which one of the following is a lecture that could be scheduled for the afternoon of day 1?

   (A) history
   (B) oils
   (C) pastels
   (D) sculpture
   (E) watercolors

14. If lithography and history are scheduled for the mornings of day 2 and day 3, respectively, which one of the following lectures could be scheduled for the morning of day 1?

   (A) fresco
   (B) naturalism
   (C) oils
   (D) pastels
   (E) sculpture

15. If oils and lithography are scheduled for the mornings of day 2 and day 3, respectively, which one of the following CANNOT be scheduled for any day?

   (A) fresco
   (B) history
   (C) naturalism
   (D) pastels
   (E) sculpture

16. If neither fresco nor naturalism is scheduled for any day, which one of the following must be scheduled for day 1?

   (A) history
   (B) lithography
   (C) oils
   (D) pastels
   (E) sculpture

17. If the lectures scheduled for the mornings are fresco, history, and lithography, not necessarily in that order, which one of the following could be true?

   (A) Lithography is scheduled for day 3.
   (B) Naturalism is scheduled for day 2.
   (C) Fresco is scheduled for the same day as naturalism.
   (D) History is scheduled for the same day as naturalism.
   (E) History is scheduled for the same day as oils.

GO ON TO THE NEXT PAGE.

Questions 18–24

The population of a small country is organized into five clans—N, O, P, S, and T. Each year exactly three of the five clans participate in the annual harvest ceremonies. The rules specifying the order of participation of the clans in the ceremonies are as follows:

Each clan must participate at least once in any two consecutive years.

No clan participates for three consecutive years.

Participation takes place in cycles, with each cycle ending when each of the five clans has participated three times. Only then does a new cycle begin.

No clan participates more than three times within any cycle.

18. If the clans participating in the first year of a given cycle are N, O, and P, which one of the following could be the clans participating in the second year of that cycle?

(A) N, O, S
(B) N, O, T
(C) N, P, S
(D) O, P, T
(E) O, S, T

19. Which one of the following can be true about the clans' participation in the ceremonies?

(A) N participates in the first, second, and third years.
(B) N participates in the second, third, and fourth years.
(C) Both O and S participate in the first and third years.
(D) Both N and S participate in the first, third, and fifth years.
(E) Both S and T participate in the second, third, and fifth years.

20. Any cycle for the clans' participation in the ceremonies must be completed at the end of exactly how many years?

(A) five
(B) six
(C) seven
(D) eight
(E) nine

21. Which one of the following must be true about the three clans that participate in the ceremonies in the first year?

(A) At most two of them participate together in the third year.
(B) At least two of them participate together in the second year.
(C) All three of them participate together in the fourth year.
(D) All three of them participate together in the fifth year.
(E) None of them participates in the third year.

22. If, in a particular cycle, N, O, and S participate in the ceremonies in the first year, which one of the following must be true?

(A) N participates in the second and third years.
(B) O participates in the third and fourth years.
(C) N and O both participate in the third year
(D) P and T both participate in the fifth year.
(E) S and T both participate in the fifth year.

23. If, in a particular cycle, N, O, and T participate in the first year and if O and P participate in the fourth year, any of the following could be a clan that participates in the third year EXCEPT:

(A) N
(B) O
(C) P
(D) S
(E) T

24. If, in a particular cycle, N, O, and S participate in the ceremonies in the first year and O, S, and T participate in the third year, then which one of the following could be the clans that participate in the fifth year?

(A) N, O, P
(B) N, O, S
(C) N, P, S
(D) O, P, S
(E) P, S, T

STOP

IF YOU FINISH BEFORE TIME IS CALLED, YOU MAY CHECK YOUR WORK ON THIS SECTION ONLY.
DO NOT WORK ON ANY OTHER SECTION IN THE TEST.

KAPLAN

Practice Test 3
Section II: Logical Reasoning

Time—35 minutes
26 questions

<u>Directions:</u> The questions in this section are based on the reasoning contained in brief statements or passages. For some questions, more than one of the choices could conceivably answer the question. However, you are to choose the <u>best</u> answer; that is, the response that most accurately and completely answers the question. You should not make assumptions that are by commonsense standards implausible, superfluous, or incompatible with the passage. After you have chosen the <u>best</u> answer, blacken the corresponding space on your answer sheet.

1. Paperback books wear out more quickly than hardcover books do, but paperback books cost much less. Therefore, users of public libraries would be better served if public libraries bought only paperback books, since by so doing these libraries could increase the number of new book titles added to their collections without increasing their budgets.

Which one of the following, if true, most seriously weakens the argument?

(A) If a public library's overall budget is cut, the budget for new acquisitions is usually cut back more than is that for day-to-day operations.

(B) Paperback books can very inexpensively have their covers reinforced in order to make them last longer.

(C) Many paperback books are never published in hardcover.

(D) Library users as a group depend on their public library for access to a wide variety of up-to-date reference books that are published in hardcover only.

(E) People are more likely to buy for themselves a copy of a book they had previously borrowed from the public library if that book is available in paperback.

2. Garbage in this neighborhood probably will not be collected until Thursday this week. Garbage is usually collected here on Wednesdays, and the garbage collectors in this city are extremely reliable. However, Monday was a public holiday, and after a public holiday that falls on a Monday, garbage throughout the city is supposed to be collected one day later than usual.

The argument proceeds by

(A) treating several pieces of irrelevant evidence as though they provide support for the conclusion

(B) indirectly establishing that one thing is likely to occur by directly ruling out all of the alternative possibilities

(C) providing information that allows application of a general rule to a specific case

(D) generalizing about all actions of a certain kind on the basis of a description of one such action

(E) treating something that is probable as though it were inevitable

3. When compact discs first entered the market, they were priced significantly higher than vinyl records. Manufacturers attributed the difference in price to the difference in production costs, saying that compact disc production was expensive because the technology was new and unfamiliar. As the technology became more efficient, the price of the discs did indeed come down. But vinyl records, whose production technology has long been established, then went up in price to approach that of compact discs.

Which one of the following most helps to explain why the price of vinyl records went up?

(A) Consumers were so enthusiastic about the improved sound quality offered by compact disc technology that they were willing to pay a higher price to obtain it.

(B) Some consumers who continued to buy vinyl records instead of compact discs did so because they were unwilling to pay a higher price for compact discs.

(C) As consumers bought compact discs instead of vinyl records, the number of vinyl records produced decreased, making their production less cost-efficient.

(D) Compact disc player technology continued to change and develop even after compact discs first entered the market.

(E) When compact discs first entered the market, many consumers continued to buy vinyl records rather than buying the equipment necessary to play compact discs.

GO ON TO THE NEXT PAGE.

4. Conservationists have established land reserves to preserve the last remaining habitat for certain species whose survival depends on the existence of such habitat. A grove of trees in Mexico that provide habitat for North American monarch butterflies in winter is a typical example of such a land reserve. If global warming occurs as predicted, however, the temperature bands within which various types of vegetation can grow will shift into regions that are currently cooler.

If the statements above are true, they provide the most support for which one of the following?

(A) If global warming occurs as predicted, the conservation land reserves will cease to serve their purpose.

(B) Monarch butterflies will succeed in adapting to climatic change by shortening their migration.

(C) If global warming occurs, it will melt polar ice and so will cause the sea level to rise so high that many coastal plants and animals will become extinct.

(D) The natural world has adapted many times in the past to drastic global warming and cooling.

(E) If global warming occurs rapidly, species of plants and animals now protected in conservation land reserves will move to inhabit areas that are currently used for agriculture.

5. Financial success does not guarantee happiness. This claim is not mere proverbial wisdom but a fact verified by statistics. In a recently concluded survey, only one-third of the respondents who claimed to have achieved financial success reported that they were happy.

Which one of the following, if true, most strongly supports the conclusion drawn from the survey results?

(A) The respondents who reported financial success were, for the most part, financially successful.

(B) Financial success was once thought to be necessary for happiness but is no longer considered a prerequisite for happiness.

(C) Many of the respondents who claimed not to have achieved financial success reported that they were happy five years ago.

(D) Many of the respondents who failed to report financial success were in fact financially successful.

(E) Most of the respondents who reported they were unhappy were in fact happy.

6. The distance that animals travel each day and the size of the groups in which they live are highly correlated with their diets. And diet itself depends in large part on the sizes and shapes of animals' teeth and faces.

The statements above provide the most support for which one of the following?

(A) Animals that eat meat travel in relatively small groups and across relatively small ranges compared to animals that eat plants.

(B) Animals that have varied diets can be expected to be larger and more robust than animals that eat only one or two kinds of food.

(C) When individual herd animals lose their teeth through age or injury, those animals are likely to travel at the rear of their herd.

(D) Information about the size and shape of an animal's face is all that is needed to identify the species to which that animal belongs.

(E) Information about the size and shape of an extinct animal's teeth and face can establish whether that animal is likely to have been a herd animal.

7. It is not correct that the people of the United States, relative to comparable countries, are the most lightly taxed. True, the United States has the lowest tax, as percent of gross domestic product, of the Western industrialized countries, but tax rates alone do not tell the whole story. People in the United States pay out of pocket for many goods and services provided from tax revenues elsewhere. Consider universal health care, which is an entitlement supported by tax revenues in every other Western industrialized country. United States government health-care expenditures are equivalent to about 5 percent of the gross domestic product, but private health-care expenditures represent another 7 percent. This 7 percent, then, amounts to a tax.

The argument concerning whether the people of the United States are the most lightly taxed is most vulnerable to which one of the following criticisms?

(A) It bases a comparison on percentages rather than on absolute numbers.

(B) It unreasonably extends the application of a key term.

(C) It uses negatively charged language instead of attempting to give a reason.

(D) It generalizes from only a few instances.

(E) It sets up a dichotomy between alternatives that are not exclusive.

GO ON TO THE NEXT PAGE.

8. Various mid-fourteenth-century European writers show an interest in games, but no writer of this period mentions the playing of cards. Nor do any of the mid-fourteenth-century statutes that proscribe or limit the play of games mention cards, though they do mention dice, chess, and other games. It is therefore likely that, contrary to what is sometimes claimed, at that time playing cards was not yet common in Europe.

The pattern of reasoning in which one of the following is most similar to that in the argument above?

(A) Neither today's newspapers nor this evening's television news mentioned a huge fire that was rumored to have happened in the port last night. Therefore, there probably was no such fire.

(B) This evening's television news reported that the cruise ship was only damaged in the fire last night, whereas the newspaper reported that it was destroyed. The television news is based on more recent information, so probably the ship was not destroyed.

(C) Among the buildings that are near the port is the newspaper's printing plant. Early editions of this morning's paper were very late. Therefore, the fire at the port probably affected areas beyond the port itself.

(D) The newspaper does not explicitly say that the port reopened after the fire, but in its listing of newly arrived ships it mentions some arrival times after the fire. Therefore, the port was probably not closed for long.

(E) The newspaper is generally more reliable than the television news, and the newspaper reported that the damage from last night's fire in the port was not severe. Therefore, the damage probably was not severe.

9. In a mature tourist market such as Bellaria there are only two ways hotel owners can increase profits: by building more rooms or by improving what is already there. Rigid land-use laws in Bellaria rule out construction of new hotels or, indeed, any expansion of hotel capacity. It follows that hotel owners cannot increase their profits in Bellaria since Bellarian hotels _____.

Which one of the following logically completes the argument?

(A) are already operating at an occupancy rate approaching 100 percent year-round

(B) could not have been sited any more attractively than they are even in the absence of land-use laws

(C) have to contend with upward pressures on the cost of labor which stem from an incipient shortage of trained personnel

(D) already provide a level of luxury that is at the limits of what even wealthy patrons are prepared to pay for

(E) have shifted from serving mainly Bellarian tourists to serving foreign tourists traveling in organized tour groups

10. Every political philosopher of the early twentieth century who was either a socialist or a communist was influenced by Rosa Luxemburg. No one who was influenced by Rosa Luxemburg advocated a totalitarian state.

If the statements above are true, which one of the following must on the basis of them also be true?

(A) No early-twentieth-century socialist political philosopher advocated a totalitarian state.

(B) Every early-twentieth-century political philosopher who did not advocate a totalitarian state was influenced by Rosa Luxemburg.

(C) Rosa Luxemburg was the only person to influence every early-twentieth-century political philosopher who was either socialist or communist.

(D) Every early-twentieth-century political philosopher who was influenced by Rosa Luxemburg and was not a socialist was a communist.

(E) Every early-twentieth-century political philosopher who did not advocate a totalitarian state was either socialist or communist.

GO ON TO THE NEXT PAGE.

KAPLAN

Questions 11–12

Harris: Currently, hybrid animals are not protected by international endangered-species regulations. But new techniques in genetic research suggest that the red wolf, long thought to be an independent species, is a hybrid of the coyote and the gray wolf. Hence, since the red wolf clearly deserves protection, these regulations should be changed to admit the protection of hybrids.

Vogel: Yet hybrids do not need protection. Since a breeding population that arises through hybridization descends from independent species, if any such population were to die out, it could easily be revived by interbreeding members of the species from which the hybrid is descended.

11. Which one of the following is a point at issue between Harris and Vogel?

   (A)   whether the red wolf descends from the gray wolf and the coyote
   (B)   whether there are some species that are currently considered endangered that are not in fact in any danger
   (C)   whether the packs of red wolves that currently exist are in danger of dying out
   (D)   whether there are some hybrids that ought to be protected by endangered-species regulations
   (E)   whether new techniques in genetic research should be used to determine which groups of animals constitute species and which constitute hybrids

12. Which one of the following is an assumption on which Vogel's argument relies?

   (A)   The techniques currently being used to determine whether a population of animals is a hybrid of other species have proven to be reliable.
   (B)   The international regulations that protect endangered species and subspecies are being enforced successfully.
   (C)   The gray wolf has been successfully bred in captivity.
   (D)   All hybrids are the descendants of species that are currently extant.
   (E)   The coyote and the red wolf are not related genetically.

13. From an analysis of broken pottery and statuary, archaeologists have estimated that an ancient settlement in southwestern Arabia was established around 1000 B.C. However, new evidence suggests that the settlement is considerably older: tests show that a piece of building timber recently uncovered at the site is substantially older than the pottery and statuary.

Which one of the following, if true, most seriously undermines the conclusion drawn from the new evidence?

   (A)   The building timber bore marks suggesting that it had been salvaged from an earlier settlement.
   (B)   The pieces of pottery and fragments of statues that were analyzed come from several parts of the site.
   (C)   The tests used to determine the age of the pottery and statuary had been devised more recently than those used to determine the age of the building timber.
   (D)   The site has yielded many more samples of pottery and statuary than of building timber.
   (E)   The type of pottery found at the site is similar to a type of pottery associated with civilizations that existed before 1000 B.C.

14. The book *To Save the Earth* is so persuasive that no one who reads it can fail to heed its environmentalist message. Members of the Earth Association have given away 2,000 copies in the last month. Thus the Earth Association can justly claim credit for at least 2,000 people in one month converted to the environmentalist cause.

Which one of the following is an assumption on which the argument depends?

   (A)   No other environmental organization gave away copies of *To Save the Earth* during the month in which the Earth Association gave away its 2,000 copies.
   (B)   The people to whom the Earth Association gave copies of *To Save the Earth* would not have been willing to pay to receive it from the Earth Association.
   (C)   The copies of *To Save the Earth* given away by members of the Earth Association were printed on recycled paper.
   (D)   None of those who received *To Save the Earth* from a member of the Earth Association were already committed to the environmentalist cause when they received this book.
   (E)   Every recipient of *To Save the Earth* will embrace the environmental program advocated by the Earth Association.

GO ON TO THE NEXT PAGE.

KAPLAN

15. Smokers of pipes or cigars run a distinctly lower risk to their health than do cigarette smokers. However, whereas cigarette smokers who quit smoking altogether sharply reduce their risk of smoking related health problems, those who give up cigarettes and take up pipes or cigars remain in as much danger as before.

Which one of the following, if true, offers the best prospects for an explanation of why the two changes in smoking habits do not both result in reduced health risks?

(A) Smokers of pipes or cigars who quit smoking thereby reduce their risk of smoking-related health problems.

(B) Cigarette smokers who quit smoking for a time and who then resume cigarette smoking do not necessarily reduce their risk of smoking-related health problems.

(C) The kinds of illnesses that smokers run an increased risk of contracting develop no earlier in cigarette smokers than they do in smokers of pipes or cigars.

(D) At any given period in their lives, virtually all smokers smoke either cigarettes exclusively or cigars exclusively or pipes exclusively, rather than alternating freely among various ways of smoking.

(E) People who switch from cigarette smoking to smoking pipes or cigars inhale smoke in a way that those who have never smoked cigarettes do not.

Questions 16–17

Production manager: The building materials that we produce meet industry safety codes but pose some safety risk. Since we have recently developed the technology to make a safer version of our product, we should stop producing our current product and sell only the safer version in order to protect public safety.

Sales manager: If we stop selling our current product, we will have no money to develop and promote the safer product. We need to continue to sell the less-safe product in order to be in a position to market the safer product successfully.

16. Which one of the following principles, if established, most helps to justify the production manager's conclusion?

(A) Companies should be required to develop safer products if such development can be funded from sales of existing products.

(B) That a product does not meet industry safety codes should be taken as sufficient indication that the product poses some safety risks.

(C) Companies should not sell a product that poses safety risks if they are technologically capable of producing a safer version of that product.

(D) Product safety codes should be reviewed whenever an industry replaces one version of a product with a technologically more advanced version of that product.

(E) In order to make building materials safer, companies should continually research new technologies whether or not they are required to do so in order to comply with safety codes.

17. The sales manager counters the production manager's argument by

(A) pointing out that one part of the production manager's proposal would have consequences that would prevent successful execution of another part

(B) challenging the production manager's authority to dictate company policy

(C) questioning the product manager's assumption that a product is necessarily safe just because it is safer than another product

(D) proposing a change in the standards by which product safety is judged

(E) presenting evidence to show that the production manager has overestimated the potential impact of the new technology

GO ON TO THE NEXT PAGE.

Questions 18–19

Each year, an official estimate of the stock of cod in the Grand Banks is announced. This estimate is obtained by averaging two separate estimates of how many cod are available, one based on the number of cod caught by research vessels during a once-yearly sampling of the area and the other on the average number of tons of cod caught by various commercial vessels per unit of fishing effort expended there in the past year—a unit of fishing effort being one kilometer of net set out in the water for one hour. In previous decades, the two estimates usually agreed closely. However, for the last decade the estimate based on commercial tonnage has been increasing markedly, by about the same amount as the sampling-based estimate has been decreasing.

18. If the statements in the passage are true, which one of the following is most strongly supported by them?

(A) Last year's official estimate was probably not much different from the official estimate ten years ago.

(B) The number of commercial vessels fishing for cod in the Grand Banks has increased substantially over the past decade.

(C) The sampling-based estimate is more accurate than the estimate based on commercial tonnage in that the data on which it relies is less likely to be inaccurate.

(D) The once-yearly sampling by research vessels should be used as the sole basis for arriving at the official estimate of the stock of cod.

(E) Twenty years ago, the overall stock of cod in the Grand Banks was officially estimated to be much larger than it is estimated to be today.

19. Which one of the following, if true, most helps to account for the growing discrepancy between the estimate based on commercial tonnage and the research-based estimate?

(A) Fishing vessels often exceed their fishing quotas for cod and therefore often underreport the number of tons of cod that they catch.

(B) More survey vessels are now involved in the yearly sampling effort than were involved 10 years ago.

(C) Improvements in technology over the last 10 years have allowed commercial fishing vessels to locate and catch large schools of cod more easily.

(D) Survey vessels count only those cod caught during a 30-day survey period, whereas commercial fishing vessels report all cod caught during the course of a year.

(E) Because of past overfishing of cod, fewer fishing vessels now catch the maximum tonnage of cod each vessel is allowed by law to catch.

20. Pretzels can cause cavities. Interestingly, the longer that a pretzel remains in contact with the teeth when it is being eaten, the greater the likelihood that a cavity will result. What is true of pretzels in this regard is also true of caramels. Therefore, since caramels dissolve more quickly in the mouth than pretzels do, eating a caramel is less likely to result in a cavity than eating a pretzel is.

The reasoning in the argument is vulnerable to criticism on the grounds that the argument

(A) treats a correlation that holds within individual categories as thereby holding across categories

(B) relies on the ambiguous use of a key term as well

(C) makes a general claim based on particular examples that do not adequately represent the respective classes that they are each intended to represent

(D) mistakes the cause of a particular phenomenon for the effect of that phenomenon

(E) is based on premises that cannot all be true

GO ON TO THE NEXT PAGE.

Questions 21–22

Mark: Plastic-foam cups, which contain environmentally harmful chlorofluorocarbons, should no longer be used; paper cups are preferable. Styrene, a carcinogenic by-product, is generated in foam production, and foam cups, once used, persist indefinitely in the environment.

Tina: You overlook the environmental effects of paper cups. A study done five years ago showed that making paper for their production burned more petroleum than was used for foam cups and used 12 times as much steam, 36 times as much electricity, and twice as much cooling water. Because paper cups weigh more, their transportation takes more energy. Paper mills produce water pollution, and when the cups decay they produce methane, a gas that contributes to harmful global warming. So they are a worse choice.

21. Which one of the following, if true, could Mark cite to counter evidence offered by Tina?

(A) The use of energy for chain saws that cut down trees and for trucks that haul logs is part of the environmental cost of manufacturing paper.

(B) Foam cups are somewhat more acceptable to consumers than paper cups because of their better insulating qualities.

(C) The production and transportation of petroleum occasions serious environmental pollution, but the energy that runs paper mills now comes from burning waste wood rather than petroleum.

(D) The amount of styrene escaping into the environment or remaining in foam cups after their manufacture is negligible.

(E) Acre for acre, tree farms for the production of wood for paper have fewer beneficial effects on the environment than do natural forests that remain uncut.

22. To decide the issue between Mark and Tina, it would first be most important to decide

(A) how soon each of the kinds of harm cited by Mark and Tina would be likely to be at its maximum level

(B) whether members of some societies use, on average, more disposable goods than do members of other societies

(C) whether it is necessary to seek a third alternative that has none of the negative consequences cited with respect to the two products

(D) how much of the chains of causation involved in the production, marketing, and disposal of the products should be considered in analyzing their environmental impact

(E) whether paper and foam cups, in their most popular sizes, hold the same quantities of liquid

23. When people experience throbbing in their teeth or gums, they have serious dental problems, and if a dental problem is serious, it will be a problem either of tooth decay or of gum disease. Therefore, since throbbing in the teeth or gums is a sign of serious dental problems, and neither Sabina's teeth nor her gums are throbbing, Sabina can be suffering from neither tooth decay nor gum disease.

Which one of the following contains an error of reasoning most similar to that made in the argument above?

(A) People who drink a lot of coffee are said to have jittery nerves. Therefore, medical students who drink a lot of coffee should not become neonatologists or surgeons since neither neonatology nor surgery should be practiced by people with jittery nerves.

(B) A legally practicing psychiatrist must have both a medical degree and psychiatric training. Thus, since Emmett has not undergone psychiatric training, if he is practicing as a psychiatrist, he is not doing so legally.

(C) Someone with severe nasal congestion has a sinus infection or else is suffering from an allergy. Therefore, if Barton does not have a sinus infection, Barton probably does not have severe nasal congestion.

(D) If a person is interested in either physics or chemistry, then that person would be wise to consider a career in medicine. Yolanda, however, is interested in neither physics nor chemistry, so it would not be wise for her to consider a career in medicine.

(E) Someone who is neither an ophthalmologist nor an optometrist lacks specialized training for diagnosing defects of the eye. Therefore, Kim must have been trained in ophthalmology or optometry, given that she accurately diagnosed John's eye defect.

GO ON TO THE NEXT PAGE.

24. A certain airport security scanner designed to detect explosives in luggage will alert the scanner's operator whenever the piece of luggage passing under the scanner contains an explosive. The scanner will erroneously alert the operator for only one percent of the pieces of luggage that contain no explosives. Thus in ninety-nine out of a hundred alerts explosives will actually be present.

The reasoning in the argument is flawed because the argument

(A) ignores the possibility of the scanner's failing to signal an alert when the luggage does contain an explosive
(B) draws a general conclusion about reliability on the basis of a sample that is likely to be biased
(C) ignores the possibility of human error on the part of the scanner's operator once the scanner has alerted him or her
(D) fails to acknowledge the possibility that the scanner will not be equally sensitive to all kinds of explosives
(E) substitutes one group for a different group in the statement of a percentage

25. Unless negotiations begin soon, the cease-fire will be violated by one of the two sides to the dispute. Negotiations will be held only if other countries have pressured the two sides to negotiate; an agreement will emerge only if other countries continue such pressure throughout the negotiations. But no negotiations will be held until international troops enforcing the cease-fire have demonstrated their ability to counter any aggression from either side, thus suppressing a major incentive for the two sides to resume fighting.

If the statements above are true, and if negotiations between the two sides do begin soon, at the time those negotiations begin each of the following must also be true EXCEPT:

(A) The cease-fire has not been violated by either of the two sides.
(B) International troops enforcing the cease-fire have demonstrated that they can counter aggression from either of the two sides.
(C) A major incentive for the two sides to resume hostilities has been suppressed.
(D) Other countries have exerted pressure on the two sides to the dispute.
(E) The negotiations' reaching an agreement depends in part on the actions of other countries.

26. If Blankenship Enterprises has to switch suppliers in the middle of a large production run, the company will not show a profit for the year. Therefore, if Blankenship Enterprises in fact turns out to show no profit for the year, it will also turn out to be true that the company had to switch suppliers during a large production run.

The reasoning in the argument is most vulnerable to criticism on which one of the following grounds?

(A) The argument is a circular argument made up of an opening claim followed by a conclusion that merely paraphrases that claim.
(B) The argument fails to establish that a condition under which a phenomenon is said to occur is the only condition under which that phenomenon occurs.
(C) The argument involves an equivocation, in that the word "profit" is allowed to shift its meaning during the course of the argument.
(D) The argument erroneously uses an exceptional, isolated case to support a universal conclusion.
(E) The argument explains one event as being caused by another event, even though both events must actually have been caused by some third, unidentified event.

STOP

IF YOU FINISH BEFORE TIME IS CALLED, YOU MAY CHECK YOUR WORK ON THIS SECTION ONLY.
DO NOT WORK ON ANY OTHER SECTION IN THE TEST.

KAPLAN

Practice Test 3
Section III: Reading Comprehension

Time—35 minutes
27 questions

<u>Directions:</u> Each passage in this section is followed by a group of questions to be answered on the basis of what is <u>stated</u> or <u>implied</u> in the passage. For some of the questions, more than one of the choices could conceivably answer the question. However, you are to choose the <u>best</u> answer; that is, the response that most accurately and completely answers the question, and blacken the corresponding space on your answer sheet.

A major tenet of the neurosciences has been that all neurons (nerve cells) in the brains of vertebrate animals are formed early in development. An adult vertebrate, it was believed, must make
(5) do with a fixed number of neurons: those lost through disease or injury are not replaced, and adult learning takes place not through generation of new cells but through modification of connections among existing ones.
(10)   However, new evidence for neurogenesis (the birth of new neurons) has come from the study of canary song. Young canaries and other songbirds learn to sing much as humans learn to speak, by imitating models provided by their elders. Several
(15) weeks after birth, a young bird produces its first rudimentary attempts at singing; over the next few months the song becomes more structured and stable, reaching a fully developed state by the time the bird approaches its first breeding season. But
(20) this repertoire of song is not permanently learned. After each breeding season, during late summer and fall, the bird loses mastery of its developed "vocabulary," and its song becomes as unstable as that of a juvenile bird. During the following
(25) winter and spring, however, the canary acquires new songs, and by the next breeding season it has developed an entirely new repertoire.
    Recent neurological research into this learning and relearning process has shown that the
(30) two most important regions of the canary's brain related to the learning of songs actually vary in size at different times of the year. In the spring, when the bird's song is highly developed and uniform, the regions are roughly twice as large as
(35) they are in the fall. Further experiments tracing individual nerve cells within these regions have shown that the number of neurons drops by about 38 percent after the breeding season, but by the following breeding season, new ones have been
(40) generated to replace them. A possible explanation for this continual replacement of nerve cells may have to do with the canary's relatively long life span and the requirements of flight. Its brain would have to be substantially larger and heavier
(45) than might be feasible for flying if it had to carry all the brain cells needed to process and retain all

the information gathered over a lifetime.
    Although the idea of neurogenesis in the adult mammalian brain is still not generally accepted,
(50) these findings might help uncover a mechanism that would enable the human brain to repair itself through neurogenesis. Whether such replacement of neurons would disrupt complex learning processes or long-term memory is not known, but
(55) songbird research challenges scientists to identify the genes or hormones that orchestrate neurogenesis in the young human brain and to learn how to activate them in the adult brain.

1. Which one of the following best expresses the main idea of the passage?

(A) New evidence of neurogenesis in canaries challenges an established neurological theory concerning brain cells in vertebrates and suggests the possibility that human brains may repair themselves.

(B) The brains of canaries differ from the brains of other vertebrate animals in that the brains of adult canaries are able to generate neurons.

(C) Recent studies of neurogenesis in canaries, building on established theories of vertebrate neurology, provide important clues as to why researchers are not likely to discover neurogenesis in adult humans.

(D) Recent research into neurogenesis in canaries refutes a long-held belief about the limited supply of brain cells and provides new information about neurogenesis in the adult human brain.

(E) New information about neurogenesis in canaries challenges older hypotheses and clarifies the importance of the yearly cycle in learning processes and neurological replacement among vertebrates.

GO ON TO THE NEXT PAGE.

2. According to the passage, which one of the following is true of the typical adult canary during the late summer and fall?

    (A) The canary's song repertoire takes on a fully structured and stable quality.

    (B) A process of neurogenesis replaces the song-learning neurons that were lost during the preceding months.

    (C) The canary begins to learn an entirely new repertoire of songs based on the models of other canaries.

    (D) The regions in the canary's brain that are central to the learning of song decrease in size.

    (E) The canary performs slightly modified versions of the songs it learned during the preceding breeding season.

3. Information in the passage suggests that the author would most likely regard which one of the following as LEAST important in future research on neurogenesis in humans?

    (A) research on possible similarities between the neurological structures of humans and canaries

    (B) studies that compare the ratio of brain weight to body weight in canaries to that in humans

    (C) neurological research on the genes or hormones that activate neurogenesis in the brain of human infants

    (D) studies about the ways in which long-term memory functions in the human brain

    (E) research concerning the processes by which humans learn complicated tasks

4. Which one of the following, if true, would most seriously undermine the explanation proposed by the author in the third paragraph?

    (A) A number of songbird species related to the canary have a shorter life span than the canary and do not experience neurogenesis.

    (B) The brain size of several types of airborne birds with life spans similar to those of canaries has been shown to vary according to a two-year cycle of neurogenesis.

    (C) Several species of airborne birds similar to canaries in size are known to have brains that are substantially heavier than the canary's brain.

    (D) Individual canaries that have larger-than-average repertoires of songs tend to have better developed muscles for flying.

    (E) Individual canaries with smaller and lighter brains than the average tend to retain a smaller-than-average repertoire of songs.

5. The use of the word "vocabulary" (line 23) serves primarily to

    (A) demonstrate the presence of a rudimentary grammatical structure in canary song

    (B) point out a similarity between the patterned groupings of sounds in a canary's song and the syllabic structures of words

    (C) stress the stability and uniformity of the canary's song throughout its lifetime

    (D) suggest a similarity between the possession of a repertoire of words among humans and a repertoire of songs among canaries

    (E) imply that the complexity of the canary's song repertoire is equal to that of human language

6. According to the passage, which one of the following factors may help account for the occurrence of neurogenesis in canaries?

    (A) the life span of the average canary

    (B) the process by which canaries learn songs

    (C) the frequency of canary breeding seasons

    (D) the number of regions in the canary brain related to song learning

    (E) the amount of time an average canary needs to learn a repertoire of songs

7. Which one of the following best describes the organization of the third paragraph?

    (A) A theory is presented, analyzed, and modified, and a justification for the modification is offered.

    (B) Research results are advanced and reconciled with results from other studies, and a shared principle is described.

    (C) Research results are presented, further details are provided, and a hypothesis is offered to explain the results.

    (D) Research findings are described, their implications are explained, and an application to a related field is proposed.

    (E) Research results are reported, their significance is clarified, and they are reconciled with previously established neurological tenets.

8. It can be inferred from the passage that the author would most likely describe the current understanding of neurogenesis as

    (A) exhaustive
    (B) progressive
    (C) incomplete
    (D) antiquated
    (E) incorrect

GO ON TO THE NEXT PAGE.

KAPLAN)

For too many years scholars of African American history focused on the harm done by slaveholders and by the institution of slavery, rath-er than on what Africans in the United States were
(5) able to accomplish despite the effects of that institution. *In Myne Owne Ground*, T. H. Breen and Stephen Innes contribute significantly to a recent, welcome shift from a white-centered to a black-centered inquiry into the role of African
(10) Americans in the American colonial period. Breen and Innes focus not on slaves, but on a small group of freed indentured servants in Northampton County (in the Chesapeake Bay region of Virginia) who, according to the authors,
(15) maintained their freedom, secured property, and interacted with persons of different races and economic standing from 1620 through the 1670s. African Americans living on the Chesapeake were to some extent disadvantaged, say Breen and
(20) Innes, but this did not preclude the attainment of status roughly equal to that of certain white plant-ers of the area. Continuously acting within black social networks, and forming economic relation-ships with white planters, local Native Americans,
(25) indentured servants, and white settlers outside the gentry class, the free African Americans of Northampton County held their own in the rough-hewn world of Chesapeake Bay.
     The authors emphasize that in this early period,
(30) when the percentage of African Americans in any given Chesapeake county was still no more than 10 percent of the population, very little was predetermined so far as racial status or race relations were concerned. By schooling themselves
(35) in the local legal process and by working prodigiously on the land, African Americans acquired property, established families, and warded off contentious white neighbors. Breen and Innes do acknowledge that political power on
(40) the Chesapeake was asymmetrically distributed among black and white residents. However, they underemphasize much evidence that customary law, only gradually embodied in statutory law, was closing in on free African Americans well before
(45) the 1670s: during the 1660s, when the proportion of African Americans in Virginia increased dramatically, Virginia tightened a law regulating interracial relations (1662) and enacted a statute
(50) prohibiting baptism from altering slave status (1667). Anthony Johnson, a leader in the commu-nity of free African Americans in the Chesapeake Bay region, sold the land he had cultivated for more than twenty years and moved north with
(55) his family around 1665, an action that the authors attribute to a search for "fresh, more productive

land." But the answer to why the Johnsons left that area where they had labored so long may lie in their realization that their white neighbors were
(60) already beginning the transition from a largely white indentured labor force to reliance on a largely black slave labor force, and that the institu-tion of slavery was threatening their descendants' chances for freedom and success in Virginia.

9. The author of the passage objects to many scholarly studies of African American history for which one of the following reasons?

(A) Their emphases have been on statutory law rather than on customary law.
(B) They have ignored specific historical situ-ations and personages in favor of broad interpretations.
(C) They have focused on the least eventful peri-ods in African American history.
(D) They have underemphasized the economic system that was the basis of the institution of slavery.
(E) They have failed to focus to a sufficient extent on the achievements of African Americans.

10. Which one of the following can be inferred from the passage concerning the relationship between the African American population and the law in the Chesapeake Bay region of Virginia between 1650 and 1670?

(A) The laws affecting black citizens were embodied in statutes much more gradually than were laws affecting white citizens.
(B) As the percentage of black citizens in the population grew, the legal restrictions placed on them also increased.
(C) Because of discriminatory laws, black farm-ers suffered more economic setbacks than did white farmers.
(D) Because of legal constraints on hiring indentured servants, black farmers faced a chronic labor shortage on their farms.
(E) The adherence to customary law was more rigid in regions with relatively large num-bers of free black citizens.

GO ON TO THE NEXT PAGE.

KAPLAN

11. The author of the passage most probably refers to Anthony Johnson and his family in order to

(A) provide a specific example of the potential shortcomings of Breen and Innes's interpretation of historical events

(B) provide a specific example of relevant data overlooked by Breen and Innes in their discussion of historical events

(C) provide a specific example of data that Breen and Innes might profitably have used in proving their thesis

(D) argue that the standard interpretation of historical events is superior to Breen and Innes's revisionist interpretation

(E) argue that a new historiographical method is needed to provide a full and coherent reading of historical events

12. The attitude of the author of the passage toward Breen and Innes's study can best be described as one of

(A) condescending dismissal
(B) wholehearted acceptance
(C) contentious challenge
(D) qualified approval
(E) sincere puzzlement

13. The primary purpose of the passage is to

(A) summarize previous interpretations
(B) advocate a new approach
(C) propose and then illustrate a thesis
(D) present and evaluate an interpretation
(E) describe a historical event

GO ON TO THE NEXT PAGE.

KAPLAN

Late-nineteenth-century books about the French artist Watteau (1684–1721) betray a curious blind spot: more than any single artist before or since, Watteau provided his age with an influ-
(5) ential image of itself, and nineteenth-century writers accepted this image as genuine. This was largely due to the enterprise of Watteau's friends who, soon after his death, organized the printing of engraved reproductions of the great bulk of his
(10) work—both his paintings and his drawings—so that Watteau's total artistic output became and continued to be more accessible than that of any other artist until the twentieth-century advent of art monographs illustrated with photographs.
(15) These engravings presented aristocratic (and would-be aristocratic) eighteenth-century French society with an image of itself that was highly acceptable and widely imitated by other artists, however little relationship that image bore to real-
(20) ity. By 1884, the bicentenary of Watteau's birth, it was standard practice for biographers to refer to him as "the personification of the witty and amiable eighteenth century."

In fact, Watteau saw little enough of that "witty
(25) and amiable" century for which so much nostalgia was generally felt between about 1870 and 1920, a period during which enthusiasm for the artist reached its peak. The eighteenth century's first decades, the period of his artistic activity, were
(30) fairly calamitous ones. During his short life, France was almost continually at war: his native region was overrun with foreign troops, and Paris was threatened by siege and by a rampaging army rabble. The dreadful winter of 1709, the year of
(35) Watteau's first Paris successes, was marked by military defeat and a disastrous famine.

Most of Watteau's nineteenth-century admirers simply ignored the grim background of the works they found so lyrical and charming. Those who
(40) took the inconvenient historical facts into consideration did so only in order to refute the widely held deterministic view that the content and style of an artist's work were absolutely dictated by heredity and environment. (For Watteau admirers,
(45) such determinism was unthinkable: the artist was born in a Flemish town only six years after it first became part of France, yet Watteau was quintessentially French. As one patriotic French biogra-
(50) pher put it, "In Dresden, Potsdam, and Berlin I have never come across a Watteau without feeling refreshed by a breath of native air.") Even such writers, however, persisted in according Watteau's canvases a privileged status as representative

(55) "personifications" of the eighteenth century. The discrepancy between historical fact and artistic vision, useful in refuting the extreme deterministic position, merely forced these writers to seek a new formula that allowed them to preserve the desired
(60) identity between image and reality, this time a rather suspiciously psychic one: Watteau did not record the society he knew, but rather "foresaw" a society that developed shortly after his death.

14. Which one of the following best describes the overall organization of the passage?

(A) A particular phenomenon is discussed, the reasons that it is atypical are put forward, and these reasons are evaluated and refined.

(B) An assumption is made, results deriving from it are compared with what is known to be true, and the assumption is finally rejected as counterfactual.

(C) A point of view is described, one hypothesis accounting for it is introduced and rejected, and a better hypothesis is offered for consideration.

(D) A general characterization is offered, examples supporting it are introduced, and its special applicability to a particular group is asserted.

(E) A particular viewpoint is explained, its shortcomings are discussed, and its persistence in the face of these is noted.

15. The passage suggests that late-nineteenth-century biographers of Watteau considered the eighteenth century to be "witty and amiable" in large part because of

(A) what they saw as Watteau's typical eighteenth-century talent for transcending reality through art

(B) their opposition to the determinism that dominated late-nineteenth-century French thought

(C) a lack of access to historical source material concerning the early eighteenth century in France

(D) the nature of the image conveyed by the works of Watteau and his many imitators

(E) their political bias in favor of aristocratic regimes and societies

GO ON TO THE NEXT PAGE.

16. According to the passage, explanations of artistic production based on determinism were unthinkable to Watteau admirers for which one of the following reasons?

(A) If such explanations were widely accepted, too many people who would otherwise have admired Watteau would cease to appreciate Watteau's works.

(B) If such explanations were adopted, they would make it difficult for Watteau admirers to explain why Watteau's works were purchased and admired by foreigners.

(C) If such explanations were correct, many artists who, like Watteau, considered themselves French would have to be excluded from histories of French art.

(D) If such simple explanations were offered, other more complex arguments concerning what made Watteau's works especially charming would go unexplored.

(E) If such explanations were true, Watteau's works would reflect a "Flemish" sensibility rather than the especially "French" one these admirers saw in them.

17. The phrase "curious blind spot" (lines 2–3) can best be interpreted as referring to which one of the following?

(A) some biographers' persistent inability to appreciate what the author considers a particularly admirable quality

(B) certain writers' surprising lack of awareness of what the author considers an obvious discrepancy

(C) some writers' willful refusal to evaluate properly what the author considers a valuable source of information about the past

(D) an inexplicable tendency on the part of some writers to undervalue an artist whom the author considers extremely influential

(E) a marked bias in favor of a certain painter and a concomitant prejudice against contemporaries the author considers equally talented

18. It can be inferred from the passage that the author's view of Watteau's works differs most significantly from that of most late-nineteenth-century Watteau admirers in which one of the following ways?

(A) Unlike most late-nineteenth-century Watteau admirers, the author appreciates the importance of Watteau's artistic accomplishment.

(B) The author finds Watteau's works to be much less lyrical and charming than did most late nineteenth-century admirers of the works.

(C) In contrast to most late-nineteenth-century Watteau admirers, the author finds it misleading to see Watteau's works as accurately reflecting social reality.

(D) The author is much more willing to entertain deterministic explanations of the origins of Watteau's works than were most late-nineteenth-century Watteau admirers.

(E) Unlike most late-nineteenth-century admirers of Watteau, the author considers it impossible for any work of art to personify or represent a particular historical period.

19. The author asserts that during the period of Watteau's artistic activity French society was experiencing which one of the following?

(A) widespread social upheaval caused by war

(B) a pervasive sense of nostalgia for an idealized past

(C) increased domination of public affairs by a powerful aristocracy

(D) rapid adoption by the middle classes of aristocratic manners and lifestyles

(E) a need to reconcile the French self-image with French social realities

20. The information given in the passage suggests that which one of the following principles accurately characterizes the relationship between an artist's work and the impact it is likely to have on a society?

(A) An artist's recognition by a society is most directly determined by the degree to which his or her works are perceived as lyrical and charming.

(B) An artist will have the greatest influence on a society that values art particularly highly.

(C) The works of an artist who captures the true and essential nature of a given society will probably have a great impact on that society.

(D) The degree of influence an artist's vision will have on a society is conditional on the visibility of the artist's work.

(E) An artist who is much imitated by contemporaries will usually fail to have an impact on a society unless the imitators are talented.

GO ON TO THE NEXT PAGE.

Faced with the problems of insufficient evidence, of conflicting evidence, and of evidence relayed through the flawed perceptual, retentive, and narrative abilities of witnesses, a jury is forced to draw inferences in its
(5) attempt to ascertain the truth. By applying the same cognitive tools they have developed and used over a lifetime, jurors engage in the inferential exercise that lawyers call fact-finding. In certain decision-making contexts that are relevant to the trial of lawsuits, how-
(10) ever, these normally reliable cognitive tools may cause jurors to commit inferential errors that distort rather than reveal the truth.

Although juries can make a variety of inferential errors, most of these mistakes in judgment involve the
(15) drawing of an unwarranted conclusion from the evidence, that is, deciding that the evidence proves something that, in reality, it does not prove. For example, evidence that the defendant in a criminal prosecution has a prior conviction may encourage jurors to pre-
(20) sume the defendant's guilt, because of their preconception that a person previously convicted of a crime must be inclined toward repeated criminal behavior. That commonly held belief is at least a partial distortion of reality; not all former convicts engage in repeated
(25) criminal behavior. Also, a jury may give more probative weight than objective analysis would allow to vivid photographic evidence depicting a shooting victim's wounds, or may underestimate the weight of defense testimony that is not delivered in a sufficiently forceful
(30) or persuasive manner. Finally, complex or voluminous evidence might be so confusing to a jury that its members would draw totally unwarranted conclusions or even ignore the evidence entirely.

Recent empirical research in cognitive psychology
(35) suggests that people tend to commit inferential errors like these under certain predictable circumstances. By examining the available information, the situation, and the type of decision being made, cognitive psychologists can describe the kinds of inferential errors
(40) a person or group is likely to make. These patterns of human decision-making may provide the courts with a guide to evaluating the effect of evidence on the reliability of the jury's inferential processes in certain situations.
(45) The notion that juries can commit inferential errors that jeopardize the accuracy of the fact-finding process is not unknown to the courts. In fact, one of a presiding judge's duties is to minimize jury inferential error through explanation and clarification.
(50) Nonetheless, most judges now employ only a limited and primitive concept of jury inferential error: limited because it fails to recognize the potential for error outside certain traditional situations, primitive because it ignores the research and conclusions of
(55) psychologists in favor of notions about human cognition held by lawyers.

21. Which one of the following best expresses the main idea of the passage?

(A) When making decisions in certain predictable situations, juries may commit inferential errors that obscure rather than reveal the truth.
(B) The views of human cognition taken by cognitive psychologists on the one hand and by the legal profession on the other are demonstrably dissimilar.
(C) When confronting powerful preconceptions, particularly shocking evidence, or complex situations, jurors make errors in judgment.
(D) The problem of inferential error by juries is typical of the difficulties with cognitive processes that people face in their everyday lives.
(E) Juries would probably make more reliable decisions if cognitive psychologists, rather than judges, instructed them about the problems inherent in drawing unwarranted conclusions.

22. Of the following hypothetical reforms in trial procedure, which one would the author be most likely to support as the best way to address the problem of jury inferential error?

(A) a move away from jury trials
(B) the institution of minimum formal educational requirements for jurors
(C) the development of strict guidelines for defense testimony
(D) specific training for judges in the area of jury instruction
(E) restrictions on lawyers' use of psychological research

23. In the second paragraph, the author's primary purpose is to

(A) refute the idea that the fact-finding process is a complicated exercise
(B) emphasize how carefully evidence must be presented in order to avoid jury inferential error
(C) explain how commonly held beliefs affect the Jury's ability to ascertain the truth
(D) provide examples of situations that may precipitate jury errors
(E) recommend a method for minimizing mistakes by juries

GO ON TO THE NEXT PAGE.

24. Which one of the following best describes the author's attitude toward the majority of judges today?

(A) apprehensive about whether they are consistent in their instruction of juries
(B) doubtful of their ability to draw consistently correct conclusions based on the evidence
(C) critical of their failure to take into account potentially helpful research
(D) pessimistic about their willingness to make significant changes in trial procedure
(E) concerned about their allowing the presentation of complex and voluminous evidence in the courtroom

25. Which one of the following statements, if true, would most seriously undermine the author's suggestion about the use of current psychological research in the courtroom?

(A) All guidelines about human behavior must take account of variations in the patterns of human decision-making.
(B) Current models of how humans make decisions apply reliably to individuals but do not hold for decisions made by groups.
(C) The current conception of jury inferential error employed by judges has been in use for nearly a century.
(D) Inferential errors can be more easily predicted in controlled situations such as the trial of lawsuits than in other kinds of decision-making processes.
(E) In certain predictable circumstances, juries are less susceptible to inferential errors than they are in other circumstances.

26. It can be inferred from the passage that the author would be most likely to agree with which one of the following generalizations about lawyers?

(A) They have a less sophisticated understanding of human cognition than do psychologists.
(B) They often present complex or voluminous information merely in order to confuse a jury.
(C) They are no better at making logical inferences from the testimony at a trial than are most judges.
(D) They have worked to help judges minimize jury inferential error.
(E) They are unrealistic about the ability of jurors to ascertain the truth.

27. The author would be most likely to agree with which one of the following generalizations about a jury's decision-making process?

(A) The more evidence that a jury has, the more likely it is that the jury will reach a reliable verdict.
(B) Juries usually overestimate the value of visual evidence such as photographs.
(C) Jurors have preconceptions about the behavior of defendants that prevent them from making an objective analysis of the evidence in a criminal trial.
(D) Most of the jurors who make inferential errors during a trial do so because they are unaccustomed to having to make difficult decisions based on inferences.
(E) The manner in which evidence is presented to a jury may influence the jury either to overestimate or to underestimate the value of that evidence.

STOP

IF YOU FINISH BEFORE TIME IS CALLED, YOU MAY CHECK YOUR WORK ON THIS SECTION ONLY.
DO NOT WORK ON ANY OTHER SECTION IN THE TEST.

Practice Test 3
Section IV: Logical Reasoning

Time—35 minutes
24 questions

Directions: The questions in this section are based on the reasoning contained in brief statements or passages. For some questions, more than one of the choices could conceivably answer the question. However, you are to choose the best answer; that is, the response that most accurately and completely answers the question. You should not make assumptions that are by commonsense standards implausible, superfluous, or incompatible with the passage. After you have chosen the best answer, blacken the corresponding space on your answer sheet.

1. James: In my own house, I do what I want. In banning smoking on passenger airlines during domestic flights, the government has ignored the airlines' right to set smoking policies on their own property.

   Eileen: Your house is for your own use. Because a passenger airline offers a service to the public, the passengers' health must come first.

   The basic step in Eileen's method of attacking James's argument is to

   (A) draw a distinction
   (B) offer a definition
   (C) establish an analogy
   (D) derive a contradiction from it
   (E) question its motivation

2. The company that produces XYZ, a computer spreadsheet program, estimates that millions of illegally reproduced copies of XYZ are being used. If legally purchased, this number of copies would have generated millions of dollars in sales for the company, yet despite a company-wide effort to boost sales, the company has not taken available legal measures to prosecute those who have copied the program illegally.

   Which one of the following, if true, most helps to explain why the company has not taken available legal measures?

   (A) XYZ is very difficult to copy illegally, because a sophisticated anticopying mechanism in the program must first be disabled.
   (B) The legal measures that the company that produces XYZ could take against those who have copied its product became available several years before XYZ came on the market.
   (C) Many people who purchase a software program like XYZ are willing to purchase that program only after they have already used it.
   (D) The number of illegally reproduced copies of XYZ currently in use exceeds the number of legally reproduced copies currently in use.
   (E) The company that produces ABC, the spreadsheet program that is XYZ's main rival in the marketplace, is well known for taking legal action against people who have copied ABC illegally.

Kim: Some people claim that the battery-powered electric car represents a potential solution to the problem of air pollution. But they forget that it takes electricity to recharge batteries and that most of our electricity is generated by burning polluting fossil fuels. Increasing the number of electric cars on the road would require building more generating facilities since current facilities are operating at maximum capacity. So even if all of the gasoline-powered cars on the roads today were replaced by electric cars, it would at best be an exchange of one source of fossil-fuel pollution for another.

3. The main point made in Kim's argument is that
   (A) replacing gasoline-powered cars with battery-powered electric cars will require building more generating facilities
   (B) a significant reduction in air pollution cannot be achieved unless people drive less
   (C) all forms of automobile transportation are equally harmful to the environment in terms of the air pollution they produce
   (D) battery-powered electric cars are not a viable solution to the air-pollution problem
   (E) gasoline-powered cars will probably remain a common means of transportation for the foreseeable future

4. Which one of the following is an assumption on which Kim's argument depends?
   (A) Replacing gasoline-powered cars with battery-powered electric cars will not lead to a net increase in the total number of cars on the road.
   (B) Gasoline-powered cars are currently not the most significant source of fossil-fuel pollution.
   (C) Replacing gasoline-powered cars with battery-powered electric cars is justified only if electric cars produce less air pollution.
   (D) While it is being operated, a battery-powered electric car does not cause any significant air pollution.
   (E) At least some of the generating facilities built to meet the demand for electricity for battery-powered electric cars would be of a type that burns fossil fuel.

Questions 3–4

GO ON TO THE NEXT PAGE.

5. Planetary bodies differ from one another in their composition, but most of those in the Solar System have solid surfaces. Unless the core of such a planetary body generates enough heat to cause volcanic action, the surface of the body will not be renewed for millions of years. Any planetary body with a solid surface whose surface is not renewed for millions of years becomes heavily pockmarked by meteorite craters, just like the Earth's Moon. Some old planetary bodies in the solar system, such as Europa, a very cold moon belonging to Jupiter, have solid icy surfaces with very few meteorite craters.

If the claims above are true, which one of the following must, on the basis of them, be true?

(A) The Earth's Moon does not have an icy surface.
(B) If a planetary body does not have a heavily pockmarked surface, its core does not generate enough heat to cause volcanic action.
(C) Some planetary bodies whose cores generate enough heat to cause volcanic action do not have solid icy surfaces.
(D) Some of Jupiter's moons are heavily pockmarked by meteorite craters.
(E) Some very cold planetary bodies have cores that generate enough heat to cause volcanic action.

6. Patient: Pharmacists maintain that doctors should not be permitted to sell the medicine that they prescribe because doctors would then be tempted to prescribe unnecessary medicines in order to earn extra income. But pharmacists have a financial interest in having a monopoly on the sale of prescription medicines, so their objection to the sale of medicines by doctors cannot be taken seriously.

The patient's argument proceeds by

(A) pointing out an unstated assumption on which the pharmacists' argument relies and then refuting it
(B) attempting to discredit a position by questioning the motives of the proponents of that position
(C) undermining the pharmacists' conclusion by demonstrating that one of the statements used to support the conclusion is false
(D) rejecting a questionable position on the grounds that the general public does not support that position
(E) asserting that pharmacists lack the appropriate knowledge to have informed opinions on the subject under discussion

7. Murray: You claim Senator Brandon has accepted gifts from lobbyists. You are wrong to make this criticism. That it is motivated by personal dislike is shown by the fact that you deliberately avoid criticizing other politicians who have done what you accuse Senator Brandon of doing.

Jane: You are right that I dislike Senator Brandon, but just because I have not criticized the same failing in others doesn't mean you can excuse the senator's offense.

If Murray and Jane are both sincere in what they say, then it can properly be concluded that they agree that

(A) Senator Brandon has accepted gifts from lobbyists
(B) it is wrong for politicians to accept gifts from lobbyists
(C) Jane's criticism of Senator Brandon is motivated only by personal dislike
(D) Senator Brandon should be criticized for accepting gifts from lobbyists
(E) one or more politicians have accepted gifts from lobbyists

GO ON TO THE NEXT PAGE.

KAPLAN

Questions 8–9

Oscar: Emerging information technologies will soon make speed of information processing the single most important factor in the creation of individual, corporate, and national wealth. Consequently, the division of the world into northern countries—in general rich—and southern countries—in general poor—will soon be obsolete. Instead, there simply will be fast countries and slow countries, and thus a country's economic well-being will not be a function of its geographical position but just a matter of its relative success in incorporating those new technologies.

Sylvia: But the poor countries of the south lack the economic resources to acquire those technologies and will therefore remain poor. The technologies will thus only widen the existing economic gap between north and south.

8. Sylvia's reasoning depends on the assumption that
   (A) the prosperity of the rich countries of the north depends, at least in part, on the natural resources of the poor countries of the south
   (B) the emergence of new information technologies will not result in a significant net increase in the total amount of global wealth
   (C) there are technologies other than information technologies whose development could help narrow the existing economic gap between north and south
   (D) at least some of the rich countries of the north will be effective in incorporating new information technologies into their economies
   (E) the speed at which information processing takes place will continue to increase indefinitely

9. The reasoning that Oscar uses in supporting his prediction is vulnerable to criticism on the ground that it
   (A) overlooks the possibility that the ability of countries to acquire new technologies at some time in the future will depend on factors other than those countries' present economic status
   (B) fails to establish that the division of the world into rich countries and poor countries is the single most important problem that will confront the world economy in the future
   (C) ignores the possibility that, in determining a country's future wealth, the country's incorporation of information-processing technologies might be outweighed by a combination of other factors
   (D) provides no reason to believe that faster information processing will have only beneficial effects on counties that successfully incorporate new information technologies into their economies
   (E) makes no distinction between those of the world's rich countries that are the wealthiest and those that are less wealthy

10. At the beginning of each month, companies report to the federal government their net loss or gain in jobs over the past month. These reports are then consolidated by the government and reported as the total gain or loss for the past month. Despite accurate reporting by companies and correct tallying by the government, the number of jobs lost was significantly underestimated in the recent recession.

Which one of the following, if true, contributes most to a resolution of the apparent discrepancy described?

(A) More jobs are lost in a recession than in a period of growth.
(B) The expenses of collecting and reporting employment data have steadily increased.
(C) More people who lose their jobs start up their own businesses.
(D) In the recent recession a large number of failing companies abruptly ceased all operations.
(E) The recent recession contributed to the growing preponderance of service jobs over manufacturing jobs.

GO ON TO THE NEXT PAGE.

Questions 11–12

Beverage company representative: The plastic rings that hold six-packs of beverage cans together pose a threat to wild animals, which often become entangled in the discarded rings and suffocate as a result. Following our lead, all beverage companies will soon use only those rings consisting of a new plastic that disintegrates after only three days' exposure to sunlight. Once we all complete the switchover from the old to the new plastic rings, therefore, the threat of suffocation that plastic rings pose to wild animals will be eliminated.

11. The argument depends on which one of the following assumptions?

(A) None of the new plastic rings can disintegrate after only two days' exposure to sunlight.

(B) The switchover to the new plastic rings can be completed without causing significant financial hardship to the beverage companies.

(C) Wild animals will not become entangled in the new plastic rings before the rings have had sufficient exposure to sunlight to disintegrate.

(D) Use of the old plastic rings poses no substantial threat to wild animals other than that of suffocation.

(E) Any wild animal that becomes entangled in the old plastic rings will suffocate as a result.

12. Which one of the following, if true, most seriously weakens the representative's argument?

(A) The switchover to the new plastic rings will take at least two more years to complete.

(B) After the beverage companies have switched over to the new plastic rings, a substantial number of the old plastic rings will persist in most aquatic and woodland environments.

(C) The new plastic rings are slightly less expensive than the old rings.

(D) The new plastic rings rarely disintegrate during shipping of beverage six-packs because most trucks that transport canned beverages protect their cargo from sunlight.

(E) The new plastic rings disintegrate into substances that are harmful to aquatic animals when ingested in substantial quantities by them.

13. Alcohol consumption has been clearly linked to high blood pressure, which increases the likelihood of developing heart disease. Yet in a study of the effects of alcohol consumption, the incidence of heart disease was lower among participants who drank moderate quantities of alcohol every day than it was among participants identified as nondrinkers.

Which one of the following, if true, most helps to resolve the apparent discrepancy in the information above?

(A) Because many people who do not drink alcohol are conscious of their health habits, they are likely to engage in regular exercise and to eat nutritionally well-balanced meals.

(B) Many of the participants identified as nondrinkers were people who had been heavy drinkers but had stopped drinking alcohol prior to participating in the study.

(C) Some of the participants who drank moderate quantities of alcohol every day said that they occasionally drank large quantities of alcohol.

(D) Some of the participants who drank moderate quantities of alcohol every day had high blood pressure.

(E) The two groups of participants were similar to each other with respect to the participants' age, sex, geographical origin, and economic background.

14. Some of the world's most beautiful cats are Persian cats. However, it must be acknowledged that all Persian cats are pompous, and pompous cats are invariably irritating.

If the statements above are true, each of the following must also be true on the basis of them EXCEPT:

(A) Some of the world's most beautiful cats are irritating.

(B) Some irritating cats are among the world's most beautiful cats.

(C) Any cat that is not irritating is not a Persian cat.

(D) Some pompous cats are among the world's most beautiful cats.

(E) Some irritating and beautiful cats are not Persian cats.

GO ON TO THE NEXT PAGE.

15. At Flordyce University any student who wants to participate in a certain archaeological dig is eligible to do so but only if the student has taken at least one archaeology course and has shown an interest in the field. Many students who have shown an interest in archaeology never take even one archaeology course. Therefore, many students who want to participate in the dig will be ineligible to do so.

The flawed reasoning of which one of the following arguments is most similar to that of the argument above?

(A) Theoretically, any jar is worth saving regardless of its size, but only if it has a lid. Therefore, since some jars are sure not to have lids, there are certain sizes of jar that are actually not worth saving.

(B) For a horse that is well schooled to be ideal for beginning riders that horse must also be surefooted and gentle. Many horses that are surefooted are not gentle. Therefore many well-schooled horses are not ideal for beginning riders.

(C) If an author's first novel has a romantic setting and a suspenseful plot, it will become a best-seller. Since many authors' first novels have neither, not many first novels become best-sellers.

(D) Any automobile that is more than a few years old is eventually sure to need repairs if it is not regularly maintained. Many automobiles are more than a few years old, but still do not need repairs. Therefore, many automobiles are regularly maintained.

(E) An expensive new building will prove to be a good investment only if it is aesthetically pleasing or provides lots of office space. However, since many expensive new buildings are not aesthetically pleasing, few expensive new buildings will prove to be good investments.

16. From the observation that each member of a group could possess a characteristic, it is fallacious to conclude immediately that it is possible for all the group's members to possess the characteristic. An example in which the fallacy is obvious: arguing that because each of the players entering a tennis tournament has a possibility of winning it, there is therefore a possibility that all will win the tournament.

Which one of the following commits the fallacy described above?

(A) You can fool some of the people all of the time and all of the people some of the time, but you cannot fool all of the people all of the time.

(B) Each of the candidates for mayor appears at first glance to possess the necessary qualifications. It would therefore be a mistake to rule out any of them without more careful examination.

(C) Each of the many nominees could be appointed to any one of the three openings on the committee. Therefore it is possible for all of the nominees to be appointed to the openings on the committee.

(D) If a fair coin is tossed five times, then on each toss the chance of heads being the result is half. Therefore the chance of heads being the result on all five tosses is also half.

(E) It is estimated that 10 million planets capable of supporting life exist in our galaxy. Thus to rule out the possibility of life on worlds other than Earth, 10 million planetary explorations would be needed.

GO ON TO THE NEXT PAGE.

17. Recent research shows that hesitation, shifting posture, and failure to maintain eye contact are not reliable indicators in discriminating between those who are lying and those who are telling the truth. The research indicates that behavior that cannot be controlled is a much better clue, at least when the lie is important to the liar. Such behavior includes the dilation of eye pupils, which indicates emotional arousal, and small movements of facial muscles, which indicate distress, fear, or anger.

Which one of the following provides the strongest reason for exercising caution when relying on the "better" clues mentioned above in order to discover whether someone is lying?

(A) A person who is lying might be aware that he or she is being closely observed for indications of lying.

(B) Someone who is telling the truth might nevertheless have a past history of lying.

(C) A practiced liar might have achieved great control over body posture and eye contact.

(D) A person telling the truth might be affected emotionally by being suspected of lying or by some other aspect of the situation.

(E) Someone who is lying might exhibit hesitation and shifting posture as well as dilated pupils.

Questions 18–19

Orthodox medicine is ineffective at both ends of the spectrum of ailments. At the more trivial end, orthodox medicine is largely ineffective in treating aches, pains, and allergies, and, at the other extreme, it has yet to produce a cure for serious, life-threatening diseases such as advanced cancer and lupus. People turn to alternative medicine when orthodox medicine fails to help them and when it produces side effects that are unacceptable to them. One of the reasons alternative medicine is free of such side effects is that it does not have any effects at all.

18. If the statements above are true, which one of the following can be properly inferred from them?

(A) Practitioners of alternative medicine are acting in bad faith.

(B) There are some medical conditions for which no orthodox or alternative treatment is effective.

(C) There are some trivial illnesses that can be treated effectively by the methods of alternative medicine.

(D) There are no effective medical treatments that are free from unacceptable side effects.

(E) Orthodox medicine will eventually produce a solution for the diseases that are currently incurable.

19. The charge made above against alternative medicine is most seriously weakened if it is true that

(A) predictions based on orthodox medicine have sometimes failed, as when a patient has recovered despite the judgment of doctors that an illness is fatal

(B) alternative medicine relies on concepts of the body and of the nature of healing that differ from those on which orthodox medicine is based

(C) alternative medicine provides hope to those for whom orthodox medicine offers no cure

(D) a patient's belief in the medical treatment the patient is receiving can release the body's own chemical painkillers, diminish allergic reactions, and promote healing

(E) many treatments used for a time by orthodox medicine have later been found to be totally ineffective

GO ON TO THE NEXT PAGE.

20. Humans began to spread across North America around 12,000 years ago, as the climate became warmer. During the same period the large mammals that were once abundant in North America, such as the mastodon, the woolly mammoth, and the saber-toothed tiger, became extinct. Thus, contrary to the myth that humans formerly lived in harmony with the rest of nature, it is clear that even 12,000 years ago human activity was causing the extinction of animal species.

The argument is most vulnerable to the criticism that

(A) it adopts without question a view of the world in which humans are seen as not included in nature

(B) in calling the idea that humans once lived in harmony with nature a myth the argument presupposes what it attempts to prove

(C) for early inhabitants of North America the destruction of mastodons, woolly mammoths, and saber-toothed tigers might have had very different significance than the extinction of mammal species does for modern humans

(D) there might have been many other species of animals, besides mastodons, woolly mammoths, and saber-toothed tigers, that became extinct as the result of the spread of humans across North America

(E) the evidence it cites is consistent with the alternative hypothesis that the large mammals' extinction was a direct result of the same change in climate that allowed humans to spread across North America

21. The town of Greenfield recently instituted a substantial supplementary tax on all households, whereby each household is taxed in proportion to the volume of the trash that it puts out for trash collectors to pick up, as measured by the number of standard-sized garbage bags put out. In order to reduce the volume of the trash on which their tax bill is based, Greenfield households can deliver their recyclable trash to a conveniently located local commercial recycling center, where such trash is accepted free of charge.

The supplementary tax provides some financial incentive to Greenfield households to do each of the following EXCEPT:

(A) sort out recyclable trash thoroughly from their other trash

(B) dump nonrecyclable trash illegally at parks and roadsides

(C) compress and nest items of nonrecyclable trash before putting them out for pickup

(D) deliver recyclable materials to the recycling center instead of passing them on to neighbors who want to reuse them

(E) buy products without packaging or with recyclable rather than nonrecyclable packaging

22. In a survey of consumers in an Eastern European nation, respondents were asked two questions about each of 400 famous Western brands: whether or not they recognized the brand name and whether or not they thought the products bearing that name were of high quality. The results of the survey were a rating and corresponding rank order for each brand based on recognition, and a second rating-plus-ranking based on approval. The brands ranked in the top 27 for recognition were those actually available in that nation. The approval ratings of these 27 brands often differed sharply from their recognition ratings. By contrast, most of the other brands had ratings, and thus rankings, that were essentially the same for recognition as for approval.

Which one of the following, if each is a principle about consumer surveys, is violated by the survey described?

(A) Never ask all respondents a question if it cannot reasonably be answered by respondents who make a particular response to another question in the same survey.

(B) Never ask a question that is likely to generate a large variety of responses that are difficult to group into a manageable number of categories.

(C) Never ask all respondents a question that respondents cannot answer without giving up their anonymity.

(D) It is better to ask the same question about ten different products than to ask 10 different questions about a single product.

(E) It is best to ask questions that a respondent can answer without fear of having gotten the answer wrong.

GO ON TO THE NEXT PAGE.

23. A certain species of bird has two basic varieties: crested and noncrested. The birds, which generally live in flocks that contain only crested or only noncrested birds, tend to select mates of the same variety as themselves. However, if a bird that is raising a flock in which all other members are crested is later moved to a mixed flock, then that bird—whether crested or noncrested—is likely to select a crested mate. This fact indicates that the birds' preference for crested or noncrested mates is learned rather than genetically determined.

Which one of the following, if true, provides the most support for the argument?

(A) Birds of other species also tend to show preferences for mates that have one or another specific physical feature.

(B) In general there are few behavioral differences between the crested and noncrested birds of the species.

(C) Both the crested and noncrested birds of the species tend to select mates that are similar to themselves in size and age.

(D) If a crested bird of the species is raised in captivity apart from other birds and is later moved to a mixed flock, that bird is likely to select a crested mate.

(E) If a bird of the species is raised in a flock that contains both crested and noncrested birds, that bird shows no preference for one variety or the other in its selection of a mate.

24. Plant species differ in that renewed growth in spring can be triggered by day length or by temperature or else by a combination of both. Day length is the same, year after year, for any given date. Therefore, any plant species that starts to grow again on widely different dates in different years resumes growth at least in part in response to temperature.

Which one of the following arguments is most similar in its pattern of reasoning to the argument above?

(A) In Xandia, medical assistant trainees must either complete a formal training course or work for one year under the close supervision of a physician. Since few physicians are willing to act as supervisors, it must be true that most medical assistant trainees in Xandia take the training course.

(B) In the Crawford area, easterly winds mean rain will come and westerly winds mean dry weather will come; winds from other directions do not occur. Therefore, since it is currently raining in Crawford, there must be an easterly wind blowing there now.

(C) Some landfills charge garbage companies by volume only, some charge by weight only, and all others use a formula sensitive to both volume and weight. So if at a particular landfill the charges for two particular loads of equal volume dumped on the same day are different, weight must determine, or help determine, charges at that landfill.

(D) Depending on volume of business, either one or two or three store detectives are needed for adequate protection against shoplifting. Therefore, if on any particular day store management has decided that three detectives will be needed, it must be because business that day is expected to be heavy.

(E) A call is more likely to be heard if it is loud rather than soft, if it is high-pitched rather than low-pitched, and especially if it is both loud and high-pitched. Therefore, anyone whose call goes unheard in spite of being at maximum loudness should try to raise the pitch of the call.

STOP

IF YOU FINISH BEFORE TIME IS CALLED, YOU MAY CHECK YOUR WORK ON THIS SECTION ONLY.
DO NOT WORK ON ANY OTHER SECTION IN THE TEST.

Practice Test 3
Writing Sample

SIGNATURE _____   /   /
                                                    DATE

LSAT WRITING SAMPLE TOPIC

Sea Coast University is hiring new faculty for its science program and has narrowed its selection to Louise Parker or the team of Joe Echevarria and Jean Mydral. Assuming the cost of hiring Parker alone or the team is comparable, write an argument supporting one choice over the other based on the following considerations:

- Sea Coast University wants to develop a science program that will attract more undergraduate science majors.
- Sea Coast University wants to increase private and public support for its scientific research.

Louise Park, an internationally recognized scientist, plans to retire in three to five years. The recipient of numerous prizes for several key discoveries, Dr. Park has published extensively in scientific journals. While many of her graduate students have become influential scientists, undergraduates often find her inaccessible. Dr. Park is eager to leave her current university for Sea Coast's warmer climate, and she will bring a large, well-equipped laboratory if she comes to Sea Coast. This year, as usual, Dr. Park has secured grants from public and private sources to support her research.

Joe Echevarria and Jean Mydral number among the most promising young scientists in the country. They have begun to publish in respected scientific journals and have received research grants from major foundations. Last year, their team-teaching approach won them a national teaching award. They recently published an article detailing their groundbreaking research on commercial uses of biotechnology; this research has attracted the attention of major corporations, several of whom are eager to fund their future work.

_____

_____

_____

_____

_____

_____

_____

_____

_____

_____

_____

_____

GO ON TO THE NEXT PAGE.

KAPLAN

STOP

IF YOU FINISH BEFORE TIME IS CALLED, YOU MAY CHECK YOUR WORK ON THIS SECTION ONLY.
DO NOT WORK ON ANY OTHER SECTION IN THE TEST.

Practice Test Three: **Answer Key**

Section I Analytical Reasoning	Section II Logical Reasoning	Section III Reading Comprehension	Section IV Logical Reasoning
1. D	1. D	1. A	1. A
2. B	2. C	2. D	2. C
3. C	3. C	3. B	3. D
4. E	4. A	4. C	4. E
5. B	5. A	5. D	5. E
6. D	6. E	6. A	6. B
7. E	7. B	7. C	7. E
8. E	8. A	8. C	8. D
9. C	9. D	9. E	9. C
10. C	10. A	10. B	10. D
11. C	11. D	11. A	11. C
12. B	12. D	12. D	12. B
13. A	13. A	13. D	13. B
14. E	14. D	14. E	14. E
15. D	15. E	15. D	15. B
16. B	16. C	16. E	16. C
17. E	17. A	17. B	17. D
18. E	18. A	18. C	18. B
19. C	19. C	19. A	19. D
20. A	20. A	20. D	20. E
21. A	21. C	21. A	21. D
22. D	22. D	22. D	22. A
23. C	23. D	23. D	23. E
24. E	24. E	24. C	24. C
	25. A	25. B	
	26. B	26. A	
		27. E	

Answers and Explanations

SECTION I: ANALYTICAL REASONING

GAME 1—Consumer Research

The Action

This game announces itself pretty obviously: the word "group" appears four times in the opening paragraph. Not surprisingly, you're asked to group eight people—to divide them into two groups of four people each. The key issues are predictable:

1) Who's in what group?

2) What people can or must be in the same group?

3) What people cannot be in the same group?

The Initial Setup

```
        F G H J K L M N

  1  |  ___   ___   ___   ___

  2  |  ___   ___   ___   ___
```

Keep this setup simple, just as you would if you were choosing up sides in everyday life. You can keep a roster of the entities, and since there are definitely four slots in each group, picture them that way:

The Rules

1) Rules like this are a blessing in grouping games: It means that you can treat two entities as a solid block, and whenever you get information about one, the other must tag along. To remember the rule, jot down "ALWAYS FJ" nearby (although chances are, you had this rule pretty much memorized before the game was half done).

2) Remember that G and M can never be present in the same group, but remember that it's best to build rules right into the picture whenever possible. And since you have eight definite slots to fill, one slot in each group is now filled, one by G, the other by M. Even if you choose to jot down "Never GM" off to the side, build

the G/M relationship into the master sketch (see below).

3) If/then rules: Not much you can do except think them through. If H is in 1, L is in 1. Remember to also think through the contrapositive. It's true that if L isn't in group 1, then neither is H, but take that further: In this game "not in 1" is equivalent to "In group 2." So you should take note of the contrapositive: If L is in 2, H is in 2. Note that this rule DOESN'T require H and L always to be in the same group—that's a common mistake and you can bet that some questions will test whether you've recognized that.

4) Same kind of deal as Rule 3. If N's in 2, G's in 1. The contrapositive: If G's in 2, N's in 1. Note that, like the preceding rule, this one has a built-in trap. It *doesn't* mean that N and G can never be together... they can in group 1.

Deductions

Despite the fact that G appears in Rules 2 and 4, the deduction that "if N is in group 2, then G is in 1 and M is in 2" is not really worth your time. If/then rules are hypothetical only: Wait for the questions to provide concrete information. Enjoy the knowledge that, thanks to your interpretation and shorthanding of the rules, the information will be there when you need it.

What *is* important, however, are the restrictions of space. You've seen that G and M take up one slot in each group. And F and J are always together (Rule 1), so you know that one of the groups will always consist of F and J; either G or M; and one other entity. And you might stop there, or go on to realize that if H and L are in group 1 (as Rule 3 says is possible), then F and J must be in group 2. Again, don't take hypothetical reasoning too far, but whenever big deductions aren't immediately accessible (as in this game), focus on space limitations and the numbers that govern the game. Often, the answers to many of the questions will be based on these.

Finally, note the play of the if/then rules and their contrapositives that you listed along with them. You can scan the "if" column only, and whenever you know that H is in group 1, or L, N, or G is in group 2, more information is provided. Recognize, however, that if you find out that H is in group *2*, or that L, N, or G is in group *1*, these rules are of no help to you. Don't commit the fallacy of affirming the consequent!

The Final Visualization

As you move on to the questions, here's what you have to work with:

1 | G/M ___ ___ ___
_____
2 | G/M ___ ___ ___
   (FJ)

If H is 1 → L is 1
IF L is 2 → H is 2
If N is 2 → G is 1
If G is 2 → N is 1

The Big Picture

- Always think through and note the contrapositive of every if/then rule. It can be your best friend, especially in games that have a limited number of options.

- When a game is largely in hypothetical (if/then) form, don't take a lot of time to work out possibilities in advance. Wait for concrete info to come along.

The Questions

1. D

For this "could be true" question focusing on group 1, you need to find the single choice that violates no rules, so check each rule against each answer choice. Rule 1 eliminates (B), which separates F and J. Rule 2 eliminates (E), which mistakenly puts G and M together, and (C), which, by omitting both G and M, force this forbidden pair into group 2. Rule 3 does away with (A)—H can't be in group 1 without L. This leaves only (D), which must be an acceptable lineup for group 1.

- This "could be true" question is basically just another type of acceptability question; as in any acceptability question, test the rules against the answer choices.

- In a grouping game containing exactly two groups, remember that a complete list of entities in one group tells you more than who's in that group; it also tells you who's in the other group.

2. B

Don't just stare at it; work it out on paper. Put K and N in one group, but don't label it yet; realize that F and J have to be in the other group (if not, Rule 2 is violated). And G and M split up, so three of the four spaces in each group are set. H and L are the only ones left. Scan the 'if' conditions in your rules: Which apply? Rule 3 does. If H is in group 1, then L is too. But no matter which group above you designate as group 1 (K, N, and G or M; or F, J, and G or M), you have no room for H and L in group 1. Therefore, H must go into group 2 and L in group 1, the former of which is (B).

(A) and (E) G and M could be in either group. The only stipulation is that they not be together in the same group.

(C) and (D) Group 1: K, N, G, L and group 2: F, J, H, M shows that neither of these choices must be true.

- Whenever you're given new information in an "if" clause, remember that this information applies for that question only. Forget it when moving on to the next question.

- Sometimes you have to start linking entities up even if you don't know exactly which group to place them in. Here, just separating the F/J group from the K/N group set forth in the stem, and then separating G and M, gives you a good head start on the question.

3. C

This is question 2 revisited, this time with different entities—F and H—grouped together. Rule 1 tells you that J joins them, and Rule 2 fills out that group with either G or M. Everybody else goes into the other group: K, L, N, and either G or M. Now—which group is which? Once again you have H and L in different groups, which means that H's group has to be group 2 (remember, if H is in 1, so is L). Group 2 is therefore F, H, J, and either G or M; group 1 is N, K, L, and either G or M. The only choice that must be true under these circumstances is (C).

(A) and (E) are possible only, whereas (B) and (D) cannot be true.

- Always take an active role in pursuing the answer. Take any new information you're given, *put it down on paper,* and see where it leads you. The worst thing you can do on test day is to sit and stare at a question. If you can't think of anything to do with the new information, then skip it; but by and large, going back to the rules armed with the new information will normally lead you to, or toward, the answer.

4. E

This one promises to be easier than the previous two because it names members of a specific group—and it *is* easier. You're asked for someone who could be in either of the groups, given L and M are in group 2. Jot that down and consider the contrapositive of Rule 3: If L is in 2—which he is—then H is in 2 as well, joining L and M.

This pushes F and J into group 1, along with G (Rule 2). This much information alone allows you to cross off choices (A), (B), (C), and (D); all these entities are fixed in one group or another. You don't even have to check to make sure that K can be in both groups. When you've narrowed it down to one choice, that's our answer. Indeed, both K and N could occupy either group, but the test makers chose K as the answer.

- Don't waste time proving that an answer works when you've confidently rejected all the others. If there's only one choice left, mark it, secure in the knowledge that there are *no* questions on the LSAT without a credited answer.

5. B

Which pair of people cannot be together in group 1? See whether any pairs in the choices have appeared together in group 1 before; if so, you can cross that pair off. (D) and (E) have—both pairs appeared together in group 1 in question 1's correct answer (D). Toss those choices. And note that in question 4, F and G—(A) here—appeared together in group 1, so (A) can be eliminated too. As for (C), the group F, L, J, G can be together in 1, leaving (B) as the answer to this "all EXCEPT" question.

- Here's another argument for doing separate scratchwork for each question and keeping your sketches "pristine"—you can use them to help you in later questions. Why duplicate your work?

6. D

L is in group 2, and you're asked for a pair that could *not* be in group 1 together. The contrapositive of Rule 3 says that if L is in group 2, then so is H; jot that down, and recognize that from there you have to put your FJ pair in group 1. Of course, each group gets the customary G or M. N and K are left over, one per group.

Now what? If you can't figure out how to apply the rules toward the answer, use trial and error: Take each pair, combine them with the other inhabitants of group 1, and see what you're left with. You'll find that if K and M join F and J in group 1 (choice D), G and N will be forced to join group 2, which is a blatant violation of Rule 4.

- When many questions go by without a certain rule being invoked, you have to figure it'll come along sooner or later. For instance, you hadn't used Rule 4 very much until question 6—a strong indication that that rule would be useful here.

GAME 2—Game Show Contestants

The Action

A really straightforward sequencing game in which you're told to schedule five people to appear on a television show, one per day from Monday through Friday.

The Initial Setup

Since your job is to assign entities to discrete slots, you can just create those slots (labeled "M T W Th F") and list the contestants off to the side:

M   T   W   Th   F
                                        H I K N V
___   ___   ___   ___   ___

The Rules

You get quite the cross-section of rule types here: one negative rule, two if/thens, and one concrete. Where to begin?

4) Sure: with the rule that gives you the most concrete help. Somewhere in this sequence the letters "VK" have to appear consecutively, in that order. So make a note to that effect. Just make sure you don't get it backward.

1) "No N" over your M for Monday will help you keep this rule in mind. Can't do much more than that: Only 1 of N's 5 prospects has been eliminated.

2) and 3) can be handled together because they're in the same logical form. Each gives you a hypothetical person/day assignment, and says that if that assignment occurs, then *another* person/day assignment will result. Jot them down off to the side, and just like the if/thens from the last game, be sure to think through the contrapositive of each:

NOTE: The sketch below is a graphic, but does not follow our current notation in that you've written out the names AND the days. People should be a single capital letter if days are going to be represented with three letter abbreviations.

Harry $_{Mon}$ → Nan $_{Fri}$ Nan $_{Tues}$ → Iris $_{Mon}$

Nan $_{not\ Fri}$ → Harry $_{not\ Mon}$ Iris $_{not\ Mon}$ → Nan $_{not\ Tues}$

Deductions

Given the nature of these rules, it shouldn't be too surprising that deductions are not in great supply here. However, do take special note of the "VK" pairing. They will always take up two out of the five possible spaces, and generally when a bloc of entities has to travel together, more than a couple of the questions hinge on whether or not there's adequate space for everyone. One thing you might notice—and it's not such a big deal—is that "If Nan not Fri" in the contrapositive of Rule 2 really means "If Nan is T, W, or Th" (since she's ineligible for Monday). Also, Kate can't be on Monday and Victor can't be on Friday thanks to Rule 4. Not earth-shattering stuff, but things worth noting before embarking on the questions. (Actually, this "VK" business turns question 7 into a huge "gimme.")

The Final Visualization

Here's all the info you should have heading into the questions:

NO N

M   T   W   TH   F   (VK)

—   —   —   —   —   H I K N V

Harry $_{Mon}$ → Nan $_{Fri}$ Nan $_{Tues}$ → Iris $_{Mon}$

Nan $_{not\ Fri}$ → Harry $_{not\ Mon}$ Iris $_{not\ Mon}$ → Nan $_{not\ Tues}$

The Big Picture:

- Don't kill yourself looking for deductions. Some games lend themselves to big deductions and some games do not. The way to figure it out is to take rules with common elements and see whether you can combine them. Steer clear of if/then's, however, when looking for deductions; since their info is purely hypothetical, you're usually better off waiting for the question stems to give you direction.

- Always try to identify the "most significant rule" or "most significant block of entities" in a game. Target them as most likely to be helpful during the questions. Here, of course, it's the "VK" block that you need to keep in mind throughout.

The Questions

7.   E

Yes, a "gimme" indeed. As you saw above, Rule 4 says that Kate is scheduled for the day *after* Victor, so Victor cannot be scheduled for the last day, Friday.

- In an "all Except" question, once you've found a choice that cannot be true, there's absolutely no reason to prove that the other choices *can* be true— you've got your answer.

- This question hinges on what one might call an "excluded ends" principle. Since V must precede K, V cannot occupy the last slot in a sequence, and for the same reason K cannot be first.

8. E

This is basically an Acceptability question, with the added information about Iris following Harry: Jot down "HI" to get started. The best way to proceed is to check each day to determine which of the days on which Harry could be scheduled. And use your pencil if you need to. (Note that there's no reason to check Monday, since it appears in every choice, it's obviously acceptable.)

If Harry is on Tuesday, Iris is on Wednesday; to slot in "VK," you need to assign Victor to Thursday and Kate to Friday. This leaves Monday for Nancy, a rule violation, so Harry can't take Tuesday after all. Cross off any choice that includes Tuesday: (A) and (D).

Now try Harry on Wednesday—no problem. Iris takes Thursday, Nancy gets Friday, and the Victor/Kate pair begin the week. Therefore, the answer must *include* Wednesday, so cross off (C).

None of the answer choices include Friday, so the last day you need check is Thursday, and again—no problem. If Harry is on Thursday, Iris takes Friday, Nancy takes Wednesday, and again the V/K pair begins the week. The answer must include Thursday, so cross off (B). The answer is therefore (E).

- Sometimes the only way to work a question is to check each choice. You can help yourself, however, by using your pencil instead of trying to work things out in your head. You can also help by looking for shortcuts (such as not bothering with Monday and Friday). These strategies can make questions like this relatively quick.

9. C

Kate is scheduled for Wednesday, so Victor takes Tuesday (Rule 4). This means that Rule 3 (Nancy on Tuesday) doesn't apply in this one. Monday is forbidden to Nancy, so she can only take Thursday or Friday. Now work with Rule 2: If H is on Monday, then N must be Friday, leaving I for Thursday—the schedule would then be "H, V, K, I, N." However, if H isn't on Monday, he must be on Thursday or Friday, with N also on Thursday or Friday, leaving I for Monday: "I, V, K, H/N, H/N" is the only other option. Checking these two options against the choices, only (C) could be true.

- Work out the implications of any new information you're given. When one entity is limited to only a few options, check them out; you may find that you can quickly cover all the bases and then simply check the choices against the schedules on your page.

- Recognize up front which rules don't apply to a given situation, and proceed to ignore them

10. C

Don't you love how these question stems keep dealing with Kate and Victor, about whom you know so much? Kate on Friday means Victor on Thursday. Now, go back to your Rules—Rule 2 states that if Harry is on Monday, then Nancy is on Friday. Can that be? No, Kate owns Friday in this one, so Harry can't be Monday, Nancy can never be on Monday (Rule 1), which means that Iris must take Monday, (C).

Nancy and Harry end up floating between Tuesday and Wednesday, so (A), (B), and (E) are *possibly* true. But (D) is definitely false.

- In games that contain only a few entities, stay conscious of who *can't* go where; often the process of elimination will tell you who *must* go where.

- Remember the hint that the question and answer choices gave you. When the question is "what must be true" and the choices are definite statements, forge ahead boldly.

11. C

Assigning Iris to Wednesday leaves two possibilities for our V/K pair. If they take Thursday and Friday respectively, you should see (by working things out with your pencil) that things break down, because no one's available for Monday—Nancy can't take Monday ever, and putting Harry in Monday for "H N I V K" violates Rule 2. So V and K will have to take Monday and Tuesday respectively, leaving Nancy and Harry to Thursday and Friday in either order. Which must be true? Check the choices in order and stop at (C). Indeed, Kate's day precedes Harry's.

- As it turned out, working through the contrapositives of Rules 2 and 3 didn't help you too much. But that's utterly beside the point. You *must* take the time to think them through, because in 99 percent of games, the contrapositive *will* help. *Any* time spent thinking through rules is time well spent.

GAME 3—Art Lectures

The Action

This hybrid game combines aspects of grouping, matching *and* sequencing. You are called upon to select six of eight lectures (the grouping part); designate on which day they are scheduled (sequencing); and figure out whether they are scheduled in the morning or the afternoon of that day (matching). The issues have to do with:

1) Which lectures are scheduled on each day?

2) Which lectures are *not* scheduled on a particular day?

3) When a lecture is scheduled for a day, is it given in the morning or afternoon?

4) Which lectures can, must, or cannot be scheduled on the same day as other lectures?

5) Which lectures can, must, or cannot be scheduled immediately preceding or following other lectures?

The Initial Setup

To take care of the grouping/selection element—the choice of the six out of eight lectures—list the entities in a roster, ready to circle the six chosen and X out the two rejected. As far as the scheduling goes, what did you do at the beginning of each semester when plotting out your weekly class schedule? You probably made a list of the days of the week and jotted the classes down accordingly. The process is even simpler here, because there are only three days involved, and exactly two classes per day, one in the A.M. and one in the P.M. Something like this:

	1	2	3
AM			
PM			

The Rules

Given that you have *three* separate though related tasks to attend to, it will be useful to think about which of those tasks is tied into each rule. For example:

1) On the face of it, this is a scheduling rule only: If O is chosen, it must be scheduled for day 2. But it has a selection element as well, which you might only see after thinking through the contrapositive: *If O can't be scheduled for day 2, then O isn't one of the six chosen.* In other words, should day 2 be occupied by two other

lectures, then O will be one of the two lectures not scheduled that week. After you've put that all together in your head, your pencil can do the rest in the same way you've jotted down other if/then rules in this section.

2) This rule is big. Two—count 'em, two—lectures can't be in the afternoon—which means that if selected, they must be scheduled in the morning. Therefore, should all the morning slots be taken, then *sculpture and watercolors would be the two rejected lectures*. All the others would be automatically selected. This rule is so big and so important to remember that it may be helpful to jot it down twice: once next to the sketch, and once *within* it (see below).

3) Like most negative rules, this one can only be jotted down nearby, as a constant visual reminder never to assign oils and lithographs, or pastels and lithographs, to the same day.

4) A two-part if/then rule—complex and information-packed, and worth spending time on for those very reasons. *Should* pastels be scheduled on day 1, then fresco and history will take day 2 (sorry, oils). And should pastels be scheduled on day 2, then the same two lectures will take day 3. (You might well ask yourself, suppose pastels are chosen for day 3? In that case, all bets are off; the rule won't apply.)

What's *truly* important here is using the contrapositive to spell out the implications of this rule. If either fresco or history is unavailable for day 2 or day 3, or if another lecture is already there, then pastels will not be able to be chosen for day 1 or 2 (respectively). And you'll see all of that come up over and over in the questions. See the sketch for a commonsense way to jot down this rule, but remember: If it ain't in your head, having it on the page won't help.

Deductions

Nothing more than hypotheses. But pay special attention, once again, to the numbers game. Since sculpture and watercolors cannot be scheduled in the afternoon (Rule 2), this game is ripe for some questions in which running out of lectures that *can* be scheduled in the afternoon should lead you right to the answer.

The Final Visualization

Here's what the master sketch looks like heading into the questions:

	1	2	3	SW always here (AM)
AM				
PM				No SW here

If $\oslash$ → Day 2

If not in Day 2 → No $\oslash$

If $P_{Day\ 1}$ → F, $N_{Day\ 2}$

If $P_{Day\ 2}$ → F, $N_{Day\ 3}$

The Big Picture

- A common mistake in matching games is not recognizing that when all of the other choices are ruled out, what's left must be the answer. As you proceed through this game, see whether you were hip to what *had* to be true when a bunch of possibilities were eliminated.

The Questions

12. B

You know what to do with an Acceptability question: Check each rule against the choices. (C) puts oils on day 1 in violation of Rule 1. (D) puts watercolors in the P.M., which Rule 2 forbids. (A)'s assignment of pastels/lithography violates Rule 3, and according to Rule 4, if pastels takes day 2, then fresco and history take day 3, and that's not the case in (E).

- Acceptability questions are quick confidence builders. Save even more time by beginning with the easiest rules. And when you've eliminated a choice, cross it out completely: Doing so makes it easier to read the remaining choices.

13. A

Think about the afternoon of day 1, which is what the question is all about. Oils is impossible for day 1, period, and sculpture and watercolors are impossible in the *afternoon,* period; so (B), (D), and (E) can be rejected. And (C)'s mentioning pastels might prompt you to check Rule

4, which lo and behold would be violated if pastels were scheduled for day 1 (here, lithography in day 2 blocks you). (A) is left as the answer.

14. E

A slightly more complicated version of the previous question, with two definite assignments made. Since the question asks what could take day 1's morning slot, cross out oils (C) right away (Rule 2); and recognize that pastels (D) is also out, since you cannot have fresco and history in day 2 as Rule 4 requires.

If you sketch out the situation—with L and H in the A.M. slots of days 2 and 3 as specified—then a little trial and error should lead you to the right answer. If either fresco or naturalism—(A) and (B), respectively—took day 1's A.M. slot, fully *three* lectures would be unavailable for selection: sculpture and watercolors, which are A.M. only, and oils, which can only take day 2 but can't be paired up with lithography. This leaves (E), sculpture, and that would be okay—the two rejected lectures would be oils and watercolors.

- See how important the numbers game can be? Whenever you seem to be "stuck" in a Logic Games question, remember to work out the numerical possibilities.

15. D

With oils in the morning of day 2 and lithography in the morning of day 3, you should recognize that pastels are forbidden to day 1 or day 2—you can't have the fresco/history day that Rule 4 requires; and pastels is blocked from day 3, as well, since lithography's there. So pastels is out of the running altogether, (D). For the record, a schedule of sculpture, oils, lithography in the AM and fresco, history, naturalism in the P.M. takes care of (A), (B), (C), and (E).

- Combine a question's new information with the old rules. Ask yourself: What rule(s) can help me here?

16. B

The most helpful "if" yet: Telling you the two rejected lectures also tells you the six that are chosen, and you can proceed to think about the day assignments. Now, since fresco is out, pastels can't take day 1 or day 2; but pastels *have* to be chosen, so day 3 it is for pastels and (D) bites the dust. In the meantime, the choices continue to try to slip oils into a day other than day 2; throw out (C). But the rule that moves you to a *positive* conclusion is Rule 3: Lithography *has* to be selected, but cannot be paired up with oils (day 2) or pastels (day 3). So it's lithography that must go to day 1, (B).

17. E

The morning lectures are fresco, history, and lithography, but *not necessarily in that order.* Well, first off, with the morning lectures decided, Rule 2 demands that the two rejected lectures are sculpture and watercolors, and all of the others must be scheduled. Jot down the list of the three afternoon lectures—gotta be oils, naturalism, and pastels. And oils must be on day 2 (Rule 1), and of course that means the afternoon of day 2 here; so naturalism and pastels will take the afternoons of day 1 and 3, in either order.

Or *is* it quite so open-ended? Can you assign pastels to day 1 or 2 in line with Rule 4? No, you cannot, because you cannot follow pastels with a "fresco/history" day. So as so often in earlier questions, pastels must take day 3, leaving naturalism for the afternoon of day 1. What's the impact on the morning schedule? Lithography will have to take the day 1 slot, or else Rule 3 would be violated. So all that's uncertain is the assignment of fresco and history—they'll take day 2 and 3, in either order—so (E) is the choice that *could* be true. All the others violate the arrangement established.

- There is a ton of information to keep track of in this question. If you had success on the first five questions, this was the one to consider putting aside if it seemed unmanageable.

GAME 4—Clans & Ceremonies

The Action

This game is a variant of the "process" games that appear rarely on the LSAT, in that it requires constant reference to the rules. (It may be more amenable to scratchwork help than the average process game.) Exactly three of five clans take part in an annual harvest ceremony.

The Initial Setup

Not much to draw here. You'll want to jot down the list of the clans, and be ready to figure out what kind of behavior they undergo, and how the rules define that behavior.

The Rules

1) Don't rush to write it down. Consider what it means, in concrete terms. One year—call it year one—three clans will take part in the ceremony. Okay, so two *don't* take part. So what about them? Well, the rule means that those two clans *have to* take part in the ceremony in year two: No clan can miss two years in a row. The third clan in that second year ceremony, of course, would be one of the clans that took part in the *first* year. Now, whether you write it down or not, you need this information clear in your mind throughout. The same holds true for:

2) "No clan takes part three years in a row." So after two years in a row, a clan takes a powder. And think about what you learned in Rule 1: This rule means that the one clan that takes part in the ceremonies in years one and two cannot also take part in year three.

3) This rule introduces the new concept of a "cycle." Once each clan has taken part in exactly three ceremonies, a cycle ends.

4) Just puts a numerical limit on the business: Within any cycle, three ceremonies is the limit for each clan.

Deductions

You have to figure that Rules 3 and 4 bear consideration in tandem (because each has to do with the number of clan appearances and the composition of a cycle). Each ceremony consists of three clans; and each clan will take part in exactly three ceremonies per cycle. Okay: There are five clans—five clans that must each take part three times in a cycle. Five clans, each taking part three times, equals 15 "appearances" in a cycle. And each ceremony allows for three participations. Fifteen divided by three equals five. Clearly, *each cycle consists of five years.*

The Final Visualization

While a customary "Final Visualization" isn't appropriate in this case—what's to draw?—it might be worth your time to do something else.

Forget the clans in the game. Think of five different clans: Call them a, b, c, d, and e. Think about and work out the five years in a possible cycle. For instance: Say that a, b, and c take part in year one of a cycle. What has to happen in year two? Well, d and e, the clans that missed out in year one, will have to take part (Rule 1), as well as one of the original three: Let's say it's a, for the time being. (Jot down each list of 3 if you like, to make it more concrete.)

Year three, what happens? Well, b and c will have to be back for the ceremony—they're not allowed to miss two years in a row. And they'll be joined by either d or e; say it's d for argument's sake. So far you've got: a b c / d e a / b c d. Get the picture? Years four and five will continue, each taking the two clans that *didn't* take part the year before, as well as a third available clan. And remember: In the end, *every clan will be named exactly three times.*

Now that you've understood the process "in the abstract," using nonsense letters, you can work with the *real* clans somewhat more confidently.

The Big Picture

- Sketchwork is never a substitute for thinking. This game is a wonderful example of the importance of making abstract concepts concrete. Once you take the time to think through the behavior of entities in process games, you have a shot to rack up points quickly and accurately.

The Questions

18. E

Your "concretization," as it were, shows you how this question has to work. If N, O, and P take part in year one, the clans that missed year one—S and T—must stand and deliver in year two. The only choice that includes both of these is (E)—and remember, *any* of the three year one clans can make a reappearance in year two.

- Don't be surprised when after a complex setup, you are given a fairly straightforward opening question. The opening question will often test whether you've deduced something basic about the game. You get a reward just for hangin' in there.

19. C

Here is where your work in the "Final Visualization" comes through for you, abetted by your usual confidence in Acceptability questions. (A) and (B) are unacceptable because each violates Rule 2, with three consecutive appearances of a clan. Next, you can try out (C), (D), and (E), searching for the one and only one possible statement; or you can recognize from your earlier thinking that a pair of clans can only take part in, at most, two ceremonies together. No pair could be together in years one, three, and five (D), or years two, three, and five (E). Try them and see. You're left with (C), which is eminently possible.

- A process game, in the unlikely event that you see one, will almost always take more time than other games, which is why time management is so important. Save such games till last.

20. A

Already calculated.

- If you waited until now to work out that each cycle consists of five years, the first two questions may have been considerably more difficult. Actively attack each game and you'll find all of them much more manageable.

21. A

What must be true about the clans that take part in the first ceremony? You could have used the earlier thinking discussed, or how about this: You could have proceeded from, and used, question 18. Why not? There you had an acceptable set of year one clans, N, O, and P: It had to be acceptable, because the test makers provided it. Well, year two (as you saw) would have to welcome S, T, and one of the first three clans; notice that (B), the only choice mentioning year two, is false.

What about year three? Two members of the original N, O, P group will be back (whichever two skipped year two), and so you see that (A) is true. In fact, (A) could go even further: *Exactly* two members of the year one group will take part again in year three. Scan the choices. You've already worked out that "at most" and exactly two of them will be back together in year three, as (A) states. Because of that, (E) is revealed as obviously false; and you needn't stop to affirm that (C) and (D), too, are impossible, although in fact, *no* trio can take part together in any two different years.

- As you move through the questions, the rules and deductions should become more and more familiar and thus easier to use. And you will find yourself getting used to making the abstract more concrete.

22. D

If N, O, and S take part in year one, Rule 2 eliminates choice (A) right away. From there you can use our "possible" cycle to try and find a situation in which the other choices aren't necessarily true. For instance, O *could* take part in years three and four, but any of the first year clans could do so instead: Cross off (B). In the same way, N and O (C) could take part together in year three, but so could N and S, and O and S, instead. Cross off (C). You're left with (D) and (E), two choices that deal with year five, and (D) turns out to be correct (which you can affirm through trial and error). There's no way to avoid a year five repairing of clans P and T—the clans not used in year one.

- Whenever you're asked for the one choice that "must" be true, remember that in order to eliminate a choice, all you have to do is find one situation in which the choice is not true.

23. C

N, O, and T are in year one's ceremony, and O and P are in year four; you're asked which clan is locked out of year three's ceremony. S and P (the two clans not used in year one) will be part of year two, and the inability of any clan to take part three years in a row makes P the clan that the question is looking for.

- Always have a game plan. Deal with any new information and then see how that new information relates to the rules.

24. E

N, O, and S are in year one's ceremony, and O, S, and T are in year three. Sneak up to year five—the topic of the question—by applying your knowledge of the rules to the concrete situation. Year two, of course, will consist of P and T and . . . ? Not O or S, who would thereby be taking part three years in a row. Year two must be P, T, N.

Year three, you've got. Year four? Clearly, N and P will take part—remember, no clan misses two years in a row; T, however, will not take part, because that would be three T's in a row. But T has to make three appearances in the cycle, and has only taken part twice so far. Therefore, T has to be one of the clans taking part in year five . . . and if you scan the choices, only one mentions T: the correct answer, (E).

- Just because a question is the last one in a game doesn't necessarily mean that it's the most difficult. Work with each question in the same way, and you'll find that the majority of questions can be answered with the same techniques. Just be ready to move along to more fertile ground if a question gets messy.

SECTION II: LOGICAL REASONING

1. D

The argument concludes that libraries can best serve their users by purchasing only paperbacks, allowing libraries to add more new titles to their collections. The assumption being made is that adding the greatest possible number of new titles is the best way to serve library users. But if library users as a group depend on the library for access to *specific* books *only* published in hardcover, then this assumption, and the argument, falls apart.

(A) makes an irrelevant comparison. Neither issue raised here—a library's overall budget and a library's budget for day-to-day operations—gets at the paperback vs. hardcover issue.

(B) and (C) are 180 choices: (B) strengthens the argument by eliminating a possible objection to the acquisition of paperbacks, while (C) suggests another advantage of the paperback over the hardcover, thus supporting the author's recommendation for libraries to move entirely to paperback.

(E) For this to be a convincing weakener, you'd have to assume that people only use public libraries for access to books that they wouldn't buy themselves.

- For Weaken questions, look for the choice that contradicts the passage's central assumption.

- Another way to weaken an argument is to look for the choice that would directly negate the conclusion. In this case, ask yourself: "Which choice makes me believe that users would *not* be better served if the library bought only paperbacks?" (D) should then jump out.

- Be wary of choices like (E), which require additional assumptions in order to complete the logic.

2. C

The evidence is a couple of general rules about when garbage is usually collected and what happens with garbage pickup after a Monday public holiday. This evidence is then applied to the specific case of garbage collection in *this* neighborhood *this* week, which leads to the conclusion in the first sentence. So as far as the author's method of argument is concerned, the author reasons from the general to the specific, which is (C).

(A) The pieces of evidence given aren't irrelevant; they're *directly* relevant to the issue of garbage pickup and thus do support the conclusion.

(B) fails because the argument establishes its conclusion *directly*, by discussing the rules about garbage pickup, not indirectly by ruling out alternative possibilities.

(D) Reasoning from the specific to the general is the precise opposite of what this argument does.

(E) The conclusion is that garbage will *probably* be picked up on Thursday; there's no inevitability element at work here at all.

- Reading the question stem first is especially handy for Method of Argument questions, since it allows you to begin to *abstract* the reasoning in the argument as you read. In other words, you know right off the bat that you'll be asked "how" the author makes her point, not "what" specific point is being made.

- Stay familiar with the common argumentative structure featured here. Arguing from a general case to a specific example (or vice versa) appears every now and then on the LSAT—in Method questions, Flaw questions, and even Parallel Reasoning.

3. C

Why did vinyl record prices go up after CD prices, which were higher to begin with, came down? The latter were higher at first because of "different production costs"—CD technology was initially more expensive to use because it was unfamiliar. But vinyl technology's not unfamiliar, so what's the deal?

(C) provides an explanation: As CDs became more affordable and more people bought them, they bought fewer vinyl records, making it less cost-effective to produce vinyl records and therefore more expensive. Notice that this doesn't contradict the explanation for initially higher CD prices: Vinyl records ended up with "different production costs," just as CDs had at first.

(A) and (D) both entirely miss the point; in fact, neither one even *mentions* vinyl. Therefore, why some people bought CDs even though they were more expensive (A) and changes in CD technology (D) are both irrelevant issues that don't help explain the paradoxical situation.

(B) is irrelevant, too. Who cares whether people kept buying vinyl records as long as they were cheaper? You want to know why vinyl records didn't *stay* cheaper.

(E) gives a reason for people to continue buying vinyl, but ignores the issue of the increase in the cost of vinyl, so it's irrelevant.

- Although there's no reference to a "paradox" or "discrepancy" in the question stem, there's one to be solved here. Whether they use these words or not, a paradox exists if a surprising result occurs that seems counter to that which should happen.

- This is a good question for using the strategy of elimination; none of the wrong choices even remotely deals with the situation you're asked to explain.

4. A

None of the statements here is a conclusion stemming from the others—it's your job to find that conclusion among the choices. Land reserves are supposed to preserve habitats that don't exist elsewhere and that are necessary for certain species' survival. What will happen to the typical land reserve if global warming occurs as predicted? A bunch of plants now there will grow elsewhere, and you can infer a bunch of plants elsewhere will start to grow *there*. In other words, the *habitat* provided by the land reserve will change, which means that the reserve will no longer serve its purpose as the only appropriate habitat for its intended species.

(B) is unsupported; first, you can't be so sure that the butterflies will adapt; second, you know nothing about the function of migration in their survival, either now or in the future.

(C) is outside the scope, first introducing melting polar ice (remember, the stimulus only spoke of the effect of warming on vegetation), then predicting a completely unsupported consequence of the melting ice.

(D) is a distortion: Just because global warming is predicted for the future doesn't mean that you can infer that the world has adapted to drastic global warming and cooling *in the past*.

(E) The *speed* of global warming is irrelevant and therefore outside the scope, as is the idea of "agricultural areas."

- Working on inference questions, watch out for choices that introduce new vocabulary; here (E) introduces the new concepts of *rapid* global warming and *agricultural* areas.

5. A

Did you catch the scope shift in this one? The conclusion is that "Financial success does not guarantee happiness." But the evidence is based on the responses of people who "*claimed* to have achieved financial success." If most

of these people were lying, then the argument falls apart for lack of evidence; (A) therefore supports the conclusion by supplying information (the people who claim financial success *are* actually financially successful) that tightens up the argument's apparent shift in scope.

(B) distorts the argument by confusing the ideas of necessity and sufficiency. The conclusion states that financial success is insufficient for happiness. Whether financial success is necessary to be happy is irrelevant.

(C) The conclusion is based on evidence concerning respondents who claimed to have achieved financial success, so the minute you see a choice beginning "many . . . who claimed *not* to have achieved financial success," you should recognize it as outside the scope and immediately cross it off. (C) also introduces a time element with no bearing on the argument.

(D) suffers from the same scope problem as (C), and therefore amounts to nothing more than useless background info: The conclusion is based on the evidence provided by the respondents who reported financial success; data about respondents who falsely claimed to be financially unsuccessful can't help strengthen the link between the author's evidence and conclusion.

(E) 180. The conclusion is based on the fact that most of the people who reported financial success also reported unhappiness. If these people were, in fact, happy, the argument would be severely weakened.

- An argument that involves a scope shift necessarily depends on the assumption that the scope shift is a valid one. To strengthen the argument, select the choice that reinforces this assumption. To weaken it, pick a choice that shows the scope shift to be invalid.

- As you practice, take note of the precise way in which the LSAT uses language. For example, if a survey shows that 25 percent of the people in a group "are happy," then you must take this evidence to mean that they actually *are* happy. But if 25 percent "*report* that they are happy," you *cannot* assume their actual happiness.

6. E

This is formal logic disguised in casual argument: Two characteristics (distance traveled by animal daily and size of group) correlate well with a third (diet); and diet correlates well with yet another characteristic, size and shape of teeth and face. (E) simply applies this to a specific case, working backward: Knowing the size and shape of an extinct animal's teeth and face should be a good clue as to what its diet was, which in turn should provide some indication as to whether or not it lived in large groups.

(A), (B), and (C) all make the same mistake of manufacturing some *specific* correlation, where the stimulus only mentioned the existence of some general connection between teeth, diet, and behavior.

(A) contains an irrelevant distinction between meat eaters and plant eaters, which is nice and all but something you can't infer.

(B) involves the effects of a special kind of diet (the results are qualities never mentioned in the stimulus).

(C) deals with the effects of the *loss* of teeth. Each of these choices goes away from the correlations outlined in the stimulus, and therefore each is unsupported.

(D) is closer than the others; at least it plays off the correlation aspect of the passage. However, it goes too far; it's a distortion. An animal's teeth and face can help determine an animal's diet, which in turn can help you figure out the distance traveled each day and the size of the group in which it lives. This in no way helps you identify the animal's *species*.

- Pay careful attention to the language of the stimulus in an Inference question. If the stimulus makes qualified assertions of a general nature (e.g., diet depends in large part . . .) you can reject any supposed inference that speaks too confidently or specifically. Learn to quickly recognize the qualified nature of an answer choice (size and shape . . . *can* establish whether . . .) that must match the tone of a qualified stimulus.

7.   B

In order to show that U.S. taxes aren't as light as they seem, the author states that U.S. tax revenues provide fewer goods and services. She goes on to say that people in the U.S. have to pay out of their own pockets for additional things such as health services, and that that's the same thing as paying a tax.

But why is it the same? The author simply extends the meaning of the word "tax" in order to make her point—which is exactly what (B) says. Essentially, her argument is that if you count *voluntary private expenditures* as taxes (although she offers no reason to believe they should be), then U.S. citizens indeed pay high taxes.

(A) A comparison of percentages is appropriate here, since the question concerns tax *rates*, not total amount of money paid in taxes.

(C) The argument is not based on "negatively charged" language; the problem isn't an appeal to emotion. And she certainly does give a reason for her view—it's just a logically flawed reason.

(D) The author doesn't generalize from her example. Instead, she uses the example to *illustrate* what she means by saying "tax rates don't tell the whole story."

(E) The only obvious alternatives the author sets up— between the U.S. being the most lightly taxed of comparable countries and the U.S. *not* being so—are indeed exclusive.

- In Flaw questions, if you have difficulty in seeing how an answer choice applies to the argument—like (E) perhaps—it probably doesn't describe the argument's flaw. In Logical Reasoning questions in general, if you find yourself having to go out of your way to justify an answer choice, then that choice is probably wrong.

8.   A

The conclusion of the stimulus, signaled by "therefore," tells you that something probably did *not* occur. There are two important terms here that have to be recognized in your characterization: Probably (versus a definite conclusion), and the *not.*

(A) and (B) both have the right form of conclusion, so hold on to them for now and see what else you can eliminate using the conclusions. If you're left with more than one option and have to characterize the evidence as well, you'll discover that (B) deviates from the original by pointing to opposing evidence—TV said damage, the paper said full destruction— and basing the conclusion on which evidence is more recent.

(C) You've got the probably, but this conclusion is positive— the fire probably *did* affect areas beyond the port. Eliminate.

(D) is tricky. It's got "probably" and "not," but this argument doesn't conclude that something probably didn't *occur.* It introduces the new element of duration.

(E) This conclusion is parallel enough to the stimulus— "damage wasn't severe" matches up acceptably to "cards weren't common"—but its conclusion is based on the *reliability* of the source of its evidence, and that knocks (E) firmly out of the running.

- Don't neglect the preliminary step, in Parallel Reasoning, of a quick scan and comparison of the six conclusions presented, in order to reduce the number of possible choices. Once you see that the stimulus conclusion is that "phenomenon X probably didn't happen [or wasn't the case]," only (A), (B), and (E) can remain in the running.

9. D

There are only two ways to increase profits: build more rooms or improve the current rooms. The second sentence says that they can't build more rooms. So if they want to increase profits, they must improve the rooms they already have. The last sentence says they *cannot* increase profits, and then asks you to provide a reason. So there's your prephrase—the correct choice must have something to do with the fact that "their rooms can't be improved." (D) is a fancy way of saying just that.

(A), (B), and (C) all offer other limits to increasing profits; that is, other reasons that Bellarian hotel owners can't make more money. However, while plausible, these reasons have nothing to do with the alternatives given in the stimulus. Even faced with 100 percent occupancy rates (A), the fixed maximum attractiveness of the site (B), and the upward pressure of labor costs (C), the hotel owners could theoretically still increase profits: by making other improvements to "what's already there." Only (D) argues otherwise.

(E) introduces a completely irrelevant distinction (Bellarian vs. foreign tourists). Who these hotels serve has no impact on the two stated alternatives for increasing profits.

- Look for clues that establish the limit of the argument's scope. Here the very first sentence tells you that there are *only* two ways to do X; once you grasp that the whole argument is built around those two alternatives, it becomes easy to reject irrelevant choices.

- On fill-in questions, take note of important keywords that lead up to the blank; this signals what *type* of statement the answer must be. For example, in this case, the word "since" tells you that the answer will be a piece of evidence that supports the conclusion in the first part of the last sentence (hotel owners cannot increase their profits).

10. A

Another formal logic stimulus, this one containing two premises: 1) All early-twentieth-century socialist and communist political philosophers were influenced by Rosa Luxemburg. 2) No one influenced by Rosa Luxemburg

(which obviously includes the philosophers mentioned above) advocated a totalitarian state. Put them together and you get (A): No early-twentieth-century socialist political philosopher advocated a totalitarian state. (No early-twentieth-century *communist* either, but the choices don't mention them.)

(B) Though no early-twentieth-century political philosopher influenced by Rosa Luxemburg advocated a totalitarian state, that doesn't mean that *only* those philosophers influenced by her failed to advocate a totalitarian state. Many others may have done so.

(C) is an unwarranted distortion. Rosa Luxemburg was certainly one person who did influence all the people in (C)'s group. However, there may have been many people besides her who influenced all early-twentieth-century communists or socialists—G.B. Shaw, Karl Marx, Aristotle, who knows?

(D) boils down to saying that among early-twentieth-century political philosophers, *only* socialists and communists were influenced by Rosa Luxemburg. But this does not follow from what you've been told; she may also have influenced early-twentieth century capitalists, distributists, anarchists, or anything else.

(E) Though you *can* infer that not every early-twentieth-century socialist and communist political philosopher advocated totalitarianism, you can't turn that around and say that every early-twentieth-century philosopher who didn't advocate totalitarianism was a socialist or communist.

- Many of the wrong answer choices in formal logic questions will make the mistake of reversing the legitimate inference. "Every socialist is against totalitarianism" doesn't mean "everyone against totalitarianism is a socialist." Learn to expect such traps when you scan the choices.

11. D

This one looks confusing, but actually boils down to something fairly straightforward: Harris argues that the endangered-species regulations should be expanded to admit the protection of hybrids. Vogel counters that hybrids do not need protection.

(A) and (C) can be ruled out immediately because Vogel never discusses the example of red wolves.

(B) neither Vogel nor Harris takes issue with the definition of the term "endangered." There may also be a very subtle scope shift at work here: The issue, as stated in (D), hinges more on what species should be protected, not necessarily which ones are "currently considered endangered."

(E) Vogel's argument is totally devoid of a "genetic research" component, so this certainly can't be the crux of the disagreement.

- The correct answer to a Point at Issue question must satisfy two criteria: 1) It must be a point that both characters address in their arguments; and 2) it must be a point about which the two characters disagree. Any choice that fails to meet either one of these criteria should be crossed off immediately.

- In essence, Point at Issue questions are testing little more than whether you've identified the topic and scope that two speakers have in common.

12. D

This one is ripe for prephrasing an answer: Hybrid species, argues Vogel, don't need protection because they can be easily revived by interbreeding the species from which they are descended. In order for this argument to fly, all the species from which hybrids are descended must still be around (extant).

(A) and (B) distort the issue by confusing what endangered-species regulations *can* do with what they *should* do. Vogel's argument is that hybrid species *should* not be protected. Whether those species can be identified (A), and whether the regulations can be enforced (B), are irrelevant.

(C) makes a useless distinction. What does captivity have to do with anything? Also, remember that Vogel's argument is very general; he doesn't get into the specifics of the red wolf and its descendants, so it's doubtful that his argument would rely on an unstated premise concerning the gray wolf.

(E) Same problem as (C): Vogel doesn't address the example of coyotes and red wolves, let alone speculate on the genetic relationship between them. Whether such a relationship exists has no bearing on his argument.

- When an argument contains a policy recommendation, watch out for choices that confuse what *can* be done with what *should* be done. For example, you may never be able to stamp out world hunger, but that doesn't mean you shouldn't want to.

- In dialogue stimuli, watch out for choices like (E)

that deal with issues raised in the wrong character's statement. This question is about Vogel's argument, so an example used only by Harris isn't likely to help.

13. A

The conclusion: The ancient settlement dates back to significantly before 1000 B.C. The evidence: A piece of building timber found at the site is substantially older than other artifacts found there which date back to 1000 B.C. Underlying this reasoning is the assumption that the piece of timber comes from, and was once a part of, the ancient settlement in question (which would, inferably, make it a valid indicator of the settlement's age). However, if the piece of timber appears to have been salvaged from an *earlier* settlement, then its usefulness as a guide to the age of the particular settlement in this stimulus becomes doubtful.

(B) provides useless background information. Nothing in the reasoning hinges on how wide an area the site occupies.

(C) makes an irrelevant comparison. The history of the tests used to determine the age of the artifacts says nothing about their relative reliability.

(D) So what? From the very beginning, the conclusion was based on only one piece of timber as evidence. The relative paucity of lumber samples is irrelevant.

(E) A strengthener: This provides additional evidence to support the conclusion that the settlement predates 1000 B.C. Always be on the lookout for 180 answer choices in Strengthen and Weaken questions—they can be tempting because the scope is right on target.

- In a weaken the argument question, it's not necessary to completely disprove the argument's conclusion. All you have to do is select the choice that makes the conclusion *significantly less likely* to be true.

- An argument is not faulty simply because it's based on limited evidence. The key is whether the conclusion logically follows from that evidence.

14. D

The keyword in this stimulus is "converted." The author concludes that at least 2,000 people were converted because 2,000 people got the book, and it's impossible to read the book and ignore the issue . . . but not ignoring the issue doesn't necessarily mean "conversion." If some of the people who received copies of *To Save the Earth* were already committed to the environmentalist cause, then the number "converted" by the Earth Association would be less than 2,000.

(A) The argument deals only with the "converted" of whom Earth Association can justly take credit. Other groups giving away copies of *To Save the Earth* are outside the scope of the argument.

(B) makes an irrelevant distinction. Whether or not they were willing to pay for it, 2,000 people got a copy of *To Save the Earth* from the Earth Association.

(C) The argument states that *To Save the Earth* is so persuasive that anyone who reads it will heed its environmentalist message. Presumably this is because of the *words* in the book, not the composition of the paper on which those words are printed. So this irrelevant and distorted choice is just silly.

(E) Two problems: First, there's a scope shift. The "environmentalist cause" in the conclusion is not necessarily the same as "the environmental program advocated by the Earth Association" in this choice. Secondly, even if these things were synonymous, (E) is closer to a restatement of the evidence in the first sentence than a necessary assumption.

- You may have noticed a fairly significant scope shift in this stimulus. The argument states that "no one who reads" *To Save the Earth* can fail to heed its message. But you have no evidence that the 2,000 people who received copies of the book from the Earth Association *actually read it*. This wasn't the key to getting the correct answer here, but being able to recognize this kind of scope shift will stand you in good stead on future LSAT questions.

- In Assumption questions, beware of choices that simply restate the evidence—some students gravitate to these because of the familiarity factor ("yeah, I recognize this idea"). But just because a choice reflects or is consistent with ideas in the argument doesn't mean that it necessarily answers the question that was asked.

15. E

A paradox: Pipe and cigar smoking is less dangerous than cigarette smoking, yet cigarette smokers who switch to pipes or cigars remain at the same level of risk as they did before they switched. A possible resolution: Former cigarette smokers inhale smoke in a different, and presumably more harmful way, than those who never smoked cigarettes.

(A), (B), (C), and (D) all provide useless background information. These choices furnish data on the effects of various types of smoking—(A), (B), and (C)—or on the habits of smokers (D), but none helps to explain why cigarette smokers remain in as much danger as before despite switching to the supposedly lower risk pipes or cigars.

- Don't let the unfamiliar wording throw you. If you're asked to resolve or explain why two pieces of evidence in the passage seem at odds, or seem to lead to a surprising conclusion or result, then it's a Paradox question.

- Sometimes a very simple, general prephrase can still lead you to the correct choice. Here, for example, you may have latched onto the notion that "there has to be a difference between the way former cigarette smokers and non–cigarette smokers smoke pipes or cigars." You wouldn't necessarily come up with the specifics, but it's enough to recognize correct answer choice (E).

16. C

The production manager's second sentence states that since the company has the technology to make a safer version of the materials, they should *only* sell the safer version. (C)'s principle is a direct restatement of that sentence.

(A) is no good because it's the *sales* manager who raises the issue of funding, not the production manager, who never mentions how the improvements will be paid for.

(B) is irrelevant because the materials in question *do* meet safety codes, as the production manager states right in his first sentence.

(D) is way off. The production manager never mentions reviewing the safety codes at all, so this principle doesn't fit. Also, (D) introduces a scope shift; it involves "technologically *more advanced*" products, but you can't be sure these are the same as the *safer* products produced with the aid of new technology.

(E) is out because while the production manager does argue for making the materials safer, he doesn't claim the company should keep researching new technologies—rather, his point is that since the company happens to already have the technology, it should use it.

- The answer to a Principle question is usually the choice that expresses the key concepts and terms left out by the other choices. In this case, (C) is the only choice that directly deals with the issue of replacing the current product with a safer one.

- In dialogues, be sure to isolate the argument each person is making. Often wrong choices, like (A), will play off the *other* person's argument.

- Like lawyers, the LSAT test makers use language very precisely, and in this way often slip scope shifts into the argument or choices. As you saw in (D), *using technology* to make safer products isn't the same thing as making *technologically more advanced products.*

17. A

The sales manager argues that stopping the sale of the current, less safe product will render the company unable to develop and promote the safer product. In other words, carrying out one part of the production manager's proposal would make the company unable to carry out the other part.

(B) The sales manager never mentions authority at all, and certainly doesn't challenge the production manager's authority.

(C) The production manager doesn't assume that the new product is safe *because* it's safer than the current one; he argues that the current product *is* relatively safe (it's met the safety standards), but the new one is even *safer.*

Besides, since the sales manager uses the terms "safer" and "less safe" in the same way as the production manager, she doesn't quibble with his conclusions about safety.

(D) As you saw in (C), the sales manager *agrees* with the production manager's conclusions about safety, so she certainly doesn't propose any new standards for judging safety.

(E) Once again, it seems as if the sales manager agrees with the product manager's conclusions about safety, so nothing indicates that she's overestimated the new technology. The only thing that she possibly overestimates is the company's ability to *sell* the new technology, but that's a different issue altogether from the one in (E).

- Avoid skipping stimuli that come with two questions. Once you've taken the time to answer one of the questions, the other one usually isn't difficult.

- In dialogues, isolate the argument each person is making and read the second argument with respect to its relation to the first.

18. A

The Grand Banks cod estimate is arrived at by averaging two other estimates: a sampling-based estimate and a commercial estimate. During the last decade, the commercial estimate increased *by about the same amount* that the sampling-based estimate decreased. Based on that, it's pretty safe to infer that the average of those two numbers—that is, the official estimate—has stayed about the same for the past 10 years.

(B) The old number vs. percent trap: The commercial estimate is based on the *rate* at which cod are caught: the number of fish caught per kilometer of net, per hour. The fact that this *rate* has increased is no reason to infer that the *number* of commercial vessels has also increased.

(C) makes an unsupported comparison between the two estimates, with no basis whatsoever in the stimulus.

(D) is even worse than (C), throwing out the commercial estimate entirely. There's absolutely no support given in the stimulus for this recommendation.

(E) is too precise to be drawn from the info in the passage. You can't infer anything about estimates that go back 20 years, because you simply don't have information regarding estimates at that time.

- Don't get caught up in details before you get a handle on the overall situation. Here, it was imperative that you first understood that there was one estimate, arrived at by averaging two other estimates. Then, when you find out that one of the base estimates increased as much as the other decreased, the correct inference should suggest itself.

- The stimulus simply *describes* a phenomenon; the likelihood that you can infer a recommendation (D) from a qualified descriptive neutral-sounding passage like this one is minimal.

19. C

The correct choice has to account for the difference between the trend in the commercial estimate and that in the research-based estimate. You may have been able to prephrase an answer here, something along the lines of: "The commercial vessels somehow got better at catching cod than the research vessels."

Even if you didn't prephrase, the improvement in fishing technology described by (C) should have cleared up the mystery for you. Bagging more large schools of cod explains an increase in the rate of fish caught per hour, and hence an increase in the commercial estimate. This may even help to explain the decrease in the research-based estimate; there may simply be fewer cod around for the research vessels to collect, given the new technology employed by the commercial vessel.

(A) Makes things worse, not better, since it would mean that the commercial vessels might be catching even more cod than you think—and you were already surprised by their numbers. In addition, if underreporting impacts the estimates, it may have impacted them all along, so this doesn't explain the *change*.

(B) Once again, the number of vessels involved is irrelevant, since you need to explain a discrepancy in averages.

(D) Useless background information. This simply elaborates on the stimulus's description of the two estimates, without connecting that information to the opposite changes they experience.

(E) suggests that there may be fewer cod around to catch, which could explain the decrease in the research-based estimate, but not how the commercial estimate could increase at the same time.

- For Paradox questions, make sure you understand precisely the paradox you're supposed to explain. Here the problem is the opposite *changes* in the estimates. Any choice not accounting for this kind of change is out.

20. A

The longer a pretzel remains in contact with your teeth, the more likely it is to cause a cavity. Likewise, a caramel that remains in contact with your teeth for a long time is more likely to cause a cavity than a caramel that remains in contact with your teeth for a short time. But that doesn't mean that a *pretzel* is more likely to cause a cavity than

a *caramel*. You have no basis for comparing caramels to pretzels, only caramels to caramels and pretzels to pretzels. As (A) wordily puts it, you can't apply the correlation between time-in-the-mouth and likelihood-of-producing-cavities across categories (e.g., pretzels and caramels).

(B) There's no ambiguity in any of the terms used. The problem isn't in language, but in logic.

(C) The argument isn't based on examples that represent classes, but rather on general information about classes (pretzels and caramels). The problem is that the argument uses information that is valid only *within* classes to draw a conclusion *across* classes.

(D) There *is* cause-and-effect here: Eating pretzels and caramels can cause cavities (the rest of the stimulus deals with a correlation: longer tooth contact to greater cavity likelihood). Does the author confuse cause with effect? If so, then the proper cause-and-effect should be "Getting cavities causes one to eat pretzels and caramels." Uh . . . no.

(E) The premises don't contradict each other, and there's no reason they can't all be true. On the contrary, they seem quite plausible. It's the conclusion drawn from them that's bogus.

- In some questions, it's difficult to prephrase an answer. Don't hesitate to jump right into the answer choices when nothing occurs to you immediately.

- The chief difficulty here lies in the phrasing of the choices. When you find the choices confusing, try to zero in on keywords. (A), for instance, focuses on the issue of "within categories" vs. "across categories," which should ring a bell. In (C), the crux is "general" vs. "particular," and "examples representing classes," neither of which fits the argument.

21. C

The key here is "to counter evidence offered by Tina." If a choice doesn't relate to Tina's evidence, eliminate it. Only (C) deals with an aspect of Tina's argument, the information on the heavy need for petroleum to make paper: (C), which explains that petroleum isn't used to run the paper mills anymore, is an effective counter to this.

(A), (B), (D), and (E) all fail on the same count; they're not specifically related to Tina's evidence. On top of that major flaw, there are other problems with these choices.

(A) and (E), if anything, provide additional evidence to support Tina's claim that paper cups are even more harmful to the environment than foam.

(B) is outside the scope: Consumer preference has no bearing on this discussion, since the consumers are incapable of altering the effects of cup production on the environment.

(D), which is all about styrene, a Mark issue, not only has nothing to do with Tina's evidence, but also hurts Mark's argument to boot.

- Decode the question stem carefully. Here, you're specifically asked to attack Tina's *evidence*, not simply to find something to weaken her argument. The right answer has to address a specific part of Tina's evidence, which allowed you to identify all of the wrong choices.

- Elimination works well as a strategy here. The correct choice wasn't easy to prephrase, but careful evaluation of the choices shows that (A), (B), (D), and (E) clearly don't satisfy the requirement of the question stem.

22. D

Mark argues for paper over plastic-foam cups; Tina argues for the opposite. Both base their respective viewpoints on the environmental damage caused by the production, transportation and disposal of foam and paper cups. So to evaluate their recommendations, you must first decide how much weight should be given to each part of the available evidence.

(A) doesn't help you decide the issue. Even if you knew how soon each of the kinds of harm cited by Mark and Tina would reach its maximum level, you would still have to evaluate which maximum level would be most harmful to the environment.

(B) conjures up an irrelevant distinction. Whether some societies use more disposable goods than others has no bearing on the relative ills of the two types of disposable goods under discussion.

(C) It may well be necessary to seek a new, alternative form of disposable cup, but even if you knew that, it wouldn't help you decide the issue in question—whether paper or foam is more harmful to the environment.

(E) is an irrelevant distinction. How much liquid each type of cup can hold has nothing to do with how much damage it does to the environment.

- To test an answer choice in a "relevant information" question, ask "If I knew the answer to this question, would I have a better understanding of the argument?" If the answer is no, eliminate it. Here, even if you weren't sure about correct choice (D), using this test would have helped you to eliminate the other four choices.

- If you encounter a question stem that seems unfamiliar and you're not sure how to approach it, don't get bogged down. Circle the question in your test booklet and move on. Come back to it after you've answered the rest and then let your common sense and your critical thinking skills guide you to the correct choice.

23. D

Begin by characterizing the flaw. Because Sabina possesses neither of two symptoms of tooth decay and gum disease, says the stimulus, she must not have either ailment—ignoring the possibility that those ailments may come with *other* symptoms that Sabina may have. The same structure is present, even more clearly, in (D): Because Yolanda is interested in neither of two branches of science that are associated with a medical career, she shouldn't study medicine—ignoring the possibility that one's interest in *other* fields might make it wise for one to go into medicine.

(A) The only real flaw here is that the first sentence doesn't exactly provide the evidence needed to make the argument work. If you were told that people who drink a lot of coffee *do* get the jitters (as opposed to "are said to have" the jitters), then the argument would be logically valid: In that case, coffee-addicted med students should indeed not go into either specialty, because neither specialty can be handled when one has the jitters. So (A) isn't 100 percent sound as written, but unlike the original stimulus and (D), in no sense does it commit the "fallacy of denying the antecedent."

(B) Besides its extraneous if-clause, (B) errs by dropping a key term (medical degree) from its conclusion, something the stimulus doesn't do.

(C) Besides its extraneous "probably," (C) also drops a key term (suffering from an allergy).

(E) Besides its positive conclusion, (E) errs in its scope shift ("specialized training" vs. "accurate diagnosis") not present in the stimulus.

24. E

The first sentence merely gives you setup information. The second sentence gives you the crux of the evidence, so paraphrase what it says to make it more concrete: If you run one hundred clean pieces of luggage past the scanner, it will wrongly sound an alert only once. The author concludes from this that in 99 out of a 100 actual alerts, explosives will be present.

Did you see the scope shift? The evidence and conclusion deal with percentages based on two different groups: The evidence involves the percentage of *clean pieces* of luggage that trigger false alerts, while the conclusion deals with the percentage of *alerts* that are accurate (meaning that the luggage does contain explosives).

(A) The argument is only interested in cases when the alert actually sounds—cases when the alert fails to do so are outside the scope.

(B) The argument doesn't base a general conclusion on a sample, it bases a conclusion about one percentage on evidence about another percentage. Also, there's no reason to suspect bias.

(C) is outside the scope, since the argument only concerns the functioning of the scanner and has nothing to do with the actions of the operator.

(D) introduces a false distinction. The argument is interested in the scanner's performance testing explosives *in general*, so it doesn't matter if some explosives are easier to detect than others.

- In questions involving percentages, keep track of what groups the percentages are based on. In a case like this, even if you can't get past the confusing statistical data, just noticing the scope shift—that is, recognizing that the groups the percentages are based on change from evidence to conclusion—should be enough to help you get to the credited answer.

25. A

When you were growing up, the phrase you used to yell when you fooled somebody was "Fake out! Fake out!" You can almost hear the test writers yelling it with regard to this question.

Each of the formal statements defines a condition necessary for a result (phrases like "unless" and "only if" signal the necessity). But just because a necessary condition has been met doesn't mean that the result must occur.

In the first sentence, cease-fire violations will occur *unless* negotiations begin soon. And negotiations *do* begin soon—the stem says so. But it's still possible that the cease-fire violations will occur, because a quick start to negotiations is only *necessary* for avoiding violations, not necessarily sufficient for doing so.

Therefore, when asked for a statement that need not be true, you have to choose (A)—it's *possible* that violations don't occur, but it's just as possible that they do. And as for all the additional conditions and clauses in the stimulus? Fake out!

(B) No negotiations can occur until the international troops have demonstrated that they can control aggression; if negotiations do begin, the international troops must have fulfilled this condition.

(C) is essentially the same inference as (B); as the last sentence says, when the international troops show they can counter aggression, they thereby suppress a major incentive for the sides to resume fighting.

(D) follows from the second sentence; negotiations can begin *only if* other countries have exerted pressure on the two sides.

(E) follows from the second part of the second sentence; an agreement will emerge *only if* other countries pressure the two sides throughout the negotiations.

- When a question stem says that all of the following EXCEPT one choice is an inference, don't bother to try to prephrase. There are infinite possibilities for non-inferences.

- If a question asks for a choice that *isn't* an inference, see if you can treat the stimulus statements in isolation and avoid getting caught up in a lengthy chain of reasoning. Look at each choice and compare it to the relevant statement or statements.

26. B

The evidence says that if Blankenship Enterprises switches suppliers, then it will not show a profit. The conclusion reverses this, and says that if Blankenship Enterprises failed to show a profit, then it must have switched suppliers.

You've come to know this as "the fallacy of affirming the consequent": You're not allowed to simply flip the "if" and "then" terms of a conditional statement. Although you know that switching suppliers would account for a failure to make a profit, it's not necessarily the only possible cause of such a failure. And that's all that (B) says, in so many words.

(A) is far from the truth: The conclusion doesn't even follow from the evidence, so it can hardly be a *restatement* of same (which is what "circular" means).

(C) There's no change in the meaning of the word "profit"— it's a constant throughout the argument.

(D) There's no universal conclusion; the author never looks beyond Blankenship Enterprises.

(E) misses the point. The issue isn't whether one event causes the other, but whether the occurrence of one event is absolutely necessary for the occurrence of a second event. Whether or not there's some basic underlying cause for the occurrence of both events is irrelevant.

- The mistake made here is one of the most common in LSAT Logical Reasoning. There are many ways to describe it—it's basically a matter of taking "if A occurs then B will also occur" to mean "B can never occur unless A does too" (or vice versa). Keep your eye open for this flaw as you do Logical Reasoning; become an expert in spotting it. It occurs in many guises and it's always wrong.

SECTION III: READING COMPREHENSION

PASSAGE 1—Neurogenesis

Topic and Scope

Neurogenesis (the birth of new neurons)—specifically, whether traditional thinking about vertebrate neurogenesis needs modification in light of research into how the process seems to work in canary brains

Purpose and Main Idea

To suggest that current thinking about vertebrate (especially human) neurogenesis needs to be modified in light of research into canary brains. The author's main idea is that the results of this research both defy the existing theory about vertebrate neurogenesis and open up the possibility that human brains may have the capability to regenerate themselves.

Paragraph Structure

Paragraph 1 outlines the traditional theory that vertebrate neurogenesis basically doesn't exist—that an adult vertebrate's brain cannot create new nerve cells. The contrast keyword "However" in line 10 signals that the passage is about to provide some evidence to the contrary and, predictably, paragraphs 2 and 3 go on to discuss in detail the behavioral and neurological evidence (from canaries) that throws the accuracy of the traditional theory into question.

In paragraph 4, the author addresses the implications of these research findings for humans. The contrast keyword "Although" in line 48 serves to distinguish the general scientific community's skeptical response from the author's much more optimistic stance that human brains may be able to regenerate themselves.

The Big Picture

- A good grasp of a passage doesn't mean assimilating all of its details (you can look them up if you have to). It means understanding what the author's doing in the text—in this case, understanding that the author's taking issue with the traditional theory of vertebrate neurogenesis (and its implications for the human brain) by providing evidence that contradicts it.

- While the author's specific main idea isn't entirely clear until you've read through the whole passage, topic, scope, and purpose are all revealed early. That makes this passage an ideal place to begin working in the Reading Comprehension section, even if you're a science-phobe. Topic, scope, and purpose, after all, are the three things you need to grab onto as quickly as possible in order to get a passage under control.

- If you suffer from "science anxiety," this passage should have come as a pleasant surprise to you. In practice, even the most jargon-filled and complex science passage won't prove very difficult if you apply the Kaplan techniques for critical reading.

The Questions

1. A

It's a Global question, so you've already done the work; (A) is a match for your prediction.

(B) focuses on a detail. Moreover, the author suggests that there's no difference between canary brains and the brains of other vertebrates in this respect—if he believed otherwise, why would he suggest that research findings about canary brains have implications for vertebrate neurogenesis in general?

(C) The author asserts precisely the opposite. Canary research breaks with the traditional theory of vertebrate neurogenesis, and supplies clues as to how researchers may discover neurogenesis in the human brain.

(D) and (E) have scope problems. Both choices have other problems as well.

(D) should have limited itself to "supply of vertebrate brain cells," not the overly broad "supply of brain cells," while (E) should have confined itself to "older hypotheses about vertebrate neurogenesis," not the more encompassing "older hypotheses."

(D) is too categorical; the author's more cautious in his conclusions. As for (E), the author never states that vertebrates other than canaries are subject to a "yearly cycle."

- Incorrect choices in global questions often include inviting familiar language. Knowing what you're looking for before you attack the choices will help protect you from being drawn in by that familiarity.

2. D

Lines 21–24 say that the canary's singing ability decreases during the late summer and fall. Lines 35–38 attribute this seasonal decrease to a 38 percent drop in the number of neurons in those parts of the brain that control singing. This is simply another way of saying that those regions of the brain decrease in size during the late summer and fall.

(A) 180: Lines 24–27 and 32–33 indicate that the canary's song repertoire matures in the *spring*.

(B) And 180 again: The new song-learning neurons are generated during the winter and spring months.

(C) distorts the text: Canaries do learn a new repertoire of songs (during the winter and spring), but there's no indication that these songs are based on the songs of fellow canaries.

(E) Canaries largely lose their ability to sing during the late summer and fall, after which they learn "entirely new" songs for the next breeding season.

- Never try to answer an explicit text question on a hunch or a vague remembrance of the text. Use the information or line reference in the question stem to find the relevant piece(s) of text and reread, reread, reread.

3. B

The ratio of brain weight to body weight is mentioned as a possible explanation for neurogenesis in canaries only. This ratio has no direct connection per se to the larger issue of general vertebrate neurogenesis, and certainly not to human neurogenesis in particular.

(A) The author's entire argument rests on the supposition that humans, like canaries, may have the capability to generate new nerve cells; thus, it's safe to infer that he'd consider research on neurological similarities to be important.

(C) The author alludes to the importance of studying infant neurogenesis in lines 54–58.

(D) The importance of understanding how long-term memory works in order to determine the possible effects of neurogenesis on long-term memory is suggested in lines 52–54.

(E) Similarly, the author suggests in lines 52–54 that it's important to understand how complex learning takes place in order to figure out the possible effects neurogenesis might have on complex learning.

- In Inference questions, beware of choices—like (B) here—that are outside the author's scope.

4. C

If it were true that birds similar to the canary have bigger brains, the author's explanation for canary neurogenesis would be placed in jeopardy. In paragraph 3, after all, he argues that canary neurogenesis occurs because the canary needs to possess a lot of information in order to sing, yet has a small brain adapted for flight. Hence its brain, with its limited storage capacity, has to generate new nerve cells every year in order for it to relearn how to sing.

(A) is consistent with the author's explanation. He suggests that canary neurogenesis is spurred in part by the canary's long lifetime.

(B) The author's basic explanation, which rests on the link between limited brain capacity and neurogenesis cycles, isn't fundamentally threatened by cyclic differences from species to species.

(D) has no impact on the author's explanation, as he draws no link between the ability to sing and the ability to fly.

(E) is consistent with the author's explanation, which suggests that singing ability is directly related to brain size.

- Don't nitpick over incorrect choices. Worrying about their precise meaning will tie you up if you're not careful. Only one choice will be categorically correct. Once you've found it, quickly discard the other choices.

5. D

Lines 12–14 draw a comparison between the way canaries learn to sing and the way humans learn to speak. Thus, the word "vocabulary" is meant to evoke a sense of this similarity by applying a concept taken from human speech to canary song.

(A) echoes the substance of the detail rather than addressing *why* the author included it in the text.

(B) and (E) go too far. Indeed, the author never even discusses "patterned groupings of sounds" in canary songs or "the syllabic structures of words" (B). Nor does the text compare the level of complexity of canary song and human speech (E).

(C) goes against the text, which reveals that canary songs are anything but stable and uniform over the course of the bird's lifetime. Lines 19–27, in fact, stress just the opposite of what (C) says.

- Questions often ask about the *why* of a detail or paragraph—that's why you've got to be most interested in "paragraph sense," not in content.

6. A

Lines 40–43 explicitly state that a long life span may help to account for canary neurogenesis.

(B) through (E) mention subjects that are connected in some way to canary neurogenesis, but none of them is ever described as a possible *cause* of same.

- If you didn't go back to the text and reread, all of the choices may have looked good to you. Rereading, contrary to what you may think, will actually *save* time, by allowing you to throw out incorrect choices in short order.

7. C

Lines 28–32 present research results. Lines 32–40 provide additional details bearing on these results. And lines 40–47 furnish a possible explanation for the results.

(A) is off target. No theory is presented, let alone "analyzed" or "modified." Moreover, this choice makes no reference to the research results and facts provided in paragraph 3.

(B), (D), and (E) are outside the scope of paragraph 3. Only one set of research results is "advanced," and there's no talk of "a shared principle" among different studies, eliminating (B). And the research results aren't applied to "a related field" (D). Both of these choices try to tempt you into seeing a connection between research on canary and human neurogenesis that just isn't in paragraph 3.

Similarly, (E) tries to tempt you by making reference to the traditional view of neurogenesis, which is brought up in paragraph 1.

- Be careful not to get hooked by choices that refer to the wrong part of the passage. Don't stray too far from the detail or paragraph in question.

8. C

Beginning in line 10, the author discusses "new evidence for neurogenesis." Furthermore, this new evidence "might help uncover a mechanism" (line 50) to promote human neurogenesis, despite the fact that "neurogenesis in the adult mammalian brain is still not generally accepted" (lines 48–49). Based on these sentiments, it's clear that the author believes that the "current understanding of neurogenesis" is "incomplete."

(A) and (B) express sentiments that are the opposite of the author's. According to him, the traditional view of neurogenesis is neither comprehensive (A), nor forward-thinking (B).

(D) and (E), on the other hand, take the author's view to an unwarranted extreme. "Incomplete" is not the same thing as "antiquated" (D) or "incorrect" (E).

- Always take the passage's "temperature." Know whether the author's got an opinion on the topic, and, if he or she does, watch for words or phrases that'll give you some insight into just how committed the author is to that opinion.

PASSAGE 2—Free African Americans in Colonial Virginia

Topic and Scope

The African American experience in colonial Virginia in the 1600s—specifically, the merits and drawbacks of Breen and Innes's book *Myne Owne Ground*

Purpose and Main Idea

The author wants to argue that while Breen and Innes "contribute significantly" to a more positive and "welcome" historical view of the lives of freed African Americans, they stumble by underemphasizing "much evidence" that, as slavery became more entrenched in the 1660s, living conditions for free blacks in colonial Virginia grew tougher.

Paragraph Structure

Paragraph 1 cites the book's strengths, associating it with "a recent, welcome shift [in historical studies]" from those centering on slaveholder-caused misery to those centering on African American–created accomplishment.

The rest of paragraph 1 and the opening of paragraph 2 specify ways in which free African Americans exercised control over their lives. Paragraph 2 moves from praise to qualified criticism: Breen and Innes overlook the fact that increasing restrictions (both "customary" and "statutory" laws) in the 1660s made Virginia inhospitable for free blacks like Anthony Johnson.

The Big Picture

This passage fits some familiar and oft-repeated LSAT patterns:

- It's a book review in which the author gives a balanced evaluation, with both praise and pointed criticism. You can bet that questions will hinge on these points.
- The opening 10–20 lines—always key—offer a classic contrast: between an outdated viewpoint and a newer, hipper perspective. This kind of contrast occurs over and over in LSAT passages. (The author's purpose, after all, is to discuss B's and I's contribution to the new perspective.)
- Note the shift between the paragraphs: paragraph 1 praises the book; paragraph two moves steadily into criticism. The distinct separation of focus eases your job—*finding the answers!*

The Questions

9. E

It's a Detail question, so go back to the passage. (E) paraphrases a point made in the first sentence: For years, scholars tended to ignore "what Africans in the United States were able to accomplish despite the effects of [slavery]."

(A) refers to irrelevant material from paragraph 2. Customary and statutory law are discussed only in relation to Breen and Innes's book.

(B), (C), and (D) are outside the passage's scope. The author never implies that most scholars have tended to deal only in "broad interpretations" (B); and note how off the wall (C) and (D) sound. Historians have focused in on "the least eventful periods"? And downplayed discussion of the economic side of slavery? Oh come now. Both sound pretty unlikely, don't you think?

- If you're careful with the opening lines, the paraphrase in (E) should snap into place. The only hassle is getting past the first four choices. Luckily, though, . . .
- Three choices—(B), (C), and (D)—have nothing whatever to do with this author's ideas. Choices like these should be skimmed and dismissed, with no further thought.

10. B

The author emphasizes the major issue of growing legal restrictions in paragraph 2, in the middle of which he states that customary and statutory law "was closing in on free African Americans well before the 1670s." During the previous decade, after a "dramatic" increase in the proportion of African Americans, Virginia began passing legal restrictions. (B) paraphrases the idea.

(A) contradicts the essential point: The pace of legal restrictions on black people was picking up during the period.

(C) sounds plausible but is never implied. Answers must jibe with evidence in the passage.

(D) is never implied and also picks up on irrelevant information (indentured servants) in paragraph 1. Paragraph 2 says nothing about them. A tempting choice only if the reference to dates in line 17 make you think the answer is to be found nearby.

(E) mentions growing numbers of blacks, but the notion that some regions adhered more rigidly to customary law is never implied.

- Long, wordy stems and choices can make questions look tougher than they really are. You can save such questions for last if you like, but note the clear similarity between (B) and the bigger point of paragraph two: Growing legal restrictions made life increasingly hard for free African Americans. Keep thinking, and reading, for "gist."

11. A

Details are usually mentioned to support bigger points. According to the passage, the Johnsons moved to escape worsening conditions in Virginia. The bigger point is that Breen and Innes underestimated those conditions. The Johnsons' situation, then, is mentioned to illustrate a shortcoming of Breen and Innes's thesis (A).

(B) is tempting, but the point is not that Breen and Innes failed to note the specific case of the Johnsons. To "underemphasize" (line 42) is not to "overlook."

(C) Distortion: The Johnsons' story is cited to criticize, not add support to, Breen and Innes's thesis.

(D) 180: According to the opening lines, the author is critical of the standard interpretation.

(E) Another distortion. The author cites a new historiographical approach (and praises Breen's and Innes's book for applying it) in the opening lines.

- Read the stem carefully, then check the relevant text in the passage and come up with a rough prephrase of the answer. Finally, scan the choices aggressively for a rough equivalent of your idea.
- With a good, solid prephrase in mind as you skim

the five choices, the correct one is more likely to snap into place, and wrong ones can be quickly dismissed.

12. D

(D) corresponds to the shift that occurs between the paragraphs: paragraph 1 praises Breen and Innes's book, and paragraph 2 then focuses on criticism. Only (D)— "qualified approval"—corresponds to the mixed review.

(A) Far too negative.

(B) Far too positive.

(C) Too negative.

(E) There's no evidence anywhere for "puzzlement."

- If you recall the outlines of the argument (the gist of each paragraph) and roughly prephrase the likely answer (the author's attitude is "mixed"), you can sidestep distracting choices like "contentious challenge" and "sincere puzzlement" and zero straight in on (D).

13. D

You've already done the groundwork here—the author's purpose was to "argue" certain things about Breen and Innes's book. The answer choices here are very general, so you have to abstract that a bit. Only (D) jibes with the fact that this is a review of somebody's book—it's as simple as that.

(A) is far too narrow; only in the opening sentence does the author "summarize previous interpretations." The focus then changes.

(B) Also too narrow. The author praises a new historiographical approach in the passage's second sentence, but then zeroes in on Breen and Innes's book, which he isn't advocating, but evaluating.

(C) The verb "propose" is wrong: The author isn't *proposing* a thesis (of his own); he's describing somebody else's.

(E) The author's discussing a book, not a "historical event."

- In Global questions, abstract-sounding choices like these needn't pose a problem. As always, add up the gists of the paragraphs and look for the corresponding choice, which should fit like a well-tailored shirt. Accept nothing less.

PASSAGE 3—Watteau's World

Topic and Scope

Eighteenth-century artist Watteau—specifically, the relationship between Watteau's work, historical events during his lifetime, and perceptions of him by 19-century writers

Purpose and Main Idea

The author's purpose is to prove that there was a "blind spot" in 19th-century books that regard Watteau as *the* guy—*the* representative of that "witty and amiable 18th century." Part one of this argument is to show that war-torn 18th-century France was anything but "witty and amiable." Part two is to offer some explanations as to why 19th-century writers so blatantly ignored the historical facts. All things considered, this passage has the air of a Logical Reasoning Paradox problem.

Paragraph Structure

Paragraph 1 describes Watteau's increasing popularity in the 18th and 19th centuries as an artist who captured the "witty and amiable" character of 18th-century life.

Paragraph 2 provides a reality check, pointing out that the early 18th century was in fact a pretty miserable period for France, notable more for its years of military defeat and disastrous famine than for its lyricism.

Paragraph 3 attempts to explain the "blind spot" in 19th-century books about Watteau: Some writers just ignored the facts, while others simply argued that artists aren't necessarily influenced by their environment. Note the final twist on this position—some writers were so pro-Watteau that they even argued that he was *predicting* the society that evolved after his death.

The Big Picture

- The purpose of this passage is typical LSAT: Some academic takes issue with a traditional, accepted

interpretation of a historical period or an artist's work (in this case, it's both) and tries to set the record straight.

- The key thing in such passages is to keep the author's opinions separate from the views of those deluded scholars he or she is attempting to refute.

- Whether you tend to be comfortable with humanities passages or not, this one practically screamed "Attack me early in the section!" That's because of that keyword emphasis signal "curious blind spot." From those three little words virtually the entire structure is revealed to you, because you know that three questions will inevitably be raised and answered: What was the blind spot? What was the real story? And *why* were the people in question deluded? And note that all by themselves, these three questions come very close to paraphrasing the contents of correct choice (E) for question 14.

The Questions

14. E

The trick here is to be clear about the paragraph topics, and that's work you should have done up front. Once again, paragraph one outlines the viewpoint of Watteau's 19th-century biographers, paragraph 2 pokes it full of holes by presenting the historical facts, and paragraph three explains why those biographers persisted in their beliefs *in spite* of the evidence. (E) fits the way this argument develops.

(A) gets the link between paragraphs 2 and 3 wrong: The author doesn't *evaluate* or *refine* the evidence presented in paragraph 2.

(B) The *author* doesn't use the passage to test an assumption. The passage does deal with 19th-century assumptions about Watteau, but it goes far beyond simply rejecting them as counterfactual.

(C) doesn't account for paragraph 2; also, the author doesn't advance 2 separate theories about the historians' "blind spot."

(D) The author provides evidence that proves the *inaccuracy* of Watteau's 19th-century image. Beware of 180 answer choices—they can be tempting because they're directly on point.

- Summing up the gist of the paragraph topics really helps when the answer choice language is abstract. If you can approach the answer choices with a *fairly*

clear idea of what each paragraph is about, you'll be less inclined to try to make the wrong answers fit the passage—a common misstep that students take in abstract questions like this one.

15. D

The end of paragraph one explains the most basic reason for Watteau's reputation. Writers, aristocrats, and would-be aristocrats ignored the historical facts because Watteau presented such a flattering picture of 18th-century French life.

(A) is tricky: According to paragraph 3, it was only the *minority* of writers who developed the sophisticated argument that Watteau was transcending reality.

(B) also refers to this minority of writers (paragraph 3) who opposed the determinist stance.

(C) is well outside the scope; no lack of historical source material is discussed.

(E) distorts the passage. Nothing as radical as a political bias towards aristocrats is mentioned.

- The keywords "Most," "those," and "Even some . . . " indicate that the passage is dealing with three different groups of Watteau admirers in paragraph 3. Take note whenever contrasting viewpoints are mentioned, because questions that hinge on them are sure to follow.

16. E

This Detail question can be answered quickly with reference to paragraph three, which explains that the determinist viewpoint was "unthinkable" to these particular Watteau fanatics because Watteau was quintessentially French, even though born in a Flemish town. (E) captures the logic of this faction—if artists *were* primarily influenced by their environment, Watteau would have produced "quintessentially Flemish" works.

(A) 180: Watteau was widely admired precisely *because* people believed in the determinist philosophy.

(B) is geographically outside the scope—the passage never discusses Watteau's popularity outside of France.

(C) can be quickly rejected because the passage never considers Watteau's *view of himself*. Watteau is of course long dead and buried during the events and viewpoints of the passage (happy 200th birthday, Pierre—see line 20).

(D) Abstruse phrasing should flag this choice as outside the scope. There's no debate about "simple" versus "complex"

explanations offered, nor is the author concerned with why Watteau's works were charming.

- Don't get sucked in by wordy choices. Go from the stem to the passage, prephrase the answer, and then scan the choices *with the author's ideas in mind*. You'll find that a lot of choices, like (B), (C), and (D) here, just don't click. The only one that's worth your time and thought is the correct one.

17. B

True to its pole position at the head of paragraph one, the "blind spot" is the problem in 19th-century scholarship that the author attacks throughout the passage. It's the "obvious discrepancy" between 19th-century writers' acceptance that Watteau portrayed his age realistically, and the historical facts mentioned in paragraph 2.

(A) and (D) misrepresent the author's position: She doesn't single out anything "admirable" about Watteau's work or accuse others of not appreciating Watteau enough.

(C) presents an even wilder distortion: No willful disregard of available evidence is cited.

(E) goes beyond the scope, since no neglected contemporaries are discussed.

18. C

The correct choice nicely paraphrases the argument in paragraph 2.

(A) 180: 19th-century admirers thought Watteau's accomplishments were extremely important.

(B), (D), and (E) all distort the passage. The author never endorses the deterministic standpoint (D) or indicates whether she finds Watteau's work lyrical and charming or otherwise (B). The extreme language in (E) ("*impossible* for any work of art to personify or represent a particular historical period") helps tag this wrong answer choice.

- Questions that ask about the author's attitude or viewpoint are *not* going to relate to minor issues or passing details. Sure, choices (A), (B), and (D) all remind you of issues raised in the passage. But they don't capture the overall thrust of the passage the way (C) does.

19. A

Paragraph 2 describes conditions in France during Watteau's lifetime: Social upheaval caused by war summarizes the "calamitous" events.

(B) describes 19th-century nostalgia for the witty and amiable past—not what actually occurred during Watteau's life.

(C) distorts paragraph one's brief mention of the aristocracy.

(D) also relates to paragraph 1, but Watteau's popularity with the aristos (and aristo wannabes) occurred *after* his death.

(E) is outside the scope—no sweeping generalizations about French society in this passage.

- If the wording of the question is specific, you can bet you're looking for a specific answer. The passage discusses several different periods of French history (during Watteau's lifetime, the late 18th century, and 19th century), so the trick here was knowing which period to look at and zeroing in on the right piece of the passage.

20. D

A tricky question that depends on your picking up on the implied reasons for Watteau's success. Paragraph 1 explains why Watteau's work had such a powerful impact on French society: Engravings of his work were made available in such numbers that his work became "more accessible than any other artist until the 20th century." No word on whether he painted dogs playing poker or clowns on velvet.

(A) focuses on a detail. Sure, Watteau was successful partly because he produced "lyrical and charming" images. But you cannot subscribe to (A)'s inference that only "lyrical and charming" works of art will achieve wide recognition.

(B) is outside the scope. Nowhere does the author suggest that French society had an exceptional regard for art.

(C) is very tricky. The passage certainly links Watteau's long-standing appeal to the perception that he had captured the essential France of his time. But paragraph 1 indicates that Watteau only became France's favorite artist because his work was so widely available, so you can't infer that capturing the true nature of your society guarantees artistic success. After all, Watteau's "lyrical and charming" engravings wouldn't have had an impact if they hadn't been resurrected and sold like hot cakes. Another problem: As you know, Watteau didn't *really encapsulate* the true nature of his time; (C) makes it sound as if he did.

(E) distorts paragraph 1's brief mention of Watteau's imitators.

- Always watch out for choices that aren't true to the spirit of the passage. In question 20, for example, the tricky choice (C) *sounds* somewhat plausible until you remember that it represents the viewpoint that the author spends most of the passage attacking.

PASSAGE 4—Trial By (Misguided) Jury

Topic and Scope

Inferential errors made by juries—specifically, how these errors come about and what should be done to prevent them

Purpose and Main Idea

The author's purpose is primarily to explain the kind of inferential errors that juries can make in certain specific trial situations. Paragraph 2 provides the real meat of the passage by listing some specific examples. The final two paragraphs only briefly suggest some measures to alleviate the problem: using cognitive psychology to assess the reliability of juries in certain situations, and making judges more aware of the issue.

Paragraph Structure

Paragraph 1 introduces the topic, explaining that juries sometimes make inferential errors in their search for the truth.

Paragraph 2 provides some specific examples of the most common errors juries make (note how clearly the keywords "For example," "also," and "finally" map out the author's presentation of evidence). You also learn that most jury errors involve unwarranted conclusions. Could the judicial system benefit from a Kaplan course in Logical Reasoning?

Paragraph 3 suggests one possible solution to the problem, using cognitive psychology to assess the reliability of juries in certain situations.

Paragraph 4 calls for greater awareness of potential jury error on the part of judges.

The Big Picture

- A very straightforward passage rounds off the set. Once again, it's a familiar passage format for the LSAT, describing a problem and offering a couple of solutions to remedy it. The only real substance to the passage is paragraph 2's detailed discussion of jury errors, but not for a moment should you get bogged down in specifics there: Skim through the paragraph, note that you're mostly getting examples of unwarranted conclusions, and expect that you're gong to be returning later to this paragraph to score some points.

The Questions

21. A

Don't let the convoluted wording of the answer choices distract you. The author's overall point is basically very simple: Juries make inferential errors in certain specific situations.

(B) is too broad—the passage is about jury error, not *human cognition*.

(C) focuses on a detail, one particular cause of jury error mentioned in paragraph three.

(D) focuses narrowly on paragraph one's passing mention of everyday inferential thinking.

(E) exaggerates paragraphs 3 and 4. The passage isn't advocating replacing judges with cognitive psychologists. Come on.

- When confronting Global questions, high on your list of choices to watch for and shoot down should be: choices that focus on details, choices that are way too broad, and choices that go beyond the scope of the relevant discussion.

22. D

Paragraphs 3 and 4 address possible reforms. (D) fits well with paragraph 4's point that judges—with their "limited and primitive" understanding of the problem—aren't always fulfilling their obligation to minimize jury error through explanation and clarification.

(A) is too extreme. An LSAT passage advocating an end to jury trials? Puhleeze.

(B) Outside the scope: Formal educational requirements is an issue often discussed in relation to juries, but isn't discussed here.

(C) Defense testimony is mentioned earlier in paragraph two, a sure sign that it's not relevant to the reform discussion (paragraphs 3 and 4). In any case, misleading defense testimony is only one of several causes of jury error mentioned, so you can infer that monitoring defense testimony wouldn't provide a broadly effective remedy.

(E) should sound distinctly *au contraire;* the passage *advocates* wider understanding of psychological research.

- Question 22 underlines the importance of knowing and referring to the gist of each paragraph. Just knowing that paragraphs 3 and 4 discuss reforms (and therefore contain the answer) enables you to eliminate (A), (B), and (C) as beyond the scope.

23. D

This answer choice deftly summarizes paragraph 2, which lists three situations in which inferential error is likely to occur.

(A) has 180 stamped all over it. If anything, paragraph 2's litany of jury errors underscores the complexity of the fact-finding process.

(B) is a bit tricky, but the author doesn't specifically argue for a more careful presentation of evidence, or indeed any change in the trial process whatsoever. The gist of the passage is that judges have to be more aware that errors *are* going to occur in these specific situations.

(C) focuses narrowly on a detail. The influence of commonly held beliefs on juries (e.g., that defendants with prior conviction must be guilty) is only one cited cause of jury error.

(E) Wrong paragraph—possible reforms aren't discussed until paragraphs 3 and 4.

- Note that the keywords "For example," "also," and "finally" provide a major assist in showing that paragraph 2 is basically a list of specific examples.

24. C

(C) Captures both the tone and thrust of paragraph 4. Judges have been guilty of having only a "limited and primitive concept of jury error" and failing to acknowledge psychologists' research into the problem.

(A) has the wrong verb; LSAT authors are rarely if ever going to sound "apprehensive." You can't recall a single instance.

(B) distorts the passage; it's the juries, not the judges, who are drawing unwarranted conclusions.

(D) is also a distortion. There's nothing in paragraph 4 that actually suggests opposition from judges, nor, as you noted in question 23 choice (B), is the passage advocating "significant changes in trial procedure."

(E) should scream "wrong paragraph." Paragraph 2 mentions excessively complex evidence, but it doesn't seem to be the judges' fault.

- A sharp take-charge attitude usually pays off with Reading Comprehension answer choices. If the verb is wrong, trash it. If the issue is beyond the scope, toss it out the window. Only the correct answer is going to satisfy your critical judgment.

25. B

Definitely a tricky question. The author's argument for using psychological research in the courtroom is based on the notion that researchers can predict the situations in which inferential error will occur (see the examples in paragraph 2). (B) would present a major challenge to that argument. If researchers cannot predict how groups will act in decision-making situations, then inferential errors by juries cannot be addressed.

(A) strengthens the author's case, since he argues that human decision making conforms to patterns whereby people react in predictable ways according to the situation.

(C) isn't an effective weakener, since the author is criticizing the existing system based on the results of recent psychological research.

(D) basically strengthens the argument by asserting or implying that human decision making is predictable in controlled situations such as trials.

(E) also fits the passage in its claim that inferential error is predictable in certain situations.

- In Strengthening/Weakening questions like this one, the wrong answers will often stay true to the spirit of the passage. Here, in (A), (D), and (E), the phrases "patterns in human decision-making," "controlled situations," and "predictable circumstances" should help you rule these choices out because they remind you of the author's basic argument.

26. A

The right choice is consistent with the overall idea that those involved in the judicial process could benefit from the insights of cognitive psychologists.

(B) is too extreme; the passage does say that "complex and voluminous" evidence is often confusing for juries, but it doesn't accuse lawyers of attempting to confuse juries.

(C) Outside the scope—the inferential abilities of judges and lawyers are never compared.

(D) is also outside the scope. The passage suggests no conscientious pursuit of the truth on the part of lawyers. (Ahem.)

(E) distorts paragraph one; the author says that lawyers call the inferential process "fact-finding," but this is far short of saying that they are unrealistic about the abilities of juries.

- Many wrong answer choices in the Reading Comprehension section are wrong because they fall outside the scope of the passage or of the relevant paragraph. That's one reason that getting a clear handle on topic and scope up front and creating tight paragraph summaries is so critical.

27. E

The right choice summarizes the cause and effect of jury error described in paragraph 2: Basically, the manner in which evidence is presented leads the jury to make various types of unwarranted conclusions.

(A) 180: "complex and voluminous evidence" most often obscures the truth.

(B) distorts the passage: The author says that the jury "may" give more weight to photographic evidence, not that the jury "usually" overestimates its value.

(C) is tricky, but it's not a generalization that the author would agree with. Remember, the passage says that preconceptions about defendants with prior convictions influence juries, not that preconceptions about defendants *in general* are problematic.

(D) contradicts the passage: Juries use inferential skills "developed and used over a lifetime" (paragraph 1).

- Be ready and eager to apply your Logical Reasoning skills to the Reading Comprehension section. If an answer choice makes a strong argument such as "the more evidence juries have, the better decisions they make," or "juries usually overvalue visual evidence," make sure it jibes with the passage.

SECTION IV: LOGICAL REASONING

1. A

James's argument consists of an analogy between his house and an airplane: Just as he can do as he pleases inside his own home, so too the airlines have the right to decide smoking policies on their own property—the planes—without government interference.

Eileen responds, essentially, by breaking this analogy. She points out that whereas James's house is for his own use, airlines serve the public and must therefore consider the public's health their priority. In other words, she draws a distinction between a house, which is primarily occupied by those who own it, and an airplane, which is primarily occupied by those who *don't* own it: the public.

(B) is dead wrong; Eileen doesn't offer anything resembling a definition.

(C) describes *James's* method of argument; as you saw, he establishes an analogy between his house and an airplane. But you want *Eileen's* method, not his.

(D) might have tripped you up if you thought Eileen's contradicting James is the same as "deriving a contradiction" from his argument. No. Although Eileen disagrees with James, she does so by attacking his analogy, not by showing that his argument contains a contradiction.

(E) Eileen doesn't address James's motivation at all; she merely points out that his analogy is poor.

- In dialogue questions, make sure you keep track of who's making which argument. Wrong choices often play off the *other* person's argument, as (C) does here.

- This kind of question illustrates the importance of reading the question stem first—it allows you to focus on structure as you read the argument.

2. C

The company that makes XYZ is aware that millions of illegal copies are in use, yet they take no legal action. Why? The key here is recognizing the current "company-wide effort to boost sales." That, as (C) says, many consumers prefer to use a spreadsheet program before plunking down hard cash, provides a solid, sales-boosting reason why the company might be willing to turn a blind eye to the illegalities.

(A) is useless background. The issue is not whether XYZ *can* be copied; obviously it can. The issue is why the company

has taken a particular tack with regard to the illegal copies that have been made.

(B) is also fairly useless. If anything, that such legal measures have been available for so long just compounds the paradox of why the company hasn't taken those measures.

(D) This is an irrelevant distinction, emphasizing the degree of the company's illegal copying problem but doing nothing to explain why the company tolerates the copying.

(E) Some students attempt to make a case for (E) as the rationale for the nonprosecutions, figuring that the XYZ makers don't want to be perceived as corporate bad guys like their competitors. However, this kind of analysis requires too much work, and too many unwarranted assumptions about the motives of the XYZ company, to be correct. Specifically, you have to work too hard to establish a connection between (E)'s implied motive and its effect on XYZ sales. (C)'s connection, by contrast, is manifest.

- We mentioned this earlier in the first Logical Reasoning section, but it bears repeating: Paradox questions have many faces. Here, the question stem doesn't characterize the stimulus for you with a word like "paradox" or "discrepancy." Don't be thrown: the logical skills you needed here were the same as those needed for a more traditional Paradox question.

- Remember, there is no "second-best" answer on the LSAT. If a choice requires you to make a lot of assumptions to complete the logic, then it's just plain wrong. Eliminate it.

3. D

Kim's conclusion or main point is nicely highlighted in the last sentence by the keyword "So." Replacing gas-powered cars with electric cars would be, at best, an even trade in terms of air pollution. And remember, the argument is framed around the claim that the battery-powered electric car *would* solve the air pollution problem. Based on the last sentence, then, you can rest assured that the author disagrees with that claim and that (D) is the main point.

(A) simply restates part of Kim's evidence. It isn't the conclusion.

(B) Kim doesn't call for a reduction in driving, for one thing; for another, maybe there are ways of reducing air pollution besides "cleaner" cars; e.g., switching from coal to hydroelectric power plants. So (B) is way off in scope and point of view.

(C) is too extreme. Kim deals only with gasoline-powered cars and electric cars, concluding that the latter isn't better for air pollution than the former. To go one step further and say that Kim's point is that *all* cars create an *equal* amount of air pollution involves a major distortion.

(E) Maybe Kim believes that gasoline-powered cars are here to stay, maybe not. You just don't know; in any case, there's no way that this can be the point she set out to prove in her argument.

- Use the one-sentence test to identify an author's conclusion. Ask yourself, "What's the one thing that the author wants me to take away from this passage?"

- Keep in mind the scope of the author's argument. All Kim says about battery-powered cars is that they aren't an improvement over gasoline-powered cars in terms of air pollution. The argument remains silent on other issues such as noise or fuel economy.

4.   E

Isolate and paraphrase the components of the argument. The evidence: 1) electric cars require (surprise!) electricity, which means building new generating facilities. 2) *Most* of our generating facilities burn fossil fuels.

Conclusion: Electric cars would cause as much fossil-fuel pollution as gasoline-powered cars. Not if the new generating facilities don't burn fossil fuels, they wouldn't—so the author must be assuming that some of the new generating facilities would, in fact, burn fossil fuels.

(A) and (D) Both of these statements can be negated without damaging Kim's logic. In fact, if the number of electric cars went through the roof (A), or if electric cars *did* cause air pollution while they're running (D), either fact would reinforce Kim's point that switching to battery-powered cars wouldn't reduce air pollution.

(B) is an irrelevant comparison. Identifying the greatest producer of fossil-fuel pollution (cars, boats, airplanes, factories) is irrelevant to this argument about whether electric cars would help solve the air pollution problem.

(C) is a distortion. One last time, Kim's argument isn't about whether to replace gasoline-powered cars with electric cars; it's about whether doing so would reduce air pollution.

- Test takers often get bogged down in fancy language and big words on the LSAT, but often it's

the *smallest* words that have the greatest impact on the logical validity of an author's points. The word "most" in the second sentence will fly by many readers, but the critical reader spots it and realizes that it means that not *all* electricity is *necessarily* generated by burning fossil fuels. This realization leads directly to the author's assumption.

- An assumption fills in an essential missing piece of the argument—a gap that must be filled in order for the argument to be logically sound.

- Be wary of choices, like (B), that implicitly question the importance of the entire argument. An argument's logic is independent from its relevance to the rest of the world. This argument is very self-contained— pointing out that there are greater sources of fossil-fuel pollution in the world than gasoline-powered cars has no relevance whatsoever.

5.   E

Any planetary body with a solid surface becomes heavily pockmarked if its surface isn't renewed for millions of years. Although Europa has a solid surface, it isn't heavily pockmarked. Therefore, you can conclude, its surface has been renewed.

You're told that a planetary body's surface can't be renewed unless its core generates enough heat to cause volcanic action. So Europa's core must generate enough heat to cause volcanic action. But Europa was described as "very cold"; therefore, the cores of some very cold planetary bodies—at least Europa's—have to generate enough heat to cause volcanic action.

(A) All you're told about the surface of the Earth's moon is that it's heavily pockmarked, which doesn't mean that it can't be icy.

(B) is a 180 choice. If a planetary body has a solid surface that's not heavily pockmarked, then its surface has been renewed and its core *must* generate enough heat to cause volcanic action. (You are told nothing about surfaces that aren't solid.)

(C) sounds vaguely plausible, but there's no evidence of the existence of such planetary bodies in the stimulus.

(D) The only moon of Jupiter that is described, Europa, isn't heavily pockmarked; you can't conclude anything about Jupiter's other moons.

- Long stimuli can sometimes be broken up into sections, making it easier to follow the flow of the logic. Here, the first section introduces the setting: planetary bodies and solid surfaces. The second section explains the idea of "renewal": what it means for a surface to be renewed and what effect renewal has. The final section gives a specific case to which to apply the principle discussed in the second section.

6. B

As the patient asserts in the last sentence of the stimulus, "pharmacists have a financial interest" in having a monopoly on selling prescription drugs; therefore, their objections to letting doctors sell prescription drugs can't be taken seriously.

So rather than directly addressing the pharmacists' argument—which is that letting doctors sell prescription drugs would tempt them to prescribe unnecessary drugs in order to make extra money—the patient impugns the pharmacists' motives for making their argument. As you know, this is bogus reasoning; regardless of the pharmacists' motives, their argument may be sound and must be addressed on its own merits.

(A) and (C) Since the patient doesn't deal with the pharmacists' argument, but rather their motives, he can't be denying any assumptions they make (A), or undermining their evidence (C). (A) and (C) describe eminently *reasonable* ways of weakening arguments, but the patient just sidesteps the pharmacists' reasoning entirely.

(D) describes an appeal to popular opinion, but while this is another poor form of reasoning, it isn't what the patient does.

(E) bears no resemblance to what the patient does. Nowhere does he claim that the pharmacists don't know what they're talking about—rather, he attacks their motives, pure and simple.

- Read critically and put arguments into real-world situations. If a friend of yours made this argument, would you swallow it, or would you wonder, "What do the pharmacists' motives have to do with whether or not they're right?"
- The LSAT test makers want to know whether you can distinguish good reasoning from bad. Although the question stem here is that of a Method of Argument question, in order to answer the question correctly you need to recognize that it's a *bad* method of argument.

7. E

Murray tries to deflect Jane's criticism of Senator Brandon by saying that other politicians have done what Senator Brandon is accused of doing; therefore, he must believe that at least one other politician has accepted gifts from lobbyists.

Jane retorts that her failure to attack other politicians doesn't excuse Senator Brandon's offense; she stands by her claim that the Senator Brandon is guilty of accepting gifts from lobbyists.

Therefore, both Murray and Jane would agree that there is at least one politician (Senator Brandon in Jane's case; "other politicians" in Murray's case) who accepts gifts from lobbyists.

(A) Murray doesn't actually admit that Senator Brandon has accepted gifts from lobbyists; his point is Jane's hypocrisy in failing to criticize other politicians for doing likewise.

(B) Murray doesn't admit that there's anything wrong with accepting gifts from lobbyists; again, his argument focuses on the motivation Jane has for singling Senator Brandon out among all the others who have done the same thing.

(C) Jane admits that she dislikes Senator Brandon, but not that her dislike is her only motivation for criticizing him.

(D) There's no evidence that Murray considers this a valid reason for criticizing Senator Brandon; in fact, he explicitly says that Jane is wrong to make this criticism.

- Just as you are careful not to read anything into the stimulus argument, be careful not to read anything into the answer choices. Here, (E) doesn't require that Murray and Jane agree about *which* particular politician accepts gifts from lobbyists (Murray hasn't admitted Senator Brandon accepts gifts, and Jane hasn't committed herself to agreeing that any other politicians accept gifts).

8. D

Sylvia concludes that the gap between the rich north and the poor south will widen because the poor southern countries can't afford to acquire the new technologies. But if the economic gap is going to "widen," then she has to be assuming that some of the rich northern countries *can* acquire the new technologies.

(A) is useless background information. All that matters for Sylvia's argument is that the southern nations be poor and the northern nations be rich.

(B) The north could incorporate the new technologies and therefore increase its wealth and the total amount of global wealth, while the south remained poor, thus widening the gap. So, it's not necessary that the technology not affect an increase overall.

(C) Outside the scope: You might think this is a 180 choice; after all, Sylvia's whole point is that the existing economic gap will *widen* with the coming of the new technologies. But she's referring specifically to information technologies; consideration of other types of technologies has no bearing on the argument.

(E) The speed of information processing is irrelevant as long has some countries have access to the new technologies and some don't.

- The correct choice here seemed so reasonable you might not have recognized it as an assumption. But assumptions as a group are neither reasonable nor unreasonable—they merely represent things that the author is taking for granted as true on their face, that fill the gap between the evidence and the conclusion.

- Let the question stem guide your reading. Often, one character's argument can be evaluated independently from the other character's.

9. C

Oscar's argument includes a slight scope shift. He says that speed of information processing will soon be "the single most important factor" in the creation of wealth. But he concludes that national wealth will be "just a matter of . . . relative success in incorporating the new technologies"—i.e., the new technologies will be the *only* factor.

Choice (C) points out this scope shift by noting that Oscar's conclusion ignores a possible combination of other factors.

(A) is a flaw in Sylvia's argument, not Oscar's. Read the question stem carefully.

(B), (D), and (E) are all true, but none of them signify a flaw in Oscar's reasoning.

(B) isn't a flaw because it's not necessary for Oscar to establish the importance of the rich-poor division in order to draw a conclusion about it.

(D) Oscar doesn't need to show that *only* countries that successfully incorporate the new information technologies will benefit; all his argument requires is that those countries benefit *more* than countries that don't succeed in incorporating the new tech.

(E) faults Oscar for failing to make a distinction between things he has no logical obligation to distinguish. His whole point is that the old distinctions of rich and poor nations will soon be eliminated; there's no need for him to bother distinguishing the wealthy from the *really really* wealthy.

- The correct answer to a Flaw question must be an actual flaw. Statements about the argument that are true but that don't indicate a hole in the author's reasoning should be eliminated.

- An author isn't obligated to throw the whole kitchen sink into her argument. The fact that an author "fails to mention this . . ." or "ignores the possibility of that . . ." only constitutes a flaw in the argument *if* that failure damages or severs the link between her evidence and conclusion.

- Read critically, using keywords to help you thread your way through wordy passages. Here, both characters' conclusions were clearly signaled by the same keyword: "thus."

10. D

You seek a reason why the number of jobs lost was underestimated in the recent recession, despite the fact that companies accurately reported their net job gains and losses to the government and the government accurately calculated those figures.

One possibility that might have occurred to you is that not all companies reported their figures to the government. This is essentially what you get in (D): Due to the recession, many companies suddenly went out of business, and it's reasonable to infer that they didn't bother to report all these job losses before shutting down, thereby leaving the government's calculations drastically underestimated.

(A) This information is not only self-evident but irrelevant. You're not interested in comparing job loss in recessions vs. growth periods, but in why job losses in *this* recession were underestimated.

(B) claims that it's gotten more costly to report employment data. Fine, but since (B) *doesn't* tell you that this increased cost caused many companies not to report their job losses, it can't help you resolve the discrepancy at hand.

(C) is irrelevant. Who cares what people do once they've lost their jobs? Remember, the discrepancy involves the number of jobs *lost*, not the overall unemployment rate, so the fact that many people who lost their jobs found something else to do is irrelevant.

(E) is also irrelevant. You're not interested in changes from manufacturing to service, but in why the number of jobs lost was underestimated. And if you thought (E) meant that, say, people who lost their jobs at the auto plant found new ones at a fast-food chain, again, the discrepancy's not about the unemployment rate, so this doesn't matter.

- In Paradox questions, the correct choice will always answer the question, "How can that be?"

11. C

There will be no danger of wild animals suffocating from entanglement in the new plastic rings, says the representative, because the new rings disintegrate after only three days of exposure to sunlight. So if you know any wild animals, you should probably say, "Hey, Fido—don't go near those nasty rings for three days, okay?"

Obviously, the assumption the representative makes, and one that you probably could have prephrased on your own, is that no wild animals will become entangled in the rings during that three-day window before they (the rings, not the animals) disintegrate.

(A) and (B) both raise side issues that have no effect on the risk of animals suffocating in the rings. You can negate both choices without affecting the conclusion one bit.

(D) The old rings are being eliminated anyway, so it doesn't matter what threats besides suffocation they pose to wild animals.

(E) has two problems; it's a distortion, and it's irrelevant to boot. It's not necessary to assume that *all* wild animals that become entangled in plastic rings will suffocate in order to say that the threat of suffocation is real. That's the distortion part. It's irrelevant because the representative isn't trying to prove that the threat is real; he's trying to show that the switch to the new plastic rings will totally eliminate the threat of suffocation to wild animals.

- Conceiving the argument's conclusion in specific terms will help you stay focused and avoid outside-the-scope answer choices. Here, the representative simply says that the old rings often caused wild animals to suffocate, and that the new rings will not. Immediately eliminate choices that deal with issues other than the relationship between the plastic rings and animal entanglement/suffocation.

- Beware of very strictly worded conclusions, such as the one here: " . . . the threat *will be* eliminated." That doesn't say "probably be," or "most likely be," or "could be," or even "will largely be"; it's a definite. Strictly unqualified conclusions like this are often based on assumptions that usually (there's an example of a nice qualifying word) involve alternative possibilities or exceptions that the author overlooks.

12. B

Once all beverage companies switch to the new plastic rings, says the representative, "the threat of suffocation that plastic rings pose to wild animals will be eliminated." As mentioned above, that's pretty strong language. What if there were still a significant number of the old rings lying around where wild animals could get at them? Then, even if the new rings were 100 percent safe, the threat would not be "eliminated." Choice (B) raises this possibility, weakening the argument considerably.

(A) Since the representative's conclusion is contingent on completion of the switchover, how long the switchover will take is irrelevant.

(C) makes a useless distinction. It's hard to see how the price of the rings affects the likelihood of animal suffocation.

(D) answers a question that is of great importance to the beverage companies (and possibly beer drinkers), but of no importance to the animals, and is therefore outside the scope of the argument.

(E) contains a scope shift. The representative doesn't claim that the new plastic rings are more eco-friendly than the old ones. All it says is that the new rings won't make animals *suffocate*.

- Arguments that make extreme-sounding claims can be weakened simply by showing that "actual results may vary." Remember, you don't have to completely disprove an argument to weaken it. You just have to pick a choice that suggests that the conclusion is less likely to be true.

- Know the test: There's lots of synergy between assumption questions and weaken the argument questions. That's because contradicting an author's assumption is a weakener.

  Question 11: What assumption does the author of the argument make? Answer—question 12 choice (B): *After the beverage companies have switched over to the new plastic rings, a substantial number of old plastic rings will not remain where wild animals could come in contact with them.*
  Question 12: What, if true, would weaken the argument? Answer—question 11 choice (C): *Wild animals can become entangled in the new plastic rings before the rings have had sufficient exposure to sunlight to disintegrate.*

13. B

Alcohol consumption, you're told, has been linked to high blood pressure and consequently to heart disease. But a study showed that heart disease was lower among those who drank a moderate amount daily than among people identified as nondrinkers. From what you were told you'd expect the results to be just the opposite, so what's the deal?

(B) asserts that many of the people identified as nondrinkers were heavy drinkers who'd quit, which raises the possibility that they had a higher rate of high blood pressure and heart disease left over from their drinking days. Notice that (B) doesn't contradict the stimulus; the stimulus referred only to people "identified as nondrinkers," which needn't mean they've been teetotalers their whole lives.

(A) says people who don't drink are healthier, but since the nondrinkers were the ones who *weren't* healthier, this is no help at all.

(C) and (D) might explain why the moderate drinkers had even higher rates of heart disease than one might expect—(C) because some of them overdo it sometimes and (D) because some have high blood pressure—but since you want to explain the *nondrinkers'* higher rate of heart disease, (C) and (D) are irrelevant.

(E) stresses the groups' similarity to one another, essentially ruling out a possible alternative explanation: that there was some *other* difference between the two groups studied that could account for the unexpectedly higher rate of heart disease.

- In Paradox questions, the correct choice will be one that resolves the discrepancy without contradicting the information in the stimulus.
- Since the key to a Paradox question is finding a reasonable explanation, any choice that contradicts a possible explanation, such as (E), should be discarded immediately.

14. E

You're told that all Persian cats are pompous and therefore irritating, but you cannot conclude that any *other* kind of cat is either pompous or irritating. For all you know, the only irritating cats in the world are Persian cats. In other words, there may be no irritating cats that are not Persian cats (and therefore, of course, no irritating and beautiful cats that aren't Persian cats). (E) is not necessarily true. On the other hand:

(A) and (B) are identical inferable statements. Since some of the world's most beautiful cats are Persian, and all Persian cats are irritating, some of the world's most beautiful cats (the Persians) must be irritating (A). Another way of putting this is that there *are* some irritating cats (the Persians) among the world's most beautiful cats (B).

(C) Since all Persian cats are irritating, it's impossible for a Persian to be nonirritating; any cat that isn't irritating isn't a Persian.

(D) works in the same way as (A) and (B). All Persian cats are pompous (that's why they're irritating), and some Persian cats are among the world's most beautiful cats, so some pompous cats (the Persians) are among the world's most beautiful.

15. B

It's a parallel Flaw question, so your first task is to characterize the flaw in the stimulus. The author in the stimulus erroneously assumes that all students who have shown an interest in archaeology want to go on the dig. Likewise, the author in (B) makes the unwarranted assumption that all of the sure-footed, non-gentle horses are also well schooled.

(A) The "theoretically" should've given you pause—where does *that* shine in?—and (A) contains only three terms (worth saving; having a life; size) where the stimulus contains four.

(C) does commit the fallacy of denying the antecedent, but that's not the flaw in the original.

(D) Isn't flawed at all, so it's automatically out of the running.

(E) This one is flawed, but in a different way…the evidence tells you that one of two things is required for a certain result, then the conclusion tells you that since you don't have one of those things, the result must not occur.

- Interrogate the stimulus; don't read passively. Why, you must ask, will many students who want to go on the dig be ineligible to do so?
- Use all information given in the stem. When the test makers tell you that a flaw is present, read the argument critically and *find that flaw.*

16. C

A Parallel Logic question with a twist: The stimulus saves you the trouble of analyzing the argument by characterizing the flaw for you. You're told exactly what kind of flaw you're looking for, and only have to recognize the answer choice that matches the description. And it's (C) that commits the flaw described.

The initial observation is that each member of a group (each nominee) could possess a characteristic (being appointed to one of three openings on a committee). The conclusion is that all of the group's members could possess that characteristic (all the nominees could be appointed to the committee). As with the example of the tennis tournament in the stimulus, it's actually only possible for a comparatively few members of the group to possess the characteristic.

(A) is off in many ways; it doesn't move from "each" to "all" members of a group, it doesn't describe a characteristic that "could" be possessed, and it doesn't conclude that all members of the group possess the characteristic described.

(B) This conclusion is qualified, unlike that of the stimulus fallacy; (B) doesn't conclude that all the candidates possess the necessary qualifications. Moreover, unlike the example of the tennis tournament, it *would* be possible for all candidates to possess the characteristic of being fully qualified.

(D) is tricky. The problem is the nature of the "characteristic" described: the *probability* of a head being tossed. This makes the flaw a mathematical fallacy (the real probability of all five tosses being heads is one divided by two to the fifth power, or one in thirty-two), which doesn't match the stimulus fallacy.

(E) doesn't jump to an "immediate conclusion" based on the original observation, but instead offers a way of testing the observation's accuracy.

- Don't be thrown by the fact that a question looks peculiar. Here the oddness, the fact that the stimulus described the fallacy in abstract terms, made it much easier—half the work of a typical parallel Flaw question was done for you.

17. D

Make the question stem work for you by actively decoding it. In a roundabout way, you're asked to weaken the argument; that is, find something that suggests that the "better clues" may not be so great. You need only concern yourself with the last two sentences, since that's where the "better" clues are described.

These clues don't specifically indicate lying; they indicate emotional arousal or distress. So a person under stress might well exhibit these clues even if he were telling the truth.

(A) and (C) can be eliminated because they don't relate to the "better" clues described in the last sentence.

(B) A person's past history has nothing to do with the argument, which is all about physical manifestations of lying.

(E) Just because hesitation and shifting posture prove to be reliable indicators of lying in some cases doesn't mean that the better clues (uncontrolled behavior such as pupil dilation) aren't reliable indicators.

- Read actively. Decoding question stems that are very specifically worded can often save you time when it comes to selecting the correct answer choice.

18. B

Orthodox medicine is not effective in treating certain medical conditions. And alternative medicine, says the author, is *never* effective. So it has to be true that there are some medical conditions for which neither type of treatment is effective.

(A) You cannot infer that practitioners of alternative medicine are acting in bad faith, because you don't know whether they believe their treatments to be effective. Their personal beliefs, in fact, are way outside the author's scope.

(C) 180: you're told that alternative medicine doesn't have any effects at all.

(D) is a distortion. You can infer that *some* effective treatments produce unacceptable side effects; that's one of the reasons people turn to alternative medicine. But saying that *all* effective treatments have unacceptable side effects is too extreme.

(E) It would be nice to believe that orthodox medicine will eventually produce cures for incurable diseases, but the author offers no such ray of hope.

- On Inference questions, think about what you know. Then think about what you don't know. The things you don't know will often show up in wrong answer choices.

- Steer clear of choices like (A) that ascribe venal or otherwise bad motives to a person or group. Such choices are usually wrong.

19. D

The charge against alternative medicine is that it has no effects. You might have expected that the way to weaken that charge would be to find positive effects in such treatments. And (D), by suggesting that the patient's belief in the treatment can help promote healing, opens up the possibility that alternative medicine *can* assist in the healing process, thus having an effect.

(A) and (E) Showing that orthodox medicine is sometimes ineffective doesn't imply that alternative medicine is therefore effective. It doesn't even damage the author's credibility, since the argument clearly *states* that orthodox treatment is sometimes ineffective.

(B) Alternative medicine may be based on different concepts than orthodox medicine, but that doesn't necessarily mean that it works.

(C) Alternative medicine may provide patients with hope, but hope is not a medical effect. To select this choice, you have to assume that hope somehow aids the healing process, and that's too big a leap—there's no evidence for it. At the same time, when you select (C) you have to find a reason why (D) must be wrong, and that's well-nigh impossible.

- Weakening an argument doesn't always mean blowing it apart completely. In fact, extreme-sounding statements (like the author's final sentence in the stimulus) can often be weakened simply by showing that other possibilities exist.

- There's a big difference between criticizing one side of an argument and supporting the other side. The old adage "the enemy of my enemy is my friend" has no logical value. In this example, you can't shore up the case for alternative medicine by breaking down the case for orthodox medicine.

20. E

The author mentions two important developments that took place in North America during the period that saw the extinction of large mammals like the mastodon, wooly mammoth, and saber-toothed tiger: the spread of human beings and climactic warming. She concludes that human activity caused the mammals' extinction. But she's ignoring an alternate possibility suggested by her own evidence—that the change in the climate caused the mammals' extinction. From what she's told you, there's no reason to choose one cause over the other.

(A) The author doesn't adopt without question the view that humans aren't *included* in nature; she attempts to disprove the view that humans lived in *harmony* with nature.

(B) The author doesn't presuppose that humans' one-time harmonious existence with nature is a myth; she draws a conclusion that she believes *demonstrates* that this idea is a myth.

(C) is irrelevant. The author's conclusion was that human activity 12,000 years ago caused the extinction of animal species; her conclusion is unrelated to the significance of that extinction to the humans of the time.

(D) would only strengthen the contention that 12,000 years ago human activity was causing species to become extinct.

- It's fairly common on LSAT Logical Reasoning for an author to err by failing to consider some alternative

possibility; noticing this error can make prephrasing very easy.

- Always read actively. Treat the stimulus as a real description of a real situation. When you read that way, you're less likely to miss the importance of details like "as the climate became warmer" above.

21. D

When Greenfield households deliver recyclable trash to commercial recycling centers, that trash is accepted *for free*. That means that homeowners don't lose money, as they would if they put out the trash for collectors to add to their trash tax, but it also means they don't *gain* any money by bringing the trash to the centers. They would do just as well financially giving their recyclable trash to their neighbors; in both cases, they avoid the tax. So there's no financial incentive for the action described in (D).

(A) Since households pay a tax for putting out nonrecyclable trash, and can dispose of their recyclable trash for free, there *is* a financial incentive to make sure they find all their recyclable trash.

(B) provides a method for avoiding the tax levied on trash put out for collection, so there's a definite financial incentive to follow this course.

(C) The trash tax is calculated based on the volume of trash put out. (C) would reduce the volume of the trash put out and therefore would reduce the tax paid.

(E) Since nonrecyclable packaging goes into the trash, using products without packaging, or with packaging that could be brought to recycling centers, would reduce the volume of trash put out and so would reduce the trash tax paid.

- This is essentially an Inference question (like question 14); given the conditions described in the stimulus, each of the choices but one describes a course of action that can be inferred to be financially advantageous.

22. A

In rather an odd survey, consumers living in an Eastern European nation are asked to rank 400 Western products according to brand name recognition and quality. But it turns out that only 27 of the products are even available in that nation. Not surprisingly, the survey results for the 27 products that are available (in terms of how name recognition correlates with perceived quality) were unlike the results for the products that aren't available.

What's the point of asking people about the quality of products they've never used? The survey violates (A):

Although all the respondents can answer the question about whether they recognize the brand names, they cannot reasonably answer the question about the quality of products that are unavailable.

(B) There's no difficulty in categorizing the responses to questions; on the contrary, the survey results can be organized neatly into two rankings.

(C) It's never stated that the survey requires respondents to give up their anonymity, so there's no evidence that (C)'s principle is violated.

(D) The survey doesn't ask many questions about a single product, but two questions about 400 products.

(E) The survey abides by (E); the respondents are asked about their personal opinions of the products in question, so how could they get the answer wrong?

- If you don't recognize the principle directly, use the process of elimination. Concentrate on the violation the survey is supposed to have committed: an unmanageable number of categories (B), violating anonymity (C), asking 10 questions about one product (D), respondents' fear of being wrong (E). Even if you had trouble following the stimulus, all of these are pretty clearly inapplicable.

23. E

Both crested and noncrested birds of this species tend to select mates of their own variety. Is this preference genetically determined or is it learned behavior (based on the fact that the birds generally live only with birds of their own variety)? The author concludes that the preference is learned, because when a noncrested bird is raised in a crested flock and later moved to a mixed flock, it's likely to pick a crested mate. Its mate selection seems to have been influenced by the environment it was raised in.

(E) supports this with similar evidence: When a bird is raised in a mixed flock, it shows *no* preference for one variety over the other when choosing a mate. Again, its choice of mate seems determined by its environment.

(A) is outside the scope—it speaks of other species instead of the species you're interested in, and it ignores the learned vs. genetic question which is the focus of the argument.

(B) Whether or not there are many other behavioral differences between crested and noncrested birds doesn't tell you whether their preference in mates is learned or genetic.

(C) is irrelevant; since you're only interested in why the birds choose crested or noncrested mates, their mates' other characteristics don't matter.

(D) is a 180 choice, since the bird described chooses a mate of its own variety without any environmental reason for learning such behavior.

- In order to understand an argument, you have to understand the function that each piece of evidence serves. When a section of the argument begins with "however," take the time to understand how it functions as counterevidence or as a counterbalance to what went before; above, the "however" introduces evidence showing a bird behaving in an uncharacteristic manner, apparently because of how it was raised.

24. C

The key to getting into and out of this question with a quick right answer is the nature of the conclusion, signaled by "therefore": It boils down to "A particular phenomenon occurs *at least in part because of* a particular factor." If you scan the five choices, the only one whose conclusion even comes close is (C)'s "weight must determine, *or help determine*, charges."

That's all you needed to see. Analyzing things further, the gist of both (C) and the stimulus is that two causes (day length and temperature/volume and weight), separately or together, bring about an effect (renewed plant growth/landfill charges); therefore, if one cause (day length/volume) is identical for all and thus taken out of the equation, then the other cause (temperature/weight) must have some influence on the effect.

(A) This conclusion hinges on "most" and "few," which aren't in the stimulus, and lacks an explicit parallel to the stimulus's "day length or temperature or both."

(B) The certainty of (B)'s conclusion (an easterly wind *must* now be blowing) is missing from the stimulus, and the "east means rain, west means dry" opposition has no parallel in the stimulus either.

(D) This "1 or 2 or 3" might seem like a clever parallel to "X or Y or both," but only mathematically. To be parallel, (D) would have to draw a conclusion about the number of store detectives needed, but instead its conclusion explains *why* a particular number is needed.

(E) This conclusion, first of all, is a recommendation ("X should try to do Y"), and that alone renders it impossible. (E) also deviates by bringing in four terms (loud, soft, low-pitched, and high-pitched) and its reference to "especially," none of which appears in the stimulus.

- Keep characterizing the choices and stimulus. Here, only if the stimulus's conclusion were a recommendation could (E) be correct. And here, since the stimulus's conclusion is an assertion of partial cause, only (C) need be considered.

PART FOUR

Getting into Law School

Chapter 8: **Law School Admissions**

- Where to apply

- When to apply

- How to apply

INTRODUCTION

I can still remember the day I received my LSAT score report in the mail. I was jubilant about my score, which put me in the top two percent of all test takers. This kind of LSAT performance, I thought—combined with my high college GPA—would surely get me into any law school I desired; all I had to do was decide which one I would deign to attend. I proceeded to apply to 10 top law schools, fully confident that I would be accepted by all 10.

Well, it didn't turn out quite that way. By the following April, I had received a meager two acceptance letters, one wait-list letter, and an appalling seven rejection letters, including ones from Harvard and Stanford. As the rejection letters rolled in, one after the other, my original hubris slowly and painfully gave way to humility.

Two weeks after the last rejection, still reeling from the shock, I had the good fortune to bump into an admissions officer from a local law school at a party. I cornered her and began peppering her with questions about what could possibly have gone wrong. She mentioned several potential problems and suggested that I call a friend of hers at one of the law schools I had applied to and ask her to critique my application. What I found out was eye-opening: My application could not have been more inept. In fact, just about everything I'd done had contributed to preventing my admission to law school, including carelessly misspelling my name on the application (fortunately, the University of Michigan Law School saw fit to let me attend despite these blunders).

> **KAPLAN) EXCLUSIVE**
>
> You have to show the admissions officers how strong and well-qualified you are—by conducting an effective, meticulously organized campaign for admission.

Today, after years of conversations with other lawyers, law students, and my Kaplan LSAT classmates, I realize that my experience was hardly unique. An astonishing number of people apply to law school without a clue about the admissions process. That's why I've made something of a career out of ensuring that others don't make the same mistakes I did. In the last several years, I've spoken to admissions officers at more than 65 schools in all regions of the country, gleaning as much information from them as I could.

One cautionary note—admission officers are human beings; they don't all think alike. Attitudes and priorities vary from law school to law school. However, the suggestions that follow are the ones I've heard over and over again, straight from the most important source—the admissions officers themselves. Stick closely to these suggestions and you'll increase your chances of getting in the law school you want to attend.

WHERE TO APPLY

The question of where you should apply has two parts. What schools should you consider, regardless of your chances, and which of these schools can you actually get into? Let's begin with the first question.

What Schools Should You Consider?

A recent article about law school education published a remarkable statistic. Upon graduation, according to one study, 58 percent of all law students end up living and working within a one-hour drive of where they went to law school. That's nearly 6 out of every 10 students!

There are many reasons for this surprising statistic. Obviously, a lot of people attend the local law school in the town where they have always lived and want to continue living. Also, since employers tend to interview and hire from nearby law schools, many recent grads stay put. Some students find that they just like the area and don't want to leave. Still others meet and marry a local person during their three years. Whatever the explanation, a majority of all law students end up spending more than just the required three years in the city or region where they attend law school.

Despite the importance of law school selection, however, it's frightening how lightly many applicants treat the whole process, even students who spend a great deal of time studying for the LSAT or working on their applications. Horror stories abound—of distant relatives convincing someone to attend State University Law School just because they themselves did 40 years ago or of a student who decides not to apply to a school because his girlfriend's cousin heard that the social life was not so hot.

This point cannot be stressed enough. *Choosing a law school is a major decision in your life and should be treated as such.* There are several factors to consider when choosing where to apply, including reputation, location, and cost.

Reputation

How much does a law school's reputation matter? The short answer is that it matters very much in your first few years out of law school, when you're looking for your first job or two. Most employers evaluating you at this time will have little else to go on and so will tend to place a lot of weight on school reputation. After a few years, when you've established a reputation and a record of your own, the importance of your alma mater's rep will diminish.

The long answer to the question of academic reputation, however, is a little more complex. Each applicant must look at his or her situation and ask several questions:

- **Am I looking to work for a law firm or to do public service work?**
  Law firms tend to put more emphasis on the reputation of the school.

- **Do I want to stay in the area or have more mobility nationwide?**
  Some schools enjoy strong local reputations as well as strong alumni bases, whereas other schools have a nationwide appeal.

- **How competitive do I want my law school experience to be?**
  Although there are exceptions, as a general rule the schools with better reputations tend to be very competitive.

- **Do I want to consider teaching as an option?**
  Virtually all law school professors come from a handful of top-notch law schools. The same also applies for the most prestigious judicial clerkships.

- **To what extent am I willing to go into debt?**
  The schools with the biggest reputations also tend to have the biggest price tags.

What's the best way to research reputation? Many publications rank law schools. How accurate these rankings are is anybody's guess, but they tend to become self-fulfilling. Once published, they're discussed over and over by students, lawyers, and faculty until they become fact. Although the methodology behind these rankings is often suspect, the results are frequently heeded by employers. Studies rank the top 50 schools, the top 15 schools, or categorize all schools into four or five levels. (Most of these books can be found in the reference section of your local bookstore.) Many law firms rely heavily on such rankings in making their hiring decisions.

But there are other methods to determine a school's reputation. Speak to friends who are lawyers or law students. Lawyers have a habit of noting who their most formidable opponents are and where they went to law school. Look through law school catalogs and see what schools the professors attended. Finally, ask the placement offices how many firms interview on campus each year, and compare the numbers. Their answers can give you a strong indication of what the law-firm community thinks of a school.

Location

Location is of prime importance because of the distinct possibility that you'll end up spending a significant part of your life near your law school—three years at the very least. Even under the best of conditions, law school will be a difficult period in your life. You owe it to yourself to find a place where you'll be comfortable. Pick cities or areas you already know you like or would like to live. Pay particular attention to climate problems. Think about rural areas as opposed to urban centers.

KAPLAN) EXCLUSIVE

Statistics show that you'll probably end up spending at least part of your working life in the area where you went to law school. So pick one in a location you can live with (and in).

Visit as many law schools as possible, your top two or three choices at the very least. You may be surprised at what you find. For example, a recent student related that his dream was to get into the law school of one particular university because he'd visited its campus several years ago and loved it. But his dream was quickly crushed when told that the university's law school is not on the campus, but rather 30 minutes away in an area closer to downtown. Spend some time researching location by visiting *when school is in session*, which is when you'll get the most accurate picture. You should also:

- Buy a local newspaper and scan the real estate ads for prices near campus; check out campus housing to determine whether it's livable.
- Check out transportation options at the law school.
- Take the school's tour so you can hear about the area's good points.
- Look at bulletin boards for evidence of activities.

Finally, don't be afraid to wander into the student lounge and just ask several law students what they think. Most are more than willing to provide an honest appraisal, but be sure to get more than one opinion.

Costs

Cost ranks at the bottom of many law students' list of criteria to consider, because law school financial aid works in much the same manner as a credit card—you get it now and pay for it later. Each year a number of students enter law school with the goal of doing some type of public service work, but then are forced to take higher-paying firm jobs in order to meet their loan payments. This is certainly understandable when you realize that many law students rack up debts of over $100,000 over the course of three years.

Among the cost issues to consider are:

- **Low-Cost State Schools**
  State schools tend to have lower tuition, particularly for in-state residents.

- **Urban Versus Rural Living Costs**
  Schools in large urban areas will almost invariably have higher living costs than those in rural areas (although the larger cities also tend to have more part-time jobs for second- and third-year students, which can offset the extra cost).

- **Special Loan Programs**
  Many schools now offer special loan repayment or loan forgiveness programs for students who take low-paying public service jobs.

- **Special Scholarship Programs**
  Many law schools offer special scholarship programs that range from small grants to full three-year rides.

KAPLAN) EXCLUSIVE

Cost should be a factor in your choice of law school. Loans have to be paid back, and a high burden of debt might force you to make a less-than-desirable career choice.

The law school application will tell you what the annual tuition was for the previous year. Many applications will even give you an estimate of living expenses. If you want to dig deeper, call the financial aid office and ask them to send you the breakdown of living expenses of the average law student. Also ask them to send information about any loan forgiveness programs and about scholarships offered by the law school.

Job Placement

With the legal job market shrinking, the proficiency of a law school's placement office is now a major factor to be considered. If interviews with law students can be believed, the competency of placement officers varies widely. Some see their job as simply setting up on-campus interviews and making sure they run smoothly. Others call and write letters on behalf of students and are constantly selling the school to employers. Some schools direct almost all of their efforts into placing students into private law firms. Other schools provide information on an entire range of opportunities. At some schools students are lucky if the placement office even provides them with a list of alumni in cities in which they'd like to live. At other schools the office calls alumni to hunt for leads.

Ask the placement office for the percentage of graduates in the most recent class who had jobs upon graduation. Don't be fooled by statistics that show 98 percent of all graduates employed. Almost all law students are eventually employed, even if they drive taxis. The key is to determine how many are placed in law jobs *before* they leave law school.

Second, stop by the placement office on your visit and look around. Ask to see the placement library and check whether it's well organized and up-to-date. Note whether it carries materials on public interest or teaching jobs and how large this section is. Also ask whether a newsletter is published to keep alumni informed of any recent job openings.

Again, talk with law students. Most have very strong opinions about the performance of their placement office. Most students recognize and appreciate when the placement office is making an extra effort.

Course Selection

One of the nicest things about law schools today is their growing number of course selections and the new areas of law that are opening up. International trade, employment discrimination, sports and entertainment, and environmental law are all areas in which schools are providing more offerings. Many law students nowadays are becoming specialists, because of both personal preference and better marketability. If you're one of the many students who enter law school without a clue about what kind of law they want to practice, look for schools that offer a lot of different areas of study.

As a rule, schools with larger student populations offer not only more classes but also a greater variety. They need more professors to handle the standard course load, and most professors also like to teach and explore new areas of law as well.

Schools list the courses most recently taught in their recruiting brochure, which they will gladly send you. One note of caution: Just because a class has been taught in the past and is listed in the brochure doesn't mean that it's taught every year or will be taught in the future. If you're interested in a particular class, call the registrar's department and find out how often the class has been taught in the past and whether it will be offered again in the future. Ask to speak with the professor who has taught the course in the past.

Social Life

Although it's an important part of the law school experience, social life should rank near the bottom of the list of factors to consider when choosing a law school. Why? Because your social life at any law school is what you make of it. Almost all law schools have monthly parties or weekly Thursday night get-togethers at local bars. And if you choose to expand that schedule, you can always find a willing accomplice. Furthermore, most schools now have a comparably full range of social organizations that cover race, religion, political affiliation, and sex.

Examine the area surrounding the law school. During your first year, locale probably won't matter much. But as you get into your second and third years, you'll likely find that you do have some free time, particularly on weekends. Think about whether you want a quiet rural area where canoeing or skiing are readily available or whether you'd prefer a larger city with a vibrant restaurant and nightlife scene.

Additional Considerations

There are a few other factors that you may want to toss into the equation when deciding which law school is right for you.

Class Size: This factor is not as important as it is when choosing a college because, despite what you may read in a catalogue, virtually all first-year classes will be large. Nevertheless, there are some differences between a school such as Georgetown, with more than 2,000 students, and a school such as Stanford, with fewer than 800. In the second and third years, the larger schools tend to have more course offerings, whereas the smaller schools focus on smaller class size and more contact between professors and students. Smaller schools also tend to encourage a greater sense of camaraderie and less competition. Larger schools, on the other hand, produce more alumni and thus more contacts when it comes time for your job search.

Attrition Rates: Law schools generally try to keep their attrition rate below 10 percent. There are exceptions, however, and if the school you're interested in has an attrition rate above 10 percent, you should ask an admissions officer why. There may be a reasonable explanation, but you should probably approach the school with some caution.

Joint-Degree Programs: These are designed to help students pursue two degrees jointly in less time than it would take to earn them separately. Some common examples are the Master of Public Policy (M.P.P.) or the Master of Business Administration (M.B.A.) combined with the law degree. These programs generally take four to five years to complete. Most schools are becoming more daring in this field—indeed, some are now encouraging students to create their own joint-degree program in any area that they choose, as long as it meets both departments' approval. It's not uncommon now to see joint degrees in law and foreign languages, music, or sociology. Check with the schools to see what joint-degree programs are routinely offered, but don't be limited by them. If you have a specialized program in mind, call the registrar's office and see how flexible they are.

Clinical Programs: Every law school in the country now offers one or more clinical programs. A clinic is a unique, hands-on opportunity that allows law students to see how the legal system works by handling actual civil cases for people who can't afford an attorney (and getting credit for it at the same time). Not only are these clinics a tremendous learning tool, but they are also the highlight of many law students' three years of study.

Usually the workload is heavy on landlord/tenant disputes or other debt-collection cases. However, many schools are branching out and offering specialized clinics in such areas as child abuse, domestic violence, and immigration. One word of caution: Clinics tend to be popular with students. In many cases, it's very difficult to get a spot in the class, and admission usually depends on the luck of the draw. As a general rule, the schools in large cities have bigger and more clinics because they tend to have more clients.

Internships: Like clinical programs, internships are becoming more popular and varied. Internship programs vary widely from school to school, and may include anything from working for an international trade organization in Europe for an entire year to getting three hours credit for part-time work at the local prosecutor's office. Internships are often overlooked by students who are afraid to veer from the traditional path. Yet they can be a welcome break from regular law studies and may also help in the later job search.

Computer Facilities and Law Library: Legal research is a big part of your three years in law school. Nothing will frustrate you more than to have a brief due the next day only to find that your library lacks essential volumes on the subject or that the few computers they have are either occupied or not working. If you make a visit to the law schools, check out their facilities. Again, don't be afraid to ask students for their opinions.

Where Can You Get In?

Let's turn to the second major question in the selection process: "Where do you have a chance of being accepted?"

Anyone who tells you that he can predict where you'll be accepted is fooling himself and, worse, fooling you. Stories of students accepted by a Harvard, Stanford, or Michigan only to be turned down by schools with far less glamorous reputations are common. Yet what is often overlooked is how well the process does work, considering the volume of applications and the amount of discretion exercised by admissions officers.

One reason the admissions process runs smoothly is that all law schools use the combined LSAT score and GPA as the most important determinant in making the decision. This provides a degree of consistency to the admissions process and gives the applicants some direction in deciding where to apply.

Those Legendary Law School Grids

Each year, LSAC publishes the *Official Guide to ABA-Approved Law Schools* (the LSAT application booklet tells you how to order it). This guide includes a wealth of information on all the accredited law schools in the United States. The schools themselves provide most of the information for the book, including the LSAT scores and GPAs of the most recently admitted class. These are generally presented in grid form and are the single most valuable tool in determining your chances of being accepted at any particular law school. The grid shown here is a hypothetical grid, similar to the ones found in the Guide.

State University Law School

	LSAT Percentile Rank						
GPA	< 40%	41–50%	51–60%	61–70%	71–80%	81–90%	91–99%
4–3.75	11/1	21/3	29/5	41/12	62/33	68/55	48/47
3.74–3.5	16/0	14/0	8/2	38/16	84/38	115/64	102/81
3.49–3.25	18/0	9/1	12/0	24/8	73/28	96/38	76/48
3.24–3.0	13/0	13/0	22/2	25/6	55/15	71/28	53/27
2.99–2.75	3/0	5/0	8/0	19/2	38/6	49/10	31/9
2.74–2.5	1/0	0/0	3/1	18/3	41/2	32/4	11/5
<2.5	1/0	1/0	3/0	9/1	9/0	6/2	3/1

Take a close look at the hypothetical grid above. Note that GPAs are divided into categories that drop .25 every line. Also note that LSAT scores are listed by percentile rank rather than by score. This is done because the scoring system for the LSAT was changed in 1991, and law schools still receive applications from students with scores under the old system. In order to use the grid, first find the line where your GPA fits in. Then read across until you find the percentage category of your existing or anticipated LSAT score. There you'll find two numbers, divided by a slash. The first number indicates the number of people in that range of LSAT scores and GPAs who applied to that school. The second number is the number accepted.

Most students apply to too few schools. According to LSAC, the average applicant applies to only about five schools. Admittedly, the cost of applications is rising, and sending out 10 or more applications can result in an outlay of $500 or more. But keep in mind that if the cost of application presents a real hardship, most schools will waive the application fee—provided you give them a good, credible reason.

Assembling a List of Schools

Using the grid numbers as a guide for determining your chances of acceptance, you should create a list of schools to apply to, dividing the list into three categories: preferred schools, competitive, and safe schools.

Preferred Schools: These are schools you'd *love* to attend, but your numbers indicate a less than 40 percent chance of admission. Apply to two or three schools in this group. Long shots rarely pay off, but daydreaming about them is always nice.

Competitive Schools: Competitive (or "good fit") schools are those where your grid numbers are in the ballpark and where, depending on the rest of your application, you have a decent chance of getting admitted. These are schools where your numbers give you a 40–80 percent chance of admission. These are the schools on which you should focus most of your attention. Applying to four to seven schools in this group is reasonable and increases your odds of getting into at least one school where you are competitive.

"Safe" Schools: These schools are not high on your preference list, but your odds of admission are excellent there. Look at the grids and determine two or three schools where your chances of getting in appear to be 80 percent or better. One suggestion for this list would be to pick schools in locations that you particularly like.

Note: Students with low numbers may need to be a little more flexible and work a little harder. Be willing to travel a little farther to go to school. Also, look at schools in areas that aren't quite as popular or that tend to draw mostly local students. Sometimes the more expensive schools are applied to by fewer applicants and can be easier to get into.

Drawbacks to Using the Law School Grids

Although the grid system is very helpful, it does have its problems. Remember that the law schools provide the grids. Some schools take the opportunity to enhance their reputation by making their numbers seem higher than they really are. This is not done by lying, but rather by the schools' selectively using pertinent information to artificially enhance the numbers. If a school's numbers don't jibe with its reputation, be skeptical.

Second, because each category in a grid covers a fairly wide range of numbers (i.e., 10 LSAT percentile points or .25 GPA points), don't be fooled into thinking that your 3.51 and 71 percent put you on the same level as the student with the 3.74 and 79 percent, even though you fall in the same place on the grids. There are wide gaps in every category.

Third, many law schools—including some of the very best—do not provide LSAC with grids. However, these schools generally will tell you the average GPA and LSAT score for the previous year's entering class. If you want to get a picture of your chances at these schools, try determining which schools are similar in reputation. You can do so using the published ranking lists discussed earlier. Then determine which one of these schools comes closest in number of applications and size of the entering class to the school in question and use that grid.

Use the application list on the following page to plot out your law school application campaign.

WHEN TO APPLY

Prior to the 1980s, the typical law school application season began in October or November with the mailing of the brochures and application forms. The schools would begin accepting applications in December or January and set a deadline for all applications to be completed by around March. Once all applications were received, the schools would begin the decision-making process, usually sending out acceptances or rejections in April, May, or June.

> **KAPLAN) EXCLUSIVE**
>
> Does it really pay to go to a lot of trouble to apply early? Yes, particularly in this era of rolling admissions. Start your campaign 18 months before you intend to step into your first law class.

Schools send out application forms in August and September, begin accepting applications in October, and start sending out acceptance letters by November. (As proof that they have a heart, most law schools will not begin sending out rejection letters until after the holiday season.) Application deadlines may be in February or March, but because the schools have begun filling their classes in the fall, it is not unusual for more than 75 percent of the anticipated acceptance letters to have been sent by the spring deadline date. This is what's known as rolling admissions, which creates the scenario of unaware applicants who proudly deliver their applications on the deadline date only to find that they have put themselves at a distinct disadvantage.

The Advantages of Early Application

Does applying early really provide you with an advantage? Yes! Here are the major reasons why.

Rising Index Numbers

The first reason has to do with index numbers. Your index number is based on the combination of your LSAT score and your GPA. At the beginning of the application process, most schools set an automatic admittance index number. Applicants whose index numbers surpass that figure are admitted quickly with only a cursory look at their application to confirm that they are not serial killers. At the beginning of the process, law schools are always afraid that they'll have too few applicants accepting their offers, which would mean less tuition money and almost certainly some complaints from the school's administrative office. Thus, they usually begin the application process by setting the automatic admittance index number on the low side. Then they gradually increase it as the admission season wears on and they discover that their fears are unfounded.

Fewer Available Places

Because schools have a tendency to be a little more lenient early in the process, they begin reaching their admission goals fairly quickly. By February, the school may well have sent out more than 75 percent or more of all the acceptance letters it plans to send. Yet, at this point, all of the earlier applicants haven't been rejected. Instead many people are left hanging, just in case better applicants don't start coming through the system. This means that if you apply in March, you're now shooting for fewer possible positions, yet you're still competing against a fairly substantial pool of applicants.

Application Worksheet

YOU SHOULD APPLY TO AT LEAST EIGHT SCHOOLS.

Preferred Schools

Chances of admission 40 percent or less. Choose two or three.

1. _____

2. _____

3. _____

Competitive Schools

Chances of admission 40–80 percent. Choose four to seven.

1. _____

2. _____

3. _____

4. _____

5. _____

6. _____

7. _____

"Safe" Schools

Chances of admission 80 percent or greater. Choose two or three.

1. _____

2. _____

3. _____

The "Jading" Effect

If they are candid, admissions officers will admit that by the time they get to the 2,000th essay on "Why I want to go to law school," they're burned out, and more than a little jaded. Essays or applications that might have seemed noteworthy in the beginning now strike the reader as routine.

The Nay-Sayers

A handful of prelaw advisors and admissions officers dispute the importance of early applications, and at a few schools, there may indeed be no special advantage. Law schools are almost always open to exceptional applicants, and will sometimes admit someone well after the deadline if the student can give a good reason for the late application. Furthermore, a few schools routinely accept applications up until a week or two before classes start.

But these are exceptions. We became convinced of the importance of early applications while working with a student a few years ago. She hadn't taken the LSAT until December and was running late on her applications, barely making the deadline at the eight law schools to which she applied. Eventually, she was rejected by seven of the schools and accepted by one. She decided to sit out a year and try again. The next time, she applied in November to the same eight schools, changed almost nothing on her application, and was accepted at five of the schools and wait-listed at two others. The only logical explanation was the timing of the application.

When to Start

For the most part, a pre-Halloween application is overdoing it. When schools are just gearing up, you run the risk of documents being misplaced. Pre-Thanksgiving is the preferable choice and assures that you'll be among the early entries. Shortly before Christmas is not as desirable, but should still hold you in good stead. After Christmas and the holidays, however, you're on the downside and may well find yourself among the last 30 percent of all applications received. And if you go with a post-Valentine's Day application—well, you'd better have strong numbers.

Remember that this discussion applies to the date on which your application is *complete*, not just the date on which the school receives your application forms. Applications are not considered complete until the LSAT score, LSDAS (Law School Data Assembly Service) reports, transcripts, and all recommendations have been received. Even though other people are sending these pieces, it's your responsibility to see that they arrive at the law school promptly. This does *not* mean calling the law school three times a week to see if they've arrived. It means prodding your recommenders or your college to send in the necessary documentation. Explain to them the importance of early applications.

If you want to have a complete application at the law schools by, say, late November, you can't start planning just a few weeks in advance. Your campaign for admission should begin 5 or 6 months before that deadline—i.e., 18 months before your first day as a law student. We've included, at the end of this section, a schedule that you can use to organize your campaign. As you'll see, you should plan to devote plenty of time to your applications the summer before they're due.

Here are some of the important things to do each season. For convenience, let's assume that you want to go to law school the fall after you graduate from college.

Spring of Junior Year

Your first step should be to register for the June LSAT. You won't need your LSAT score for a while yet, but if you take the June test and bomb out, you'll be able to retake the test in October. Get a copy of the *LSAT/LSDAS Registration and Information Book* at any local college or law school admissions office or at any Kaplan Center. The registration booklet will tell you not only about the LSAT but also about the LSDAS. The LSDAS is the organization that will be sending your LSAT scores and transcripts to the law schools you apply to. You'll want LSDAS to open a file on you as early as possible. The book will explain exactly how to do this and how much it will cost (yes, they charge for their mandatory services).

You can buy the *Official Guide to ABA-Approved Law Schools*, which contains those grids we talked about, as well as other information about American law schools. If you can't find it in your local bookstore, you can order it from LSDAS.

The Summer Before Senior Year

Start thinking about a "theme" for your application, which can serve as a way to stand out from the crowd and as an organizing principle for personal statements, recommendations, and everything else in your file. Think about how you'd like to be identified. As the environmentalist who plays oboe recitals for the local recycling center? Of course, you don't *have* to have a theme, but any kind of "high concept" will help your application stick in the minds of admissions officers. You should also be assembling your list of schools at this point. Visit as many of them as you can. Send for their catalogues and applications.

Early Fall of Senior Year

This is when the action really starts. Applications will start arriving. (In filling them out, follow the procedures outlined in the "How to Apply" section.) Line up your recommenders. Make sure they have everything they need to write you a great letter. (More on how to do so in the "How to Apply" section.) Take the October LSAT, if you've decided to do so. Revise your personal statement. Revise it again. And again.

Late Fall of Senior Year

Complete and submit your applications. Prod recommenders so that your applications are complete before Thanksgiving.

Applying to law school is a time-consuming process that tests your organizational skills and your attention to detail. Students who believe that they can simply plot out four hours on a weekend to complete this ordeal are kidding themselves. Plan to set aside some big blocks of time well in advance to work intensively on this important step in achieving your admission goals.

An Ideal Law School Application Schedule

Your campaign for law school admission should start up to 18 months before you step into your first law classroom. Here's a schedule of what you should be doing when:

SPRING OF JUNIOR YEAR

❏ Get the *Official Guide to U.S. Law Schools.*

❏ Register for the June LSAT (you can retake it in October if you blow it).

❏ Prepare for the LSAT.

❏ Subscribe to LSDAS (they take care of sending your transcript and LSAT scores to each school you apply to).

SUMMER BEFORE SENIOR YEAR

❏ Take the June LSAT.

❏ Start drafting your personal statement.

❏ Think about whom you'll be asking for recommendations.

❏ Make a list of schools you'll be applying to, using the grids from the *Official Guide* as an aid.

❏ Send away for applications, and start visiting as many schools as you can.

❏ Register for the October LSAT if you're not satisfied with your June score.

EARLY FALL OF SENIOR YEAR

❏ Familiarize yourself with the applications as they roll in.

❏ Make a checklist and schedule for each application, and photocopy all forms.

❏ Send transcript request forms to all undergraduate and graduate schools you've attended.

❏ Line up your recommendation writers. Give them the specific info they need to write an outstanding recommendation of you.

❏ Revise your personal statement. Tailor it to specific essay topics, if any, on individual applications.

MID-FALL OF SENIOR YEAR

❏ Finalize your personal statements.

❏ Transfer application information from the photocopies to the actual application forms.

❏ Make sure your recommendation writers are on board.

❏ Take the October LSAT (if necessary).

❏ Send in your applications. (Make sure you don't mix up the mailings!)

LATE FALL OF SENIOR YEAR

❏ Remind your recommendation writers to send in recommendations ASAP.

❏ Get Master Law School Report from LSDAS, summarizing transcripts, etcetera.

Winter and Spring/Summer after Senior Year

❏ Receive monthly updates from LSDAS, telling you which schools your records have been sent to.

❏ Cross your fingers while you wait for the acceptances to roll in.

❏ Decide which offer to accept.

❏ Send in acceptance.

❏ Apply for financial aid.

Fall after Graduation

❏ Start your first semester at the law school of your choice.

LSDAS Checklist

☐ Get the LSAT/LSDAS *Registration and Information Book*.

To order a free copy, call LSAC at (215) 968-1001, or email your request to lsacinfo@lsac.org.

The book is also available at law school admission offices and prelaw adviser offices.

☐ Subscribe to LSDAS by completing the registration form in the *Registration and Information Book*.

You can subscribe to LSDAS on the same form you use to register for the LSAT.

☐ Use transcript request forms (they're in the Information Book) to request transcripts from all undergraduate and graduate institutions you've attended.

They will send transcripts directly to LSDAS.

☐ Receive LSDAS Subscription Confirmation.

☐ Receive Master Law School Report—summarizing your academic information.

They get sent shortly after LSDAS receives your transcripts.

Check it carefully; report any inaccuracies to LSAC.

☐ If you've decided to apply to more schools than you originally planned to, order extra reports from LSDAS and pay an additional fee.

☐ Receive monthly reports from LSDAS.

Check them for accuracy or discrepancies.

☐ If necessary, renew your LSDAS subscription after 12 months.

HOW TO APPLY

After you've made the decision to apply to law school and have decided where and when to apply, you need to order the application forms from the various schools you've chosen. This can be done by mail, but the quickest way is just to call the admissions offices around July and get put on their mailing lists. Once the applications begin arriving (usually around Labor Day) you'll notice one thing quickly: No two applications are exactly alike. Some require one recommendation, others two or three. Some ask you to write one essay or personal statement, while others may ask for two or even three. Some have very detailed forms requiring extensive background information; others are satisfied with your name and address and very little else.

Despite these differences, most applications follow a general pattern with variations on the same kinds of questions. So although not all of this section is relevant to all parts of every application, these guidelines will be valuable for just about any law school application you'll encounter.

KAPLAN **EXCLUSIVE**

You won't be writing 10 different applications so much as 10 variations on a single application.

The most important thing to keep in mind about your law school application is that it is, above all else, a sales pitch. The application is your single best opportunity to sell yourself. Remember, every person who applies will have strengths and weaknesses. It's how you *present* those strengths and weaknesses that counts. *You* are in control of what that admissions committee sees on your application and how they see it.

So what's the best way to sell yourself? We all know that some people are natural-born sellers in person, but the application process is written, not spoken. The key here is not natural talent but rather organization—carefully planning a coherent presentation from beginning to end and paying attention to every detail in between. But be careful not to focus so much on the overall theme that you neglect the details. That can be disastrous.

Getting Organized

You must first put together a checklist of the forms that each of your chosen schools requires, double-checking to make sure you don't overlook anything. Some schools may require you to fill out residency forms or financial aid forms in addition to the regular application forms. Don't ignore these and put them off until last. Schools may require proof of residency or income verifications that you might not have readily available.

Next, make photocopies of all forms before you complete them. Changes and corrections will have to be made no matter how careful you are. These changes should not be made on the original form, which will go to the school. Almost every admissions officer we have spoken with explicitly prizes neatness. The feeling is that if the application is sloppily prepared, the student is not very serious about attending that law school. Work on your photocopied rough draft until you are sure you are ready to transfer to the original application.

The Application Form

For the most part, filling out the application form requires simply putting down factual information. But even in something so apparently mindless, you can still make sure you present yourself as a thorough, organized person who can follow directions.

The key to filling out the application form can be summed up in a single sentence: *Don't make the admissions officers do more work than they have to.* Make sure that they have all of the information they need at their fingertips. If they have to hunt down your statistics, if your application is full of unexplained blanks, if they can't read what you've written—all of these things will just serve to annoy the very people you want to impress.

One key to not annoying the admissions people is to make sure you answer *all* of the questions asked on the application form. If some questions don't seem to apply to you, type in "not applicable"; leave nothing blank. If the admissions officers see blank spaces, they don't know whether you found the question not applicable, just didn't want to answer it, or overlooked it. Many schools will return the application if even a single question is left blank. This can be a real problem, because it may be a month or more before the application is looked at and returned and then filled in and looked at again. That kind of delay can easily turn an early application into a late one.

Along these same lines, don't answer questions by saying "see above" or "see line 22." Most applications will ask you for things like your address or phone number more than once. Go ahead and fill them in again. Remember that law schools are flooded with documentation and may separate parts of the application. They don't appreciate having to find what you wrote back on line 22 if they've asked you for that information again on line 55.

As long as we're talking about practices that annoy the decision makers, another is the failure to follow directions on the forms. If the form says, "Don't write below this line," then don't write below the line. You are not an exception to this rule. If they ask for an explanation in 150 words or less, then don't give them 300 words. One admissions officer remarked that the comment, "He couldn't even follow directions," is heard several times a year in committee meetings.

Addendums

An important part of the application form will not be in the package sent from the law school. These are your addendums. Addendums (or *addenda*, if you want to be fancy) are the additional page or pages that you staple onto the forms when the space they give you to answer a question is too small.

This is where an addendum comes in. Simply write "continued on addendum" on the application form after you've used their space up, and then clearly mark what you are listing at the top of the addendum. Staple this addendum at the back, and you've solved a tricky problem. Law schools appreciate addendums because they're much neater than attempts to cram things into a limited space—*and* they show careful organization. But don't overdo it. One or two addendums should be sufficient for any application.

Addendums can be used to preserve neatness when the application blanks are of insufficient length. But they can also be helpful if an answer requires further explanation. For example, if you won the Grant R. Humphrey Science award, it's not enough just to list it. You need to explain what it is, what it's given for, and possibly how many others were competing for it or how prestigious it is.

Honesty

One final topic about the application form that needs to be discussed is honesty. If you think you can get by with a lie or two on your application—well, you may be right. Law schools as a rule don't have the resources to verify all aspects of every application. But before you go overboard and decide to put down that you were once the Prince of Wales, you should realize that you're taking a big chance.

KAPLAN EXCLUSIVE

Admissions officers are human beings. Many of them will be looking for any little excuse to reject yours and get on to the next one. Don't give them that excuse. Make sure that nothing about your application is annoying to them.

First of all, many schools are beginning to devote more time to checking up on applicants' claims. Recently, the president of an undergraduate prelaw society told us that she regularly gets calls from law schools verifying membership of applicants. Secondly, there's always the chance that, if you lie, some other part of your application will contradict the lie and get you booted.

Finally, even if you fool the law school, get in, and graduate with honors, you'll find that any state in which you apply to take the bar exam will do a much more extensive background check than that done by the law school. This check very well might include looking for contradictions in your law school application. Lying on your law school application, in fact, is considered grounds for refusing admittance to a state bar.

Additional Points

Here are a few more things to take note of when filling out the application form:

Be sure to type the application from start to finish. A surprising number of applicants still handwrite the application—something that, according to admissions officers, costs you dearly.

Don't use application forms from previous years. Most applications change from year to year, often substantially. Also, don't use other school's forms because you lost the form of the school you're applying to (yes, people have done that, believe it or not).

Staple extra sheets to the forms. Don't use paper clips unless told to do so. Paper clips—and the pages they attach—tend to get lost.

Always double- and triple-check your application for spelling errors. You lose a certain amount of credibility if you write that you were a "Roads Scholar."

Check for accidental contradictions. Make sure that your application doesn't say you worked for a law firm in 1997 when your financial aid forms say you were driving a cab that year.

Prioritize all lists. When a question asks you to list your honors or awards, don't begin with fraternity social chairman and end with Phi Beta Kappa. Let the admissions committee know that you realize what's important—that is, always list significant scholastic accomplishments first.

Craft your list of extracurricular activities. Don't list every event or every activity you ever participated in. Select the most significant and, if necessary, explain them.

Don't mention high school activities or honors. Unless there's something very unusual or spectacular about your high school background, don't mention it, even if it means you don't take note of the fact that you were senior class president.

Clear up any ambiguities. On questions concerning employment, for instance, make sure to specify whether you held a job during the school year or only during the summer. Many applications ask about this, and it may be an important point to the admissions officer.

The Personal Statement

There are about as many theories on what constitutes a winning personal statement as there are theories on the Kennedy assassination—and, unfortunately, many of them have about the same validity. To begin with, how can you tell 85,000 annual applicants with 85,000 different personalities and backgrounds that there is one correct way to write a personal statement? Furthermore, if even a small percentage of those applicants read and come to believe that a certain way is the correct way, it automatically becomes incorrect, because law schools despise getting personal statements that are familiar—that are, in other words, *im*personal.

For that reason, this section on personal statements has been broken down into two parts. First, we'll look at the procedure of putting together a personal statement. Then we'll look at a list of DOs and DON'Ts that admission officers most frequently mention.

KAPLAN EXCLUSIVE

Next to your numbers, your personal statement is probably the most important part of your application, particularly at the top schools (where so many applicants have great numbers).

Putting Together an Outstanding Personal Statement

Next to your LSAT score and GPA, the personal statement is probably the most important part of your application. If your numbers are excellent or very poor, the essay may get only a cursory glance. But if your numbers place you on the borderline at a school, then it may very well make the difference between acceptance and rejection.

What Kind of Essay to Write: The personal statement is exactly what its name implies—a statement by you that is meant to show something about your personality and character. But that doesn't mean you are to create a lengthy essay detailing every aspect of your life since birth. Nor is the personal statement intended to be a psychological profile describing all of your character attributes and flaws. Several admissions officers have said that the best essays are often only remotely related to the applicant. The point is that you need not write an in-depth personality profile baring your innermost soul. Admissions officers are adept at learning what they want to know about you from your essay, even if it doesn't contain the words *me, myself,* and *I* in every sentence.

One exception, however, should be noted. Although most schools still provide wide latitude in their directions about what the personal statement should be about, some schools are becoming more specific. The problem with specific requirements like these is that you may well have to write a separate essay for that school alone. Be sure to check the instructions carefully and follow them closely. If a law school asks for a specific type of essay and you provide them with a more general one, they'll likely feel that you're not very interested in attending that particular school.

But take heart. Most schools provide few restrictions on what you can write about, so unless you're very unlucky, you should be able to limit the number of essays you must write to two or three.

How Long an Essay to Write: How long should the personal statement be? Some schools place a word limit on the essay; others specify one or two typed pages. Always follow the specific directions, but you should be in good shape with virtually all schools if your essay is one and a half to two pages in length.

Writing the Essay: The personal statement shouldn't be done overnight. A strong personal statement may take shape over the course of months and require several different drafts. One practice that many have found particularly effective is to write a draft and then let it sit for four to six weeks. If you leave it alone for a significant period of time, you may find that your first instincts were good ones. On the other hand, you may shudder at how you could ever have considered submitting such a piece of garbage. Either way, time lends a valuable perspective.

KAPLAN EXCLUSIVE

Start drafting your personal statement now, so that you'll be able to put it aside for a while. You'll be amazed at how different it will look when you go back to it.

Try to start the essay sometime during the summer before you apply. Allow at least three months to write it, and don't be afraid to take it through numerous drafts or overhaul it completely if you're not satisfied. Get several different perspectives. Ask close friends or relatives to scrutinize it to see if it really captures what you want to convey. Be sure to ask them about their initial reaction as well as their feelings after studying it more carefully. Once you've achieved a draft that you feel comfortable with, try to have it read by some people who barely know you or who don't know you at all. If certain criticisms are consistently made, then they're probably legitimate. But don't be carried away by every suggestion every reader makes. Stick to your basic instincts because, after all, this is *your* personal statement, no one else's.

Proofreading is of critical importance. Again, don't be afraid to enlist the aid of others. If possible, let an English teacher review the essay solely for spelling and grammar mistakes.

Essay Content: As stated earlier, there's no one correct way to write an essay, but admissions officers do provide some helpful tips about what they like and don't like to see in a personal statement. Let's begin with a list of the things that officers most often mentioned they disliked seeing.

Personal Statement DON'Ts

Don't turn your personal statement into a résumé. This is the personal statement that begins at birth and simply recites every major (and sometimes minor) event of the person's life. Most of this information is repetitive since it's included on other parts of the application. But worse than that, it's just a boring format.

Avoid the "why I want to go to law school" essay. Although this can be a *part* of any law school essay, too many people make it the entire focus of their statement. The problem is that there are not many new variations on this theme, and the admissions officers have likely heard them all before, probably many times.

Avoid talking about your negatives. The personal statement is not the place to call attention to your flaws. Don't forget that you're selling yourself, and the personal statement is your most prominent sales tool.

Don't be too personal. Stories of abuse or trauma are often very moving and can be particularly effective if tied into a person's reason for wanting to practice law. Several admissions officers, however, have noted a trend towards describing such problems in graphic detail in personal statements. This kind of confessional essay can easily cross the line and become too personal.

Don't discuss legal concepts. Along those same lines, don't try to impress the reader with how much you already know about the law. The school assumes that they can teach you what you need to know, regardless of the level at which you start. By discussing a legal concept, you also run the risk of showing a certain amount of ignorance about the subject while at the same time appearing arrogant enough to have tried to discuss it.

Don't put down lawyers or the legal profession. Although it may seem that spewing cynicism about the legal profession is a clever device, trust us when we tell you that it isn't. Once you become a member of the legal profession, you can make as many lawyer jokes as you want. Until then, watch your step.

Don't try to cover too many subjects. Focus on one or two areas you really want to talk about. One of the worst mistakes applicants make is writing essays that ramble from one subject to another and back again. Fight the desire to talk about every highlight of your life.

Now that you've got a sense of what not to do in your personal statement, let's turn to a list of suggestions for things that you *should* do.

Personal Statement DOs

Tell stories. Readers respond much better to a concrete story or illustrative anecdote than to an abstract list of your attributes. Instead of just writing how determined you are, for instance, tell a story that demonstrates it. Stories stick in people's memories. The same holds true when you're trying to make sure the admissions officers remember you.

Be funny—if you can pull it off. Humor, particularly self-deprecating humor, is a very effective device. Admissions officers appreciate occasional flashes of irony. However, be careful in your use of humor. Don't overdo it—a couple of funny lines or a funny story can be great, but include too many jokes and you start to sound flippant. Finally, think about using *self-deprecating* humor. Law schools often complain about the lack of humility among students and appreciate those who show some.

Be unique. The term *unique* has been overused. Even some applications now ask you to describe what is unique about you. Applicants rack their brains trying to figure out how they're different from the other 5,000 people applying to that law school. Or worse, some interpret *unique* to mean disadvantaged and rack their brains trying to think how they have suffered more than others. But what the admissions officers want to know is what qualities or experiences in your life would make you a particularly valuable member of a law school class.

Start strong. In private moments, admissions officers will often admit that they don't read every essay carefully. They may just glance at an essay to get a general impression. That's why it's important to grab them from the beginning. Tell the ending of a story first and make them want to read on, to see how it all started, for example.

> **KAPLAN) EXCLUSIVE**
>
> Admissions officers try to assemble a law school class that includes a rich variety of perspectives. Let them know what you could contribute to the diverse intellectual atmosphere they're trying to achieve.

The above points are as much general advice as one can responsibly give about the personal statement in a book such as this. We hope that they'll provide you with some ideas or keep you from making some costly mistakes. In the end, however, it *is* a personal statement, and it must come from you.

Recommendations

During the last 10 years, as law school applications have increased dramatically and the odds against being accepted at any particular school have increased, applicants have taken various approaches to stand out from the crowd. Too often overlooked in this mad pursuit, however, is one of the very best ways for an applicant to stand out—that is, by getting terrific, vividly written recommendations.

Because so many recommendations tend to be blasé, an outstanding recommendation that goes beyond the standard language can really make an applicant stand out. Not only does such a recommendation serve the purpose of pointing out an applicant's strengths, it also shows that the recommender thought enough of the person to put time and effort into carefully writing it.

What Makes a Recommendation Outstanding?

Outstanding recommendations can vary in format, but there are several qualities they all tend to have in common.

An outstanding recommendation must be personal: By far the most common mistake made by applicants is believing that the prestige or position of the recommender is more important than what that person writes. Admissions officers tend to treat recommendations from senators, governors, and chief executive officers of major corporations with a great deal of skepticism, because very few applicants have a truly personal relationship with such people. To make matters worse, these officials tend to respond with very standard recommendations that rarely offer any real insight into the applicant's character; in a worst-case scenario, they may even be computer-generated.

Find people who truly know you and are able to make an honest assessment of your capabilities. This means that it may be better to have the teaching assistant with whom you had daily contact write the recommendation, rather than the prestigious professor you spoke to once during the year.

 EXCLUSIVE

Discrepancies between your personal statement and a recommendation can undermine the credibility of your entire application. Make sure your recommendation writers know who you are and what you're about.

An outstanding recommendation compares you to others: When an admissions officer reads a recommendation, he or she often has to put into perspective the meaning of overused phrases—such as *hard-working* and *quick mind*—as they relate to the applicant. A much better format, and one that admissions officers appreciate, is the comparison recommendation, one that compares the applicant to other people that the recommendation writer previously knew in the same position, or (in a best-case scenario) to people he or she has known who are alumnae of that particular law school.

An outstanding recommendation tells stories: A concrete and specific recommendation stands out. Rather than merely listing attributes, a good recommendation engages the reader by telling an insightful story about the applicant. Recently, a professor of political science chose not to submit the standard phrase about what a quick study a student was. Instead, he related a story about the student in class. It seems the professor introduced a new and difficult concept in class that the student discussed intelligently and actually took further than the professor was prepared to do. That kind of story sticks in a reader's mind.

An outstanding recommendation focuses on scholastic abilities: Although recommendations often cover a lot of ground, from the applicant's attitudes about school to his or her personality traits, admissions officers focus on comments about a person's scholastic ability. Obviously, this means that a strong recommendation from a professor carries a great deal of weight. However, a lot of people are in a position to observe a person's intellectual aptitude. Employers, friends, clergy, and workers at volunteer agencies are all usually able to discuss an applicant's scholastic abilities—and should.

An outstanding recommendation will contain some negative comments: In many ways, this is the trickiest area of writing a recommendation, yet it can also prove to be a vital component. A recommendation that is only laudatory, failing to mention a single negative thing about an applicant, may lose credibility. By pointing out a small character flaw or a potential weakness, the recommender gains credibility with the admissions officers and tends to make them less skeptical about the preceding positive comments.

One word of caution, though. Admissions officers universally hate "fake" negatives—for example, "If Suzy has one fault, it is that she works just too darn hard." Much more appreciated are such comments as, "Joe can afford to improve his attention to detail." Combined with effusive praise for the applicant's strong points, this sort of comment impresses admissions officers as being straightforward and helpful.

How to Ensure You Receive Outstanding Recommendations

Now that you know what makes for an outstanding recommendation, all you have to do is ensure that each of your recommenders produces one. While you can't actually write the recommendations yourself, you *can* have a great deal of influence over how accurate and persuasive they are.

Choose the right people to recommend you: What are the qualities of a good recommender? Obviously, you should choose someone who likes you and who thinks you're good at what you do. This doesn't mean that you have to be intimate pals, but sworn enemies don't often write good recommendations. It helps if the person is a good writer so that he or she can clearly express an opinion about you.

Most, if not all, of your recommendations for academic programs should come from professors or other academic faculty. If you've been out of school for a few years and haven't kept in touch with your professors, call or write the admissions offices of the schools to which you're applying. Don't assume that it's okay to send fewer letters than required or to substitute other kinds of information for recommendation letters. Most likely, schools will allow you to submit recommendations from employers or from other nonacademic people with knowledge about your background, skills, and goals.

Balance your list of recommendation writers: Three professors from your undergrad major department probably will have similar things to say about you, so why not include someone from another field who can speak to your thinking and writing skills?

Be considerate of your recommendation writers: As soon as you decide to go to law school, you should start sizing up potential recommenders and letting them know that you may ask them for a letter. This will give each plenty of time to get to know you better and to think about what to say in the letter. Once they've agreed, let them know about deadlines with plenty of lead time to avoid potential scheduling conflicts. The more time they have, the better the job they'll do recommending you.

Make sure your recommendation writers know what they need to know: Once someone has agreed to consider writing a letter for you, you should arrange an appointment to discuss your background and goals for your future. If you live thousands of miles away from your recommender, arrange a telephone appointment.

> **KAPLAN) EXCLUSIVE**
>
> When asked whether you want to see what your recommendation writers have written about you, say no! If admissions officers know that you'll be seeing your recommendations, they'll discount much of what is said in them.

Bring to the appointment copies of appropriate documentation such as your transcript, papers you've written, your résumé or curriculum vitae, your personal statement, and a sheet of bullet points that you plan to feature in your application and essay. Supply the appropriate form or forms, as well as stamped, addressed envelopes and a copy of your home address and phone number.

Keep the appointment relatively brief—you're already taking up enough of their time. Give your recommenders a good idea of why you want to go to law school. Play up your good points, of course, but be reasonably humble. If you have a very specific "marketing" image that you're trying to project, let your recommenders in on it—they may want to focus on some of the same points you're trying to stress. But don't tell your recommenders what to write—don't even give them the impression that you're doing so! Recommenders tend to resent any attempts at manipulation, and may, as a consequence, refuse to write your letter. What recommenders *do* appreciate, however, is some direction as to what you'd like to see.

Keep your recommendation writers on schedule: Finally, make sure your recommenders know how important it is to complete the letters as early as possible. If they procrastinate, gently remind them that their deadline is approaching and be sure to remind them of the importance of early applications.

Common Questions About Recommendations

Here are other points about recommendations that should be considered.

How Long Should a Recommendation Be?

Like the personal statement, the recommendation should be short and concise. A one-page recommendation is usually sufficient. In any case, it should be no longer than two to two and a half pages.

Should I Request to Look at the Recommendation?

Easy answer—NO! Almost all schools have a box you check to indicate whether or not you would like to be able to see the recommendation once it's provided to the school. Just say no! If the school believes that the recommender cannot be completely honest for fear of offending the applicant, the school will heavily discount what is written, no matter how laudatory.

Can I Send More Recommendations Than the School Requests?

Be careful. Law schools may request anywhere from one to four recommendations from an applicant (the recent trend is towards fewer recommendations). Invariably, the situation arises in which a student has three good recommendations, but the school only asks for two. Some schools are very specific in their instructions that they will not accept more than the exact number requested. If the application doesn't spell out how the school handles it, call the school and ask to make sure.

Should I Use the Letter of Recommendation Service?

The Letter of Recommendation Service is set up by LSAC as a convenience. Basically, the service allows your recommenders to send letters to LSAC, who then forwards them to the law schools. Note that the same letter is sent to each school, and so school-specific letters should not be sent through this service. For more information, check out the latest *LSAT/LSDAS Information Book*, or contact your target schools to see if they prefer that you use the service.

A Final Check

After you've completed everything and are getting ready to place it in a manila envelope and mail it, make sure you go through one more time and check each document. Law schools frequently receive documents that were intended to go to another law school. With all of this paperwork, it's easy to see how that can happen, and the law schools expect a certain amount of it. However, it can be embarrassing if you've written in your personal statement that ABC Law School is the one and only place for you—and then you accidentally send it to XYZ Law School instead.

Application Checklist

The three major parts of your law school application:

1. The application form
2. The personal statement
3. Recommendations

THE APPLICATION FORM

- ☐ Working photocopies of applications made
- ☐ Information/addresses/other data gathered
- ☐ Addendums (if any) written
- ☐ Information transferred to actual application
- ☐ Application proofread
- ☐ Final check done

THE PERSONAL STATEMENT

- ☐ Theme finalized
- ☐ Readers selected and notified
- ☐ First draft written
- ☐ Self-evaluation made
- ☐ Second draft written
- ☐ Comments from readers received
- ☐ Final draft written
- ☐ Final statement proofread

RECOMMENDATIONS

- ☐ Recommendation writers chosen
- ☐ Recommendation writers on board
- ☐ Informational meeting with recommendation writers conducted
- ☐ Reminders to all recommendation writers sent
- ☐ Notice of complete application received

Chapter 9: **Special Note for International Students**

In recent years, U.S. law schools have experienced an increase in inquiries from non-U.S. citizens, some of whom are already practicing lawyers in their own countries. This surge of interest in the U.S. legal system has been attributed to the spread of the global economy. When business people from outside the United States do business with Americans, they often find themselves doing business under the American legal system. Gaining insight into how the American legal system works is of great interest around the world.

This new international interest in the U.S. legal system is having an effect on law schools. Many schools have developed special programs to accommodate the needs of this special population of lawyers and students from around the globe. If you are an international student or lawyer interested in learning more about the American legal system, or if you are considering attending law school in the United States, Kaplan can help you explore your options.

Getting into a U.S. law school can be especially challenging for students from other countries. If you are not from the United States, but are considering attending law school in the United States, here is what you'll need to get started.

- If English is not your first language, you'll probably need to take the TOEFL® (Test of English as a Foreign Language), or provide some other evidence that you are proficient in English. Most law schools require a minimum computer TOEFL score of 250 (600 on the paper-based TOEFL) or better.

- Depending on the program to which you are applying, you may also need to take the LSAT® (Law School Admissions Test). All law schools in the United States require the LSAT for their J.D. programs. LL.M. programs usually do not require the LSAT. Kaplan will help you determine if you need to take the LSAT. If you must take the LSAT, Kaplan can help you prepare for it.

- Since admission to law school is quite competitive, you may want to select three or four programs and complete applications for each school.

- You should begin the process of applying to law schools or special legal studies programs at least eighteen months before the fall of the year you plan to start your studies. Most programs will have only September start dates.

In addition, you will need to obtain an I-20 Certificate of Eligibility from the school you plan to attend if you intend to apply for an F-1 Student Visa to study in the United States.

Kaplan English Programs*

If you need more help with the complex process of law school admissions, assistance preparing for the LSAT or TOEFL, or help building your English language skills in general, you may be interested in Kaplan's programs for international students.

Kaplan English Programs were designed to help students and professionals from outside the United States meet their educational and career goals. At locations throughout the United States, international students take advantage of Kaplan's programs to help them improve their academic and conversational English skills, raise their scores on the TOEFL, LSAT, and other standardized exams, and gain admission to the schools of their choice. Our staff and instructors give international students the individualized attention they need to succeed. Here is a brief description of some of Kaplan's programs for international students:

General English Self-Study

For students needing a flexible schedule, this course helps improve general fluency skills. Kaplan's General English Self-Study course employs the communicative approach and focuses on vocabulary building, reading, and writing. You will receive books, audio, and video materials as well as three hours of instructor contact per week.

TOEFL and Academic English

Kaplan has updated its world-famous TOEFL course to prepare students for the new TOEFL iBT. Designed for high-intermediate to advanced-level English speakers, our new course focuses on the academic English skills you will need to succeed on the new test. The course includes TOEFL-focused reading, writing, listening, and speaking instruction, and hundreds of practice items similar to those on the exam. Kaplan's expert instructors help you prepare for the four sections of the TOEFL iBT, including the new Speaking Section. Our new simulated online TOEFL tests help you monitor your progress and provide you with feedback on areas where you require improvement. We will teach you how to get a higher score!

LSAT Test-Preparation Course

The LSAT is a crucial admission criterion for law schools in the United States. A high score can help you stand out from other applicants. This course includes the skills you need to succeed on each section of the LSAT, as well as access to Kaplan's exclusive practice materials.

Other Kaplan Programs

Since 1938, more than 3 million students have come to Kaplan to advance their studies, prepare for entry to American universities, and further their careers. In addition to the above programs, Kaplan offers courses to prepare for the SAT®, GMAT®, GRE®, MCAT®, DAT®, USMLE®, NCLEX®, and other standardized exams at locations throughout the United States.

Applying to Kaplan English Programs

To get more information, or to apply for admission to any of Kaplan's programs for international students and professionals, contact us at:

Kaplan English Programs
700 South Flower Street, Suite 2900
Los Angeles, CA 90017
Phone (if calling from within the United States): 800-818-9128
Phone (if calling from outside the United States): 213-452-5800
Fax: 213-892-1364
Email: world@kaplan.com
Web: www.kaplanenglish.com

FREE Services for International Students

Kaplan now offers international students many services online—*free of charge!* Students may assess their TOEFL skills and gain valuable feedback on their English language proficiency in just a few hours with Kaplan's TOEFL Skills Assessment. Log onto www.kaplanenglish.com today.

---

*Kaplan is authorized under federal law to enroll nonimmigrant alien students. Kaplan is accredited by ACCET (Accrediting Council for Continuing Education and Training) and is a member of FIYTO and ALTO.

CD COMPANION COPYRIGHT AND PERMISSION NOTICES

SOFTWARE LICENSE/DISCLAIMER OF WARRANTIES

The Key to 1L Success

You made it to law school! The success you have had as an undergrad will translate into law school. Right? Not so fast. No matter what your background and success habits were as an undergrad, law school is different. It is as different as college was from high school. The faster you embrace the differences the better your chances are of success in law school. You may be smart, but so is everyone else.

Don't let this unnerve you. You've got Kaplan PMBR on your side to help you succeed. We provide invaluable guidance for all three years of law school, and *then* we help you pass the Bar Exam. Kaplan PMBR offers the most realistic, complete, up-to-date, and effective bar review prep through live courses, home study material, and small group tutorials. The following pages provide just a small preview of the insights and advice, tools and tactics that you'll receive in Kaplan PMBR's 1L Success Program. Visit our website at kaplanpmbr.com to learn more!

Your law school experience is likely to be the most challenging academic process of your life. Just remember, it can be done. Kaplan PMBR will help you do it. Good luck and we will see you on campus!

WHAT IS A "1L"? WHAT IS YOUR "SOL" ON YOUR "COA"? WHO IS THE "π"? WHO IS THE "Δ"?

If you answered these questions with a "Huh?" that is perfectly normal. Law school has its own language. A 1L is simply what first year law school students are called. "SOL" stands for statute of limitations. "COA" is your cause of action. π is shorthand for "Plaintiff", and Δ is shorthand for "Defendant". At first, it is a lot like learning Klingon, but you will learn quickly, and it is a language that will last you a lifetime. With a large legal dictionary in hand, you can create your own shorthand for note-taking and start using words like negate, moot, or sua sponte!

BE PROFESSIONAL

At first glance, law school seems to be very much like college. There are social events, a lot of studying, and new friends. However, keep in mind you are building a professional reputation that will follow you through the rest of your legal career. Your professors and classmates are learning who you are and those impressions last. Make sure they are good ones, and enjoy the process of becoming an attorney along the way.

NIGHT OWLS VS. EARLY BIRDS

Just because you've made it to law school doesn't mean you have to reinvent the wheel. In fact, don't. What and how you studied worked for you. If you study best at night, keep up that practice. If you study best first thing in the morning, continue to do so. Your study patterns have long been established and law school doesn't necessarily require you to change them. Stick with what works!

STUDY GROUPS AND STUDY MATERIALS

Two important issues you will face are whether you should join a study group, and when and how to use study aids.

Study Groups

Early in law school people usually scramble to get together to form study groups with other students. They are completely optional. Some groups will go fast, others slow. Others will study more of the social conditions in law school rather than anything substantive. To get the most from a study group, you must position yourself in the best group *for you*—should you chose to join one.

Study Materials

There are as many opinions about study aids. Used correctly, study aids can help you understand your class notes, let you see how things relate to each other, provide focus on the rationale of cases, and in the end, help you better understand the topic of law covered in class. Commercial outlines are prepackaged outlines in skeletal form of the law you need to know for a particular course. Hornbooks are the comprehensive and expansive overview of the particular course. They are also referred to as treatises.

Finally, there are the bar review programs. Don't let the term "bar review" fool you. True, Kaplan PMBR is a bar review company, but we also are a *law student* company. We have materials for first years, second years, third years, and *then* we help you pass the Bar Exam. For example, Kaplan PMBR offers substantive black letter law course outlines, and audio CDs to help you prepare for classes. These are resources you will turn to again and again—throughout law school and beyond. Visit our website at kaplanpmbr.com to learn more or to enroll.

OUTLINES

What goes into an outline? Essentially, it contains the rules of law, exceptions, and defenses to it. As a brief example, a Battery is a harmful or offensive touching of another with Intent. Consent is a defense to battery.

You might choose to incorporate some of your professor's pet topics or the like to keep them in the front of your mind. They very well could show up on the exam. Sometimes students split up different sections of the course with each creating an outline for her or his portion. However, if you focus on only one portion of the course, you will likely have a good understanding of only that one area and must rely on someone else's perception of their section of the course. Make your own outlines for each course. This allows you to understand the material and how it relates together.

THE EXAM PROCESS

Your exam can include multiple choice questions, short answer, and most popular, essay questions. Your grade depends on how you perform on the exam. However, it is what you do prior to exam day that will have the most impact on your success. Developing a good outline, learning to spot issues, honing your exam skills by practicing on old exams, and designing your test strategy are all solid ways to get ahead of the game and likely many of your classmates as well.

Issue spotting

The first step is knowing the law. The next—issue spotting—is a real time test of your ability to identify legal issues or causes of action. Your professor will test you on material you covered in class and material you were assigned but didn't cover in class. Every law school exam is invented using complex situations that may involve multiple lawsuits or defendants, and usually the professor will ask multiple questions. Truly, some facts are trash while some are treasure. You'll have to decide which is which.

Practice Exams

Practice exams are an essential tool to building your law school success. Sample exams are an underappreciated and under utilized tool. Too often, in the heat of preparing for exams, they are overlooked or ignored due to time constraints. Not only are they are a great barometer of the issues the professor likes, the style of the exam, but you could luck out and one those questions could end up on your actual final exam. Remember to allocate the time to use them!